Higher Education in Canada

Edited by
Charles M. Beach
Robin W. Boadway
R. Marvin McInnis

JOHN DEUTSCH INSTITUTE FOR THE STUDY OF
ECONOMIC POLICY, QUEEN'S UNIVERSITY

Published in cooperation with
McGill-Queen's University Press
Montreal & Kingston • London • Ithaca

ISBN: 1-55339-069-5 (bound)   ISBN: 1-55339-070-9 (pbk.)
© John Deutsch Institute for the Study of Economic Policy
Queen's University, Kingston, Ontario K7L 3N6
Telephone: (613) 533-2294   FAX: (613) 533-6025
Printed and bound in Canada

Library and Archives Canada Cataloguing in Publication

Higher education in Canada / edited by Charles M. Beach,
Robin W. Boadway and R. Marvin McInnis.

Includes bibliographical references.
ISBN 1-55339-069-5 (bound).--ISBN 1-55339-070-9 (pbk.)

1. Education, Higher–Canada. I.Beach, Charles M. II. Boadway,
Robin, W., 1943- III. McInnis, R. Marvin IV. John Deutsch Institute
for the Study of Economic Policy.

LA417.5H53 2005   378.71   C2004-907100-9

Table of Contents

Section V:
Student Financing and Postsecondary Education

Section VI:
Wrap-Up Panel on Alternative Perspectives, Directions and Innovations

Contributors

Preface

The papers and commentaries in this volume were almost all originally presented at the John Deutsch Institute conference on "Higher Education in Canada" held at Queen's University on February 13–14, 2004. The conference was organized by Charles Beach, Robin Boadway and Marvin McInnis in the Department of Economics at Queen's. Funding for the conference came from the John Deutsch Institute, the Ontario Council on Graduate Studies, the Canada Millennium Scholarship Foundation, and the Queen's University Faculty of Education. The organizers thank these latter organizations for helping to make the conference possible.

The objectives of the conference were threefold. First was to provide a timely input on identifying the major issues to government re-examinations of postsecondary education policies in Canada generally and specifically in Ontario where the Rae Review taskforce has been charged with making major recommendations in this area. Second, the conference and this subsequent volume have pulled together some major original research studies with Canadian data to help inform public debate on the key issues around underfunding of the sector and product quality, student access and affordability, and on-coming faculty shortages. Third, the studies provide a number of concrete proposals for reform and alternative policy options that would help address these major problems facing the postsecondary education sector in Canada.

The co-editors and conference organizers benefited from the assistance of a number of people in both the operation of the conference and the production of this volume. We especially wish to thank Sharon Sullivan of the John Deutsch Institute for her assistance throughout the project, for her excellent job in the planning and managing of the conference, and for her exceptional editorial and development work in producing this volume. Marilyn Banting and Mark Howes of the Queen's School of Policy Studies provided excellent creative and editorial services for the volume. We also gratefully acknowledge the very helpful contributions of a large number of others who contributed to the project by providing advice or assistance and/or served as discussants, chairs or manuscript reviewers: Robert Best, William Bruneau, Rosa Bruno-Jofré, Ian Clark, Chad Gaffield, Sean Junor, William Leggett, David Leyton-Brown, Kevin McQuillan, Ken Norrie, Herb O'Heron, Bonnie Patterson, Ross Paul, Abigail Payne, Marilyn Rose, Donald Savage, France St-Hilaire, Arthur Sweetman, and Richard Van Loon.

Finally, we wish to acknowledge the marvellous cooperation we received from the contributors to this volume.

Charles M. Beach   Robin W. Boadway
Director   Queen's University
John Deutsch Institute

R. Marvin McInnis
Queen's University

Introduction

Charles M. Beach, Robin W. Boadway and R. Marvin McInnis

Background Context and Major Issues in Postsecondary Education in Canada

Higher education has been under strain for a number of years in Canada and has reached the point where the system is fraying. Years of underfunding have threatened the quality of university education and research. Large increases in student tuition levels have threatened access to a university education in Canada and dramatically increased student debt levels upon graduation. And there is a looming shortage of new faculty to sustain the system as large numbers of older faculty retire over the next ten years.

Governments in Canada and abroad are re-examining their policies towards higher education. Ontario has recently set up the Rae Review to report in January 2005 on the design and funding of Ontario's post-secondary education system, the largest in Canada. This follows the earlier oft cited Smith Report, *Excellence Accessibility Responsibility: Report of the Advisory Panel on Future Directions for Postsecondary Education* (Smith, 1996). Other comprehensive reviews have been recently undertaken in the United Kingdom *(The Future of Higher Education* [2003] White Paper on postsecondary education reform), as well as in Australia, New Zealand and the Organisation for Economic Co-operation and Development (OECD). In 2004, the United Kingdom passed legislation to bring in major changes to student support and the funding of their university system. In the

United States, cut-backs in state budgets have forced re-examination of how public universities there are funded and their implications for access, and a full issue of the *Journal of Economic Perspectives* has been devoted to a symposium on "The Economics of Higher Education" (Winter 1999).

Several major trends or factors are driving this re-examination and are discussed in the papers in this volume. Governments and analysts are paying much greater attention to possible linkages (and the channels through which these linkages operate) between growth of colleges and universities on the one hand and innovation, productivity, and economic growth on the other, so a healthy postsecondary education sector is viewed as a contributor to prosperity and economic growth in the country, both locally and to the economy at large. As the economy shifts away from traditional primary sectors and old-line heavy manufacturing, individuals increasingly see the growing need of a postsecondary education to get ahead and make use of the new job opportunities opening up in the economy, so that college and university enrolment rates among university-age cohorts have been steadily rising in Canada, the United States, and other industrialized countries. Thus even for a stable population, there is a growing demand for college and university training. Between 1990–91 and 2000–01, university participation rates among Canadians aged 18 to 24 rose from 15.4% to 18.4%.[1] There is also a great deal of evidence — across all these countries — that the graduates of colleges and universities benefit substantially from their education through better jobs, higher earnings, and less time unemployed. So in a period of severe pressures on the public purse, graduates should be expected to help shoulder the costs of their postsecondary education. Studies have also documented a growing shift of emphasis in university research towards science, technology, and medical areas and of rising costs of equipment and personnel in these areas. Universities thus face rapidly rising costs of just maintaining quality of research and training. If external research funding does not fully cover these costs, then incentives arise to reallocate internal funds to support these activities which can have the effect of increasing student-faculty ratios and reducing quality of education elsewhere in the universities.

In Canada itself, additional factors are at work. Provincial government budgets are being continually squeezed by the growing costs of health care and other infrastructure and social needs while trying to maintain competitive tax rates, so the proportion of their budgets being allocated to

---

[1]Specific figures in this section come from the *CAUT Almanac of Post-Secondary Education in Canada, 2004.*

higher education has been declining for some years. This has meant the real value of government funding per capita to universities has markedly declined and the costs of program delivery are increasingly being borne by students through rapidly rising tuition fees. At the same time, provincial student support programs have become less generous, student financing options are becoming complex when linked with federal sources, and the students are increasingly turning to private sector borrowing and are graduating with dramatically higher debt loads than even a few years ago. Canadian universities face competition from United States schools for top talent and have experienced a considerable brain drain of their best scholars to the United States as they have been hobbled by ongoing provincial funding cuts and a low Canadian dollar. Provincial funding rules are also geared to squeezing more students into the classrooms rather than improving the quality of the education that is delivered, and support uniformity of product rather than differentiation and specialization of universities into different areas or missions. There is also a large number of older faculty at Canadian colleges and universities who will be retiring over the next decade and the Canadian postsecondary education system is simply not producing enough replacements for them. Where the needed new faculty will be found is a very severe problem that has not at all been adequately planned for.

A number of recent studies and commentaries have highlighted various of these concerns. In the United States, concern has been raised about the growing commercialization and marketing of universities (Bok, 2003; Kirp, 2003). In the United Kingdom, *The Economist* (2002, 2004) has repeatedly highlighted the situation of British universities. In Canada, a flock of recent books has drawn attention to the growing problems in Canadian universities (Axelrod, 2002; Bercuson, Bothwell and Granatstein, 1997; Laidler, 2002, including Paul Davenport's commentary on the challenge of accessibility and quality, 2002; and Pocklington and Tupper, 2002), an entire issue of *Policy Options* (September 2003) has been devoted to papers on concerns about Canadian universities (e.g., Shapiro, 2003), and *Maclean's* magazine, the source of Canada's annual university rankings, has repeatedly raised the alarm about declining quality on Canadian campuses (e.g., Johnston, 2002a,b).

The major problems facing higher education in Canada, and the motivation for the research studies appearing in this volume, can be gathered under three broad headings: underfunding, student access, and faculty shortage. First is the funding shortfall under which the postsecondary sector — and especially universities — in Canada have been operating for more than a decade now. Provincial funding transfers to universities and colleges have significantly declined in real (inflation-adjusted) per-student terms, in per capita terms, as a percent of the gross domestic product (GDP), and most markedly relative to public universities in the United States. Indeed, funding levels in Ontario have slipped from being among the highest in Canada to being at the bottom among all provinces and among the lowest across all ten provinces and 50 states in the United States. Since the early 1980s, real per-student funding transfers in Canada as a whole have fallen by about 30% while increasing by about 20% in the United States. In Ontario, for example, between 1992–93 and 2002–03, provincial (real dollar) transfers to colleges and universities per full-time equivalent (FTE) student enrolment fell by 36%. As a result, classes are overcrowded, numbers of full-time faculty have declined or barely held constant, student-faculty ratios have shot up dramatically, and methods of teaching have shifted to accommodate large student numbers, so that quality of under-graduate education has noticeably declined. For example, between 1991–92 and 2000–01 university students per full-time faculty rose in Canada from 17.5 to 22.5 while the number of full-time university teachers declined from a peak of about 33,000 to under 30,000 by the late 1990s. Universities could not offer positions to all those students seeking entrance and, with student fees being capped, rationing of positions has been done on the basis of entrance grades, so that entering grade point averages have risen to historic levels, particularly at the most selective institutions. Growing Canada-US faculty salary gaps and reduced resources and opportunities in Canada have resulted in many of the best faculty being attracted to positions in the United States — especially in the mid-1990s and especially in the most internationally marketable disciplines such as computer science and economics. When scholars left the country, moved out of academics or retired, their positions were often closed down in the name of salary savings. Many of the faculty leaving or retiring were experienced researchers and supervisors. There are distinct signs of slippage in the quantity and quality of research produced again in the most marketable disciplines. As the economy prospered and offered lots of jobs to university graduates, fewer students carried on for doctoral training with an eye for academic work. In order to be sustainable without continuing severe declines in quality, clearly greater resources need to be directed to the operations of the postsecondary education sector in Canada.

The funding environment also came with non-neutral incentives. Universities faced tuition caps and uniform funding rules which inhibited differentiation of focus and specialization of programs, so institutions could not readily compete on the basis of price and product delivery and concentrate on what they could do best. Recent federal research funding has largely been concentrated in the science/technology/medical areas and not in the humanities and social sciences where most students are located. Federal programs such as the Canada Foundation for Innovation or provincial programs such as Ontario's Super-Build and its Research and Development Challenge Fund require universities to find funding partners or matching grants such as from the private sector (so-called public-private partnerships) or internal funds. These have the effect of privileging applied practical scientific research, diverting funds away from fundamental and long-horizon research, leveraging university activities to become more aligned with specific corporate research priorities, and shifting resources from non-science/technology/medical areas which have traditionally provided liberal education training and where most undergraduates and faculty are located. Granting council policies that do not fully cover overheads and indirect costs again require universities to short-change undergraduate training in order to ease up funds for prestige research projects. It has also long been the case that it is easier to raise funds for bricks and mortar than for people, programs, and general operating expenses.

The second broad set of issues that needs to be addressed revolve around student access and affordability of a postsecondary education. On average, tuition fees have more than doubled over the past decade in Canada, with even higher increases in some provinces. Between 1991–92 and 2003–04, average undergraduate arts tuition rose by 122% for Canada as a whole, by 138% in Ontario and by 187% in Alberta. But the job opportunities and income benefits of a higher education are so great that it is still an excellent investment in the future to graduate from a college or university. So the problem is how to allow all qualified students the opportunity to gain these benefits in spite of the greatly increased expense. The worry is that a postsecondary education may simply be unaffordable for students with the requisite ability, so the higher fees (and associated costs of books, computers, residence fees, etc.) will limit access. As well, students from low-income households may face psychological barriers to taking on heavy debt loads in order to meet these high costs. Comparing Canada and the United States, Swail (2004) finds that, while the post-secondary participation rates are very similar between the two countries, university participation rates are considerably higher in the United States (29.4 versus 22.8% in 2000). He also finds that, while costs of attendance at universities are still considerably lower in Canada, student aid (from all sources) covers only 48% of the bill in Canada compared to 60% in the United States, so that out-of-pocket expenses to be covered by the student (and family) are 25% higher in Canada than in the United States.

This situation has both an efficiency cost to the economy if some of the most productive members cannot attain their full potential, an equity concern if access is effectively unavailable to the poor and even middle class, and an individual dimension if one of the most traditional channels of personal advancement and improvement and social inclusion falls into jeopardy. Modern advanced economies are all experiencing a rising demand for postsecondary education by a growing fraction of their university-age workforce, and now is not the time for Canada to throttle down this advance by restricting student access through unaffordable fees. This is not to say that if postsecondary graduates are the principal beneficiary of such training, they should not make a major contribution to covering its cost. Indeed, it has been argued that making tuition fees the major source of postsecondary funding would make universities and colleges more responsive to student needs and work to provide better quality programs as they compete for student revenue.

The issue should be how to overcome credit constraints and help students to afford a postsecondary education. The current system of overlapping provincial and federal student support programs is inadequate to the current level of fees, overly complex, and in the case of Ontario's Student Assistance Program (OSAP) has faced substantial funding cuts and more restrictive eligibility criteria. A number of suggestions should be examined. While again we need to be mindful of overlapping federal-provincial roles, one should work towards a simpler student funding program that would include, perhaps, a mix of grants, fellowships, and publicly provided loans that would meet certain criteria. For example, initial funding for each eligible student could be in the form of a grant (with fellowships available for the most able) and additional support in the form of government loans. Repayment conditions on the loans could be made income-contingent and payable by graduates. The size of the initial grant, for example, could be means-tested for family income as reported in income taxes, so students from poorer family backgrounds benefit from a degree of progressivity in the system. Just such a system has been passed into law this year in Great Britain and extensive discussions have undertaken on variations of such a scheme.

The relationship between colleges and universities should also be re-examined. Colleges (with their lower fees and less academic admission requirements) could serve some students as conduits into the university system where they might not go in directly. This could involve rethinking the greater differentiation of programs, possibly wider eligibility for student support at colleges, and broader university recognition of some college programs. Income-tax-based educational saving incentives, such as the current Registered Education Savings Plan (RESP), could be enhanced, again perhaps with a progressive component. Finally, Canada could do a

Charles M. Beach, Robin W. Boadway and R. Marvin McInnis

better job of attracting international students and enhancing foreign-exchange programs so that Canadian schools and programs become better known internationally.

The third major concern is the challenge of faculty renewal over the next decade. Retirement of the large wave of faculty hires in the 1960s and 1970s has already begun, indeed it began early because of early-retirement buy-out packages offered by universities in the name of salary savings in the 1990s. On the other hand, rising numbers of postsecondary students are being driven by the demographics of the baby-boom echo and ongoing large immigration flows, especially in the large cities, and by rising Canadian participation rates in postsecondary education. Projected demand figures for new faculty have been estimated at 30,000 to 40,000 by 2020. But where are the new faculty to come from? While the number of undergraduates has burgeoned, the number of doctoral degrees awarded by universities in Canada over the last decade has barely remained constant and in many disciplines has significantly declined since PhD-training is very resource-intensive. Of these numbers, a large fraction of Canadian-produced PhDs have moved to the United States where there has been much more faculty hiring due to greater resources at American universities and to a stronger and slightly earlier baby-boom echo than in Canada. Also, a substantial proportion of new PhDs in more marketable disciplines move out of academics to better job opportunities elsewhere. Thus there is a problem of retention as well as production of PhDs in the Canadian academic sector. Also as already noted, in the fields where most students and faculty are, funding incentives have been to shift resources away from them, and many graduate-training capabilities in these programs have been significantly weakened. Recreating good graduate-training programs does not happen over night and may take years of effort to rebuild. American schools have already started on renewal programs to hire new young faculty, so international competition for new young scholars will be a challenge to Canadian schools.

Incentives and initiatives need to be put in place as soon as possible to attract good students into PhD programs in Canada and to help retain them in academics once they graduate. For example, the number and value of doctoral fellowships could be increased and they could be made more readily available to non-Canadian citizens so as to attract more international graduate students to Canadian universities. If some form of income-contingent loan system is brought in, more generous and flexible terms could be made available to those who continue studying for a PhD and enter academic positions (Great Britain currently does this to attract young people into the teaching profession). More generous university funding grants could be directed to graduate faculties or graduate programs, so it becomes worthwhile for universities to build up their capacity to run such programs.

The papers in this volume have been selected to throw light and further policy debate on these three major sets of issues.

Overview of the Contributing Papers

In setting the scene, the two contributions by Ronald Ehrenberg and David Laidler identify some key issues facing higher education in the United States and incentive concerns facing universities in Canada. Academic trends in the United States provide a background academic environment within which Canadian schools must operate and compete. Ehrenberg points out four major trends affecting higher education in the United States. Tuition and costs in the postsecondary education sector have for some while been rising at rates significantly higher than the rate of inflation. The increased costs are being driven by higher costs of technology, student services and financial aid, increasing institutional contributions to scientific research and the ongoing withdrawal of state support to public schools of higher education. Second, the share of state governments' budgets going to public academic institutions has declined over time as states devote a greater share of their higher education expenditures to providing grant aid directly to students, and increasingly this aid is non-needs based. This affects who gets higher education and increasingly students from lower-income families are being financially forced to enter higher education through public two-year colleges rather than directly into universities. Third, scientific research — in areas such as genomics, advanced materials, and information technology — has grown in importance in American universities with real average research and development expenditure per faculty member doubling since 1971. Over the same time, average institutional expenditures per faculty member paid out by the universities themselves has more than tripled. So individual academic institutions are bearing a greater share of the rising costs of the scientific research activity. In order to do so, they have increased student-faculty ratios and substituted part-time and full-time non-tenure-track faculty for tenure-track faculty. Ehrenberg's work suggests that these changes result in higher under-graduate attrition rates and lower student graduation rates, not signs of increased quality of undergraduate training. Fourth, a major problem facing American higher education is where the next generation of faculty will come from to replace the wave of on-coming retirements since the total number of PhDs produced in the United States has been declining and the share of Americans among out-coming PhDs has also been declining, and quite dramatically so in key science areas. Consequently, there will be a rising demand by US institutions to hire faculty from abroad to fill their own needs.

David Laidler focuses on incentives facing Canadian universities within the current funding environment. He notes the shift in basis behind government funding of universities towards arguments around the "knowledge economy" and an economic productivity agenda. While such a linkage has yet to be convincingly demonstrated in the research literature, this shift in argument has resulted in a broad shift in funding emphasis towards science and technology fields. It has also created worrisome incentives for resource reallocations within universities as emphasis is focused on applied and results-oriented research, interdisciplinarity and a corporatist agenda as government research and building grants require matching funds from other sources such as the business sector. Science and technology research also involves substantial overheads and maintenance budgets which result in resources being drawn away from elsewhere within universities. This sets up incentives to operate humanities and social science programs, possibly at lower academic standards as "cash-cow" sources of internal subsidies to support activities favoured by governments and donors.

Laidler also considers ways to foster greater efficiency in resource allocations in universities. Allowing tuition revenue to become the main source of universities' income would allow students to seek out good quality academic programs and universities to compete more directly to offer such programs as a counterweight to current reliance on government and business sectors in setting universities' priorities. Allowing fees for different programs to better reflect actual program costs while allowing students to choose among these differently priced programs would end up allocating resources within universities efficiently without the need for central or ministry direction. This would also foster greater differentiation and specialization across different universities with students playing a significant role in this resource-allocation process. If the higher tuition fees in such an approach were addressed by some form of income-contingent loan scheme, the scheme would also need to be supplemented with student grants that vary with the students' income background so that qualified students from low-income backgrounds are not priced out of the system by unaffordably high tuition levels.

Michael Skolnik in his paper reminds us that, in the recent attention to performance and financing of postsecondary education, an earlier concern for what should be the make-up of the postsecondary sector by type of institution may have slipped out of view. This issue is now reasserting itself as governments are being pressured to alter the structure without consideration of the whole picture. Skolnik draws our attention mainly to two issues. One is accrediting the granting of degrees by private, mainly for-profit institutions. The other is the blurring of the lines between universities and community colleges. Both are being driven by demands for more technically sophisticated, market-oriented education in the postsecondary sector.

Throughout the world, and notably in Canada, there is a burgeoning demand for accreditation and technically-sound, marketable training at a level sufficiently advanced to claim degree status. Private, for-profit organizations claim to be able to provide that. Governments have come under pressure to allow them, and first steps are being taken in several Canadian provinces.

The second issue concerns the division of postsecondary education between traditional universities and community colleges. Two models of the latter have been pursued. British Columbia has opted for a model that is well-developed in the United States in which the colleges offer a cheaper and more convenient way of providing the first two years of university-level education. They accord a modest accreditation to some of their students and pass others on to the universities to complete the baccalaureate. An alternative model has been pursued by Ontario and other Canadian provinces. There the colleges were intended to offer more technically-based, career-oriented training beyond secondary school. Some of the programs have been eminently successful in doing just that. Yet, overall, college graduates appear to have lower earnings than university graduates. That has led some critics to argue that Ontario, especially, has overinvested in colleges and underinvested in universities. But the debate does not adequately take into account that universities have long had a strong career-orientation and still have a lock on preparation for the traditional, high-paying professions — medicine, law, engineering, and accountancy. The colleges have picked up on the technical side of career preparation. The question remains: How far should the general education go of students who wish to pursue fairly specific technical careers? Many students should perhaps do two years of liberal arts at a university and then transfer to a college for technical training. That would strengthen the claim that colleges would like to make on the offering of baccalaureate degrees.

At present, the colleges turn out some well-trained, technically-oriented graduates. They also keep up their enrolments by accrediting students in trade courses that formerly were offered by high schools and by proprietary colleges. The large number of these lower-level accreditations serves to considerably depress the reported earnings of college graduates. For many students the college has been made the vehicle for a significant economic transfer as it provides publically subsidized training of a sort that formerly was done, for a price, by the private sector. The upshot is that the colleges are providing a mix of outcomes that have not yet been fully evaluated by careful economic analysis.

As Skolnik points out, the assessment of resources directed to post-secondary education calls for good estimates of rates of return to investment in both university and community college education. For economists, the natural way to look at the allocation of resources to higher education is in an investment framework. It focuses on whether the rate of return to resources invested in college and university education compares favourably with what might be returned in other uses. A complication is that the higher education sector turns out two products — educated graduates (human capital in current parlance) and new knowledge. These are joint products and there is no unambiguous way of separating the costs of the two functions. The more developed literature concerns the rate of return on instruction. That is reviewed in the paper by Herb Emery who offers an overview and synthesis of a relatively large number of estimates of the rate of return to postsecondary education.

Emery tackles the subject first by examining the component elements of rate-of-return estimates. Those are the employment and income benefits to graduates, and the costs of becoming graduates. Previous studies have almost all found postsecondary education to be worthwhile in purely economic terms. Emery's concern is more with trends. Has the rate of return on higher education declined as the number of graduates increased so greatly? His answer is "no". The returns to university education may have sagged a bit after the big enrolment increases of the 1960s and early 1970s, but in recent years they have risen. A rise in the ratio of earnings of university graduates to those who had only completed high school has enhanced the income gains from a university degree while at the same time lowered the opportunity cost of acquiring the degree. From the point of view of the individual prospective student, a university degree is a worthwhile investment and has become even better in recent years. That is, the private rate of return to university education remains strong. The labour market has not, evidently, become overly-crowded with university graduates, as some observers have supposed.

University education is quite heavily subsidized. Tuition costs are well below the overall costs of instruction. Hence, what Emery calls the "total" returns to higher education are lower than the private returns. These total rates of return are still well above what could be obtained on alternative investments generally and so publically supported higher education appears still to be a worthwhile use of resources. The qualifications that one might apply to Emery's calculations suggest that the, albeit healthy, rates of return that he reports may be lower-bound estimates. There are two reasons for this. One is that there are consumption benefits to a university education. Few who have had the experience would deny that it carries with it considerable enjoyment. Those benefits are overlooked in the calculation. The second reason is that, at least in the opinion of many observers, there are intangible and probably unmeasurable benefits to society of having a highly educated population. A skeptic might want to see a more careful and thorough articulation of those supposed benefits. They do not lie just in the provision of highly educated manpower to private and public enterprises. Those benefits are very largely captured by the educated persons and are counted in the income gain. What is also involved are uncounted spillover effects. One suspects that many of the claims made for them are overblown. Nevertheless, they are frequently claimed by commentators on higher education so we should presume that they have positive value at least. If so, the true "social rate of return" on university education would be above the levels that Emery reports as the "total rate of return". His principal conclusion is that, however one looks at it, university education continues to be a worthwhile investment.

Much less has been done in the way of estimating rates of return to community college education. College programs are highly varied and so it is especially difficult to generalize about them. Emery makes a stab at it by using very aggregate information. He points out that in recent years public funding has shifted away from universities towards colleges. This has been in response to a widespread perception that college programs are "more relevant", particularly as viewed in the labour market. The rates of return reported by Emery do not support that. Universities still appear to be the superior investment. What we do not know is the extent to which the overall rate of return to a college diploma is pulled down by the inclusion of shorter, vocational courses that used to be offered by high schools, such as secretarial training. There are other popular, but relatively low-paying programs offered by the colleges, such as infant daycare and hair dressing, although the shorter duration and lower costs of some of those may offset the smaller income gain. There are also some college programs that may be as remunerative as university education. What is seriously needed is a thorough study of the outcomes of narrowly specified college courses.

Universities also produce new knowledge. It is widely recognized in the economics literature that therein lies the major rationale for their subsidization. That much is well known, although it has not yet effectively permeated Canadian policy on the support of universities. The external benefits of university research accrue to the nation as a whole (or for that matter to the world as a whole). That should make the support of research a federal government responsibility. It should be pointed out that the facts of the case in Canada have not really been carefully explored. That could well be the topic for further research.

Quite apart from the broad national, or even international, benefits from university research, there has been increasing recognition that university research may have important local benefits as well. That is the topic taken up by Julian Betts and Carolyn Lee in their contribution. They identify five avenues or pathways by which universities may benefit the local economies in which they are situated: as a trainer of skilled young graduates; as an innovator through the direct generation and commercialization of knowledge (working fairly independently of the private sector); as a partner to the private sector through providing technical know-how, consulting advice or joint ventures; as a regional talent magnet that increases the general attractiveness of a region to bringing in talented and innovative personnel; and as a facilitator to foster networking among those involved in the local high-tech community. The last four of these involve primarily the role of universities as producers of new knowledge. The first is that universities may contribute to the local supply of highly educated manpower. The authors review the evidence for each of these pathways and find extensive circumstantial evidence supporting the four knowledge pathways — "in short, universities appear to matter importantly". But the evidence leads them to be skeptical about the training effect. The mobility of highly educated manpower is high, and in the absence of other attractions, local universities see their graduates readily drain away to other locales. Universities' local impact, then, is largely through their research function.

However, Betts and Lee point out that there appears to be no single or simple recipe for success. They put considerable emphasis upon the interaction between cutting-edge research and the transmission of knowledge to local workers and entrepreneurs. They draw evidence from the experience of the successful case of San Diego, California, where the University of California, San Diego is located. More broadly, in the United States, universities have attracted talent at the faculty level who have played an important role in local industrial development. This has often been by spawning new enterprises through the entrepreneurial activities of either faculty members themselves or persons with whom they have direct interaction. Just having a research university is not sufficient. Some American universities have stimulated their nearby economies much more than others. There are some great research universities that have had little local impact in the way of generating new, high-tech, economic activity.

Others have done famously. Quite evidently it is not research output per se that matters but the interaction between research success and other factors "such as smart sources of financing that understand the needs of emerging high-tech firms, managerial talent savvy in these industries, as well as the scientists and engineers who innovate in these firms. Technology commercialization is a very different beast than knowledge creation; a region needs *both* to survive. To be blunt, if anything, there is a tendency in the literature to perhaps overplay the role of universities and underplay the role of the private sector in generating innovative technology clusters".

The postsecondary education sector relies heavily on both the federal and provincial governments for financial support. This support comes in a variety of ways and has a significant influence on the way that post-secondary educational services are delivered. The next set of papers address various dimensions of the role of governments in postsecondary education. A prerequisite for any assessment is to have accurate and transparent information on the sources and adequacy of finance, a topic that is explored by Ken Snowdon for the university sector. He begins by expressing caution about the quality of data that is available on university financing. This generally leads to an understatement of the already precarious financial position of universities. For example, costs of raising trust revenues and the requirement for a portion of fee increases to be devoted to student aid have not been included: university finances are in worse shape than they appear to be. This leads him to plea for better financial accounting of university financing, with more consistency imposed across institutions and sources of finance.

Nonetheless, some trends and stylized facts can be discerned from the data that is available. Snowdon focuses on three funds: operating funds, trust funds, and research funds. Operating funds, which in Canada are mostly provincial grants and tuition fees, have grown considerably less than research funds, and much less than trust funds. By source of funds, federal finance, which is largely devoted to research support, has increased relative to provincial government finance, which tends to support operating expenditures. A serious concern of this is that research funding carries with it additional overhead and indirect costs that encroach on operating costs. This, combined with the fact that provincial operating grants are not even keeping up with inflation, puts considerable financial pressure on the university sector. Moreover, as governments provide more and more financing to the universities, the demand for accountability increases. Snowdon argues that universities would do well to take it upon themselves to improve their financial reporting.

The role of the federal government in postsecondary education and the manner in which federal funding has been made available are chronicled in the contribution by David Cameron. Despite the fact that education is a provincial responsibility in the Canadian federation, the federal government has over the postwar period used its spending power to provide financing directly to universities and to students, and indirectly via transfers to the provinces. The national interest in postsecondary education arises from the fact that there are interprovincial spillover benefits from postsecondary education. Students and graduates are mobile among provinces: residents of any one province may attend postsecondary institutions in any other, and graduates of institutions in one province can seek employment in any other. Moreover, research undertaken in one province creates knowledge that is available to residents in other provinces. More generally, the constitutional commitment of provincial and federal governments to equality of opportunity implies a federal interest in postsecondary education.

Federal support has evolved over the years. Originally, the federal government made direct contributions to postsecondary institutions and operated training programs. During the 1970s, direct contributions gave way to virtually unconditional grants to the provinces in support of post-secondary education, and later the federal government began to withdraw from the training field in favour of the provinces. More recently, un-conditional grant support has waned, but the federal government has increasingly taken an array of more direct initiatives. These include direct support for students (e.g., the Canada Millennium Scholarship Foundation), tax assistance for educational financing, enhanced student loans, the competitive funding of faculty research chairs, and increased support for research and infrastructure.

Cameron cautions that, with the federal government having set the agenda for universities in recent years and the universities having willingly accepted that, the provinces might have ceded too much responsibility. In the end, it is they who have the legislative responsibility for postsecondary education, and it is they who will ultimately bear the cost if federal funding takes another abrupt turn for the worse.

Accountability for university spending is the theme of David Leyton-Brown's paper, with the focus on quality assurance. He argues that quality assurance is a necessary feature of university governance. Not only does it serve as a check that value for money is being achieved, but it also encourages those persons, units or institutions being evaluated to discover ways of improving the work they undertake and the programs they offer. He sets out in a systematic way the role of quality insurance, the activities to whom it should apply, the authority responsible for quality assurance, and the elements of good quality-assurance processes, including best practices. Above all, quality assurance will work best when those being evaluated believe in the benefits of the process and participate in it with enthusiasm rather than resentment.

Problems of financing postsecondary education are universal, and lessons might be learned from experience elsewhere. A particularly pertinent case is that of the United Kingdom, where universities have faced comparable funding problems to those in Canada. Nicholas Barr outlines the recent comprehensive reforms undertaken in the UK to improve the quality of the universities and their financial viability and to improve student access to the postsecondary system, and to do so in a way that is fair to those who do and do not attend while ensuring that financial constraints do not preclude able students from attending. His discussion reviews the lessons from the UK debate. The approach taken by the reforms is multi-faceted. It reduces the central direction of universities by allowing them freedom to set their own fees. It commits more public resources to universities while at the same time allowing fees to rise. Most significantly, it introduces an income-contingent loan system whereby a generous amount of loan financing is made available so that students can obtain upfront funds to cover the cost of fees and living costs, with repayment based on a fixed proportion of earnings after graduation. Barr identifies a well-designed student loan program as having three core characteristics: income-contingent repayments, loans that are large enough to cover all fees and student living costs, and a repayment interest rate that is broadly equal to the government's cost of borrowing. Finally, there are supplementary grant funds and fee remissions available to students from low-income families to ensure their access. He sees income contingency of the loan repayment as fundamental to the politics of implementing such a reform. People making low earnings after graduation make low or even no monthly repayments, so that repayments operate like an income tax or payroll deduction. Student loans should thus be regarded not as a lump-sum debt but as a tax on future earnings. Barr outlines carefully the rationale for such a system and compares it with alternatives. He comes down foursquare in favour of the UK reforms.

In a commentary on the session, Clément Lemelin offers some cautionary views about income-contingent loan schemes such as that introduced in the United Kingdom. He wonders, for example, if the scheme is self-financing as an insurance scheme would be, and if not, who is responsible for the payment of unpaid loans, which could be sizable. He asks some pertinent questions about the details of the scheme, such as what interest rate should be charged on the loans, what income should be used as the basis for repayment, whether all students should be forced to participate, and whether the funding terms should differ by type of study. These are all details that need to be addressed explicitly when designing such a scheme.

The next four papers examine, in different ways, factors affecting access to, demand for, and participation in postsecondary education in Canada. The study by Miles Corak, Garth Lipps and John Zhao looks at the relationship between family income and participation of youth (age 18–24) in postsecondary education, and how this has changed since the 1980s. Using several Statistics Canada data sources, the authors find that overall participation rates (in higher education) reached historic highs, but their rates of growth have flattened or stalled over the 1990s, particularly for universities, while college participation rates have continued to grow. In response to rapidly rising tuition fees during the 1990s, student debt levels rose significantly; and for male students there was a tendency to choose (lower-cost) community colleges rather than universities as university participation rates for men declined steadily after 1993 and college attendance went up.

Their Figures 9 and 10 document participation rate changes by level of (real) family income. University participation rates increase with family income. Participation rates in the top broad family income group ($100,000 or more) varied from year to year at around 40%, but have not changed much since the later 1980s. The lowest income group ($25,000 or less) participation rates are much lower but have been rising fairly steadily over the entire period — from less than 10% in the early 1980s to 19% by 1997. So the gap in participation rates between top and bottom income groups has noticeably narrowed. University participation rates among the three middle income groups, however, trended up through the 1980s then stopped growing in the early 1990s and have noticeably declined since 1993. Thus the fall off in university participation rates over the 1990s was felt most among middle-class families. The pattern for college participation is very different. College participation rates are quite similar across family income groups. And while college rates are not as closely tied to family income as university participation rates, it is again the case that the lowest income group experienced the most consistent growth over the full period. The authors also use regression analysis to find that the association between family income and university participation became stronger over the 1980s up until the early to mid-1990s. But from the mid-1990s, when borrowing limitations were eased on a number of loan programs, the strength of the relationship weakened.

The second paper on family background effects on access to post-secondary education by Ross Finnie, Eric Lascelles and Arthur Sweetman acts as a companion piece to that of Corak *et al.*, but takes a more structural approach of identifying direct and indirect channels through which family background effects can operate. Using Statistics Canada's 1991 School Leavers Survey and its 1995 Follow-Up Survey of youth aged 18 to 20 in 1991, the authors find that family background variables such as parental education levels, family type, ethnicity, and location have important direct and indirect effects on postsecondary participation. The indirect effects of family background operate through a set of intermediate variables including high-school outcomes (such as grades) and related attitudes and behaviours. They look at both university participation and all postsecondary participation and find much stronger effects on university participation. For example, "each additional year of parental education increases the likelihood of university attendance ... as much as about five percentage points. The relative university attendance rates for those whose parents have a high-school diploma and those with at least some university education are 29 versus 53% in the case of men, and 37 versus 65% for women (holding other factors constant)". Approximately 40% of these effects operate indirectly through the various intermediate variables. The major direct effects indicate a continuing role for policy measures to expand postsecondary opportunities for those from less privileged backgrounds. The sizeable indirect effects point to important inequalities being generated during high school and even before, consistent with postsecondary access being affected by social and economic factors well before issues of affordability arise at time of entrance to postsecondary education.

Richard Mueller and Duane Rockerbie look at how *Maclean's* magazine rankings of Canadian universities affect students' choices and hence enrolment demand at the universities. They develop a simple demand-supply model where tuition does not adjust to clear the market for university admissions resulting in excesss demand for university positions. As a result, rationing is based on high-school grades to fill the limited number of positions relative to demand. The authors estimate their model from applications and admissions data over seven years for Ontario, and find that the *Maclean's* rankings do have a statistically significant and strong effect in determining excess demand for positions across universities and hence the height of average high-school entrance grades among universities. An "improvement in the ranking increases the mean grade point average and thus improves the average quality of admitted students ... The effect is the strongest for medical/doctoral schools where a one-position improvement in the ranking increases the mean GPA of those admitted by 0.96 percentage points for males and 0.85 percentage points for females. The effect of the ranking is reduced as we move to comprehensive schools (0.70 percentage points for males and 0.60 percentage points for females), then primarily undergraduate schools (0.33 percentage points for males and 0.29 percentage points for females) ... The *Maclean's* rankings appear to have a strong effect on where students choose to apply to (and end up)".

The study by Nicole Fortin looks at access restrictions arising from *both* sides of the higher education market — both higher tuition fees and lower university funding levels are found to have restricted enrolment rates at Canadian universities. Underlying these policy levers are the ongoing demographics of the changing size of the college-age population and the upward trending demand for greater postsecondary education by the college-age population. Fortin uses US state and Canadian provincial data over 1973–99 in a reduced-form regression analysis to obtain estimates of the effects on university (four-year college) enrolment rates of (i) higher tuition fees and (ii) provincial/state funding levels to universities, while controlling for ongoing demographic shifts. Her analysis looks both at demand-side effects for university positions by potential students for whom higher tuition levels may result in a reduction in demand for university positions, and at supply-side effects on university positions by the university system itself for which reductions in provincial funding levels (their largest revenue source) result in fewer university positions being made available than otherwise. Fortin notes that total enrolment at Canadian universities increased at an annual rate of 4.1% from 1973 to 1990, but basically stalled to no growth in the 1990s. In the United States, on the other hand, enrolment growth at four-year colleges continued to grow over the 1990s though at a lower rate than in previous decades. Like Mueller and Rockerbie, she takes the higher education system to be in disequilibrium where tuition does not adjust to clear the market, rationing of university positions is done on the basis of grades, and total enrolment rates are determined by the short side of the market. If tuition levels are too low to clear the market because of the high demand, the short side of the market will be the supply side and provincial/state funding to universities will, in effect, determine enrolment rates.

Fortin estimates that (i) an increase of 1% in university tuition levels reduces university enrolment rates by about 0.15%, while (ii) a 1% decrease in provincial funding levels to universities (measured by provincial funding per college-age person in the population) yields a 0.25% decrease in enrolment rates. The negative funding effect to universities is almost twice as large as the negative tuition effect on students. The latter effect on students is found to be virtually the same in Canada and the United States. The negative funding effect on universities, however, is found to be about three times larger in Canada than in the United States. So a 50% increase in (real) tuition levels is estimated to reduce university enrolments by about 7%, and a 20% reduction in (real) university funding levels is estimated to reduce enrolments by about 5%. She thus finds that supply-side institutional restrictions had a major constraining effect on enrolment growth of Canadian universities in the 1990s, quite different from the experience in the United States over this period where student-faculty ratios actually declined.

Students are bearing an increasing financial burden in meeting the costs of postsecondary education, and there is no indication that this is likely to change. At the same time, there are a large number of ways that provincial and federal government policies mitigate these costs. These include direct grants and scholarships, loans at preferred rates, and a number of measures in the tax system, including tax credits, tax deductions, and tax-assisted schemes to save for postsecondary education. Naturally there is concern with the effectiveness of these measures. Do all able students have adequate access to funds so that they are not deterred from higher education? Do the schemes systematically favour some groups over others? Will students be left with large levels of debt on graduation that they will find burdensome to repay? To what extent are those fortunate enough to attend postsecondary education to be subsidized by those who are not? Will the current schemes be able to support the increased tuition costs that are likely to be imposed on students in the future? The next set of papers assess the current complex system of student financing, and propose some alternatives.

The careful study by Kirk Collins and Jim Davies focuses solely on the manner in which the tax system influences the incentive to undertake postsecondary education. The tax system includes some specific measures aimed at supporting the financial costs of education, including educational tax credits, Registered Educational Savings Plans (RESPs), and Canada Educational Savings Grants (CESGs). At the same time, since a significant part of the cost of education is foregone earnings and part of the reward for education is increased earnings, the manner in which the system of personal and other taxes impinges on earnings can influence the incentive to undertake higher education. Collins and Davies devise measures that capture the cumulative effect that the tax system has on the incentive to invest. In fact, they devise two such measures. One, the effective tax rate (ETR), measures the difference between the before- and after-tax rate of private return to education, comparable to effective tax rates that have been calculated for physical investments. The ETR measures that disincentive or distortion that the tax system imposes on the private decision to invest in human capital, taking into account only the private costs of education. The second measure, the effective subsidy rate (ESR), measures the difference between the public versus private return to education, now taking into account the costs borne by the public sector. The difference between ETR and ESR measures the overall net effect of the fiscal system on the incentive to invest on higher education.

Collins and Davies find that private rates of return on education are lower than in previous studies, and are lower for males than for females, but that the ETR is higher for males. Moreover, between 1998 and 2003, ETRs decreased substantially — from about 19% to 11% for males and from 13% to 8% for females — owing both to the introduction of CESGs and the flattening of the income-tax structure, which reduced the penalty from increased future earnings. At the same time, the ESR exceeds the ETR, implying that there is a net subsidy on higher education. The authors discuss at some length the sources of these effects and their consequences for student financing policy.

In a commentary on the Collins-Davies paper, John Burbidge puts the tax treatment of human capital accumulation into a broader context by noting that tax support for human capital investment is part of a larger system of incentives for asset accumulation that includes Registered Retirement Savings Plans and Registered Pension Plans. He argues that taking account of how these programs interact with incentives for human capital accumulation may well mitigate the incentive effects of the ETRs that Collins and Davies have measured. Moreover, he argues that RESPs may in fact serve to distort household asset accumulation decisions by contradicting the effects of tax-sheltered retirement-savings systems.

Kevin Milligan studies RESPs and CESGs from the perspective not of their effect on the incentive to invest in human capital — that is, their efficiency effect — but of their effect on households of different income, wealth, and family types. Using very detailed data from the Survey of Financial Security, he finds that the use of RESPs, and therefore CESGs, is highly concentrated in high-income households and in households in which parents are highly educated. He argues that this is in direct conflict with the intent of the program of increasing access to postsecondary education, as well as with the goals of the Canadian Opportunities Strategy, which is to direct aid to lower-income families. His results constitute a serious indictment of these programs as vehicles for improving access to higher education. He suggests, provocatively, that Canada might be better served by abandoning CESGs and diverting the funds saved to those who truly need them.

Lorne Carmichael's paper is also concerned with both accessibility and fairness. He explores an innovative approach to student financial assistance that is designed to ensure that all students who are capable of achieving a postsecondary education have the resources to do so, and that the burden of financing those resources is primarily borne by those who stand to benefit rather than society at large. The idea is disarmingly simple in concept. Students would have access to a sufficient sum of money to finance their education (or at least that part of their education that is deemed to provide private benefits to them rather than general benefits to society). This sum would be provided by the government directly to the student, who would then be responsible for making tuition payments to the institution in which they enrol. Then, on graduation, all students would pay a "graduate tax" that would be based on their earnings. The tax rate would be such that the scheme is self-financing, so the burden is borne by those who take advantage of postsecondary education. Carmichael makes a persuasive case for such a system, which bears much resemblance to an income-contingent loan system discussed earlier.

A final paper by Ross Finnie, Alex Usher and Hans Vossensteyn takes a very broad and ambitious perspective. They argue that the existing system of financial support to students is unnecessarily complicated. It includes far too many different elements that taken together do not succeed in meeting the basic objectives of ensuring accessibility to all potential and able students regardless of need. They propose a sweeping overhaul — what they refer to as a "new architecture" — in which the myriad of existing programs is replaced by an overarching one that targets funds better to those in need and ensures that all able students have sufficient funds to cover the full costs of attending a postsecondary institution. The program would first assess each student's financial need, taking account both of the costs they bear as a result of attending a postsecondary institution and the resources, including parental, that they potentially have. This would be made available to all students by a combination of loans and grants. They discuss the details of such a scheme, including how the federal government and the provinces could be persuaded to accept a single comprehensive scheme in place of their currently very different and fragmented ones.

The volume wraps up with the reflections of a panel of persons with substantial experience in the Canadian postsecondary scene. There was a common note of concern for the present state of affairs and for the little public concern for the deteriorating quality of the universities. Peter George, the president of McMaster University, and speaking from the viewpoint of the chair of the Council of Ontario Universities' Task Force on Quality and Financing, describes the endeavour of the task force to articulate the dimensions of quality. He also recounts optimistically the findings of an Ontario Task Force on Competitiveness, Productivity, and

Economic Progress which has placed a strong emphasis on the value of higher education. One may hope that his optimism is borne out with beneficial changes in government policy.

John Chant, a panelist with long experience at several Canadian universities, raises the matter of research quality in Canada. But as Chant points out, the overriding concern of governments, and with public discussion of the university issue, has been access, and the policies being pursued are aimed at promoting access at the expense of a continuing dilution of the university education being offered. Little attention has been devoted to the question "access to what?".

Panelist John Greenwood takes up the question of access in a more narrowly focused way. His concern is with ways of assuring access by those with low-income backgrounds who tend to think of university as not being an option. He sketches two experimental approaches to drawing in students who might otherwise not attend university. The issue is not just one of transcending financial barriers but of inducing people to think beyond those barriers.

Elizabeth Parr-Johnston, having completed terms as presidents of two universities in Atlantic Canada, reviews some problems that have already been identified as well as raising several other important issues on the direction in which we are headed. She argues that we are no longer in a world where there will be large increases in government funding. It is a world in which governments are determined to play a more directive role. In that context she raises an issue, where a greater emphasis is being placed on applied research of ownership of intellectual property which will become increasingly important.

All of the panelists agree that the universities currently are seriously underfunded. Peter George explains that one of the main objectives of the task force which he chairs is to generate proposals for appropriately augmenting the funding of the universities. John Chant argues, however, that the real problem lies in the centrally-directed, overly-regulated nature of the Canadian university system. Major pressures are being exerted by provincial governments whose objectives are more concerned with seeing that large numbers of young people get admitted to some sort of higher education and that they receive substantially subsidized education which has broad voter appeal.

Chant's point is that, in the area of higher education, Canadian governments continue to engage in central planning long after the failure of central planning has been made evident. The simple solution that Chant puts forward is for governments to fund students, not universities. In his role as final speaker, Douglas Auld, president of an Ontario community college, concurs with Chant and sees value in incorporating more market-type influences into the higher education system. Auld also raises the matter of the mix of institutions. Sorting out the division of resources between colleges and universities is not something that can be satisfactorily done by central planning. A task for economic policy analysts will be to convince governments that competitive market-like solutions have some advantages in getting resources efficiently allocated. However, access to higher education is strongly influenced by the existing distribution of income and it has an important bearing on the future distribution. It is only appropriate, then, that much of the attention of the presentations is directed to mechanisms for better financing of students so as to ensure that they obtain the type and extent of higher education that allows them to achieve their opportunities.

The scope of topics that can be covered in a two-day conference on which this volume is based is necessarily limited. We have chosen to focus on those topics that are of immediate interest to current policy debates, and that therefore are amenable to remedial action. There remain, however, some overriding issues that, even if they are not resolved, should inform that debate. One concerns the very role of the public sector in the financing and delivery of postsecondary education. In principle, education could be left to the private sector. Arguments for public intervention ultimately rely on failure of the private sector to achieve socially acceptable outcomes. Such arguments include (i) classic market failures arising from external benefits provided to society from the dissemination of knowledge associated with university education, whether resulting from research or embodied in graduates; (ii) shortcomings in credit markets or markets for risk-sharing that inhibit potential students from acquiring a postsecondary education; and (iii) social objectives like equality of opportunity and redistributive equity that private provision cannot address. Then, given that a case is made for public intervention, what are the most appropriate forms of that intervention? Should postsecondary institutions be public, private, or some combination of both? Should finance be directed to students or to institutions, or both? To what extent should universities be regulated? More generally, what kinds and mixes of services should these institutions provide? Finally, given that postsecondary institutions are partly publicly funded, how should they be made accountable for the use of those funds? This raises issues of university governance that the conference only briefly addressed. What policies can ensure that the interests of universities are aligned with those of all other stakeholders, including the students? This volume only scratches the surface of these important issues. Clearly there is more work to be done.

References

Association of Universities and Colleges of Canada (AUCC). 2002. *Trends in Higher Education*. Ottawa: AUCC.

Axelrod, P. 2002. *Values in Conflict: The University, the Marketplace, and the Trials of Liberal Education*. Montreal: McGill-Queen's University Press.

Barr, N. 2004. "Higher Education Funding", *Oxford Review of Economic Policy* 20(2), 264-283.

Barr, N. and I. Crawford. 2005. *Financing Higher Education: Lessons from the U.K.* London: Routledge.

Bercuson, D., R. Bothwell and J.L. Granatstein. 1997. *Petrified Campus: The Crisis in Canada's Universities*. Toronto: Random House of Canada.

Bok, D. 2003. *Universities in the Marketplace: The Commercialization of Higher Education*. Princeton, NJ: Princeton University Press.

Canadian Association of University Teachers (CAUT). 2004. *CAUT Almanac of Post-Secondary Education in Canada, 2004*. Ottawa: CAUT.

Card, D. 2003. "Canadian Emigration to the United States", in C.M. Beach, A.G. Green and J.G. Reitz (eds.), *Canadian Immigration Policy for the 21st Century*. Kingston: John Deutsch Institute, Queen's University, 295-312.

Chant, J. and W. Gibson. 2002. "Quantity or Quality? Research at Canadian University", in D. Laidler (ed.), *Renovating the Ivory Tower: Canada University and the Knowledge Economy*. Policy Study No. 37. Toronto: C.D. Howe Institute.

Council for Employment, Income and Social Cohesion. 2003. *Education and Redistribution*. Paris.

Council of Ontario Universities (COU). 2003. *Advancing Ontario's Future through Advanced Degrees*. Report of the COU Task Force on Future Requirements for Graduate Education in Ontario. Toronto: Task Force.

Davenport, P. 2002. "Universities and the Knowledge Economy", in D. Laidler (ed.), *Renovating the Ivory Tower: Canadian Universities and the Knowledge Economy*. Policy Study No. 37. Toronto: C.D. Howe Institute.

Drummond, D. 2004. "TD Economics Special Report on Post-Secondary Education in Canada", *T.D. Financial Group*, March 11.

The Economist. 2002. "Britain's Universities: On the Road to Ruin" and "Higher Education: The Ruin of Britain's Universities", November 16.

_____. 2004. "Universities: Pay or Decay" and "Special Report: Financing Universities — Who Pays to Study?" January 24.

Ehrenberg, R.G. 2003. "Studying Ourselves: The Academic Labor Market", *Journal of Labor Economics* 21(2), 267-287.

_____. 2004. "Prospects in the Academic Labor Market for Economists", *Journal of Economic Perspectives* 18 (Spring), 227-238.

_____, ed. 2004. *Governing Academia: Who is in Charge at the Modern University?* Ithaca: Cornell University Press.

Johnston, A.D. 2002a. "A Lament for Quality", *Maclean's*, May 6.

_____. 2002b. "The Crisis in Quality", *Maclean's*, June 10.

Journal of Economic Perspectives. 1999. "Symposium: The Economics of Higher Education", Vol. 13 (Winter).

Junor, S. and A. Usher. 2004. *The Price of Knowledge: Access and Student Finance in Canada.* Montreal: Canada Millennium Scholarship Foundation.

Kirp, D.L. 2003. *Shakespeare, Einstein, and the Bottom Line: The Marketing of Higher Education.* Cambridge, MA: Harvard University Press.

Laidler, D., ed. 2002. *Renovating the Ivory Tower: Canadian Universities and the Knowledge Economy.* Policy Study No. 37. Toronto: C.D. Howe Institute.

Linsenmeier, D.M., H.S. Rosen and C.E. Rouse. 2002. "Financial Aid Packages and College Enrollment Decisions: An Econometric Case Study". NBER Working Paper No. 9228. Cambridge, MA: National Bureau of Economic Research.

Pocklington, T. and A. Tupper. 2002. *No Place to Learn: Why Universities Aren't Working.* Vancouver: UBC Press.

Shapiro, B. 2003. "Canada's Universities: Quantitative Success, Qualitative Concerns", *Policy Options* (September).

Smith, D.C. 1996. *Excellence Accessibility Responsibility: Report of the Advisory Panel on Future Directions for Postsecondary Education.* Toronto: Ontario Ministry of Colleges and Universities.

Spencer, B.G. 2002. *The Double Cohort and the Shortage of Faculty: How Big Are the Problems?* Backgrounder No. 64. Toronto: C.D. Howe Institute.

Statistics Canada. 2003. "Changing Patterns of University Finance", *Education Quarterly Review* 9(2).

Swail. W.S. 2004. *The Affordability of University Education: A Perspective from Both Sides of the 49th Parallel.* Washington, DC: Educational Policy Institute.

United Kingdom. Department of Education and Skills. 2003. *The Future of Higher Education.* London: HMSO.

Section I

Introduction: Key Issues in Postsecondary Education

Key Issues Currently Facing American Higher Education

Ronald G. Ehrenberg

To paraphrase the title of one of my books, "Tuition Keeps Rising" in the United States — during the last quarter of a century undergraduate tuition and fees have risen at annual rates exceeding the rate of inflation by an average of 2.5 to 3.5 percentage points (Ehrenberg, 2002). This has led one key Congressman to propose that institutions that raise tuition by more than twice the rate of inflation for several years in a row should be penalized by the government; fortunately his colleagues in Congress rejected this idea (Burd, 2004). Faculty salary increases are not the major cause of increases in tuition — average faculty salaries at four-year colleges and universities in the United States have risen at only about 0.5 to 1.0% a year more than the rate of inflation during the period (Ehrenberg, 2004).

The reasons for tuition increases differ in public and private higher education. In the private sector, factors include the increased costs of technology, student services, and institutional financial aid; the unrelenting competition to be the best in every dimension of an institution's activities; and, at the research universities, the increasing institutional costs of scientific research (to which I will return). In public higher education, all

The Cornell Higher Education Research Institute (CHERI) is financially supported by the Atlantic Philanthropies (USA) Inc. and the Andrew W. Mellon Foundation. As Director, I am grateful to them for their support.

these factors are also important, however, another important driver is the withdrawal of state support.

In his Cornell PhD dissertation, Michael Rizzo documents that the share of state budgets going to higher education has shrunk by over one-third over the last 30 years (Rizzo, 2003). Although there is no reason why higher education's share should remain constant over time, the net result of this decline is that per capita state appropriations per full-time equivalent student at public higher education institutions rose in constant dollars from $5,622 in FY1974 to $6,717 in FY2004 — an average increase of only 0.6% a year. This occurred during a period when the real costs faced by higher education institutions were rising much more rapidly and when private higher education institutions were relentlessly annually increasing their tuitions by a much greater percentage than state appropriations were increasing. Public higher education institutions responded to their diminishing state support by increasing their tuition levels at slightly higher percentage rates than the private institutions did. However, because public tuition rates started at much lower levels, the public institutions generated less income from these increases than their private counterparts did from theirs. Thus, the resource base of public academic institutions fell relative to the resource base of private academic institutions.

As a result, while the average professor at a public doctoral university earned about 91% of what his counterpart at a private doctoral university earned in 1978–79, by 2003–04 the percentage had fallen to about 74% (Ehrenberg, 2004). Increasingly public institutions are having great difficulty attracting and retaining high-quality faculty, which surely influences the standard of what is going on in public higher education where the vast majority of our students are educated.

In the face of persistent rates of increase in tuition that exceed inflation, the changing pattern of financial aid in the United States has had an effect on who gets a college education. In 1982–83, over 50% of federal financial aid was in the form of grant aid, but by 2002–03, this had fallen to 40% (College Board, 2003b, Figure 6). Most federal financial aid now comes in the form of loans and research suggests that students from lower-income families are less willing than other students to take on large loan burdens to finance their higher education. Federal grant aid has not kept up with increases in college costs. During the mid-1970s the average Pell grant received by students was about 46% of the average costs (including room and board) of attending a public higher education institution. Last year, the ratio was under 30% (the ratio is much lower at private institutions, but they have more institutional resources for financial aid) (ibid., Figure 7).

Ronald G. Ehrenberg

The Bush administration has proposed increasing loan limits (which private higher education institutions applaud), but has shown little interest in increasing Pell grant levels.

The share of states' higher education budgets that go to public academic institutions has also declined over time — putting added pressure on public tuitions — as states are now devoting a greater share of their higher education expenditures to providing grant aid to students (Rizzo, 2003). Moreover, increasingly, this grant aid is non-need based. As late as 1993, less than 10% of all state grant aid to students was non-need based, but the growth of programs such as the Hope Scholarship program in Georgia, which started in 1993, raised this to almost 25% by 2001 (ibid., Figure 10). Today there are 12 other states that have Hope-type programs. More and more, financial aid at private colleges and universities in the United States is also "merit" rather than needs-based, as private institutions use financial aid for enrolment management purposes (to attracting a class with "desirable characteristics" at least cost) rather than to permit lower-income students access to them. Probably less than 15 to 20 private academic institutions provide financial aid based solely on students' financial need today.

As a result, the United States has not achieved its goal of reducing educational inequality based upon family income levels — differentials in college enrolment by family income quartiles are almost as large today as they were 30 years ago (College Board, 2003a, Figure 11). Moreover, more and more students from lower-income families are being forced, for financial reasons, to enter higher education through public two-year colleges. Given projections of growing college-age populations during the next decade, primarily from underrepresented groups, and limitations on state resources for both operating and capital expenses, we may increasingly see limitations on access to college (such as is happening in California) and disparities in college attainment, by income and race/ethnicity, may worsen in the United States in the years ahead.

The importance of scientific research has grown at American universities fuelled by major advances in genomics, advanced materials and information technology, and by dramatic increases in governmental and private funding for research. However, in spite of the latter, a little known fact is that the costs of research are increasingly being borne by the universities themselves out of their institutional resources. The share of universities research and development expenditures coming out of their own pockets grew from 11.2% in 1972 to almost 21% in 2000 (Ehrenberg, Rizzo and Jakubson, 2003).

There are many reasons for why universities are increasingly bearing the costs of their faculty members' research, but one important one is the magnitude of the start-up cost packages needed to attract new faculty members. At the Research I universities, these costs average $300,000 to $500,000 for assistant professors and often well over a $1 million for senior faculty. While universities properly view these costs as investments in their faculty members' scientific research productivity, where they get the money to fund these investments is of great concern. Public universities, more often than private universities, sometimes leave faculty positions vacant until salary savings can generate necessary start-up cost funds; these vacant faculty positions surely have an impact on the quality of undergraduate education at the public institutions (Enrenberg, Rizzo and Condie, 2003). Researchers at CHERI have found evidence that the increasing institutional costs of research have led both public and private institutions to increase student-faculty ratios and substitute part-time and full-time non-tenure-track faculty for tenure-track faculty.

In fact, throughout American higher education, institutions are increasingly relying on part-time and full-time non-tenure-track faculty. During the 1990s, the share of full-time faculty not on tenure tracks and the ratio of part-time to full-time faculty grew significantly. Moreover, the share of newly hired faculty not on tenure tracks grew to over 50% (Ehrenberg and Zhang, 2004). Preliminary research findings suggest that as the share of part-time faculty grows at an institution, undergraduate students' attrition rates rise and their graduation rates fall. As the share of non-tenure-track faculty increases, the demand for full-time, tenure-track faculty declines and the attractiveness of entering PhD study also declines for American college graduates.

This may be one of the factors that explain the increase in the share of PhDs granted by American universities going to temporary residents of the United States. During the last 30 years, this share rose from 10.4 to 26.3%. In key science areas the increase was more dramatic. In 2002, almost 40% of all PhDs in the physical sciences and 55% of those in engineering were awarded to temporary residents (Hoffer et al., 2003, Table 11). As higher education institutions improve around the world, there is no guarantee that foreign students will want to continue to pursue PhD study in the United States and no guarantee that those who do will remain in the United States for employment. Given the decline in the number of PhDs produced in total by US universities in recent years and the large share of American faculty rapidly approaching retirement ages, a major problem facing American higher education is who will be our next generation of professors.

References

Burd, S.J. 2004. "Rep. McKeon is Expected to Drop Effort to Penalize Colleges that Raise Tuition Too Much", *Chronicle of Higher Education*, March 3 (daily electronic edition, available to subscribers at www.chronicle.com).

Ehrenberg, R.G. 2002. *Tuition Rising: Why College Costs So Much.* Cambridge, MA: Harvard University Press.

_____. 2004, "Don't Blame Faculty for High Tuition: The Annual Report on the Economic Status of the Profession: 2003-2004", *Academe* 90 (March/April), 22-33.

Ehrenberg R.G. and L. Zhang. 2004. "The Changing Nature of Faculty Employment". CHERI Working Paper No. WP44. Ithaca, NY: Cornell Higher Education Research Institute. Paper available at www.ilr.cornell.edu/cheri.

Ehrenberg, R.G., M.J. Rizzo and S.S. Condie. 2003. "Start-Up Costs in American Research Universities". CHERI Working Paper No. WP33. Ithaca, NY: Cornell Higher Education Research Institute. Paper available at www.ilr.cornell.edu/cheri.

Ehrenberg, R.G., M.J. Rizzo and G.H. Jakubson. 2003. "Who Bears the Growing Cost of Science at Universities". CHERI Working Paper No. WP35. Ithaca, NY: Cornell Higher Education Research Institute. Paper available at www.ilr.cornell.edu/cheri.

Hoffer, T.B. *et. al.* 2003. *Doctorate Recipients from United States Universities: Summary Report 2002.* Chicago: NORC at the University of Chicago.

Rizzo, M.J. 2003. "A (Less than) Zero Sum Game? State Funding For Public Higher Education: How Public Higher Education Institutions Have Lost". CHERI Working Paper No. WP42. Ithaca, NY: Cornell Higher Education Research Institute. Paper available at www.ilr.cornell.edu/cheri.

College Board. 2003a. *Trends in College Pricing.* Washington, DC: Washington Office of the College Board.

_____. 2003b. *Trends in Student Aid.* Washington, DC: Washington Office of the College Board.

Incentives Facing Canadian Universities: Some Possible Consequences

David Laidler

Introduction

In Canada, debates about postsecondary education and health care have much in common. Both activities are largely in the public sector, their provision being the responsibility of provincial governments, albeit with significant federal financial input. In the political domain, debates about both systems focus on funding and accessibility, but, in both cases, economists must also be concerned with the implications for the systems' efficient functioning of the incentives inherent in decisions taken about funding and accessibility. Widespread ideological opposition to allowing the very special structures inherent in market-based activity to play important roles in these sectors has, however, distracted attention from the fact that *any* way of organizing them will create incentives that profoundly influence the outcomes they deliver, and that no rational policy choices can be made without their careful analysis.

Though much has been written by economists on these matters, their arguments have yet to make much headway with the public. There is nothing to be done about this but to keep trying: hence the motivation for this brief essay. It will concentrate on universities, for no better reason than that this is the area of postsecondary education with which I am familiar. The paper will discuss, in turn: the incentives that have rendered no longer viable the provisions that Canada made from the 1960s onwards for the funding of a widely accessible university sector; the incentives that have both driven and are inherent in the arrangements that have emerged piecemeal in the last decade or so, and some of their probably baleful consequences; and it will then offer some suggestions for changing the incentive structures currently at work in directions that might improve the system's performance. The use of the phrase "possible consequences" in my title reflects a profound sympathy with the warning issued by Clément Lemelin (2005) that when it comes to tinkering with any system as complicated as the universities, the devil may indeed lurk in the details. I am more confident that I am raising at least some of the right questions about this sector than that I am offering the right answers to them.

Some Basic Trade-offs

Let me begin with the assertion that there is something to be said for a university system that provides space at close to zero cost for all suitably qualified applicants. Canada created such a system in the 1960s and 1970s, and it seemed to work rather well for a while. In the nineteenth century we learned to accept the idea that primary education was sufficiently important to an individual's ability to be a fully contributing member of society that its provision should be in significant measure a social responsibility and mandatory for all potential recipients into the bargain. As the twentieth century progressed, society became richer and more complicated, the skills needed to function therein became more extensive, and we accepted the widening of this case to cover secondary education, though we stopped short of making school attendance mandatory up to the point of high-school graduation. No doubt this line of argument becomes a harder stretch as we extend it to the community college and university levels, particularly if we honestly face the difficulties inherent in deciding how to, and who should, draw the line between "suitably qualified applicants" and the others, but it does not become irrelevant. Traditional arguments for the collective provision of educational opportunities surely retain considerable validity beyond the age of 18.

The trouble is, however, that Canada's universities have been extraordinarily successful in adding value to what in earlier times would have been regarded as some extremely unpromising raw material, and that the resources required for them to go on doing in the twenty-first century what

David Laidler

they did so successfully for a while in the twentieth on a significantly smaller scale, have large opportunity costs in terms of other worthwhile activities. These costs require that difficult choices be made on important margins, and, obviously, the incentive structures that face decisionmakers will determine how those choices will be made.

As far as university funding is concerned, and particularly long-term funding for base budgets, the primary decisionmakers are provincial governments. Thus the alternative uses of resources, which are always and everywhere visible when decisions are made, are in health care, primary and secondary education, and in providing consumption opportunities to those whose disposable income would be reduced by tax increases. The visibility of these particular margins extends well beyond the bureaucrats and politicians who must make the spending and taxation choices, moreover. Given Canada's demographics, not to mention the public's rather newly developed, but already seemingly deeply entrenched, distaste for higher taxes, these facts make it inconceivable that there can be any hope for a system of public funding for universities that would support the system of its present scale but with the generosity that ruled in the 1970s; nor, on the other hand, does there seem to be any constituency for a significant cut in the size of the university sector.

The piecemeal movement away from a university system almost completely and generously supported by provincial governments, that we have seen over the last two decades, has not been the product of some deep-laid ideological plot that will be foiled once revealed, nor even of a series of episodes of political opportunism whose effects can be easily reversed. It is, rather, the result of political responses to incentives created by fundamental socio-economic forces — some of them the outcome of the very success of the expansion of the university sector itself. The configuration of the political framework through which these effects are now playing out in Canada is influencing many specific characteristics of the overall process, and frequently not for the better, but the process itself cannot be reversed. To argue that it can be, and to urge that we try to go back to the university system of the 1970s, but on a larger scale, is to be irrelevant. The only appropriate response to the underlying pressures on Canada's universities as they currently exist is to analyze their effects with a view to ensuring that those institutions face an incentive structure that is more likely to produce constructive rather than destructive outcomes for the sector.

The Productivity Agenda

Universities are institutions whose business it is to create and disseminate knowledge. As Douglas Auld (1996) has reminded us, they are places where researchers teach and teachers do research, and they are neither research institutes nor teaching colleges. This does not mean that every course that a university offers should be, or indeed ever has been, always taught by a researcher, or that every researcher attached to a university must regularly devote a significant fraction of his or her time to the classroom, but it does mean that, in a university, students and researchers alike should routinely encounter one another as members of a community devoted to the advancement of knowledge. That is what happened in Canadian universities, albeit on a small scale, before their expansion got under way in the 1960s, and it is this characteristic that makes them potentially important players in what it has become fashionable to call the "knowledge economy" of the present day. Even so, there is an all important difference between attitudes then and now. The perception that creating and acquiring knowledge for its own sake was not just a privately, but also a socially, valuable activity and therefore deserving of public subsidy, has been replaced by the idea that these activities are materially productive and worthy of support for that reason.

This change in some measure reflects the outcome of developments within economics. It has long been understood that, if the gains from university research or education, whether these take the form of an agreeable consumption activity or the creation and acquisition of marketable skills, accrue only to the individuals directly involved in these activities, then there is no strong case for subsidizing them, and that the case for their public support must therefore rest on the existence of externalities of one sort or another. Evidence of externalities has been extremely hard to find up till now, however, and, though the climate of opinion might shift in future in the light of new evidence such as that recently surveyed by James Davies (2003), the case for public support of the generalized pursuit of knowledge for its own sake made on the basis of their existence currently finds few takers among economists.

On the other hand, the ideas that new knowledge in science and technology is materially productive, that it becomes a public good once created, and hence that it is likely to be inefficiently under-provided by any system that relies on private incentives alone, are nowadays extremely popular. So is the related idea that a labour force well trained in these areas is needed to exploit such knowledge. And in addition, it is widely held that many of these benefits accrue at the national rather than provincial levels. Small wonder, then, that Canadian university administrators in search of new and more effective arguments to attract public funding have responded to the federal government's "productivity agenda", and have welcomed funding increases heavily biassed towards supporting research and advanced training in science and technology.

It is hard to look a well-endowed gift-horse in the mouth, particularly when its presentation signifies that the donor believes the recipient to be of vital national importance and also comes with assurances that the transaction is well justified by the current state of economic knowledge. But there is room for worry that the rush by Canadian universities to participate in the knowledge economy owes more to their desire to replace the provincial funding they have recently lost than to well-founded confidence that more research and teaching in science and technology will produce faster technical progress, a higher rate of growth of labour productivity, and therefore, more rapidly expanding living standards for the population at large. If the universities fail to deliver here, they will invite a backlash and the evidence that they will be able to deliver is a good deal more fragile than is commonly supposed.

To begin with, it is, as noted by Laidler (2002) all too easy to confuse the *level of productivity* with its first time derivative, the *rate of productivity growth,* and, as noted by Jeffrey Smith (2002), equally easy to confuse *average* with *marginal* productivity. The evidence that the material returns accruing to those educated at universities in science and technology subjects are comfortably positive, and higher than those in the arts and humanities, is overwhelming. Even if this did imply that a labour force with more rather than fewer workers trained in these fields would generate higher level of productivity, it would imply precisely nothing about the capacity of such a labour force to generate productivity that rises faster. However, the results that we have for rates of return to education in various fields are for their average and not their marginal values. It may well be that, for the student currently enrolled in the humanities who has, among his or her peers, the best prospects of success in the sciences or technology, there is no difference in the rates of return to be expected in the two fields. That is, indeed, the outcome that a system in which well-informed students pick their own programs on the basis of expected material rewards would tend to produce.

If we were starting from such a point, then policies designed to over-ride students' choices and expand science and technology programs would not increase, and might even decrease, the economy's overall level of productivity, let alone its growth rate. Now, I hasten to add that I have not the faintest idea whether either of the two conjectures upon which this conclusion is based is true or false, but the point I wish to make is that nor does anyone else. In the current state of knowledge, neither government nor universities have a secure basis for any claim that an expansion of programs in science and technology at the expense of those in other fields will have positive effects on either the level or rate of growth of Canadian living standards. Given the evident strength of their incentives to make such a claim, however, let us hope that they get lucky.

Matters are no different when it comes to university research. Perhaps more research in science and technology will indeed lead not just to more efficiency in productive processes, but to a more rapid rate of growth in that efficiency too. We have seen some dramatic instances of this apparently happening — in electronics and bio-technology, for example. But we must be careful not to fall into a "reefer madness" interpretation of innovation-driven productivity growth. To show that the tragic decline of a single drug-crazed homicidal maniac began with a single puff of marijuana does not tell us much about the likely effects of a widespread increase in experimentation with that substance among young people. There are many more clusters of universities, some of them even equipped with research parks, than there are Silicon Valleys. It would be nice to know why this is so, but at present we do not.

Though modern endogenous growth theory of the type accessibly surveyed by Paul Romer (1994) has attracted widespread academic attention and admiration, its central features, namely that the creation of a public good called "knowledge" can overcome diminishing returns, and its apparent implication that by subsidizing that creation, government can contribute to perpetual economic expansion, seem hard to square with empirical evidence about how productivity growth actually comes about. It may be possible for this approach to meet the challenge implicit in Arnold Harberger's (1998) "Vision of the Growth Process", which arises from his finding that "real cost reduction", as he calls it, seems to be a bottom-up phenomenon, whose appearance is more akin to the random sprouting of mushrooms, than the generalized rising of yeast. However, the challenge has not yet been met: if university research generates public goods which are so widely accessible once created that the activity requires public subsidy, the activity should surely lead to across-the-board productivity increases, if only within specific sectors, but it does not.

And, incidentally, if productivity-enhancing knowledge is a public good, perhaps the taxpayers of a smallish open economy like Canada would

David Laidler

be better off not subsidizing its production, but free-riding on the efforts of others. This, moreover, is to say nothing of an awkward analytic result generated a little while ago by Philippe Aghion and Peter Howitt (1992) to the effect that, if innovations cannot be instantaneously replicated by competitors, and if those who make them can capture for a while not just the benefits arising from their own advance but also the profits that had been accruing to those using the previous "state of the art" technique, then market mechanisms might produce not too little technical progress, but too much of it relative to the resources devoted to bringing it about.

Now as with my doubts about the extent of university teaching's potential to contribute to Canada's success in the "knowledge economy", so it is with my skepticism about the productivity payoffs from research in science and technology: I would not deny that there is a potential for such payoffs that can support a case for subsidizing such activities; but my point is that there are other arguments, at least as plausible, that point in the opposite direction and that these are currently getting insufficient attention.

Incentives Within Universities

Canada's universities are hardly to be blamed for responding to the incentives presented to them by a changing political marketplace. At the very time that the provincial audience for their older arguments for public support has been losing its enthusiasm, the federal government has grown increasingly attentive to a new case, and one that just might, after all, be valid. But it is hard to avoid the conclusion that the universities are currently taking a gamble on over-selling themselves, and that serious losses are in prospect if their gamble fails.

The losses to which I am referring here go far beyond the simple damage that will be done among the general public to universities' reputations should the productivity agenda produce disappointing results. They also involve changes that are taking place within universities as a consequence of their having signed on to that agenda which will be hard to reverse if they prove to have been for the worse. Universities are nowadays paying more attention to science and technology and less to what we must now learn to call the "humane sciences", and also, within both areas, the emphasis has shifted towards applied research on practical problems whose payoffs are likely to be reasonably sure, not to mention visible.

These tendencies are not simply a result of changes in the incentives associated with public support. The business sector is an increasingly important source of funding for universities, whether in the form of research contracts or donations. That sector has its own obvious interest in results-oriented research, and it also exerts influence through its lobbyists on governments' expenditures at all levels. In some jurisdictions, indeed, a corporatist agenda of public-private partnerships that impinges heavily on the universities has been actively adopted by government: Ontario's Super-Build Program and its Research and Development Challenge Fund are two cases in point.

The increasing attention paid to interdisciplinarity, not just among funding agencies but also within universities, provides striking evidence of the above-mentioned shift of emphasis, and the universities' response to it. Practical problems seldom respect the boundaries of academic subjects, and it should go without saying that research designed to have a relatively early payoff can also have considerable value. Cooperation among disciplines is often vital to achieving such a payoff, moreover, and there can be no harm in helping researchers adopt the best means available to meet their ends. But research councils and universities now make inter-disciplinarity an end in itself, as John Polanyi, as quoted by John Chant and William Gibson (2002, p. 147) has pointed out, and in so doing, they also *ipso facto* privilege applied and policy-oriented work over basic research.

We can be sure that the faculty and graduate students of these institutions will respond to the incentives that they thereby have created, and that those who are particularly interested in basic research will consider making a move to other jurisdictions, to be replaced by those of a more practical bent. One does not have to take a position on whether basic discipline-based work has been over- or under-emphasized in the past to conclude that these current trends must be changing not just the balance of the research that gets done in universities, but also of the teaching. After all, universities are, or should be, places where the bulk of the teaching is done by researchers.

Other incentives inherent in current ways of financing universities also impinge with particular force on their teaching activities. Research in science and technology of the type that best meets the productivity agenda tends to be building and equipment intensive, and it is a platitude among university fundraisers that it is easier to raise private money for new buildings than for other causes such as maintenance budgets. Even after recent changes in their rules, however, grants from the federal research councils do not fully cover the overheads of the projects they support, while certain public programs (eg., Ontario's Super Build Fund), not to mention some private donations, devoted to financing new buildings and equipment, require that matching funds be provided by the university. Moreover, the ongoing provincial funding programs on which universities rely for their base budgets, those from which they are expected to meet their long-term commitments to provide laboratories and equipment as well as to pay the salaries of tenured and tenure-track faculty and career members of support staff, are typically based on student numbers. Though they weight students by the academic level of their programs, they do not generally differentiate among disciplines, while the scope available to universities to set different fees for their programs based on the costs of providing them vary considerably across provinces and is severely limited in all of them.

The interactions here face universities with strong incentives to expand their activities in relatively expensive areas, even though the direct funding available is not sufficient to meet all the costs of that expansion, and the key to understanding how this can be lies in their ability to support the expansion of activities that are attractive to government and other donors by internal subsidies drawn from surpluses in operating grants and tuition revenue generated elsewhere within the institutions. Such cross-subsidization is, of course, a time-honoured practice. Twenty or 30 years ago, no one expected that provincial government grants nominally attached to enrolments in arts and social science faculties would all be spent within those units. It was understood that medical schools and faculties of science and engineering, for example, had particular needs for equipment and supplies and that the overall levels of provincial grants had been set with this in mind. So long as the latter condition held, an untidy system of internally determined redistribution was workable and even desirable, which is why such a well-informed commentator as Claude Montmarquette (2004) still regards it with some favour.

But provincial grants have long ceased to be adequate, and the desires of governments and business donors to see expansion of expensive operations have simultaneously become more intense. That is why universities now face the temptation to abuse the mechanisms that permit the internal redistribution of funds by running courses, or even whole programs, not to meet academic goals but to generate revenue out of which other operations can be supported. Hard information on what is actually happening on this front is difficult to come by, but there is anecdotal evidence that such abuse is already taking place, particularly in the humane sciences, where the costs of providing instruction are, in any case, low. Rubenstein and Clifton (2002), for example, suggest that some universities are turning a blind eye to falling academic standards in undergraduate programs in the humanities because of their desire for the revenue that these generate.

A little speculation with round numbers will, in any event, reveal the incentives nowadays faced by universities seeking to meet the need for matching funds, or to cover the overheads of research projects that are attractive in the political and business circles on which they rely for so much of their support. Suppose that the physical and administrative structure of a faculty of arts or social science is already in place, that it costs $40,000 in direct outlay to staff one full course, and that five such courses make up a full student load. If the average class size is 50 students, and each student pays $4,500 in tuition fees and brings in $3,500 in government grants, then the mark-up on the marginal student is $4,000 per annum. Readers may make their own calculations about the effects on this figure of, for example, (a) employing sessional instructors at a cost of about $25,000 per course, (b) operating with average class sizes of 75 or 100, (c) accommodating more students by increasing the sizes of already existing classes, from, say, 50 to 100, or (d) they may substitute their own assumptions. The point of this example is not to provide exact estimates of anything that might now be happening in any particular institution, but merely to illustrate the possibilities open to any one of them should it decide to turn one or more of its academic units into what is sometimes referred to as a "cash-cow".

It is not conducive to the maintenance of academic standards in Canadian universities to expose their hard-pressed administrators to such incentives, not least, it might be noted, because, when it comes to the matter of replacing established faculty with sessional instructors in the classroom, they invite a weakening of that essential characteristic of a university, namely that it be a place where researchers teach and teachers carry out research.

Accountability of Universities

Accountability has become something of a buzzword in Canadian universities, and the line of responsibility to which it seems to refer runs from faculty members and other employees, through administrators, to donors, bureaucrats and politicians. Politicians in turn, being elected to office, are presumed to represent the interests of the general public in this scheme of things. There is some logic to this approach. Donors are surely entitled to keep an eye on how their money is spent if they so wish, and a university that does not want to allow them such a privilege is always free to reject their gifts. Furthermore, if significant amounts of taxpayers' money are being used to support universities' teachers and researchers, then the case for making them answerable for their activities to the elected representatives of those taxpayers is surely iron-clad.

Even so, something important is all too often missing from current discussions of the accountability of universities, namely an acknowledgement of their direct responsibilities to their students for the quality of the instruction that they offer. Matters are in flux here at the moment, however, because tuition fees have been rising, and already constitute a significantly larger fraction of university budgets than they once did. Some programs indeed, often but not solely in professional schools, are already operating on what amounts to a full cost-recovery process. The central theme of the foregoing discussion has been that universities seem to respond to the desires of those who provide them with the resources they need to operate, and if the importance of students in this respect is increasing, then they are likely to get more attention.

The continuation of the trend towards greater reliance on tuition income is eminently feasible because of the positive returns that accrue to recipients of university education. It would also be well worth encouraging because, as I have argued at some length elsewhere (Laidler, 2002), it is in this trend that we seem to have the best chance of finding a meaningful counter-weight to the universities' excessive reliance on the business sector, and a government sector motivated by a productivity agenda. To be sure, students' decisions, based on their own information and desires, might in fact reveal that the doubts that I have expressed above about the desirability of the current balance of activities in universities, and of ongoing changes therein, are misplaced; but then again, they might not; and in either case we could have a great deal more confidence in the social desirability of the outcome than we do now.

To allow the fees of different programs to reflect the costs of providing them, and to have students themselves pay those fees — where they might get the wherewithal to do so is an issue I shall take up in a moment — would address many difficulties inherent in current arrangements, which have already been touched upon. Such a system would draw for us the line between suitably qualified applicants and others. Those whose perceptions of the benefits likely to accrue to them from going to university were such that they were willing to pay the costs of going would apply, and the others would not. And any individual university's own perception of any applicant's likelihood of success would determine who, among the applicants, got admitted. There would be no need for bureaucrats to engage in research in order to make decisions about these issues from the centre of the system.

Similar processes would also work to determine the allocation of students among disciplines within universities, and among discipline-based and interdisciplinary programs too. There would no longer be any need for bureaucrats to worry about their ignorance of discrepancies between average and marginal returns to various programs as they made decisions about how many places to provide in them, nor would they then need to design measures to get those places filled. Those decisions would no longer be made centrally, but by the interactions among individual students and university teachers and administrators, once more with students' own information and desires playing an important part in the process. To the extent that the outcomes here were in accord with currently held ideas about the likely payoffs from the "productivity agenda", they would encourage the latter; and to the extent that they did not, they would inhibit its over-enthusiastic pursuit. In either case, it would be much harder to argue about the desirability of the outcome than it is under current circumstances.

A decision would also be likely to emerge from such a system about a matter that is often discussed, but about which those currently in charge seem unwilling to make up their minds: namely, whether Canada should seek to concentrate scarce academic talent in a few universities, and allow others to operate at lower standards, or whether to seek equality among all institutions. At the moment, no one seems willing to make up their minds about this matter and we have a system in which, obvious differences notwithstanding, myths about the universality of high quality still persist, at least in the domain of political rhetoric. Such a state of affairs would not long survive in a framework in which the choices of well-informed students played a significant role in the allocation of resources within the country's university system.

But, of course, everything in the last few paragraphs hinges on the assumption that the students making the choices would be "well-informed". On this contentious point, I must confess to the economist's usual optimism about peoples' ability to seek out information and to use it wisely — when faced with the right incentives, it should go without saying. Even now, the amount of attention given to the information about Canada's universities provided by *Maclean's* survey suggests that there is a great deal of interest in getting their decisions right among potential students. To judge from some recent anecdotal evidence, they are also acting on the data this survey provides to the point of inducing responses from universities, not all of them to their credit. A system in which students paid more of the costs of their programs than they now do would create a demand for more and better information than is now available. It is hard to believe that the market would not provide it, and even harder to believe that such a state of affairs would not represent an improvement over the *status quo.* Would "cash-cow" courses and programs (if indeed they do exist under present circumstances) long survive the scrutiny of well-informed, full-fee-paying students?

Even so, the well-known trouble with making universities rely on tuition fees for a substantial portion of their revenue is that, if undertaken in isolation, such a measure would not only limit access to them, but would do so in a socially divisive way: richer students would attend and poorer ones would not. Here, it is important to recall that this well-known problem has complicated roots, not all of which lie in economic inequality. There is a well-understood gap in the capital market that arises from the fact that a loan taken now cannot be secured by offering a claim on the human capital it will be used to create should the borrower later default. And there are also well-understood solutions to this problem involving government intervention in the educational-loan market. If there were no more to the matter than this, there would be no case for making subsidies a part of any such intervention.

There is more to it, however. Though the payoff from university education is undoubtedly high enough to make financing its acquisition through unsubsidized loans an attractive prospect *on average*, we also need to worry about what happens *on the margin.* The payoff from this particular investment is risky for any individual, and in some instances, it does *ex post* fall below a value that would justify having undertaken it. This considera-tion suggests the desirability of an insurance market in this area, and the widely-held belief that those from poorer families are more averse to such risks than others adds greater weight to the case for providing such insur-ance by making the repayment of student loans income-contingent. But, of course, wherever there is insurance, there arise questions about adverse selection and moral hazard. Beyond noting that income-contingent loan schemes can come in many shapes and sizes, and that extremely careful attention be paid to the incentives implicit in the alternatives before a choice is made, space prevents me carrying discussion of this important matter any further.

Even the best of income-contingent loan programs will still leave the children of richer families with easier access to university education than the children of poorer families. Of course, having better or worse access to all sorts of things is what being richer and poorer are all about in the first place, but in the case of university education this observation cannot be the end of the matter. Inequalities of income and wealth among agents may be tolerable to the extent that they reflect the outcomes of the efforts of the agents in question. But if such inequalities impinge upon the educational choices of their children, they create distasteful inequalities of opportunity. That is why it may be desirable to supplement any program of loans whose repayment is contingent upon borrowers' *future* economic status with a program of grants that are contingent upon their *current* economic status. Here too, though, there are incentive effects to be considered that impinge on household labour supply and savings decisions, not to mention on the very process of household formation itself, that require much more discussion than space permits here.

Concluding Comment

I remarked at the outset of this brief essay that there is still something to be said in favour of the old arguments for the public support of postsecondary education in general and universities in particular based on ideas of promoting equality among agents in their opportunities to participate fully in society. And to this I would add that an important aspect of that participation involves the promotion of constructive and critical thought about social and political issues. As I noted in Laidler (2002), the fact that economic analysis is not well adapted to discussing considerations such as these does not mean that they are of minor importance. Rather it means that there is much more at stake in the current debate about universities than economic matters. Accessibility, and the provision of funding to ensure that what is accessible is also socially worthwhile, are indeed important and need to be debated as the ethical and political issues that they are.

But universities use materially productive resources, and they create them as well, and for these reasons alone, economics must play a part in any debate about them. Economics is not useful only for discussing the material aspects of social issues, however. It also yields insights into the role played by the incentives that exist within any form of organization in determining what outcomes, material and otherwise, it is likely to generate. This is the matter I have tried to emphasize in this brief essay and I hope that I have shown that it must be an important part — though only a part, nevertheless — of our ongoing debate about the future of our universities.

David Laidler

References

Aghion, P. and P. Howitt. 1992. "A Model of Growth Through Creative Destruction", *Econometrica* 60 (March), 322-352.

Auld, D. 1996. *Expanding Horizons: Privatizing Universities*. Toronto: University of Toronto Press.

Chant, J. and W. Gibson. 2002. "Quantity or Quality? Research at Canadian Universities", in D. Laidler (ed.), *Renovating the Ivory Tower: Canadian Universities and the Knowledge Economy*. Toronto: C.D. Howe Institute.

Davies, J. 2003. "Empirical Evidence on Human Capital Externalities". Working Paper No. 2003-11. Ottawa: Department of Finance.

Harberger, A.C. 1998. "A Vision of the Growth Process", *American Economic Review* 98 (March), 1-23.

Laidler, D. 2002. "Renovating the Ivory Tower: An Introductory Essay", in D. Laidler (ed.), *Renovating the Ivory Tower: Canadian Universities and the Knowledge Economy*. Toronto: C.D. Howe Institute.

Lemelin, C. 2005. "Thoughts on Financing Postsecondary Education", in this volume.

Montmarquette, C. 2004. "Post-secondary Educational Institutions' Adjustments to Labour Market Changes: Major Concerns and Key Research Issues". Issue Paper prepared for the Roundtable on "Adjustments in Markets for Skilled Labour in Canada", CIRANO and Université de Montréal, March 22. Unpublished paper.

Romer, P.M. 1994. "The Origins of Endogenous Growth", *Journal of Economic Perspectives* 9 (Winter), 3-22.

Rubenstein, H. and R. Clifton. 2002. "University Access is No Guarantee of Learning", *Fraser Forum* (December), 31-33.

Smith, J. 2002. "Comments", in D. Laidler (ed.), *Renovating the Ivory Tower: Canadian Universities in the Knowledge Economy*. Toronto: C.D. Howe Institute.

Section II

Role of Colleges and Universities and
the Value of Postsecondary Education

The Case for Giving Greater Attention to Structure in Higher Education Policy-Making

Michael L. Skolnik

The primary focus in higher education policy discussions in Canada for the past 25 years has been on the topics of funding levels and mechanisms, accountability, accessibility, and quality. To be more precise, the focus has been on these topics in relation to existing postsecondary education institutions as each of them continues to perform within the framework of its existing institutional mission.

The recent focus in higher education policy discussions contrasts with the focus in an earlier era, from the early 1960s to the early 1970s. In that decade, the emphasis was not so much on the performance of the individual institution, as on the structure of emerging and developing systems of higher education. By structure, I mean the distribution of postsecondary institutions by size, mission and type, and geographic location. In that earlier period, across Canada much attention was directed towards the question of what was the optimal, or at least the most appropriate, structure for higher education systems. The outcomes of these efforts included some remarkably articulate and cogent visions for provincial higher education systems, such as the Macdonald Report in British Columbia, the Parent Commission in Quebec, and the Deutsch Commission in New Brunswick (Dennison, 1997, pp. 36-38; Donald, 1997, pp. 164-167; Brown, 1997, pp. 200-202; Skolnik, 1997, pp. 329-333). Planning and design initiatives like the ones just cited determined the shape of Canadian higher education for several decades to follow.

The question to which I wish to draw attention is whether three to four decades after the foundations were laid for our present structures, those structures are still the most appropriate for the twenty-first century, or whether they are in need of significant renovation. At the highest level of generality, we can say that the effectiveness of higher education in meeting societal needs is a function of two distinct factors: first, how effectively each higher education institution performs its role; and second, how effectively the mix of different types of institutions conforms to what is needed. The preoccupation in recent years with the first of these factors is understandable, especially insofar as policy discussion is driven by the concerns and interests of existing institutions which want simply to be given the resources and freedom to continue doing what they have been doing without interference or competition. However, no matter how well each institution does its job, the net result will be less than optimal if the whole configuration of institutions is inappropriate. Thus, it is sometimes important to stand back from the trenches and look at the big picture. In view of changes that have occurred in the environment of higher education over the past few decades, now may be one of those times.

Some of the important changes in the environment of higher education in recent decades that ought to have implications for the appropriate structure of higher education are: the development of a technologically oriented, knowledge society; globalization; commercialization of teaching and research; advances in information technology and virtual education, and changes in skill and knowledge requirements that have increased the educational needs in most occupations. The next section summarizes the most important of these changes in the environment of higher education. I then note some aspects of the structure of Canadian higher education that may warrant examination in the context of the changes in the environment identified. The remainder of the paper concentrates on one of these aspects, the relationship between the university and the non-university sectors of higher education.

The Changing Environment of Higher Education

The elements in the environment of higher education that have potentially significant implications for some reshaping of it are many, and their inter-relationships are complex. Perhaps the most important interrelationships are among the phenomena connoted by the terms: knowledge economy, technological change, and globalization. The implication of the first two of these concepts for the university was aptly summarized by David Laidler:

> the key to securing a rising standard of living at the turn of the millennium lies in the creation and dissemination of knowledge, particularly technological knowledge. The "new economy" is said to be a "knowledge economy", and within it, universities are often presented as having special roles to play as creators of new ideas in their research function and as producers of human capital capable of exploiting those ideas in their teaching function. In this way of looking at things, the output of universities is a vital input into the material progress of the market economy. (Laidler, 2002, pp. 7-8)

The knowledge economy and associated developments in technology take on a different significance for higher education in the context of globalization than would be the case in a closed economy.

Globalization refers to a process in which nations are integrated into a highly competitive international economic system in which the perceived ability of each nation to compete economically in this system becomes the driving force in public policy not only in the economic sphere, but increasingly in the cultural and social spheres as well, including especially postsecondary education.

Globalization has had two major types of impact on postsecondary education. First, it has caused increased emphasis on the economic contribution of education relative to its other objectives. Postsecondary education has always had diverse objectives that can be broadly classified as economic and non-economic. The economic objectives include preparing people to be productive workers in professional and other occupations and research which results in new products, new technologies, and greater economic efficiency. As important as these objectives are, they stand in contrast to the cultural, moral, civic, and broader intellectual purposes of education. There has been a perennial tension between these two sets of objectives, and arguably a society is best served when there is a healthy balance between the two. Globalization threatens to upset this balance, as governments use financial and other policy levers to get universities to give the dominant emphasis to the economic objectives of their activities. Even without this steering, the unprecedented opportunities for institutional and individual profit-making that the knowledge society has brought may, as former Harvard University President Derek Bok — and countless other observers of higher education — has warned, lead to the erosion of traditional academic values and the substitution of self-interest and pecuniary gain as dominant motivating forces in academe (Bok, 2003).

The other way in which globalization has impacted postsecondary education is through marketization, and what some refer to as commodification of education. While postsecondary education has in some countries for a long time been, at least in part, a commodity supplied and purchased on the market and subject to normal market forces, this has not been the case in Canada, except for a portion of non-degree vocational training. Rather, university education has been treated as a public good in much the same way that health care in Canada has been, provided by government in a manner determined by public policy. As globalization has proceeded, there has been a shift in the way that postsecondary education is perceived, towards being a commodity for which the conditions of its provision and acquisition are determined by autonomous providers and consumers. While it is perhaps not necessarily so, marketization of postsecondary education has been accompanied by privatization which has meant that more of the funding of postsecondary education, including research funding, has come from private sources (students and donors), and more of the suppliers of postsecondary education are private, for-profit organizations.

The worldwide growth in demand for forms of higher education that are more explicitly linked to the labour market has led increasingly to viewing higher education as an internationally traded commodity. Although restriction on the international exchange of services in higher education has long been a feature of Canadian educational policy, increased mobility of labour, capital, and knowledge stimulated by reduction in trade barriers and advances in electronic technology has made this policy position obsolete. As former president of the University of Michigan, James Duderstadt, has pointed out, whereas in the past most colleges and universities served local populations, increasingly they themselves are operating in a global context (Duderstadt, in press).

Coinciding with the weakening significance of political borders limiting the movement of higher education, there has also been an associated movement to reduce other kinds of borders affecting the provision of higher education. Recently, the term "borderless education" has been coined to refer to a situation in which those educational and related institutions and organizations that have the desire to provide various types of educational programs are no longer constrained by the traditional boundaries that defined their former sphere of activity. The dimension of borderless education that has attracted the most attention is that in which the lucrative market for career-related degree education is invaded by new providers of higher education, crossing into what was formerly regarded as the preserve of public and private not-for-profit universities.[1] The so-called new providers include: university programs given by other educational sectors (like community colleges and technical institutes); corporate universities (public sector employers); private, for-profit universities; media and publishing businesses; educational brokers; regional and international consortia of universities; virtual universities; and other forms of transnational postsecondary education (Middlehurst, 2002).

An indicator of the seriousness with which mainstream universities view these new developments is that the association of universities in the United Kingdom has established an Observatory on Borderless Higher Education.[2] There is, of course, a question of whether the newer forms of higher education described here will operate only on the periphery of higher education or become a substantial force. In response to this question, Middlehurst begins his discussion of these developments with the caution that "overestimating change in the short term and underestimating it in the long term is a common phenomenon when revolutions are underway" (ibid., p. 1).

Responses by Higher Education Systems

In general, the predominant response by higher education systems to the types of challenges and opportunities described briefly in the preceding paragraphs could be in one of two directions. In one direction, all universities would become substantially more market driven and commercially

---

[1]The concept of borderless higher education appears to have originated in a document produced by the Australian Department of Education, Training and Youth Affairs (Cunningham *et al.*, 1998), and was elaborated in much greater detail in subsequent documents produced by the Australian and UK Governments, respectively (Cunningham *et al.*, 2000; Committee of Vice-Chancellors and Principals, 2000).

[2]The Observatory provides access to relevant national and international documents like those cited in the previous note, and presents information on new initiatives such as new partnerships between private companies and universities. The Observatory is operated by Universities UK, formerly the Committee of Vice-Chancellors and Principals of UK Universities. It can be accessed at http://www.obhe. ac.uk.

oriented, and invest in distance education, virtual education, and other innovative forms of education. Some institutions, particularly "brand name institutions", might be quite successful financially in adopting such a strategy, but for each winner, there would likely also be losers. The result could be a widening of the resource gap between better and poorer funded institutions, and a lot of duplication of activities and consequent waste of resources.

The other direction in which systems might respond is that of increased institutional differentiation in which some institutions move very aggressively to take advantage of new commercial opportunities, or new institutions are created or existing ones in other fields allowed to cross previously existing borders in order to address new needs. Other institutions might move moderately to respond to new opportunities, but they would retain their essential academic character.

Traditional theories of institutional differentiation in higher education, which are based upon population ecology or resource dependency models, suggest that such differentiation would come about naturally as different institutions seek different niches (Hannan and Freeman, 1977; Birnbaum, 1983). However, more recent literature, which emphasizes the influence of isomorphic forces in producing organizational homogeneity (DiMaggio and Powell, 1983), suggests that institutional differentiation is "largely the product of political competition and state sponsorship" (Rhoades, 1990; see also Huisman, 1998). An implication of these newer theories is that if institutional differentiation is thought to be a desirable property of higher education systems, public policy must be directed towards that end — because that is the only way that it will be achieved.

There have been some recent examples in Canada of provincial governments attempting to make their higher education systems more responsive to the needs of globalization and the knowledge society through increased institutional differentiation. One is in regard to enabling private degree-granting institutions to operate. For a long time, private university level institutions were generally not allowed in Canada, except in a very limited way in Alberta through the Private Colleges Accreditation Board which was established in 1984. Recently, there has been legislation in British Columbia (Degree Authorization Act, 2002) and Ontario (Post-Secondary Choice and Excellence Act, 2000) to enable the establishment of private degree-granting institutions, and Alberta has opened the door more widely for private institutions under the Postsecondary Learning Act, 2003.

Michael L. Skolnik

The rationale for these moves has been to provide residents greater choice in the realm of degree level postsecondary education. These new frameworks for regulation of degree granting are designed to make it possible for nearly all types of new providers of degree level education in the world of borderless higher education to operate if they meet appropriate quality standards. It is most unlikely that any new private institutions will be large, well endowed, ivy league types that offer traditional academic programs. Rather, most will likely be small, typically for-profit, institutions that concentrate on particular areas of career-related education, frequently delivered in a way that makes use of state-of-the-art instructional technology.[3] A newly emerging private degree-granting sector that is market driven, commercially focused, and technologically oriented would increase institutional differentiation in Canadian higher education. Adding a private sector would also increase the amount of private funding going into Canadian higher education (Task Force on Competitiveness, 2003, p. 23).

Another recent structural change in Canadian higher education was the opening in Fall 2003, of the University of Ontario Institute of Technology (UOIT). The special mission of the UOIT is to provide "career-oriented university programs" that are responsive to "the market-driven needs of employers" (UOIT Act, 2002). Whether the establishment of a public university with a mission this distinct from those of the other universities will divert pressure away from the others to behave in the same market-driven way as is expected of UOIT remains to be seen. It also remains to be seen whether UOIT will be better able to keep to its task than Canada's other technical universities.[4] The Technical University of British Columbia, which had a similar mandate to UOIT, was closed in 2002 only five years after it was established. In the same year that the BC university was established, the Technical University of Nova Scotia was closed and some of its programs transferred to Dalhousie University. Also in 2002, the former Ryerson Polytechnical University completed its journey towards

---

[3] The other significant category of new private degree-granting institutions will likely be religious institutions seeking to offer secular degree programs.

[4] A considerable part of the rationale for the establishment of UOIT was to improve access to university for residents of the rapidly growing Durham region. However, many of the people in this region will probably want the same types of opportunities as residents elsewhere in the province rather than a special niche institution, and this will likely be a constant source of pressure on UOIT to become more like other Ontario universities. In the language of the literature on institutional differentiation, this would be an example of a mimetic isomorphism.

becoming a conventional university and removed the word Polytechnical from its name.

The Relationship Between the University and Community College Sectors

The potentially greatest changes in the structure of Canadian higher education are those that involve altering the relationships between the major sectors of higher education, the universities, and the community colleges.[5] Until recently, one of the fundamental defining characteristics of this relationship was that the universities were authorized to award degrees and the colleges were not. In the context of the present discussion, the two primary functions of community colleges may be described as: (a) offering first and second year courses in the same fields as universities for transfer credit; and (b) offering certificate or diploma programs of study of an applied nature in fields where there is no corresponding university program for direct entry into the labour market.

The first substantial alteration in the binary structure of Canadian higher education was in 1989 in British Columbia when initially three (now five) community colleges were converted into university colleges.[6] These hybrid institutions offer programs of both the type traditionally associated with the community college and those associated with the university, including baccalaureate degree programs. In regard to the distinction in the previous paragraph, the original emphasis in the university college was on adding the third and fourth years of university-type programs for which the colleges had already been offering the first two years. Later was added the

---

[5]What I refer to as the community college sector also includes post-secondary institutions that traditionally have not offered baccalaureate degrees but are known by other names, such as institute of technology, or in Quebec, college d'enseignement general et professionel.

[6]As this paper was being finalized, the Government of British Columbia announced that one of the university colleges, Okanagan, was going to be replaced by a new University of British Columbia Okanagan and a new Okanagan College (Government of British Columbia, 2004).

Michael L. Skolnik

notion of *applied* baccalaureate degrees in fields that had no directly corresponding university program.[7] In 1996, Alberta community colleges also were given the opportunity to offer applied baccalaureate programs, and in 2000, a similar provision was incorporated into the Postsecondary Education Choice and Excellence Act in Ontario, the same piece of legislation that enabled the establishment of private degree-granting institutions in that province. As of 2004, about a third of the community colleges in Canada will be able to offer baccalaureate degrees.

A similar movement has been occurring in the United States, but on a relatively smaller scale. Presently, community colleges have been empowered to offer baccalaureate degrees in a handful of states, including Texas and Florida (Floyd, 2005). In both countries, there have been two distinct models of, or purposes for community college baccalaureate programs (Skolnik, 2005). One purpose is to improve access to the types of programs typically offered by universities. This is particularly important for placebound students, but serves also to overcome other economic, cultural, and learning style barriers that may prevent community college students from continuing on to complete a baccalaureate degree at a university.

The idea for the university colleges in British Columbia came from a provincial study of access, and their original and primary purpose was to improve access to the types of programs typically offered by universities. Access has been the primary motivation for the community college baccalaureate in the United States too, but with a twist. One of the first areas that has been targeted for the community college baccalaureate in the United States is teacher education. This responds *both* to limitations on access to university teacher education programs *and* to national concerns about shortages of teachers.

The other purpose of the community college baccalaureate is to provide programs of an applied nature that are designed to meet specific workplace needs. The rationale for this type of degree is that because of changes in technology and advances in knowledge, workers in many of the occupations for which labour market preparation is provided by community colleges now require more advanced education. Though this education has

---

[7]The first four university colleges (Cariboo, Okanagan, Malaspina, and Fraser Valley) were mandated to offer traditional degrees in arts and sciences. Subsequently, in 1995, Kwantlen College became a university college with a mandate to offer applied degrees, not traditional degrees in arts and sciences (Carr, 2001). However, recently the restriction on the types of degrees that Kwantlen University College could offer was lifted and Kwantlen is now permitted to offer academic degree programs, the first being in Psychology (Charlton and Hamilton, 2004).

a strong applied focus, the increased level of complexity and sophistication of the curriculum, advocates for the change argue, warrants the awarding of a baccalaureate degree. The colleges are still providing training for the same types of jobs that they used to, it is just that the college programs are changing commensurately with the changes in the knowledge and skill requirements of those jobs.

Except for the university colleges in British Columbia, in Canada the community college baccalaureate has been used exclusively for workforce development. This is the thrust of the applied degree programs in Alberta and Ontario, and apparently will be the case also under a new policy that will allow community colleges in British Columbia, as distinct from university colleges, to offer baccalaureate programs. A few examples of titles of applied degree programs may help give the reader a sense of the applied nature of these programs: Bachelor of Applied Information Science (Information Systems Security); Bachelor of Applied Technology (Advanced Manufacturing Technologies: Wood and Composite Products); Bachelor of Applied Petroleum Engineering Technology. Some American community colleges are now offering what they call workforce baccalaureate degrees in such areas as manufacturing technology and information technology, but these are a minority of community college baccalaureate degree programs in the United States.

In the first model of the community college baccalaureate degree described above, where the community college offers a complete baccalaureate program in areas where universities offer programs, there is a definite blurring of the traditional boundary between the sectors, and in that regard, an alteration of the structure of the postsecondary education system. It is not clear that the second model, that of the applied baccalaureate degree, constitutes a change in the structure of postsecondary education. Enhancing the curriculum of the former applied diploma programs in community colleges could be viewed as similar to the continual enhancement of university degree programs to take account of advances in knowledge. In principle, the differentiation between the community college's applied degrees and university degrees is of the same type as the differentiation between the former's diplomas and the latter's degrees. In practice, however, the distinction that I have drawn between two types of baccalaureate degrees may be difficult to apply, especially as universities become more market driven and workplace oriented, a point to which I will return later. Also, even if the applied baccalaureates represent only an intensification of the type of programs that the colleges have been offering, the new degrees could foster a change in the culture and identify of the colleges (Laden,

Michael L. Skolnik

2005). However, even with the introduction of a relatively small number of baccalaureate programs in community colleges in some provinces, the predominant focus of the community college is likely to remain as it is for the foreseeable future. For example, the Government of Alberta has made the following unequivocal statement on this issue:

> Public colleges and technical institutes offering applied degree programs will not become universities, nor will they confer degrees in traditional university programs ... The intention of the applied degree demonstration project is to allow public colleges and technical institutes greater flexibility to fulfill their traditional mandate which is providing career and technical education and training to Albertans at the certificate and diploma level. (Government of Alberta, 2003, p. 2)

Insofar as the binary structure of postsecondary education in Canada is likely to be a continuing feature, an important question is: What should be the balance in scale between the two sectors?

The Balance Between Sectors

Several documents emanating from the Institute for Competitiveness and Prosperity (ICP)[8] in Toronto in the past few years have argued that the present allocation of investment between community colleges and universities in Ontario is economically inefficient (ICP, 2003, 2004; Task Force on Competitiveness, 2003; Martin and Milway, 2003). For example, a Working Paper from the ICP states that:

> Another key issue we think Ontarians should focus on is the respective roles of colleges and universities in raising the competitiveness and prosperity of Ontarians. We are concerned that Ontarians may be under-investing in the latter relative to the former. (ICP, 2003, p. 43)

---

[8]The Institute for Competitiveness and Prosperity is described in its documents as an independent not-for-profit organization established in 2001 to serve as the research arm of Ontario's Task Force on Competitiveness, Productivity and Economic Progress. The mandate of the task force "is to monitor Ontario's competitiveness, productivity, and economic progress compared to other provinces and U.S. states and to report to the public on a regular basis". The institute is funded by the Government of Ontario through the Ministry of Enterprise, Opportunity and Innovation.

The focus of the ICP has been Ontario, but in some places the arguments are generalized to Canada as well. The crux of the ICP argument is that compared to the United States, Ontario invests more in community colleges relative to universities, but since the returns to investment are greater for universities than for community colleges, Ontario's relative over-investment in community colleges contributes to the prosperity gap between Ontario and the United States.

Rather than focusing on comparative levels of public funding between the sectors, the data that the ICP provides pertain mostly to enrolment and educational attainment. For example, one document presents data that compares educational attainment for people aged 25 and over in urban Ontario compared to the urban population of 14 American states deemed appropriate for economic comparisons. The data shows that the percentage of people with a university degree as highest academic credential is smaller for Ontario (23%) than the average for the American states (27%); whereas the reverse is true for the category, "Some Postsecondary", which would include a community college credential (ICP, 2003, p. 21).

This result is consistent with comparisons of educational attainment for the working-age population between Canada and the United States. According to Organisation for Economic Co-operation and Development (OECD) figures for the year 2000, Canada had the highest proportion of working-age population (25–65) with a postsecondary credential of any member country, 41% (Statistics Canada, 2003, p. 10). The highest level of educational attainment was a university degree for 20% of Canadians of working age, and it was a community college certificate or diploma for 21%. Though highest in total, Canada did not have the highest figure for either sectoral category. In the community college category, Canada was second to Ireland at 22%. In the university category, Canada was fourth, after the United States, 28%; Norway, 26%; and the Netherlands, 21%. The university degree attainment figure for the United States was significantly higher than Canada's, and the community college attainment figure for Canada, 21%, was substantially higher than the figure for the United States, 9%.[9]

---

[9]Paul Davenport, president of the University of Western Ontario, cites similar OECD figures for 1996, as well as other labour market outcomes, in his critique of a journalist's observation that the Canadian public is beginning to realize that education at a college or vocational school is more valuable than a university degree (Davenport, 2002, pp. 46-49).

Michael L. Skolnik

Another way of looking at the relative size of the two sectors is in terms of the number of postsecondary institutions in each sector. The numbers reported by Statistics Canada are 76 universities and 204 community colleges, a ratio of 2.7 of the latter to the former.[10] In the United States, the Carnegie classification manual for 2000 (McCormick, 2000) shows 1,406 universities and 1,184 community colleges, a ratio of 0.84 community colleges to universities.[11] Even allowing for issues of comparability of definitions, it does seem that there is quite a disparity between Canada and the United States in the relative numbers of the two types of postsecondary institutions.

However, when one looks at enrolment figures, one gets quite a different picture. Fall 2000 enrolment in community colleges accounted for 39.3% of total enrolment in institutions of higher education in the United States (derived from Table B, National Center for Education Statistics, 2002). In Canada the corresponding figure for 1999 was 37.4% (derived from Tables D1.8 and D1.10, Statistics Canada and Council of Ministers of Education Canada, 2003, Tables). In Ontario, enrolment in community colleges comprised 33.8% of total postsecondary enrolment, whereas the average for the 14 states used in the ICP's studies was 34.1% (derived from Table 48, National Center for Education Statistics, 1998). Thus, in terms of relative enrolment in the two sectors, it does not appear that Canada is overemphasizing community colleges relative to the United States or that Ontario is doing so relative to peer states.[12] The difference appears to be

---

[10]These figures are from Orton (2003, p. 7). This paper, by a senior Statistics Canada official in the area of postsecondary education statistics, discusses the difficulties involved in providing a definitive answer to the question of how many community colleges and universities there are in Canada and presents some alternative ways of answering that question.

[11]For comparability, these figures exclude private, for-profit institutions, of which there were 15 universities and 485 Associate's Colleges in 2000. The Canadian figures given above exclude comparable non-university-type institutions. I have also excluded the 46 combination Baccalaureate-Associate's Colleges in the United States because of ambiguity about which sectoral category they should be included in, although as of 2000 they were mostly university-type institutions. Also excluded are specialized institutions like free-standing medical schools and Tribal Colleges and Universities.

[12]It should be noted that the figures given here are for different years for Canada and the United States. The latest figures that the author was able to access were for 1999 for Canada. However, national figures for the United States were

that relative to the United States, Canada has fewer and larger universities, and more and smaller community colleges.

A study by DesRosiers posted on the Web site of the Association of Colleges of Applied Arts and Technology of Ontario (DesRosiers, 2003) provides some additional figures that refute the ICP's assertion that Ontario is overemphasizing community colleges relative to the United States. DesRosiers shows that for the youngest age group, 25–34, Ontario has a slightly higher percentage of the population with a university degree, 28.7%, than the 14 American states, 28.2% (2003, p. 6). This suggests that the historical gap in educational attainment between Ontario and the United States is being eliminated. DesRosiers shows also that, based on the population aged 18–21, Ontario has a higher university participation rate than the United States (43.0% to 41.1%), and a lower community college participation rate (25.6% to 36.1%, p. 8).[13]

The next part of the ICP argument alludes to the "increased productivity from higher levels of education", that is, from attending university compared to attending community college. The suggestion is that because of the higher productivity of university than community college graduates, Ontario's income per capita relative to the United States would increase if the province had fewer community college and more university graduates. The difference in productivity is inferred from the estimate that on average, for the 14 American states, Ontario, and Quebec, annual earnings are 26% higher for university than for community college graduates (ICP, 2003,

---

available for 1998 or 2000, not for 1999. The latest state level figures for the United States were for 1996. While there have been some short-term fluctuations, year-to-year discrepancies have not been sufficient to alter the broad conclusion that enrolment in community colleges as a percentage of total postsecondary enrolment is certainly not higher in Canada than in the United States, and is probably lower. It is also noteworthy that the range in community college enrolment as a percentage of total enrolment in the 14 peer states used in the ICP studies is enormous, from California at nearly 60% to Indiana at about 13%.

[13]Another comparison presented by ICP pertained to flows of students from Grade 9 to postsecondary education five years later. The ICP data showed that the transition rates to community college were higher for Ontario than the United States and the reverse for transition rates to university (ICP, 2003, p. 22). However, DesRosiers pointed out that the raw data is not comparable between countries because the US data includes both full-time and part-time students while the Ontario data includes only full-time students. When adjusted for this discrepancy, the transition rates for both sectors are substantially higher for Ontario than for the United States (DesRosiers, 2003, p. 9).

p. 20). Of course, on average, the university graduates may have up to two years more of postsecondary education than the community college graduates, and the additional years of schooling could be expected to have an impact on earnings whatever the type of institution. In the United States, Grubb reported that after controlling for other variables, the average increase in earnings *per year* of postsecondary study is about the same for graduates of both types of institutions (Grubb, 1997).

A more precise way to look at the relative influences of the different educational sectors would be to focus on rates of return to different levels of education rather than just the earnings side of the equation. Until recently, most rate-of-return studies in Canada concentrated on the university sector, but now we are starting to get more studies that look at both sectors. As the comparison of different rate-of-return studies is a complex undertaking because of differences in definitions, assumptions, methods, and data sources I will offer just a few tentative observations here.

First, there is likely a big difference in employment outcomes between persons who enter the labour market after completing a career education program and those who complete an academic program and then enter the workforce instead of transferring to a university. Research in the United States shows that while on average, the rate of return per credit is about the same in community colleges as in universities (Kane and Rouse, 1995, p. 601), the Academic Associate Degree is not a good investment for students who fail to transfer to university (Grubb, 1997, p. 238; Pascarella, 1999, p. 11). For community college transfer students who do not transfer, the appropriate comparison would be with students who drop out of university after two years rather than with university graduates. I do not know of any studies that provide this type of comparison. Another important gap in the literature is the absence of provincial level data. This is especially important for Ontario, because community colleges there have since their founding had a stronger emphasis on career education than colleges in other provinces (or states), and are unique among North American colleges in offering a wide range of three-year career programs. It is impossible to assess the validity of the ICP's argument without data on earnings and rate of return for graduates of these three-year programs.

Second, while earlier Canadian estimates tended to show moderately to slightly lower rates of return for community colleges than for universities, some recent estimates show the reverse. For example, Vaillancourt's 1996 study showed private rates of 18.4% for community college women compared to 16.1% for university, and for men 16.3% for community college compared to 12.3% for university (cited in Boothby and Rowe,

2002, p. 26). Boothby and Rowe estimated rates of return in the 26 to 27% range for community colleges, and 15 to 16% for universities (ibid., p. 26). Of course, private rates of return have been relatively higher than total rates in the university than community college sector because of the relatively higher university tuition fees. And these are only two studies. Still, it is far from clear that, on average, rates of return are higher to investment in university than in community college programs. Having earlier refuted the ICP's assertion that Ontario is over-investing in community colleges relative to the United States, we cannot support their argument that the present allocation of resources between the two sectors is economically inefficient.[14]

Implications and Conclusions

Even if the ICP's argument for reallocation of resources from the community college to the university sector is not valid, the changes that are occurring in both sectors make it important to consider the appropriate relationship between these sectors. Even if the enrolment distribution between sectors is about the same on average in Canada as in the United States, one cannot help but ask whether the present balance between sectors in either country is appropriate for a society whose future is intimately tied to the creation, dissemination, and application of knowledge. Intuitively, one senses that anything close to the present balance between sectors makes sense only if the college sector, like the university sector, is on the cutting edge of knowledge. But if colleges aim to do this — as no doubt, all would maintain is their goal — that could raise another troubling question: In the

---

[14]In this volume, Emery cites two earlier studies that show higher rates of return for university bachelor's degrees than for college programs. Also cited is one study that shows large, negative returns for trades training. Emery reports that total expenditures on community colleges for Canada increased by 14% between 1993 and 1998, and expenditures on trades training increased by 41%, while expenditures on universities increased by only 4%. He thus concludes that the expansion of trades training and community college education relative to universities has not reflected a socially efficient use of resources. This approach of focusing on the relationship between incremental returns relative to costs for different sectors within a jurisdiction is an alternative to the ICP approach of focusing on relative returns and costs between jurisdictions. Both approaches require finer data on rate of return in the college sector than has been available to date.

process of continually making advances in the education they provide, are colleges becoming universities?

This, of course, refers to the issue of academic drift, a process in which institutions strive to become more like institutions at the next rung of a hierarchical system of postsecondary education. Except with respect to the BC university colleges, which are intended to be hybrid institutions, provincial governments have stated explicitly that offering baccalaureate degrees is not a step on the way to becoming a university. Earlier, I cited a strong statement by the Government of Alberta on this point. However, subsequent to that statement being posted on the government Web site, new legislation made it possible for community colleges to apply to the minister responsible for postsecondary education to have their institutional mission and status changed (Tetley, 2004).

Moreover, anyone who has studied the history of higher education may rightfully be skeptical about the ability of any government to honour in the long run, or in today's climate perhaps even in the medium run, a pledge to absolutely prohibit academic drift. A common theme in this history is that of postsecondary institutions that started off as something quite distinct from universities evolving into universities. A large-scale transformation of this type that some believe has relevance to what is now happening in North American community colleges was when the polytechnics in the United Kingdom were converted into universities (Ward, 2001). Prior to that conversion, there had been quite articulate statements of the rationale for differences between the applied degrees awarded by the polytechnics and the academic degrees awarded by the universities (Matterson, 1981). On the other hand, a big difference between the situation of the UK and Canada's was the exceedingly low university participation rate in the UK that existed prior to the wholesale conversion of the polytechnics into universities, whereas Canada has had one of the highest in the world.

Another factor that is important to consider when looking at historical analogies is the knowledge society-technology-globalization context of higher education today, as described briefly earlier. How qualitatively different is the environment of the university today, and the university's response to it, from anytime in the past? Writing about higher education today is replete with criticisms, like that of Derek Bok's cited earlier, of the extent to which the universities have become economically oriented and market driven, and in the process are failing to perform other important functions properly. James Downey, former president of Waterloo University, recently suggested that universities have become "too economy-centric in our focus, at the expense of some other values and considerations that go to the heart of our enterprise, notably the qualitative aspects of undergraduate education and the role of universities in a civil society, as distinct from in a knowledge economy" (Downey, 2003, p. 29). In a similar vein, Fisher and Rubenson have asserted that the increased vocationalism and utilitarianism in the university have contributed to a blurring of the boundary between universities and community colleges (Fisher and Rubenson, 1998, pp. 94-95).[15]

Insofar as such a blurring of the boundaries is actually occurring through the behaviour of institutions in both sectors, I would offer two observations. First, in such a context, not only is the community college a credible institution to offer bachelor's programs of an applied nature in selected areas, but this may be an economically efficient way to help increase the number of baccalaureate graduates. In fact, within the constellation of *new* providers of baccalaureates described earlier, the community college may be the most credible in regard to dedication to academic quality and serving student and community needs. In the context of the ICP argument about the importance economically of producing more baccalaureates, research is needed on the comparative benefits, relative to costs, of additional university and community college baccalaureates.

The second observation is that as community colleges assume more responsibility for higher level technical training, this could allow universities to concentrate more on their unique role in society, a role that observers like Derek Bok and James Downey feel is in danger of being neglected due to universities becoming too economy-centric in their focus. Many of the postsecondary institutions in the non-university sector, such as the CAATs in Ontario, were established for the express purpose of addressing the knowledge and skill needs of industry. The more that

---

[15]One of the examples that Fisher and Rubenson give is of an advanced wood processing program at the University of British Columbia. A comparison of university and college Web sites suggests that this program has a lot in common with the applied degree program in advanced technologies for wood and composite products that is offered by Conestoga College in Ontario. For example, the Conestoga program "offers a detailed study and evaluation of the principles, methods and applications needed for making technically sound decisions in manufacturing processes, physical properties of materials, advanced computer applications, a solid foundation in business considerations, and an exposure to liberal arts disciplines" (Conestoga College, n.d.). The UBC program "teaches state-of-the-art manufacturing processes, as well as the structure of successful businesses. Students learn valuable workplace skills that are important to employers, and vital for those wanting to successfully start and run their own businesses" (UBC Forestry, n.d.).

Michael L. Skolnik

institutions that were established for this purpose can be enabled to do so in a deeper and wider manner, the more can institutions that have other substantial reasons for being fulfill their promise. Such an allocation of roles would be consistent with Abraham Flexner's advice that universities should not do everything, but rather concentrate on doing "supremely well what they almost alone can do" (Flexner, 1930, p. 27). In this connection, there is more than a little irony in the fact that the period of introduction of applied baccalaureate degrees in many of Canada's community colleges coincides with the period of demise of most of Canada's technical universities. It may well be that in the future, community colleges with the most technically advanced programs will play the role formerly played by technical universities.

What specifically might the developments described in this paper mean for the future of the binary structure of postsecondary education? One implication is that the practice of differentiating between the two sectors on the basis of the ability to award a baccalaureate degree or by the types of programs offered may no longer be viable. Does this mean that the binary idea should be abandoned, as some other jurisdictions have done, or that a different principle should be employed as the basis of differentiation between sectors? Perhaps the key basis of distinction between sectors should be that one is highly regulated by, and responsive to, government, while institutions in the other sector have considerable autonomy.[16]

I have attempted to describe some of the ways in which both community colleges and universities, but particularly the former, are changing in response to changes in their environment. To a considerable extent, these changes have been the consequence of responses of individual institutions to market forces rather than the result of government planning. That experience suggests that one possible stance for public policy would be to step aside and let market forces reshape our system of higher education. However, the environment in which universities and, more so, colleges operate is only partially market determined; it is still controlled significantly by government regulation. Unless governments are prepared to eliminate most of this regulatory apparatus — for example, let all public and private, provincial and out-of-province institutions compete equally — the structure of higher education must be determined by public policy. The issues pertaining to the structure of higher education described in this paper seem to me at least as compelling candidates for the higher education

---

[16]I am indebted to my departmental colleague Dan Lang for this observation.

policy agenda as the other higher education issues that governments have been addressing in recent years.

References

Birnbaum, R. 1983. *Maintaining Diversity in Higher Education*. San Francisco: Jossey-Bass.

Bok, D. 2003. *Universities in the Marketplace: The Commercialization of Higher Education*. Princeton, NJ: Princeton University Press.

Boothby, D. and G. Rowe. 2002. "Rate of Return to Education: A Distributional Analysis Using the Life Paths Model". Ottawa: Applied Research Branch, Human Resources Development Canada.

Brown, S.A. 1997. "New Brunswick", in G.A. Jones (ed.), *Higher Education in Canada: Different Systems, Different Perspectives*. New York: Garland Publishing, Inc.

Carr, B. 2001. "The University College System in British Columbia, Canada", *CCBA Beacon* 2(1), 2-7.

Charlton, S. and K. Hamilton. 2004. "The First Two Years of a New Under-graduate Psychology Degree: Problems and Solutions". Paper presented at "It's About Access", fourth annual conference of the Community College Baccalaureate Association, San Francisco, CA, February 28 – March 1.

Committee of Vice-Chancellors and Principals and Higher Education Funding Council for England. 2000. *The Business of Borderless Education: UK Perspectives*. London: CVCP and HEFCE.

Conestoga College. no date. "About the AMT-WCP Program". At www.conestoga.on.ca/jsp/programs/schoolengit/degree/wood/aboutamt.jsp.

Cunningham, S., S. Tapsall, Y. Ryan, L. Stedman, K. Bagdon and T. Flew. 1998. *New Media and Borderless Education*. Canberra, ACT: Department of Education, Training, and Youth Affairs.

Cunningham, S., Y. Ryan, L. Stedman, S. Tapsall, K. Bagdon, T. Flew and P. Coaldrake. 2000. *The Business of Borderless Education*. Canberra, ACT: Department of Education, Training, and Youth Affairs.

Davenport, P. 2002. "Universities and the Knowledge Economy", in D. Laidler (ed.), *Renovating the Ivory Tower: Canadian Universities and the Knowledge Economy*. Toronto: C.D. Howe Institute.

Dennison, J.D. 1997. "Higher Education in British Columbia, 1945-1995: Opportunity and Diversity", in G.A. Jones (ed.), *Higher Education in Canada: Different Systems, Different Perspectives*. New York: Garland Publishing, Inc.

DesRosiers, E. 2003. "A Comparative Analysis of the Balance Between College and University Enrollment in the United States and Ontario". Toronto:

Michael L. Skolnik

Association of Colleges of Applied Arts and Technology of Ontario. At http://www.acaato.on.ca.

DiMaggio, P.J. and W.W. Powell. 1983. "The Iron Cage Revisited: Institutional Isomorphism and Collective Rationality in Organizational Fields", *American Sociological Review* 48(2), 147-160.

Donald, J. 1997. "Higher Education in Quebec: 1945-1995", in G.A. Jones (ed.), *Higher Education in Canada: Different Systems, Different Perspectives.* New York: Garland Publishing, Inc.

Downey, J. 2003. "The Heart of Our Enterprise", *University Affairs*, December, 27-30.

Duderstadt, J.J. in press. "The Future of Higher Education in the Knowledge-Driven, Global Economy of the 21st Century", in G.A. Jones, P. McCarney and M.L. Skolnik (eds.), *Creating Knowledge, Strengthening Nations: The Changing Role of Higher Education.* Toronto: University of Toronto Press.

Fisher, D. and K. Rubenson. 1998. "The Changing Political Economy: The Private and Public Lives of Canadian Universities", in J. Currie and J. Newsom (eds.), *Universities and Globalization: Critical Perspectives.* London: Sage Publications.

Flexner, A. 1930. *Universities: American, English, German.* New York: Oxford University Press.

Floyd, D.L. 2005. "Community College Baccalaureate: Models and Programs in the United States", in D.L. Floyd, M.L. Skolnik and K.P. Walker (eds.), *The Community College Baccalaureate: Emerging Trends and Policy Issues.* Sterling, VA: Stylus Publishing, LLC.

Government of Alberta. 2003. *The Applied Degree — Frequently Asked Questions.* At http://www.learning.gov.ab.ca/college/AppliedDegree/faq.asp.

Government of British Columbia. 2004. News Release: "New UBC Okanagan to Help Add 5,500 Student Spaces". Victoria: Office of the Premier, March 17.

Grubb, W.N. 1997. "The Returns to the Sub-baccalaureate Labor Market, 1984–1990", *Economics of Education Review* 16(3), 231-145.

Hannan, M.T. and J.H. Freeman. 1977. "The Population Ecology of Organizations", *American Journal of Sociology* 82(4), 929-964.

Huisman, J. 1998. "Differentiation and Diversity in Higher Education Systems", in J.C. Smart (ed.), *Higher Education: Handbook of Theory and Research*, Vol. 13. New York: Agathon Press.

Institute for Competitiveness and Prosperity (ICP). 2003. *Missing Opportunities: Ontario's Urban Prosperity Gap.* Working Paper No. 3. Toronto: ICP.

_____. 2004. "Partnering for Investment in Canada's Prosperity". Presented at the Annual Meeting of the World Economic Forum, Davos, Switzerland, January.

Kane, T.J. and C.E. Rouse. 1995. "Labor Market Returns to Two- and Four-Year College", *American Economic Review* 85(3), 600-614.

Laden, B.V. 2005. "The New ABDs: Applied Baccalaureate Degrees in Ontario Colleges", in D.L. Floyd, M.L. Skolnik and K.P. Walker (eds.), *The*

Community College Baccalaureate: Emerging Trends and Policy Issues. Sterling, VA: Stylus Publishing, LLC.

Laidler, D. 2002. "Renovating the Ivory Tower: An Introductory Essay", in D. Laidler (ed.), *Renovating the Ivory Tower: Canadian Universities and the Knowledge Economy.* Toronto: C.D. Howe Institute.

Martin, R. and J. Milway. 2003. "Ontario's Urban Gap", *National Post*, FP 11, July 4.

Matterson, A. 1981. *Polytechnics and Colleges.* New York: Longman, Inc.

McCormick, A.C., ed. 2000. *The Classification of Institutions of Higher Education, 2000 Edition.* Menlo Park, CA: The Carnegie Foundation for the Advancement of Teaching. At http://www. carnegiefoundation.org/Classification/CIHE2000.

Middlehurst, R. 2002. "The Developing World of Borderless Higher Education: Markets Providers, Quality Assurance and Qualifications". Paper presented at the first Global Forum on International Quality Assurance, Accreditation and the Recognition of Qualifications in Higher Education, UNESCO, Paris, October 17-18.

National Center for Education Statistics. 1998. *State Comparisons of Education Statistics: 1969–70 to 1996–97.* Washington, DC: Office of Educational Research and Improvement, US Department of Education.

_____. 2002. *Enrollment in Postsecondary Institutions, Fall 2000 and Financial Statistics, Fiscal Year, 2000.* Washington, DC: Office of Educational Research and Improvement, US Department of Education.

Orton, L. 2003. *A New Understanding of Postsecondary Education in Canada: A Discussion Paper.* Catalogue No. 81-595-MIE. Ottawa: Statistics Canada.

Pascarella, E.T. 1999. "New Studies Track Community College Effects on Students", *Community College Journal* 69(6), 8-14.

Rhoades, G. 1990. "Political Competition and Differentiation in Higher Education", in J.C. Alexander and P. Colony (eds.), *Differentiation Theory and Social Change: Comparative and Historical Perspectives.* New York: Columbia University Press.

Skolnik, M.L. 1997. "Putting It All Together: Viewing Canadian Higher Education from a Collection of Jurisdiction-based Perspectives", in G.A. Jones (ed.), *Higher Education in Canada: Different Systems, Different Perspectives.* New York: Garland Publishing, Inc.

_____. 2005. "The Community College Baccalaureate in Canada: Its Role in Enabling Provincial Systems of Postsecondary Education to Address Accessibility and Workforce Needs in Ontario Colleges", in D.L. Floyd, M.L. Skolnik and K.P. Walker (eds.), *The Community College Baccalaureate: Emerging Trends and Policy Issues.* Sterling, VA: Stylus Publishing, LLC.

Statistics Canada. 2003. "Education in Canada: Raising the Standard", 2001 Census, analysis series. Ottawa: Statistics Canada, March.

Statistics Canada and Council of Ministers of Education Canada. 2003. *Education Indicators in Canada: Report of the Pan-Canadian Education Indicators Program 1999.* Ottawa: Statistics Canada.

Task Force on Competitiveness, Productivity and Economic Progress. 2003. *Investing for Prosperity. Second Annual Report.* Toronto: Task Force.

Tetley, D. (with files from S. Hill). 2004. "Mount Royal Eager to Grant Degrees", *Calgary Herald*, March 18. Accessed March 19 at http://CalgaryHerald.com.

UBC Forestry. no date. "B.Sc. Wood Products Processing". At www.forestry.ubc. ca...ms/undergrad/prospective/WPP-learn.html.

University of Ontario Institute of Technology Act. 2002, S.O. 2002, c. 8 Sched. O.

Vaillancourt, F. 1996. "The Private and Total Returns to Education in Canada, 1990". Montreal: Centre de rescherche et développement économique, Université de Montréal. Unpublished paper.

Ward, C.V.L. 2001. "A Lesson from the British Polytechnics for American Community Colleges", *Community College Review* 29(2), 151-163.

Total and Private Returns to University Education in Canada: 1960 to 2000 and in Comparison to Other Postsecondary Training

Herb Emery

Total full-time university undergraduate enrolment has grown from 69,000 students in 1956 to 600,000 students today. Over the same period, the ratio of full-time university enrolment to the Canadian population aged 20 to 24 increased from 0.04 to 0.29. Along with the expansion of Canada's university enrolment, up until 1980 there were large increases in public expenditures and public investment that resulted in growing resources per full-time student (Davenport, 2002). Since 1980, enrolment growth has outstripped the growth of university revenues, particularly from public sources, such that the real level of resources per student in universities has declined. In addition, public funding of universities resulted in falling tuition costs for students until 1984 and since that time, with the squeeze on public funds for universities, tuition costs for students have climbed to the point that tuition costs per student today are in real terms higher than at any time since 1950. As we look to the future, there are three important resource issues for university and postsecondary education. First, should resources for university education be restored to the levels of the late 1970s, or should they be allowed to decline? Second, should the large amount of resources used for "general education" within universities be reallocated to programs training students for specific skills and specific knowledge that are currently in high in demand, offered by universities, community colleges and trade/vocational schools? Third, who should pay for university education, the individual receiving the education or Canadian taxpayers?

A common concern with the "squeeze" on Canada's universities has been that, in order to accommodate enrolment growth after 1980, the quality of education has been compromised and will likely be diminished further unless resources for universities are increased, or enrolment growth is slowed. With this view, the cause of the decline in public funding for universities is attributed to causes external to universities themselves such as the perception that the opportunity cost of public funds increased after 1980.[1] An alternative view of the squeeze on university funding is that its causes were rooted in universities and what they provide. It was argued that the value of university education has declined in general since 1970 and society would be better served by allocating resources towards trades/vocational training.[2] Canadian workers are viewed as over-educated relative to society's human capital needs, hence the level of public spending on postsecondary education is too high. Thus, diverting resources away from universities to other uses represented a desirable reallocation of public funds. Finally, as most Canadians believe that the private benefits to postsecondary education are high, it seemed reasonable to shift the burden of financing education away from the general taxpayer and onto the individual who benefits from the investment.

Riddell and Sweetman (2000) distinguish between two views of the importance of educational attainment for society through two explanations for the rise of participation in postsecondary education in Canada. First, the

---

[1] For example, Laidler (2002) argues that government spending on universities in Canada competes directly with spending on health care, at least in the mind of the electorate. Thus, as government spending tightened after the 1980s, it was inevitable that university funding from governments would tighten in order to maintain spending levels on health care that benefit a wider segment of society than postsecondary education.

[2] See Allen (1998), Laidler (2002), or Davenport (2002) for a discussion of this perspective on university education. This point of view gained credence through theoretical alternatives to the human capital model, in particular, signaling and sorting theories. Alternatively, there was a perception that government "subsidies" encouraging greater participation in postsecondary education resulted in over-investment in education (Texeira, 2000).

"relative demand shift" view sees technical change, or structural change in Canadian labour markets, increasing the demand for higher skilled workers relative to lower skilled workers. Thus, growing employment opportunities for highly educated workers signal the need for increased educational attainment to meet the growing demand for this type of labour and to prevent an increase in unemployment that would be associated with declining demand for less skilled labour. The contrasting view is the "over-education/underemployment" view that increased educational attainments are the result of poor labour market opportunities for youth and young adults. Thus, young Canadians invest in postsecondary education to improve their chances at getting a good job, and employers facing a glut of applications for their vacancies upgrade their workforce. In this view, there is a substantial unemployment and underemployment among the well educated. Rising educational attainment is a waste of society's resources (time and money), as the education received is unnecessary since high human capital workers occupy jobs that do not require a university level of education. In addition, what universities do in terms of programs offered has been brought into question to the extent that many believe that universities are training workers ill-suited for the current labour market at a high social cost.

Labour market outcomes (employment, earnings premia, and quality of jobs) indicate that the relative demand shift is a better description of the Canadian situation of the reasons for the rise in participation in university education (Allen, 1998; Beaudry and Green, 2000; Riddell and Sweetman, 2000; and Davenport, 2002). Rising university enrolments and allocation of resources to university education were driven by labour market demands. This alone, however, cannot tell us if the university system has had too many resources allocated to it, or too few. As Allen (1998) argues, we need to know the costs and benefits of resources allocated to universities which are summarized by the internal rates of return (IRR) to investments in university education. If Canadian society has allocated too many resources to university education, then we should see that the rate of return to the investment of those resources is low. If "squeezing" universities by reducing per student resources has diminished the quality of education, then we should see that the rate of return to a university education has fallen. If trades and other forms of vocational training are better uses for society's resources, then we should see rates of return to those postsecondary credentials exceeding the rates of return to university degrees.

This paper addresses the three resource issues identified above by examining the evolution of university participation in Canada and by surveying the literature on the rate of return (cost/benefit) to resources allocated to university education in Canada. My investigation of the private and total rates of return to bachelor's degrees over the last 40 years suggests that the university system had an unnecessarily high level of resources by the mid-1980s. While the earnings premium of bachelor's degree holders over high-school graduates has been stable since 1981, the total rate of return to a bachelor's degree has increased while the resources per university student have declined. In addition, while private costs have increased and reduced the private rate of return to university education, university education remains a good investment for the individual acquiring the education and there is still considerable scope for raising tuition fees. Finally, even if resources per student are squeezed further, the rate of return to university education for the individual and society will rise due to the expected contraction of the supply of highly educated workforce that will arise with the aging of Canada's population.

The Evolution of Participation in University Education

Figure 1 shows the size of full-time undergraduate enrolment in Canadian universities since 1860.[3] Over a 140 year period, 1960–70 and 1980–90 stand out as two notable decades as full-time university undergraduate enrolment increased by 200,000 students in both of these decades. Owram (1996) notes that between 1963 and 1968, Canadian university enrolment increased as much as it had between 1913 and 1963.

Some of the increase in full-time undergraduate university enrolment was due to the demographics of the baby boom, but the majority of the increase was due to increases in participation in university education amongst Canadians aged 18–26 (CAUT, 2003, Figure 5.2). The baby-boom generation with its sheer size also resulted in increases in enrolment, but as the peak of the baby boom entered university around 1979, university enrolments were expected to plateau, if not fall, through the 1980s. Foot and Stoffman (1996) argue that increased participation of Canadians over age 25 in university education fuelled the growth of enrolments in the late 1980s and early 1990s. Thus, through the 1980s as the traditional supply of

---

[3]University enrolment accounts for 60% of total postsecondary enrolment (CAUT, 2003).

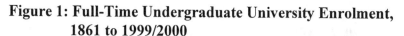
Figure 1: Full-Time Undergraduate University Enrolment, 1861 to 1999/2000

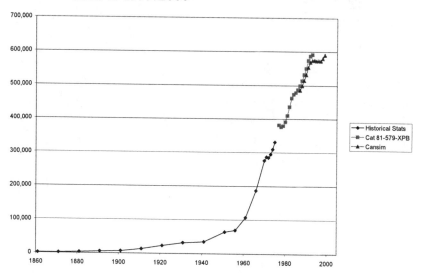

19 to 24-year-olds declined in Canada, entrance standards fell and competition to attract students increased. Foot and Stoffman contend that baby boomers facing a bottleneck in traditional career ladders returned to university to retrain for new labour market opportunities, though this was largely increasing part-time postsecondary enrolment and graduate program enrolments. The most notable feature of the growth of full-time university undergraduate enrolments is lack of change in the age group that has gone to university. The highest participation rates in university education are amongst Canadians aged 20–24. Thus, the growth of enrolment reflects the choices, behaviours, and opportunities for this age group as opposed to changing behaviours, choices, and opportunities of Canadians over the life cycle (CAUT, 2003, Figure 5.2).

Owram (1996) notes that in 1951, 1 in 20 18-year-olds went on to university. By the mid-1960s, it was one in ten, and by the early 1970s it was one in six. Participation rates have been highest for Canadians aged 20–24, and Figure 2 shows that the ratio of university enrolment in Canada to population aged 20–24 increased from less than 0.02 from 1860 to less than 0.04 in 1940. From 1940 to 1956 the ratio increased to 0.06. By 1970, the ratio had increased to 0.14. From 1970 to 1980, the ratio only increased by 0.02 to 0.16, thus enrolment increases in this decade were largely a

Figure 2: Full-Time University Enrolment to Population Aged 20–24, 1861–2001

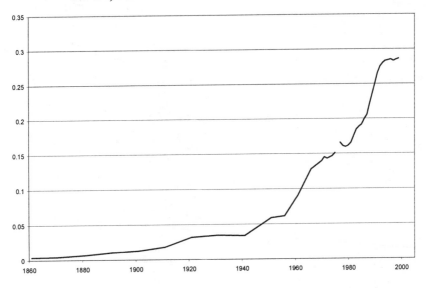

function of the baby-boom cohort entering the traditional ages for attending university. From 1980 to 1990 the ratio of enrolment to 20 to 24-year-old population increased by 0.09 to 0.25, but from 1990 to 2000 only increased by 0.04 to 0.29.

Within the 20 to 24-year-old age group, a notable development over the last half-century has been the increasing proportion of females choosing to pursue university education to the point that since 1988, females represent a larger share of undergraduate enrolment than males (Easton, 2002). Although the rising proportion of women in full-time undergraduate enrolment has been increasing for the last century, it is the post-1960 expansion in participation that is the remarkable development. In 1911, female enrolment to male enrolment was 0.25 and by 1950 the ratio had reached 0.28, and by 1960 it reached 0.33. By 1970, the ratio was 0.58 and by 1977 it was 0.8. In 1988 there were as many females as males enrolled in full-time university undergraduate study in Canada, and in 1999/2000 the ratio of female students to male students is 1.25.

Figure 3 shows that while the size of university undergraduate enrolments has increased enormously, in broad terms, what universities teach

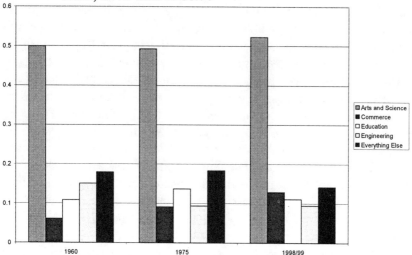

has not changed a great deal.[4] In 1960, half of enrolment was in Arts and Science and by the end of the century, half of total university enrolment was still in Arts and Science. The only discernible shifts in enrolment patterns over the last 40 years have been the relative rise of enrolment in commerce and business administration, and the decline in enrolment shares of Education, Engineering, and everything else that universities teach.[5] To

---

[4]Data for enrolments by field is from Historical Statistics of Canada for 1960 and 1975. The data for 1998/99 is from the 2003 CAUT *Almanac of Post-Secondary Education in Canada*. Arts and Science includes enrolment in Bio-sciences (excluding Agricultural Science, Veterinary Science, and Household Science), Arts and Science, Humanities (excluding Religious Studies and Theology), Math and Physical Sciences and Social Sciences (excluding Commerce and Business Administration and Law). "Everything Else" includes Fine Arts, Health Sciences (including Medicine), Household Science, Law, Religion and Theology, and Veterinary Medicine.

[5]While the distribution of undergraduate enrolments has not changed a great deal, one important change over the last 40 years has been the growth of graduate student enrolment relative to undergraduate enrolment. In 1998–99, graduate program enrolment represented less than 14% of total university full-time equivalent enrolment (CAUT, 2003, Table 5.3).

see such stability in the distribution of enrolment over 40 years of dramatic changes in Canadian labour markets may be one reason that what universities do has come into question. In particular, in the 1990s many observers argued that universities needed to re-orient towards training graduates to have tangible, specialized educations to match up with labour market needs. Allen (1998) describes the view that emerged in Canada in the 1990s that university programs in the humanities and social sciences were irrelevant for success in the global economy because graduates of these programs lacked necessary "specific skills" to find jobs. Thus, the general "Arts and Science" education most Canadian university students acquire was seen to be obsolete and impractical for the contemporary labour market. Foot and Stoffman suggest that by the mid-1980s, many younger Canadians chose not to attend university due to a combination of higher fees and possibly "because they doubt that a degree will help much on the job market" (1996, p. 155). Allen (1998) notes that the policy implications of these perspectives was that money would be better spent on technical and vocational training programs, or other university programs that taught specific, relevant skills to students.

The Labour Market for University Graduates over the Long Run

Why did participation in postsecondary education increase so dramatically after World War II, particularly after 1960? World War II and the launch of Sputnik in 1957 are often given as explanations for some of the expansion of the university system (Owram, 1996; Laidler, 2002). In particular, government support for returned veterans from the war to attend university reduced the cost of doing so, and Sputnik raised the perceived benefit to Canadian society of having a highly educated workforce, particularly in science and engineering. Whatever impact World War II or Sputnik had on university enrolments paled in comparison to what happened after 1960.

Up until World War I, agricultural employment was the dominant activity for Canadian workers, but the share of employment in agriculture had been declining since the nineteenth century. In the 1950s, strong employment growth in the area of resource extraction and resource processing, in particular, pulp and paper, oil and gas, and other minerals was driven by export demands in the United States. By the late 1950s, however, technological change in forestry and mining reduced labour needs in the primary sector. By the 1960s, the share of total employment in primary industries was declining, while the service sectors had a rapidly growing share of total employment (Norrie, Owram and Emery, 2002).

Owram (1996, p. 179) identifies the expansion of white-collar positions in administration, finance, and in the public sector between 1950 and 1980 as the trend behind the increased participation of Canadians in university education. Canada needed more teachers, civil servants, nurses, doctors, and bankers; and university education was increasingly a prerequisite for obtaining employment in these occupations.[6] Owram also argues that most of the emerging white-collar jobs required a general education in Arts and Science as opposed to "specialist training". The existence of a post-1960 relative demand shift is not in itself a complete explanation as it is not obvious why a university degree became a necessary credential for obtaining these jobs. Barber (1962) noted that a relative demand shift towards white-collar employment in favour of skilled, or more highly educated, workers was put forward as a cause for the rising unemployment rate in Canada in the late 1950s, as it was observed that many of the unemployed workers did not have the necessary skills or education. Barber argues that the largest increases in employment since 1949 were in the skilled, professional white-collar occupations, but the skill requirement to "wear a white collar" was far from clear. If the relative demand shift was a full explanation, then university enrolments should have taken off after 1949, not 1958. It must be the case that higher education levels were required over time to obtain white-collar employment. Thus, some of the rise of university education must have been due to employers upgrading the educational requirements of their workforce.

Figure 4 shows the effects of the changes in the Canadian labour market as reflected in unemployment rates of 20 to 24-year-olds and workers over 24 years of age. While 20 to 24-year-olds have always had higher unemployment rates than older age group workers, from 1946 to 1958 the gap was not large and overall measured unemployment was low. Strong employment opportunities were driven by exports of minerals,

---

[6]Owram (1996) cites that the number of government workers rose from 318,000 in 1951 to 710,000 in 1971. Similarly, the number of teachers in 1951 was 153,000 but over 250,000 by 1971.

Figure 4: Unemployment Rates by Age Group, 1946–2002

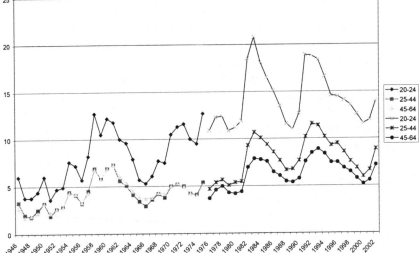

particularly oil and gas, and pulp and paper, and the coincident investment boom.[7] The 1958 recession coincided with the end of this investment boom and unemployment increased, particularly for 20 to 24-year-olds. Unemployment rates for workers over age 24 returned to a "normal" level of 5% by the early 1960s, but for 20 to 24-year-olds, unemployment rates were generally double that and stubbornly high. The next notable change in the unemployment rates was during the 1982 recession when all age groups experienced large increases in measured unemployment, but for 20 to 24-year-olds the unemployment rate reached 20% in 1983. Similarly in the early 1990s, Canadians of traditional university attendance age faced high unemployment rates. Thus, by the early 1960s, the opportunity cost of attending university for young Canadian workers fell.

While there were clearly improvements in employment prospects for university educated males in the 1960s, by the 1970s a perception emerged that employment prospects of university educated workers were declining,

---

[7]During the 1950s, gas and oil pipelines, the St. Lawrence Seaway, and the TransCanada Highway were notable projects during this boom (Norrie, Owram and Emery, 2002).

possibly due to an over-supply of university educated workers. The Canadian workforce after 1970 was thought to be increasingly "over-educated" relative to labour market needs. For example, Statistics Canada noted that while the less educated had always had more severe employment problems than the highly educated, the "rapid expansion of the supply of highly educated job-seekers could affect this relationship" (Statistics Canada, 1978, p. 168). It was also argued that overexpansion of university education, or over-education of workers, resulted in the situation that many university graduates could not find work, or they were forced down the job ladder to work in jobs that did not require a university education.[8]

This has not turned out to be the case. Riddell and Sweetman (2000) argue that the increasing level of human capital investment of Canadian workers has been in response to relative shift in the demand for labour towards demand for highly educated workers. The body of evidence apparent in employment, unemployment, and earnings outcomes over-whelmingly supports their view. While labour market conditions after 1970 worsened for all workers, they worsened by relatively less for university graduates. Allen (1998) finds that while the supply of university educated workers expanded, by the 1990s university educated workers have main-tained their place on the occupational hierarchy, have had lower unemploy-ment rates and higher earnings than less educated workers. Figure 5 shows that it is also the case that since at least 1969, university graduates have had lower unemployment rates than workers without university education (although the relative advantage for university degree holders has been in decline since 1993).[9] As Allen notes, this is true for graduates of the Humanities and Social Sciences, which suggests that general educations remain economically relevant. Allen concludes that the university system in Canada did not overexpand, and instead kept pace with the growth in demand for highly educated workers. Beaudry and Green (2000) show that since 1970 there has been a deterioration in employment outcomes for men in Canada with less than a university education, while for university

---

[8]See Allen (1998, p. 13); Riddell and Sweetman (2000); and Davenport (2002) for discussions of this point of view.

[9]Unemployment rates are from Statistics Canada (1978, Table V-8), and Cansim V2582457 and V2582460.

Figure 5: Unemployment Rates for Workers with Secondary Education and University Degrees, 1969–77 and 1990–2002

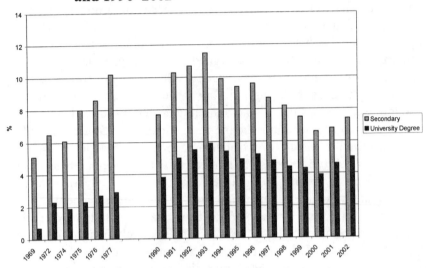

educated men, once cyclical effects are controlled for, there has been no deterioration in employment prospects.[10]

Despite the large expansion in the Canadian workforce with university education, with the exception of the first half of the 1970s, there has been no decline in the earnings premium of males with university degrees over males with high-school diplomas (Dooley, 1986; Riddell and Sweetman, 2000; Bar-Or *et al.*, 1995; and Burbidge, Magee and Robb, 2002). Census earnings data for 1961, 1971, 1981, 1991, 1995 and 2000 suggests that the "education premium" associated with a university degree increased from 1961 to 1971, but has been stable since (see Figure 6). Studies that look at ratios of weekly earnings from the Survey of Consumer Finance, the Labour Force Survey and the SLID, reveal the same overall behaviour of the education premium. Bar-Or *et al.* (1995) find that the ratio of median weekly earnings of males aged 25–64 with a university degree to the median weekly earnings of males in the same age group with a high-school

---

[10]Beaudry and Green (2000) find no evidence of increased work instability for females generally; thus, the changes in the Canadian labour market since the 1950s have largely impacted Canadian males with high-school education or less.

Herb Emery

Figure 6: Ratio of Average Annual Earnings of Workers with University Degree to Workers with Completed High School, 1961–2001 (census data)

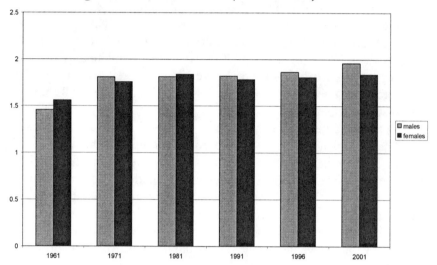

education fell from over 1.35 in 1971 to 1.3 in 1977. The ratio increased to over 1.35 in 1981 and it remained between 1.35 and 1.4 to 1991. For females, the ratio of median earnings for university and high-school educated females was 1.7 in 1971, fell to 1.55 in 1975 and then trended towards 1.65 in 1990. Burbidge, Magee and Robb (2002) look at the ratio of weekly earnings of the university and high-school educated in Canada for the period 1981 to 2001 and find that for males the ratio has remained between 1.35 and 1.4 for the entire period. For females, the earnings ratio has declined from 1.65 in 1981 to 1.5 in 2001. These studies of the education premium are informative for understanding the relatively large increase in female participation in university education. As Easton (2002) shows, the returns to university education have been persistently higher for females than for males, but it would appear that the growth of the supply of female workers with university education is starting to reduce the education premium towards that observed for males.

With the exception of the first half of the 1970s, there does not appear to be any problem with the growth of supply of highly educated workers exceeding the growth in demand for them. It would appear that the expansion of enrolment in universities, even with its orientation towards "general education" has matched the growth of labour market demands. It is also worth noting that the education premium since 1970 has been much higher than it was in 1960 prior to the expansion.

Figure 7 shows that the real costs of tuition fell to its historic lows in the mid-1980s and they have since climbed to historic highs by 2001.[11] The ratio of fee revenues to total university operating expenditures is less today than it was in 1960 (Figure 8), but this is largely explained by relatively low operating expenditures of universities before 1960 (Figure 9). Resources per university student increased until the early 1980s but have declined since that time.

Operating expenditures per student increased from 1960 to a peak in 1978, after which time growth in enrolment outpaced the expansion in university revenues. Between 1977 and 1993, general operating expenditures per full-time equivalent enrollee in universities fell from $13,500 to $11,000 (constant 1993 dollars) (Canadian Education Statistics Council, 1996, Chart C6). While tuition fees have risen since the mid-1980s, the increased fee revenue has not offset the lack of growth, and in many cases, reductions in the values of grants to universities from the provincial governments (Davenport, 2002; CAUT, 2003). Davenport (2002) shows that in 1998, public funding per student (in constant dollars) was 70% of its 1980 level. From 1980 to 1985 the decline in per student public funding to 90% of its 1980 value reflected enrolment growth outpacing the growth of government funding. After 1990, the precipitous drop in per student resources from public sources reflected dramatic reductions in provincial operating grants to universities.

What is not clear is whether the real level of resources to universities and postsecondary education should be restored to 1970s levels, be maintained at current levels, or reduced back to 1960 levels. While faculty of universities and students may complain about lower resources that result in larger classes, higher tuition fees and stagnant salaries, Canada allocates a higher share of resources to formal education than other OECD countries and has one of the most highly educated workforces in the world. Thus it may be that Canada is investing too many resources in postsecondary education. Riddell and Sweetman (2000, p. 87) show that in 1994, Canada's expenditures on education represented 7.2% of gross domestic

---

[11]For a detailed tuition fee picture, see Figure 5.4 in the CAUT Alamanc that shows Average Annual Cost of University Tuition in Canada (2001$), 1972–2002 for five different degree categories.

Herb Emery

Figure 7: Average University Tuition Fees in Canada, 1961–2001 (Constant 1992 $)

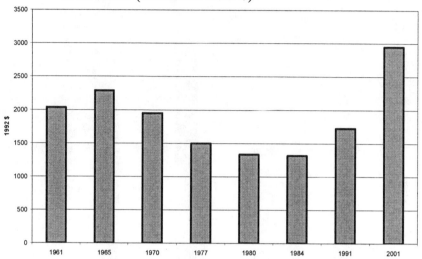

Source: Data compiled from Statistics Canada (1961/62, various years); Canadian Education Statistics Council (1996).

Figure 8: Tuition Fee Revenue as a Share of Total University Operating Expenditures, 1951–1993

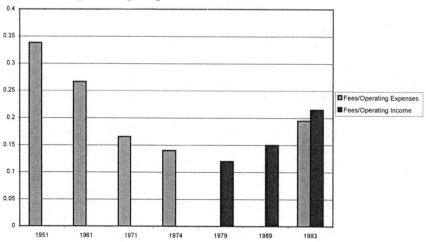

Source: Data compiled from Statistics Canada (1975) and Canadian Education Statistics Council (1996).

Total and Private Returns to University Education in Canada   *91*

Figure 9: Total Operating Expenditures per Full-Time University Student, 1951, 1961, 1971 and 1993 (Constant 1992 $)

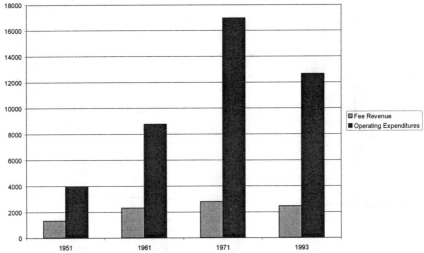

Source: Data compiled from Statistics Canada (1975) and Canadian Education Statistics Council (1996).

product (GDP) compared to the OECD average of 6.3% of GDP. Public sector spending on education was 6.7% of GDP compared to the OECD average of 5.2%. Riddell and Sweetman show that the United States spends 6.8% of GDP on education, but public sector spending on education in the United States only amounts to 4.9% of GDP. While the share of GDP that Canada expends on education and the reliance on public sector resources are high, the level of resources per student is considerably lower than in postsecondary education in the United States (Riddell and Sweetman, 2000; Davenport, 2002). In 1994, the United States had postsecondary expenditures per student of US$16,262 compared to Canada's US$11,471. The United States also has a higher proportion of its population with a university degree (25%) than Canada (17%). Thus, it is not clear if Canada should be allocating fewer resources to formal education to be more in line with the rest of the OECD, or increasing the resources to postsecondary education to keep up with the world's leading economy, the United States.

While it is clear that the Canadian labour market has increasingly demanded workers with higher levels of education since 1960, there is still the issue of the resource cost of investment in university education, and whether the benefits of the educational investment justify the allocation of resources towards university education. It may be that the education premium is stable, but it is at too low a level given the cost to society of educating the workers. The earnings of university graduates may be higher than those of high-school graduates, but is the gain in productivity enough to justify the investment of resources in those workers?

The Returns to University Undergraduate Education, 1960–2000

In this section, I examine the trends in published rates of return to bachelor's degrees over the period 1960–2000. Enrolment in programs towards a bachelor's degree, and full-time enrolment in particular, constitutes the largest part of postsecondary education in Canada and from a policy perspective, it is the component that is being questioned as a socially worthwhile investment.

Estimation and analysis of rates of return to education have been the standard approach for cost-benefit analysis of investment in postsecondary education (Weale, 1993). The standard measure for the rate of return to education is to compare a "snap-shot" of average earnings at different stages of the working life for people with different educational attainments. The rate of return is calculated as the interest rate (discount rate) that would be required to equate the present value of the incremental increases in earnings associated with the education level expected over the remainder of the working life with the present value of the costs incurred in acquiring the education. Rates of return that are intended to represent the value of an education level to society are referred to as *total rates of return*, or *social rates of return*, or *public rates of return*. Rates of return that represent the profitability of an educational investment for the individual acquiring the human capital are referred to as *private rates of return*.

Rates of return are calculated with an income-based approach. For private rates of return, the increase in income associated with the educational attainment represents the benefit for the educated individual. For total rates of return, the validity of the income-based approach for representing the gains to society from an educational investment requires that earnings are determined by market mechanisms. If we assume that the wages/earnings of workers reflect their productivity (value of what they produce for society), then the earnings of an individual reflects the value of their labour services to society. Thus, the gain to society from individuals acquiring postsecondary education are represented by the gain in income that the individual can expect to earn with the education level compared to what he or she would have earned without the education level. If we assume that a worker's increase in income from the education reflects an increase in the value of their marginal product of labour, then the increase in a worker's income represents the increase in gross domestic product attributable to the educational investment.

Weale (1993) discusses the potential biases associated with an income-based approach for valuing educational investments. The higher earnings of university educated individuals will reflect the influence of the education on productivity, and the potentially higher abilities of individuals choosing to acquire a university education. Rates of return attributed to university education that are based on average earnings of individuals with different educational attainments will be biased upwards as they will in part reflect a return to the innate ability of the individual. Rates of return based on an income approach are also potentially biased downward since income does not necessarily capture non-pecuniary (consumption) benefits of an education or the benefits of increased civic participation that are associated with higher levels of education; or productivity increases of lesser educated workers arising from the interaction with higher educated workers; or productivity increases associated with improved health outcomes associated with increasing levels of educational attainment.

If we wish to assess the value of an education, we need to assess the present value of the stream of net benefits that the educated worker will produce from now until they retire. The present value of a dollar received in t years, is the amount of money that you would have to invest today at interest rate r to receive the one dollar in t years. This reflects that a dollar received in t years has a value of less than one dollar today due to the opportunity cost of money.

$$NPV = \sum_{t=1}^{T} \frac{B_t - C_t}{(1+r)^{t-1}}$$

B_t and C_t are the benefits and costs accruing to the investment in each year t. The net present value of an investment is a sum of the present value of net benefits from each year t over the remainder of the working life. The internal rate of return (IRR) to the investment is the value of r which sets the net present value of the investment to 0. The IRR compares the stream of benefits from investment in education to the stream of costs from the time that the investment begins to the time at which the degree-holder is assumed to retire. The IRR is determined by using the following:

$$\text{IRR} = r^* \text{ such that } \sum_{t=1}^{T} \frac{B_t - C_t}{(1 + r^*)^t} = 0$$

The IRR is interpreted as the real annual rate of return to the investment which is directly comparable to annualized rates of return to other investments like stocks, bonds or real estate.

To do this calculation, age-earnings profiles associated with populations with different levels of education are represented as the average earnings of individuals with a specified level of education at each age. For total/social rates of return, the before-tax incomes of a representative university degree-holder provide the B_t stream, and measures of the resources allocated towards teaching an individual while in university plus the foregone before-tax earnings of a representative high-school graduate provide the C_t stream. The resources allocated to teaching an individual student are often proxied by an estimated share of university operating expenses that goes towards teaching and allocated on a per student basis. For the total rate of return, tax incidence and tuition fees are irrelevant to the calculation since they merely apportion the benefits and costs between the individual student and society.[12] Typically, for the private rate of return, after-tax incomes of a representative university degree-holder are the B_t stream, and the foregone after-tax earnings of a representative high-school graduate, and the costs of tuition and books incurred while in university are included in the C_t stream.[13]

---

[12]To the extent that subsidies for postsecondary education, and the taxes imposed on individuals not currently acquiring postsecondary education, are distortionary, the economy will experience some drag due to deadweight losses of the taxes and subsidies. Vaillancourt and Bourdeau-Primeau (2002) argue that the omission of these costs will bias the rate of returns upwards.

[13]It is also possible to adjust incomes to account for the benefits of non-wage/fringe benefits. The incomes used typically correspond to workers who worked full-year and full-time. Housing costs, food, etc. are not included since it is assumed that these costs are borne whether the individual invests in the education

Because average earnings for education levels are used, these rates of return are referred to as average rates of return and these need to be distinguished from marginal rates of return that would be based upon the increase in earnings from an education associated with the last or marginal individual admitted into the educational program.[14] Calculated IRRs are "risk-free" rates of return since they typically do not incorporate unemployment, mortality, child-bearing or health risks that may interrupt a worker's time in the labour force.[15] For married females, the assumption that the working careers will be uninterrupted from ages 23 to 65 is not a particularly good one to make and may lead to unrealistically high calculated IRRs. As cross-sectional earnings data is used to construct age-earnings profiles for the calculations, it is also a maintained assumption that there is no expected productivity growth (general increases in real wages in the economy), and as inflation does not influence the cross-sectional calculation, the IRRs are interpreted real annual rates of return to the investment.

Figure 10 presents the estimated total rates of return to university degrees from 21 studies published between 1968 and 2002 plotted against

---

or not. Vaillancourt and Bourdeau-Primeau (2002) discuss two other maintained assumptions of these approaches. First, a single year of earnings information is representative of what an individual can expect to earn over the remainder of their working life. Second, it is common to assume that all workers retire at the same age. To the extent that retirement behaviour differs across workers with different educational attainments, this assumption will bias the rates of return.

[14]Marginal rates of return are likely much lower at this time than the estimated average rates of return. Consider that at the University of Calgary, only two-thirds of students who were admitted to the university in Fall 1990 went on to graduate by 2000 (University of Calgary, 2001). One-third of first-year students incur education costs with no associated benefit of the education which means for them, admission to university has a negative rate of return.

[15]Calculations by the author show that if the gap in unemployment rates between high-school graduates and university degree-holders is six percentage points as was the case in 1981, then the IRR adjusted for this gap will be 1.4 percentage points higher than the risk-free rate.

the year for which they were calculated.[16] Figure 11 presents the estimated private rates of return to university degrees from the same studies. The figures demonstrate many of the conclusions about investment in university education. First, both the private and total rates of return to university education are high for the entire 1960 to 2000 period, with private rates of return typically being over 10% and social rates of return over 6%. Second, there appears to have been some reduction in the rates of return to university education in the late 1970s and early 1980s, but by 1985, the rates of return resumed their high levels of the 1960s and 1970s.

Typically the estimates presented in Figures 10 and 11 are presented as a defence of continued investment in university education in the sense that they are used to address the perception that the returns have been falling over time, and may have declined to levels at which it makes little sense to continue investing in university education. What has not been established is the long-run trends for the total and private rates of return to university education, and what these trends may suggest about the likely rates of return in the future. To that end, I compiled a list of rates of return found in the literature and the characteristics of the studies (year published, for males/females/both, for Canada or a province, whether Census earnings data was used, and whether taxes were accounted for in the calculation of the private rates of return).[17] Then the rates of return were regressed on the set of study characteristics to establish the expected rate of return by year for Canada and for males and for females. Time and time-squared were included to account for any trends.

The fitted rates of return shown in Figure 12 highlight the declining total rates of return to university education after 1960 up until the mid-1980s. Even at the low point, however, in the late 1970s, for males the rate of return was above 7.8% and 8.8% for females. While total rates of return

---

[16]Some data points on the figures correspond to estimates for males and females from the same study. Where studies reported rates of return by specific bachelor's degree programs, shares of total enrolments in those programs in Canada were used to calculate an "average rate of return" to correspond to a general "bachelor's" degree. Some studies report rates of return for specific provinces as opposed to Canada.

[17]The rates of return and study characteristics are largely from Vaillancourt (1995, Table 1) and Vaillancourt and Bourdeau-Primeau (2002, Table 1), supplemented with some other studies that they did not include in their surveys. The data-set is presented in Appendix 1.

Figure 10: Published Estimates of the Total Rates of Return to Bachelor's Degrees in Canada for the Period 1960–1995

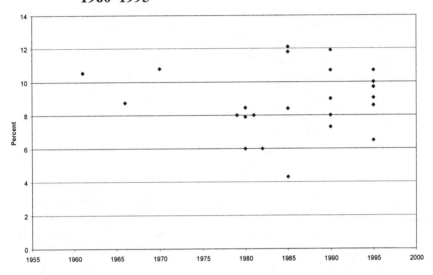

Figure 11: Published Estimates of the Private Rates of Returns to Bachelor's Degrees in Canada for the Period 1960–1998

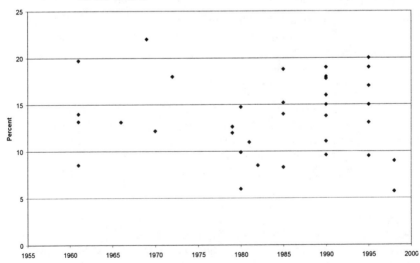

Herb Emery

Figure 12: Fitted Rates of Return to Bachelor's Degrees, Canada, 1960–2000

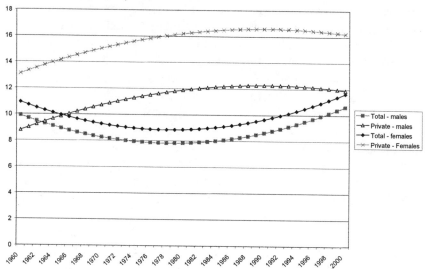

were at their lowest, the private rates of return were at their highest when resources per student were high and the real cost of tuition was low. It is not difficult to see why policymakers saw that there was scope for students to pay more for their education and lower public expenditures on universities. By 2000, total rates of return are high and private rates of return have fallen by two percentage points from their peak values of 12.3 and 16.6% in 1990. Clearly, the bachelor's degree has been, and continues to be, a worthwhile investment for society and for the individual acquiring the education.

The higher rates of return for females is probably due in part to the upward bias associated with the assumption of full-time employment from the date of graduation to retirement, the higher education premium for females, and tax differences associated with income levels.

The direction of change in the fitted private rates of return would seem to support the view that rising tuition fees, and consequently student debt loads, are eroding the incentive for Canadians to invest in university education at a time when the benefit to Canadian society from having them do so is rising. The levels of the private rates of return to university degrees, however, remain high, suggesting that tuition fee increases of the last 16 years have not rendered university education a poor investment. The rates of return are high enough that there is still room for tuition fees to rise. Stager (1996) finds that increasing the private share of the direct university teaching costs to 40%, via a doubling of tuition fees from $1,950 to $3,900, would reduce the private rate of return to bachelor's degrees by only three percentage points. Rathje and Emery (2002) estimate that there is still considerable room for tuition fees to rise as it would take an increase of over $10,000 in annual tuition fees for social science programs over the current levels to render a private rate of return of 4.25%.[18]

Perhaps the most interesting implication of these changes in the total rates of return to bachelor's degrees concerns what these findings suggest about whether more resources should be allocated to university education. As the earnings premium of university graduates has been stable since 1970, the changes in the total returns to bachelor's degrees are driven by changes in resource costs of education and potentially the distribution of who pays the cost. The total returns fell as the per student resources increased and tuition fees fell. The private return increased in the 1970s despite a falling wage gap due to the falling costs for the individual. The reversal of the 1970s trends, with rising total returns and falling private returns arose from diminishing resources per student in universities and rising tuition fees, as earnings ratios of university degree-holders to high-school graduates have been stable through the 1980s and 1990s as shown above. Given the stability of the bachelor's degree earnings premium, it would appear that the Canadian labour market has not identified students educated in larger classes and with fewer resources as being less productive than earlier cohorts of university graduates. This suggests that universities have responded to the squeeze on resources by using up excess capacity in the university so as to exploit scale economies in undergraduate instruction. In addition, universities have exploited the availability of Web-based teaching and library resources, and have substituted sessional/part-time for more expensive full-time tenured professors' teaching time, particularly for large enrolment, lower level of curriculum, first-year courses. This suggests that earlier cohorts of university graduates were beneficiaries of unnecessarily high resources allocated to universities, and the squeeze on university funding since the 1980s has not had high social costs for Canadians.

---

[18]Davenport (1996), Stager (1996), and Rathje and Emery (2002) also show that there is considerable scope for differentiating fees and fee increases by program.

What Will Happen to Returns to University Education in the Future?

Since the earnings premium of university graduates over high-school graduates in Canada has been stable since 1970, the changes in the rates of return to university education over the last 30 years were largely driven by changes in resources allocated to university education over time and changes in tuition fee levels. Canada is on the verge of a dramatic change in its labour supply as the workers of the baby-boom generation reach the normal age of retirement. While there are reasons to believe that the labour force participation rates of baby boomers in their 60s could rise due to policy changes (e.g., increased age of eligibility for pension benefits), sluggish returns from capital markets, restructuring of work arrangements to accommodate preferences of older workers; and possibly due to improved health status at higher ages, it is inevitable that the supply of labour in Canada will not grow to keep pace with the growth in labour demand. In all likelihood, this slower growth of labour supply will result in rising real wages paid for labour services (Emery and Rongve, 1999; Scarth, 2002; Merette, 2002).

Merette (2002) is of the view that the growth in the demand for labour will be biased towards high human capital workers, but it is not obvious that this will occur. If Merette is correct, then the earnings premium of university graduates over high-school graduates will rise and dominate any increases in education resource costs resulting in increasing private and total rates of return to university education. If the rise of participation in postsecondary education reflected the relative rise in demand for high education workers over lower education workers, then when the baby boomers retire, the premium of university graduate earnings over high-school graduates' earnings and hence the returns to investment in post-secondary education should rise. Riddell and Sweetman (2000) come down on the side of the latter hypothesis and work by Beaudry and Green (2000) documents that employment opportunities for university graduates have been greater than for high-school graduates and such conditions will likely persist. Thus, while the social and private rates of return to university education are high in 2004, the aging Canadian labour force could result in higher rates of return to university education.

On the other hand, if the relative rise in demand for labour increases wages for all skill/education levels, and if the resource costs of post-secondary education rise, then it is also possible that the rates of return to human capital could fall. If university education is largely useful for helping employers choose between workers in ways that result in unnecessarily high education levels required for jobs, then as the baby boomers retire, the general labour scarcity will diminish the ability of employers to maintain their high requirements for education to fill the job due to the increased competition for workers and the earnings premium of university graduates would fall.

What About "Other Postsecondary" Programs?

Allen (1998) and Davenport (2002) describe how in the 1990s a belief emerged that a technical education at a community college or vocational school was more valuable than a university degree, particularly when the degree was in the humanities or social sciences. Full-time undergraduate university study accounts for 60 to 65% of total postsecondary enrolment in Canada today. In 1998, expenditures on university education accounted for 21% of total education spending in Canada and 49% of total postsecondary education expenditures. Expenditures on trade level education accounted for 32% of total postsecondary spending and community colleges accounted for 19%. Since 1993, total expenditures on community colleges in Canada increased 14% and trades level education had total expenditures increase by 41%. Over the same period, total expenditures on university education increased by only 4% (Statistics Canada, 2000). Thus, recent policy changes in Canada have directed resources to "other postsecondary" programs as opposed to university education, with the one caveat that many community colleges have expanded their university transfer programs and in some cases have evolved into bachelor's degree-granting institutions. Perhaps what is most striking is the commitment of resources to training Canadians in trades. This allocation of resources away from the general education of universities to training for specific skills reflects what Allen (1998) and Laidler (2002) identify as a declining belief in the relevance of university education in today's labour market. Is this direction a desirable one for Canada's postsecondary education system to take?

On the premise that incremental resources should be allocated to the use that yields the highest return, it would appear that the expansion of trades and community college education is not a socially efficient use of resources. Allen (1998) and Davenport (2002) show that earnings of university graduates, employment prospects and unemployment rates reflect superior labour market outcomes for university graduates over college diploma holders and trades people in Canada. Default rates on student loans are lower for universities than any other class of postsecondary institution. The picture emerges that there is an education-based hierarchy in the Canadian labour market with high-school leavers and graduates at the bottom and university degree-holders at the top. College diploma holders and graduates of trade vocational schools sit in the middle of the hierarchy. While there has been a perception that the lofty position of university degree-holders has declined, Allen (1998) shows that it has not. University graduates in the mid-1990s had far better labour market outcomes and status than any other education level. Whatever deterioration in the labour market for university degree-holders occurred was less severe than the deterioration in labour market prospects for workers with other levels of education (other than graduate degree-holders).

Two studies that estimate the rates of return to college diplomas, trades training and bachelor's degrees support the view that the highest returns for students and Canadian society arise from resources allocated to universities. Figure 13 summarizes the rates of return to college education, trades training, and bachelor's degrees calculated by Vaillancourt (1995) for 1985 and Rathje (2000) for 1995. Both studies indicate that the private and "public" (total, social) rates of return to bachelor's degrees have exceeded other postsecondary education in 1985 and 1995 for males and females. Given the enormous expansion of resources towards trades training since 1993, Rathje's finding that the IRR for trades training were so large and negative as to be "undefined" should trouble policymakers. For the individual and society, the investment in these programs would appear not to be worthwhile. This could help to explain why the default rate of student loans for students in trades programs was 30% in Ontario in 1996 and 1999 when the default rate for students graduating from universities was 10% or less. These rates of return can also help explain why demand for university transfer programs has grown in community colleges over the last decade and why community colleges have been evolving towards traditional bachelor's degree institutions specializing in the humanities and social sciences programs. Both studies support Allen (1998) and Davenport (2002) who conclude that university education is considerably more valuable than that provided by colleges and vocational schools.

Figure 13: Public and Private Returns to College Diplomas and Bachelor's Degrees 1985 and 1995

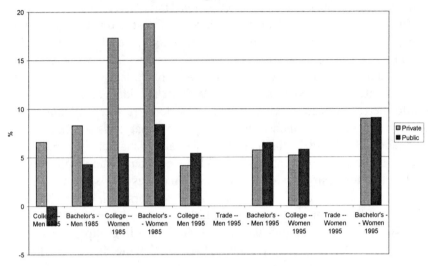

Policy Directions for Postsecondary Education in Canada

This paper posed three general policy questions for postsecondary education in Canada. First, do the levels of resources for postsecondary education need to be increased, and perhaps restored, to the per student levels of the 1970s and early 1980s? Second, should the majority of postsecondary resources for teaching continue to go to "general education" as associated with Arts and Science programs in universities, or should resources be diverted to "specific skills training" associated with professional degree programs, vocational programs, and trades training? Third, who should pay for postsecondary education, Canadian taxpayers or the individual receiving the education? The answer to the second question is clearly "yes". The rates of return to investment in bachelor's degrees are higher for the individual acquiring the education and for the society in which they live than the rates of return for investments in vocational and trades training.

The answer to the first question is not so clear. The review of total rates of return to university education suggests that there has been no social cost to date of reducing per student resources in universities since the mid-

1980s. In all likelihood, this has reflected the disappearance of some of the excess capacity in the university system with growing enrolments and efficiency gains in universities associated with substitution to lower cost teaching inputs and exploitation of scale economies in undergraduate teaching. How much further universities can go in accommodating the squeeze on resources in future is uncertain, and in all likelihood, requires some significant structural changes in the university system. First, the excess capacity that remains in the university system is largely in universities that are in urban centres remote from the large populations of 18 to 24-year-olds, and/or in urban centres with declining populations. If the demand for university space is high in Toronto, but not in Peterborough, St. Catherines, Sudbury or Thunder Bay, then to accommodate further growth in university enrolment, it may be necessary to have a geographic rationalization of university resources. Similarly, most universities in Canada have a dual mission of research and teaching. It may be that unless resources per student are maintained, then it may be necessary to have a small number of universities specialize as research institutions, and the majority of universities take on the role of pure teaching colleges.

Presuming that universities need more resources, there is the issue of where the additional resources would come from. It is unlikely that governments will restore the level of public funding per student for universities to the levels of the late 1970s and early 1980s, particularly as health-care budgets grow to take a bigger share of provincial government budgets. This means that student fees will need to rise considerably in future to increase university resources. Private rates of return to bachelor's degrees suggest that the good news for universities is that there is still considerable room for raising fees without discouraging prospective students so long as the necessary capital markets are in place for students to borrow. With the retirement of the baby-boom generation, it is also likely the case that the scope for raising fees will increase over the next 30 years.

Appendix 1: Data for Regression for Figure 12

Author	Year Published	Year of Returns	Private Return	Total Returns	Male	Female	Both	Not Specified	Canada/ Province	Census Data Only	Tax Treatment
Podoluk	1968	1961	19.7	na	1	0	0	0	0	1	0
Stager	1968	1961	13.2	10.55	0	0	1	0	1	1	1
Dodge and Stager	1972	1966	13.15	8.75	1	0	0	0	0	0	0
Crean	1972	1961	8.55	na	0	0	1	0	0	1	1
Mehmet	1977	1961	14	na	0	0	1	0	0	1	0
Mehmet	1977	1969	22	na	0	0	1	0	0	0	0
Mehmet	1977	1972	18	na	0	0	1	0	0	1	0
Belanger and Lavallee	1980	1979	12	na	0	0	0	1	2	0	0
Cousineau	1984	1979	12.65	8	0	0	0	1	2	0	1
Vaillancourt and Henriques	1986	1981	11	8	1	0	0	0	0	0	1
Vaillancourt and Henriques	1986	1982	8.5	6	0	0	1	0	2	0	1
Cousineau and Vaillancourt	1987	1980	14.75	8.45	0	0	0	1	0	1	1
Vaillancourt, Carpentier and Henriques	1987	1980	6	6	1	0	0	0	0	1	1
Stager	1989	1985	14	12.1	1	0	0	0	1	1	1
Stager	1989	1985	15.2	11.8	0	1	0	0	1	1	1
Stager	1989	1970	12.2	10.8	1	0	0	0	1	1	1
Stager	1989	1980	9.9	7.9	1	0	0	0	1	1	1
Vaillancourt	1995	1985	8.3	4.3	1	0	0	0	0	1	1
Vaillancourt	1995	1985	18.8	8.4	0	1	0	0	0	1	1

continued

Stager	1996	1990	13.8	10.7	1	0	0	0	1	1	1
Stager	1996	1990	17.8	11.9	0	1	0	0	1	1	1
Dickson, Milne and Murrell	1996	1990	9.6	7.3	0	0	1	0	3	1	1
Stager	1998	1995	13.1	9.7	1	0	0	0	1	1	1
Stager	1998	1995	19	10.7	0	1	0	0	1	1	1
Vaillancourt	1997	1990	15	9	1	0	0	0	0	1	1
Vaillancourt	1997	1990	18	8	0	1	0	0	0	1	1
Demers	2000	1990	11.1	na	0	0	0	1	2	1	1
Demers	2000	1995	9.5	na	0	0	0	1	2	1	1
Bourdeau-Primeau	1999	1995	17	10	1	0	0	0	0	1	1
Bourdeau-Primeau	1999	1995	15	10	0	1	0	0	0	1	1
Bourdeau-Primeau and Vaillancourt	2002	1990	16	8	1	0	0	0	0	1	1
Bourdeau-Primeau and Vaillancourt	2002	1990	19	8	0	1	0	0	0	1	1
Bourdeau-Primeau and Vaillancourt	2002	1995	17	10	1	0	0	0	0	1	1
Bourdeau-Primeau and Vaillancourt	2002	1995	20	10	0	1	0	0	0	1	1
Allen	1998	1995	na	8.6	0	0	1	0	0	0	0
Rathje and Emery	2002	1995	na	6.5	1	0	0	0	0	1	1
Rathje and Emery	2002	1995	na	9.05	0	1	0	0	0	1	1
Rathje and Emery	2002	1998	5.73	na	1	0	0	0	0	1	1
Rathje and Emery	2002	1998	8.98	na	0	1	0	0	0	1	1

Appendix 2: Estimated Coefficients and P-Values for Rates of Return Regressions

	Dependent Variable – Total Rate of Return	Dependent Variable – Private Rate of Return
Independent variable	Coefficient Estimate (P-value)	Coefficient Estimate (P-value)
Time	−0.22 (0.11)	0.23 (0.38)
Time squared	0.006 (0.07)	−0.004 (0.53)
For females	1.01 (0.12)	4.3 (0.02)
For males and females	−0.82 (0.48)	1.76 (0.47)
Sex not specified	1.54 (0.23)	2.96 (0.37)
Used census earnings data	−1.1 (0.27)	0.04 (0.99)
Accounts for taxes	- -	−5.7 (0.02)
For Ontario	2.8 (0.00)	0.9 (0.58)
For Quebec	−1.2 (0.42)	−5.2 (0.15)
For New Brunswick	0.57 (0.76)	−4.5 (0.33)
Constant	9.9 (0.00)	14.5 (0.00)
Number of observations	29	36
R-squared	0.64	0.44

Note: The constant represents the Canada-wide rate of return to university education for males in 1960.

References

Allen, R.C. 1998. "The Employability of University Graduates in the Humanities, Social Sciences, and Education: Recent Statistical Evidence". Discussion Paper No. 98-15. Vancouver, BC: Department of Economics, University of British Columbia.

Barber, C. 1962. "Canada's Unemployment Problem", *Canadian Journal of Economics and Political Science* 28(1), 88-102.

Bar-Or, Y., J. Burbidge, L. Magee and A.L. Robb. 1995. "The Wage Premium to a University Education in Canada, 1971-1991", *Journal of Labor Economics* 13(4), 762-794.

Beaudry, P. and D.A. Green. 2000. "Employment Outcomes in Canada: A Cohort Analysis", in W.C. Riddell and F. St. Hilaire (eds.), *Adapting Public Policy to a Labour Market in Transition*. Montreal: Institute for Research on Public Policy.

Burbidge, J.B., L. Magee and A.L. Robb. 2002. "The Education Premium in Canada and the United States", *Canadian Public Policy / Analyse de Politiques* 28(2), 203-217.

Canadian Association of University Teachers (CAUT). 2003. *CAUT Almanac of Post-Secondary Education in Canada 2003.* Ottawa: CAUT.

Canadian Education Statistics Council. 1996. "Index of General Operating Expenditures and Full-Time Equivalent (FTE) Enrolments and General Operating Expenditures per FTE, Constant 1993 Dollars, Canada, 1977-1993", *A Statistical Portrait of Education at the University Level in Canada*. Catalogue No. 81-579-XPB. Ottawa: Statistics Canada.

Davenport, P. 1996. "Deregulation and Restructuring in Ontario's University System", *Canadian Business Economics* 4(4), 27-36.

_____. 2002. "Universities and the Knowledge Economy", in D. Laidler (ed.), *Renovating the Ivory Tower: Canadian Universities and the Knowledge Economy*. Toronto: C.D. Howe Institute.

Dooley, M.D. 1986. "The Overeducated Canadian? Changes in the Relationship among Earnings, Education, and Age for Canadian Men: 1971-1981", *Canadian Journal of Economics* 19(1), 142-159.

Easton, S.T. 2002. "Do We Have a Problem Yet? Women and Men in Higher Education", in D. Laidler (ed.), *Renovating the Ivory Tower: Canadian Universities and the Knowledge Economy*. Toronto: C.D. Howe Institute.

Emery, J.C.H. and I. Rongve. 1999. "Much Ado About Nothing? Demographic Bulges, The Productivity Puzzle, and CPP Reform", *Contemporary Economic Policy* 17(1), 68-78.

Foot, D.K. and D. Stoffman. 1996. *Boom, Bust & Echo: How to Profit from the Coming Demographic Shift*. Toronto: Macfarlane, Walter & Ross.

Laidler, D. 2002. "Renovating the Ivory Tower: An Introductory Essay", in D. Laidler (ed.), *Renovating the Ivory Tower: Canadian Universities and the Knowledge Economy*. Toronto: C.D. Howe Institute.

Mehmet, O. 1977. "Economic Returns on Undergraduate Fields of Study in Canadian Universities: 1961 to 1972", *Relations Industrielles/Industrial Relations* 32(3), 321-339.

Merette, M. 2002. "The Bright Side: A Positive View on the Economics of Aging", *Choices* 8(1). Montreal: Institute for Research on Public Policy.

Norrie, K., D. Owram and J.C.H. Emery. 2002. *A History of the Canadian Economy,* 3rd edition. Toronto: Thompson-Nelson.

Owram, D. 1996. *Born at the Right Time: A History of the Baby Boom Generation.* Toronto: University of Toronto Press.

Psacharopoulos, G. 1989. "Time Trends of the Returns to Education: Cross-National Evidence", *Economics of Education Review* 8(3), 225-231.

Rathje, K.A. 2000. "Rates of Return to Advanced Education". Calgary: Department of Economics, University of Calgary. MA thesis.

Rathje, K.A. and J.C.H. Emery. 2002. "Returns to University Education in Canada Using New Estimates of Program Costs", in D. Laidler (ed.), *Renovating the Ivory Tower: Canadian Universities and the Knowledge Economy.* Toronto: C.D. Howe Institute.

Riddell, W.C. and A. Sweetman. 2000. "Human Capital Formation in a Period of Rapid Change", in W.C. Riddell and F. St. Hilaire (eds.), *Adapting Public Policy to a Labour Market in Transition.* Montreal: Institute for Research on Public Policy.

Scarth, W. 2002. "Population Aging, Productivity and Living Standards", in A. Sharpe, F. St-Hilaire and K. Banting (eds.), *The Review of Economic Performance and Social Progress: Towards a Social Understanding of Productivity.* Montreal: Institute for Research on Public Policy.

Stager, D.A.A. 1996. "Returns to Investment in Ontario University Education, 1960-1990, and Implications for Tuition Fee Policy", *The Canadian Journal of Higher Education* 26(2), 1-22.

Statistics Canada. 1961/62. *University Student Expenditure and Income in Canada 1961-62.* Catalogue No. 81-520. Ottawa: Statistics Canada.

_____. 1975. *Historical Compendium of Education Statistics from Confederation to 1972.* Catalogue No. 81-568. Ottawa: Statistics Canada.

_____. 1978. "Spring Unemployment Rate by Educational Level, Canada, 1969-77", in *Out of School - Into the Labour Force: Trend and Prospects for Enrolment, School Leavers and the Labour Force in Canada – The 1960s Through the 1980s.* Catalogue No. 81-570E. Ottawa: Statistics Canada.

_____. 2000. *Education in Canada, 2000.* Catalogue No. 81-229. Ottawa: Statistics Canada.

_____. Various Years. *Tuition and Living Accommodation Costs at Canadian Degree-Granting Universities and Colleges.* Catalogue No. 81-219 for 1965–66 to 1970–71, and 1993–94. Ottawa: Statistics Canada.

Texeira, P.N. 2000. "A Portrait of the Economics of Education, 1960-1997", in R.E. Backhouse and J. Biddle (eds.), *Toward a History of Applied Economics,*

Annual Supplement to Volume 32 *History of Political Economy*. Durham and London: Duke University Press.

University of Calgary. 2001. *A Profile of Full-Time Frosh at the University of Calgary*. Analysis Report No. 571. Calgary: Office of Institutional Analysis.

Vaillancourt, F. 1995. "The Private and Total Returns to Education in Canada, 1986", *Canadian Journal of Economics* 28(3), 532-554.

Vaillancourt, F. and S. Bourdeau-Primeau. 2002. "The Returns to University Education, 1990 and 1995", in D. Laidler (ed.), *Renovating the Ivory Tower: Canadian Universities and the Knowledge Economy*. Toronto: C.D. Howe Institute.

Weale, M. 1993. "A Critical Evaluation of Rate of Return Analysis", *Economic Journal* 103(418), 729-737.

Universities as Drivers of Regional and National Innovation: An Assessment of the Linkages from Universities to Innovation and Economic Growth

Julian R. Betts and Carolyn W.B. Lee

Introduction

Job growth, innovation, and an abundance of well-paying high-tech jobs —
is there a politician anywhere who would want less of these things in his or
her region? It is not surprising, then, that regional planners worldwide have
tried to develop a recipe for replicating the economic success of Silicon
Valley in their home region (see Kenney, 2000; Lee, Miller and Hancock,
2000; Rosenberg, 2002). Many commentators have speculated that one of
the key ingredients in this recipe is the presence of a strong university
system (see Smilor, Kozmetsky and Gibson, 1998; Etzkowitz, Webster and
Healey, 1998).

This paper will selectively review the literature on universities as
determinants of regional and national innovation, focusing first on potential

The authors would like to acknowledge the able assistance of Solace Shen
and Rick Switzer. Funding for this work was provided in part by the University of
California's Industry-University Cooperative Research Program and the California
Council on Science and Technology.

pathways through which universities might act as drivers of innovation, and then on the empirical evidence. We find circumstantial evidence from around the world that universities can and do play an important role. These individual pieces of evidence collectively become more compelling than any piece of evidence viewed on its own. But perhaps the most important message from the literature is that there are many ways to boost scientific innovation locally, and universities can play dominant or subsidiary roles in that process. What seems most clear is that a university acting entirely on its own cannot do much to boost regional innovation unless a multi-faceted entrepreneurial infrastructure is in place locally. This includes a complex and subtle set of complementary physical, political, and organizational inputs. In short, universities appear to matter importantly, but there is no single recipe for success.

The next section outlines the theoretical pathways through which the presence of universities could boost the rate of innovation locally, followed by an examination of the conceptual problems that confront research in this area. Subsequent sections examine the importance of the supply of skills generated by university graduates, direct evidence of the impact of universities on innovative activity itself, and less direct evidence from the burgeoning literature on high-tech clusters. We make frequent references to research on "what makes Silicon Valley tick", and in addition provide a case study of the rapid rise of San Diego as a cluster for biotech and wireless communications technology.

Basic Mechanisms and Problems of Interpretation

There are at least five mechanisms through which the presence of a university could boost the amount of research and development (R&D) or the creation of high-tech jobs more generally:

University as Trainer. This mechanism refers to the university's role in providing to the local economy a steady and ample supply of skilled young university graduates.

University as Innovator. This mechanism refers to direct generation and commercialization of knowledge by universities working fairly independently of the private sector.

University as Partner. The university as partner provides technical know-how to local or national firms through fee-for-service agreements, less formal consulting on the part of university professors, and more formal joint ventures which often involve a private concern helping university researchers to commercialize the product of a university-owned patent. In addition, there is the possibility that a private firm licenses an existing patent owned by a university and pays royalties, but does this at arm's length rather than working collaboratively with university personnel.

University as a Regional Talent Magnet. By "talent magnet" we mean any way in which the presence of a university in a region increases the attractiveness of the region as a whole to talented innovative entrepreneurs, scientists, and engineers. For example, in the hopes of establishing working relationships with professors, a high-tech firm may decide to open an office in a city that boasts a strong team of university researchers. More subtly, a top university often recruits skilled senior scientists and engineers from other regions, only to have these individuals leave after some time to work locally in the private sector. The university may have acted as a magnet to attract such workers to a region in the first place, and so can claim some of the credit for subsequent innovations made by its former employees who remain in the local labour market.

University as Facilitator. Another role that universities can play is to create a venue to facilitate networking among those involved in the high-tech community from the private and public sector. While acting as a convener is not an obvious comparative advantage of the university, we will document evidence that both Stanford University and the University of California San Diego (UCSD) have facilitated networking with visible and positive effects on the local high-tech private sectors.

Problems of Interpretation

Our definitions of the university as trainer, innovator, partner, regional talent magnet, and facilitator of networking are in themselves somewhat vague. But these problems of definition are dwarfed relative to the problems inherent in observing these patterns in the real world. Accordingly, in this paper, the best we can do is to create a collage of evidence from many countries. A third difficulty, and perhaps the greatest of all, is that of assigning causation. The existing literature takes two broad approaches. The first is to focus on one aspect of innovation, say, patenting, and to estimate statistically the impact of universities on local patent rates. These studies are very useful but are limited in the sense that the "economic production function" that maps the many inputs that go into innovative activity into the "output", in this case patents, is not clearly measurable. Many inputs into the process, such as the quality of personnel and the purchase of consulting time, will often be poorly measured or completely unmeasured.

A second approach, which has gained currency in the last decade and a half, is qualitative analysis of high-tech clusters (Council on Competitiveness, 2001). This approach seeks to find cause and effect by looking for a common set of factors that underlies successful regional clusters. This more informal analysis, which relies on spatial correlations, is obviously even more prone to errors of interpretation. The most dangerous risk is that it becomes easy to overstate the role of the university. If high-tech clusters tend to exist only in major cities where universities exist, then can we claim that universities *cause* high-tech clusters to arise? If proximity is the sole criterion then perhaps we should also conclude that universities "cause" the creation of international airports, professional sports teams, drug abuse, homelessness, and inner city decay more generally! We believe that cluster analysis has much to tell us about causation, but only when it is backed up by evidence about the thickness of local high-tech networks, and the extent to which universities are embedded in those networks.

Evidence on the Link between a Local Supply of College Graduates and Innovation

The University as Trainer

The role of "university as trainer" seems obvious. Industries that experience rapid technological change require highly educated workers to implement these changes, and universities and community colleges provide these workers to the economy. Econometric studies have shown that technological change is skill-biased (that is, skill-using). (See, e.g., Berman, Bound and Griliches, 1994 for the United States; Betts, 1997 for Canada; and Berman, Bound and Machin, 1998 for evidence from a wide array of countries.) More concretely, Bartel and Lichtenberg (1987) document that in the United States industries with newer capital stocks (and hence newer technologies) tend to employ greater shares of highly educated workers. Further afield, studies in developing countries establish that farmers with greater levels of education are likely to adopt new technologies before other farmers (e.g., Binswanger *et al.*, 1978).

Cross-country studies such as that by Bils and Klenow (2000) show that countries that have experienced more rapid output growth tend to have more highly educated labour forces. However, levels of education can explain only about one-third of the variation across countries. Hanushek and Kimko (2000) find a strong link across countries between output growth and test scores on international tests of student achievement. This sort of evidence is perhaps less persuasive than within-country studies because the former could be contaminated by unobserved differences among countries, but the evidence is nonetheless suggestive.

Direct evidence on the link between the supply of university graduates and rates of innovation at the national level seems to be more scarce, but does point in the same direction. For instance, Arora, Gambardella and Torrisi (2004) study the rise of successful high-tech clusters in Ireland and India and conclude that a key facilitating factor was an ample supply of well-educated workers with a science and engineering background. Further, they argue that an overabundance of such workers relative to demand from non-high-tech sectors spurred the creation of high-tech clusters in these countries.

None of this evidence, of course, establishes that a thick network of universities is either necessary or sufficient for a country to experience rapid innovation and productivity growth. Some countries might easily obtain ample supplies of skilled labour through immigration. De Fontenay and Carmel (2004) contend that immigration of Russian scientists and engineers to Israel has done much to foster high-tech clusters in that country, and that the military in Israel does much to generate supplies of well-trained technicians.

What about at the regional level within a country: Is it sensible to claim that the individual region must have one or more strong universities in order to innovate? Gibbons (2000), from his vantage point as a dean of engineering at Stanford, argues that local educational infrastructure in the Bay Area has been one of the key elements in the Silicon Valley success story. He cites not only the graduate training provided by research power-houses such as Stanford and Berkeley, but the other local universities that provide the lion's share of baccalaureate engineers, the technical programs within community colleges and the entrepreneurship programs provided by the business schools at several local universities. Indeed, virtually every analysis that we have read about the sources of vigour in Silicon Valley mention the importance of the supply of skilled workers generated locally.

Another benefit provided by the postsecondary education sector not mentioned by Gibbons is coursework provided by universities' "Extension" or "Extended Study" systems. By responding to the needs of local employers, such systems can provide short courses, which allow already skilled workers to update and extend their knowledge. Our case study of San Diego will show that in that city at least, extended studies offers technical courses to surprisingly large numbers of individuals each year.

And yet, in spite of the large numbers of workers who gain technical skills at local universities, if some countries such as Israel can succeed by importing skilled workers from other countries, then surely individual regions within countries can play the same game. In addition to attracting immigrants, individual regions can import skilled workers from other regions within the same country. In some ways, as Betts (2000) points out, this approach can benefit local government coffers because importation of university graduates from other regions and countries in essence allows the local government to "free-ride" on the subsidies that governments elsewhere have provided to students while they pursued their studies. This is not necessarily a wise policy, as it places the individual region at the mercy of far-flung labour markets. But it does raise important questions about the extent to which local universities are truly a prerequisite to local high-tech success.

Indeed, there is now ample evidence that Silicon Valley, and California more generally, have relied heavily on importing workers from elsewhere. Saxenian (1999) documents the prominent role that foreign-born immigrant entrepreneurs have played in creating some of the leading high-tech companies in the San Francisco/San Jose area. More broadly, Betts (2000) has estimated that between 1970 and 1990, California's community colleges and universities produced only about one-half of the net observed increase in the number of working-age adults in California holding post-secondary degrees. California has been a massive importer of talent from elsewhere.

The fact that university graduates are free to migrate loosens the reliance of net importer regions on the supply of graduates from their local universities. The flip side of the coin, of course, is that regions that habitually lose graduates to other areas must recognize that only a fraction of local graduates will remain available to local employers.

These migration effects can be significant. Groen and White (2004) use a panel dataset of university students to estimate interstate mobility in the United States. In 1996, 16 years after graduation, the probability that a student from in-state remains in the same state is 55% for public colleges and 51% for private colleges on average.[1]

In Canada, interprovincial mobility of university graduates is quite large as well, especially when considering the more sparsely populated provinces. Burbidge and Finnie (2000) examine the mobility of samples of bachelor's graduates from the time they enter university to the fifth year after graduation. The main focus of this paper is net mobility from the "pre-university" province, but we can still infer that in some provinces large percentages of graduates move to different provinces after graduation. For instance, for Canada as a whole, of graduates in 1990 who graduated from university in their home province, 9.1% moved to another province within five years of graduation. This masks some much bigger numbers for some provinces. As Figure 1 shows, both Saskatchewan and Nova Scotia lost about one-third of their "homegrown" university graduates within five years.

As large as they are, these figures on interprovincial and interstate migration understate the risk that a region will lose graduates from its local postsecondary institutions because typically we think of regions as small portions of provinces or states. In other words, a University of Toronto graduate may well stay in Ontario, but move away from Toronto, weakening the link between the university and the skill set of workers in the Toronto region.

Conversely, if we are interested primarily in the impact of universities on the supply of skilled workers nationally, regional migration within the country is of less concern. But then we need to consider the possibility that a country as a whole is a net exporter of technically trained workers. Arora, Gambardella and Torrisi (2004) report that emigration of scientists and engineers from India to other countries, primarily the United States, potentially threatens the growth of high-tech clusters in India.

Similarly, in Canada, many observers have raised concerns about the brain drain to the United States that appears to have accelerated in the last 10 to 15 years. Card (2003) shows that between 1940 and 2000, Canadians who had emigrated to the United States were more highly educated than

---

[1]The authors provide these calculations for "marginal" students who would probably not be admitted if the universities increased their admission requirements.

Figure 1: Percentage of 1990 Bachelor's Graduates Who Remain in Home Province for University, but Who Move Within Five Years of Graduation

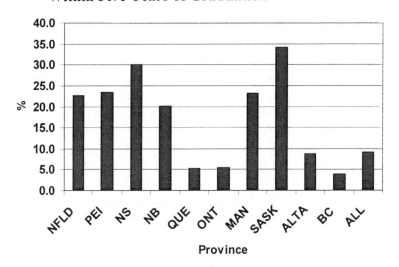

Source: Calculated from Table 4 of Burbidge and Finnie (2000).

native-born Americans. Over the last two decades it has also been the case that Canadian emigrants to the United States have been substantially more highly educated than Canadians remaining in Canada. For instance, Card estimates that in 2000, 44.3% of Canadians in the United States held a university degree and 8.1% held an advanced degree, compared to just 16.0% and 1.1% of Canadians in Canada. In addition, he shows that between 1980 and 2000 the earnings premium earned by Canadian emigrants to the United States relative to Americans has risen even after controlling for observable characteristics, which could mean that Canadian emigrants have become increasingly self-selected with respect to unob-served skills. Clearly, emigration of highly educated Canadians has become a real issue.

A second cautionary note: we cannot think of the university and community college systems as the only providers of skilled workers. The educational pipeline begins in each region's elementary and secondary school systems, and these local school systems typically provide the majority of students for the local public universities. A public university that seeks students mainly from its own region has no hope of producing large numbers of qualified engineers and scientists if the local school system fails to prepare high-school students adequately.

Ironically, California is a hub of innovative activity *in spite* of its K–12 system. A recent study by the California Council on Science and Technology (2002) identified problems in the state's schools as a key limiting factor to high-tech growth in the state. One report prepared for this project found that the percentage of grade 9 students who ultimately graduate from high school having taken the required number of courses in the "a-f" subjects needed for admission to the University of California or the California State University System is surprisingly low (Betts, 2002). Table 1 illustrates the leakages quite clearly. For instance, in 1999–2000 high-school graduates who had fulfilled the course requirements needed for public university eligibility represented only 24.5% of enrolment in grade 9 three years earlier. Dropouts during the high-school years combined with the low percentage of graduates who have taken sufficiently rigorous courses explain this disappointingly low figure. With problems like this in a state's public schools, universities will be limited in the supply of qualified graduates that they can produce.

Overall, what are we to conclude? There is considerable evidence that innovative activity requires skilled labour, including university graduates, and that universities are a key provider. But we need to be skeptical about claims that a region with a weak local supply of university graduates can never succeed at innovation. The quality of local schools that act as feeders to universities also matters. Even more important, the private sector can and often does draw university graduates from outside the local region, from other parts of the country and from other countries as well. Ultimately, some of the largest high-tech clusters, often in the United States, appear to have such an advantage through agglomeration effects that they can reliably attract skilled workers from around the world.

The University as "Talent Magnet"

Some of the most compelling evidence for our "talent-magnet" hypothesis comes from stories of the development of clusters in individual cities. Not only are these places talent magnets for young, high-tech workers, but they are also magnets for senior level scientists and engineering pioneers, the stars of their field. If Frederick Terman had not encouraged his students,

Table 1: Enrolment and Graduates as Percentage of Grade 9 Students Three Years Earlier in California

Year	Grade 12 Enrolment	Graduates	Graduates Fulfilling a-f with Grade of C or Better
	(%)	(%)	(%)
1991/1992	88.4	79.6	26.5
1994/1995	82.6	73.9	23.9
1995/1996	81.7	73.1	25.6
1996/1997	81.0	71.0	25.3
1997/1998	79.8	68.7	24.9
1998/1999	81.3	68.7	25.1
1999/2000	79.9	68.8	24.5

Note: "a-f" refers to the course requirements that high-school students must fulfill in order to be eligible for admission to the University of California and the California State University System.
Source: Betts (2002).

William Hewlett and David Packard, to start their own company in Palo Alto in 1938, instead of joining established firms on the East Coast, Hewlett-Packard would never have come into being. Hewlett-Packard is widely regarded as the pioneer company that gave rise to Silicon Valley (Saxenian, 1994). Furthermore, if William Shockley, father of the transistor, had not been encouraged by Fred Terman, Dean of Stanford's engineering school, to start up Shockley Semiconductor Laboratories in 1955, in Palo Alto, next to Stanford's campus, the young physicists and engineers that Shockley recruited would never have been lured to the region from the East Coast and Europe. Eight of the most talented young recruits subsequently defected to start Fairchild Semiconductor, which then begat all the "Fairchildren" firms (including Intel) which gave rise to what is now Silicon Valley (Lee, Miller and Hancock, 2000).[2]

---

[2]There are others who argue that the rise of Silicon Valley can be traced even further back to the turn of the century. See Sturgeon (2000).

Julian R. Betts and Carolyn W.B. Lee

Two other similar examples relate to the meteoric rise of San Diego's biotech and wireless communication sectors. Ivor Royston, founder of Hybritech, San Diego's first biotech firm and the original firm that spawned San Diego's biotech industry, was lured to UCSD as a professor, but left the university to found the firm. Irwin Jacobs, Chairman of Qualcomm, was also a UCSD professor who left to found Linkabit, the precursor to Qualcomm and the original firm that gave rise to San Diego's wireless communications industry.[3] It has been well documented that both these pioneering firms have spawned more than 40 firms *each* in the past two decades. Begetting charts reveal fourth and fifth generation "children" firms in the San Diego area that have been started by founders of Hybritech and Linkabit (UCSD CONNECT). The presence of Hybritech and Qualcomm subsequently led other major biotech and wireless technology companies such as Johnson & Johnson, Nokia, and Ericsson to open up substantial R&D operations in San Diego. In a very real sense, it is hard to imagine any of this happening had Ivor Royston and Irwin Jacobs not been lured to UCSD in the first place. This view has been reinforced in interviews with key players in San Diego's high-tech industries:

> One interviewee told us that San Diego attracted pioneers. Faculty who left places such as Harvard, Penn, and NIH were attracted to UCSD because they were scientific entrepreneurs. *(Project interview #12)* Others told us in informal conversations that people came to UCSD, Scripps, and Salk not just because of the research money offered but also because of the freedom to work on what interested them, including interdisciplinary work or research in fields outside their original fields. We also heard that a large number of the early faculty were divorced and looking for new beginnings, although we know of no easy way to confirm or disconfirm these anecdotes. (Walshok *et al.*, 2001, p. 17)

Additionally, a small but growing body of evidence suggests that universities can also serve as magnets to attract younger workers to the region as students who then stay after graduating.

For instance, Betts (2000) shows, using 1990 Census data for California, that a significantly higher share of young college enrollees in California were born in other states or are immigrants compared to a

---

[3]In the 1970s, UCSD did not encourage entrepreneurial faculty to stay. Both Royston and Jacobs left UCSD when told by the university administration that their consulting commitments conflicted with their university appointments.

slightly younger cohort. People originating out of state comprise 42.4% of the young college-attending population, compared to just 34.4% of the age group 13–17. He interprets this as a "college magnet effect".

Groen and White (2004) show that students who graduate from a university in a given state are more likely to live in that state 16 years after graduation. Some of this effect, they argue, is self-selection. In other words, a high-school student from Minnesota who yearns to live in California is likely to apply to many universities in California, and we cannot necessarily think of the fact that he or she does graduate from a California university as *causing* the graduate to remain in California for his career. But even after attempting to control for this self-selection, the authors find that for both public and private universities attendance increases the chance that the student will remain in the same state by about 10%, an estimate quite close to that of Betts for California.

In Canada, data in Burbidge and Finnie (2000, Table 4) suggests that of all 1990 bachelor's graduates in their sample, 3.5% leave their home province to attend a university in another province and have not returned home to work by five years after graduation. For smaller provinces, the outflows are significantly greater. The four highest rates of outflows are 24.7% for Prince Edward Island, 9.8% for New Brunswick, 8.7% for Nova Scotia, and 8.2% for Manitoba. Not surprisingly, the largest provinces have the lowest rates of "permanent" outflows to universities elsewhere: 1.7% for Ontario and 2.8% for Quebec.[4]

---

[4]All these studies beg the question, besides the university, are there other factors that help attract and keep university graduates in a region? The most talented graduates, especially PhD graduates from a top university, are the most mobile workforce in the world. Richard Florida would argue that "creative workers" are drawn to "creative centers [that] provide an integrated eco-system or habitat where all forms of creativity — artistic and cultural, technological and economic — can take root and flourish" (2002, p. 218). However, in the case of Palo Alto in the 1950s or San Diego in the 1970s, neither locale presented an urban, sophisticated environment teeming with nightlife and culture that would attract members of "the creative class". Other than good weather and the presence of a university, several decades ago neither locale would have registered high on Florida's list of creative-class attractions. This fact should be of some comfort to technologically "have-not" regions.

Evidence on the Direct Impact of Universities on Private Sector Innovation

The University as Innovator and Partner to the Private Sector

Two of the university's roles that we identified earlier are as an innovator and a partner to private sector innovation. In practice, the boundary between these two roles is quite blurry, and in this section we present evidence on both aspects of universities' direct role in innovation.

Researchers have used quantitative measures of the impact of universities on innovation including patent counts, patent royalties, and the number of firms created as spin-offs or start-ups. Much of the US evidence based on this sort of data suggests a sobering truth: *transferring technology from the university to the private sector is a very difficult task.*

Feldman's (2003) review of data related to technology transfer offices (TTOs) at American universities is quite revealing. These organizations exist to facilitate a variety of means of technology transfer, including patenting and licensing of patents in return for fees or royalties, and administering sponsored research. Feldman reports that in 1999 only 140 American universities had established TTOs, up from only 25 in 1980. She also summarizes evidence that "for every one hundred invention disclosures, ten patents and one commercially successful product result". Although TTOs executed 3,295 technology licences in 1999 this is highly skewed towards a handful of universities. Most TTOs seek to be self-funding through the royalties and fees that they garner for their universities, but the majority still lose money.

What about licensing from the point of view of industry executives? Feldman cites a survey showing that 66% of industry respondents had not yet licensed technology from a university. The two most common reasons for not licensing were the beliefs that university research is typically at too early a stage of development and that it is not related to the respondent's industry.

Further evidence on the importance of universities to innovation comes from university-awarded patents in the United States. The data in Table 2 shows that the number of patents awarded to universities has greatly increased in recent years, and that the share of universities in overall US origin patents awarded in the United States has also risen. But overall, universities account for only about 3–4% of US patents awarded per year to inventors in the United States. (Public universities typically account for

Table 2: Statistics on Importance of US Universities in Patent Awards

Year	# Patents Awarded to US Universities	% from Public Universities	University Patents as % Total US Origin Patents	% of University Patents Claimed by Top 100
1982	464	51.9	N/A	83.2
1983	437	51.3	N/A	81.7
1984	552	46.9	N/A	82.8
1985	589	52.3	N/A	81.8
1986	670	53.3	1.8	81.8
1987	820	48.4	1.9	84.9
1988	814	49.9	2.0	86.5
1989	1228	53.4	2.4	88.8
1990	1184	56.8	2.5	91.0
1991	1340	59.3	2.6	90.4
1992	1542	58.9	3.0	92.1
1993	1620	58.0	3.0	91.7
1994	1780	60.0	3.2	91.8
1995	1879	63.3	3.4	91.2
1996	2155	62.1	3.5	91.4
1997	2436	61.7	3.9	92.2
1998	3151	57.9	3.9	92.7

Source: Authors' calculations based on National Science Board (2002), Appendix Tables 5–56 and 6–12. N/A indicates data not available.

slightly over half of these university patents.) The final column of the table shows that the top one hundred universities account for roughly 80–90% of all patents earned by American universities. This skewed pattern suggests that many universities do not participate much in the patent game, if at all. Again, this provides an indication of how difficult it can be to create what Rosenberg (2003) refers to as the "entrepreneurial university".

Data on the number of firms created as university spinoffs or start-ups is more encouraging, but again suggests that technology transfer occurs only slowly over time. Feldman cites a survey showing that 275 university-related start-ups opened in 1999, an average of about two companies per university. Again, Feldman reports, the data is right-skewed, indicating that a small number of universities account for a disproportionate share of these start-ups.

A third type of technology transfer is sponsored research, through which a firm subsidizes or wholly finances university research in return for preferential access to the results of the research. In absolute terms, the flow of funds is large, at $2 billion in 2000, but this represents only about 7% of all university research funding (Feldman, 2003). The $2 billion in sponsored research is also small relative to total R&D and investments made by "angel" investors and venture capitalists in the private sector, estimated by Auerswald and Branscomb (2003) to have totaled $266 billion in 1998.

Why don't we see more transfer of technology from American universities? Auerswald and Branscomb (2003) develop the following line of argument: there is a wide gulf between basic research and a marketable product. The intermediate stages include proof of concept, early stage product specifications, and actual product development, followed by production and marketing. They argue that a university professor alone is unlikely to possess more than a few of the many skills needed to bring to fruition the idea for a new product based on research. The need for *teams* to bring an idea to market creates all sorts of informational asymmetries between the many parties involved, including the original research team, angel investors who typically fund early research and provide mentoring based on their own entrepreneurial experience, and venture capitalists who typically fund the later stages of product design and development. Compounding the difficulties are the intrinsic risks facing innovators. Auerswald and Branscomb (2003) estimate that of the roughly 200,000 "technology ventures" in the United States, in a given year only about 10% receive funding from angel investors, only about 0.25% of technology ventures receive heftier venture capital investments, and a similar or smaller percentage make initial public offerings on the stock market.

One reason why our literature review suggests a fairly limited impact of universities on innovation is that our focus on innovations directly linked to universities (through university-owned patents and so on) seriously undercounts the impact of university scientists and engineers. Faculty often consult with firms, and this may produce innovations that are not directly measurable as coming from the university. However, it is notoriously difficult to measure university collaboration with the private sector because faculty consulting is not tracked by formal university means. A study by Boyd and Bero (2000) of University of California San Francisco (UCSF) faculty consulting uses Conflict of Interest forms. This data suggests that not much consulting occurs. The discrepancy probably results from massive underreporting by professors of these activities. Between 1980 and 1999, there were only 488 positive disclosures from 225 UCSF researchers.[5] Only 37% of researchers had more than one positive disclosure but the variance is huge: one researcher had 28 positive disclosures but most had less than four. A third of these disclosures related to speaking honoraria received from speaking engagements, another third arose from consulting arrangements, and the final third from participation in company-scientific advisory boards or on company boards of directors.

University as Facilitator

A fifth potential role of universities is to act as a facilitator for private sector innovators in the region. This can include creation of science parks, which often are associated with local universities. Wallsten (2004) reports that between 1980 and 1998 the number of science parks in the United States soared from 16 to 135. Often these parks are subsidiaries of universities or at least have an affiliation with one or more local universities. Two of the most famous and highly regarded examples are the Stanford Research Park and the Research Triangle Park in North Carolina, the latter is near a number of leading universities. However, Wallsten shows that, in general, counties with a science park have not shown greater growth in either high-tech employment or in venture capital funding than a comparison group of similar counties without science parks. Clearly, science parks succeed to varying degrees.

A more subtle but perhaps more important way in which universities can facilitate local innovation in the private sector is to create a meeting ground in which seasoned professionals from the high-tech industry can rub shoulders as well as mentor less experienced scientists and entrepreneurs as they attempt to create thriving start-ups of their own. A number of organizations like this have sprung up in the United States. Our case study of San Diego will provide a detailed discussion of UCSD CONNECT, a program that acts as a catalyst for local high-tech entrepreneurship.

---

[5]UCSF has over 17,000 faculty and staff with 1,137 principal investigators.

Julian R. Betts and Carolyn W.B. Lee

Indirect Evidence from the Literature on High-Tech Clusters

Over the last 15 years, the idea that industries tend to agglomerate in certain regions has come to the forefront of regional planning. Michael Porter has spearheaded much of this research, arguing that the availability of certain inputs, including skilled labour, can help to explain why industries agglomerate in some countries and within certain regions of a given country. (See, for instance, Porter, 1990 and 1998.)

In the context of the present paper, this leads to a central question: Is the main impact of a university on innovation felt locally or at the national level? Put differently, does the presence of universities lead to local agglomeration of high-tech innovation?

This question parallels our earlier analysis in which we concluded that a substantial fraction of graduates from a university in a given region are likely to be "lost" to other regions or even other countries. However, our conclusions regarding the direct contributions of universities to regional innovation through patenting, spinoffs and licensing are quite different. The evidence tentatively suggests that the local area may gain much of the direct impact of universities on innovative activity. If the university actively chooses to engage in activities to boost regional economic development, then this effect can be greatly augmented (Tornatzky, Waugaman and Gray, 2002).

There are a number of reasons for this. Inventors typically need to team up with networks of funders who can provide a variety of technical, financial, and marketing services. This reliance on others for business expertise appears to concentrate product development work fairly close to the location of the initial investor. Auerswald and Branscomb (2003) cite studies by Sohl (1999) and Wong (2002) who establish that in the United States more than half of angel investors surveyed reported that they restricted their investments to locations within 50 miles, ostensibly in order to keep tabs on the receiving organization and to avail it of the angel's network of business partners.

Related evidence based on citations establishes that local innovations spill over to other entities in the same area, so that a university's innovative activity is likely to boost the local private sector in indirect ways. Jaffe (1989) models the location of US inventors who are granted patents and finds that the amount of both university R&D and industrial R&D are strong predictors of private sector patents granted by the state. The implication is that university research stimulates local innovation. Supporting evidence comes from his finding that university research appears to stimulate industrial research in the same state. Jaffe, Trajtenberg and Henderson (1993) show more generally that the applications for new US patents tend to cite other patents issued to entities in the same state and even metropolitan area to a high degree. Again, this suggests that local knowledge, once generated, sends ripple effects through the local R&D community that are far larger than the ripples felt in distant regions.

Supporting these statistical analyses is a wealth of evidence from case studies of high-tech clusters.

First and foremost, recent observations about Silicon Valley back up the notions that high-tech product development will occur in geographically concentrated areas, and, more importantly, that these areas will often centre on major research universities. Gibbons (2000) argues that in 1996 the one hundred companies initiated with Stanford "teams and technology" accounted for 65% of Silicon Valley revenues, or about $65 billion.

Not only has Stanford directly created many successful spinoffs locally, but it continues to sustain high-tech companies in the immediate area. Gibbons (2000) quotes Ed McCracken, Chairman and CEO of Silicon Graphics, as follows: "We drew a ten-minute commute circle around Hoover Tower [on the Stanford campus] to define acceptable locations for our company." McCracken cites the company's reliance on Stanford's research, faculty, and graduate students as the reasons for locating so close to Stanford.

Gibbons also quotes Gordon Moore, chairman emeritus of Intel, as follows: "The most important contribution Stanford makes to Silicon Valley is to replenish the intellectual pool every year with new graduate students."

Our case study of San Diego in the next section will document a similar and particularly remarkable clustering of high-tech start-ups around the campus of UCSD and nearby research institutes.

A recent study by Lee and Walshok (2003) attempted to analyze a confidential dataset of California Small Business Innovation Research (SBIR) applicants for links to local research universities in the company's vicinity.[6] SBIR applications contain extremely detailed information about

---

[6]The federally funded Small Business Innovation Research (SBIR) Program provides funding for the commercialization of new technology by small firms. SBIR funds feasibility studies and prototype development, not basic R&D.

a company's business plans. From these plans, it is possible to document a variety of what Lee and Walshok call "Know-How/Know-Who" linkages. These linkages range from university researchers as founders, to local alumni as senior managers, to local industry executives and local investors serving as board members. These links also influence funding decisions; there is a positive correlation between the total number of links between companies and university academics and the funding received. Collectively, these indicators represent statistically significant relationships between teams of *local* academic researchers and *local* industrial scientists and engineers working jointly on product-development activities. Firms are leveraging local university expertise through more than research collaborations and faculty consulting activities. They also benefit from local university resources through equipment rental and access to specialized facilities. Companies utilizing university facilities and tapping into faculty expertise are also likely to be more reluctant to locate corporate facilities far from the academic research centre as travel time between the sites could cut down on the productivity of scientific/engineering personnel. None of these activities are quantifiable transactions that can be easily measured because these are frequently transactions with no formal reporting requirements. Hence, the results reported in the Lee and Walshok study provided a first, quantitative look at how California's high-tech firms and research universities are embedded in a local milieu that shapes their interactions, their co-location, and multiple individual relationships between university and industry counterparts.

Evidence from clusters in other countries seems to corroborate the idea that universities tend to anchor innovative regions. In their examination of Israel high tech, de Fontenay and Carmel (2004) produce a map that illustrates quite vividly that multinational high-tech companies and home-grown high-tech companies alike tend to locate nearby some of the country's leading universities. Arora, Gambardella and Torrisi argue that part of the agglomeration of high-tech firms in India reflects the pre-existing location of universities. They conclude that: "The distribution of engineering colleges, concentrated in the western and southern regions, closely mirrors the distribution of the software industry" (2004, p. 104). The same authors cite examples of Irish high-tech firms that were formed

---

This public venture capital is vital to small technology firms as it provides critical gap funding to develop an innovative technology to the point where a company can attract private venture funding.

by university professors and are located near their universities. In addition, they summarize results from surveys they performed of 28 domestic firms and 13 foreign-owned high-tech firms. Both surveys showed that the availability of skilled Irish workers was by far the most important factor leading the firms to locate operations in Ireland.

San Diego as a Case Study

This section has three goals: (a) to provide an overview of San Diego's rapid rise to prominence in biotech and wireless communications, (b) to examine the links between local universities and San Diego's high-tech growth, and (c) to showcase some new methods for studying the diverse ways in which universities can support the development of a local high-tech private sector.

In the past two decades, the San Diego region has transformed itself into one of the most innovative regions in the United States (see Palmintera, 2000). The University of California at San Diego (UCSD), together with other major research centres such as the Salk Institute for Biological Studies, the Scripps Research Institute (TSRI), the Neurosciences Institute and the US Navy's Space and Naval Warfare Systems R&D Center (SPAWAR)[7] among others, garners close to a billion dollars in basic research annually, with nearly half of that coming from the Department of Health and Human Services (mostly National Institutes of Health [NIH] funding) for basic research in the life sciences (See Figure 2). While UCSD is the largest recipient of federal research dollars,[8] San

---

[7]SPAWAR's San Diego Center (SSC San Diego) is the US Navy's research, development, test and evaluation, engineering and fleet support centre for command, control and communication systems, and ocean surveillance. SSC San Diego provides information resources to support the joint warfighter in mission execution and force protection.

[8]In FY2001, UCSD received over $485 million from federal funding sources, on an annual basis, and ranked sixth in the nation for federal funding in 2001 according to NSF. According to UCSD's *Annual Report*, UCSD outranked all other campuses of UC in terms of federal support for programs. For 2003, the campus received $627 million in federal funding, the latest year for which figures are available. Federal support has been growing at over 14% per year, and has doubled over the past decade.

Figure 2: San Diego County's Unrestricted Federal Funding for R&D, in FY2001

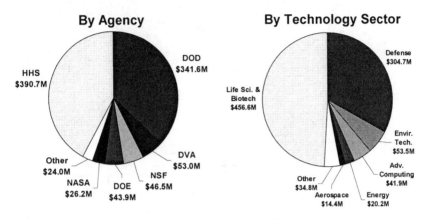

Note: Acronyms for the US federal agencies in the left-hand pie chart are:
HHS — Department of Health and Human Services, mostly funding from the
      National Institutes of Health (NIH)
DOD — Department of Defense
DVA — Department of Veteran's Affairs
NSF — National Science Foundation
DOE — Department of Energy
NASA —National Aeronautical and Space Administration
Source: The Rand Corporations's RaDiUS database.

Diego's other research institutions also add significantly to the regional funding picture. In addition to this federal funding, San Diego high-tech firms receive on the order of $1 billion annually in private venture funding (See Figure 3).[9]

A first striking pattern that emerges from our analysis of San Diego is the remarkable extent of geographical clustering. Location appears to matter pivotally for high-tech and biotech start-ups in San Diego, with most of them situated less than three miles from world-class centres of academic research, all located within a mile of each other. More than a thousand high

---

[9]PWC's *Moneytree Report* indicated that San Diego received a total of 107 venture funded deals worth $964 million in 2002, down from a high of $2.32 billion in 2000, at the height of the Dot-Com bubble.

Figure 3: Private Venture Capital to San Diego, by Industry Sector

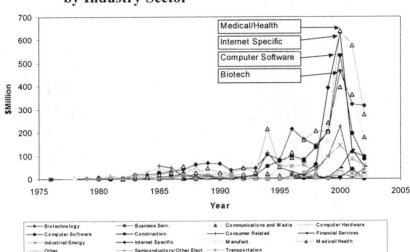

Source: Thomson Financial/Venture One.

technology and biotechnology companies have sprung up in Torrey Pines Mesa and Sorrento Valley, areas neighbouring UCSD, the Scripps Research Institute and the Salk Institute, over the past two decades. As one illustration of this clustering, Figure 4 provides a map of San Diego's Small Business Innovation Research (SBIR)-funded emerging high-tech firms — these are the newest firms in the cluster. We believe that the firms' desire to locate close to the aforementioned research institutions is the primary explanation of the clustering of activity around UCSD/Salk/Scripps. At the same time, it is important to acknowledge that two important facilitating factors were the availability of land to the north and northeast of UCSD in the 1980s and early 1990s and the fact that these areas were zoned appropriately for light industrial development decades earlier. Indeed, in other studies of SBIR-funded firms in Greater Philadelphia and Indiana, we have shown that urban geography can be key to the lack of agglomeration.

Philadelphia: In the absence of planned zoning, Philadelphia's SBIR-funded emerging biotech firms are located in a elongated 60-mile long stretch of Philadelphia suburbs and exburbs, anchored solely by an interstate freeway that runs through the area, and not by the University of

Julian R. Betts and Carolyn W.B. Lee

Figure 4: 1999–2001 SBIR-Funded Companies in San Diego County Cluster Around UCSD, on Torrey Pines Mesa and Sorrento Valley

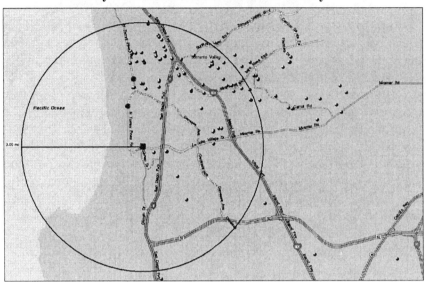

Source: Rand RaDiUS.

Pennsylvania, which has a world-class medical centre in downtown Philadelphia (Switzer, Walshok and Lee, 2003). Rush hour traffic jams on area freeways would preclude these suburban biotech firms from having the close ties to Philadelphia's world-class universities, which are all located downtown.

Indiana: Indiana and Purdue Universities are major research institutions in Indiana, but the main campuses for both university systems are located in small, college towns (Bloomington and Lafayette respectively) outside Indianapolis, the state's main metropolitan centre. Yet, the schools' main medical campus is located in downtown Indianapolis.[10] While Purdue University has created a science park next door to the university and

---

[10]Indiana University and Purdue University share one campus in Indianapolis (IUPUI). The campus grants mostly professional degrees in the medical sciences.

Indiana University is encouraging the development of a biotech sector, the number of SBIR-funded biotech firms near both Bloomington and Lafayette campuses have been extremely small. The number of SBIR-funded biotech firms in Indianapolis is larger than either Bloomington or Lafayette but again, there is no agglomeration near the main health-care campus (IUPUI) because the campus is located in downtown Indianapolis while the emerging firms are located around the major freeways that ring Indianapolis' suburbs (Lee, Walshok and Switzer, 2002).

A second striking pattern is that in San Diego, private sector high-tech investment and employment have both grown very quickly from low initial levels. Figure 3 shows that private venture capital investments in San Diego were virtually zero in 1980 but have grown quickly since then, with steady growth in the 1980s giving way to much more rapid, if volatile, growth in the 1990s. Over the course of a decade (1990–2000), San Diego created over 37,000 jobs in high-tech industries, which more than made up for the decline in the defence industry sector which declined by nearly 27,000 jobs after the end of the Cold War. See Figure 5.

Figure 5: San Diego's High-Tech Employment, by Industry Cluster

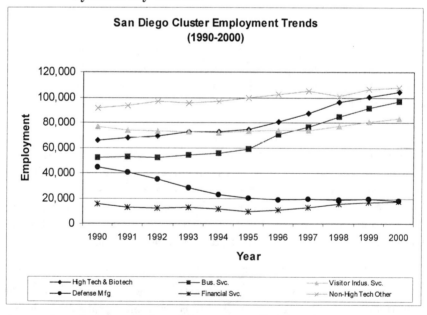

Source: San Diego Association of Governments (SANDAG).

Julian R. Betts and Carolyn W.B. Lee

How has San Diego engineered such a transformation? Little more than 15 years ago, the region was still dominated by three major industries: (a) defence contracting, (b) tourism and visitor services, and (c) real estate development. The various economic crises in the late 1970s to mid-1980s necessitated a regional shift in direction. Regional civic and business leadership, in collaboration with local research institutions including UCSD, sought the means to assist the region's economy to diversify into knowledge-based industries. Prompted by the end of the Cold War, the downturn in the defence contracting sector hit San Diego's regional economy particularly hard in the early 1990s; that sector's employment has never recovered to Cold War highs. Because the region had already put into place mechanisms to assist high-tech entrepreneurs, San Diego's economy rebounded shortly afterwards and rose to new heights during the late 1990s.

While many observers view the creation of Silicon Valley as a happy accident that cannot be recreated, there is a perception that San Diego engineered its current success through planning, with UCSD and the CONNECT program playing central roles in revitalizing a moribund regional economy (see the Appendix for a description of CONNECT). Indeed, extensive interviews with key business, government, and academic leaders involved with San Diego's high-tech transformation reinforce this view (Walshok et al., 2001).

If one were to probe into the data presented above and ask what is the direct role of UCSD in spinning off new technology companies, the picture becomes murkier. According to the US Patent and Trademark Office (USPTO), patent counts for the San Diego metropolitan statistical area (San Diego MSA) have risen steadily over the late 1990s (see Table 3). Yet, only 149 patents or 2% of all patents awarded in the San Diego County during this period originated with inventors at UCSD. Nor is it clear that UCSD affects mainly local innovation. Of the 162 companies currently listed on UCSD's Technology Transfer & Intellectual Property Services (TechTIPS) Web site as having licensed technology from UCSD, only 58 (or 36%) are San Diego companies. Yet UCSD's technology transfer track record makes it a star among UC campuses (see Table 4).

What is less understood is how the university interacts with the sur-rounding region to prime the innovation pump. Much of this activity is not captured on national datasets either because it involves informal trans-actions that are not easily rendered into quantitative data and/or they arise out of self-funded, self-supporting outreach activities that the university undertakes with no formal reporting requirements. Some of these will be

Table 3: Patents Awarded in San Diego County, by Organization, 1995–1999

Rank	Organization	1995	1996	1997	1998	1999	Total (1995–99)
1	Hewlett-Packard Co.	56	51	66	71	92	336
2	Qualcomm, Inc.	19	43	35	69	90	256
3	Isis Pharmaceuticals, Inc.	8	27	36	37	68	176
4	The Scripps Research Institute	31	25	25	54	40	175
5	UCSD	20	24	28	39	38	149
6	US Navy	26	30	31	27	30	144
7	The Salk Institute of Biological Studies	8	17	27	27	20	99
8	Gen-Probe, Inc.	6	9	30	32	21	98
9	La Jolla Cancer Research Foundation	3	16	26	27	23	95
10	Eastman Kodak Co.	16	27	22	19	10	94
11	Solar Turbines, Inc.	17	15	12	8	5	57
12	General Instruments Corp.	9	10	11	12	13	55
13	Mycogen Corp.	9	5	19	8	10	51
14	Sony Corp.	-	9	7	15	20	51
15	Cymer, Inc.	-	-	4	13	24	41
16	Corvas International, Inc.	-	4	11	10	15	40
17	Medtronic Inc.	6	6	7	10	11	40
18	Agouron Pharmaceuticals, Inc.	1	3	9	13	12	38
19	Huges Aircraft Co.	18	12	5	3	-	38
20	SIBIA Neurosciences Inc.	-	2	8	15	11	36
	All Others	398	490	573	848	850	3,159
	Individuals	257	290	243	316	345	1,451
	Total	908	1,115	1,235	1,673	1,748	6,679

Julian R. Betts and Carolyn W.B. Lee

Table 4: UCSD's Technology Transfer Activities

	UCSD's Technology Transfer Activity	Rank among the 9 Campuses of UC[a]
2002 Invention Disclosures	255	1
Total Invention Portfolio	1,274	1
Total Patents Portfolio	392	3
2002 Licences Executed	181	2
2002 Licensing Revenue	$12,690,000	3

Note: [a] The nine campuses of the University of California (UC) System include: UC Berkeley, UC Davis, UC Irvine, UC Los Angeles (UCLA), UC Riverside, UC San Diego, UC San Francisco, UC Santa Barbara, and UC Santa Cruz.

Source: University of California's Office of Technology Transfer Annual Report (2002).

detailed below, along with first attempts to measure the impact that each can have on the regional innovation process that is on-going in San Diego.

Technology Commercialization through CONNECT, UCSD's "Incubator Without Walls"

Founded in 1985 at the urging of San Diego's business community, San Diego's version of high technology business incubation is embodied in a program called UCSD CONNECT. CONNECT's private model of incubation differs significantly from that of most public incubators. There is no physical incubation space provided at a subsidized cost to the firm, nor is there public funding from local, regional, state or national governments. Instead, CONNECT's success in building high-tech industry clusters come from the numerous and frequent networking activities that are underwritten by memberships, sponsorships, and event registration fees. CONNECT acts as a resource to assist entrepreneurs throughout the San Diego region, not just for university spinoff companies and faculty entrepreneurs.

Without a clear understanding of how CONNECT builds quality business networks in a learning community, it is tough to see how CONNECT has come to play such a pivotal role in driving firm agglomeration into industry clusters in San Diego. Yet, how does one quantitatively measure a social phenomenon such as "networking" or the formation of a "learning community" and what does one mean by "quality"? To the casual observer, it appears that all CONNECT does is to put on events that do not differ from many industry-sponsored investor forums. Delegations from around the world have asked repeatedly to see the CONNECT facilities, only to be disappointed by the odd collection of standard cubicles clustered in rented office space located just off UCSD's main campus. Here then, is a first attempt to quantify some of the factors that lie behind CONNECT's model of virtual incubation.

One of CONNECT's signature programs is Springboard which assists high-tech entrepreneurs with business formation (see the Appendix for a more detailed description of this program). Between 1995 and 2002, over 202 San Diego companies have graduated from this program. Sixty percent of these companies are still going concerns in 2002. Forty percent of these companies raised capital within two years of Springboard graduation. Of the companies raising capital within two years of Springboard graduation, 88% are still alive. Together, these 202 Springboard companies have raised cumulatively in excess of $581 million, with nearly $325 million within the first two years of graduation. See Tables 5 and 6 and Figure 6.

The evidence above suggests that Springboard is quite effective at mentoring entrepreneurs. Hidden from these statistics is how senior business leaders are networking with each other before and after the event, and evaluating their peers during the question and answer part of the event. We would argue that this peer evaluation is just as important for building and maintaining the strength of regional networks as the feedback and mentoring assistance provided to the entrepreneurs because this "donation" of volunteer time by local executives to the common goal of boosting start-up firms in San Diego builds trust among the major players in the region.

When negotiating a deal, it is of paramount importance to the deal-makers that there be a certain level of trust established. If trust between the players has already been established, then this can lend speed and ease to the process of concluding a deal. If the major actors in a region have built up this trust repeatedly, then over time the overall speed with which deals can be concluded increases and this can lead to the regional competitive

Julian R. Betts and Carolyn W.B. Lee

Table 5: Tracking UCSD CONNECT's Springboard Graduates, 1995–2002

a. All Springboard Graduates (1995–2002)

	No. of Firms	% of Firms
In business	120	59
Acquired	18	9
Out of business	66	33
Total	202	100

b. Springboard Firm Survival Rates

Survival Time	No. of Firms (Total=202)	Survival Rate (%)
1 year or more	161	80
2 years or more	120	62
3 years or more	93	57
4 years or more	73	54
5 years or more	49	42

c. Springboard Firms' Ability to Raise Capital

	No. of Firms (Total=81)	% of Firms (Total=81)
Still alive	71	88
Out of business	10	12
Raised capital and survived 3+ years	48	59
Raised capital and survived 5+ years	31	38

Note: Out of 202 graduates, 81 firms (40% of all graduates) were able to raise capital within two years.

Data in this table are right censored. That is, the table measures survival rates as of 2003. Some of the firms in the sample participated in Springboard as late as 2002, so cannot have had a survival duration of more than one year as of 2003. Therefore, in panel b survival rates for x or more years are calculated as the number of firms alive in 2003 divided by the number of firms that presented at Springboard x or more years before 2003.

Table 6: Capital Raised by CONNECT's Springboard Graduates, 1995–2002

a. Total Capital Raised by Springboard Graduates (Total=202 cos.)

Springboard Graduation	$ Million
Pre-1995 & 1995	128.1
1996	62.2
1997	76.7
1998	89.4
1999	102.4
2000	91.7
2001	30.4
2002	0.6
Total	581.5

b. Capital Raised by all Companies Within 2 Years of Graduation (Total=81 cos.)

Springboard Graduation	$ Million
1995	34.8
1996	14.7
1997	49.9
1998	19.8
1999	82.7
2000	91.7
2001	30.4
2002	0.6
Total	324.6

Julian R. Betts and Carolyn W.B. Lee

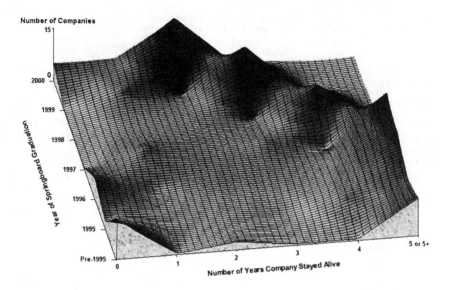

advantage observed by Porter and others. Springboard and other CONNECT events are designed to foster repeated peer-to-peer networking with substantive feedback in a forum where nothing more than reputations are at stake. The social capital accumulated by the panelists comes into play after a CONNECT event when they conduct business with each other, refer each other's clients to trusted members of this network and introduce new members to the network. None of these activities can be captured by conventional measures of transactions. Yet, anecdotally, interviewees tell us time and again, that without CONNECT's fostering of social networks, San Diego's high-tech industries would never have taken off (Walshok et al., 2001).

Even if one cannot quantify what happens during or after a networking event such as a Springboard panel presentation, one could quantify the number of interactions between key players in an industry cluster. An examination of the attendance roster of all Springboard presentations between 1996 and 2002 yields a total of 1,597 panelists representing a variety of senior managers at local firms (see Table 7). This total count of 1,597 panelists consists of 807 individuals who attended between one and as many as 19 Springboard presentations each. Approximately two-thirds

Table 7: Managerial Function of Springboard Panelists, 1996–2002

	1996	1997	1998	1999	2000	2001	2002	Total (1996-2002)	%
Firm executives/senior managers	66	92	56	58	71	123	49	515	32
Management consultants	28	40	32	32	32	37	14	215	13
Attorneys	29	32	26	12	26	51	38	214	13
Financing/loan officers	19	26	21	19	22	15	14	136	9
Venture capitalists	10	13	11	11	23	38	11	117	7
Angel investors	5	6	5	15	16	28	28	103	6
Marketing/PR professionals	4	24	12	10	17	18	4	89	6
High-tech industry/member organization representatives	5	2	2	3	7	15	28	62	4
University administrators	4	5	3	1	7	2	9	31	2
Others*	3	8	4		6	2	6	29	2
Headhunter/HR professionals	3	6	3	4	1	9	2	28	2
University faculty	2	8	4		3	3	2	22	1
Commercial real estate/ insurance brokers	1	4	3	1	7	5		21	1
Unknown		3	1	2	2	6	1	15	1
Total	**179**	**269**	**183**	**168**	**240**	**352**	**206**	**1,597**	**100**

Note: These individuals include federal, state, local government officials, as well as press and members of foreign delegations that expressed a high interest in CONNECT and were invited to be observers at a Springboard event.

of these 807 individuals served on a panel once, but another third served two or more times (see Table 8). If as we postulate, peer evaluation, the development of trust among key business players and fostering the growth of a common community are important, then the high percentage of panelists who served more than once on a Springboard panel is a revealed preference for the value ascribed to serving on a Springboard panel.

Suppose one were to ascribe a conservative estimate that each of these 807 individuals who served as Springboard panelists each knew five other peers of the same managerial function, and could refer each other's clients

Julian R. Betts and Carolyn W.B. Lee

Table 8: Frequency of Participation as Springboard Panelists, 1996–2002

Frequency of Springboard Panel Participation	No. of Springboard Panelists Who Participated at this Frequency Level
1	539
2	117
3	49
4	32
5	19
>5	51
Total	**807**

to these five others, if occasion arose, then the number of people in this network who are indirectly affected by CONNECT would quickly snowball. If one were to ask, in a "six degrees of separation" fashion, how many members of San Diego's current high-tech business leaders were personal friends of Bill Otterson, CONNECT's now deceased founding executive director, there would be few members of this club who would be more than a degree or two separated from a "friend of Bill". Indeed, one of the interview findings from San Diego's high-tech leaders (Walshok *et al.*, 2001) reveals that doing business in San Diego these days is like operating in a small town — everyone knows everyone else — hence, technology and deals get "shopped around" very quickly. Without this dense, informal business network nurtured through CONNECT, early technology entrepreneurs found the process of accessing capital and expertise a "hit or miss" process. In other words, the social networks that have grown up in San Diego's high-tech industries over the past two decades have conveyed a competitive advantage for doing business in the region, but we are just beginning to understand how this process works and how it can be recreated elsewhere.

High-Tech Workforce Training through UCSD Extension

As San Diego's high-tech industries have been growing and maturing, there has been a continuing need to train and re-train the workforce required by these growing companies. In San Diego, both UCSD and San Diego State University (SDSU)[11] have been dominant institutions in providing the bachelor's, master's and PhD degree credentialing for the high-tech workforce. Less well known is the role that UCSD Division of Extended Studies (UCSD Extension) and SDSU's College of Continuing Education have played in providing workforce training for San Diego's burgeoning high-tech industries and how this affects regional competitive advantage. These self-funded programs "fly under the radar screen" of most national and state policymakers because there are few reporting requirements. Yet, without a full accounting of the numbers of students who participate in relevant continuing education programs, one would not obtain a true accounting of the amount of education and training that is taking place in a region. A recent study by Lee and Walshok (2002) examined UC's Extension Divisions and CSU's Colleges Extended Studies to determine populations served and the types of training provided. See Table 9 for a comparison of regular degree enrolments and Extension/Continuing Education enrolments (ibid.). Extension enrolments are large and at UC in particular, far larger than even regular degree enrolments.

Given that UC Extension courses do not carry college credit and serve a post-baccalaureate working adult population, one could ask what kinds of courses are offered, and why are working adults taking these courses in such droves? A more detailed survey of UCSD Extension students in San Diego (a "high-tech" regional economy) versus UC Riverside Extension students in Riverside/San Bernardino counties (a "low-tech" regional economy) revealed that fully 75% of Extension enrollees in San Diego held post-baccalaureate degrees with a significant minor fraction holding PhDs; two-thirds of students were employed in high-tech sectors and two-thirds

---

[11]San Diego State University is the largest and one of the oldest campuses of the California State University (CSU) system.

The California public university system consists of a three-tiered system. The nine campuses of UC confer advanced degrees such as MA/MS and PhD while the 23 campuses of the California State University (CSU) system confer BA/BS and master's but no PhD degrees, except in conjunction with a UC campus. There are also 108 community colleges that confer two year associates' degrees.

Table 9: UC and CSU Regular Full-Time Enrolment Compared to Extension Program Enrolments

a. University of Califormia

Year	UC Regular Full-Time Enrolment[a]			UC Continuing Education[b,c]		
	Under-graduate	Graduate	Total FT Enrolment	Extension Enrollees	Concurrent Enrolment	Total Enrolment
1996	120,198	26,328	146,526	431,231	12,145	443,376
1997	122,453	26,267	148,720	441,331	11,997	453,328
1998	125,040	26,595	151,635	451,738	11,724	463,462
1999	128,883	26,607	155,490	433,301	11,191	444,492
2000	132,712	27,008	159,720	409,011	10,470	442,631

b. California State University System

Fiscal Year	CSU Regular FT Enrolment[d]			CSU Continuing Education[e]			
	Under-graduate	Graduate	Total FT Enrolment	Extension Enrolment	Open University	Special Session	Total Enrolment
1995–96	264,968	62,747	327,715	98,074	44,272	57,478	199,824
1996–97	272,480	65,695	338,175	124,417	43,552	61,101	229,070
1997–98	275,164	69,438	344,602	133,230	44,041	70,262	247,533
1998–99	279,656	73,219	352,875	125,155	44,021	66,670	235,846
1999–00	286,176	76,570	362,746	143,922	48,394	70,332	262,648

Note: [a] 1995–2000 UCOP Statistical Summary of Students and Staff, UC Office of the President, Budget Office. Post-baccalaureate students are students pursuing education/ teaching credentials. These enrolments are typically small, less than two hundred students per year per campus.

[b] 1999–2000 UCOP Annual Statistical and Financial Report on University of California Extension and Statewide Programs.

[c] UC Extension courses serve a post-baccalaureate working adult population and are non-college credit professional development courses that carry continuing education credit units. These credits are non-transferrable to degree-granting programs. Concurrent enrolment refers to members of the local community who occasionally register in degree-granting courses, without pursuing a degree, but on a space availability basis and with the permission of the instructor. There are restrictions on how many courses a student can take under concurrent enrolment before s/he must apply to for regular admissions into the university.

[d] 1995–2000 CSU Annual Statistical Reports, CSU Chancellor's Office, Analytical Statistics Division.

[e] CSU's Continuing Education serves a working adult population seeking a mix of degree credentialing and workforce training. Extension courses consist of professional development courses that provide continuing education credit units only. Open University provides access to CSU regular degree courses without formal admission to the university (same as UC's Concurrent Enrolments). Non-admitted residents and those who have been disqualified and/or denied admission at CSU may participate in Open University. Special Session courses are approved courses offered by the university's academic departments. Special Session courses meet residence requirements and may be applied towards a degree program. Admission to the university is not required.

of students were reimbursed for their course-taking by their employers. In comparison, only 56% of UC Riverside Extension students held bacca-laureate degrees or higher; only a quarter of students were employed in high-tech sectors and only half of students were reimbursed by employers.[12] See Figure 7.

Furthermore, UC Extension has demonstrated that continuing education programs can be very effective workforce training programs for a region that has aspirations to become a high-tech hotspot, if these programs are implemented as that region's high-tech companies are in rapid expansion stage. UCSD's Extension enrolments have more than doubled over the course of the 1990s, from approximately 20,000 enrollees to the current level of over 40,000. The nature of the course offerings has evolved over

Figure 7: UCSD and UC Riverside Extension Students Employed in High-Tech Industry Clusters

San Diego County
"High-Tech" Region

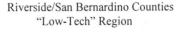

Riverside/San Bernardino Counties
"Low-Tech" Region

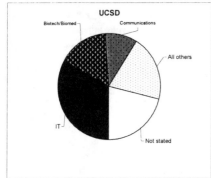

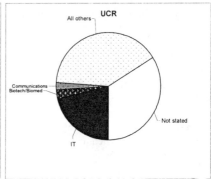

Source: Lee and Walshok (2002).

---

[12]UC and CSU's Continuing Education efforts have slightly different thrusts. UC's programs concentrate on providing non-credit, professional develop-ment courses to a post-baccalaureate working adult population. CSU's programs concentrate on providing regular college credit courses to a working adult popula-tion lacking degree credentials. The survey probed regional efforts on high-tech workforce training and therefore highlighted UC Extension students over those at CSU.

time as well. The current catalog lists nearly 60 courses in bioscience, and nearly 100 courses in CDMA and related engineering, all geared to post-graduate level scientists and engineers in the biotech and wireless communications industries. These courses did not exist five to ten years ago and were developed in response to specific industry needs for trained workers.[13]

Finally, because UCSD Extension's student population consists of working adults in the local community who are pursuing course-taking activities on a part-time, evening basis, the turnover in UCSD Extension enrollees from one academic year to the next is almost 100%. Contrast this with the low turnover rates in UCSD's regular, undergraduate student population who are on campus for four or more years on average; a significant fraction of these students come from outside the region and may not settle in the San Diego area after they graduate. Over a decade, a strong, regional continuing education program such as UCSD Extension can impact a significant fraction of the post-baccalaureate, working population in San Diego County. Without a full understanding of the extent of these university-based workforce training programs, one would be grossly under-estimating the full impact of a major research university in any region.

Concluding Thoughts

Our goal in this paper has been to document the extent to which universities spur both local and national innovation through their multiple roles as trainer, innovator, partner, regional talent magnet, and facilitator of net-working. Evidence on all counts is mostly circumstantial, but collectively suggests that universities can and do play major roles in all of these ways. Although the last two of these roles are the least studied, the "talent magnet" and "facilitator" effects are potentially as important as the more obvious roles for the university that we have studied.

---

[13]While this study has highlighted the UCSD Extension role in high-tech workforce training in San Diego, UC Santa Cruz serves a similar function for workers in Silicon Valley. UC Santa Cruz has over 50,000 enrollees pursuing non-college credit professional development courses in a variety of campuses throughout Santa Clara County and the East Bay.

So what is the bottom line? How important are universities to the creation of innovative economies? Even in the best of all worlds, in which all of the claims that we have documented are true, a "have-not" region could invest in universities in each of our five domains, only to find that local high-tech growth remains dismally low. Broadly speaking, there are two reasons for potential failure. The first reason is simply that a university could produce outstanding graduates, only to see them leave for more thriving areas. Spatial agglomeration is very real, and we have documented how this works to the benefit of the "technology-have" regions and to the detriment of the "technology-have-not" regions in both the United States and Canada.

But there is a second and more fundamental reason why it is probably wrong to think of universities in isolation as a magic key to high-tech growth. Universities can function as the knowledge creation anchor for a region, but the university is not sufficient in and of itself to drive the creation of a knowledge-intensive industry cluster. There are other vital pieces that need to be connected such as smart sources of financing that understand the needs of emerging high-tech firms, managerial talent savvy in these industries, as well as the scientists and engineers who innovate in these firms. Technology commercialization is a very different beast than knowledge creation; a region needs *both* to thrive. To be blunt, if anything, there is a tendency in the literature to perhaps overplay the role of universities and underplay the role of the private sector in generating innovative technology clusters.

Increasingly, in knowledge-intensive industries such as biotech, it is not firms competing in a global marketplace, it is also *regions* competing with each other for the attraction of major corporate research establishments and promising start-up firms. Whether a region tries to grow its own power-house firms from scratch or tries to lure branch plants and R&D centres to its region, success with these regional strategies is couched on truly under-standing a region's competitive advantage and then being able to sell this advantage to entrepreneurs, corporate executives and financiers of these industries. The university is but one of several actors that help to determine the competitive advantage of the region.

Predictably, we end this paper with the usual call for "more and better data". Our own analysis and summary of that of others based on national measures of R&D or skilled labour are an important first step, but do not reveal the subtleties at work on the regional level. In this paper we have highlighted some recent attempts to gather and interpret data on actual linkages between universities and firms. This approach, while time consuming and costly, promises to tell us much that is new about the full extent of university-industry interactions and the resulting impact on innovation in both settings. We also need to develop new datasets that track new indicators of success, that is, the agglomeration of intellectual property lawyers in a region over time, the development of indigenous venture capital funding in a region that had none, and the agglomeration of scientists and engineers of particular sub-specialities (e.g., neuroscientists in San Diego). Armed with better data, preferably at the city, metropolitan or county levels, there is greater hope that we can perform studies that carefully delineate between cause and effect.

Appendix

UCSD CONNECT, San Diego's Program for High Technology Entrepreneurship

CONNECT Program History and Mission

Founded in 1985 at the urging of San Diego's business community, San Diego's version of high technology business incubation is embodied in a program called UCSD CONNECT. CONNECT's private model of incubation differs significantly from that of most public incubators. There is no physical incubation space provided at a subsidized cost to the firm, nor is there public funding from local, regional, state or national governments. Instead, CONNECT's success in building high-tech industry clusters comes from the numerous and frequent networking activities that are underwritten by memberships, sponsorships, and event registration fees. The university provides some administrative overhead by hosting the program in the Division of Extended Studies and Public Programs (UCSD Extension), the academic unit for continuing education studies.[14]

CONNECT acts as a resource to assist entrepreneurs throughout the San Diego region, not just for university spin-off companies and faculty entrepreneurs. CONNECT also relies heavily on volunteers from the local business service-provider community. These business service-providers not only sponsor CONNECT's activities, but the senior partners of local law firms, management consulting companies, venture capitalists, and angel investors also serve on numerous committees to mentor entrepreneurs, review business plans, select candidate companies for CONNECT's investment forums, and choose the winners for the region's Most Innovative Products

---

[14]The Division of Extended Studies and Public Programs (UCSD Extension) operates at the interface between the university and the community. All of its programs are self-supporting, in that there is no federal, state or local support for any of its activities. UCSD Extension operates on a tuition-fee-based, cost-recovery basis. CONNECT is one of several public programs housed in Extension; others include a TV station (UCSD TV), San Diego Dialogue, the San Diego Civic Collaborative, UCSD Summer Session, Academic Connections and the Cross-Border Health Initiative.

of the Year Award. Besides assisting a larger number of companies than a typical physical incubator, CONNECT's programs also serve to build and strengthen a growing network of savvy business service-providers who understand the needs of the emerging high-tech firms in their midst. The privately funded model allows CONNECT to remain close to its regional membership in tailoring its events and activities. The dense and multiple levels of networking that occur in this "learning community" fuel San Diego's competitive advantage as a region where technology deals are concluded quickly and efficiently, experienced management teams can be put in place fast, and the local service-providers are specialized and knowledgeable about high-tech issues.

CONNECT's Role in Technology Commercialization

Spinning off technology from a university academic setting involves two different processes, technology transfer of intellectual property (IP) ownership from the university and subsequent commercialization of this IP by a private entity other than the university. After transferring the intellectual property (IP) rights from the university to a start-up company, the company's founders must still seek funding to further the development of the technology into a product that sells. University technology transfer offices typically do not engage in these technology commercialization and business incubation activities that lie downstream from the technology transfer process. Some universities have built physical incubators to assist with technology commercialization activities, but the success of these incubators are debatable as the throughput of companies being incubated is not high enough to jumpstart the agglomeration of firms in a particular industry that gives rise to regional industry clusters (Lewis, 2001; Tornatzky, Sherman and Adkins, 2003). CONNECT, on the other hand, acts downstream of the Technology Transfer Office, and is concentrated solely on assisting high-tech entrepreneurs on capital formation, management team building and workforce issues. The lack of physical incubation space was not an issue at the program's inception, as San Diego's regional economy in 1985 was reeling from the fallout of the Savings and Loans crisis. In retrospect, this also gave CONNECT an advantage, as the number of companies that it could assist was not limited by CONNECT's own office space, as would be the case for a physical incubator. CONNECT's throughput remains much higher than that of physical incubators.

CONNECT's Springboard Program Assists Emerging Firms

CONNECT's Springboard program mentors entrepreneurs with business plan writing and strategic planning. After 8 to 12 weeks of one-on-one coaching by CONNECT staff, graduation consists of a presentation of the polished business plan by the entrepreneurs to a review panel of business service-providers, seasoned entrepreneurs, and potential angel and venture capital investors. The panelists, serve on a volunteer basis and provide honest feedback to the entrepreneurs during a two-hour breakfast meeting.[15] If a panelist wishes to pursue further discussions with an entrepreneur, that is solely at the two parties' discretion. CONNECT, having served the role of an honest broker in convening the Springboard panel, steps aside. While there are anecdotes of companies being directly funded out of a Springboard panel, this is not the norm. Rather, the program is designed to introduce promising entrepreneurs to San Diego's business networks while providing business leaders an opportunity to network with each other while they are mentoring the next generation of business leaders in their midst.

References

Arora, A., A. Gambardella and S. Torrisi. 2004. "In the Footsteps of Silicon Valley? India and Irish Software in the International Division of Labor", in T. Bresnahan and A. Gambardella (eds.), *Building High Tech Clusters: Silicon Valley and Beyond.* Cambridge: Cambridge University Press, 78-120.

Auerswald, P.E. and L.M. Branscomb. 2003. "Start-ups and Spin-offs: Collective Entrepreneurship between Invention and Innovation", in D.M. Hart (ed.), *The Emergence of Entrepreneurship Policy: Governance, Start-ups, and Growth in the U.S Knowledge Economy.* Cambridge: Cambridge University Press, 61-91.

Bartel, A.P. and F.R. Lichtenberg. 1987. "The Comparative Advantage of Educated Workers in Implementing New Technology", *Review of Economics and Statistics* 69, 1-11.

---

[15]Panelists are typically senior partners in law and accounting firms, CEOs, and senior decisionmakers in the firms they serve. Junior staff from these firms are never tapped to be volunteers for CONNECT events, although they may be invited by the senior partner to observe on an occasional basis.

Berman, E., J. Bound and Z. Griliches. 1994. "Changes in the Demand for Skilled Labor within US Manufacturing Industries: Evidence from the Annual Survey of Manufactures", *Quarterly Journal of Economics* 109(2), 367-397.

Berman, E., J. Bound and S. Machin. 1998. "Implications of Skill-Biased Technological Change: International Evidence", *Quarterly Journal of Economics* 113(4), 1245-1280.

Betts, J.R. 1997. "The Skill Bias of Technological Change in Canadian Manufacturing Industries", *Review of Economics and Statistics* 79(1), 146-150.

_____. 2000. *The Changing Role of Education in California*. San Francisco: Public Policy Institute of California.

_____. 2002. *Critical Path Analysis of California's S&T System: California's K-12 Sector*. Riverside: California Council on Science and Technology.

Binswanger, H.P. and V.W. Ruttan *et al.* 1978. *Induced Innovation: Technology, Institutions and Development*. Baltimore: Johns Hopkins University Press.

Bils, M. and P.J. Klenow. 2000. "Does Schooling Cause Growth?" *American Economic Review* 90(5), 1160-1183.

Boyd, E.A. and L.A. Bero. 2000. "Assessing Faculty Financial Relationships with Industry: A Case Study", *Journal of the American Medical Association* 284(17), 2209-2214.

Burbidge, J. and R. Finnie. 2000. "The Geographical Mobility of Baccalaureate Graduates: Evidence from Three Cohorts of the National Graduates Survey, 1982, 1986, 1990", *Canadian Journal of Regional Science* 23(3), 377-401.

California Council on Science and Technology. 2002. *Critical Path Analysis of California's S&T System: California's K-12 Sector*. Irvine: California Council on Science and Technology.

Card, D. 2003. "Canadian Emigration to the United States", in C.M. Beach, A.G. Green and J.G. Reitz (eds.), *Canadian Immigration Policy for the 21st Century*. Kingston: John Deutsch Institute, Queen's University, 295-312.

Council on Competitiveness. 2001. *Clusters of Innovation Initiative*. At http://www.compete.org.

de Fontenay, C. and E. Carmel. 2004. "Israel's Silicon Wadi: The Forces behind Cluster Formation", in T. Bresnahan and A. Gambardella (eds.), *Building High Tech Clusters: Silicon Valley and Beyond*. Cambridge: Cambridge University Press, 40-77.

Etzkowitz, H., A. Webster and P. Healey, eds. 1998. *Capitalizing Knowledge: New Intersections of Industry and Academia*. Albany, NY: SUNY Press.

Feldman, M.P. 2003. "Entrepreneurship and American Research Universities: Evolution in Technology Transfer", in D.M. Hart (ed.), *The Emergence of Entrepreneurship Policy: Governance, Start-ups, and Growth in the U.S. Knowledge Economy*. Cambridge: Cambridge University Press, 92-112.

Florida, R. 2002. *The Rise of the Creative Class: And How It's Transforming Work, Leisure, Community and Everyday Life*. New York: Basic Books.

Gibbons, J.F. 2000. "The Role of Stanford University: A Dean's Reflections", in C.-M. Lee, W.F. Miller and M.G. Hancock (eds.), *The Silicon Valley Edge: A Habitat for Innovation & Entrepreneurship*. Stanford, CA: Stanford University Press, 200-217.

Groen, J.A. and M.J. White. 2004. "In-State versus Out-of-State Students: The Divergence of Interest Between Public Universities and State Governments", *Journal of Public Economics* 88(9-10), 1793-1814.

Hanushek, E.A. and D.D. Kimko. 2000. "Schooling, Labor-Force Quality, and the Growth of Nations", *American Economic Review* 90(5), 1184-1208.

Jaffe, A.B. 1989. "The Real Effects of Academic Research", *American Economic Review* 79, 957-970.

Jaffe, A.B., M. Trajtenberg and R. Henderson. 1993. "Geographic Localization of Knowledge Spillovers as Evidenced by Patent Citations", *Quarterly Journal of Economics* 108(3), 577-598.

Kenney, M., ed. 2000. *Understanding Silicon Valley: The Anatomy of an Entrepreneurial Region*. Stanford, CA: Stanford University Press.

Lee, C.-M., W.F. Miller and M.G. Hancock, eds. 2000. *The Silicon Valley Edge: A Habitat for Innovation & Entrepreneurship*. Stanford, CA: Stanford University Press.

Lee, C.W.B. and M.L. Walshok. 2002. *Critical Path Analysis of California's S&T System: Alternative Paths to Competency through Continuing Education and Lifelong Learning*. Riverside, CA: California Council on Science and Technology.

_____. 2003. *Total Links Matter: The Direct and Indirect Effects of Research Universities on Regional Economies*. A report for the University of California's Industry-University Cooperative Research Program.

Lee, C.W.B., M.L. Walshok and B.R. Switzer. 2002. "An Overview of the R&D Capacity of Indiana's Top Six Metropolitan Statistical Areas". A report for New Economy Strategies and Central Indiana's Life Science Initiative.

Lewis, D.A. 2001. "Does Technology Incubation Work? A Critical Review". A report to the US Economic Development Administration.

National Science Board. 2002. *Science and Engineering Indicators*, Volume Two: Appendix Tables. Arlington, VA: National Science Foundation.

Palmintera, D. 2000. *Developing High-Technology Communities: San Diego*. A report to the US Small Business Administration's Office of Advocacy.

Porter, M. 1990. *The Competitive Advantage of Nations*. New York: The Free Press.

_____. 1998. "Clusters and the New Economics of Competition", *Harvard Business Review* (November-December), 77-90.

Rosenberg, D. 2002. *Cloning Silicon Valley: The Next Generation High-Tech Hotspots*. London: Pearson Education Ltd.

Rosenberg, N. 2003. "America's Entrepreneurial Universities", in D.M. Hart (ed.), *The Emergence of Entrepreneurship Policy: Governance, Start-ups, and*

Growth in the U.S Knowledge Economy. Cambridge: Cambridge University Press, 113-137.

Saxenian, A.L. 1994. *Regional Advantage: Culture and Competition in Silicon Valley and Route 128*. Cambridge, MA: Harvard University Press.

_____. 1999. *Silicon Valley's New Immigrant Entrepreneurs*. San Francisco: Public Policy Institute of California.

Smilor, R.W., G. Kozmetsky and D.V. Gibson. 1988. *Creating the Technopolis: Linking Technology Commercialization and Economic Development*. New York: HarperCollins.

Sohl, J.E. 1999. "The Early-Stage Equity Market in the U.S.A.", *Venture Capital* 1, 101-120.

Sturgeon, T.J. 2000. "How Silicon Valley Came to Be", in M. Kenney (ed.), *Understanding Silicon Valley: The Anatomy of an Entrepreneurial Region*. Stanford, CA: Stanford University Press, 15-47.

Switzer, B.R., M.L. Walshok and C.W.B. Lee. 2003. "Greater Philadelphia's Research Capacity and Dynamism". A report prepared for New Economy Strategies and Innovation Philadelphia.

Tornatzky, L., H. Sherman and D. Adkins. 2003. *A National Benchmarking Analysis of Technology Business Incubator Performance and Practices*. A report by the National Business Incubation Association to the US Department of Commerce, Technology Administration.

Tornatzky, L.G., P.G. Waugaman and D.O. Gray. 2002. *Innovation U: New University Roles in a Knowledge Economy*. A Southern Policies Growth Board Report, Research Triangle Park, NC.

University of California. 2002. *Office of Technology Transfer Annual Report*. Oakland: University of California.

Wallsten, S. 2004. "The Role of Government in Regional Technology Development: The Effects of Public Venture Capital and Science Parks", in T. Bresnahan and A. Gambardella (eds.), *Building High Tech Clusters: Silicon Valley and Beyond*. Cambridge: Cambridge University Press, 229-279.

Walshok, M., C. Lee, E. Furtek and P. Windham. 2001. *Networks of Innovation: Contributions to San Diego's Telecommunications and Biotech Clusters*. A report for the University of California's Industry-University Cooperative Research Program.

Wong, A. 2002. "Angel Finance: The Other Venture Capital". Chicago: University of Chicago Graduate School of Business. Unpublished manuscript.

Section III

Role of Government in Financing and Overseeing Postsecondary Education

"Muddy" Data: University Financing in Canada

Ken Snowdon

Introduction

Queen's University is a fitting place for this timely review of higher education in Canada. This university has a long and storied history of involvement in higher education in Ontario and Canada — especially since the expansion era of the 1960s and 1970s. Principals Corry and Deutsch were instrumental in establishing the current funding regime and were major forces to be reckoned with as Ontario struggled with the weighty issues of postsecondary education expansion to accommodate the "baby boom". Principal Watts and Principal Smith left their marks on Queen's and the university system in Ontario and, at the national level, played prominent roles in the higher education sector. Peter Leslie (1980)[1] produced "the" authoritative study on university financing for the Association of

---

I would like to express my appreciation to H. O'Heron, R. Best and C. Lemelin for their thoughtful comments and insights.

[1]Dr. Leslie's study should be required reading for all individuals interested in higher education funding. His findings and recommendations on such issues as provincial/federal roles in higher education, the support of university research, the funding of indirect costs, and income-contingent loan repayment programs are as topical and valid today as they were 25 years ago.

Universities and Colleges of Canada and there are numerous other examples of Queen's persons — Roderick Fraser, president of the University of Alberta and a former member of the Department of Economics at Queen's — who continue to play significant roles in furthering higher education in the country.

The task today is to examine trends in postsecondary financing with an emphasis on the federal/provincial roles. My focus will be on "direct" university financing, although it is readily acknowledged that college systems also have a major role to play in Canadian higher education. The term "direct" applies to revenue received by the universities and thus this paper excludes financing associated with government student aid programs.[2] Nor does it attempt to enter into the murky world of federal/provincial fiscal arrangements such as the Canada Health and Social Transfer (CHST).

This review of federal/provincial funding of Canadian universities started out as a relatively straightforward exercise but quickly turned into a review of university financial reporting. Based on the premise that sound policy should be informed by solid, reliable information, there are some major "data" issues that must be addressed if policymakers are to develop a true picture of the state of university financing.

This paper begins by outlining some of the major data "challenges" emerging from a review of two reports providing information on university financing in Canada; the recent *Education at a Glance: OECD Indicators* report by the Organisation for Economic Co-operation and Development (OECD) (2003), and a Statistics Canada report *Changing Patterns of University Finance* (2003). A number of data issues are identified here, raising some doubt about the reported findings and speaking directly to the need for the university community to focus more attention on the information used to inform policymakers.

Informed by some of the shortcomings associated with financial data, the paper then proceeds to examine basic trends in university finance in Canada, identifying key sources of revenue and the changes therein over the past 30 years. The findings suggest major shifts in the sources of funding over the period with private revenue — tuition, investment income, and donations/grants — increasing markedly in contrast to government

---

[2]Individuals interested in a survey of government student aid programs and the level of government expenditures, see Junor and Usher (2002).

Ken Snowdon

funding.[3] However, it is instructive to note the important increases in both provincial and especially federal funding over the past few years. Further, it is important to recognize that governments are, by far, still the major funding source of universities.

University Financing in Canada: Recent Interpretations

In Canada, the major source of university financial information is an annual report entitled *Financial Information of Universities and Colleges* compiled by Statistics Canada based on a survey of all Canadian universities. The survey is actually administered by the Canadian Association of University Business Officers and is generally referred to as the CAUBO report. The CAUBO report is used by Statistics Canada as the source for higher education financial data and is a major part of the information that finds its way into the OECD publications. As such it plays an exceedingly important role in helping governments, researchers, and individuals understand the financial situation of Canadian universities.

We begin by looking at two recent reports, one from the OECD and one from Statistics Canada, that both use the data from the CAUBO report. These reports provide interpretations of the overall level of funding for higher education in Canada versus other countries and point to trends in Canadian university financing.

A recent OECD study ranks Canada second in *total* "tertiary education" spending per student and third, behind the United States and Switzerland

---

[3]There are clearly regional differences in the proportion of provincial government funding provided to universities, largely due to differences in tuition policies. For example, provincial grants constitute about 70% of operating revenue in Quebec and Newfoundland — two provinces that have adopted policies of lower tuition, while in provinces like Nova Scotia and Ontario, provincial operating grants represent about 45–50% of operating revenue and then have higher tuition and fees to help compensate for lower provincial grants.

Figure 1: International Comparison of Expenditure on University Programs

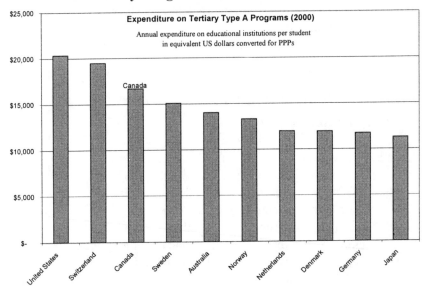

Source: OECD (2003, Table B1.1).

in spending on Tertiary Type A programs (primarily universities).[4] More-over, the study concludes that Canada is one of the few countries where spending on tertiary education has actually kept pace with gross domestic product (GDP) growth over the five-year period (1995–2000). As Figure 1 illustrates, the OECD report paints a reasonably good picture of the *relative* financial position of higher education in Canada compared to other OECD countries.

Turning to Canada specifically: What do we know about trends in university funding? In 2003, a Statistics Canada report, *Changing Patterns of University Finance*, indicated that:

---

[4]The table is derived from OECD data, which in the case of some countries (US) does not distinguish between levels of tertiary education. In fact, the gap between Canada and the United States for "universities" is considerably greater as reported in AUCC *Trends in Higher Education.*

- Government is accounting for a smaller proportion of universities' operating revenue over time;
- All sources of private revenue are increasing — tuition increases are by far the largest source of private revenue;
- Total operating revenue (after adjusting for inflation) on a full-time equivalent (FTE) basis increased by over $1,000 or over 8% from 1986 to 2000.

Table 1 provides a summary directly from the Statistics Canada report. The report noted that smaller universities "experienced a greater decline per FTE in government support for operating revenue than the large universities". At the same time it was noted that "Over the same 15 year period, small universities experienced an increase of 48% in operating revenues double the 24% recorded increase for large universities. However, enrolment for the small universities increased by 51% compared with 14% for the large universities" (2003, p. 13).

Taken together, the preceding analyses suggest overall funding increased in real terms on a per student basis *and* Canada's relative position is reasonably good. Based solely on those two documents, cries of underfunding from the university community may be perceived as a bit "hollow", although the Statistics Canada report does suggest smaller universities are being disadvantaged relative to larger institutions.

Table 1: Operating Revenue by Source Per Full-Time Equivalent Student, 1986–87 and 2000–01

	1986–87	*2000–01*	*Change*	*% Change*
	$ constant 2000–01 per FTE			
Government	10,091	8,190	(1,901)	−18.8
Student fees	2,029	4,525	2,496	123.0
Bequests, etc.*	47	135	88	187.2
Investment	156	343	187	119.9
Miscellaneous**	83	251	168	202.4
Total "private" revenue	2,315	5,255	2,940	127.0
Total operating revenue	12,406	13,444	1,038	8.4

Notes: *Includes bequests, donations and non-government grants and contracts.
**Includes commissions, royalties, rentals, and library and similar fines.

In fact, there are a host of issues and concerns swirling around the findings from reports like the preceding Statistics Canada report and the OECD report.

First, in both cases, the analyses are based on "dated" information. Significant increases in enrolment, alone, have occurred since 2000/01 and would have a major impact on the "findings".

Second, in both studies, the financial information does not appear to account for factors that may overstate the financial situation by hundreds of millions of dollars. For example, the analyses fail to recognize major increases in university-funded student assistance expenditures. These are mandated by government and effectively reduce the actual amount of income available for instruction, research, and services (core operations). In the case of OECD comparisons, some, if not all, of those student assistance expenditures would be the purview of government, not universities. In Canada, as governments have "off-loaded" student assistance costs to the universities, the more recent revenue data overstates the value of tuition revenue and its contribution to core operations.

In a similar fashion, the more recent CAUBO information employs the concept of "gross" reporting rather than "net", resulting in an "accounting induced" increase in both revenue and expenditures in more recent years relative to the past. In the past, for example, "sales-of-service" revenue was largely confined to ancillary operations where universities operated residences, book stores, and food services. In other parts of the university, revenue from sales of service was "netted" against the expenditures associated with those sales. Since CAUBO made the change to "gross" reporting in the late 1990s, the data is simply not comparable year over year and overstates the actual revenue and expenditures by at least $500 million (2001/02). The Statistics Canada report acknowledged the change in reporting and excluded sales-of-service revenues from the analysis. However, other users of the report may not be aware of the change and it is unclear how the more recent CAUBO information is being treated for OECD purposes.

The analyses also fail to recognize the substantial investment required to support a strategy of enhanced revenue diversification, increasingly, a characteristic of Canadian universities. To the extent that Canadian universities have been successful in increasing income from sources other than government (grants) and students (tuition and other fees), there is no recognition of the costs associated with generating those funds. Accordingly, the increase in revenue and the revenue figure itself could be seen as misleading, especially in comparison with other countries where funding systems may rely much more heavily on government grants.

Third, the CAUBO data — despite best intentions — has a number of institutional reporting "quirks" that cumulatively have a major impact on the overall levels of funding being reported, and thus the interpretations that may follow. For example, since the mid-1990s Queen's University has been reporting the government grant from the Ministry of Health for the Alternative Funding Plan (AFP) in the School of Medicine, in the same fashion as the provincial operating grants from the Ministry of Training, Colleges and Universities. What appears to be an increase in provincial funding is really just a change in funding practice employed by the provincial government. Prior to the AFP those funds — essentially direct payment for service fees to physicians — would have either not shown in the university's financial documents or only a small portion would have shown in the Special Purpose Trust fund.[5] Lest one think those sums are relatively small and "get lost in the noise", the Queen's AFP figure, alone, is in the order of $50 million annually.

Another example of institutional policies/practices affecting the comparability of data over time and among institutions is the move towards a more comprehensive definition of the "operating fund". At one time the operating fund focused principally on government operating grants, tuition fees, and a relatively minor amount of "other income" from sales of services and investment income on operating cash flow. Universities themselves had a vested interest in keeping the "other funds" — donations and endowment income, for example — segregated in a separate "fund", usually special purpose trust funds. The intent was to clearly identify the activities and income under the purview of the province (grants and tuition) to ensure other funds generated by the university would not be taken into consideration by the government in computing institutional operating grants.

Over time, what had been a fairly simple distinction has become blurred for a variety of reasons: accounting regulations, government

---

[5]Usually in the form of "ceiling payments". Individual physicians associated with the university would have a remuneration ceiling established based on physician fee-for-service incomes in the province. If the physician earned more than the agreed "ceiling" through fee-for-service income, the extra funds were paid to a trust fund in the physician's department and used to help finance academic activities such as research projects.

directives, new revenue sources, increased private-giving, institutional initiatives, greater organizational complexity, the impact of *Maclean's* rankings, and the increasing recognition that the university *is* the sum of its parts — whether restricted or not. The long-standing argument from the academic community about the synergy between teaching and research, or the value of the "broader learning environment" highlights the fact that separating university finances, or at least some of them, into specific "baskets" may have been a somewhat artificial exercise. In the last decade individual institutions have taken steps to include other sources of income in the operating fund for a variety of reasons, including internal transparency and a desire to provide a more consolidated picture of the university's financial situation.

Regardless of the merits of consolidation, however, the result is an overstating of university revenue (and expenditures) relative to past information. Accordingly, some portion of the change in general operating funding over a given period of time may well be caused by changes in the definition of the "general operating fund".[6] To the extent that historical analyses focus on operating funds (e.g., the Statcan report cited earlier) there is an "apples to oranges" effect that overstates the revenue increases.

While the focus of this paper is financial, the reality is that data issues spill over to other information often used to construct ratios or "$ per" measures. For example, the use of a simple full-time equivalent (FTE) enrolment measure does not recognize differences in the discipline composition of the enrolments, nor the undergraduate/graduate "mix" of students. Why does that matter? There are differences in program cost (and

---

[6]Universities tend to operate, financially, with two basic "baskets" of income and expense: general expendable funds and restricted expendable funds. The distinction is driven by restrictions established, usually, by external funders — research councils, foundations, donors, and government. Restricted expendable funds are exactly that — spent according to restrictions set by an external "funder". Those monies contribute to the overall financial health of the university, but are not generally available for the basic operation of the institution. General expendable funds, on the other hand, are spent according to policies and decisions made by the university. Within the two preceding baskets are a number of smaller baskets — restricted expendable includes special purpose trust, sponsored research and capital, while general expendable includes operating, ancillary and non-credit programs. The preceding is the essence of fund accounting — monies are received in one "fund" according to specific purposes and spent for those purposes in that same "fund".

revenue) associated with programs and level of instruction. To the extent that comparisons are being made it is important to recognize those differences. Statistics Canada (2003) noted funding per FTE declined more for smaller universities than for larger universities and attributes the difference, implicitly, to the change in the number of students. While changes in the number of students may have affected that funding result, another factor was very likely that larger institutions had more expensive per student costs and hence larger provincial grants per FTE student. Those institutions have greater proportions of graduate enrolments, professional program enrolments, and specialized programs — all of which tend to be more expensive on a per FTE basis — than direct entry undergraduate education. If Statistics Canada had constructed a "weighted FTE" measure factoring in differences in program costs, the cited differences would have narrowed considerably.

The preceding examples are not intended to be exhaustive. Rather, the intent is simply to illustrate the primary source of financial data being used by policymakers at both the provincial and federal levels, Statistics Canada, the Council of Ministers of Education (CMEC), and provided to the OECD has some reporting discontinuities and inconsistencies that overstate the actual revenue situation for Canadian universities by *hundreds of millions* of dollars relative to earlier years. Not surprisingly, then, government officials may have quite a different view of university finances than members of the university community. Further, it is not at all clear how the financial data is actually translated into the OECD comparisons. Efforts must be made to ensure greater transparency in the production of those figures.

CAUBO is in the process of trying to address one part of the problem — improving the year-to-year consistency and comparability of the financial information and noting major reporting changes.[7] However, how financial data is then interpreted and used by agencies such as Statistics Canada and government ministries and how it is used for international comparisons poses another set of challenges for the university community that must be addressed as well. "Muddy" data is part of the higher education landscape, so tread carefully as you use it.

----

[7]In fact, the current CAUBO guidelines that accompany the survey instrument are intended to draw attention to the limitations of the financial data and users of the report are encouraged to read the limitations carefully.

University Financing: An Historical Review

With the preceding as background, this paper now turns to a review of university financing with a focus on changes in revenue over the past approximately 30 years. Notwithstanding the preceding comments about "muddy" data, the use of the financial data for highly aggregated "trend" analysis is much more acceptable.[8] To provide a more comprehensive picture and account for some changes in reporting definitions and institutional practices, the focus in this section of the paper is on three funds (see footnote 6 previously for a description of fund accounting) — general operating (operating), special purpose trust (trust) and sponsored research (research). Those three funds constitute what might be considered the "core activities" of teaching and research and related services and constitute almost 90% of total university revenues as illustrated in Figure 2.

Since the early 1970s there have been marked differences in the rate of growth in each of those funds; with the trust fund increasing from about $15 million to almost $950 million (a factor of over 60 times), the research fund increasing from $167 million to almost $3.8 billion (a factor of over 20 times), and the operating fund increasing from about $1.1 billion to almost $9.9 billion (a factor of nine times). Analyses of university finances tend to focus on the general operating fund and sponsored research fund as two separate entities. While there is reference to the special purpose trust fund it is often not factored into the overall financial equation.[9]

What accounts for the major differences in the rate of growth by fund? The simple answer is the composition of each fund (in terms of income sources) and the differential rates of growth in those income sources. Table 2 illustrates the different composition of the funds. Income in the operating fund is generated primarily from provincial grants and fees. Income in the trust fund is derived from gifts and donations as well as a host of other

---

[8]The CAUBO guidelines specifically note that: "The data is most useful when aggregated and used for trend analysis. As users move from aggregated data to data that directly compares institutions, either individually or even between provinces or regions, the comparability of the data has limitations" (2000/01, p. 2).

[9]See, for example, Association of Universities and Colleges of Canada (2002). The financial figures in *Trends* differ a bit from the numbers in Table 2 because the AUCC analysis excludes the university colleges in British Columbia — yet another factor that leads to the "muddy" data noted earlier.

Figure 2: Income by Fund 2001/02 ($ billions), All CAUBO Institutions

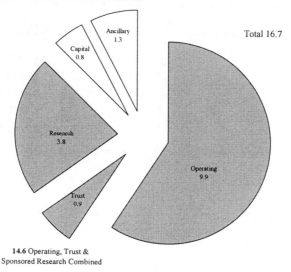

Total 16.7

Ancillary 1.3

Capital 0.8

Research 3.8

Operating 9.9

Trust 0.9

14.6 Operating, Trust & Sponsored Research Combined

Table 2: Distribution of Income by Fund ($000s) 2001/02

	General Operating	% of Total	Special Purpose Trust	% of Total	Sponsored Research	% of Total	Total Combined	% of Total
All fees	$3,246,203	33	$34,110	4	--	0	$3,280,313	22
Provincial	$5,824,935	59	$176,565	19	$728,692	19	$6,730,192	46
Federal	$69,662	1	$76,019	8	$1,686,420	45	$1,832,101	13
Gifts and donations	$74,072	1	$351,164	37	$1,098,778	29	$1,524,014	10
Investment income	$149,818	2	$102,860	11	$43,852	1	$296,530	2
All other	$521,141	5	$208,185	22	$212,787	6	$942,113	6
Total	$9,885,831	100	$948,903	100	$3,770,529	100	$14,605,263	100
% of Total	68%		6%		26%		100%	

sources. Sponsored research is funded principally by federal monies, gifts, donations and non-government grants and contracts, and by provincial grants.

Table 3 indicates that relative to 1971/72, provincial grants and contracts is the only income source where the proportion has actually

Table 3: Distribution of Total Combined Income by Source

	1971/72	% of Total	2001/02	% of Total
All fees	$209,598	16	$3,280,313	22
Provincial	$928,838	69	$6,730,192	46
Federal	$119,894	9	$1,832,101	13
Gifts and donations	$40,051	3	$1,524,014	10
Investment income	$27,108	2	$296,530	2
All other	$24,716	2	$942,113	6
Total	$1,350,205	100	$14,605,263	100

decreased.[10] As noted earlier, there has been a significant difference in the rate of change in the three funds.

Figure 3 provides a review of the income sources since 1971/72. The changes since 1971/72 are adjusted for inflation and portrayed as an index to better illustrate the relative change. Gifts, donations, and non-government grants have increased markedly over the period and help to explain the increase in the trust fund as well as part of the increase in the sponsored research fund.[11] A significant portion of that funding is from non-government foundations and companies contributing to research — not basic operations. Moreover, it is difficult to establish the actual "net" revenue associated with some of the components of this particular income source because of the varying costs of what is referred to as "advancement" — the actual fundraising operation that must be paid for from somewhere in the organization.[12] Nevertheless, the change over time is impressive and

---

[10]The source of this data is the CAUBO report. Although it is recognized there are discontinuities in the data, including the addition of some university colleges in British Columbia over the time period, the basic trends remain valid.

[11]A portion of the increase in sponsored research is due to changes in reporting in the mid-1990s involving the inclusion of affiliated hospital research funding.

[12]Estimates of the cost of fundraising range from 10% to 25% of all dollars raised depending on whether the institution is in the midst of a campaign or in-between campaigns and depending on whether alumni relations activities are

Ken Snowdon

Figure 3: Indexed Change in Income by Source (Adjusted for Inflation)

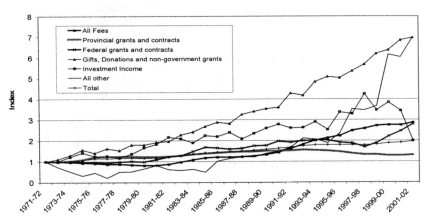

a function of concerted effort by the university community to increase private funding from alumni and other donors, companies and foundations. Governments have also played a major role by encouraging private contributions through changes in tax legislation, introducing matching programs whereby the government matches contributions for specific purposes and by requiring private contributions as a condition of receiving government monies.

Investment income increased over the period, although the downturn in investment returns in the most recent year (2001/02) indicates the volatility associated with that income source. Nevertheless, it provides a valuable addition to the revenue stream of many institutions and is responsible for contributing to the significant increase in the trust fund

---

included in the numerator. In many cases the cost — whether it is 10% or 25% of every dollar raised — is actually funded by a combination of direct subsidy by the university, a portion of the investment income earned on donation cash flow and perhaps endowments, an overhead levied on donations and the retention of some (or all) of the profits from affinity programs such as university credit cards, insurance, travel, and sales of institutional branded goods.

where it comprises about 11% of the total income.[13] While the increases in the preceding two major income sources have been significant it is important to remember the relative size of each of those sources of income. Gifts, donations, and non-government grants account for about 10% of total income and investment income accounts for about 2%.

Much of the change in the "All other" category is actually due to the change from net to gross reporting that occurred in the latter part of the 1990s, thus the apparent shift in the proportion of funding is, in fact, largely illusory.

Fee income has increased by a factor of three times over the period with steady increases from 1990 onward. Federal funding (grants and contracts) increased through the 1980s, decreased for part of the 1990s and then increased markedly from 1998/99. Provincial funding peaked in the early 1990s and then declined through to the end of the 1990s before turning up slightly.

The contrast between federal and provincial funding is notable and highlighted in Figure 4. That particular graph could be the subject of a separate analysis that would highlight major changes in federal/provincial funding agreements. For example, federal/provincial funding arrangements changed in 1977 and within a very short time thereafter direct federal support to sponsored research began to increase. Interestingly, 1977 also marks the date that the university sector tends to use as the starting point to chronicle the decades long decline in provincial grants per student (adjusted for inflation) (AUCC, 2002, Figure 4.6, p. 61).

However, the most significant difference between federal and provincial funding is the marked change in federal funding beginning in the late 1990s. The introduction of direct funding programs, such as the Canada Foundation for Innovation and the Canada Research Chairs, along with major increases in funding to research councils and a major contribution to the indirect costs of research has, to quote AUCC *Trends* "transformed the funding landscape for research in Canada" (ibid., p. 43). In fact, because of the magnitude of the increases in federal funding, and the way the federal government decided to allocate the increased funds the *entire* funding landscape for university education has changed.

----

[13]Readers should keep in mind that the investment income is generated from university endowments — which have grown to approximately $6.4 billion (2002) — as well as investment of cash flow (CAUBO, 2004).

Figure 4: Indexed Change in Federal and Provincial Income

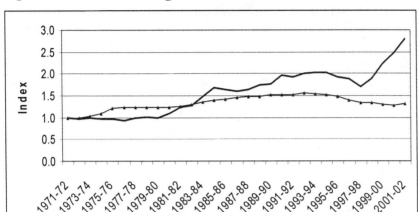

Figure 5 focuses on the last five years and examines the absolute changes in funding levels from the federal government, provincial governments, and tuition — the three largest sources of funding. In absolute terms, the provincial contributions have increased by approximately $1.4 billion, the federal contribution by $0.9 billion with tuition and other fees adding an additional $1 billion. Virtually all of the federal increase is in the research area and almost 30% of the provincial funding increase is also in the research area — the latter generally in the form of "matching" funds for CFI or targeted to specific provincial research initiatives. A significant portion of the remaining increase in provincial grants is related to specific enrolment expansion programs rather than general increases to address on-going cost increases. The "fee increase" of $1 billion yields considerably less in discretionary income for core operations once institutional student assistance is taken into account.[14] Nevertheless, investments by both levels of government (taxpayers) and by students represent a significant increase in revenue over the past several years. In light of those investments it is not

---

[14]Over those five years, expenditures on student assistance in the general operating fund and special purpose trust fund increased from approximately $300 million to $650 million per year.

Figure 5: Operating, Trust and Sponsored Research Funding (Major Income Sources)

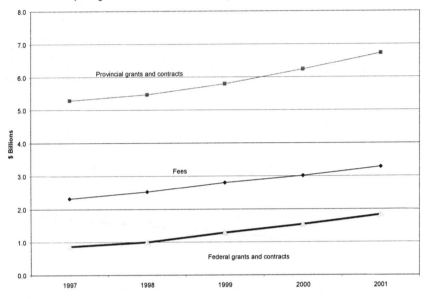

surprising there are increased calls from government for strengthened accountability.

Considerations

The significant increase in overall funding to universities over the past five years signals a major change in the federal presence. But the impact of direct federal investment carries with it added costs. At a time when universities are dealing with record numbers of students, the federal investment is requiring direct subsidies to support the increased research effort — despite the advent of some research overheads. Also, a significant amount of the provincial funding increase (approximately $400 million) is actually being directed to research, some to meet federal contributory requirements and some to demonstrate that the provinces have their own research agendas.

Ken Snowdon

Core provincial operating grants are not keeping pace with inflation and enrolment change. This reality, significant pressure on *core operations funding*, is the most worrying aspect of higher education funding. Since 1997/98 there have been major increases in enrolment — almost 80,000 FTE in the period 1997/98 to 2001/02, an increase of about 12% (AUCC estimates).

The federal investment is carefully considered by provincial governments as they craft their own budgets and the steering effects of the federal investments have not gone unnoticed by the provinces nor the universities. Moreover, the impact on campuses in terms of priority-setting and increasing concerns about "the haves" and "the have-nots" contributes to the unease associated with constraints on institutional autonomy.

Finally, it is important to note that the allocation mechanisms for the federal monies are considerably different than for provincial grants and fees. In the case of provincial grants and fees there is a direct link to students — and the institutions receive those monies based, largely, on enrolment levels. In the case of the federal monies the allocation mechanisms are largely driven by past research performance. The result is that the significant infusion of federal monies, while welcome, are having differential impacts across the country, an area that deserves further research to fully understand the implications for higher education in Canada.

Would universities be just as well off if the major increases in federal funding for CFI and CRCs had been added as an earmarked transfer payment to the provinces and allocated through a provincial grants mechanism? Would there be a demonstrable difference in research performance? Would the university community be in a better position to increase capacity and accommodate the significant increase in projected student demand? If the goal is to secure appropriate levels of funding for *both* teaching *and* research, should we be considering major changes in the way the teaching and research are funded — the United Kingdom model? Is it time for the provinces and the federal government to strike a post-secondary education accord, simplify the funding flow, and introduce an accountability framework that satisfies the needs of both levels of government and the universities? Perhaps it is naïve, as some have suggested, to think the federal government would even consider allocating the funds (or some portion thereof) through the provinces in light of the federal/provincial squabbles that seem to be the characteristic of Canadian federalism. Nevertheless, the questions should be asked; the answers and further considerations are better left to the informed opinion of individuals such as David Cameron (2001) who have studied the federal/provincial dynamic in higher education for many years.

Concluding Comments

Dealing with "muddy data" is a major problem for Canadian universities. The "muddiness" contributes to misinterpretation at all levels — institutional, provincial, federal, and international — and may, in fact, leave policymakers with the mistaken perception that university financing is actually in pretty good shape. The university community would be well-served to devote some time, attention, and resources to ensuring that financial information (and other information such as student enrolments and numbers of faculty) provides an accurate, comparable, and consistent picture of higher education in the country. The university community has a great story to tell, but it needs to be based on good data.

The federal/provincial funding relationship has changed dramatically in the past several years, in particular as the federal government — having cut the transfers to the provinces in the mid-1990s — has "reinvested" through a series of funding vehicles focused on research. Whether that is ultimately in the best interests of Canadian higher education is a matter of debate. What is clear, however, is that investment in research, while very welcome, has highlighted the funding shortcomings in core operations. Surely the time has come to begin considering the efficacy of the federal initiatives and workable options that may strengthen the federation and prepare Canada's universities to meet the many challenges associated with increased enrolment pressures, faculty recruitment in a global market, the provision of a learning environment — at both the undergraduate and graduate levels — that ranks with the best in the world, and the building of institutional capacity to translate the goals of the federal government Innovation Strategy (Industry Canada, 2002) into reality.

The last several years have witnessed a significant increase in investment from the major funders of Canadian universities — governments (taxpayers), students, and the private sector. Nevertheless, in light of the actual enrolment increases of the past few years, and projected enrolment increases well into the future, and, in light of the federal government's desire to improve the relative international position of Canadian research, additional resources will be required. With continuing concern about affordability (and accessibility), greater levels of public investment will be required to meet the resource challenge. How both levels of government respond — in terms of the level of funding and the mechanisms used to allocate the funds — will have a long-standing impact on higher education in Canada. One development is clear, however. Governments will demand greater accountability for that investment and the university community would be well served to take a proactive stance on financial reporting and telling the higher education story in ways that emphasize both transparency and outcomes.

References

Association of Universities and Colleges of Canada (AUCC). 2002. *Trends in Higher Education*. Ottawa: AUCC.

Cameron, D.M. 2001. "Postsecondary Education and Canadian Federalism: Or How to Predict the Future", *Canadian Journal of Higher Education* 31(3).

Canadian Association of University Business Officers (CAUBO). Various Years. *Financial Information of Universities and Colleges*. Ottawa: Statistics Canada.
_____. 2004. "Canadian University Investment Survey for Endowment and Pension Funds", *University Manager* 12(4), 19-38.

Industry Canada. 2002. *Achieving Excellence: Investing in People, Knowledge and Opportunities*. Ottawa: Industry Canada.

Junor, S. and A. Usher. 2002. *The Price of Knowledge, Access and Student Finance in Canada*. Millennium Research Series. Montreal: Canada Millennium Scholarship Foundation.

Leslie, P. 1980. *Canadian Universities and Beyond, Enrolment, Structural Change and Finance*. AUCC Policy Studies Study No. 3. Ottawa: AUCC.

Organisation for Economic Co-operation and Development (OECD). 2003. *Education at a Glance OECD Indicators*. Paris: OECD.

Statistics Canada. 2003. "Changing Patterns of University Finance", *Education Quarterly Review* 9(2).

Financing Higher Education: Commentary on the 2004 UK Higher Education Act

Nicholas Barr

Introduction

A White Paper on higher education in England and Wales (UK. Department for Education and Skills, 2003), published in January 2003, was the basis of the United Kingdom Higher Education Act, which received Royal Assent in July 2004. The act brings in major changes to the financing of higher education in England and Wales, to address very similar problems of underfunding of universities and problems of student access to post-secondary education faced also in Canada and elsewhere. This paper argues that the act gets things very largely right for the United Kingdom, and provides helpful lessons for other countries, including Canada. The act helps universities, which get more resources to improve quality, and helps families and students because of its emphasis on improving access. The present discussion reviews lessons from the UK debate.

This paper is updated from the author's presentation "Financing Higher Education in the UK: The 2003 White Paper" before the UK House of Commons' Education and Skills Committee, Session 2002–03, appearing in *The Future of Higher Education, Fifth Report of Session 2002–03,* Volume II, *Oral and Written Evidence*, HC 425–II, (TSO, 2003), pp. Ev 292–309.

This introduction establishes the background and sets out three central lessons from economic theory. The next section assesses the system prior to the act and puts forward a strategy for addressing the problems of that system. The third section assesses the act's core strategy, arguing that it redistributes from better- to worse-off and to some extent moves away from the central direction of higher education. Section four discusses what needs to be done to ensure that the strategy is translated successfully into action. The fifth section addresses a series of worries about the changes, arguing that they are understandable but misplaced. The final section summarizes the key elements of the act.

This paper focuses on recent experience in the United Kingdom. The studies by Peter George (2005) and by Ross Finnie, Alex Usher and Hans Vossensteyn (2005) in this volume provide useful background to the Canadian context.

Higher education in England and Wales (and to a lesser extent in Scotland) faces three fundamental and widely agreed problems: universities are underfunded, students are poor, and the proportion of students from the lowest two socio-economic backgrounds has not changed significantly in 40 years. In 2002, 81% of children from professional backgrounds went on to higher education; the comparable figure for children from unskilled backgrounds was 15% (Education and Skills Select Committee, 2002, p. 19). There is also agreement about two core objectives: strengthening quality and diversity, both for their own sake and for reasons of national economic performance; and improving access, again for both efficiency and equity reasons.

Economic theory offers three strong sets of messages for the finance of higher education: the days of central direction have gone; students should contribute to the cost of their degrees; and well-designed student loans have core characteristics.[1]

The days of central direction of higher education have gone. The argument against central direction, rooted in the economics of information, is fundamental to the strategy in the act and to the debate about the nature of higher education. To illustrate the essence of the argument, consider the following stylized facts about health care: consumers are imperfectly

---

[1]On the theoretical underpinnings, see Barr (2001, chs. 10–13; 2004c) or, more briefly, Barr (1998).

Nicholas Barr

informed since health care is a highly technical subject;[2] the need for treatment is usually a result not of choice but caused by an external event, for example, breaking a leg; and where someone needs treatment, there is only limited choice about what type of treatment. Much of the efficiency case for the national health service is based on these facts. With food, the story is very different. We are generally well informed about what we like and its costs, hence we can do our own shopping. And though food is a biological necessity, there is enormous choice over how we meet those needs. These *technical* differences explain why we ensure access to health care by giving it to people (largely) free through the national health service; with food, in contrast, we ensure that a person (e.g., granny) has access to nutrition by paying her a pension and allowing her to buy her own food at market prices. This respects her freedom of choice. In contrast, food subsidies would be highly regressive.

Within this stylized context, the question is whether education is more like food or more like health care. My view is that school education is more like health care. Small children are not well informed. The need for education is externally imposed by legal compulsion. And, especially for younger children, the range of choice over curriculum is constrained. Hence, there is a compelling case for publicly funded school education. Higher education, in contrast, is more like food. Students are generally well informed and can (and should) be made better informed. There is genuine choice about whether or not to go to university — it is precisely that fact that has made taxpayer funding of higher education so regressive. Finally, the choice of which subject to study and at which university is large and growing.

On the demand side, therefore, it can be argued that students are well informed, or potentially well informed, consumers, and hence better able than planners to make choices that conform with their personal interests and those of the economy. Though that proposition is robust for the generality of students, there is an important exception: students from poorer backgrounds might not be fully informed, with important implications, discussed below, for access in general and debt aversion in particular. On

---

[2]There is an important distinction between an information problem, soluble by giving more information, and an information-processing problem, where the problem is technically too complex for a layperson to solve even if given the necessary information. Health care faces significant information-processing problems.

the supply side, central direction, whether or not it was ever desirable, is no longer feasible. In response to technological change, advanced countries increasingly have mass higher education, meaning more universities, more students, and greater diversity of subject matter. Thus the myth of parity of esteem and relative parity of funding is no longer sustainable. In principle, differential funding allocations could be made by an omniscient central authority, but the problem is too complex for that to be the sole mechanism: mass higher education requires a funding regime in which institutions can charge differential prices to reflect their different costs and missions.

The second lesson from economic theory is that students should contribute to the cost of their degree. There are strong arguments that higher education creates benefits to society above those to the individual — benefits in terms of growth, social cohesion, the transmission of values, and the development of knowledge for its own sake. These arguments suggest that taxpayer subsidies to higher education should be a permanent part of the landscape. I support those arguments. Equally, however, there is overwhelming evidence that students receive a significant private benefit from their degrees. Thus it is efficient and equitable that they should bear some of the costs.

This leads to the third set of lessons — the design of student loans. Well designed student loans have three core characteristics.

- *Income-contingent repayments*, repayments calculated as $x\%$ of the borrower's subsequent earnings, collected alongside income tax, are essential. In efficiency terms, they protect the student from excessive risk; and because repayments are collected alongside income tax, they also protect the borrower from the risk of making an unsecured loan. In equity terms, the loan protects access because it has built-in insurance against inability to repay. Income-contingent repayments have a profound effect on higher education finance, one that is insufficiently understood by politicians and the public, and a topic discussed in detail in the fourth section.
- *Large enough to cover all fees and all living costs*, solving student poverty and promoting access by making higher education free at the point of use. Nobody has to make any upfront payments; nor are students forced to rely on their parents.
- *An interest rate broadly equal to the government's cost of borrowing.*

Where Things Stood Before the Act: A Wedding and Four Funerals

Before the Act

The UK government has done one thing triumphantly right: since 1998 student loans have had income-contingent repayments collected by the tax authorities. The bad news is that the current system has at least four strategic flaws: central direction continues; the system is very complex; loans are too small; and loans attract an interest subsidy.

Central direction continues in several guises. First, there is price control in the form of a centrally-determined tuition fee (£1,200 in 2005/06) for UK and European Union (EU) students. There is also quantity control, that is, control of student numbers, albeit recently slightly relaxed. Not the least of the resulting anomalies is that successful universities can be penalized by exceeding their recruitment targets. The central authority is heavily bureaucratic. For example, the process for assuring teaching quality during the latter part of the 1990s involved vast amounts of paper-work; it also bore another hallmark of central direction — a counter-productive one-size-fits-all set of procedures.[3]

The system of student support is so complicated that few understand it.[4] The problem was exacerbated by the government's failure to explain the system and, in particular, to explain the nature of income-contingent loans. Complexity has major ill-effects: few can understand the system; it is a nightmare to administer; and complexity, per se, impedes access.

The full loan to students is too small to cover living costs; in addition, not all students get the full loan; and there is no loan to cover fees, so that there are upfront charges. As a result, students are poor, forcing them to rely on their parents, to use expensive credit card debt, and/or to spend long hours earning money. These factors all impede access.

The interest rate on student loans in the United Kingdom is equal to the inflation rate, that is, a zero real rate, and thus provides an interest subsidy

---

[3]The objection is not to teaching quality assurance, an important activity, but to the nature of the inspection process.

[4]As an example of complexity, see the notes about the operation of the income test by which a student's loan entitlement and tuition fees are assessed (UK. Department for Education and Skills, 2001).

to loan recipients. This is a policy design that achieves not a single desirable objective.[5]

- The subsidy is enormously expensive, currently around at £800 million per year.
- It impedes quality. Student support, being politically salient, crowds out the funding of universities.
- It impedes access. Loans are expensive, therefore rationed and therefore too small.
- It is highly regressive.

The Barr-Crawford Proposals

Iain Crawford and I have long advocated a financing strategy with three elements.[6]

Deferred variable fees. Universities should be free to vary their tuition fees, subject to a cap. This brings in additional resources to improve quality, benefiting students and restoring the sector's considerable export potential. Students should be helped to pay the charges as described below. Of central importance, charges should be deferred: thus graduates make repayments, not students. Thinking on fees can be muddled. Many people agree that higher education is a right, but it does not follow that it must always be free (food, equally, is a right, yet nobody demonstrates outside shops or restaurants). Another confusion is between social elitism, which is abhorrent, and intellectual elitism, which is both necessary and desirable. There is nothing inequitable about intellectually elite institutions. The access imperative is a system in which the brightest students are able to study at the most intellectually demanding institutions irrespective of their socio-economic background.

Adequate and universal income-contingent loans. The loan should be large enough to cover fees and realistic living costs in full and should be

---

[5]In contrast, the interest rate charged on Ontario Student Assistant Program (OSAP) loans in Ontario is the prime rate plus 2%.

[6]This section draws on Barr (2002, p. 21).

available to all students. This package eliminates upfront fees (the Student Loans Company would send the fee payment directly to the university), so that higher education is free at the point of use, as in Scotland. It ends student poverty. It does away with parental contributions. It is simple for students and their parents to understand. And it is vastly simpler to administer than current arrangements. Even more fundamentally, as discussed below, the package is equivalent to restoring grants.

Active measures to promote access. A strategy for access has two elements: getting people into university, and helping low earners after university. On the first, there are two causes of exclusion: financial poverty and information poverty. The latter is important and inadequately understood: as discussed earlier, students from poorer backgrounds may systematically be less well informed, not the least of the resulting problems being debt aversion. Any strategy to encourage people to enter university, therefore, needs both to provide financial support and to increase information and raise aspirations. Scholarships (e.g., higher education maintenance allowances) are vital; so are financial incentives to universities to widen participation; and so are extra resources to provide intellectual support at university for access students to make sure that, once they arrive, they get the support necessary to make the transition.

The Government's Strategy

Key Elements of the Higher Education Act

This section summarizes the key funding elements in the 2004 act. Seen through the eyes of lurid press coverage, the proposals look horrible: high fees, large debts. That view is thoroughly misleading. The strategy has two elements, each enormously important.

First, it redistributes from better-off to worse-off. Those who can afford to pay more do so, releasing resources to improve quality and promote access, where "can afford" refers to their income as a graduate, not to their family circumstances as a student. This approach is entirely consistent with the first and third legs of the Barr-Crawford strategy.

Economic theory is particularly useful at this stage to explain what is going on. The act brings in two sets of actions (see Figure 1):

- A price increase, raising the average tuition fee from p_0 to p_1. This leads to a movement *along* the demand curve from a to b. Taken alone, this action obviously reduces demand and harms access. However, the fees are deferred for everyone, and there are also:
- Targeted transfers to groups for whom access is fragile. This moves their demand curve *outward*, increasing their demand to c.

Thus, the strategy is deeply progressive. It shifts resources from today's best-off (who lose some of their fee subsidies) to today's worst-off (who receive a grant) and tomorrow's worst-off (who, with income-contingent repayments, do not repay their loan in full). The argument is explored in more detail below.

Second, the strategy ends central direction, replacing it with a mixed economy. Earlier discussion outlined the extent to which UK higher education is centrally directed. Variable fees reduce the power of the central authority by (i) giving universities an independent source of income, and (ii) strengthening incentives to competition. The act shifts the balance from the central authority and the producers to the consumers — the students and employers. Both elements of the strategy depend fundamentally on the prior existence of income-contingent loans.

Figure 1: The Twofold Strategy to Promote Access

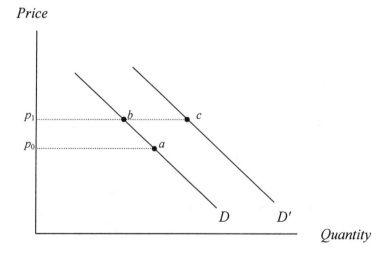

Summary of the Act

The act and surrounding policy is wide-ranging. Discussion here is limited to the funding proposals.

1. *Fees.* The term "top-up fees" conflates three separate questions: Should fees be the same at all universities or different? Should students pay fees upfront or deferred? and Should universities receive fees upfront or deferred? The act answers all three questions correctly: from 2006 on:
    *   fees will no longer be fixed at £1,200 per year, but variable between 0 and £3,000, with institutions able to set their own fee levels within those limits.
    *   However, there will no longer be an upfront charge, since fees will be fully covered by a loan. Thus the proposal is for deferred variable fees.
    *   Universities, however, will receive the fee income upfront.

2. *Access.*
    *   The act restores a grant of up to £2,700 per year where family income is low.
    *   Universities charging the maximum fee of £3,000 will be expected to offer bursaries of at least £300 to students who are eligible for a full grant, and *pro rata* for students eligible for a partial grant.
    *   An access regulator will check that universities planning to charge fees above £1,200 have well-designed plans to widen access and carry those plans out.

3. *Student Support.*
    *   The existing arrangements for maintenance loans (i.e., loans to cover living costs) continue. The maximum loan remains unchanged, and entitlement continues to be income tested, that is, parental contributions continue.
    *   Loans attract a zero real rate of interest, that is, interest subsidies continue.
    *   The threshold at which loan repayments start will be raised (in 2005) to £15,000.

4. *Public spending* on universities is set to increase significantly in the years to 2008.

The Strategy 1: Promoting Access

This section argues that deferred variable fees are a fundamental element in a strategy to promote access. To clear the ground, it is helpful first to develop three sets of arguments: the real barriers to access arise earlier in the system; other ways of paying for higher education are unfair; and there are other ways of thinking about the contents of the act.

The first point concerns the real barrier to university access. Of those with A levels good enough to go to university, 90% do so, with no socio-economic gradient — about 90% of middle-class people go on to university and about 90% of working class people. Thus, the great disparity in participation occurs when people leave school at age 16. A strategy for access therefore needs a range of interventions, including outreach to schools to raise the information available to and the aspirations of schoolchildren, additional resources to improve school education, and additional resources much earlier, for example, at nursery education. In short, £1 million spent raising GCSE scores does more for access than subsidizing fees for people who would have gone to university anyway.

The second point is that other ways of paying for higher education are unfair. A graduate tax, that is, an additional x pence tax on income tax until retirement (or for a fixed period, such as 25 years), is unfair, and hence politically difficult, since repayments are unrelated to the cost of a person's degree. Also flat fees — charging the same fee at all universities — are unfair for two reasons. First, it is unfair if a student at Bash Street College pays the same fee as one at Oxford. Second, a flat fee will continue the erosion of quality at the best universities, which face the biggest shortfalls. If this policy continues, the result will be to deprive British students of the chance of an internationally cutting-edge undergraduate degree in one of two ways. The quality of the best institutions might fall; British students could still get places, but the quality of the degree would be less. Alternatively, the best institutions will largely stop teaching British under-graduates (for whom they receive on average £5,000 per year) and will use the fees from foreign undergraduates (around £10,000 per year) to preserve their excellence.

Tax funding has at least four problems.
- It does not work. As discussed earlier, access remains woeful.
- It will not happen. Higher education will always lose out to the national health service, nursery education, and school education.
- It should not happen. Higher education confers a benefit on society as a whole and to that extent has received, and should continue to receive,

tax funding. Beyond that, however, tax funding is deeply regressive. If the money comes from general taxation, the taxes of the hospital porter pay for the degree of the old Etonian. A counter-argument from some quarters is to make direct tax more progressive. Suppose government raised an extra £2.5 billion that way. The question that proponents of tax funding must then answer is: Why should that money be spent on the best and the brightest who will disproportionately go on to become the richest, rather than on nursery education, vocational education, action to improve the staying-on rate post-16, and more generous grants?

- It is not regressive by accident. Some people argue that higher education should be treated as a tax-funded social good which a civilized country should offer. This is a beguiling vision, which was possible when higher education was a consumption good for a small number of people. But those times have gone. There are three steps in the argument: technological advance means that mass higher education is essential for national economic performance. We live in a free society, so that people can choose how hard to work and can emigrate. Both facts impose limits on taxation, and those limits are reinforced by international capital mobility. Finally, mass higher education, which is expensive, plus limited taxation lead to rationing of places and of funding. The sharp elbows of the middle class come into play, leading to disproportionate middle-class use. Thus, systematically and predictably, excessive reliance on tax funding is regressive.

It is possible to approach the reforms from a number of very different perspectives than their high-fees, high-debt portrayal in the press. One way is to view them as restoring universal grants. This perspective starts from the fact that higher education is largely free to students. The Student Loans Company squirts money into the student's bank account to cover living costs, and into the university's bank account to cover tuition fees. Thus, no one is forced to pay any fees at the time he or she goes to university. The taxpayer continues, quite rightly, to pay part of the cost. But some of the costs, again rightly, are met by the income-contingent repayments of graduates. These repayments differ from a tax in only two ways: they do not go on forever, and they are paid only by people who have been to university and benefited financially from their degree. This is not a cheap intellectual stunt — income-contingent loans are logically equivalent to a grant financed by an income-related graduate contribution.

A second way of viewing the new regime is in terms of a capped graduate tax. A graduate tax and income-contingent loan repayments are both payments levied on top of income tax. From the viewpoint of the individual graduate, the only difference is that with a graduate tax the duration of payment is fixed, and with an income-contingent loan they are variable. Thus, loan repayments can be thought of as a capped graduate tax: a tax that is switched off once the graduate has paid a set contribution towards the cost of the degree (see Smith, 2002). Colloquially, graduates pay extra tax until each has paid his or her "fair share".

Yet another perspective is to think of student loans as a modern example of the Beveridge principle of social insurance. With pensions, we pay national insurance contributions now in order to get our pension later. Pensions are an example of consumption smoothing — a device that allows people to redistribute to themselves over their life cycle. Student loans are exactly that, students receive a "pension" now to pay for their university education, repaid by their own contributions later in life.

Several arguments establish a strong case for the equity of the strategy. First, consider what is not happening. Nobody is talking about making students pay the entire cost of their degree. Currently the maximum student contribution is 25% of average teaching costs in the United Kingdom. Public spending on higher education in 2002–03 (UK. Department for Education and Skills, 2002, Table 4.1) was £6.6 billion; fee income was of the order of £400 million. All the act does is to change that balance somewhat. Nor is anyone proposing up-front fees. The act introduces *deferred* fees — a deliberate and fundamental part of the pro-access strategy. The equity case itself rests on several points:

- Variable fees resolve the serious inequities of tax funding, a graduate tax or charging flat fees.
- Those who can afford to pay a larger contribution to the cost of the higher education do so (where "can afford" refers to their income after graduation, i.e., to outcomes).
- The system protects access in two ways: students face no up-front charges, and graduates repay only if their earnings warrant.
- The system actively promotes access because it frees resources to increase the staying-on rate post age 16 and to restore grants, thus focusing resources on those who need help most, rather than spending wastefully on blanket subsidies.
- The core of the proposals in short is two sets of actions — a price increase and targeted income transfers — as illustrated in Figure 1, not

just a move along the demand curve, but a deliberate outward shift of the demand curve of poorer people.

The Strategy 2: The End of Central Direction

As well as being fair, variable fees have other major implications. If fees are set by government and are the same at all institutions, rising fee income can be offset by falling taxpayer contributions. Thus, government controls the total volume of resources going into higher education — funding is closed-ended. Australia is a graphic example: government introduced centrally-set fees in 1989 to address a funding crisis; the system is now back in crisis. Equally, the introduction of fixed fees in the United Kingdom in 1998 has not netted any extra money. Funding is closed-ended also with a graduate tax; government controls the volume of resources going into higher education, and universities compete in a zero-sum game. With variable fees, in contrast, if tax-funding falls, each university has a policy response under its own control. Universities have an independent income source. The central authority no longer controls the funding envelope of the state-owned enterprise.

Variable fees also introduce competition and enhance diversity and choice. They expose universities to more competition, empowering the choices of students, and indirectly of employers. The change in the balance of power is fundamental to creating a diversified system of higher education fit for purpose in a technological age. This is not an argument for law-of-the-jungle competition. Government has an important continuing role, but as regulator and setter of incentives, not as central planner.

The resulting changes will be significant. The days are gone when higher education consisted almost exclusively of three or four years of full-time academic study in institutions devoted to teaching and fundamental research. Diversity today has many dimensions:

- *Period of study.* It should be possible to study part-time (e.g., evenings), while staying in one's current job. Equally, accelerated study should be possible — studying over the summer to complete a degree in two or three years, reducing living costs during the degree and facilitating earlier return to the labour market.
- *Level of degree.* There should be a seamless line of progression from sub-degree work to undergraduate and postgraduate degrees. Work to strengthen the integration of further and higher education should continue.

- *Coverage of subject area.* Degrees can and should cover increasingly diverse areas.
- *Type of training.* Degrees can offer academic training, vocational training, or both. This is nothing new: medical degrees are high-quality vocational training.
- *Type of research.* Research can be fundamental, or applied, or to assist local economic development. All are important; all are properly part of higher education.

Students, like Poles in 1990 right after the collapse of communism, see prices rising, but not yet any of the resulting benefits in terms of quality and range of products. Once the changes are in place, students should enormously prefer the new system, which transforms their power. The preferences of the consumer (students and employers) will have more weight than under central direction. Universities will face strong incentives to give them such things as accelerated courses, part-time courses, and evening teaching.

A further welcome element in the strategy is the use of targeted loan write-offs, an excellent social policy tool. When applied to nurses and teachers, loan write-offs respond to low pay. If applied to doctors working in the national health service, write-offs could be used to address the issue of large loans resulting from long courses. Interestingly, the resulting incentives are strongest for people with larger debts. Therefore, graduates of the best universities will have stronger incentives than currently to go into teaching.

Making the Strategy Work

The previous section argued that the strategy in the Higher Education Act is simultaneously equitable, promoting access by transferring resources from better-off to worse-off people, and efficient, promoting competition and hence diversity. This section discusses what needs to be done to make sure that the strategy is translated into action.

Actions to Promote Student Access

Action is needed in at least three areas if the reforms are to succeed in widening access: (i) publicizing *much* more effectively what income-contingent loans mean for individual students, (ii) improving further the student support package, and (iii) ensuring proper powers and terms of reference for the access regulator.

First, what is needed is a major public education campaign. It should include the following points.

• Most of the cost of teaching is still paid by the taxpayer. This needs to be stated firmly and repeatedly. Reducing the fee subsidy frees resources for use in better targeted ways to promote access.

• Income contingency changes everything. The government has been woeful in explaining this fact; and the absence of such explanation has created a vacuum filled by a misplaced obsession with headline debt figures, fanned by lurid newspaper articles and at times, it has to be said, by scaremongering. The result is what health economists call the "worried well" — people who are worried that they are ill, though in reality they are not, but whose worries lower their quality of life. At least some debt aversion is of this sort. At a minimum, many parents worry about their child's debt in a way that they would not worry about their child's future tax liability.

The point about income contingency is fundamental to the politics of reform, and bears amplification. Any campaign should explain the following facts about income-contingent loans: repayments are like income tax in that people with low earnings make low repayments or no repayments, and repayments instantly and automatically track changes in a person's pay packet. A larger loan has no effect on monthly repayments, only on duration; thus higher fees do not affect monthly repayments, and larger maintenance loans do not affect monthly repayments; equally a higher interest rate does not affect monthly repayments.

Ministers should stop talking about debt. Instead they should firmly establish the resulting key messages: it is a payroll deduction, not debt. Students get their higher education free — it is graduates who make repayments, and then only to meet part of the costs, and only if their earnings warrant. If it is unfair to ask graduates to pay more of the cost (as the proponents of tax funding argue), it is even more unfair to ask non-graduate taxpayers to do so. Do not exaggerate the size of the debt. Repaying a £20,000 loan is not that large when compared with other expenditures. It only seems large because people (and newspapers) focus on the *stock* of debt, rather than the *flow* of repayments. Yet we mostly think about expenditure in flow terms, so that cumulative totals seem shocking. On plausible assumptions over a 40-year career a current graduate will pay (in cash terms) about £850,000 in income tax and national insurance contributions, £0.5 million on food, and £25,000 if the basic rate of income tax rises by a penny in the pound.

Quite rightly, no student loses sleep over a career tax debt of approaching £1 million, because he or she looks at such figures through the other end of the telescope — that is, in terms of monthly, income-related repayments rather than cumulative totals. Student debt, given income-contingent repayments, should not be regarded as any different. Repayments should be thought of as a payroll deduction, not a final demand notice.

A second action to promote access involves improving student support. This task has several elements.

Improve the system of grants. Since students from poor backgrounds may be less well informed and hence debt averse, grants are an essential element in a strategy to promote access. Though the political dialogue between publication of the White Paper and the passage of the act produced a welcome increase in the size of the grant, the threshold for eligibility could properly be increased. In addition, anyone receiving an Educational Maintenance Allowance[7] should automatically receive a grant. This policy promotes access by giving young people certainty at age 16 that they will receive financial support once they get to university; it is also administratively cheaper, reducing the need for a separate income test when a person starts university. Thought should be given to some "super grants" which pay the *entire* costs (tuition fees and all living costs) for the first year of a degree. Students from poor backgrounds may be unsure about whether university is right for them or about whether they are bright enough to cope. Super grants would give them a free first year, giving them the chance to become well informed about their aptitudes and prospects. At that stage, students would have more confidence in taking out a loan to cover the rest of their degree.

Increase the maintenance loan. Again, negotiations leading to final passage of the act resulted in a welcome increase in the loan to cover living

---

[7]An income-tested benefit to encourage people past minimum school leaving age to stay on till A level.

costs. Even so, the full loan is probably still somewhat too small and, separately, the loan continues to be income tested, so that parental contributions remain. Both features are regrettable. Where loans are not enough to pay realistic living costs, students face a combination of poverty, heavy and expensive indebtedness via credit cards/overdrafts, and excessive hours in part-time work. Debt aversion arises in part because student loans and credit-card debt become conflated in people's minds. The maintenance loan should be increased. However, as discussed above, the continuing interest subsidy makes any such move costly. One way out is as follows:

- Suppose realistic living costs outside London are £7,000.
- The government should offer *all* students a second maintenance loan of £x, where £x is the amount that brings a student's total maintenance package to (say) £7,000, eliminating student poverty and getting rid of compulsory parental contributions.[8]
- The interest rate on the second loan should equal the government's cost of borrowing.

A final element — restoring debt forgiveness after 25 years, thus giving well-targeted protection to people with low lifetime earnings — was introduced in the act, though missing in the White Paper.

A third action to promote student access involves ensuring proper powers and terms of reference for the access regulator. Improving access has various dimensions, including (i) increasing the aggregate number of people from poor backgrounds at university and (ii) improving their distribution across universities. Different mechanisms are needed for each of these tasks: incentives are much more likely to deliver the policy objectives than excessive use of regulation and bureaucratic forms of control.

Defining the access regulator's powers and terms of reference is therefore complex, and should take cognizance of points like the following:

- Universities can decide to whom to make an offer but cannot control who actually turns up (many applicants do not meet the conditions). The access regulator might therefore want to focus on offers as well as registrations.

---

[8]Though beyond the scope of this paper, similar loans should be offered to postgraduate students.

- Universities have little information about applicants' backgrounds. Perhaps the regulator should ensure that the university admissions service collects the necessary data and, subject to safeguards, that universities have access to it.
- What variables should the regulator use to define targets: social class, type of school, race? If all are relevant, what are the relative weights for each?

Some of the regulator's tasks are clearer. One is to ensure that a system of credit transfer is in place. Second, the regulator should mandate universities to publish on their Web site timely and accurate data allowing prospective students to make informed choices. This data should include dropout rates and the fraction of graduates who find relevant employment within a given period after graduation. Such transparency has two sets of benefits: information enables students to make better choices, and information is generally a more powerful and cost-effective form of quality assurance than bureaucratic procedures.

Actions to Promote Other Objectives

The second leg of the reform strategy is a more competitive environment for higher education. Ensuring that the policy intent takes place requires: consideration of the fees cap and a sustained real funding increase over the medium term.

The fees cap "will apply throughout the life of the next Parliament, and it will rise annually in line with inflation so that it keeps its real value" (White Paper, para. 7.31). The fees cap needs to be:
- High enough (i) to pay the best universities the rate for the job, and (ii) to bring in competition.
- Low enough (iii) to ensure that the act is politically sustainable: the issue here is to give students and their parents time to adjust, and (iv) to give universities time to put in place management suitable for a competitive environment.

Given these criteria, the initial cap of £3,000 is probably right. However, its duration — the life of the next Parliament — is too long. If the cap is too low for too long, a critical bulk of universities will charge the maximum, approximating a system of flat fees. The result will be both to reintroduce closed-ended funding and to restore central administration by the back door. Change must be irreversible.

Second, government should ensure a sustained increase in university income. In the medium term, the mechanism for achieving more resources to universities is through variable fees. However, taxpayer clawback over the next ten years (as in Australia) puts quality at risk. From 2006, students will face higher fees than their predecessors. If the quality of their student experience fails to match those higher fees, the new arrangements could come under political threat. Generous tax funding during the initial phase is therefore essential.

A further element in the way forward is to reduce the interest subsidy in student loans, whose costs considerably dilute the redistributive power of the proposals. What is wrong with the interest subsidy? As discussed earlier, the blanket subsidy achieves not a single desirable objective: it is enormously expensive; it impedes quality, since expensive student support tends to crowd out the funding of institutions; it impedes access, since it is the cost of the interest subsidy which is the direct cause of loans being too small; and it is deeply regressive, the main beneficiaries being successful professionals in mid-career.

Addressing Public Concerns

Students, their parents and politicians have a series of understandable and legitimate worries, which is precisely why the public information campaign advocated in the previous section is so vital. This section outlines those worries and tries to show that, for the most part, they should not be exaggerated.

- The new system will leave students with large debts.
- Higher participation lowers the return to getting a degree.
- Student debt will make it harder to get a mortgage.
- Variable fees are inequitable.
- Variable fees will harm access.
- Variable fees will create a two-tier system.
- It is morally wrong to charge for higher education.

Worries about Debt

The new system will leave students with large debts. As discussed above:

- Income-contingent loans change everything because monthly repayments are exactly matched to the graduate's income. Thus, student debt should be regarded as a payroll deduction, not a final demand notice.
- The debt is not large — it only seems large because of the misplaced emphasis on the headline debt figure. Under plausible assumptions a graduate will pay £850,000 in cash terms in income tax and national insurance contributions over a 40-year career. People do not lose sleep over that. Nor do they lose sleep over an increase in the basic rate of tax by a penny in the pound, though in cash terms it adds £25,000 to a person's tax bill over 40 years.
- Student loans are not like a bank overdraft, since repayments are added to income tax. Therefore, it is just as plausible to regard the new arrangements as a universal grant, repaid out of subsequent taxation if the graduate's earnings are high enough; or as a graduate tax that is eventually switched off; or as a form of national insurance contribution.

Higher participation lowers the return to getting a degree, leaving people with unsustainable debt. It is true that rising supply generally leads to a fall in price. But that is not true if demand rises as well. There are strong grounds for arguing that in an information age the demand for skills is higher than ever and rising, which is why the graduate earnings premium has thus far shown no signs of falling. However, since repayments are income-contingent, if earnings are lower than expected, loan repayments will also be lower. In addition, it is worth noting that the graduate earnings premium leaves out non-monetary returns like job satisfaction, a particular feature of graduate employment.

Student debt will make it harder to get a mortgage. Lenders are normally interested in a person's income net of deductions like income tax, national insurance contributions, and similar outgoings such as loan repayments. Thus, on the face of it (i) loan repayments would reduce borrowing capacity, but (ii) not by much since a graduate's monthly repayments, by definition, are a relatively small fraction of his/her earnings. On the other hand, (iii) a graduate's income will generally be higher because he/she has a degree and (iv) lenders regard graduates as good risks; for both reasons, even allowing for loan repayments, a person's borrowing capacity will generally be higher with a degree than without. Finally, it should be remembered that non-graduates also have debt, for example, for cars.

Worries about Variable Fees

Variable fees are inequitable. There are weighty counter-arguments.
- The core reason why variable fees are fair is that, by levying a larger contribution from people who can afford to pay, they make it possible to target transfers on people for whom access is most fragile.
- Variable fees also contribute to diversity and choice. This is efficient. And it also contributes to access: for example, universities will respond to demand by putting on part-time and evening courses, making it easier and cheaper to get a degree.
- It is efficient and equitable for the taxpayer to finance the social benefits and the beneficiary to finance his private benefits. Since the latter are higher at some universities than others, students at those universities should pay more.
- Excessive reliance on tax funding is unfair. Tax funding has done nothing to improve the social mix in higher education. Beyond a certain point, it is deeply regressive. The revenue from higher taxation promotes access most powerfully if spent on nursery education and action to improve the staying on rate post 16 years.
- Flat fees are unfair. They discriminate against British students getting into the best universities; and it is unfair to charge a student at Bash Street College the same as one at Oxford.
- A graduate tax is unfair — what a person repays bears no relation to the cost of his or her degree.

Variable fees will harm access, particularly to the best universities. Again, the counter-arguments are weighty.
- They are not up-front fees, but deferred fees. Higher education is free to the student. Only graduates makes repayments.
- The reform strategy has two elements: higher fees, which on their own would reduce demand, particularly of people from low-income backgrounds, *plus* grants and fee remission and similar targeted transfers to students from poor backgrounds, shifting their demand curve outwards.
- Subsequent loan repayments are income-contingent; thus going to a better university does not affect the size of monthly repayments (which are determined by postgraduation income), but their duration.

- Universities are interested in bright students, not rich students. It is in their interests to have scholarships. And such activities will be buttressed by the access regulator.
- Ninety percent of people with good enough A levels go on to university; the key factor harming access is leaving school at 16.
- The argument that variable fees will deter students is to some extent patronizing: it implies that middle-class students are bright enough to understand the value of going to one of the best universities, but poorer students are not.

Variable fees will create a two-tier system. This argument is based on a myth: we already have a one hundred-tier system. To pretend that all universities are equally good is a case of the Emperor's new clothes. We know that some universities are better than others, and that some degrees confer greater earning power than others. Not only is it a myth; it is a dangerous myth. If we continue to treat Oxford and Bash Street College as the same, the risk is that they will become the same. This would lead to exactly the result the reform sets out to avert — handing over the UK research base to the United States.

It is morally wrong to charge for a basic right like higher education. I agree with the value judgement that access to higher education is a basic right, but that does not mean that it has to be free. Access to nutrition is a basic right, yet nobody argues that it is wrong to charge for food. The moral imperative is not about *instruments* (e.g., prices) but about *outcomes*, that is, the imperative that a bright person should be able to go to the best university irrespective of his or her current financial circumstances.

More positively, diversity and choice are good things in their own right. Fifty years ago, transatlantic flights were the province of a rich elite, with all seats first class. Today mass aviation has made world travel an everyday reality. It is true that the cheaper seats are less roomy and the food less good, but economy passengers travel in the same plane and arrive at the same time as first class passengers — they do not fly in dangerous "rust buckets" or only on slow planes. The effect has been to widen enormously the opportunities for many more people. The analogy with higher education is apt.

Summary of the Act

The Higher Education Act received Royal Assent in July 2004.[9] It followed the proposals in the White Paper closely and in some provisions went beyond them. The strategy to improve quality in and promote access to universities has three elements. The first is variable tuition fees that are capped at £3,000. The second is loans that cover tuition fees and realistic living costs. The act abolishes the current up-front tuition charge to the student and increases the loan to cover reasonable living costs. Thus, university is largely free for students, it is the graduates who make repayments. The Student Loans Company pays the universities on the student's behalf and pays money into the student's bank account for living costs. Repayment by graduates is through a payroll deduction of 9% of earnings above an earnings level of £15,000 a year, collected alongside income tax. Therefore, someone earning £18,000 will repay £270 per year or £5.19 per week as a deduction on his or her payslip along with income tax deductions. Also, any loan not repaid after 25 years will be forgiven.

Third, the act incorporates an access package that benefits students from poor backgrounds even more than the initial proposals in the White Paper by bringing in grants of £2,700 per year for students from poor backgrounds. Where a university charges the full £3,000 tuition, it is obliged to award poor students a bursary of at least £300, so that the total up-front support package for the worst-off students is £3,000 per year. No student from a poor background is made worse-off by the reforms.

The act is not perfect. More needs to be done on outreach to schools, and the badly targeted blanket interest subsidy on student loans remains and will need eventually to be refined. But the act should be applauded as a coherent, forward-looking package.

References

Barr, N. 1998. "Towards a 'Third Way': Rebalancing the Role of the State", *New Economy* 4(2), 71-76.

_____. 2001. *The Welfare State as Piggy Bank: Information, Risk, Uncertainty and the Role of the State*. Oxford and New York: Oxford University Press.

---

[9]This section follows from Barr (2004a, p. 21 and 2004b, p. 21).

_____. 2002. "Making Universities Universal", *Financial Times*, November 22.

_____. 2004a. "A Good Deal for All the Family", *Times Educational Supplement*, January 23.

_____. 2004b. "Variable Fees are the Fairer Route to Quality", *Financial Times*, March 30.

_____. 2004c. *The Economics of the Welfare State*, 3rd edition. Oxford: Oxford University Press and Stanford, CA: Stanford University Press.

Education and Skills Select Committee. 2002. *Post-16 Student Support*. Sixth Report of Session 2001-2002, HC445. London: TSO.

Finnie, R., A. Usher and H. Vossensteyn. 2005. "Meeting the Need: A New Architecture for Canada's Student Financial Aid System", in this volume.

George, P. 2005. "Financing Quality in Ontario Universities", in this volume.

Smith, A. 2002. "A Fair and Flexible Tax on Graduates", *Financial Times*, December 6.

United Kingdom. Department for Education and Skills. 2001. *Higher Education Student Support in England and Wales 2001/02,* Chapter 6, "Assessing Financial Entitlement". At http://www.dfes.gov.uk/studentsupport/ss_admin/content/dsp_section_29.shtml.

_____. 2002. *Annual Report*. London: TSO. At http://www.dfes.gov.uk/deptreport2002/.

_____. 2003. *The Future of Higher Education*. Cm 5735. London: TSO. At http://www.dfes.gov.uk/highereducation/hestrategy/.

Collaborative Federalism and Postsecondary Education: Be Careful What You Wish For

David M. Cameron

In their 1999 contribution to the third edition of James Bickerton and Alain-G. Gagnon's *Canadian Politics*, Ian Robinson and Richard Simeon (1999) characterize the contemporary phase of Canadian federalism as collaborative. But at the same time they signal their own doubts as to the accuracy of this characterization by adding a question mark to their heading. Collaborative federalism, with a question mark, does seem to capture an important dimension of the current state of play in federalism and federal-provincial relations, especially as they are embodied and reflected in postsecondary education. There are some significant, even dramatic, changes taking place. But at the same time there is cause for concern that many of these changes may turn out to be superficial and short-lived, that the fundamentals of federalism and postsecondary education remain problematic. It is worth taking a closer look at recent developments in this area, in order to shed further light on the emerging pattern of both Canadian federalism and postsecondary education in Canada.

Federal Involvement in Postsecondary Education and Research

The federal government began to take an interest in postsecondary education and research early in the twentieth century (Cameron, 1991). Before that, what public involvement there was had been left to provincial governments. The first federal initiative was addressed to instruction in agriculture, and took the form of a conditional grant to the provinces to encourage programs in this area. Following the 1913 report of the Royal Commission on Industrial Training and Technical Education, but after a delay occasioned by World War I, the federal government expanded its reach with the introduction of the Technical Education Act of 1919. That same year marked the establishment of the National Research Council (NRC) and, with it, the beginning of federal grants to universities for the support of research.

Both of these federal initiatives were unopposed by the provinces even though they might have been seen as encroaching upon provincial constitutional responsibility for education. Technical education, which would later blossom into a full-fledged *cause célèbre* in federal-provincial relations, was initially perceived even by provincial officials as having more to do with economic development than with education. And research, except in very specific and applied fields, did not attract active provincial interest. Federal pre-eminence, which would grow significantly over the years, was largely ceded by default.

It was not until World War II that federal and provincial activities in postsecondary education actually began to overlap. Beginning in 1945, the Veterans Rehabilitation Act, covering the cost of tuition and living allowances for veterans entering or returning to university, as well as a per-student payment to receiving universities, led to such a massive increase in enrolment that existing universities were often hard pressed to accommodate the numbers. And no sooner did the war-induced influx of veterans begin to abate than a new crisis began to take shape for Canada's postsecondary institutions.

The fact was that civilian enrolment had also been increasing, something that had been largely masked by the overwhelming influx of veterans. University officials, seeking to capitalize on the special relationship that had been forged with the federal government during the war and immediate postwar period, hoped to parlay that alliance into continuing federal support. The Massey Commission, which reported in 1951,

David M. Cameron

provided the ideal vehicle, composed as it was of people closely associated with universities. It recommended that the federal government begin making unconditional grants directly to Canada's universities and colleges. The government accepted the recommendation almost immediately and began making payments totalling fifty cents per capita, divided among the provinces in proportion to their populations and then among the institutions in proportion to their shares of enrolment in each province.

The crisis continued unabated, however. It was fuelled by a combination of an increasing participation rate, the result of the growing popularity of postsecondary education as the key to employment and higher earnings, and the bulge in the population of 18 to 21 year-olds associated with the postwar baby boom. When an official with the federal Dominion Bureau of Statistics told university officials in 1955 that they could expect a doubling of university enrolment over the next decade, the universities were galvanized into action. They mounted a major public relations effort designed to secure expanded federal support. And they achieved considerable success. By 1965 the fifty-cent per capita grant had increased to $5.00.

Federal involvement expanded in other areas as well. Research grants, which had reached $1 million annually by 1945, rose to over $40 million by 1965. The Canada Council, established in 1951 at the same time as federal grants to universities and colleges were introduced, received an endowment of $50 million for university capital construction. Another $50 million was made available in 1960 through the Central (now Canada) Mortgage and Housing Corporation (CMHC) for the purpose of loans to universities for student housing. This amount was subsequently doubled to $100 million and then increased again to $150 million. In 1964, the old Dominion-Provincial Student Aid Program was replaced by the much more generous federal Canada Student Loans Program. A year later the Bladen Commission went so far as to recommend the appointment of a federal minister of education.

That was too much for the provinces. They moved quickly to form the Council of Ministers of Education of Canada (CMEC), a wholly provincial body designed explicitly to resist further federal incursions into provincial jurisdiction. Indications of federal-provincial disharmony had been growing incrementally. Not surprisingly, Quebec was the first to take overt action. After allowing its universities and colleges to accept federal per capita grants in 1951, it blocked them a year later. The impasse lasted until 1959 when, after a change of government in both Ottawa and Quebec City, an accommodation was worked out. It represented a significant retreat by the federal government, one in which the grants that elsewhere went directly to postsecondary institutions would, in the case of Quebec, go to the provincial treasury instead. The province would then finance the universities and colleges. It was the first ever instance of a province opting out of a wholly federal program. Other provinces were also chafing under the growing influence of the federal government. Ontario, for example, started advising its universities of their total government grant, a total that included the federal per capita contribution. It was, however, the federal government that pulled the plug on its relationship with universities and colleges. Research grants and student aid would remain, but the rest was swept away in a dramatic policy shift announced at a federal-provincial conference in 1966.

Shaking the Foundations

The new arrangement had two main components. First, existing federal per capita grants to universities and colleges were replaced by unconditional transfers to the provinces, through a combination of cash and tax points. In effect, the rest of Canada now joined Quebec in terms of federal involvement in supporting the operating costs of postsecondary institutions. Universities, at least in English Canada, could hardly believe what had happened. Henceforth, they would have to rely on provincial funding decisions alone for their general operating support (along with tuition revenue), and they would soon discover that provincial funding could fall far short of satisfying their growing appetites. The new federal scheme was entirely unconditional. The provinces could use the transferred resources, half of which were actually taxes they levied themselves (plus equalization for qualifying provinces), any way they chose.

The second federal shoe that fell in 1966 was no less dramatic in its consequences for Canadian federalism and postsecondary education. In this case, the federal government decided to scrap its long-standing provision of financial support for technical and vocational education, or training, through conditional grants to the provinces, and substitute a wholly federal program of occupational training for adults. It was a dramatic initiative, intended to bring under direct federal control all aspects of program design, including the selection, counselling, and training of adults already out of school and in the labour force. It was truly a grand design, but it ran head on into the emerging provincial community college systems, which did most of the actual training. In the event, the federal government was never able to achieve what it set out to accomplish, while some of the provinces managed to exercise considerable control over where the training took place, thus securing continued federal support of provincial colleges. It was not a very happy intergovernmental relationship (Dupré et al., 1973).

Then disaster struck for the provinces. Plagued by chronic deficits and mounting debt, the federal government finally decided to trim its fiscal sails and cut its spending commitments. Part of its plan, announced in its 1995 budget, was to combine transfers to the provinces for postsecondary education and health, known collectively since 1977 as Established Programs Financing (EPF) with the Canada Assistance Plan (CAP) into a single transfer to be known as the Canada Health and Social Transfer (CHST). The CHST was intended to cover federal contributions to health, welfare and postsecondary education, but the transfer, apart significantly from the health component, was still entirely unconditional. Indeed, post-secondary education was not even mentioned specifically in the name of the program. And with that, the total amount of the federal contribution to the new CHST was cut by $6 billion. The provinces, of course, had to make up the fiscal shortfall somehow, and one inviting target was to restrain expenditures on universities and colleges. Postsecondary institutions, universities in particular, took the obvious course of action and began to in-crease tuition fees. Despite policies in several provinces limiting increases in university tuition fees, their proportionate contribution to university revenues has doubled in recent years. They now contribute almost a third (31%) of total operating income (AUCC, 2002a, p. 61). This, of course, has led to greater borrowing by students and thus rising levels of debt.

Determination to reduce federal expenditures was part of the explanation for a dramatic announcement by the federal government in 1996 to devolve to the provinces much of its involvement in labour market training, reversing the bold 1966 initiative by which it asserted federal jurisdiction over this activity. The more compelling reason for this reversal appears to have been the near win by the Parti Québécois in its sovereignty referendum. Ottawa had earlier offered to withdraw from most of its programs in this policy area when it signed on to the Charlottetown Accord. That was, of course, under a different prime minister. Indeed, the federal offer was strongly opposed at the time by Jean Chrétien. In any case, that offer collapsed with the defeat of the Accord. Now Chrétien, as prime minister, was forced to offer an even more generous transfer of jurisdiction. Quebec was quick to accept the deal, negotiating further limitations on the remaining federal role. Some of the other provinces were less sanguine about the prospects of assuming greater responsibilities in this area, with the result that a variety of arrangements were negotiated, creating a situation that Herman Bakvis, quoting Pierre Trudeau, calls "checkerboard federalism" (Bakvis, 2002). Five provinces and two of the territories (Alberta, Manitoba, New Brunswick, Northwest Territory, Nunavut, Quebec, and Saskatchewan) chose to accept the devolution option. Three provinces and one territory (British Columbia, Newfoundland and Labrador, Prince Edward Island, and Yukon) chose a co-management arrangement. Nova Scotia entered into a "strategic partnership", while Ontario did not sign any agreement, leaving the situation essentially unchanged.

While this appeared to be a major concession on Ottawa's part, Rodney Haddow argues that it by no means represents a withdrawal from the field of labour market training. Rather, the federal government has simply found other means of expressing its interests in training and postsecondary education. Nor have federal-provincial relations in this area become noticeably less complex (Haddow, 2003).

The experience of the 1995 cuts in federal transfers had left a lasting mark on federal-provincial relations and provincial officials began to look for ways to rein in the federal government's use of the so-called spending power. The federal spending power, drawing on the historic, prerogative right of the Crown to make gifts to its citizens, enables the federal government to spend money in areas of provincial legislative jurisdiction. It has been a powerful instrument in extending the reach of federal authority and has certainly increased the flexibility of Canadian federalism. But for the provinces it has also been the source of great frustration, because what the Crown grants, the Crown can also take away. Time and again, the provinces have found themselves lured into expensive spending commitments by the offer of federal matching funds, only to be left holding the fiscal bag when federal priorities or circumstances change. The CHST was particularly galling if only because of the magnitude of the cut. The provinces united around two objectives: to get back the money withdrawn in 1995, now seen almost exclusively in terms of health care, and to put limits on the use of the federal spending power.

The upshot, after months of intense negotiations, was the Social Union Framework Agreement (SUFA), signed by Ottawa and all the provinces and territories except Quebec in February 1999. Quebec's refusal to sign bore eloquent testimony to the failure of the first ministers to reach agreement on any effective curtailment of the federal spending power, which had been a key demand of the government of Quebec. It had also been part of the unanimous provincial position going into the negotiations, but all but one of the other provinces and territories were prepared to abandon in return for a pledge of federal dollars. Quebec, typically, got its share of the money without signing the agreement.

The money amounted to a commitment of an additional $11.5 billion, to be spread over five years, $2.0 billion in 1999–2000 and 2000–2001, and $2.5 billion in the three succeeding years. With that, the federal minister of finance, Paul Martin, was able to claim that "when the increase in funding reaches $2.5 billion in 2001–02, federal support for health care will be as high as it was before cost-cutting in the mid-1990s" (Canada. Department of Finance, 1999). This was a tad disingenuous. It was true in the narrow sense that the absolute amount of the federal transfer, including both cash and tax points, would have reached the 1994–95 level, but as a proportion of total expenditures on health care, the federal contribution had fallen dramatically.[1] What is more significant for our purposes, while the increased transfers were to be included as part of the CHST, they were explicitly targeted for the health-care component alone. None was even nominally intended for postsecondary education.

That said, it was the SUFA that held out the promise of a more collaborative federal-provincial relationship. What was contained in this framework agreement? The short answer is very little. But on closer examination, it may well turn out to represent a signal of more significant changes. The so-called social union encompasses the social policy dimensions of Canadian federalism. The framework agreement, SUFA, incorporates a goodly number of verbal commitments to cooperation among governments. Most are assertions of good intentions, without the means of enforcement. Three aspects of the agreement stand out as particularly significant.

Perhaps the most important feature of SUFA was the willingness of the provinces and territories, again noting the absence of Quebec, to recognize the legitimacy of a substantial federal role in social policy. This was the first time the constitutional division of legislative responsibilities had been so openly set aside in a federal-provincial agreement. That agreement does not in any way alter the constitution, but it represents an important, if largely symbolic, victory for the federal government. It grants legitimacy

---

[1]The provinces, which have never considered the transferred tax room as a federal transfer, calculated that in 2000–01 the federal contribution to provincial health expenditures had fallen to 13.8%. See Provincial and Territorial Ministers of Health (2000).

to a host of current and potential future federal initiatives in the realm of social policy. Once conceded, this recognition will be difficult to withdraw.

Second, SUFA failed to restrain the federal government's ability to employ, essentially unfettered, its spending power in areas of provincial jurisdiction. Indeed, it affirmed the contribution of this instrument in the development of Canada's social union. The ability of the federal government to transfer money to provincial governments has, it stated, enabled the federal government to "support the delivery of social programs and services by provinces and territories in order to promote equality of opportunity and mobility for all Canadians and to pursue Canada-wide objectives". In terms of future conditional grants, the agreement pledged the federal government only to "proceed in a cooperative manner that is respectful of the provincial and territorial governments and their priorities" (Canada, 1999). And in terms of future Canada-wide initiatives in health care, postsecondary education, social assistance, and social services funded through intergovernmental transfers, the federal government would only proceed with the agreement of a majority (i.e., six) of provincial governments. All governments agreed to give each other advance notice of major changes in social programs, while the federal government agreed to provide a year's notice before renewing or making significant changes in existing transfers.

Finally, the agreement contained commitments by the provinces to remove any existing barriers to interprovincial mobility, and not to erect new ones. This has particular resonance for postsecondary education, where higher tuition fees for out-of-province students are now explicitly forbidden. It should be noted that Quebec, which of course was not a signatory to SUFA, does have higher out-of-province fees. This, however, is at least consistent with the spirit of the agreement since tuition fees in Quebec, by government policy, are held well below those of other provinces. Quebec's out-of-province fee is set at the average charged in provinces other than Quebec, so that students from other provinces studying in Quebec are treated much the same as they would be if they studied at home.

The tuition-fee policy does raise a particular problem for a province like Nova Scotia, which has a disproportionate number of out-of-province students, more than any other province in the country. This results in a situation where, for years, Nova Scotia has had one of the highest levels of support for its universities, if calculated on a per capita basis, but one of the lowest if calculated on a per student basis. The necessary consequence is that despite its high level of support, its students must bear the highest level

David M. Cameron

of tuition fees in the country. The reason is simply that the out-of-province students bring no provincial or federal support with them. Since the CHST is calculated on an equal per capita basis, it does not recognize or compensate for this disparity.

In conclusion, SUFA may indeed represent the confirmation of a more collaborative federal-provincial relationship. But it is hard to disagree with Alain Noël that it is a decidedly one-sided form of collaboration.

> The SUFA leaves the provinces in a subordinate role, imposes stricter mobility rules, does not integrate a strong and credible federal commitment to sufficient, stable and predictable funding, creates weak dispute-resolution mechanisms, and hardly constrains the use of the federal spending power. (Noël, 2002, pp. 17–18)

Indeed, the federal spending power has recently afforded Ottawa opportunities for a truly massive expansion of its involvement in many aspects of postsecondary education, an expansion that also raises some troubling questions about the future of Canadian federalism.

Recent Federal Initiatives

The financial crisis that gave rise to the cuts in federal expenditures, including transfers to the provinces, proved to be remarkably short-lived. By 1997–98 the federal balance sheet was coloured black and was destined to move quickly into substantial surplus. The provinces wanted a share of the new-found largesse and, as we have just seen, most of them were prepared to accept a strengthened federal hand in social policy in order to get it. In the ensuing years, the federal government would unilaterally transform its role in postsecondary education, putting together a battery of new spending initiatives that Robert Pritchard, former president of the University of Toronto, described as collectively constituting a new paradigm (Prichard, 2000). None of these initiatives was brought within the collaborative purview of SUFA.

First came the Canada Foundation for Innovation (CFI), introduced in 1997. What was most remarkable about the CFI was the manner of its management and financing. Instead of relying on annual appropriations, approved by Parliament, the CFI was established as a private corporation, drawing down funds paid to the corporation as a lump-sum endowment.

This novel management approach was defended on the grounds that it would give the corporation greater flexibility in negotiating partnerships with universities and other participants, but it has raised the ire of Canada's auditor general and others, for playing fast and loose with the principle of parliamentary accountability (Auditor General of Canada, 2000; see also Aucoin, 2003).

The CFI began operations with an endowment of $800 million from the federal government. This was subsequently increased several times, to $3.65 billion. But the real magic of the CFI initiative is the requirement that recipients of its grants obtain matching funds from provincial or private agencies or corporations. Indeed, the contribution from the CFI to a particular project is limited to 40% of the total cost. This means that CFI funds are able to lever more than $9 billion in total expenditures. This money, which is slated to last until 2010, is to be used for research infrastructure, including equipment, facilities, and installations. It is available to both universities, colleges, and associated institutions.

The CFI addressed a real problem for universities in Canada. Years of expenditure restraint by both orders of government had left universities with limited capacities to replace worn out equipment or to acquire the supplies and equipment and related infrastructure needed to keep abreast of technological developments and new research priorities. At the same time, it also confirmed the federal government's pre-eminence in the financing of university research, and added a powerful instrument in support of the government's attempts to tilt university research towards the applied end of the scale, especially in cooperation with industry. This shift in focus had begun under the Mulroney government when it introduced its matching grants program in 1986, tying future increases in funding through the federal granting councils to matching contributions from non-governmental sources. That had been followed in 1988 when the Networks of Centres of Excellence (NCEs) were established. The idea behind this innovation had been developed by Fraser Mustard and embodied in his Canadian Institute for Advanced Research. It had subsequently been extended by Ontario, and it was Ontario's experience that inspired the program introduced by Mulroney. Significantly, when the Chrétien government introduced the CFI, it simultaneously confirmed the mandate of the NCEs and increased their funding.

The CFI, with its reliance on public-private partnerships, presented universities in Atlantic Canada with a special problem. With a smaller and relatively weak private sector, they were disadvantaged by a scheme that hinged government support on their ability to obtain contributions from the

David M. Cameron

private sector. To overcome this disadvantage, the federal government introduced the Atlantic Innovation Fund within the Atlantic Canada Opportunities Agency (ACOA). Through this mechanism, the federal government provides an additional $300 million for investment in the region's infrastructure, much of it going to universities and research institutions (Atlantic Canada Opportunities Agency, 2000).

What is unique about the Atlantic Innovation Fund is the use of federal dollars to compensate for the weakness of the private sector in the region. By this means, it ameliorates the region's competitive disadvantage in attracting federal research dollars. Elsewhere in Canada, it has become common practice for provincial agencies to play a direct role in assisting their universities in this effort. Quebec has been especially aggressive in this regard. The CFI has encouraged other provinces to adopt similar strategies. From this has emerged a pattern of federal-provincial-private sector collaboration in university research, with the federal government playing the leading role.

Next in the litany of federal initiatives came the Canada Millennium Scholarship Foundation (CMSF), introduced in 1998. Once again, it used the device of an independent corporation, financed by means of a one-time endowment of $2.5 billion, designed to last for a period of ten years. The name of the new foundation is a tad misleading. Only a small portion of its annual expenditures (5%) goes in the form of scholarships, awarded on the basis of merit. The remainder (95%) is in the form of bursaries, awarded on the basis of need. And it is in the administration of these bursaries that the foundation got into its rather odd relationship with the provinces.

The CMSF was conceived in the prime minister's office and has been described as part of Jean Chrétien's legacy. It was put together in considerable haste, in order that the first cheques could be issued before the end of 2000. There was some initial confusion as to the purpose of the program. The enabling legislation says it is "to grant scholarships to students who are in financial need and who demonstrate merit, *in order to improve access* to postsecondary education in Canada so that Canadians can acquire the knowledge and skills needed to participate in a changing economy and society" (Canada. Department of Finance, 1998b, emphasis added). But when then Finance Minister Paul Martin described the scheme in his 1998 budget, the stated purpose was not improving access but reducing student debt:

> This investment will provide over 100,000 scholarships to low- and middle-income students each and every year over the next decade. The

scholarships will average $3,000 each, per year. As a result, a student receiving a scholarship over four years *will see his or her debt load cut by $12,000, half what it otherwise would have been.* (Canada. Department of Finance, 1998a, emphasis added)

Reducing the debts of students already in the postsecondary system is hardly likely to increase access, except indirectly and to a very limited extent.

Conflicting objectives aside, the push to get the money into students' hands quickly also compelled the new foundation to work through the provinces. It could have set up an independent administrative apparatus, but that would have entailed costly duplication. As it was, there already existed the means of assessing student need through the federal government's Canada Student Loan Program (CSLP), which used provincial needs assessment criteria. The decision was taken early on to piggy-back the millennium scholarship program onto existing provincial administrative processes.

This decision yielded two significant outcomes. First, the implementation of the bursary program differed somewhat from province to province (the merit-based scholarships were administered directly by the foundation, using a small army of volunteers, and consequently were essentially uniform across the country). Several patterns emerged. A number of provinces, specifically Nova Scotia, New Brunswick, Prince Edward Island, Saskatchewan, Manitoba and, initially Ontario, insisted that the bursaries be paid directly to the student's bank, under the CSLP, reducing his or her student debt. In most of the remaining provinces and territories, and later Ontario, the awards go directly to the student as a cash grant. Newfoundland and Labrador adopted a mixture of the two approaches. Quebec is distinct in that the federal grants replace provincial grants.

Herein lies the second significant outcome. Unless further action were taken, the impact of the new federal bursaries would simply have been to displace provincial loans or grants with federal grants. To avoid this, the foundation negotiated agreements with each of the provinces, indicating that they would re-direct at least some of the displaced money to other priorities in postsecondary education. In this, the foundation explicitly cited the SUFA to support its case (Institute of Intergovernmental Relations, 2003, p. 30). The commitments entered into by the provinces varied considerably, and it remains a moot point as to how positive the net effect has been for students.

There is also a future problem that faces the student aid system as a result of the CMSF. The foundation's endowment will be exhausted by 2010. If it is not renewed, future students will be left in the lurch. Federal surpluses may not continue, of course, which would make renewal of the program difficult, to say the least. But simply allowing the program and foundation to disappear will almost certainly place a severe strain on federal-provincial relations, given that the provinces have, in varying degrees, become dependent on the program, using it to displace their own expenditures on student aid.

Yet another federal initiative, announced in the 1999 budget and confirmed in legislation the following year, was the transformation of the Medical Research Council, one of the three federal granting councils, into the Canadian Institutes of Health Research (CIHR). This transformation was accompanied by a doubling of funds to almost $500 million, subsequently increased to $620 million. The CIHR is currently seeking a further increase to $1 billion (Bernstein, 2003). The new agency incorporated a new organizational structure as well. It is not a single research council, but rather a collection of 13 distinct institutes, each pursuing a distinct line of research. This approach is reminiscent of the innovative approach pioneered by the Canadian Institute for Advanced Research and then the Networks of Centres of Excellence, in drawing leading researchers from a variety of universities and disciplines to focus on a defined problem area.

The federal government took one of its boldest steps in the 1999 Speech from the Throne, announcing its intention to establish a program of Canada Research Chairs (CRCs). This was set up as a limited five-year program, although to be financed from the Consolidated Revenue Fund. The program will pump $900 million into hiring 2,000 professors over a five-year period. Half the appointments will be at senior levels, known as Tier 1 Chairs, funded at a level of $200,000 each. The other half will be junior appointments, called Tier 2 Chairs, costing $100,000 each.

The CRCs are distributed amongst Canada's universities in an interesting combination of equity and demonstrated research strength. Every institution gets at least one appointment, although this does not include federated and affiliated institutions. The rest go to institutions in proportion to their success in winning grants from the three granting councils. The government did not follow this principle through to the allocation of chairs among the disciplines represented by the three councils. Instead, it raised the share going to the social sciences and humanities from about 12% (their share of research dollars awarded) to 20%. The health sciences received 35% of the money and the natural sciences and engineering 45%. Still, the Canadian Association of University Teachers (CAUT) complained that the social sciences and humanities should have received more, reflecting the fact that 42% of the current faculty complement are employed in these disciplines. There is, of course, merit in both positions; the disparity is largely explained by the fact that research in the social sciences and humanities employs more professors but costs less (or, at least, is supported at lower levels). The upshot is that most of the chairs will go to the three most research-intensive universities: Toronto, McGill, and University of British Columbia.

The CRCs are administered by a steering committee consisting of the heads of the three granting councils, plus the head of the CFI, plus the deputy minister of Industry Canada. This committee is advised by a College of Reviewers, consisting of panels of internationally recognized researchers. Considerable long-term significance must be attached to the fact that under this program, holders of a Canada Research Chair will be expected to teach as well as perform research, a fact that draws the federal government into direct support of university teaching, a responsibility heretofore considered the preserve of the provinces and the universities themselves. The federal reach extends even further. Each university, in applying for its quota of chairs, is required to submit for approval by the steering committee, a detailed research plan.

The CRCs were designed as a partial response to two looming problems. One is a coming shortage of professors, a shortage fuelled in part by growth in student numbers, especially in British Columbia, Alberta, and Ontario, and in part by the pending retirement of the cohort of professors hired back in the 1960s and early 1970s during the last great hiring boom. The AUCC estimated in 2002 that Canada might need to hire as many as 40,000 new faculty members by 2011, more than the entire current crop of professors (AUCC, 2002a, p. 22). The AUCC now says this figure may be a conservative one (Giroux, 2003, p. 11). The second problem arises from evidence that many of Canada's top professionals, including academic researchers, are being lured away by higher salaries in US universities. The CRC program was designed to bring some of them back while persuading others to stay.

The federal government's expanding role and influence in post-secondary education and research was given a further boost in 2001. Indeed, this may prove to be the most significant step of all. After years of equivocation on the issue, Ottawa finally agreed to recognize and address the burden it was imposing on some universities by its refusal to pay the indirect costs of research. The step was initially a tentative one, a one-time commitment of $200 million, paid on a sliding scale inversely related to the value of research grants received through the three granting councils. As a result, universities with the most funded research receive the least proportionate compensation for indirect costs.

The reason this decision is so important is that it recognized and began to remove one of the most critical impediments to research productivity. Indirect costs are those not directly and immediately connected to the production of research. They include overheads, such as administrative expenses, and such things as heat, light, and depreciation. But they also include the portion of professors' salaries devoted to research. These costs have been estimated at 40% or more of the direct costs of research, which are currently covered by research grants (Brochu, 1996, p. 24). Paying for at least a portion of these indirect costs reduces the penalty imposed on Canada's universities, a penalty that increased in proportion to their research intensiveness and their success in winning research grant competitions. It is hard to imagine a more counter-productive policy. The United States has long paid the indirect costs of sponsored research, and this practice has had much to do with supporting and sustaining that country's outstanding record in research. Not paying for these costs put Canada's universities at a comparative disadvantage compared with their American cousins. Together with the CRC program, the decision to pay for at least a portion of the indirect costs of research will undoubtedly help to develop a tier of distinctively research-intensive universities in Canada. And perhaps most important, it is a policy that rewards rather than penalizing demonstrated excellence as measured by success in attracting research grants. The 2001 initiative was secured in 2003, with a commitment of $225 million per year, announced in that year's budget. The program continues the practice of paying a higher ratio of indirect costs to institutions performing lower proportions of research, and is administered by SSHRC. The arrangement is to be reviewed after three years of operation (Canada, 2004).

Federal initiatives in support of postsecondary education continue to expand. The 2004 budget, for example, included several relevant announcements. These included the introduction of the Canada Learning Bond for low-income families. It also announced the expansion of the Canada Education Savings Grant for low- and middle-income Canadians saving for their childrens' future postsecondary education. The Canada Student Loans program (CSLP) will be enriched, increasing the maximum loan from $165 to $210 per week, while reducing the contribution expected from parents.

Finally, low-income students will now qualify for an up-front grant as part of the CSLP, designed to cover half the cost of tuition in their first year (Canada. Department of Finance, 2004).

Ottawa's growing importance in postsecondary education and research was given added point and purpose in its two-part, ten-year policy paper entitled *Canada's Innovation Strategy*, released in 2002. The two parts, respectively authored by Industry Canada and Human Resources Development Canada, set out an ambitious set of goals intended to put Canada in the top rank of countries in terms of competitiveness in the global knowledge economy, as well as the steps needed for Canadians to acquire the skills and attitudes appropriate to an innovative society. The goals are nothing if not ambitious. By 2010, Canada should rank among the top five countries in the world in research and development, and rank among the world leaders in terms of Canada's share of private sector sales from innovations. To get there, the paper sets a target of at least doubling the federal government's investment in R&D, and raising the per capita value of venture capital investments, to prevailing levels in the United States (Industry Canada, 2002). On the training and education side, the strategy sets equally ambitious goals. By 2010 every high-school graduate should have the opportunity to participate in some form of postsecondary education, 50% of those 25 to 64 should have completed a postsecondary degree or diploma, and the number of Canadians admitted to master's and doctoral programs should increase by 5% per year (HRDC, 2002).

These are certainly ambitious targets. The question is not just whether we can get there from here, but what are the implications of doing so, or not, for Canada's universities and colleges and for Canadian federalism. It is to a consideration of some aspects of these questions, as well as the other related federal initiatives, that we now turn.

Reflections, Implications and Questions

What are we to make of these federal policy and spending initiatives? While not necessarily developed from a single, coherent strategy, they nonetheless constitute a mutually reinforcing package, with considerable potential to transform Canada's postsecondary system, especially its university component. Federal policy can be expected to continue to emphasize research, both because this is the key to innovation, and there-fore to Canada's capacity to compete in the global economy. Research will be even more skewed in favour of applied and marketable products, although there is no indication that basic research will be sacrificed in order to achieve this.

We are likely to see greater differentiation among universities in the coming years, as federal support for infrastructure and the indirect costs of research, as well as the Canada Research Chairs program, channel resources into universities with proven track records of research excellence in specific areas. Institutions will make their own choices as to their selected areas of specialization, but the necessity of making choices will be accentuated. We are not likely to go all the way to the American model of a distinct tier of research-intensive universities, but we are moving in that direction.

As for university students, the prospect is for tuition fees to continue to increase, not only because a university degree remains such a sound economic investment, but also because the federal government lacks the authority to do anything about it, while the provinces seem unwilling, at least in most cases, or for long, to pay the price of more stringent regulation. That price, of course, would be paid either through increased grants or by running the risk of reduced quality.

There is no question the federal government has grabbed the lead in shaping postsecondary education in Canada. The AUCC, the collective voice of Canada's university presidents, has enthusiastically bought into the new federal vision. In July of 2002 they published their response to the federal government's Innovation Strategy. Entitled "A Strong Foundation for Innovation: An AUCC Action Plan", it announced that Canada's universities

> are ready and willing to build on their already impressive contribution. They are eager to perform more research, to produce even more highly-qualified graduates, and to play an even more central role in empowering their communities through knowledge and innovation. (AUCC, 2002b, p. 2)

They signed on to meet all of the specific targets set out in the Innovation Strategy adding, by way of *quid pro quo*, that to meet these targets will require substantially increased funding from both federal and provincial governments, as well as from business and industry.

The federal government and university presidents then consummated their emerging consensus by signing a *Framework of Agreed Principles on Federally Funded University Research*, signed on November 18, 2002. In that framework agreement, the parties acknowledged AUCC's commitments as spelled out in the action plan, while the federal government accepted that it "is responsible for providing the necessary levels of investment in university research to achieve these aims, including ongoing contributions to the indirect costs of research" (Government of Canada and Association of Universities and Colleges of Canada, 2002, p. 2).

This is certainly going to be an expensive enterprise. In a recent issue of *Policy Options* dedicated almost entirely to Canadian universities, Robert Giroux, president and CEO of the AUCC, put the price tag for meeting the federal targets, as well as responding to projected enrolment increases and making up for the erosion of quality caused by the underfunding of the recent past, at a staggering $25 billion over the next decade (Giroux, 2003, pp. 13-14). Whether or not this is either a realistic or achievable estimate, it provides a useful yardstick against which to assess the recent federal initiatives.

It may be unwise to look this gift horse in the mouth, but prudence demands that we at least reflect on its possible implications, both for post-secondary education and for federalism. There are some positive implications to be sure, even beyond the simple fact of more money for colleges and universities. The decision to pay at least a portion of the indirect costs of research stands at the top of the list. Not only does it address a perennial deficit for universities, but it alleviates pressure on the provinces to compensate for this federal neglect, a pressure to which several provinces had already responded. The CRC program also deserves to be singled out because of its explicit recognition and reward of demonstrated research excellence. In that context, the possibility of federal direct encroachment into the teaching and priority-setting prerogatives of universities has so far not materialized. The expansion of medical research to encompass a much broader definition of health, with added resources, needs also to be noted.

One area that cries out for reform is student aid, the essential antidote to rising tuition. Properly framed, an effective system of student aid can ensure that access to postsecondary education is not a function of wealth. At present we have a hodgepodge of grants, loans, debt remission, tax credits, and savings grants. We also have overlapping federal and provincial programs, not to mention conflicting federal objectives. Ross Finnie recently proposed a radical streamlining of the student aid system, arguing that the existing array of programs "often miss the mark and ... don't necessarily deliver enough money where it is needed while providing funds to others (i.e., wealthier families) who don't necessarily need the money to make postsecondary schooling a viable option" (2003, p. 51). His recommendation is to consolidate these various elements into "one program that does the job well" (Finnie, 2003, p. 51). That may be an overly ambitious goal, given the competing and vested interests involved, but it surely points in the right direction. The federal government, in the Throne Speech delivered in February 2004, promised a full review of student aid. In the budget that followed shortly thereafter, it made even more ad hoc additions. Hopefully, at least some rationalization will result from the forthcoming review.

There are also some broader questions that warrant concern. One is surely the tendency on the part of the federal government to limit its funding commitments to one-shot injections. The CRC program falls into this category, as does the CFI and the Millennium Scholarships. Of course, public funding must always be subject to changing circumstances and priorities, while parliamentary principles limit multi-year budgeting. Still, one-time commitments provide a weak foundation on which to build long-term plans. After all, 1995 and its federal cuts in fiscal transfers is not exactly beyond living memory. Nor, at least for some of us, is 1966 and the federal decision to terminate direct grants to universities.

Indeed, we know at least that the CHST will not survive beyond this year, although what exactly will replace it has not, at the time of writing, been announced. We do know that health is to be split off as a separate transfer, while the postsecondary community, speaking with a rare collective voice, has suggested that postsecondary education should be separated from the remaining social programs.[2] Whatever the outcome of that debate, the successor to the CHST is not likely to remain the benign, indeed no-purpose, transfer that currently exists. The federal government will almost certainly seize this opportunity to inject greater point and purpose into federal expenditures for postsecondary education.

The federal government has been increasing its leverage across the board in its recent initiatives. One need only mention the CFI, the CMSF and the CSLP, the CRCs, and the Indirect Costs Program to appreciate how far into postsecondary education federal influence now penetrates. The

---

[2]Joint letter to Prime Minister Martin signed on behalf of the Association of Canadian Community Colleges, the Canadian Alliance of Student Associations, the Canadian Federation for the Humanities and Social Sciences, the Association of Universities and Colleges of Canada, the Canadian Association of University Teachers, and the Canadian Federation of Students. Ottawa: December 19, 2003.

Innovation Strategy puts the icing on the cake, so to speak. And where are the provinces in all of this?

In a recent article in *University Affairs*, the official organ of the AUCC, two senior officials with Industry Canada, Chummer Farina and Ken Hart, observed that "the federal policy for research in the universities is on a collision course with, at a minimum, provincial treasuries" (2004, p. 32). The provinces long ago accepted, at least tacitly, a legitimate federal role in university research. Indeed, more recently they have actively supported that role, taking steps and money to assist their universities in maximizing their potential revenue from federal research support. But it is one thing to support a specific federal role in university research. It is quite another to invite the federal government to assume a pervasive role in shaping post-secondary policy. That seems to be the not-so-thin edge of the wedge embodied in recent federal initiatives. The implications for Canadian federalism are not entirely sanguine.

Farina and Hart go on to turn their attention to universities, suggesting a triangular relationship among universities, federal, and provincial governments.

> Dialogue between the two levels of government on this issue could be improved, and, as the "meat in the sandwich", it would be in universities' interest to catalyze a more systematic, analytic and ongoing dialogue. (Farina and Hart, 2004, p. 32)

Appetizing as the analogy may be, suggesting that universities provide the substantive content for this intergovernmental relationship misses an important point. The fact is that the university "meat" is something of a dog's breakfast of ingredients. It is one thing for the AUCC to buy into the federal strategy. It is quite another to infer that the AUCC brings with it the consensus opinion of all universities.

Universities are, in fact, seriously divided within themselves. The most serious division is that between senior administrations, whose interests the AUCC does represent, and faculty members, now almost everywhere represented by certified trade unions. And then there are the students and the question of where they fit in this imaginary sandwich.

What we desperately need is to develop a new consensus, a new common sense of how the several elements comprising "the university", along with its benefactors and beneficiaries, will work collectively for the common good. Others have tried to articulate a similar objective. Frank

Rhodes, former president of Cornell University, refers to a "community of inquiry".

> Only in community, in dialogue, across the boundaries that now divide them, can universities regain their full effectiveness. Only in dialogue can they fulfill their obligations to the society that supports them. (2001, p. 54)

John Evans, former president of the University of Toronto, speaks of the idea of a social contract between the university and society (Evans, 2001). And Donald Kennedy, president emeritus of Stanford refers to the public trust that must underpin the university's relationship with its society (Kennedy, 1997).

There once existed this kind of public trust or social contract. It was perhaps most eloquently expressed in the Flavelle report on the University of Toronto back in 1906. Flavelle's contract embraced the public, the university faculty, and the university administration. To each he assigned specific responsibilities in university governance: the public interest through a board of governors, the faculty through a university senate, and the administration through the university president, who provided leadership and integrity to the whole enterprise. Ian Clark reminds us of another version of this idea of a social contract, also framed in Ontario. In 1966, then Premier William Davis put it bluntly:

> provided that universities can meet the responsibilities of our times we should undoubtedly be better off if they were allowed to operate with ... autonomy. On the other hand, if they cannot or will not accept those responsibilities ... there will inevitably be a demand ... that government move in and take over. (cited in Clark, 2002, pp. 411-412)

We need a new social contract for postsecondary education in Canada. It must be an accord that embraces the interests of students, faculty, administration, and the general public. Most important, it must accommodate the distinctive public interests represented by and expressed through our federal and provincial governments, while recognizing the primary constitutional roles of the provinces. It will not be an easy undertaking. Universities seem too divided within themselves to speak with a united voice. Students can hardly be expected to take the lead, although their interests certainly need to be incorporated. Leadership has fallen to the federal government, largely by default, but it is a partial leadership at best. The provinces must step forward, however constrained they are in terms of resources. It is only they who have the breadth of constitutional jurisdiction to respond to the full gamut of interests and opportunities, including the governance of universities, as well as colleges. Obviously, the federal government has a role to play. But to cede responsibility to the federal government alone, for charting the future of postsecondary education, is to accept a blinkered view of the roles of universities and colleges. In leaping to embrace the recent flood of federal dollars, we should perhaps be mindful of what it portends for postsecondary education and for federalism. Do we really know enough about what tune the piper is playing?

References

Association of Universities and Colleges of Canada (AUCC). 2002a. *Trends in Higher Education*. Ottawa: AUCC.

_____. 2002b. "A Strong Foundation for Innovation: An AUCC Action Plan". Ottawa: AUCC. July.

Atlantic Canada Opportunities Agency. 2000. News Release: *Atlantic Investment Partnership*. Ottawa: ACOA, June 29.

Aucoin, P. 2003. "Independent Foundations, Public Money and Public Accountability: Whither Ministerial Accountability as Democratic Governance?" *Canadian Public Administration* 46(1).

Auditor General of Canada. 2002. "Placing the Public's Money Beyond Parliament's Reach". Report of the Auditor General. At www.oag.bvg.gc.ca.

Bakvis, H. 2002. "Checkerboard Federalism? Labour Market Development Policy in Canada", in H. Bakvis and G. Skogstad (eds.), *Canadian Federalism: Performance, Effectiveness, and Legitimacy*. Toronto: Oxford University Press.

Bernstein, A. 2003. "Presentation to the Standing Committee on Finance Pre-Budget Hearing". Ottawa: Canadian Institutes of Health Research, October 2.

Brochu, M. 1996. "Indirect Costs of Federal Research Contracts to Universities". Discussion paper prepared for the Canadian Association of University Research Administrators and Industry Canada.

Cameron, D.M. 1991. *More than an Academic Question: Universities, Government, and Public Policy in Canada*. Halifax: IRPP.

Canada. 1999. "A Framework to Improve the Social Union for Canadians", February 4.

_____. 2004. *Indirect Costs Program*. Accessed January 30, 2004 at http://www.indirectcosts.gc.ca.

Canada, Department of Finance. 1998a. *Budget 1998*. Ottawa: Government of Canada, February.

_____. 1998b. *Budget Implementation Act, 1998*, Part 1, Article 5(1). This can also be found under the Department of Justice Canada Web site.

_____. 1999. "Strengthening Health Care for Canadians: Budget 1999". At www.fin.gc.ca/budget99.

_____. 2004. *Budget 2004.* Accessed April 21, 2004 at http://www.fin.gc.ca/budget04.

Clark, I.D. 2002. "Comments on 'The Challenge of Change: Canadian Universities in the Twenty-first Century' by David M. Cameron", *Canadian Public Administration* 45(3).

Dupré, J.S. *et al.* 1973. *Federalism and Policy Development: The Case of Adult Occupational Training in Ontario.* Toronto: University of Toronto Press.

Evans, J. 2001. "Higher Education in the Higher Education Economy: Towards a Public Research Contract". 2001 Killam Annual Lecture.

Farina, C. and K. Hart. 2004. "The Counting Game", *University Affairs* 45(2).

Finnie, R. 2003. "A New Architecture for the Canadian Student Financial Aid System", *Policy Options* 24(08), 50-53.

Giroux, R.J. 2003. "Looking Down the Road by the Numbers: Challenges to Universities in the Next 10 Years", *Policy Options* 24(08), 10-14.

Government of Canada and Association of Universities and Colleges of Canada. 2002. *Framework of Agreed Principles on Federally Funded University Research.* Ottawa: Supply and Services Canada.

Haddow, R. 2003. "Canadian Federalism and Active Labour Market Policy", in F. Rocher and M. Smith (eds.), *New Trends in Canadian Federalism*, 2nd edition. Peterborough: Broadview Press.

Human Resources Development Canada (HRDC). 2002. *Knowledge Matters: Skills and Learning for Canadians.* Canada's Innovation Strategy. Ottawa: HRDC.

Industry Canada. 2002. *Achieving Excellence: Investing in People, Knowledge and Opportunities.* Canada's Innovation Strategy. Ottawa: Industry Canada.

Institute of Intergovernmental Relations. 2003. *Canada Millennium Scholarship Foundation: Evaluation of the Foundation's Performance, 1998-2002.* Kingston: Institute of Intergovernmental Relations, Queen's University.

Kennedy, D. 1997. *Academic Duty.* Cambridge, MA: Harvard University Press.

Noël, A. 2002. "Without Quebec: Collaborative Federalism with a Footnote?" in T. McIntosh (ed.), *Building the Social Union: Perspectives, Directions and Challenges.* Regina: Saskatchewan Institute of Public Policy.

Prichard, J.R. 2000. "Federal Support for Higher Education and Research in Canada: The New Paradigm". 2000 Killam Annual Lecture.

Provincial and Territorial Ministers of Health. 2000. *Understanding Canada's Health Care Costs: Final Report.* Ottawa: Supply and Services Canada.

Rhodes, F.H. 2001. *The Creation of the Future: The Role of the American University.* Ithaca: Cornell University Press.

Robinson, I. and R. Simeon. 1999. "The Dynamics of Canadian Federalism", in J. Bickerton and A.-G. Gagnon (eds.), *Canadian Politics.* Peterborough: Broadview Press.

Demystifying Quality Assurance

David Leyton-Brown

Academic quality assurance often appears mysterious and/or threatening to some faculty members in the classroom. Professors who care deeply about their teaching and their students often resent or even fear exercises that assess the academic quality of the programs in which they teach. Quality assurance reviews may appear to be time-consuming distractions from the teaching and research to which they would rather devote themselves, and to provide little if any benefit from the exercise to faculty and students in the program. Low expectations of the return from the effort involved can be self-fulfilling, and can lead to an attempt simply to get through the exercise with minimal aggravation. At worst it is sometimes charged that quality assurance processes have a misleading or mistaken fixation on easily measured performance indicators that are of only secondary importance to the real quality of teaching and learning, and so can actually have damaging or counterproductive consequences by basing conclusions on the "wrong" factors. Even those sincerely eager for quality improvement can be reluctant to be openly self-critical in a quality assurance exercise because of a fear that admission of weaknesses could lead to a loss of resources in favour of programs that are stronger, or that more successfully minimize or conceal their weaknesses.

Nevertheless, quality assurance pervades academic life. The professoriate is constantly subject to external quality assurance in the form of peer review of research funding applications, manuscript submissions, and tenure and promotion. If we take for granted the review and assurance of quality of our research programs, our publications, and even the progression of our careers, including evaluation of the quality of teaching in individual courses, why should similar review and assurance of the quality of the programs in which we teach be mystifying?

Quality assurance can be a useful tool for universities, departments, and individual faculty. However, to take fullest advantage of that tool, and use it to best effect, it is important to understand what it is, and how it works.

Academic quality assurance takes many forms in the many places in which it is found, and any classification of approaches must acknowledge several overlapping dichotomies. There are many cases of internal quality assurance mechanisms, in which individual universities (and individual departments and indeed individual instructors) act to assure and improve the quality of their own academic offerings. Often internal quality assurance processes are focused on the academic unit (i.e., the department) rather than the academic program per se, as the university administration seeks to assess the relative performance of different units, and the possibility and desirability of reallocation of resources. Such internal reviews may be conducted on a regular planning cycle, or on the occasion of the end of the term of an outgoing chair or dean, or on some other basis. But the common characteristic is that the review is conducted under the authority and direction of, and at the initiative of, the institution itself. The alternative to internal quality assurance is of course where the quality review is under the authority of, and managed by, a body external to the university. External quality assurance mechanisms are of two broad types — those in which governments regulate the academic quality and those conducted by collectivities of universities as an exercise in academic self-regulation. Both state-regulated and academically self-regulated types of quality assurance can address the entire institution or the individual academic program (or department) as the unit of analysis. Despite the wide range of types of quality assurance, faculty criticism, confusion, and resentment typically concern external quality assurance, which will be the focus of this chapter.

This paper will explain the various approaches to external academic quality assurance, the key components present in all well-regarded quality assurance processes worldwide, important characteristics found to be successful and effective, and examples of the standards, factors, and elements on which familiar quality assurance processes are based. References will be made to quality assurance processes in the United States, Europe and elsewhere, but most of the focus will be on the two long-standing operations in Ontario universities — the quality appraisal of graduate programs by the Ontario Council on Graduate Studies (OCGS), and the audit of undergraduate program reviews by the Undergraduate Program Review Audit Committee (UPRAC) of the Ontario Council of Academic Vice-Presidents (OCAV). The details of these two quality assurance mechanisms will not be described here, as the documents outlining their processes and standards are available on the Web.[1] Rather, various important features of each will be used to illustrate the general components, characteristics, and standards being discussed.

Purposes of Quality Assurance

Quality assurance measures of various kinds have arisen for two principal reasons. Universities for many years have been concerned to assess, ensure, and enhance the quality of their academic programs. The internal academic approval process typically establishes standards for new programs and many universities have long been determined to ensure that existing programs continue to meet those standards. In that context, program or departmental reviews can be an important tool in making budget and resource allocation decisions, especially in times of fiscal constraint and scarce resources, when it is not possible to provide every program with all the resources it could put to good use. Nevertheless, it is the quality-improvement dimension, rather than simply confirmation of meeting minimum standards, that offers the greatest benefit and interest to academics. After all, even the best of programs can be made even better, and continuous quality improvement is a distinguishing feature of the most renowned programs and institutions in the higher education community. However, that purpose is often in tension with the other driving force behind the recent increase in quality assurance processes in many jurisdictions — namely the increasing government pressure for public accountability. Governments in many countries are pressing for demonstration that their funding for higher education is well spent, that desired

---

[1]The OCGS By-Laws and Procedures Governing Appraisals are located at http://www.cou.on.ca/ocgs/HOME/By-laws/BY-LAWSANDPROCEDURES 30Oct2003WWEBVERSION.pdf. The UPRAC Review and Audit Guidelines are available at http://www.cou.on.ca/affiliates/affiliates/UPRAC/UPRACGuidelines 2003.pdf.

outcomes are achieved, and that quality is assured. Accountability purposes can lead to celebration or defence of the status quo, rather than the active search for change and improvement.

The Unit of Analysis: Institutions or Programs

Quality assurance mechanisms typically address two different units or levels of analysis. Some processes, like US institutional accreditation, assure the quality of the entire institution, while others address individual programs (as in professional accreditation, or program assessment in most European countries). While institutional quality necessarily includes the ability to deliver quality programs, other structural issues also come into play, such as financial stability, effectiveness of governance and administration, student services, academic policies, overall faculty numbers and qualifications, etc. While program quality requires institutional context and infrastructure, much more detailed examination of the design, human, financial and physical resources, and outcomes of the program are involved. Good institutions can have individual programs that are weaker than others, or even below standard. Weak institutions can have individual programs that are strong. As with any level of analysis problem, values are not necessarily transitive across levels. Different approaches to institutional and program quality assurance will be illustrated below.

The Authority for Quality Assurance

External quality assurance measures operate under two different kinds of authority — governmental regulation and academic self-regulation. Some governments directly engage in quality assurance processes themselves, by reviewing and approving the quality of institutions or programs, or by establishing and mandating agencies to do so. Governmental regulation involves demonstration of compliance with specified minimum quality standards. The alternative to government regulation is self-regulation on the part of the university community. While internal quality assurance measures are also a form of academic self-regulation, since the university undertakes to review its own programs or departments, the more meaningful distinction is with groups of universities that collectively create and submit to an external quality assurance regime. Collective self-regulation tends to accord more respect to institutional diversity and autonomy, and to have at least the possibility of more emphasis on quality improvement than compliance with minimum quality standards. The major approaches of each type will be outlined.

Government Regulation

The first way in which governments regulate the quality of university education is at the institutional level, by approving the institutions that offer it. In Canada, where constitutional authority for education is vested in the provincial and territorial governments, public universities have been established by legislation, and some provincial governments have enacted legislation that has created boards or agencies to advise the government on the creation or entry of private and/or out-of-province institutions. The governments of Ontario, British Columbia, and Alberta have created organizations (the Postsecondary Education Quality Assessment Board, the Degree Quality Assessment Board, and the Campus Alberta Quality Council, respectively) to fulfill this function by reviewing the organizational quality of the applicant and the academic quality of the proposed degree program(s).

A second approach to government regulation is the approval of all proposed new degree programs, even from public universities. In Canada, a larger number of provincial governments do this, formally or informally. In British Columbia and Alberta the bodies described above also assess the academic content and quality of each proposed degree program from the existing public universities against specified criteria. In Ontario, what the government approves is eligibility of the program (and its enrolled students) for public funding rather than the implementation of the program per se. But since in almost all cases a public university cannot afford to offer a program for which no public funding is received, funding approval is *de facto* approval of the program. The funding eligibility decision does not involve an academic quality review by the government, since the outcome of OCGS appraisal of proposed new graduate programs or internal academic approval of proposed new undergraduate programs by the university's senate or other academic governance structure is accepted as sufficient assurance of quality. Nor is it required any longer that extensive documentation be submitted on other factors such as student demand, societal need, and program uniqueness or justifiable duplication, but universities must certify that such documentation has been considered and could be produced if required. In Quebec there is a joint needs assessment mechanism of the Ministry of Education and the Conference of Rectors and Principals of Quebec Universities (CREPUQ) for new programs. New Brunswick, Nova Scotia, and Prince Edward Island have created the Maritime Provinces Higher Education Commission (MPHEC) to review all new program and program modification proposals. In Manitoba, the Council on Post-Secondary Education reviews proposals for new and significantly changed undergraduate and graduate programs for quality, need, organization, and finances.

The third approach to government regulation is the assessment of the academic quality of existing programs. The best-known example is probably that of the United Kingdom, where the Quality Assurance Agency has systematically reviewed all degree programs in all British universities, but similar undertakings can be found in some American states and in some other countries, such as the Netherlands or Denmark.

An alternative to government-conducted program review is the audit by government or a government-appointed body of the reviews conducted by universities themselves. The audit mechanism will be described more fully below.

Finally, many governments, without reviewing the quality of programs directly, require that specified outcomes be achieved, and monitor the performance of universities on specified quantitative indicators. On some occasions public funding is tied to these performance indicators. Among the quantitative performance indicators adopted in various jurisdictions are: graduation rates, student retention or attrition, time-to-degree, student entry and exit testing, pass rates on licensing and certification examinations, postgraduation employment rates and employer satisfaction, etc. (Council for Higher Education Accreditation, 2003a, p. 18). Without analyzing exhaustively the methodological and conceptual merits of performance indicators, it is worth noting that a recurrent theme in the quality assurance literature is whether particular performance measures actually measure academic quality and the quality of student learning, or whether they are simply easy, though possibly misleading, to count. For example, Braskamp and Braskamp (1997, p. 4) contend that a common indicator such as graduation rates may reflect more about institutional enrolment policies than about student learning.

Self-regulation

External academic self-regulation operates at both the institutional and program levels. Institutional accreditation in the United States is an example of the former, while university-mandated (rather than government-regulated) external quality assessment of individual programs across a region or university system is an example of the latter. Another recent form of self-regulation is the audit of the processes by which autonomous universities exercise their responsibility to ensure academic standards and improve quality.

Self-regulation of institutional quality is not a feature of quality assurance in Canada, but it is the centrepiece of the voluntary and non-governmental institutional accreditation system in the United States. Eight regional accreditation commissions operate in six accreditation regions to recognize institutions according to standards and criteria that have been developed over time in conjunction with the university community. The accreditation commissions are independent private bodies which receive self-assessments and conduct peer evaluations to ensure the quality of institutions and programs, encourage quality improvement of institutions and programs that have already met basic standards, and certify institutional or program sufficiency as required for the receipt of public funds and for institutional licensure by state governments, and as a partial basis for decisions about the transfer of academic credit (Council for Higher Education Accreditation, 2003a, pp. 3-4). There are also various national accreditation bodies for particular types of institutions in the United States and elsewhere (e.g., faith-based institutions, independent or professional institutions, etc.). Accreditation is a voluntary rather than required process, though governments have accepted it as an essential part of the higher education system, by limiting to accredited institutions the payment of federal student assistance funds, or state licensure in some states.

The outstanding example of academic self-regulation at the program level in Canada is the OCGS appraisal process. The publicly-assisted universities of Ontario are bound that they will not implement any new master's or doctoral program unless and until it has been appraised by OCGS and found to be of good quality and approved to commence. Thereafter, all existing graduate programs are periodically reappraised on a seven-year cycle, and any program that is found not to be of good quality must cease operation. Since by far most graduate programs are of good quality, the periodic appraisal process not only provides public assurance and accountability of that fact, but it provides the occasion for self-assessment and feedback from external consultants and the Appraisal Committee aimed at quality improvement.

A relatively new, but increasingly widespread approach to academic self-regulation is the academic audit, whereby an external body audits not the quality of the academic program, but the policies, criteria, and procedures by which the university reviews the quality of its individual programs. The audit does not assess the quality of those programs selected for the audit — that review was previously conducted by the university. Nor does the audit second-guess the university review, or serve as a court of appeal for program members who hope for a better deal. Rather, the audit tests for the compliance of the university's program review policies with the standards, schedules, procedures, and other aspects enunciated by the external body, and for whether the actual reviews examined by the auditors were actually implemented fully in accordance with the letter and spirit of the university's policy. Thus the audit is concerned with process rather than direct assessment of academic quality. Its contribution to public accountability rests upon its demonstration that the quality of every program in the university is regularly reviewed according to transparent and sound procedures and standards that are verified by external audit. Its contribution to quality improvement rests upon the cyclical reviews of each individual program, and upon the logic that an improvement in quality assurance processes and attention of program members to quality issues will lead to improved academic outcomes (Dill, 2000, p. 203).

In some jurisdictions academic audits are conducted by government-appointed, quality assurance organizations, and so can also be another form of government regulation. However, academic audits have a number of features that respect and reinforce institutional autonomy, support institutional diversity, are flexible and least intrusive, and may be an alternative (or even antidote) to competition (Woodhouse, 2003, p. 136). As a consequence, audit approaches particularly lend themselves to academic self-regulation, where a collectivity of universities is so inclined.

Academic audit procedures are now in place in Ontario (for under-graduate programs), Quebec, and the Maritime provinces (New Brunswick, Nova Scotia, and Prince Edward Island). In each case, universities under-take to review the academic quality of their academic programs according to standards established by the external body responsible for the audit (UPRAC, CREPUQ and MPHEC respectively).

Key Components of Quality Assurance Processes

Experience worldwide demonstrates that effective quality assurance processes contain the following three key components:

Self-study: Program review or appraisal is not something done only by outsiders to the program. It rests in the first instance on the self-appraisal by members of the program. A necessary part of any self-appraisal (or external assessment) is the collection, presentation, and analysis of relevant data about the program. In an attempt to avoid intrusiveness and to allow programs to determine for themselves what data is most relevant to their program, some quality assurance processes have left it to the university to decide for itself what data to collect and address in the review. However, Dill found that open-ended requests for documentation produce large volumes of material less likely to be effective for the institution and its program, and for the external reviewers, than defined material upon which the members of the program have reflected carefully (Dill, 2000, pp. 196-197). The OCGS By-Laws and Procedures Governing Appraisals and the UPRAC Review and Audit Guidelines both require that the process begin with a self-appraisal, and identify the elements to be addressed and the information to be provided and interpreted in the self-study document.

UPRAC auditors have concluded that nothing is more important to the successful review of any program than the self-appraisal by its members. However, nothing is more variable in its quality and effectiveness than that self-appraisal. Ineffective self-appraisals are descriptive rather than reflective, analytical, self-critical and evaluative; loaded with data that is presented rather than analyzed; defensive or self-justifying rather than aimed at quality improvement; prepared in a formulaic or mechanical way, as if completing a checklist rather than demonstrating that the members of the program are sensitive to and thinking about the context, mission, and objectives of the program; and written by the chair without evidence of buy-in (or sometimes even knowledge) of faculty and students rather than resulting from a participatory self-critical process. Ineffective self-appraisals are most unlikely to lead to quality improvement, while good self-studies necessarily address quality improvement, and make the reports of external reviewers more useful to that purpose.

Peer Review: External quality assessment necessarily involves external review. Effective quality assurance processes, whether external or internal, involve one or more external reviewers who report on a site visit. Some program-review processes also use an internal reviewer, from the institution but from a different program. Such internal reviewers normally serve as members of the site visit team, and thus contribute to the joint review team's report, but may in some processes visit and report separately.

Judgement/decision: Effective quality assurance reaches closure. A decision is made by the responsible body (whether that is external, as in the OCGS Appraisal Committee or an Accreditation Commission, or internal, as in a senate committee or the vice-president academic or dean) as to the quality of the program and any needed remedial actions. It is important that quality improvements indeed occur, rather than linger in some limbo of wishful thinking. There needs to be a mechanism for action to determine which of the recommendations arising from the self-study and the reviewers' reports will be implemented to what extent, and by whom, and on what schedule.

Characteristics of Good Practice

Effective quality assurance processes have several common characteristics.

First, they are *mission-based.* They respect the diversity and autonomy of institutions and programs by assessing quality against their mission and objectives rather than against some inflexible standard. At the same time different missions and objectives do not become an excuse for inadequate performance, because the standards of the discipline are brought to bear by the external reviewers. Mission-based assessment means that it is important, and possible, to have high standards without standardization.

They seek *quality improvement* as well as assurance that threshold standards are met. Government regulatory approaches are focused more on compliance with rules, codes and regulations, and while they may use the vocabulary of quality improvement, their practices more frequently require demonstration that specified standards are met, not that improvements above those standards are being suggested and implemented. Professional accreditation varies considerably, but in general is primarily concerned with preparation of the graduate for professional practice, and so the quality of the program is seen as an instrumental means of achieving the intended outcome of producing professionally competent graduates, rather than as an end. In both cases the goal of the exercise for those being reviewed or accredited is all too often to "pass" by meeting the standards, rather than to improve.

They are *cyclical* rather than indefinite. Program quality is not to be determined once and then never reconsidered. Good intentions may not be fulfilled. Key faculty can depart or shift interests, and curriculum and equipment can become outmoded. Furthermore, quality improvement requires recurring review. Some programs, and some faculty members, may indeed review and improve their quality on an ongoing basis, without the stimulus of a program review or appraisal. But experience clearly demonstrates that the occasion of a scheduled program review or appraisal concentrates the mind. The maintenance and improvement of quality is more likely to be the focus of collective attention in the context of a program review or appraisal than if left to occur spontaneously amid all the other pressures of academic life.

They serve a public *accountability* function. Students and taxpayers invest substantial amounts of money in higher education, and there are increasing public pressures on universities to demonstrate that the quality of the education resulting from that investment is of high quality, and that desired outcomes are being achieved. Accountability is served by the demonstration that every program is subject to review according to appropriate standards of quality and specified procedures. Accountability is not validated by the number of programs that fail to meet standards, and so are closed or sanctioned, but by the seriousness of the standards and procedures by which all programs are assessed, and by the quality of the programs that have been successfully reviewed.

They emphasize student learning, and the *learning objectives and outcomes* of the program. Earlier quality assurance processes placed great importance on inputs, and there were, and continue to be, excellent reasons for doing so. Inputs are essential to the quality of any program, and can be objectively measured and assessed. Without a sufficient number of qualified faculty members, a program cannot succeed. Without a suitable research environment, driven by faculty researchers who are intellectual leaders in the discipline in question, the program lacks intellectual vitality. Without a suitable library, or laboratory facilities and equipment, or learning and study space, or other inputs, intended learning outcomes cannot be achieved. But it must also be recognized that similar resource inputs can be put to different use by different programs and institutions. Some may make the most of relatively scarce resources, while others may squander their abundance. Inputs alone are necessary but not sufficient for quality. Similarly, outputs such as the number, rate, and average time to completion of graduates are crucial measures, but may be correlates rather than consequences of the quality of the program. The graduation rate tells us how many students completed the program, but not how much they learned from it. The employment rate of graduates may tell us more about the state of the economy than about the quality of the program. In recent years increasing attention has been paid to learning objectives and learning outcomes as central to quality assurance.

Those who have been concerned with student learning began with the assessment of skills or competencies possessed by graduates. However, an absolute level of competence may not be an appropriate indicator of the quality of a program, because that competence may be independent of the program, that is, it may have existed before entry to the program, or have been achieved despite rather than because of the program. Attention then turned to assessment of the learning that actually occurred in the program, or the "value-added" by the program. But that too is an inadequate indicator of quality if, despite the amount of learning, the intended learning objectives were not realized. For example, Braskamp and Braskamp have pointed out that substantial progress in flight training may be of cold comfort if a pilot has become much better at getting a plane to take off, but still hasn't mastered the intricacies of a safe landing (1997, p. 6). Accordingly, the quality assurance world is increasingly concerned with learning objectives and learning outcomes.

The simplest way to understand learning objectives and learning outcomes is by the question: "What do you want graduates of your program to have learned and/or accomplished, and how will you know that they have learned and/or accomplished it?" Self-appraisal should engage every member of the program in formulating a collective answer to that question, and every individual instructor should pose and answer that question in the context of his or her course.

So what are appropriate learning objectives and outcomes, and what evidence suitably shows that they have been achieved? In identifying learning outcome indicators, it is important to remember that the unit of analysis in quality assurance is the program, not the student. Program quality is not demonstrated by more and more testing of students, but by the relationship of a program's faculty expertise, curricular content, admission requirements, mode of delivery, bases of evaluation of student performance, and commitment of resources to its goals, learning objectives and intended learning outcomes. Programs that know what they intend their students to achieve have a better chance of having their students actually achieve what is intended, and of understanding whether those intended outcomes can be achieved more effectively. There is a vast difference among disciplines, and it is much easier to define and measure learning outcomes in disciplines with specific observable skills than in disciplines marked by more subjective kinds of knowledge and understanding. Evidence that certain outcomes have been achieved is often accompanied by the assumption that other desirable but less observable outcomes are also achieved — but this is only an assumption, and indicators must be carefully and appropriately chosen to make that assumption explicit. It is important to remember that performance indicators are only indicators, and do not exhaustively encompass and measure all the complex aspects of student learning. But it is also important to remember that the most important aspect of incorporating learning objectives and outcomes into the quality assurance process is to raise the consciousness among all faculty members about the learning objectives in their courses and programs, and about even partial indicators that the intended outcomes have been achieved. Remember the question "What do you want graduates of your program to have learned and/or accomplished, and how will you know that they have learned and/or accomplished it?"

A workshop on student learning outcomes summarized the types of direct and indirect evidence of learning outcomes that is increasingly being considered in US accreditation processes (Council for Higher Education Accreditation, 2002). Indirect evidence may include portfolios and work samples, follow-up of graduates, employer ratings of graduates, and self-reported growth by graduates. Direct evidence of student learning outcomes is the result of a process deliberately designed for that purpose, and may include capstone performances, professional or clinical performances, third-party testing (e.g., licensure or professional certification examinations), and faculty-designed examinations. The workshop offered the following principles:

- Comprehensiveness: submitted evidence should cover knowledge and skills throughout the course or program.
- Multiple judgements: submitted evidence should involve more than one source or involve multiple judgements of student performance.
- Multiple dimensions: submitted evidence should provide information on multiple dimensions of student performance — i.e., they should yield more than a summative grade.

- Directness: submitted evidence should involve at least one type based on direct observation or demonstration of student capabilities — i.e., they should involve more than simply a self-report (ibid., p. 2).

These components and characteristics are evident in the *Principles of Institutional Quality Assurance in Canadian Higher Education* approved by the Board of Directors of the Association of Universities and Colleges of Canada in January 2004.

Standards, Factors and Elements

Well-regarded quality assurance processes define the standards or criteria that must be addressed both during the self-appraisal and by external reviewers. However, in some cases what are called standards are actually factors to be taken into consideration, while elsewhere there have been systematic attempts to define degree level standards or classification frameworks. For purposes of comparison, the standards and policies of US regional accreditation will first be described. This will be contrasted with the international trend towards degree level standards. Then more thorough attention will be given to the OCGS and UPRAC processes.

US regional accreditation standards encompass such major higher education activities as: curriculum, faculty, academic standards, student services, academic support for students, financial capacity, facilities, organization and governance, and expected student achievement (i.e., student learning outcomes). Accreditation also addresses expected university policies on such issues as conflict of interest, academic freedom, release of information, general education, institutional autonomy, and collegial governance (Council for Higher Education Accreditation, 2003b). As will become evident, there is great commonality in the factors and elements addressed in other quality assurance processes, but government quality assurance agencies in many non-North American countries consider that US-style institutional accreditation lacks explicit academic standards.

By contrast, elsewhere in the world the trend is towards program accreditation or assessment, involving the definition of degree level standards that provide a framework in which to place proliferating institutions, programs and credentials, and to facilitate classification of programs, as well as transfer credit and credential recognition.[2] These standards in most countries have been developed at government initiative, and have been built both from the bottom up (i.e., from specific bodies of knowledge, competencies, and skills to more generic ones), and from the top down (i.e., degrees of separation from the creation of new knowledge). The governments of Europe have set a target date of May 2005 for the development of a common Europe-wide qualifications framework.

The UPRAC Guidelines (section 3.3) specify that the review of undergraduate programs should address the following elements:

1. consistency of the program with the general objectives of the institution's mission and academic plans, and with the standards, educational goals, and learning objectives of the degree;
2. appropriateness and effectiveness of the admission requirements, for example, preparation and achievement, for the learning objectives of the institution and the program;
3. appropriateness of the program's structure and curriculum to meet its learning objectives;
4. appropriateness and effectiveness of the mode of delivery including, where applicable, distance or online delivery, to meet the program's learning objectives;
5. appropriateness of the methods used for the evaluation of student progress and, where possible, consideration of the effectiveness of the methods used;
6. the level of achievement of students, consistent with the educational goals for the program and the degree, and institutional standards;
7. appropriateness and effectiveness of the utilization of the existing human/physical/financial resources;
8. definition of indicators that provide evidence of quality of faculty, student clientele (applications and registrations), student quality, and the outcomes of the program (graduation rate, length of studies, etc.) and achievement of its learning objectives. (The indicators are invariably best developed by the unit whose program is under review, but examples of possible indicators could be provided in the institutional

---

[2]For example, the Australian Qualifications Framework has guidelines for the Bachelor Degree, the Graduate Certificate, the Graduate Diploma, the Master's Degree and the Doctoral Degree, while the Irish National Framework of Qualifications has 23 different steps.

policy for undergraduate program reviews. Data on indicators should be collected over an extended time period rather than simply once each review cycle, and the results should be discussed in the self-study as a means to enhance program quality and student satisfaction.)

The purpose of the UPRAC audit is to look for assurance that the university's policies and practices explicitly address these elements, and the objectives and structures described in other sections, and that each specified component is covered in the university's policy. The audit does not assess the quality of programs themselves, or judge the "correctness" of any particular objective or outcome, but rather assesses the extent to which the institution's quality assurance policies and practices comply with these guidelines.

The OCGS By-Laws and Procedures Governing Appraisals specify that following criteria of good quality:

- The program's objectives are appropriate and are being met.
- The core faculty provide intellectual leadership in the disciplinary area(s) of the program through active engagement in research and scholarship.
- The faculty complement is appropriate for the level and scope of the program and its identified fields of strength, and there are appropriate provisions and/or plans for its continuing vitality.
- The curriculum design is appropriate.
- The resources, such as laboratories, libraries, computer facilities and research support, are appropriate.
- Enrolments are commensurate with the resources available.
- Students complete the program in a timely fashion.
- There is evidence of appropriate financial support for students.
- There is demonstration of the quality of the educational experience of students, including intellectual development and the acquisition of relevant skills.

It is clear from the words used in these criteria, such as "appropriate" and "commensurate", that OCGS appraisal is not simply a mechanical exercise of data description. Data is essential, and the by-laws specify the nature and format of that data. But the data must be analyzed and interpreted, and academic judgement exercised, in the light of the defined learning objectives of the program. Several examples may be useful.

David Leyton-Brown

First, the criterion that students complete the program in a timely fashion rests upon the analysis of data concerning graduation rates and times to completion. But the interpretation of the data is not self-evident. There are differences among disciplines, especially with regard to average times to completion. There are differences of program structure and intended duration. It is commonly considered that many graduate programs take too long on average to complete, and that average times to completion should be reduced. However, shorter times to completion are not always preferable. It might be widely agreed that seven years to complete a PhD is too long, and that six years would be preferable, and, other things being equal, five years even better. But would four years be better still? What about three years, or two, or even one? Are the e-mail spam offers of a PhD "from prestigious non-accredited universities" in one or two months the standard of quality we should all seek to emulate? Obviously not. Clearly judgement must be exercised about the reasonable length of time in which appropriate learning and learning outcomes can be achieved.

Another example is the criterion concerning the appropriate faculty complement for the program. There is no simple mathematical formula to define how many faculty are "enough". That depends upon many factors, such as the level and scope of the program and its identified fields of strength, but also the research accomplishments and experience of the faculty, the extent to which their graduate teaching and supervision is concentrated in this single program, and within the program in a single field of strength, or dispersed across more than one field or even more than one program. However, judgements about the appropriate critical mass of faculty to sustain the quality and viability of a program, and of each of its identified fields of strength, have been made since the inception of the appraisal process in 1965. Those judgements rest upon the premise that, if students are attracted to the program because of the advertising of an area of strength in which they want to work, those students had better find that strength in place when they arrive. There should be courses available in the program's curriculum that relate to the identified field, and opportunities for thesis research with adequate supervision on issues in that field. And the critical mass of faculty should be sufficient to sustain that strength even in the light of sabbaticals or other leaves, administrative release for some faculty, etc. Thus the appropriate faculty complement is not a simple head count exercise, but an analysis requiring academic judgement.

Finally, consider the criterion concerning the quality of the educational experience of students, including intellectual development and the acquisition of relevant skills. This obviously calls for the identification of learning objectives regarding the nature and level of intellectual development and of relevant skills. However, it does even more than this. The quality of the educational experience of graduate students recognizes that a graduate program is more than the courses taken, and even the research conducted. A quality graduate educational experience requires intellectual interaction with faculty and other students outside class as well as in class. It requires a meaningful intellectual community in which the culture of research and scholarship is advanced. In one particular standard which has become a "line in the sand" for the appraisal process, it recognizes that the graduate learning experience is different than that at the undergraduate level — not only more advanced, but more equal and interactive. A different learning experience is found when a group of six graduate students cover advanced material in a seminar setting with their professor, than when those same six graduate students cover that same material with the same professor in a class that also includes 20 or 30 undergraduate students. As a result, the OCGS by-laws (section 10.4.4) famously require that the number of combined courses in which undergraduate students predominate should be no more than one-third of the total number of courses required for the degree.

Complicating Factors

Academic quality is a good thing, and the assurance of that quality should also be a good thing, especially if it conforms to the characteristics of good practice above. However, it must be recognized that there are tensions that complicate this situation.

First, members of a program or department being reviewed understandably confront mixed or even conflicting incentives. University administrations may find quality assurance processes of great use in clarifying areas of academic strength and weakness, and in examining the effective use of existing resources (e.g., the appropriate balance between undergraduate and graduate teaching, the fit between faculty appointments and enrolment, etc.). Program reviews or appraisals can identify areas of strength on which to build, or weaknesses in need of strengthening. Some faculty members see program reviews as the periodic opportunity to argue for additional resources, and seek to impress external reviewers with the need for such improvements. But this practice can be akin to riding a tiger — reviewers, and administrations, can be given the impression that not only are improvements (and additional resources) needed, but that in the absence of those improvements the program is not of acceptable quality. What is more, in times of fiscal constraint when university administrations are making difficult decisions about where to allocate or reallocate scarce resources, a self-critical examination of weaknesses to be improved may run the risk of loss of resources from a department perceived to be weakening in favour of one that sounds more positive and forward-moving (and possibly one where external financial resources may also be available, such as higher deregulated tuition or matching private sector funding). Academic decisions should be made for academic reasons, but administrators are charged to administer. Core academic programs (such as an undergraduate program in English or Mathematics) must be offered, and so identified weaknesses must be corrected. But other programs, such as those with low or declining enrolments, may not enjoy the same sense of insulation from resource reductions. External authorities like the OCGS Appraisal Committee, and university administrators often state that a program is likely to be viewed more favourably if it openly identifies its problems and presents considered plans for improvement, than if it conceals or denies those problems. However, at the departmental level, faculty members may fear to run that risk.

Second, engagement in quality assurance processes requires time and effort. Even those characteristics of good practice discussed above are demanding, and there are horror stories in some jurisdictions of enormously burdensome exercises that delivered outcomes far less than would have been warranted by the work involved. Even under the best of conditions, faculty members may experience "review fatigue", because of the possible multiple requirements for an undergraduate program review, graduate program appraisals, one or more professional accreditations, repeated university academic planning exercises, and at least one end-of-term review, all within five to seven years. While some of the data required for these different quality assurance processes may be the same (though needing annual updating), some data, and certainly some analysis will be different. Trying to synchronize two or more of these exercises can multiply the workload to unmanageable levels, but spreading them out can make the work never-ending. Quality assurance may be a good thing, but too much of a good thing is not.

Concluding Remarks

It should be clear that quality assurance processes, and especially those of academic self-regulation, are founded upon the same academic values that characterize universities. Their standards are real, but their effect can be more profound in the improvement of quality than in the certification that quality standards have been met. There are solid academic reasons for the data that is required for the key components and good practice characteristics described above. Most importantly, quality assurance processes such as OCGS appraisal or UPRAC undergraduate program review provide structured opportunities for members of a program to reflect upon their success in reaching their program's learning objectives, and to benefit from advice and feedback from noted experts in the discipline. If quality assurance processes are welcomed rather than resented, and all members of a program actively engage in the self-analysis and articulation of learning objectives and learning outcomes, then chances are greatly increased that they will be positive and productive experiences. Even more important, chances are greatly increased that the result will be the assurance and improvement of quality.

References

Braskamp, L.A. and D.C. Braskamp. 1997. "The Pendulum Swing of Standards and Evidence", *The CHEA Chronicle* 1(5).

Council for Higher Education Accreditation. 2002. "Student Learning Outcomes Workshop, March 4, 2002", *The CHEA Chronicle* 5(2), 1-4.

_____. 2003a. *CHEA Almanac of External Quality Review 2003*. Washington, DC.

_____. 2003b. "The Value of Accreditation: Four Pivotal Roles", *CHEA Letter from the President*, May.

Dill, D.D. 2000. "Designing Academic Audit: Lessons Learned in Europe and Asia", *Quality in Higher Education* 6(3).

Woodhouse, D. 2003. "Quality Improvement Through Quality Audit", *Quality in Higher Education* 9(2).

Thoughts on Financing Postsecondary Education

Clément Lemelin

I have been asked, among other things, to provide you with a Quebec perspective. It is difficult for me to show any originality: people from Quebec belong to the same Canadian federation as people from Nova Scotia, they use the same data as people from Ontario and, mind you, some of them are advocates of a system of income-contingent loans.

A federal parliamentary committee on higher education will convene next week in Quebec. Among the themes it wishes to consider are the sources of, and the federal government's involvement in, university funding. A consensus among witnesses, one of those consensuses that people in Quebec are so fond of, can be predicted. University administrators, students, and professors will all agree that, compared to the rest of Canada, universities in Quebec are underfunded by no less than $375 million, a figure reached by a working committee of representatives of the Conference of Rectors and Principals of Quebec Universities and the Ministry of Education.

It is also expected that most of the witnesses will ask the Quebec government to increase its subsidies to universities by $375 million, an obvious *non sequitur*. If in comparison with the rest of Canada, $375 million are lacking in Quebec universities, it is also true that the government already spends $255 million *more*. But the witnesses have, so to speak, been invited to make this request by the minister of education, who renewed the government's pledge to keep student fees frozen at their less than $1,700 level per year. Such is the world!

What could the members of the parliamentary committee and their witnesses learn from the three texts presented at this session?

The first lesson to draw from Mr. Snowdon's text is, of course, to be cautious when using data. That being said, I was not utterly shocked when reading the first part of his paper. Last year, as a member of a committee on the financing of adult education in Quebec, I considered using data on vocational training published by Statistics Canada. I gave up quickly. If data on university education is muddy, what is the word to characterize data on trade education?

Mr. Snowdon shows the change in the relative importance of sources of revenue over the past 30 years. The share of provincial governments has decreased from 70 to 45%. Even though the figures are probably different in Quebec, this should be used as a reminder that the Quebec government cannot anymore pretend to be able to bear most if not all the direct costs of university education.

Mr. Snowdon's data also shows a recent increase in the share of the federal government, which leads us to David Cameron's paper.

Members of the parliamentary committee would, of course, have read this paper with much interest, since the involvement of federal government in university funding is one of the five themes submitted to its witnesses. Mr. Cameron's description of this involvement in recent years is impressive; it should remind us that university resources should not be evaluated by referring only to provincial subsidies for general operating expenditures.

That being said, I must confess that I have had trouble in gauging Mr. Cameron's opinion on this involvement. While reading the first part of his paper, I had the impression that for more than 40 years Quebec had been an *empêcheur de danser en rond*. How do we say it in English? A spoilsport? A wet blanket? But then, while reading the second part of his paper, I realized that according to Mr. Cameron, the federal involvement should be received with mixed blessings. I am not clear about why he has reservations. Is it because it brings instability to universities with its one-shot injections or commitments? Is it because it changes the balance between teaching and research? Or is it because, with its emphasis on subsidizing individuals, it could tip the balance of power between providers and users, in favour of the latter? This question leads us to Nicholas Barr's paper.

By the way, the cause of the involvement of the federal government in university education and various other provincial jurisdictions has been given a name in Quebec: fiscal imbalance.

I have read Mr. Barr's various texts with much interest. I agree with most of his analysis but, following the rules of the game, I will insist on my main point of disagreement, the income-contingent loans proposition.

This proposition, which is a very old one in the economic literature, has, at times, received support from both the left and the right, which is sufficient to lead us to beware. The problem with income-contingent loans is that they can be given many different forms. They therefore mean different things to different people. Mr. Barr is well aware of this problem. In one of his texts, he shows that interest subsidies cost no less than £800 million a year in Great Britain.

There is a sort of double talk over income-contingent loans. To take an example from Quebec, where students are deeply divided over this issue, some students at times say that they are ready to pay a larger share of the direct cost of their studies. When one starts asking for further details, one quickly discovers that what students have in mind is simply the possibility of being exempted from repayment of their loans if their income is not large enough. But who will then pay these unpaid loans? The rest of society or the rest of former students? This question is of great importance since the proposed systems of income-contingent loans are supposed to be universal. They could become very costly to taxpayers if students are responsible only for their own loans. I did not find the word mutualization in Mr. Barr's texts. Perhaps it does not exist in English.

Many questions are to be asked, and answered, before even contemplating implementing such a system. For example:

- Which interest rate should be used?
- Are students to be charged interest from the moment they borrow?
- What income should be considered as the basis for repayment?
- Is there a minimum income below which no reimbursement is made?
- Is all income or only that part above the minimum used as the basis for repayment?
- Is the system self-financed? In other words, are borrowers collectively responsible for repaying their debt in its entirety?
- Is there a limit to the period of reimbursement?
- Is there a maximum to the reimbursement: 110, 125, 150% of the value of the loan?
- Is there a limit to the loans and what needs should be covered?

- Is the system universal or selective? Are all students allowed to participate?
- Are students forced to participate, which raises the question of adverse selection?
- What do we do with dropouts?
- Does the rate of reimbursement vary with the sector of study and/or the amount lent?

All these questions matter, since important distributive effects can be generated by income-contingent loans, between former students and the rest of society, or among different borrowers if loans are mutualized. In the latter case, the main beneficiaries will, of course, be those people who have a high debt-income ratio. But it does not mean that people with low income will necessarily benefit from such a system. As students accumulate years of schooling, their expected earnings increase, but at a rate that is much lower than their loans (see Caron, 2000).

One should therefore be very careful before implementing such a system: it can become very costly. Is it the devil or God who hides in the details? I do not know. But one thing is sure: hell is paved with good intentions.[1]

References

Caron, G. 2000. "Des prêts aux étudiants remboursables selon le revenu: une perspective québécoise". Montreal: Département des sciences économiques, Université du Québec à Montréal. Mémoire de maîtrise.

---

[1] In his 2004–05 budget speech, the minister of finance announced that a system of income-contingent loans will be implemented in Quebec. At the same time, he announced that more than $60 million will be cut in financial aid to students.

Section IV

Problems Faced by Postsecondary Education Sector in Canada

Family Income and Participation in Postsecondary Education

Miles Corak, Garth Lipps and John Zhao

Introduction

In no policy area is the interplay between the social goals of efficiency and equity as evident as in education. A highly skilled workforce has long been seen as important in promoting economic prosperity, with theorists and policymakers alike emphasizing the contribution of human capital to economic growth. Many observers feel this is becoming increasingly so. At the same time it is very hard to abstract from social goals related to equality of opportunity and a more inclusive society, and for many an important goal of the education system is to promote citizenship and active participation in society. For example, the federal government's innovation strategy

An earlier version of this paper was presented to the Statistics Canada Economic conference and the Canadian Employment Research Forum conference both held in Ottawa in May 2003, to the Canada Millennium Scholarship Foundation Conference held in Ottawa in October 2003, to the University of Guelph Task Force on Access to Post-secondary Education, and to the John Deutsch Institute conference on Higher Education in Canada. Comments from Michael Baker, Kevin Bishop, Dwayne Benjamin, Nicole Fortin, David Gray, Herb O'Heron, Gary Solon, Alex Usher, and the editors of this volume are appreciated. The responsibility for the content of this paper rests solely with the authors and in particular should not be attributed to Statistics Canada or to UNICEF.

highlights both of these goals, emphasizing the importance of skills and learning in fostering innovation and growth in an era of the so-called "knowledge" economy, but in a way that encourages the full participation of all groups in society (Canada, 2002). This implies there are two possible directions for the future of the education system: one in which the concerns of the marketplace are traded off against those of citizenship and inclusion, and another in which trade-offs are somehow not made and both goals are pursued simultaneously. Access to postsecondary education is one area that offers the clearest reflection of these two options: do we want higher education to promote excellence in a way that focuses resources on the few; do we want it to be universal and offer everyone the opportunity to participate; or can we have both excellence and inclusion?

In fact, the federal government has pledged that among other things "one hundred percent of high school graduates have the opportunity to participate in some form of post-secondary education" (Canada, 2002, p. 34). This milestone promises universal access to postsecondary education and as such speaks most directly to a growing worry that — at the very time its private and social returns are perceived to be increasing — higher education will become the domain of those from more privileged backgrounds. On the one hand, about 85% of Canadian parents hope their children will pursue postsecondary studies. This aspiration is shared across the income distribution, with 80% of those parents with less than $30,000 of income also holding this expectation (Statistics Canada, 2001a). On the other hand, the climate surrounding the financing of postsecondary education has changed significantly, with the 1990s witnessing notably sharp increases in university tuition fees. In this climate, lower-income families may not be as well positioned as higher-income families to realize their expectations. Statistics Canada (ibid.) also reports that less than one-fifth of families with incomes of less than $30,000 are saving for the post-secondary education of their children, but about two-thirds of those with more than $80,000 are doing so. For both these reasons — high expectations of participation and increases in the potential financial burden — "access" has become an important policy issue in understanding how higher education can promote growth and efficiency, and at the same time equality of opportunity and social inclusion.

The objective of our research is to inform this understanding by examining the relationship between family background, particularly family income, and the participation of the young in postsecondary education. What is the nature and strength of the relationship between postsecondary participation and family income, and how has it changed over the course of the last two decades or so? In other words, is higher education increasingly the purview of the well-to-do? This obvious and relevant question is surprisingly difficult to answer, in large part because of data limitations. We use two complementary approaches in the hope of overcoming these limitations and offering an accurate estimate of the correlation between family income and postsecondary participation. In addition, it should be noted that we use the term access to refer very broadly to participation in postsecondary education and at times more specifically to university. As such our analysis does not refer to the particular constraints that students may face in choosing their institution or field of study. The question as to whether the relationship between family background and entry into particular disciplines or institutions has changed would relate to a much narrower sense of the term access and is beyond the scope of our study.

In the next section we begin by documenting the extent of the changes in university tuition fees, and in a limited way some of the possible responses of students. As an example, average arts tuition started increasing significantly in 1990 and by the 2000/01 academic year was 86% higher. At the same time the 1990s also witnessed a significant variation in fees across provinces, across fields of study, and even between institutions. The most notable response by students has been to increase borrowing, particularly by those from parts of the country other than Quebec. This in part reflects an easing of borrowing limitations introduced to the Canada Student Loan program in 1994.

In the following section we review a number of Canadian studies that examine the relationship between family background and postsecondary participation, most notably that by Christofides, Cirello and Hoy (2001). The major limitation of this body of work is that it pertains to a period during the 1980s or early 1990s before the introduction of a higher tuition climate. It also does not make a distinction between participation in colleges and vocational schools on the one hand and universities on the other, nor does it distinguish the experience of young men from young women. Our analysis is intended to examine these three dimensions. In this section we also discuss the methods and data we employ. We use two alternative datasets and approaches, each with certain weaknesses, but which taken together may offer, we argue, an accurate estimate of the association between family income and postsecondary participation and how it has changed from the 1980s up to 2000.

Section four offers the results of our estimations and attempts to address a number of concerns inherent in our definitions, data, and approach. Our principle findings are three in number. First, we document slight increases in the participation of individuals from lower-income households in university. Individuals from higher-income families are certainly much more likely to be university students. But this has been a long-standing tendency, and if anything the gap between high- and low-income participation rates has narrowed slightly. This in part reflects not just rises in the participation rates of those from the lowest-income families, but also declines in the rates of those from middle-income families. In contrast, there are no significant differences in college participation rates across income classes. Second, the association between parental income and university participation did in fact become stronger, but only to about the mid-1990s just after tuition fees first experienced substantial increases. The strength of the relationship has weakened since then. According to one set of estimates we produce, every 10% increase in parental income was associated with a 2.7% increase in the probability of university attendance during the mid-1980s; with a 4.3% increase in 1994; but with only a 2.5% increase in 2000. Further, the results are more muted when the broader postsecondary system — including colleges and vocational institutions — is analyzed. However, these results pertain to women, and our third major finding has to do with the fact that the patterns for young men are different. In particular, the run-up in the correlation is not as great, and the subsequent decline is quicker.

In sum, we find no evidence that the association between family income and postsecondary participation has increased during the latter half of the 1990s, indeed just the opposite. This may reflect the fact that students have responded in a number of different ways, most notably by borrowing more. If there was a period of a tighter link between family income and participation it was in the early 1990s when tuition fees began increasing, but during which policy changes easing borrowing limits and offering increases in other forms of financial assistance had not yet been put into place. We also find a tendency for men to choose college education over university education. As a result, the latter part of the 1990s should not be characterized as a period in which the university system has become the domain of the relatively more privileged any more than it has been in the past, but rather a period in which the costs of higher education have shifted at least in part onto students. This is also a period in which the system has become more differentiated as the costs of programs varied more substantially between provinces, fields of study, and institutions. If there is a growing concern to be dealt with in terms of access, future research should examine the consequences of this differentiation. Even though globally all Canadians have access to some form of postsecondary education, are particular institutic s and particular fields of study — perhaps those more valued in the labour market — the domain of students with higher income backgrounds? Future research should also focus on the factors earlier in the lives of young people that place them in the fortunate circumstance during their late teens of having to choose whether or not to participate in postsecondary education.

The Evolution of University Financing and the Responses of Students

The main source of revenue for universities comes from provincial grants and contracts, and the two panels of Figure 1 illustrate that there have been three distinct periods in the evolution of this funding. The first is a period of steadily declining funding on a per student basis, reflecting stable funding in absolute terms during a period of rising enrolments. This began in the mid-to-late 1970s and continued to the 1985/86 academic year, when enrolments went from about 240,000 to 472,000. Throughout this period universities received in real terms about $6.3 billion annually, but on a per student basis this reflected a decline from about $20,000 to $13,000. The second period is characterized by increases in funding levels and a resulting plateauing of per student funding. This period ends in 1992/93 when increases in absolute transfers peaked at about $7.3 billion after seven consecutive annual increases. During this period the number of full-time equivalent university students increased from 472,000 to 575,000. The third period begins thereafter, and is characterized by declines in both absolute and per student funding. By the end of the 1990s, per student funding, at just under $11,000, is almost half of what it was 25 years earlier and reflects a return to absolute funding levels of the 1980s and late 1970s.

In this context universities have, among other things, increased the fees they charge students, the most important element of which is tuition for credit courses. As an example, Figure 2 charts developments in tuition fees for arts programs, which fell in real terms during the 1970s, remained flat during the 1980s, and then began to increase sharply after the 1989/90 academic year to reach historic highs by the end of the 1990s. Average weighted arts tuition fees for the entire country (expressed in $2001) rose from $1,866 in 1990/91 to a peak of $3,456 in 1999/00, after which they remained relatively constant. These Canada-wide developments mask the

Figure 1: University Revenues from Provincial Grants and Contracts, 1972/73 to 1998/99

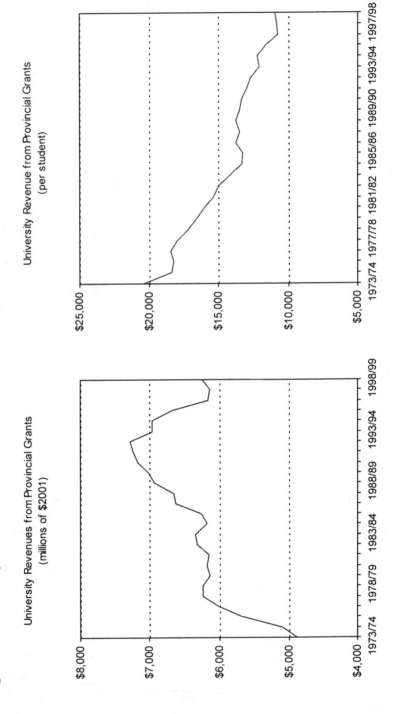

Figure 2: Average Arts Tuition Fees, Canada Provinces, 1972/73 to 2001/02 (weighted and expressed in $2001)

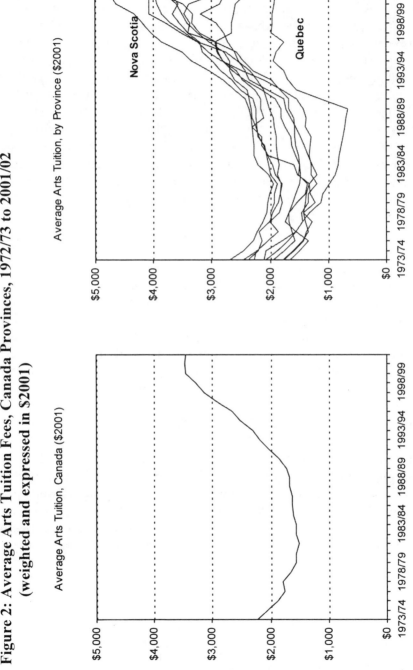

Average Arts Tuition, by Province ($2001)

Average Arts Tuition, Canada ($2001)

fact that fees are significantly different between the provinces and have increased at different rates. They rose in all regions during the early 1990s, but students in Nova Scotia have consistently paid the highest fees and have also faced the largest increases. Particularly sharp increases also occurred in Ontario and Alberta. Students from Quebec experienced steadily declining fees (from $2,215 in 1972/73 to a low of $663 in 1989/90) followed by a near doubling between 1989/90 and 1990/91. But with an average tuition of just under $2,000 in 2001/02, students in Quebec still pay the lowest tuition for arts programs. Towards the end of the period, average arts tuition in British Columbia, Manitoba, and Newfoundland and Labrador all declined, but continued to increase elsewhere. These changes led to a substantial increase in the dispersion of tuition fees between provinces. In 1978/79 the difference between the highest and lowest tuition was $1,130; by 2001/02 it had grown to $2,820.

A similar story can be told by field of study and even by institution. University tuition fees have increased for all fields but not uniformly, with some professional programs experiencing particularly sharp increases during the 1990s. Between 1995/96 and 2001/02 average fees in dentistry more than doubled (increasing from $3,389 to $8,491), while those for medicine went from an average of $3,207 in 1995/96 to $6,654 in 2001/02. During the 1990s increases in fees for law and graduate studies closely mirrored increases in overall arts tuition fees, and while those for education increased during the 1990s they did so to a relatively much smaller degree (from $1,887 in 1990/91 to $2,892 in 2001/02). On average, education students paid the lowest tuition fees of any field of study between 1991/92 and 2001/02. At the same time it should be noted that not all institutions responded in the same way. To cite only one example, between 1994/95 and 2001/02 tuition fees for dentistry at the University of Toronto quadrupled (increasing from $3,235 in 1994/95 to $13,230 in 2001/02), but the fees charged by the University of British Columbia actually dropped (from $4,300 in 1994/95 to $3,740 in 2001/02). Similarly, tuition for medicine at the University of Toronto more than tripled from $3,484 in 1995/96 to $11,550 in 2001/02, while at the University of British Columbia they fell over the same period from $4,399 to $3,740.[1]

---

[1]The source for this data is Statistics Canada, Tuition Fees and Living Accommodations at Canadian Universities Survey. Detailed information on tuition fees is available from this source for a host of disciplines for each degree-granting institution in Canada from 1979 to 2002.

Miles Corak, Garth Lipps and John Zhao

How have students responded to these changes? Some of the possible responses include: choosing a different field of study or a different institution, borrowing more from public or private sources, working more during the summer or during studies, pursuing part-time studies or otherwise taking longer to complete studies, saving on other aspects of education costs like living arrangements by living at home longer, deciding not to pursue university education and going instead to college, or finally, not pursuing postsecondary education at all and entering the labour market sooner. It may well be that access to particular institutions or fields of study has changed and that the burden of adjustment has fallen more on students from some income groups than others. The result may be that the relationship between family income and participation is now different by field of study or institution. We do not use the term access in this narrow sense, nor do we offer a full assessment of all the possible changes in student behaviour. Our focus is rather on access in the broadest sense of the term: has participation in higher education changed and how is this related to family income after all of these choices and adjustments have been made.

The final outcome of the decisions students have made in response to all of the factors — not just tuition fees — they consider when choosing their level of education is illustrated in Figure 3. Overall participation rates in postsecondary education for 18 to 24-year-olds are plotted from 1979 to 2002. In this chart postsecondary participation refers to a combination of information on current school attendance and highest level of education attained. For example, University participation refers to those who have completed a university degree or certificate at some point between the ages of 18 to 24 or who are currently enrolled in university. The definition is similar for College (which refers more specifically to community college, CEGEP or trade-vocational school participation), while dropouts are those who report having some postsecondary education but who have not completed a degree or diploma and are not currently enrolled. Overall participation in higher education is at historic highs, but the rates of growth have slowed significantly during the 1990s. University participation rates increased steady during the 1970s and 1980s and peaked in 1993 at 24%. There is a distinct drop of two percentage points between 1993 and 1994, and since that time participation rates have been flat at 22 to 23%. College rates also increased throughout the 1970s and 1980s, but display a slightly different pattern during the 1990s by continuing to grow (albeit at a much reduced rate). The dropout rate has not changed much in the last two decades, perhaps even falling a bit during the 1990s. In short there is little

Figure 3: Participation Rates in Higher Education for 18 to 24-Year-Olds

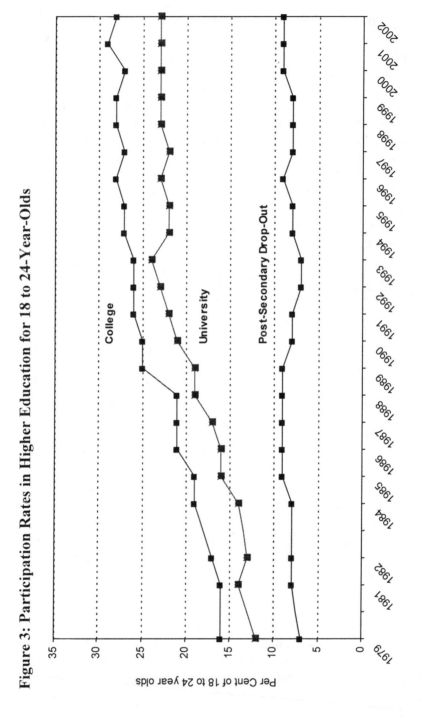

Source: Calculations by authors using Statistics Canada's Labour Force Survey.

Miles Corak, Garth Lipps and John Zhao

evidence to suggest that dropout rates have increased, some evidence to suggest that college may have been chosen over university by a small fraction of postsecondary participants, and while the rate of growth of university participation has stalled, there is no evidence to suggest declines below the levels experienced in the late 1980s and early 1990s before the sharp run-up in tuition fees.

These patterns are somewhat different by gender, as depicted in Figure 4. Participation in university declined between 1992 and 1993 for both men and women, but the pattern thereafter is different. University participation rates declined steadily for men after 1993, while community college attendance steadily increased. If there is a tendency for students in the 1990s to choose community college over university in response to high tuition fees this is almost totally a phenomenon associated with men. There was a temporary increase in college attendance by women during the early to mid-1990s, matched by a temporary fall in university attendance. But after 1995 female university participation returned to a path of steady growth and college participation stagnated, with the result that by 2002 the participation rates were about the same.

The strong majority of university students do not work while studying, but this changed slightly after about 1993 and particularly after 1997. Figure 5 shows that during the 1980s an average of 63% of university students did not work while studying, but this fell from 65% in 1993 to 59% in 1995 reflecting an equivalent percentage point increase in the fraction working part-time. Things have not changed much since that time with the fraction not working at all standing at 58% in 2002 and those working part-time at 34%. There is a greater tendency for college students to be working during their studies. In contrast to university students, only 50 to 60% of college students do not work while studying. Like university students there has been a tendency for this to fall through time, but the decline has been a long-term trend. With the exception of a possible jump in the fraction working part-time between 1996 and 1997, this tendency does not seem any more pronounced during the 1990s than it did earlier. By 2002, 43% of college students were working part-time, and less than 50% were not working at all during their studies. In contrast, the majority of university students do not work while at school, but there was a small discrete increase in part-time work among university students between 1993 and 1995.

The living arrangements of students have not changed very much during the last two decades and in particular there are no noticeable changes during the 1990s. Figure 6 offers the proportions of university and

Figure 4: Participation Rates in Higher Education for 18 to 24-Year-Olds by Gender

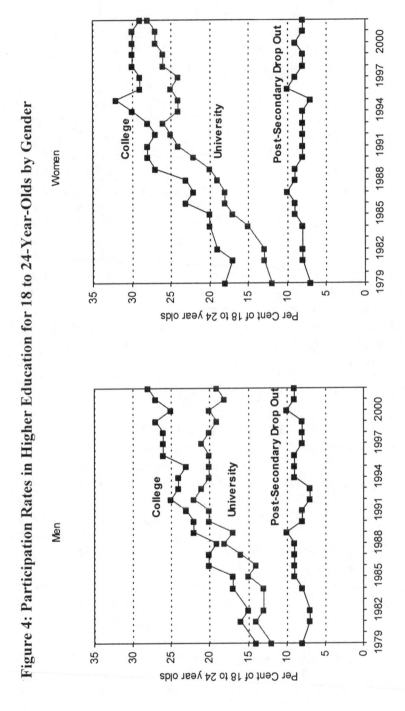

Source: Calculations by authors using Statistics Canada's Labour Force Survey.

Miles Corak, Garth Lipps and John Zhao

Figure 5: Proportion of Students Working While Studying (for those 18 to 24 years of age)

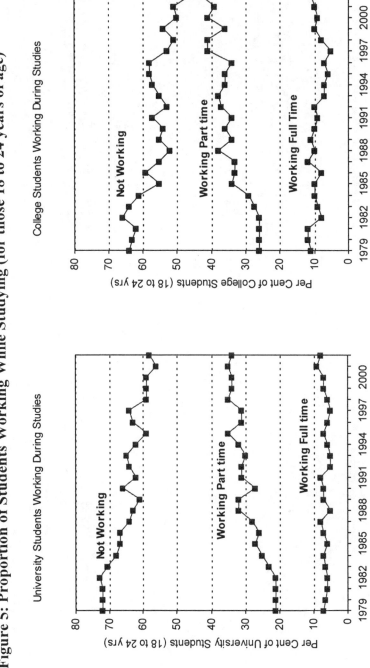

University Students Working During Studies

College Students Working During Studies

Source: Calculations by authors using Statistics Canada's Labour Force Survey.

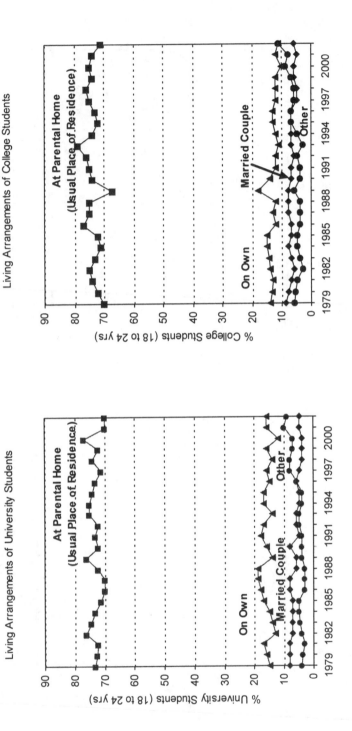

Figure 6: Living Arrangements of Students (for those 18 to 24 years of age)

Living Arrangements of University Students

Living Arrangements of College Students

Miles Corak, Garth Lipps and John Zhao

college students living at home, on their own, as a married couple, or in other arrangements. The fraction at home has hovered between 70 and 80% since 1979, and is about the same for the two groups. A certain caution is needed, however, in interpreting this data. The "At Home" category refers, strictly speaking to those whose "usual place of residence" is stated as being that of their parents. "Usual place of residence" is a construct of the survey-taking process and refers to "the dwelling in Canada where a person lives most of the time" (Statistics Canada, 2001b, pp. 141-142). This does not necessarily imply that these students are living at their parents' residence while studying. Some fraction may in fact be doing so, but another fraction may be attending an institution in another locale and returning to their parents' home during the summer while continuing to refer to it as their usual place of residence. Bowlby and McMullen (2002) find that approximately 43% of first-year university students live with their parents during the school year and 41% reported living in a university residence. It may well be that the relative shares in these two groups have changed through time. This implies that in spite of the information in Figure 6 it may be the case that students are choosing to attend institutions closer to home in order to save on moving and living expenses.

The most notable change in the decisions of those attending post-secondary schools has been with respect to borrowing. Between academic years 1986/87 and 1988/89 the number of borrowers fell by about 15%, but this trend was reversed in the 1990s so that the total number of borrowers increased from just over 300,000 at the beginning of the decade to over 500,000 by the end (Junor and Usher, 2002, p. 105). Further, during the 1990s the average student loan increased considerably (Figure 7). More precisely, between the 1992/93 academic year and the 1993/94 academic year the average amount borrowed through the provincial loans programs and the Canada Student Loan program went from about $5,000 — where it had been since the early 1980s — to over $7,500. It increased a bit further thereafter, ending the 1990s at $7,680. This information, however, refers only to those students living in provinces other than Quebec.[2] In Quebec, there has been only a modest tendency for the amount of the average student loan to increase, with no discrete changes in this relationship

---

[2]Quebec, Nunavut, and the Northwest Territories have opted out of the Canada Student Loan Program and administer similar programs on their own. Quebec's program functions in a manner similar to the Canada Student Loans Program but with different levels of support.

Figure 7: Average Amount of Student Loans by Region

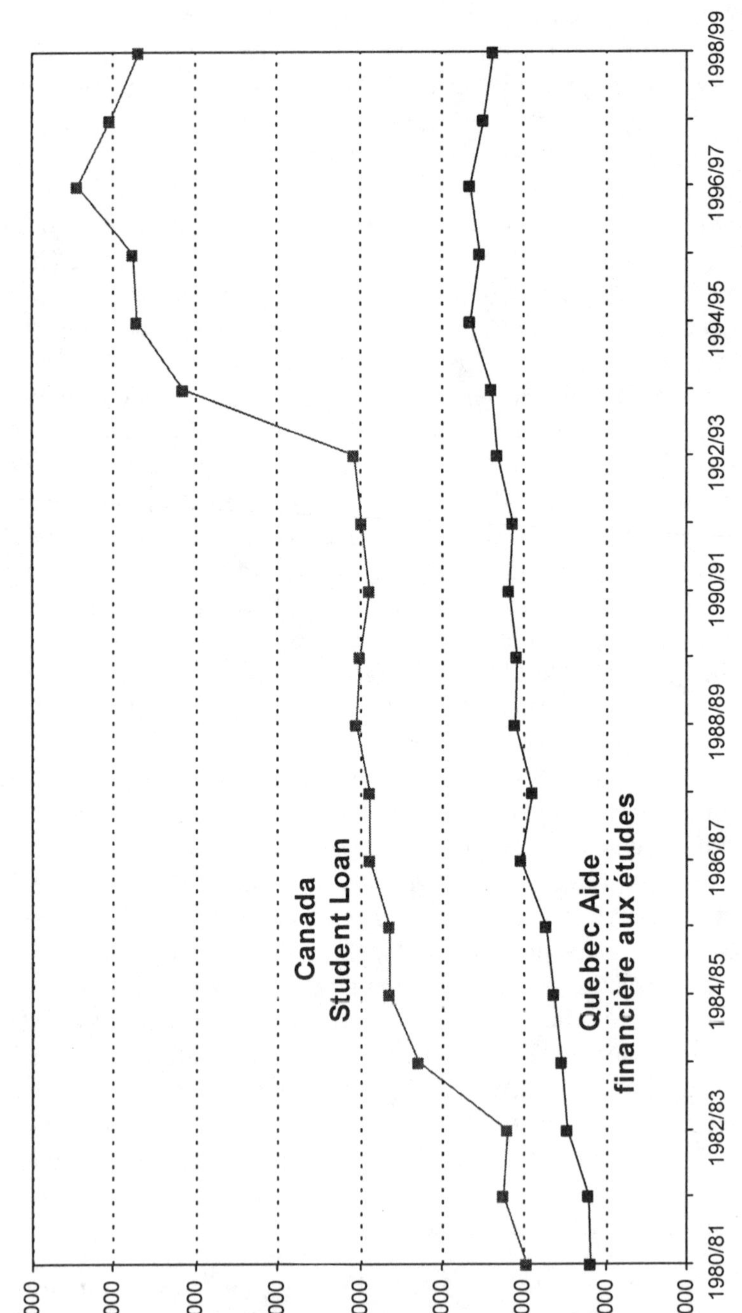

Source: Junor and Usher (2002).

Miles Corak, Garth Lipps and John Zhao

during the 1990s. At the end of the decade this figure was $3,360. The very sharp jump in student loan amounts between the 1992/93 and 1993/94 academic years reflects in part an administrative change that increased the limit on the maximum CSLP loan amount from $105/week to $165/week in 1994. Provinces that took part in the CSLP were obliged to match this increase according to a 60–40 ratio. This shift in policy also led to an increase in the number of students receiving provincial student loans since participating provinces previously only provided loans and grants to those whose need exceeded $105/week, and the policy change prompted many provinces to end their grant programs and convert them to loan-granting programs. Junor and Usher (2002, p. 110) also report that within one year the maximum allowable loan went from $105 per week to $275 per week in many provinces.

Methods and Data

Our major objective is to offer an accurate estimate of the strength of the relationship between parental income and child postsecondary participation. The issue of family background and postsecondary participation is a long-standing concern in both academic and policy circles, with Bouchard and Zhao (2000) and Knighton and Mirza (2002) offering two recent Canadian examples. Their analyses, however, are focused on the socio-economic status of families, measured as an index related to parental education and occupation. Our focus is explicitly on family income and can be summarized as follows. Let Y_i represent the postsecondary status for a young individual labelled i, which we will consider to be those 18 to 24 years of age. Y takes on the value of 1 if the individual has a postsecondary degree or diploma or is attending a postsecondary institution and 0 otherwise. In addition let X_i represent the permanent income of individual i's parents. We wish to obtain accurate estimates of β_1 in the following equation.

$$Y_i = \beta_0 + \beta_1 X_i + \varepsilon_i \qquad (1)$$

This is estimated using least squares. Equation (1) is a linear probability model of postsecondary participation, and when parental income is expressed in natural logarithms the coefficient β_1 indicates the change in the chances of postsecondary schooling for each percentage point change in income.[3] A larger coefficient implies a larger impact of differences in parental income on postsecondary participation. (The term β_0 is a constant and ε_i is a random component.) Under certain assumptions β_1 can be thought of as the correlation between postsecondary participation and parental income, though it is more accurate to refer to it as an elasticity.

Only a limited number of studies have directly analyzed the correlation between family income and postsecondary participation. In part this may reflect data limitations. There are very few surveys that contain information on parental income and the postsecondary participation of children. One possibility is to use longitudinal surveys in which family income is collected while high-school students still reside in the parental home, and then observe these students through time as they leave and make their way either into postsecondary education or into the labour market. Zhao and de Broucker (2001, 2002) use the Survey of Labour and Income Dynamics in this way to document the relationship between family income and the postsecondary participation of 18 to 21-year-olds between 1993 and 1998. They find that about 19% of youth from families with incomes in the lowest 25% of the income distribution attend university and that double that fraction do so for families in the top 25%. College attendance rates are just under 30% regardless of the position in the income distribution. Because of the need to observe young people leaving the family home, the sample size for any given year can be quite small. The authors are therefore forced to pool all 18 to 21-year-olds over the entire six years of longitudinal data available to them in order to obtain reliable estimates. As such there is no scope to illustrate how the relationship between income and post-secondary participation has changed.

The starting point for our analysis is a study by Christofides, Cirello and Hoy (2001), which uses a different approach. The major issue they explore relates to the observation that between 1975 and 1993 the post-secondary participation rate of children from families in the lower end of

---

[3]Moffitt (1999) offers an overview of the use of empirical methods for binary dependent variables, and in particular highlights the limits and appropriate use of the linear probability model, stressing that traditional objections need not always apply. Following his analysis we use the linear probability model, as opposed to probit or logit models, since there is little possibility of predications outside the 0–1 range, our concern is with an overall correlation and not with under-lying structural parameters, and since non-linearities are less likely to be a problem given the probabilities of concern are likely in the lower tail of the distribution.

Miles Corak, Garth Lipps and John Zhao

the income distribution increased much more than those in the higher end. For example, children whose families were in the top fifth of the income distribution in 1975 were almost three times as likely to be engaged in higher education than those from the bottom fifth, but in 1993 they were only 1.6 times as likely. The authors seek to examine the extent to which this reflects a disproportionately greater change in the demand for higher education among those in the bottom of the income distribution as their real income increases. They find that while income levels are certainly an important factor determining postsecondary participation, income changes do not have a disproportionate influence on the schooling choices of lower-income groups.

We address three issues raised by their study. First, our interest has less to do with their specific hypothesis than with the nature of the relationship between absolute income levels and postsecondary participation, and how this has changed. They document that children from higher-income families are much more likely to attend postsecondary education, but that lower-income groups have experienced relatively greater increases in participation over time. This finding, however, refers only to the period up to 1993 just as the significant changes in postsecondary began.[4] We update these patterns to the late 1990s. Second, they make no distinction between university education and community college education. The relationship between family income and postsecondary participation could be very different across these levels, and as alluded to in Figure 3, changes in enrolment and substitution between the two levels could be an important dimension of access. We make a distinction between university and college in our analysis. Finally, the authors offer no distinction in participation rates by gender. As illustrated in Figure 4, there are important differences across gender, with women more engaged in university education than men. It may well be that access issues play themselves out differently by gender, and to the extent possible we offer information along these lines.

Christofides, Cirello and Hay (2001) use information on parental income for a series of cross-sectional surveys over a period of almost 20

---

[4]Indeed, in some of their modelling Christofides *et al.* attempt to examine the role of tuition fees in explaining participation rates but find no significant relationship. They explain this by referring to the fact that during the period of their study tuition fees did not vary much over time and across provinces. Raymond and Rivard (2003) use different data for 1999 when there was substantial variation in fees across the provinces and they are led to the same conclusion.

years. Their information comes from the Survey of Consumer Finances (SCF) in which income information is obtained from the household head, who also reports the educational status of all family members continuing to call the home their usual place of residence. In this way they obtain a reliable link between family income and postsecondary education of the young for a relatively large sample, but at the price of missing those students who are living independently either on their own, in a partnership with others, or in some other arrangement. We alluded to this issue in discussions of Figure 6. This information suggests that between 70 and 80% of postsecondary students consider their parents' home as their usual place of residence and that this has not changed. If the likelihood of no longer living at home is the same across income levels the fact that parental income information is missing for 20 to 30% of students should not introduce a bias to their work. However, if postsecondary students from high-income backgrounds are more likely to leave home then the correlation between income and participation may be understated. It would be overstated if the opposite were the case. The fact that there have been no significant changes in this proportion over time suggests that the degree of the bias will not be changing.

This still leaves unaddressed the experiences of those who do not attend university or college. In fact, studies of the living arrangements of the young suggest that a slightly different pattern occurs for the entire population of young people (Meunier, Bernard and Boisjoly, 1998; Boyd and Norris, 1999). This is illustrated in Figure 8 for all 18 to 24-year-olds. Between 50 and 60% of this group refer to their parents' home as the usual place of residence, with a tendency for this proportion to be increasing through time, particularly after 1990. This suggests that parental income will not be as well reported for those who decide not to attend a post-secondary institution, but that the extent of this bias is falling through time. It reflects substantial declines in the fraction of 18 to 24-year-olds who live as a married couple. If children from lower-income families are more likely to leave the parental home earlier, then the sample of non-attendees actually used in the analysis will be overrepresented with higher-income groups and the correlation between family income and postsecondary participation will be understated. This bias should be falling with time.

With this in mind we also make use of the SCF to estimate equation (1) since it is the only source of information that directly links parental income with educational status of the young over the time period of interest. However, one further important limitation of this information should also be noted. The income measure provided is annual income for only one year.

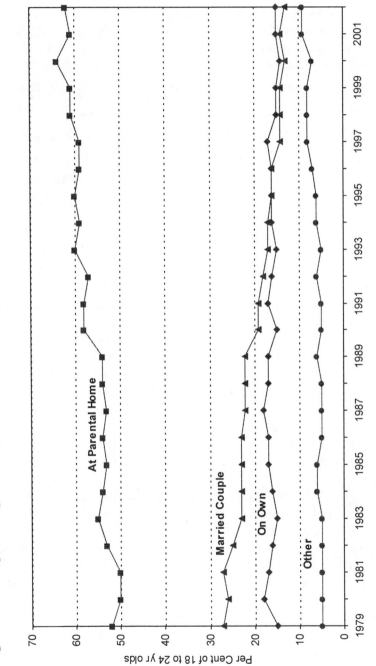

Figure 8: Living Arrangements of All 18 to 24-Year-Olds, 1979 to 2002

Annual incomes may fluctuate from year to year, and may not reflect at any point in time the true financial resources parents have to support their children's education. The use of annual income rather than a measure of permanent income will lead the correlation between family income and postsecondary participation to be understated. For example, if we actually observe $\widetilde{X}_i = X_i + v_i$, where v_i represents a transitory shock to income, this results in an error in variables problem leading the estimated coefficient ($\widetilde{\beta}_1$) to be less than the true coefficient according to a factor determined by the ratio of the variance of v_i to that of X_i, so that $\widetilde{\beta}_1(1 + \sigma_v^2 / \sigma_X^2) = \beta_1$ (Greene, 1997, pp. 436-438). Further, if the variability of the transitory component of income is increasing through time this bias will become more important. Baker and Solon (2003) report that for 40 to 50-year-old men the permanent component accounts for about two-thirds of the total variance of income. There has been a tendency for the variability of income to increase through time, stepping up particularly after business-cycle recessions, with the variance in the permanent and transitory components increasing by about the same amount. Their study is based upon data between 1976 and 1992. This would suggest that estimates of β_1 resulting from measures of annual income should be inflated by about 50%, and that the extent of the bias has not changed much. Beach, Finnie and Gray (2003) offer broadly similar conclusions for 25 to 54-year-old men over a period that extends from 1982 to 1997. They suggest that the proportion of variance due to the permanent component may have increased more. On the whole we expect substantial understatement of the true value of β_1 using the SCF — possibly in the order of 50% — and while the extent of the bias may have diminished we do not expect it to be the major source of changes through time.

We use a complementary approach to work around these two difficulties with the SCF. Generally, students and young adults tend not to be questioned in cross-sectional surveys on the income levels of their parents in large part because they may not be in a position to respond accurately. But information easier to recall is sometimes collected. In particular, many surveys ask about parental education and occupation, variables that are often used to develop indicators of socio-economic status and are strong predictors of income. Information on self-reported income, education, and occupation can be made use of in combination with the parental background information. The methodology is related to a literature that estimates intergenerational income correlations, and is in turn related to

Miles Corak, Garth Lipps and John Zhao

instrumental variables (IV) and two-sample split IV methods (Angrist, 1999; Angrist and Krueger, 1995; Björklund and Jäntti, 1997; Fortin and Lefebvre, 1998; Grawe, 2004; Zimmerman, 1992). The procedure involves two steps. The first is to estimate an income equation for a subset of survey respondents who because of their ages represent the cohort of parents of 18 to 24-year-olds. This uses self-reported information on incomes, age, occupation, and education. The second stage uses the estimated coefficients from this equation and parental education and occupation information reported by each child to ascribe to each a predicted parental income.

To be more specific we use information from the General Social Surveys (GSS) of 1986, 1994, and 2001. This is a representative survey of the entire population in which all respondents are asked to report, among other things, their incomes, occupations, and education levels. In addition, respondents are asked to recall the occupation and education levels of their parents. In the GSS, parental occupation refers to the occupation of the parent when the respondent was 15 years of age. For all those male respondents between the ages of 40 and 60 — those who can roughly be taken to represent fathers of 18 to 24-year-olds — we estimate equation (2), an earnings equation using self-reported information on occupation (Z_{1i}) and education (Z_{2i}).

$$X_i = \gamma_0 + \gamma_1 Z_{1i} + \gamma_2 Z_{2i} + \mu_i \qquad (2)$$

The estimated coefficients $\hat{\gamma}_0$, $\hat{\gamma}_1$ and $\hat{\gamma}_2$ can then be used to predict parental permanent incomes for the group of 18 to 24-year-olds in the data using the information they provide on the occupation and education of their fathers. These predicted incomes, $\hat{X}_i$, are then used as the income measure in an estimation of equation (1).

In this way all young people are captured regardless of their current living arrangements and by offering a more accurate estimate of permanent income based upon its major determinants, the bias associated with transitory income fluctuations is eliminated. At the same time, however, this two-stage approach introduces another sort of bias that will lead to an overstatement of β_1. This occurs because the influence of parental occupation and education on the postsecondary decisions of children is channelled entirely through their relationship with income. If these factors play an independent role in determining higher schooling, as they most surely do, then the influence of income on those decisions will be overstated. A formal exposition of this intuition is offered in Solon (1992).

In sum, this implies that our first method using direct information on incomes from the SCF will understate the postsecondary participation-family income relationship, but that our second method using indirect income information from the GSS will overstate it. By relying on both approaches we put an upper and lower bound on the true value of β_l, limit the role of other biases inherent in each of the surveys, and assess the robustness of any changes observed through time.

Results

Details of how we create our analytical datasets and the definitions of our key variables are offered in the working paper version of this paper.[5] With respect to the analysis based on the Survey of Consumer Finances, total income is defined as income from all sources for the household head and the spouse of the household head. The sample sizes range from a low of 4,817 individuals aged 18 to 24 in 1995 to a high of 7,695 in 1982; the sample sizes for economic families range from 3,868 to 5,601.[6] Figure 9 uses this data, and depicts the trends in university participation rates by broad groupings of family income. In the neighbourhood of 40% of 18 to 24-year-olds from families with incomes of $100,000 or more have a university degree or are enrolled in university. This percentage ebbs and flows a bit, but for the most part has not changed since the early to mid-1980s. This is a rate that is substantially and perennially higher than those for lower-income groups. The participation rate for 18 to 24-year-olds from families with more than $75,000 to $100,000 is also notably higher than for lower-income groups, ranging between 20 to 30%, but the pattern of change

---

[5]Available from www.statcan.ca as Statistics Canada, Analytical Studies Branch Research Paper No. 210, or from www.iza.org as IZA Discussion Paper No. 977.

[6]There were changes in the implementation of the survey in 1980 and 1983 that significantly lowered the sample sizes in these years. Preliminary analysis found this data to not be reliable for our purposes and they are not used in the analysis that follows.

Miles Corak, Garth Lipps and John Zhao

Figure 9: University Participation Rates of 18 to 24-Year-Olds by Parental Income

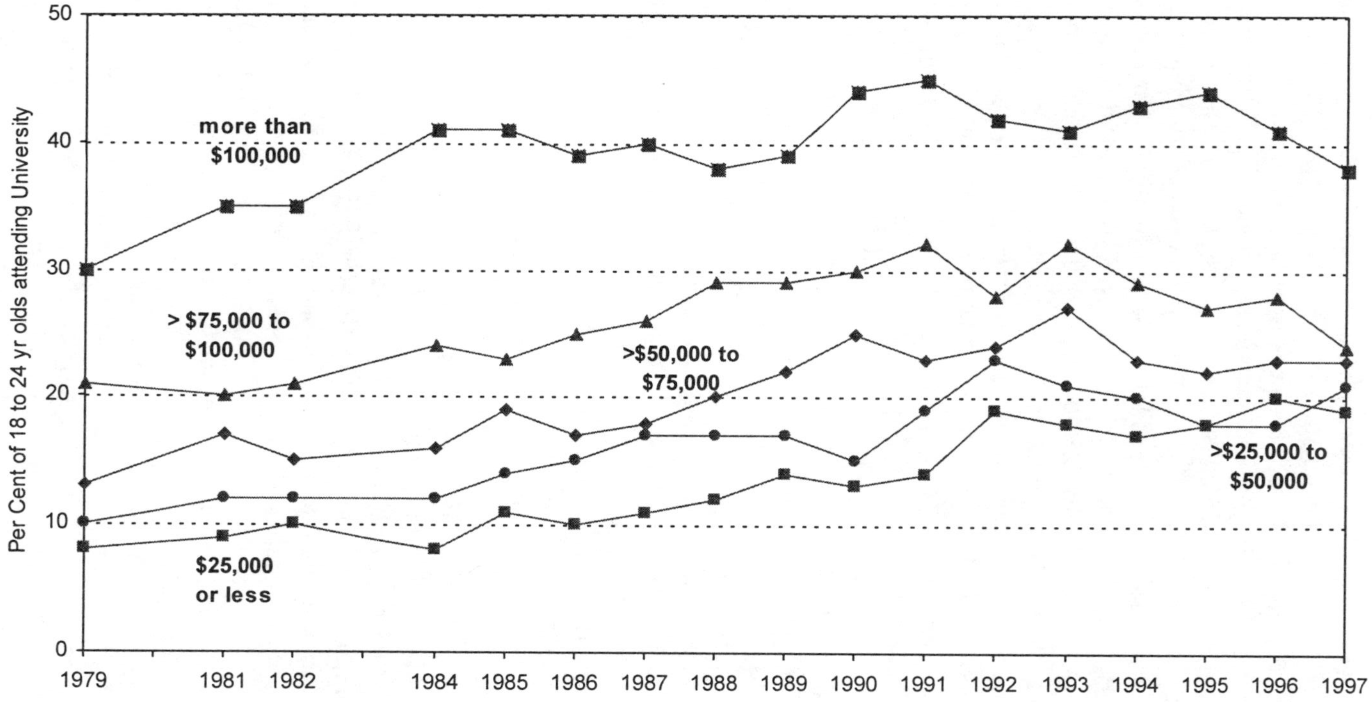

Per Cent of 18 to 24 yr olds attending University
0
10
20
30
40
50
1979
1981
1982
1984
1985
1986
1987
1988
1989
1990
1991
1992
1993
1994
1995
1996
1997
more than $100,000
> $75,000 to $100,000
>$50,000 to $75,000
>$25,000 to $50,000
$25,000 or less

Source: Calculations by authors using Statistics Canada's Survey of Consumer Finances.

does not vary too much once family income exceeds $25,000. Participation rates trended up throughout the 1980s and then stopped growing and even declined during the 1990s. The peak in participation rates seems to have occurred in 1991 or 1992. Only in the case of individuals from the lowest income families — $25,000 or less — has there been a steady progress in participation rates throughout the period under study: starting at less than 10% during the early 1980s and rising to 19% by 1997. Young people with this income background are by 1997 as likely to be attending university as those whose parents had $25,000 to $50,000 in income, and not much less likely as those whose parents had up to $100,000.

Figure 10 offers similar information for college participation. Here the patterns are very different. The participation rates are similar across family income groupings, differing only by about one to three percentage points. Further, there has been steady growth in participation, starting at about 15 to 20% in the early 1980s and rising steadily to about 20 to 25%. While college participation is not at all as closely tied to family income as university participation, it is the case that the lowest-income group has once again experienced the most consistent growth. In addition, for middle-income groups there has been steady if slight increases through the 1990s.

Figure 11 presents an overall summary of these patterns by offering the estimates of β_1 from a least squares regression of equation (1) for university and college participation. As mentioned, these estimates understate the true parameter because they are based on annual income rather than permanent income. Also the extent of the bias may diminish through time if there have been increases in the fraction of total income variance accounted for by permanent income. There could be other biases associated with changes in living arrangements, but it is difficult to determine the direction of these. With this in mind the results reveal that the elasticity between family income and the probability of university participation is quite low, less than 0.1 for most years. Our best guess might be to inflate this value by 50% as a correction for the use of annual income. This would suggest that a 10% increase in parental income raises the chances of university attendance for an 18 to 24-year-old by no more than 1.5%. However, it is the pattern of change that is particularly relevant to us, and it would appear that the estimated elasticity hovered between 0.08 and 0.1 before 1990, peaked in 1990 and 1991 at between 0.11 and 0.12, then fell substantially, particularly after 1995. Further, there is essentially no correlation between family income and college participation. The highest estimated value is only 0.03, and the coefficients are not statistically different from zero in 1989 and all

Figure 10: College Participation Rates of 18 to 24-Year-Olds by Parental Income

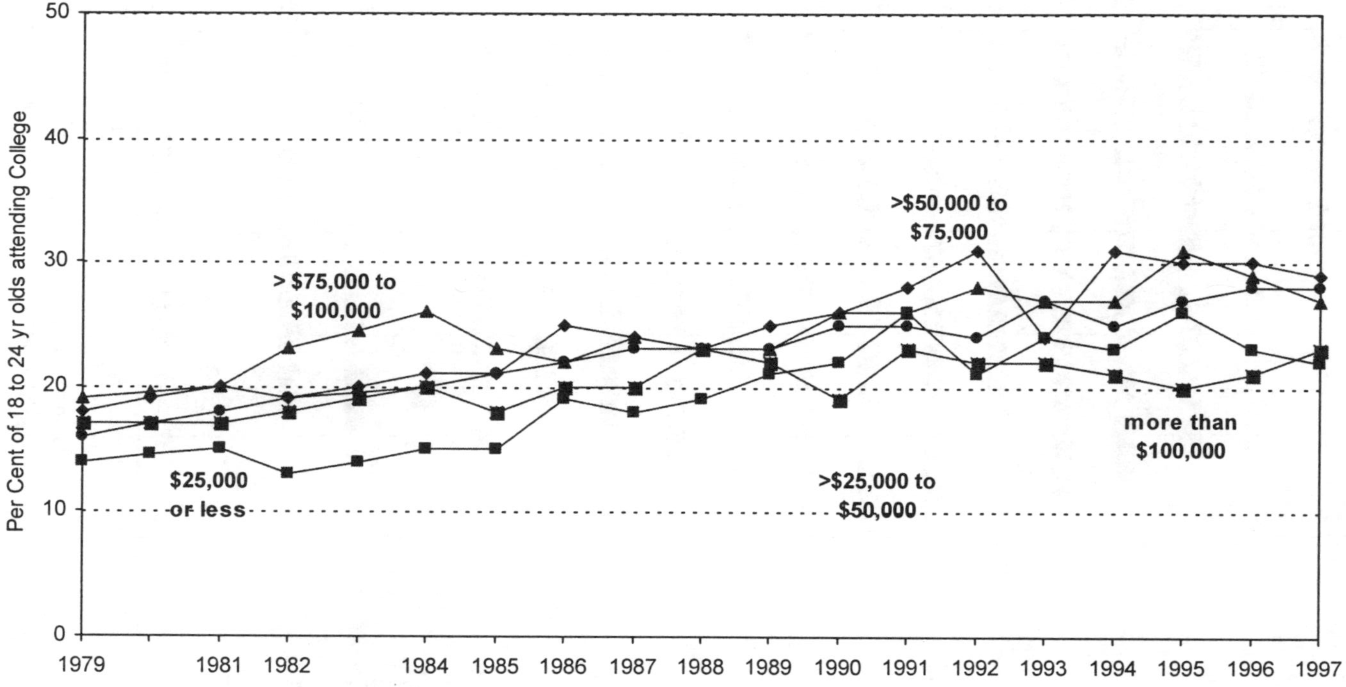

Source: Calculations by authors using Statistics Canada's Survey of Consumer Finances.

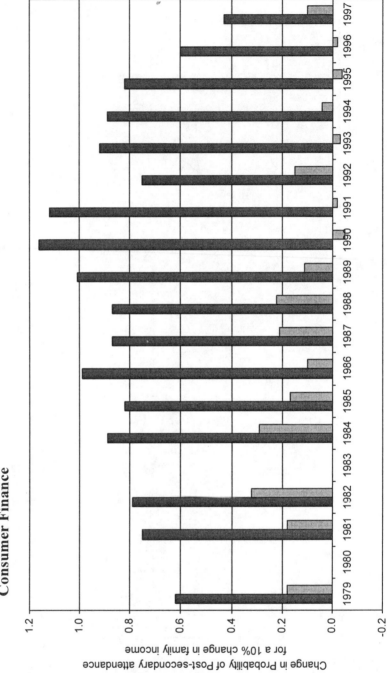

Figure 11: The Relationship Between Parental Income and Participation in University and Community College, Using Annual Parental Income from the Survey of Consumer Finance

■ University □ College

Miles Corak, Garth Lipps and John Zhao

subsequent years. This said, there is a clear drop off in the values in 1990 and after from the range of 0.02 to essentially zero.

The relationship between university participation and family income tends to be stronger for women, the elasticity being higher than that for men in 11 of the 15 years under study. (See Tables A2 and A3 in the Appendix.) The general pattern of change for university participation is also the same for men and women, a rise in the elasticity during the early 1990s followed by a fall to earlier levels during the latter part of the decade. The run-up, however, seems to have been higher for women and to have lasted longer. During the early 1990s the elasticity for women is above 0.1 for three consecutive years and only appears to have clearly fallen and returned to 1980 levels after 1994. For men the elasticity rises sharply in 1990, but falls off immediately and steadily in subsequent years, this being the only year it is above 0.1.

The GSS does not suffer from any of the possible biases in the SCF, but does differ conceptually in a number of ways. Most notably the GSS analysis is based exclusively on father's income, rather than parental income. We are not able to incorporate maternal information because a large number of young respondents do not report the occupations of their mothers, likely reflecting maternal labour force participation decisions at the time the individual was 15 years of age. The first-stage regressions used to develop a measure of predicted income for the analysis and other issues of data construction are based upon samples of men aged 40 to 60 years. These range from 1,144 in the 1986 data to 2,711 in 2001. Further, for reasons of sample size we do not separately distinguish college participation, using rather university participation and a broader definition that incorporates both university and college (which we simply refer to as post-secondary participation). It should be noted that there are some differences between the three years of the GSS in the way in which occupations and incomes are coded, and our corrections to make the data comparable as well as the associated descriptive statistics are also discussed in the working paper version.

Figure 12 offers the results of interest from the second stage regressions of equation (1), based upon estimates of father's permanent income from equation (2). As expected, the coefficient estimates of father's income are all higher than those based on annual income measures, by a magnitude of three to four. That being said the pattern of change is roughly similar. For 1986, every ten-percentage-point increase in paternal income implies a three-percentage-point increase in the probability of university attendance, rising to four percentage points in 1994, but falling to 2.6 in

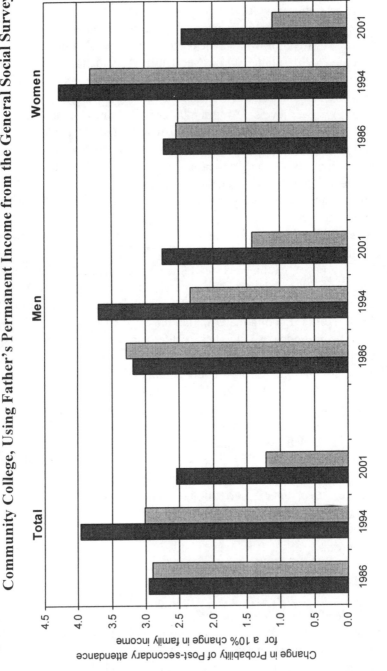

Figure 12: The Relationship Between Family Income and Participation in University and Community College, Using Father's Permanent Income from the General Social Survey

Miles Corak, Garth Lipps and John Zhao

2001. When college participation is also included in the definition of participation the magnitudes of the coefficients are muted, but the same pattern persists.

Once again there are some differences between men and women. Most notably when the broader definition of participation is used the coefficients for men display successive declines in the value of the estimated elasticity. These are the only results that do not rise between the 1980s and early 1990s, and then fall afterward. This may reflect the observation in Figure 4 that men may have had more of a tendency to opt for community college over university, particularly if this were so for those from upper-income families. As such the results suggest that for men, participation in the post-secondary system as a whole — university and colleges together — has become more loosely tied to family background in large part because of the option to pursue studies in community colleges.

The estimated elasticities tend to be lower for women, with the exception of 1994 when they are substantially higher. This difference relative to the analysis based on the SCF may reflect the fact that only the father's income (as opposed to income from both parents) is being used in the GSS analysis. It may be that father-son intergenerational correlations are stronger than father-daughter, and likewise that mother-daughter correlations are stronger than mother-son. If this is the case then the exclusive use of paternal income in the GSS analysis would lead to higher father-son correlations and lower father-daughter correlations than if paternal and maternal income were combined. That said, the only elasticity estimated to be greater than 0.4 is for university participation by women in 1994. This reflects a substantial increase from 0.27 in 1986 and is well above the 0.37 estimate for men. A similar pattern is observed when college participation is included. In this sense the results also accord with the SCF findings that the postsecondary participation decisions of women are more closely tied to family income than for men.

Conclusion

The postsecondary climate has changed significantly for Canadian students during the 1990s. On the one hand, perceptions of the return to higher education have increased. A very high proportion of Canadians from all income backgrounds view higher education as the pathway to higher earnings and over four-fifths of families expect their children to attend a postsecondary institution. On the other hand, the costs of higher education have also increased substantially with, for example, the average annual undergraduate arts tuition rising by more than 85% and fees in some disciplines and institutions rising even more. In this context "access" to postsecondary education has become an important public policy concern. As important and obvious the concern, there is surprisingly little information available to directly address whether the Canadian postsecondary system is increasingly dominated by those from relatively higher income backgrounds. In order to speak to this concern, our analysis uses two different data sources in a novel way to examine changes in the relationship between postsecondary participation and family income over the course of the last two decades.

At the most general level we find that postsecondary education at the end of the 1990s was no more the domain of the relatively better off than it was during the 1980s. It is certainly the case that children from higher-income families are more likely to attend university, but this has not changed dramatically during the 1990s with the introduction of higher tuition fees. But behind this overall finding lie a number of developments that shed light on how young people have adapted to the changed financial environment, and how the institutional structure of postsecondary education and other aspects of public policy have influenced their decisions. Post-secondary participation is at historic highs, and we find no strong evidence that dropout rates have increased. That said, it is true that the rate of growth in participation stalled during the 1990s, but this is more clearly the case for university participation than it is for college. There has been a tendency for some students, particularly male students, to increasingly choose community college over university. But the other more notable change in behaviour has been higher borrowing. The 1990s witnessed a significant increase in the average amount of a student loan. This reflects policy changes in the mid-1990s that increased the maximum permissible loan under the Canada Student Loan Program, and which in turn signalled increases in other forms of student loans and financial support.

The option to choose lower-cost community colleges and in particular to borrow more are probably the two most important factors that have influenced the relationship between family income and postsecondary participation. College participation is not related in any significant way to family income. Our estimates suggest a very small positive correlation before the 1990s, and essentially zero correlation afterwards. Young men have shown a strong tendency to choose community college over university beginning in the early 1990s and throughout the remainder of the decade.

Miles Corak, Garth Lipps and John Zhao

Young women displayed a tendency of this sort but only for two or three years when tuition fees first started increasing. By the mid-1990s college participation rates of women fell and remained flat for the rest of the decade; participation rates in university on the other hand increased and returned to earlier rates of growth. There is a clear positive association between parental income and university attendance, and this association in fact became stronger during the early to mid-1990s when tuition fees began increasing significantly. This change reflected declines in participation rates of youth from middle-income families, those with incomes ranging from $25,000 to $100,000. The strength of the association, however, weakened during the latter half of the decade reflecting rises in participation of those from the lowest-income groups. This pattern is consistent with the fact that the changes in the Canada Student Loan Program raising the maximum amount of a loan occurred only after tuition fees had already begun to rise.

In summary, our analysis offers no evidence that the tie between family income and postsecondary participation is stronger at the end of the 1990s than it was at the beginning. That said, the costs of higher education have certainly increased and in part these costs have been shifted onto students, as reflected in much higher levels of borrowing and the decline in university participation rates of those from middle-income families. At the same time it should be noted that the costs of postsecondary education have also become more differentiated. There is greater variation of fees across provinces, disciplines, and even institutions. Our analysis refers to a very broad notion of access to higher education, whether students are less likely to attend according to their family background. It may well be that students and other stakeholders will increasingly be concerned with access in a more narrowly defined sense, access to particular institutions or fields of study. Some of our results hint at this possibility, particularly the suggestion that men have been increasingly more inclined to choose community college over university. If there has been a switch in attendance between these broad categories of the postsecondary system then it may also be important to document the extent to which there have been changes at more detailed levels within the university system. Future research relating family background to the more specific choices students make in deciding upon an institution and a field of study may shed light on aspects of access not addressed in our research. In particular, our work sheds no specific light on the rules universities use in making their acceptance decisions. Research in this area may also be important in understanding the issue of access. Our findings are consistent with other work finding that tuition fees have had little impact on postsecondary attendance, but we also suggest that the reason for this may have to do with concomitant — albeit lagging — increases in the level of financial support available to students. The impact of higher tuition fees cannot be judged in isolation of changes in the level of support available to students from governments and other institutions. In the 1990s both tuition fees and financial support have gone up. In this context it may be that the most important factor determining access are changes in admission requirements. A rise in admission standards would lead to stronger links between family background and postsecondary participation in particular institutions or fields of study if children from higher-income families are more likely to have the skills to fulfill the requirements. This might play a role in understanding the gender differences highlighted in our analysis, and also suggests one further area for future research. It might be fruitful to in general examine non-financial barriers to accessing higher education, particularly the circumstances earlier in the lives of young people that place them in the fortunate situation of choosing to continue their education after high-school graduation.

Appendix

Table A1: Least Squares Regression Results of the Elasticity Between Postsecondary Participation and Family Income for 18 to 24-Year-Olds, Using Annual Income from the Survey of Consumer Finances

	University			College			Sample Size
	Intercept	*In* (Parental Income)	R^2	Intercept	*In* (Parental Income)	R^2	
1979	−0.515	0.062	0.020	−0.030	0.018	0.002	7,055
1981	−0.640	0.075	0.025	−0.009	0.018	0.001	7,354
1982	−0.686	0.079	0.027	−0.157	0.032	0.004	7,684
1984	−0.784	0.089	0.038	−0.118	0.030	0.004	6,759
1985	−0.647	0.076	0.028	0.025	0.023	0.002	6,213
1986	−0.770	0.087	0.030	0.003	0.023	0.002	5,286
1987	−0.672	0.079	0.025	−0.060	0.029	0.003	6,919
1988	−0.655	0.078	0.023	−0.083	0.031	0.003	5,554
1989	−0.869	0.101	0.032	0.118	0.011	0.000	5,992
1990	−1.020	0.116	0.043	0.298	−0.005	0.000	6,653
1991	−0.961	0.112	0.034	0.274	−0.002	0.000	6,025
1992	−0.542	0.075	0.019	0.101	0.015	0.001	5,418
1993	−0.728	0.092	0.024	0.280	−0.003	0.000	5,524
1994	−0.714	0.089	0.026	0.215	0.004	0.000	5,674
1995	−0.642	0.082	0.023	0.312	−0.004	0.000	4,817
1996	−0.405	0.060	0.014	0.289	−0.002	0.000	4,882
1997	−0.225	0.043	0.007	0.161	0.010	0.000	4,828

Note: Table entries are least squares estimation results from equation (1) described in the text using Survey of Consumer Finance Data, Statistics Canada. The coefficients on *In* Income for university participation are all statistically significant with t-statistics ranging from 5.74 in 1997 to 17.3 in 1990. Those for college participation are not statistically different from zero for 1989 and all subsequent years.

Table A2: Least Squares Regression Results of the Elasticity Between Postsecondary Participation and Family Income for 18 to 24-Year-Old Men, Using Annual Income from the Survey of Consumer Finances

	University			College			Sample Size
	Intercept	ln (Parental Income)	R^2	Intercept	ln (Parental Income)	R^2	
1979	−0.562	0.065	0.024	−0.017	0.015	0.001	4,178
1981	−0.616	0.072	0.025	−0.043	0.020	0.002	4,298
1982	−0.609	0.071	0.024	−0.136	0.028	0.003	4,513
1984	−0.770	0.086	0.038	−0.096	0.026	0.003	3,984
1985	−0.682	0.072	0.030	0.018	0.017	0.001	3,587
1986	−0.727	0.080	0.034	−0.079	0.028	0.003	3,065
1987	−0.707	0.081	0.028	−0.127	0.033	0.004	3,956
1988	−0.659	0.078	0.022	−0.021	0.022	0.002	3,182
1989	−0.729	0.085	0.025	0.094	0.011	0.000	3,399
1990	−1.144	0.125	0.056	0.104	0.010	0.000	3,804
1991	−0.789	0.093	0.026	0.073	0.014	0.001	3,469
1992	−0.676	0.084	0.026	−0.188	0.040	0.006	3,038
1993	−0.749	0.090	0.026	0.168	0.006	0.001	3,138
1994	−0.516	0.067	0.016	0.032	0.019	0.001	3,146
1995	−0.644	0.079	0.026	0.201	0.003	0.000	2,713
1996	−0.522	0.067	0.020	0.256	0.000	0.000	2,617
1997	−0.186	0.037	0.005	0.135	0.011	0.000	2,712

Note: Table entries are least squares estimation results from equation (1) described in the text using Survey of Consumer Finance Data, Statistics Canada. The coefficients on ln Income for university participation are all statistically significant with t-statistics ranging from 5.17 in 1997 to 13.8 in 1990. Those for college participation are not statistically different from zero for 1989 and all subsequent years with the exception of 1992.

Miles Corak, Garth Lipps and John Zhao

Table A3: Least Squares Regression Results of the Elasticity Between Postsecondary Participation and Family Income for 18 to 24-Year-Old Women, Using Annual Income from the Survey of Consumer Finances

	University			College			Sample Size
	Intercept	ln (Parental Income)	R^2	Intercept	ln (Parental Income)	R^2	
1979	−0.446	0.057	0.016	−0.031	0.021	0.001	2,877
1981	−0.671	0.079	0.024	0.068	0.013	0.001	3,056
1982	−0.793	0.091	0.030	−0.170	0.036	0.004	3,171
1984	−0.795	0.092	0.038	−0.137	0.034	0.005	2,775
1985	−0.675	0.081	0.027	0.090	0.032	0.004	2,626
1986	−0.788	0.091	0.031	0.139	0.013	0.001	2,221
1987	−0.597	0.075	0.020	0.062	0.020	0.001	2,963
1988	−0.651	0.079	0.024	−0.154	0.041	0.005	2,372
1989	−1.018	0.119	0.040	0.164	0.009	0.000	2,593
1990	−0.881	0.107	0.032	0.532	−0.023	0.002	2,849
1991	−1.123	0.131	0.042	0.589	−0.027	0.002	2,555
1992	−0.338	0.060	0.011	0.489	−0.020	0.001	2,380
1993	−0.728	0.098	0.024	0.413	−0.013	0.001	2,386
1994	−0.944	0.115	0.038	0.446	−0.014	0.001	2,528
1995	−0.607	0.083	0.019	0.518	−0.018	0.001	2,104
1996	−0.267	0.052	0.009	0.328	−0.004	0.001	2,266
1997	−0.235	0.048	0.008	0.205	0.007	0.000	2,116

Note: Table entries are least squares estimation results from equation (1) described in the text using Survey of Consumer Finance Data, Statistics Canada. The coefficients on ln Income for university participation are all statistically significant with t-statistics ranging from 4.02 in 1997 to 10.6 in 1991. Those for college participation are not statistically different from zero for 1979, 1982, 1984, 1985, 1988, 1990, 1991.

Table A4: Two-Stage Least Squares Regression Results of the Elasticity Between Postsecondary Participation and Family Income for 18 to 24-Year-Olds, Using Father's Permanent Income Estimated from the General Social Survey

	University			Postsecondary			Sample Size
	Intercept	In (Father's Income)	R^2	Intercept	In (Father's Income)	R^2	
1. Total							
1986	−2.85	0.296	0.053	−2.43	0.290	0.040	1,423
1994	−3.85	0.396	0.068	−2.54	0.302	0.038	750
2001	−2.42	0.255	0.025	−0.67	0.121	0.005	1,677
2. Men							
1986	−3.07	0.319	0.055	−2.84	0.329	0.048	669
1994	−3.60	0.369	0.064	−1.86	0.234	0.023	344
2001	−2.67	0.275	0.031	−0.94	0.141	0.006	735
3. Women							
1986	−2.61	0.272	0.050	−2.04	0.253	0.032	754
1994	−4.15	0.427	0.072	−3.33	0.380	0.062	406
2001	−2.27	0.245	0.021	−0.51	0.110	0.004	942

Note: Table entries are least squares estimation results from equation (1) described in the text using General Social Survey, Statistics Canada and relying on predicted parental income as estimated from equation (2). The coefficients on In Father's Income for university participation are all statistically significant at the 0.99 level with t-statistics ranging from 3.51 in 1986 to 5.88 in 1994. The coefficients on In Father's Income for overall postsecondary education participation are all statistically significant at the 0.95 level, except in 2001 analyses for men and women when the significance level is 0.90. The t-statistics for overall postsecondary education participation range from 1.66 in 2001 to 5.28 in 1986.

References

Angrist, J.D. 1999. "Estimation of Limited Dependent Variable Models with Dummy Endogenous Regressors: Simple Strategies for Empirical Practice", *Journal of Business and Economic Statistics* 19(1), 2-16.

Angrist, J.D. and A.B. Krueger. 1995. "Split-Sample Instrumental Variables Estimates of the Return to Schooling", *Journal of Business and Economic Statistics* 13(2), 225-235.

Baker, M. and G. Solon. 2003. "Earnings Dynamics and Inequality among Canadian Men, 1976-1992: Evidence from Longitudinal Income Tax Records", *Journal of Labor Economics* 21(2), 289-322.

Beach, C.M., R. Finnie and D. Gray. 2003. "Earnings Variability and Earnings Instability of Women and Men in Canada: How Do the 1990s Compare to the 1980s", *Canadian Public Policy/Analyse de Politiques* 29, Supplement S41-S63.

Björklund, A. and M. Jäntti. 1997. "Intergenerational Income Mobility in Sweden Compared to the United States", *American Economic Review* 87(5), 1009-1018.

Bouchard, B. and J. Zhao. 2000. "University Education: Recent Trends in Participation, Accessibility and Returns", *Education Quarterly Review* 6(4). Catalogue No. 81-003. Ottawa: Statistics Canada.

Bowlby, J. and K. McMullen. 2002. *At the Crossroads: First Results for the 18 to 20 Year-old Cohort of the Youth in Transition Survey*. Catalogue No. 81-591. Ottawa: Statistics Canada.

Boyd, M. and D. Norris. 1999. "The Crowded Nest: Young Adults Living at Home", *Canadian Social Trends*. Catalogue No. 11-008-XPE, Spring, No. 52. Ottawa: Statistics Canada.

Canada. 2002. *Knowledge Matters: Skills and Learning for Canadians*. Ottawa: Human Resources Development Canada.

Christofides, L.N., J. Cirello and M. Hoy. 2001. "Family Income and Post-Secondary Education in Canada", *Canadian Journal of Higher Education* 31(1), 177-208.

Fortin, N.M. and S. Lefebvre. 1998. "Intergenerational Income Mobility in Canada", in M. Corak (ed.), *Labour Markets, Social Institutions, and the Future of Canada's Children*. Catalogue No. 89-553. Ottawa: Statistics Canada.

Grawe, N. 2004. "Intergenerational Mobility for Whom? The Experience of High and Low Earnings Sons in International Perspective", in M. Corak (ed.), *Generational Income Mobility in North America and Europe*. Cambridge: Cambridge University Press.

Greene, W.H. 1997. *Econometric Analysis*. 3rd edition. Upper Saddle River, NJ: Prentice Hall.

Junor, S. and A. Usher. 2002. *The Price of Knowledge: Access and Student Finance in Canada*. Montreal: Canada Millennium Scholarship Foundation.

Knighton, T. and S. Mirza. 2002. "Post-Secondary Participation: The Effects of Parents' Education and Household Income", *Education Quarterly Review* 8(3). Catalogue No. 81-003. Ottawa: Statistics Canada.

Meunier, D., P. Bernard and J. Boisjoly. 1998. "Eternal Youth? Changes in the Living Arrangements of Young People", in M. Corak (ed.), *Labour Markets, Social Institutions, and the Future of Canada's Children.* Catalogue No. 89-553. Ottawa: Statistics Canada.

Moffitt, R.A. 1999. "New Developments in Econometric Methods for Labor Market Analysis", in O. Ashenfelter and D. Card (eds.), *Handbook of Labor Economics.* Volume 3A. Amsterdam: North-Holland Elsevier.

Raymond, M. and M. Rivard. 2003. "Have Tuition Fees in the Late 1990s Undermined Access to Post-Secondary Education in Canada?" Paper presented to the Canadian Employment Research Forum conference on Education, Schooling and the Labour Market, Carleton University, Ottawa.

Solon, G. 1992. "Intergenerational Income Mobility in the United States", *American Economic Review* 82, 393-408.

Statistics Canada. 2001a. "Survey of Approaches to Educational Planning, 1999", *The Daily.* Ottawa: Statistics Canada, April 10.

_____. 2001b. *2001 Census Dictionary.* Catalogue No. 92-378-XIE. Ottawa: Statistics Canada.

Zhao, J. and P. de Broucker. 2001. "Participation in Postsecondary Education and Family Income", *The Daily.* Ottawa: Statistics Canada, December 7.

_____. 2002. "Participation in Postsecondary Education and Family Income", *The Daily.* Ottawa: Statistics Canada, January 9.

Zimmerman, D.J. 1992. "Regression Toward Mediocrity in Economic Stature", *American Economic Review* 82, 409-429.

Who Goes? The Direct and Indirect Effects of Family Background on Access to Postsecondary Education

Ross Finnie, Eric Lascelles and Arthur Sweetman

Introduction

Access to postsecondary education is an important policy issue for two principal reasons. At the individual level advanced schooling is a critical determinant of individuals' career and economic success, and at the societal level it is fundamental to the nation's economic performance. "Who goes", therefore, impacts economic efficiency, but individual access, or lack of access, also has substantial equity implications. The twin issues of social justice and economic efficiency comprise a potent policy context for discussions of access to postsecondary education and the role of family background in this dynamic.

Much of the current Canadian debate regarding access to post-secondary education focuses on tuition levels and student financial aid; this, typically, follows from the assumption that affordability is an

The authors are grateful to Christine Laporte for her participation in related work and to our colleagues at Statistics Canada and Queen's for comments. Financial support for Sweetman from SSHRC is gratefully acknowledged. An earlier version of this paper was produced with the support of Statistics Canada.

important barrier to access and that family background operates largely through this factor. As will be discussed, there is an emerging body of evidence suggesting that affordability may not currently be the principal reason that individuals do not go on to postsecondary education, and that family background — while very important to access — operates more through factors other than financial ones, although postgraduation student debt is clearly impacted by financing.

Most studies of family background include a limited number of basic characteristics such as family income, parental education, family type, and place of residence. These studies provide important information regarding the overall degree to which these factors affect postsecondary access, but they do not tell us how these factors operate, or what other factors are important. Does parental education, for example, serve chiefly to improve individuals' performance in high school and otherwise prepare them for college or university, or does it affect participation after controlling for such factors (e.g., through financing or an understanding of the benefits of higher schooling)? Or is it some combination of the two? As far as we are aware, no research using Canadian data considers the direct and indirect mechanisms by which background variables operate.

In this paper we attempt to address these broader issues using Statistics Canada's School Leavers Survey, which is uniquely rich in background information including high school and related outcomes. We seek to identify the relative importance of pre-postsecondary intermediate outcomes in mediating background factors to affect postsecondary participation. Family background characteristics include parental education, family type, place of residence, language, and ethnicity. Pre-postsecondary intermediate outcomes and attitudes include elementary school success, high-school academic outcomes, school-related behaviour, attitudes towards school of the individual, the students' peer group and parents, and outside work during school.

We exploit these data by employing a block recursive approach which consists of first including only our set of background personal and family characteristics in the model, then adding the set of high-school and related "intermediate" variables, so-named because they occur subsequent to the family background variables and lie (chronologically) "between" these and the final outcome of interest (i.e., access). Our first ("short") model thus identifies the total effects of our measures of family background on postsecondary participation in a manner comparable to other analyses of this type. Our second ("long") model then gives a more complete view of the various determinants of postsecondary participation, including the effects of family background once the other intermediate factors are taken into account. Thus, the long regression allows us to see the effect of each regressor that is independent of the effects of the other regressors. Finally, comparing the coefficients on the family background variables in the two models allows us to break the total effects of the family background characteristics into those that operate through individuals' observed high-school outcomes and the other intermediate outcomes, and those that operate directly, after taking those other influences into account. We round out the recursive model approach by showing how some of the intermediate outcomes, such as high-school grades, are themselves determined by family background.

This exercise is carried out for men and women for two different outcomes: (i) postsecondary participation at any level, from trade school through community college up to and including university, and (ii) university participation only. We find, first of all, that family background is an important determinant of postsecondary access. We also find, how-ever, that many of the intermediate outcomes have substantial effects on postsecondary participation and, further, that the family background effects are significantly attenuated when these variables are added. Otherwise put, our results indicate that a substantial portion of the family background effects operates through their influence on other pre-postsecondary factors, such as high-school marks, attitudes towards higher schooling, the pro-pensity to work while in high school, and so on. Not surprisingly, the findings are stronger for university attendance than the broader post-secondary participation measure. We close by discussing some of the policy implications of these findings.

The Literature

Government policy involving access to postsecondary is frequently associated with the idea that liquidity constraints are a major barrier to postsecondary access and loans and grants programs are seen as a response, although reducing student debt is sometimes seen as a goal of such programs in its own right. The existing Canadian research is surveyed by Looker (2001), and Junor and Usher (2002) paint a broader portrait of the current postsecondary education system that includes a significant dis-cussion of access issues. However, a large literature, sometimes said to follow from the Coleman Report (1966) for the United States, points to the importance of family background in predicting educational outcomes. Haveman and Wolfe (1995) review the American literature on children's attainment, which clearly shows that family background starts to influence educational and related outcomes well before the transition to post-secondary. This is also a well-established empirical finding in the Canadian literature and recent work by, for example, Ma and Klinger (2000), and Willms (1999), find that socio-economic status (SES) is a key determinant of outcomes in high school. It is difficult to disentangle the effect of SES that operates directly on postsecondary access, perhaps through financing, and the part that occurs regardless of financing.

Recently, a distinction has been forcefully made in considering the relevance of family wealth or income on postsecondary access by Carneiro and Heckman (2002), and Cameron and Taber (2004). They point out that even if a correlation between financial resources and access is observed, it is not synonymous with causation because SES is also highly correlated with early school achievement and it is not clear what mechanism is causing the observed correlation. Using indirect methods, since individual credit constraints and returns to education cannot be observed, they argue that, in the United States, there is little evidence that borrowing costs hamper access. This is not to say that students do not accumulate debt, or that the current level of support is not required, but that the current environment is such that financing is not a key issue on the margin. These results are, of course, controversial, and the models employed define post-secondary access as being restricted only if not attending implies a reduction in lifetime earnings. That is, access is not taken to be hampered if, for the marginal person, it is not a good economic investment. Kane (2001) disputes these findings by showing differences in postsecondary enrolment rates across family income quartiles, even when test scores, high-school grades and parental education are held constant. Dynarski (2002), and Heller (1997) focus on the effects of price and student aid on access.

Some Canadian evidence in accord with the argument that financing is not crucial comes from work by Christofides, Cirello and Hoy (2001) who find that tuition fees do not seem to affect the pattern of postsecondary participation by social background. These ideas imply a reinterpretation of claims by students reported in, for example, Foley (2001) that educational costs *are* a major deterrent to their pursuit of postsecondary education. Student claims that high costs are preventing their attendance can also be taken to imply their expected personal low economic rates of return to education, and, therefore, for these students it is not a good investment. Of

Ross Finnie, Eric Lascelles and Arthur Sweetman

course, this interpretation ignores non-economic rationales for pursuing higher education.

A different, but starker, finding follows from a number of recent studies focusing on financial issues. They suggest that family income is no longer a crucial, or at least is a declining, determinant of postsecondary access in Canada. Corak, Lipps and Zhao (2003) report that although individuals from higher-income families are significantly more likely to attend university (although not college) in recent decades, the participation gap between high- and low-income families narrowed substantially through the early and mid-1990s until 1997, at which point their data stops. The authors suggest that this convergence may be explained by an increased take-up in student loans over this period. Zhao and de Broucker (2001, 2002) report relatively small differences in participation by family income when all levels of postsecondary education are considered, but much larger gaps when just university attainment is considered. Finnie and Laporte (2004) use the recently available Post-Secondary Education Participation Survey to find essentially no difference in participation rates by family income level, but large differences with respect to parental education, although the former finding is tempered by sample issues which also characterize some of the other papers on this subject (i.e., family income is measured for only individuals classified as living "at home").

Turning to more specific Canadian studies, Butlin (1999) uses the School Leavers Survey and identifies a wide range of simple correlations between postsecondary education, family background, and high-school outcomes. De Broucker and Lavallée (1998a) use the International Adult Literacy Survey (IALS) to examine whether parental education affects child outcomes. They find that "inherited intellectual capital" has a strong effect; that is to say, higher parental education tends to result in higher education levels in children. Using the School Leavers Survey (1998b), they find that parents' occupation and the degree to which they support the education of their children are significant influences on educational attainment. Knighton and Mirza (2002) show, using the Survey of Labour and Income Dynamics (SLID), that both parental education and family income are significant determinants of postsecondary participation, but that parental education has a larger effect.

When broader background indicators are employed, however, a different picture emerges. Bouchard and Zhao (2000) compare changes in university participation rates over time using the General Social Survey (GSS) from 1986 and 1994. They find that participation rates increased for all levels of SES, but climbed the most for those in the middle rank, less for those at the top, and least for those at the bottom — thus twisting comparative rates in an uneven pattern across family types. The changes are, however, complicated by whether one focuses on absolute or relative gaps, and the comparisons are tempered by smallish sample sizes and the data for the two periods not being perfectly comparable. Finnie, Laporte and Lascelles (2004) use the School Leavers Survey in 1991 and the Youth in Transition Survey in 2000, and employ parental education as the background indicator. They report that the participation gap, as measured by parental education, generally widened over this period, especially at the university level. This change was driven principally by significant increases in postsecondary participation for those with university-educated parents. Frenette (2002, 2003), also using the SLID, investigates distance-to-school effects, and determines that postsecondary participation rates, especially for university, are strongly influenced by the distance an individual lives from a postsecondary institution, particularly for low-income students for whom the associated financial barriers would presumably be more pertinent.

That SES affects access is not in dispute, but the mechanism is the subject of heated debate. We contribute to this literature by focusing on the importance of family background's effects on intermediate variables, which in turn influence access. This broader model of postsecondary participation for Canada identifies a wider set of influences, and disentangles the direct, which includes financing, and indirect effects of family background.

The Model

We model the relationship between family background and the other factors that affect postsecondary participation with the following set of equations:

$$x_{2i} = F_{1i}(x_1, e_1) \tag{1}$$

and

$$y = F_2(x_2, x_1, e_2) = F_2\left(\sum F_{1i}(x_1, e_1), x_1, e_2\right). \tag{2}$$

Equation (1) represents the relationship between a set of intermediate variables, x_{2i} (e.g., high-school outcomes — subscript i indexes the set of intermediate variables) and a vector of background variables, x_1 (parental education, etc.). The second equation formalizes the notion that since both the family background variables (x_1) and the intermediate variables (x_2) affect postsecondary access (y), and the background variables also affect the intermediate variables, the background variables operate in two ways on access: indirectly (through the intermediate variables), and directly (after the intermediate variables and other factors are taken into account). The e's represent unobserved variables and idiosyncratic shocks affecting the dependent variable (i.e., stochastic error terms).

The key distinction between the background and intermediate variables is that, chronologically, the background variables occur first (i.e., they are pre-determined) and influence the intermediate variables, while the reverse is not true, and, in turn, they both influence the final outcome — post-secondary attendance. This permits us to use a block recursive estimation strategy (see, e.g., Greene, 2003, pp. 383 and 411).

Since there is a common dependent variable and common regressors, ordinary least squares (OLS) coefficients on the background variables for this recursive model have the property:

$$Direct\ Effect + Indirect\ Effect = Total\ Effect, \qquad (3)$$

which follows from the linearity of OLS.[1] For the results presented below, we rely heavily on this simple relationship.

Assuming a single intermediate variable to simplify the notation, the empirical model can be written in OLS form as:

$$\text{Intermediate:} \quad x_2 = \alpha_0 + \alpha_1 x_1 + e_1 \qquad (4)$$

---

[1] While we have a dichotomous dependent variable, and probit (or logit) models are often considered to be superior when dealing with such outcomes, we elect to use OLS estimation. Moffitt (1999) makes a convincing argument that OLS is in fact the preferred specification when one is interested in obtaining coefficient estimates, as opposed to predictions, because probit and logit models are more prone to misspecification and are inconsistent in the presence of heteroskedasticity, whereas OLS is more robust. Furthermore, the non-linear models do not have the (exact) "adding-up" property with respect to direct and indirect effects depended upon here. Although we do not present the results, the direct effect regressions were estimated using probits, and in general the results were very similar to those shown here.

Direct: $\qquad y = \beta_0 + \beta_1 x_1 + \beta_2 x_2 + e_2$. $\qquad\qquad$ (5)

Substituting equation (4) into (5):

$$y = \beta_0 + \beta_1 x_1 + \beta_2 (\alpha_0 + \alpha_1 x_1 + e_1) + e_2 \qquad (6)$$

$$= (\beta_0 + \beta_2 \alpha_0) + (\beta_1 + \beta_2 \alpha_1) x_1 + (\beta_2 e_1 + e_2) \quad (7)$$

Total: $\qquad\qquad = \gamma_0 + \gamma_1 x_1 + e_3 \qquad\qquad\qquad (8)$

where α represents the parameters in the intermediate equation, β represents the direct effects, and γ represents the total effects.

Intermediate effects regressions are estimated initially (one for each element of the vector x_2), and selected sets of estimates are presented to provide some insight into the relationship between the background and intermediate variables. However, for OLS there is no need to actually estimate the intermediate relationships to obtain the indirect effects of the background variables on the final outcome, or to compare these to the total effects. Instead, only equations (5) and (8) are estimated, and the indirect effects are obtained by subtracting. Restating equation (3) using our OLS notation,

$$\beta_1 + Indirect = \gamma_1 \qquad\qquad\qquad (9)$$

$$\therefore Indirect = \gamma_1 - \beta_1 . \qquad\qquad\qquad (10)$$

Standard errors for the indirect effect are obtained by bootstrapping the difference between the direct and intermediate regressions' coefficients.

Note that the indirect effect can also be expressed as

$$Indirect = (\beta_2 \alpha_1 + \beta_1) - \beta_1 = \beta_2 \alpha_1 . \qquad\qquad (11)$$

This has a simple intuitively appealing interpretation: the background variables impact the final outcome (postsecondary access) through the intermediate variables inasmuch as they affect the intermediate variables (i.e., α_1) and the intermediate variables subsequently impact the final outcomes (i.e., β_2). It is worth pointing out that the direct effect of the background variables estimated using this approach should be interpreted as an upper bound on the "true" background effect if there exists at least one independently relevant intermediate variable (x_2) that is omitted from the specification and is also correlated with the background variables. Adding intermediate variables that are caused by the background variables, and in turn influence access in ways not accounted for by the other intermediate variables will reduce the direct effect. Note also that the intermediate variables do more than mediate the background variables. The intermediate realization, on average, matters for the subsequent access. Note also that there exist background variables (e.g., parents' income is not measured in our dataset) that are omitted. Inasmuch as these are correlated with the included background variables, the estimated coefficients will be affected (e.g., omitting parents' income may make education appear more influential).

Data

We use Statistics Canada's 1991 School Leavers Survey (SLS) and 1995 School Leavers Follow-up Survey (SLFS). The SLS was conducted between April and June of 1991 among youth aged 18 to 20 years old. Its main objectives were to determine high-school dropout rates in Canada and to compare three categories of secondary school students: those still attending, successful completers, and dropouts. The SLFS, conducted between September and December 1995 among the same young people, then aged 22 to 24, was aimed at education, training, and labour market experiences beyond high school.

The SLS sampling frame was based on five years (1986 to 1990) of Family Allowance files, believed to provide the most complete listing of youth under 15 in Canada. An initial sample of 18,000 individuals was selected, of which 10,792 were traceable and 9,460 were interviewed. For the SLFS, 6,284 individuals were located and completed the second interview.[2] These surveys represent a unique source of information on the

---

[2] See Appendix A of *Leaving School* for the SLS, and Appendix A of *High School May Not be Enough* for the SLFS for information on the weighting methodology. All the results reported here reflect the sample weights meant to make the sample representative of the underlying population.

transition from secondary to postsecondary education in Canada.[3] The original SLS contains the background information that generates the explanatory variables used in our models, while the follow-up allows us to identify which individuals have gone on to postsecondary education, and if so, at what level.

The two dependent variables used in this analysis are indicators of (i) any postsecondary education, consisting of those who enrolled in a trade-vocational, college, or university program; and (ii) university attendance, consisting of those who enrolled in a bachelor's, graduate or professional program at that level. We thus look at a wider definition of access, and then a more restricted definition.[4] It might be expected that family background would play a more significant role in access to university than for the more comprehensive measure, which includes courses as short as a few months, available at a much greater number of institutions across the country, and at lower cost. Comparing results across the two models allows us to detect such differences. These variables indicate *participation* at the indicated level, the usual definition of access in the literature. This treatment also best suits the data, since continuing in a program and completion are separate issues which would require following individuals over time in a manner for which the SLS and SLFS are less appropriate. The age range of the respondents (all 22, 23 or 24 years old at the second survey date) means that they have had a reasonable opportunity to start postsecondary

---

[3]Statistics Canada's Youth in Transition Survey (YITS) will eventually offer new data of this type, but it does not yet follow respondents long enough to have had a full opportunity to pursue postsecondary studies (i.e., individuals are but 18–20 years old in the older wave).

[4]A number of SLFS postsecondary categories have been excluded from our definition of postsecondary education, affecting 193 responses. These are diplomas or certificates recognized only by an employer or business, and education taken towards a diploma, certificate, or licence from a professional association. Our definition essentially corresponds to the one used by the Canada Student Loans Program and its provincial counterparts. Individuals who have enrolled in both university and trade-vocational or college programs are counted as having gained access to the former.

schooling, but avoids the problem of individuals still being in secondary school, which arises when more youthful samples are employed.[5]

Table 1 reports the complete set of variables used in the regression analysis. It includes as comprehensive a list of factors that might affect postsecondary participation as possible.[6] The key background variable is parental education.[7] Except where otherwise stated, we employ a combined parental education indicator representing the maximum of the father's and mother's education (where both are present, otherwise we use the education of the single parent), instead of separate variables for the father and mother. When neither parent's education is reported the linear education measure is set to zero, and the "don't know" indicator is used. This eliminates the intrinsic difficulty of disentangling the effects of a missing parent's education from the family-type effects related to single-parent families, although we test the effects of mother's versus father's education in a separate analysis of two-parent families. It should be noted that family income, a possibly interesting background variable, is not available and this may influence the interpretation of the coefficient on education given their positive correlation. Note that family income is not available in the data. This implies that, inasmuch as it is correlated with both the dependent variables and parents' education, it will bias the coefficient on parents' education. It is likely that the estimated coefficients on education will be larger than they would be were family income included as a regressor if

---

[5]Postsecondary participation rates rise sharply to about age 20, then become much flatter, rising only slightly after this.

[6]This said, we did not want the models to include an excessive number of variables, and some of those used represent aggregates of the corresponding underlying variables (i.e., we combined categories where appropriate), while other variables found to have little influence were dropped from the analysis.

[7]Two points are worth noting about the parental education measure. First, in the survey questionnaire a parent was placed in the high-school category only if a diploma was obtained, while they were counted in the college or university category simply by having participated at that level of schooling, without necessarily having finished. These definitions therefore extend to our study. Second, parents' education was gathered only for those with whom the respondent was living at the time of the survey, thus excluding non-custodial divorced and separate parents.

Table 1: Descriptive Statistics and Participation Rates

A) Dependent Variables

Postsecondary Attainment	Mean Male	Mean Female
None	0.318	0.233
Any postsecondary	0.682	0.767
University	0.309	0.389
Sample Size	2671	2998

B) Background Variables

Variable	Mean Male	Mean Female	Any Postsec. Male	Any Postsec. Female	University Male	University Female
Parental education						
Years of father's education	9.100 [0.170]	9.026 [0.170]	na	na	na	na
Years of mother's education	9.738 [0.155]	10.015 [0.146]	na	na	na	na
Years of parent's education	11.072 [0.148]	11.124 [0.142]	na	na	na	na
Don't know	0.086	0.048	0.478	0.703	0.104	0.184
No high school	0.203	0.232	0.522	0.703	0.174	0.162
High school	0.274	0.245	0.663	0.732	0.256	0.336
College	0.158	0.172	0.739	0.883	0.302	0.445
University	0.233	0.228	0.858	0.885	0.573	0.659
Family type (lived with ...)						
two parents	0.821	0.794	0.712	0.800	0.333	0.420
father	0.036	0.022	0.620	0.851	0.145	0.380
mother	0.097	0.109	0.552	0.696	0.247	0.289
other	0.047	0.075	0.457	0.507	0.141	0.203
Province at age 15						
Newfoundland	0.029	0.032	0.706	0.710	0.304	0.284
Prince Edward Island	0.005	0.006	0.613	0.755	0.327	0.368
Nova Scotia	0.038	0.036	0.711	0.762	0.372	0.454
New Brunswick	0.032	0.033	0.570	0.643	0.238	0.345
Quebec	0.227	0.238	0.624	0.824	0.249	0.367
Ontario	0.370	0.376	0.738	0.785	0.319	0.420
Manitoba	0.043	0.041	0.577	0.694	0.317	0.454
Saskatchewan	0.042	0.041	0.687	0.758	0.370	0.473
Alberta	0.099	0.090	0.675	0.705	0.323	0.391
British Columbia	0.115	0.105	0.676	0.722	0.361	0.291
Urban/rural						
Urban	0.755	0.763	0.702	0.781	0.342	0.408
Rural	0.245	0.237	0.621	0.723	0.208	0.326
Language						
Majority	0.931	0.932	0.681	0.762	0.313	0.386
English speaker in Quebec	0.035	0.028	0.683	0.872	0.269	0.499
French speaker outside Quebec	0.021	0.024	0.700	0.862	0.238	0.368
Other primary language	0.013	0.015	0.694	0.768	0.275	0.373

Ross Finnie, Eric Lascelles and Arthur Sweetman

Table 1 *(continued)*

Ethnicity

North & West Europe	0.539	0.511	0.672	0.772	0.291	0.393
South & East Europe	0.101	0.097	0.740	0.841	0.386	0.461
Canada	0.135	0.164	0.621	0.721	0.240	0.306
Asian	0.029	0.029	0.926	0.900	0.750	0.468
Native	0.039	0.039	0.568	0.496	0.198	0.290
Other	0.026	0.020	0.605	0.907	0.372	0.385
Mixed	0.078	0.093	0.774	0.828	0.354	0.516
Unknown	0.053	0.048	0.671	0.697	0.276	0.275

Age

22	0 311	0.336	0.665	0.764	0.275	0.399
23	0.335	0.329	0.696	0.770	0.356	0.374
24	0.354	0.335	0.684	0.769	0.296	0.394

C) Intermediate Variables

	Mean		Any Postsec.		University	
			\multicolumn{4}{}{Participation Rate}			
Variable	**Male**	**Female**	**Male**	**Female**	**Male**	**Female**
High school type						
Private	0.081	0.106	0.789	0.889	0.443	0.564
Public	0.919	0.894	0.672	0.753	0.298	0.368
Elementary school success						
Failed grade	0.206	0.084	0.443	0.481	0.075	0.048
Never failed	0.794	0.916	0.744	0.794	0.370	0.420
High school grades						
A average	0.199	0.290	0.881	0.896	0.631	0.648
B average	0.407	0.466	0.732	0.779	0.323	0.361
C average	0.311	0.181	0.578	0.607	0.151	0.157
D or F average	0.050	0.021	0.333	0.474	0.035	0.071
Don't know average	0.034	0.042	0.377	0.591	0.117	0.059
Skip high school classes						
Skipped	0.608	0.556	0.673	0.745	0.294	0.352
Didn't Skip	0.392	0.434	0.696	0.796	0.333	0.434
Job during high school						
No job	0.341	0.381	0.677	0.738	0.362	0.377
Worked < 10 hours / week	0.117	0.130	0.763	0.846	0.390	0.502
Worked 10-20 hours / week	0.316	0.362	0.743	0.811	0.322	0.409
Worked 20+ hours / week	0.226	0.127	0.563	0.654	0.172	0.251
Math outcome in high school						
No difficulty	0.608	0.536	0.723	0.801	0.365	0.471
Difficulty	0.391	0.461	0.618	0.728	0.223	0.295
N/A	0.001	0.002	0.625	0.935	0.350	0.000
Science outcome in high school						
No difficulty	0.723	0.695	0.726	0.794	0.349	0.428
Difficulty	0.248	0.278	0.598	0.720	0.216	0.312
N/A	0.029	0.027	0.285	0.579	0.130	0.160

Table 1 *(continued)*

English outcome in high school						
No difficulty	0.724	0.840	0.733	0.787	0.364	0.421
Difficulty	0.276	0.159	0.547	0.664	0.167	0.219
N/A	0.001	0.001	0.210	0.302	0.000	0.000
High school enjoyment						
Enjoyed	0.832	0.862	0.723	0.797	0.341	0.415
Didn't enjoy	0.168	0.138	0.480	0.580	0.155	0.227
Class participation in high school						
Low	0.114	0.108	0.573	0.669	0.258	0.289
Medium	0.679	0.662	0.663	0.758	0.269	0.345
High	0.208	0.229	0.803	0.843	0.470	0.562
Interest in high school classes						
Found interesting	0.733	0.799	0.703	0.780	0.317	0.407
Uninterested	0.267	0.201	0.622	0.719	0.290	0.317
Parents' opinion of importance of HS						
High	0.938	0.949	0.695	0.785	0.325	0.407
Medium	0.058	0.048	0.492	0.436	0.072	0.059
Low	0.004	0.002	0.407	0.382	0.002	0.000
Friends' opinion of importance of HS						
High	0.708	0.798	0.736	0.813	0.359	0.436
Medium	0.252	0.168	0.581	0.604	0.206	0.204
Low	0.038	0.033	0.367	0.523	0.066	0.190
Physical disability						
Yes	0.046	0.062	0.518	0.626	0.238	0.178
No	0.954	0.938	0.690	0.777	0.313	0.403
Relationship with teachers in HS						
Didn't get along	0.049	0.020	0.359	0.431	0.113	0.169
Got along	0.951	0.980	0.698	0.774	0.320	0.393

Note: Rates not applicable (na) for continuous variables.

family income has any effect on access. This caveat needs to be borne in mind in interpreting the results below.

Two general sets of models are estimated, reflecting our treatment of parental education. In the first, it is captured by a single "years of parental education" variable. In the second, a series of categorical (dummy) variables is used: less than high school completed, high school completed, some or completed college, some or completed university, unknown. The variables in the latter model thus correspond to the information available in the survey data, while the linear variable is derived from these

Ross Finnie, Eric Lascelles and Arthur Sweetman

categories.[8] The first model thus captures the effects of parental education in a single parameter, while the second identifies some non-linearities of interest in these relationships.[9]

Sample restrictions were kept to a minimum so that the results would be as representative of the underlying population as possible. Individuals who migrated to Canada after the age of ten or who obtained most of their schooling outside Canada were deleted, since the relationship between educational attainment and family background is likely to be different for this group. We also eliminated the relatively few unclear responses, missing values, and certain "don't know" and "do not apply" responses. The resulting sample contains 5,669 (or 90.2%) of the initial 6,284 observations.

Descriptive Statistics

Dependent and Background Variables

Descriptive statistics for the variables used in the analysis are shown in Table 1. The dependent variables, background variables, and intermediate

---

[8]The linear variable was derived by assigning the following values: no high school: 8, less than high school completed: 10, high school completed: 12, some or completed college: 14, some or completed university: 16. The first two categories were combined in the indicator variables because differentiating them added nothing to the model. Unknown education receives its own dummy variable.

[9]In the linear specification, if parental education was not available, the variable was assigned a value of zero. In addition, if the respondent was in a family type with at least one parent and that information should, therefore, have been available, a "don't know" indicator variable was created. This allows the parental education coefficient to be interpreted as the effect for those for whom the information is available. For those in "other" family types (i.e., there was no parent present and hence no parental education information available), this extra variable was not assigned because the family-type indicator captures the whole missing parental education effect along with the family type effect (i.e., it is impossible to separate the two influences since they are perfectly correlated).

variables are shown in Panels A, B, and C in turn.[10] Almost all the explanatory variables are dichotomous and the table shows the percentage of individuals with each characteristic, and the associated postsecondary education participation rates (not being dichotomous, the linear parents' education variable has no associated rates defined). These univariate relationships are interesting and identify some of the patterns to watch for in the regression analysis to follow.

As shown in Panel A, 68% of the male respondents and 77% of the females in our samples (aged 22–24) had participated in some form of post-secondary education, while 31 and 39%, respectively, had gone to university. The rates of going to trade-vocational school or college as opposed to university are (obtained by subtraction) 37% for males, and 38% for females. Females have significantly higher overall postsecondary participation rates than males, driven by their higher rates of university attendance, which are 26% greater than that for the males.[11]

Acquiring postsecondary education is strongly related to parental education as seen in Panel B. Both males and females with university-educated parents are more than twice as likely to go to university themselves than those whose parents stopped after high school, and the gap is wider still when the comparison is made with those whose parents did not complete high school. The differences are much smaller, however, for the any postsecondary measure, thus indicating that a substantial number of children with less-educated parents manage to make it into the college and trade-vocational system, especially in the case of females.[12]

---

[10]The place of residence variables (province, urban-rural), are treated as background variables because they represent where the individual lived while in high school. Urban-rural status could be viewed as an intermediate variable in alternative interpretations, but this makes no substantive difference.

[11]There are many ways to measure postsecondary participation, and for different populations, so these figures will not necessarily compare directly to other published data on postsecondary participation. They seem reasonable, however, when placed against others.

[12]Although not presented, the data indicates that going to community college (not combined with university) is negatively related to parental education (youth with less-educated parents are more likely to go to college). But the effects of parental education on college participation are both positive and negative: having more highly educated parents is related to higher postsecondary participation at

Ross Finnie, Eric Lascelles and Arthur Sweetman

Postsecondary participation is also significantly related to family type. For example, 42% of all female respondents who lived in a two-parent family went to university, whereas only 29% of those who lived in a mother-only family did so. The less common situations of living in a father-only family or with others (i.e., neither parent) are associated with rates of 38 and 20%, respectively. For males, the patterns are a little different, but the higher rate for two-parent families persists, at 33%, versus 25, 15, and 14% for the other family types (mother-only, father-only, and other). We shall see that this gender pattern, interestingly, persists in the regression findings below. The patterns vary somewhat for the any postsecondary education measure, but the two-parent family advantage again holds.

By province (representing where the individual lived while in high school), the any postsecondary attendance rate in Quebec (francophones, anglophones, other language types together) is especially high among females, reflecting to at least some degree the inclusion of CEGEP students (Quebec's amalgam of community college and pre-university preparation which substitutes for the last years of high school in other provinces). In this respect, it is perhaps surprising that the rate is not higher for Quebec males, who are in the low-middle range of the provincial ordering. University attendance among Quebec females is in the middle rank in comparison to the other provinces, and low for males. Individuals from Nova Scotia, Newfoundland, and Ontario generally have high any post-secondary attendance rates, while Saskatchewan and Nova Scotia have the highest university attendance rates among both males and females. Those from urban backgrounds are somewhat more likely to go on to some sort of postsecondary education, and are far more likely to go to university, consistent with Frenette (2002, 2003).

In terms of minority language (anglophones in Quebec, francophones and other primary languages elsewhere), English-speaking females in Quebec have the highest rate of postsecondary participation by both measures of any group. The same dominance is not seen, however, for anglophone males in Quebec. Francophones in other provinces have high rates of any postsecondary participation, but more average rates of university participation in comparison to the anglophone majorities. Individuals brought up with other languages have average participation rates.

---

some level (a positive effect), but a greater chance of going to university rather than college among those who go (a negative effect).

Respondents of Asian background are uniformly more likely to attend all types of postsecondary institutions (any postsecondary, university) than any other ethnic group, for both genders. Asian women, however, although still the most likely female ethnic group to attend university, do not enrol in nearly the numbers that their male counterparts do (47% versus 75%). In contrast, Native (First Nations) Canadians are less likely to go to a university or postsecondary institution than any other ethnic group.

Intermediate Variables

Panel C of Table 1 shows the intermediate variables representing school performance, attitudes, and related outcomes, along with the associated postsecondary participation rates. Brief titular descriptions of each variable are provided in panel C, as are the range of values each may take. It is interesting to observe that girls failed fewer grades, had higher averages, skipped fewer classes, were more interested in school, participated more, and were more likely to get along with their teachers. They also had less difficulty in English, whereas boys did better in math and sciences by these measures. Females graduating high school with 'A' averages had a 65, and males a 63, percent rate of university attendance. By contrast, substantially fewer than 10% of those with 'D' or 'F' averages went to university,[13] and the rate is just 15–16% for 'C' average students. The relationship between grade average and any postsecondary participation is much weaker, reflecting the Canadian system where access to trade-vocational schools or community colleges is open even to those with minimal qualifications.

The other relationships offer no surprises, but their magnitudes are interesting, coming as they do from a representative sample of young people followed into their postsecondary years. Rates of postsecondary participation, especially at the university level, are higher for those who went to private school, who did not skip classes, who had no difficulty in math, science, or English (French for francophones), who enjoyed school, participated more, found classes interesting, and got along with their teachers, who had parents or friends that attached a strong importance to high school (almost the entire sample in the case of the former), or who had

---

[13]The latter rates might seem high, and could represent either the mis-reporting of grades, or perhaps "mature students" going to university after a stint in the workforce, when grades are less important for meeting entrance requirements.

no physical disability. Finally, working a small number of hours at a job while in high school is associated with the highest any postsecondary and university participation rates. This roughly corresponds to Bushnik (2003) who finds that working a moderate number of hours in school decreases the likelihood of dropping out, while Ruhm (1997) finds that a moderate work commitment in high school is positively correlated with future earnings.

Regression Results

The Direct Effects Models

Tables 2 through 5 present the any postsecondary and university access model results for males and females where parental education is represented by a single "years of schooling" measure. The direct effect ("long") models based on equation (5) above, where both the background and intermediate variables are included, are presented in the first columns of numbers in these tables. The total effect models and the implied indirect effects take up the rest of the tables. Since the sample sizes are modest for some of the intermediate and background variable categories, we estimated models, which we do not present to conserve space, similar to those presented but with a male indicator variable added and the two sexes combined. This approach resulted, in general, in more precise estimates and some of the variables with marginally statistically significant coefficients became statistically significant. It also led to a masking of the differences between the sexes. Overall, the pattern observed was similar to those presented and supports the interpretations below.

Parental Education and Family Type. Parental education has a strong direct effect on postsecondary participation in all models. Since the parental education variables are also interacted with the single-parent family indicators ("live father" and "live mother"), the coefficients on the "years of par educ" variable taken alone represent the relationship between parental education and postsecondary participation for two-parent families, while the interactions pick up the differences in these effects (if any) for the other family types. Each year of parents' education for the baseline two-parent family type is associated with approximately a 2% increase in the

Table 2: Male Any Postsecondary OLS Regression Results

Variable	Direct Effect Coef.		Std.Err.	Total Effect Coef.		Std.Err.	Indirect Effect Coef.		Std.Err.	% Indirect
Parents' Education and Family Type										
Years of par educ	0.022	***	[0.006]	0.040	***	[0.006]	0.017	***	[0.003]	43%
Par educ DK	0.146	*	[0.088]	0.276	***	[0.097]	0.129	***	[0.050]	47%
Yrs par educ & live fath	-0.009		[0.028]	-0.019		[0.032]	-0.010		[0.012]	53%
Yrs par educ & live moth	-0.006		[0.017]	-0.005		[0.019]	0.001		[0.008]	-13%
Par educ DK & live fath	0.237		[0.369]	0.140		[0.420]	-0.097		[0.169]	-70%
Par educ DK & live moth	-0.076		[0.241]	-0.115		[0.274]	-0.039		[0.126]	34%
Live father	0.106		[0.335]	0.143		[0.382]	0.037		[0.150]	26%
Live mother	-0.007		[0.211]	-0.045		[0.241]	-0.038		[0.104]	85%
Live other	0.107		[0.097]	0.230	**	[0.109]	0.123	**	[0.048]	53%
Place of Residence										
Newfoundland	-0.002		[0.045]	0.032		[0.047]	0.034		[0.022]	105%
Prince Edward Island	-0.057		[0.056]	-0.065		[0.058]	-0.008		[0.024]	13%
Nova Scotia	0.010		[0.041]	0.010		[0.042]	0.000		[0.018]	-5%
New Brunswick	-0.117	**	[0.053]	-0.126	**	[0.055]	-0.009		[0.025]	7%
Quebec	-0.101	**	[0.039]	-0.056		[0.041]	0.046	*	[0.024]	-81%
Manitoba	-0.113	***	[0.044]	-0.149	***	[0.046]	-0.036	**	[0.018]	24%
Saskatchewan	-0.043		[0.043]	-0.017		[0.045]	0.026		[0.020]	-155%
Alberta	-0.059		[0.040]	-0.083	**	[0.041]	-0.023		[0.019]	28%
British Columbia	-0.077	*	[0.040]	-0.075	*	[0.042]	0.002		[0.018]	-3%
Rural	-0.022		[0.031]	-0.033		[0.034]	-0.011		[0.016]	34%
Language and Ethnicity										
English in Quebec	0.070		[0.070]	0.004		[0.091]	-0.065		[0.052]	-1506%
French outside Quebec	0.072		[0.069]	0.124	*	[0.069]	0.052		[0.039]	42%
Other language	0.020		[0.105]	0.017		[0.122]	-0.003		[0.057]	-16%
South & East Europe	0.068		[0.045]	0.093	*	[0.051]	0.026		[0.022]	27%
Canadian	-0.004		[0.040]	-0.017		[0.042]	-0.013		[0.018]	75%
Asian	0.129	***	[0.041]	0.230	***	[0.041]	0.101	***	[0.023]	44%
Native	0.020		[0.071]	-0.067		[0.075]	-0.087	**	[0.038]	130%
Origin other	-0.053		[0.086]	-0.088		[0.111]	-0.035		[0.056]	40%
Origin mixed	0.079	*	[0.042]	0.086	*	[0.046]	0.006		[0.021]	7%
Intermediate Variables										
Private HS	0.053		[0.039]							
Failed elem school	-0.163	***	[0.034]							
A average	0.059	*	[0.031]							
C average	-0.070	**	[0.031]							
D/F average	-0.201	***	[0.066]							
Skip class	0.002		[0.026]							
Short work	0.031		[0.036]							
Medium work	0.022		[0.028]							
Long work	-0.084	***	[0.032]							
Math is difficult	-0.006		[0.027]							
Science is difficult	-0.042		[0.030]							
English is difficult	-0.031		[0.030]							
Enjoy school	0.085	**	[0.040]							
Low class part.	-0.013		[0.043]							
High class part.	0.032		[0.029]							
Find class interesting	-0.027		[0.030]							
Med parent opinion	0.014		[0.056]							
Low parent opinion	-0.072		[0.227]							
Med friend opinion	-0.059	*	[0.031]							
Low friend opinion	-0.111		[0.081]							
Limited activity	-0.115	*	[0.069]							
Not along w teacher	-0.113	*	[0.066]							
R^2	0.257			0.110			N/A			

Notes: Robust standard errors in brackets: * 10% significance; ** 5% significance; *** 1% significance.
N=2671   Regressions also include indicator variables for non-response as listed in Table 1.

Table 3: Female Any Postsecondary OLS Regression Results

Variable	Direct Effect Coeff.		Std. Err.	Total Effect Coeff.		Std. Err	Indirect Effect Coeff.		Std. Err.	% Indirect
Parents' Education and Family Type										
Years of par educ	0.018	***	[0.005]	0.031	***	[0.005]	0.014	***	[0.003]	44%
Par educ DK	0.202	**	[0.090]	0.307	***	[0.095]	0.105	**	[0.043]	34%
Yrs par educ & live fath	0.030		[0.022]	0.030		[0.022]	0.000		[0.011]	0%
Yrs par educ & live moth	-0.010		[0.017]	-0.008		[0.018]	0.002		[0.007]	-31%
Par educ DK & live fath	0.324		[0.380]	0.142		[0.465]	-0.183		[0.213]	-129%
Par educ DK & live moth	-0.120		[0.265]	-0.112		[0.268]	0.008		[0.104]	-8%
Live father	-0.327		[0.312]	-0.315		[0.325]	0.012		[0.147]	-4%
Live mother	0.096		[0.214]	0.034		[0.219]	-0.062		[0.094]	-183%
Live other	0.042		[0.086]	0.143		[0.089]	0.100	**	[0.045]	70%
Place of Residence										
Newfoundland	0.027		[0.042]	0.016		[0.043]	-0.011		[0.021]	-70%
Prince Edward Island	0.062		[0.046]	0.015		[0.049]	-0.047	**	[0.022]	-303%
Nova Scotia	0.059		[0.037]	0.031		[0.039]	-0.028		[0.018]	-89%
New Brunswick	-0.099	*	[0.050]	-0.127	**	[0.052]	-0.028		[0.023]	22%
Quebec	0.073	*	[0.038]	0.096	**	[0.039]	0.022		[0.021]	23%
Manitoba	-0.067	*	[0.039]	-0.077	*	[0.042]	-0.010		[0.017]	13%
Saskatchewan	0.006		[0.037]	0.001		[0.040]	-0.005		[0.019]	-412%
Alberta	-0.051		[0.037]	-0.088	**	[0.038]	-0.037	**	[0.018]	42%
British Columbia	-0.009		[0.041]	-0.045		[0.041]	-0.036	**	[0.017]	80%
Rural	-0.014		[0.025]	-0.007		[0.028]	0.006		[0.013]	-86%
Age										
Age 23	0.000		[0.026]	0.009		[0.027]	0.008		[0.012]	99%
Age 24	0.028		[0.027]	0.024		[0.030]	-0.004		[0.014]	-17%
Language and Ethnicity										
English in Quebec	-0.055		[0.071]	-0.049		[0.068]	0.006		[0.027]	-13%
French outside Quebec	0.171	***	[0.061]	0.186	***	[0.057]	0.015		[0.027]	8%
Other language	0.012		[0.096]	-0.060		[0.110]	-0.072		[0.046]	120%
South & East Europe	0.086	**	[0.042]	0.126	***	[0.044]	0.040	**	[0.016]	32%
Canadian	-0.024		[0.032]	-0.064	*	[0.037]	-0.040	**	[0.019]	62%
Asian	0.102	*	[0.055]	0.126	**	[0.060]	0.024		[0.023]	19%
Native	-0.140	**	[0.063]	-0.219	***	[0.071]	-0.079	**	[0.033]	36%
Origin other	0.110	**	[0.049]	0.125	***	[0.045]	0.015		[0.030]	12%
Origin mixed	0.072	**	[0.036]	0.066	*	[0.038]	-0.006		[0.015]	-9%
Intermediate Variables										
Private HS	0.037		[0.036]							
Failed elem school	-0.154	***	[0.052]							
A average	0.045	*	[0.025]							
C average	-0.072	**	[0.035]							
D/F average	-0.139		[0.104]							
Skip class	0.009		[0.022]							
Short work	0.038		[0.033]							
Medium work	0.037		[0.025]							
Long work	-0.032		[0.047]							
Math is difficult	-0.004		[0.026]							
Science is difficult	0.005		[0.027]							
English is difficult	-0.002		[0.034]							
Enjoy school	0.100	**	[0.042]							
Low class part.	-0.045		[0.042]							
High class part.	0.025		[0.028]							
Find class interesting	-0.037		[0.030]							
Med parent opinion	-0.215	***	[0.078]							
Low parent opinion	-0.020		[0.164]							
Med friend opinion	-0.086	**	[0.035]							
Low friend opinion	-0.099		[0.081]							
Limited activity	-0.060		[0.057]							
Not along w teacher	-0.151	*	[0.087]							
R^2	0.212			0.110			N/A			

Notes: Robust standard errors in brackets: * 10% significance; ** 5% significance; *** 1% significance.
N=2998 Regressions also include indicator variables for non-response as listed in Table 1.

Who Goes? Access to Postsecondary Education   *315*

Table 4: Male University OLS Regression Results

Variable	Direct Effect Coeff.		Std. Err.	Total Effect Coeff.		Std. Err	Indirect Effect Coeff.		Std. Err.	% Indirect
Parents' Education and Family Type										
Years of par educ	0.033	***	[0.006]	0.054	***	[0.006]	0.022	***	[0.003]	40%
Par educ DK	0.248	***	[0.083]	0.464	***	[0.089]	0.216	***	[0.049]	47%
Yrs par educ & live fath	-0.039	**	[0.015]	-0.052	***	[0.016]	-0.013		[0.009]	25%
Yrs par educ & live moth	-0.007		[0.016]	-0.015		[0.017]	-0.008		[0.009]	53%
Par educ DK & live fath	-0.325		[0.221]	-0.534	**	[0.246]	-0.209	*	[0.127]	39%
Par educ DK & live moth	-0.002		[0.203]	-0.214		[0.206]	-0.212	*	[0.125]	99%
Live father	0.402	**	[0.193]	0.482	**	[0.207]	0.080		[0.112]	17%
Live mother	0.080		[0.191]	0.149		[0.199]	0.068		[0.106]	46%
Live other	0.329	***	[0.084]	0.502	***	[0.091]	0.173	***	[0.053]	35%
Place of Residence										
Newfoundland	-0.004		[0.042]	0.088	**	[0.041]	0.092	***	[0.021]	105%
Prince Edward Island	0.093	*	[0.048]	0.102	*	[0.054]	0.009		[0.025]	9%
Nova Scotia	0.103	***	[0.038]	0.112	***	[0.040]	0.009		[0.018]	8%
New Brunswick	0.001		[0.042]	0.025		[0.047]	0.024		[0.024]	94%
Quebec	-0.084	**	[0.039]	0.021		[0.038]	0.105	***	[0.024]	497%
Manitoba	0.044		[0.039]	0.018		[0.041]	-0.026		[0.019]	-145%
Saskatchewan	0.050		[0.043]	0.104	**	[0.048]	0.054	***	[0.021]	52%
Alberta	0.006		[0.036]	-0.021		[0.039]	-0.027		[0.018]	128%
British Columbia	0.029		[0.041]	0.022		[0.044]	-0.007		[0.018]	-29%
Rural	-0.061	***	[0.023]	-0.073	***	[0.026]	-0.012		[0.015]	16%
Age										
Age 23	0.057	**	[0.029]	0.091	***	[0.029]	0.035	**	[0.014]	38%
Age 24	0.028		[0.028]	0.041		[0.030]	0.012		[0.016]	31%
Language and Ethnicity										
English in Quebec	-0.029		[0.071]	-0.093		[0.071]	-0.064		[0.043]	69%
French outside Quebec	-0.058		[0.054]	0.030		[0.078]	0.089	**	[0.043]	292%
Other language	-0.060		[0.132]	-0.044		[0.146]	0.016		[0.055]	-35%
South & East Europe	0.154	***	[0.048]	0.177	***	[0.055]	0.023		[0.024]	13%
Canadian	0.017		[0.031]	-0.019		[0.034]	-0.036	**	[0.018]	188%
Asian	0.272	***	[0.087]	0.414	***	[0.084]	0.142	***	[0.029]	34%
Native	0.022		[0.057]	-0.062		[0.055]	-0.085	***	[0.030]	136%
Origin other	0.090		[0.083]	0.061		[0.102]	-0.030		[0.050]	-49%
Origin mixed	0.042		[0.049]	0.031		[0.053]	-0.011		[0.023]	-36%
Intermediate Variables										
Private HS	0.049		[0.048]							
Failed elem school	-0.124	***	[0.026]							
A average	0.192	***	[0.036]							
C average	-0.122	***	[0.028]							
D/F average	-0.176	***	[0.044]							
Skip class	-0.006		[0.024]							
Short work	-0.016		[0.041]							
Medium work	-0.074	***	[0.029]							
Long work	-0.149	***	[0.031]							
Math is difficult	-0.009		[0.025]							
Science is difficult	-0.022		[0.027]							
English is difficult	-0.036		[0.025]							
Enjoy school	0.031		[0.030]							
Low class part.	0.036		[0.037]							
High class part.	0.056	*	[0.032]							
Find class interesting	-0.061	**	[0.030]							
Med parent opinion	-0.087	**	[0.044]							
Low parent opinion	-0.106	*	[0.063]							
Med friend opinion	-0.052	**	[0.026]							
Low friend opinion	-0.072		[0.055]							
Limited activity	-0.032		[0.049]							
Not along w teacher	-0.040		[0.037]							
R^2	0.317			0.154			N/A			

Notes: Robust standard errors in brackets: * 10% significance; ** 5% significance; *** 1% significance.
N=2671 Regressions also include indicator variables for non-response as listed in Table 1.

Ross Finnie, Eric Lascelles and Arthur Sweetman

Table 5: Female University OLS Regression Results

Variable	Direct Effect Coeff.		Std. Err.	Total Effect Coeff.		Std. Err	Indirect Effect Coeff.		Std. Err.	% Indirect
Parents' Education and Family Type										
Years of par educ	0.041	***	[0.006]	0.065	***	[0.006]	0.024	***	[0.003]	37%
Par educ DK	0.463	***	[0.094]	0.625	***	[0.101]	0.163	***	[0.050]	26%
Yrs par educ & live fath	-0.041		[0.035]	-0.028		[0.038]	0.013		[0.015]	-47%
Yrs par educ & live moth	-0.015		[0.017]	-0.023		[0.017]	-0.007		[0.010]	32%
Par educ DK & live fath	-0.557		[0.499]	-0.546		[0.508]	0.011		[0.242]	-2%
Par educ DK & live moth	-0.239		[0.240]	-0.271		[0.232]	-0.031		[0.137]	12%
Live father	0.536		[0.482]	0.350		[0.499]	-0.187		[0.197]	-53%
Live mother	0.145		[0.210]	0.198		[0.202]	0.053		[0.123]	27%
Live other	0.411	***	[0.095]	0.619	***	[0.092]	0.207	***	[0.050]	34%
Place of Residence										
Newfoundland	-0.014		[0.044]	-0.006		[0.044]	0.008		[0.027]	-143%
Prince Edward Island	0.044		[0.046]	0.000		[0.052]	-0.043		[0.027]	-10661%
Nova Scotia	0.121	***	[0.039]	0.099	**	[0.044]	-0.022		[0.023]	-22%
New Brunswick	0.034		[0.048]	-0.007		[0.050]	-0.041		[0.027]	581%
Quebec	-0.067	*	[0.040]	0.000		[0.042]	0.068	***	[0.024]	14674%
Manitoba	0.042		[0.041]	0.040		[0.044]	-0.002		[0.022]	-5%
Saskatchewan	0.031		[0.040]	0.058		[0.045]	0.027		[0.026]	46%
Alberta	0.009		[0.039]	-0.064		[0.041]	-0.073	***	[0.022]	114%
British Columbia	-0.069	*	[0.041]	-0.132	***	[0.041]	-0.064	***	[0.021]	48%
Rural	-0.055	**	[0.028]	-0.030		[0.029]	0.025	*	[0.015]	-81%
Age										
Age 23	-0.020		[0.027]	-0.023		[0.029]	-0.004		[0.015]	16%
Age 24	0.015		[0.029]	0.012		[0.032]	-0.003		[0.016]	-29%
Language and Ethnicity										
English in Quebec	0.014		[0.086]	0.028		[0.089]	0.014		[0.038]	50%
French outside Quebec	-0.009		[0.083]	0.046		[0.078]	0.055		[0.040]	121%
Other language	0.041		[0.114]	-0.031		[0.138]	-0.072		[0.055]	232%
South & East Europe	0.101	**	[0.050]	0.164	***	[0.055]	0.063	***	[0.022]	38%
Canadian	-0.010		[0.034]	-0.060		[0.037]	-0.050	**	[0.020]	84%
Asian	0.003		[0.074]	0.042		[0.076]	0.039		[0.030]	94%
Native	0.059		[0.058]	-0.025		[0.062]	-0.085	**	[0.035]	334%
Origin other	-0.080		[0.090]	-0.062		[0.104]	0.019		[0.043]	-30%
Origin mixed	0.102	**	[0.042]	0.092	*	[0.048]	-0.010		[0.021]	-11%
Intermediate Variables										
Private HS	0.104	**	[0.046]							
Failed elem school	-0.144	***	[0.036]							
A average	0.175	***	[0.033]							
C average	-0.129	***	[0.033]							
D/F average	-0.122	*	[0.071]							
Skip class	-0.021		[0.026]							
Short work	0.017		[0.041]							
Medium work	-0.022		[0.030]							
Long work	-0.102	***	[0.039]							
Math is difficult	-0.079	***	[0.028]							
Science is difficult	0.000		[0.029]							
English is difficult	-0.033		[0.034]							
Enjoy school	0.043		[0.041]							
Low class part.	-0.001		[0.041]							
High class part.	0.076	**	[0.033]							
Find class interesting	-0.013		[0.032]							
Med parent opinion	-0.131	***	[0.048]							
Low parent opinion	0.070		[0.148]							
Med friend opinion	-0.061	*	[0.032]							
Low friend opinion	-0.044		[0.074]							
Limited activity	-0.110	**	[0.045]							
Not along w teacher	0.046		[0.073]							
R^2	0.2943			0.1475			N/A			

Notes: Robust standard errors in brackets: * 10% significance; ** 5% significance; *** 1% significance.
N=2998 Regressions also include indicator variables for non-response as listed in Table 1.

likelihood of any postsecondary attendance, and a 3 to 4% increase in the likelihood of University attendance. The four-year conventional difference between high school and university is thus worth about an 8% increase in doing any postsecondary schooling, and a 12 or 16% increase for university. These are large effects. What makes these impacts important is that they are direct effects and exist after controlling for all the other background variables available in our data and the measures of high-school outcomes, behaviour, and attitudes. Thus, parental education plays an important role in determining who goes on to postsecondary education, and at what level, even after accounting for a wide range of other factors, though, as mentioned, this is an upper bound if omitted intermediate variables are important.

Turning to the other family types, we first see that those who do not know their parents' education have low average rates of postsecondary participation, equivalent to those whose parents have about seven to ten years of schooling on average.[14] Further, although they are only sometimes individually statistically significant, the general pattern of the parental education-family type interactions suggests that the access gaps between two-parent and single-parent families grow somewhat with the level of parental education. That is, most of the interactions are negative — which are set against the general years of parental education variable just discussed. Seen from another perspective, the relationship between parental education and access appears to be in most cases weaker for single-parent families than two-parent families, and in some cases appears to be essentially flat, although the smaller sample sizes contribute to a general lack of precision of these estimates, especially for single-father families.

The family type indicators for lone-mother and lone-father families are not particularly interesting on their own, since the reduced effects of parents' education just mentioned need to be taken into account when making comparisons of access rates across family types (i.e., the models allow both the intercept and the slope on parental education to differ by family type). Table 6 shows predicted participation rates, based on the model coefficient estimates, by family type at various levels of parental education, and indicates that children from lone-mother families (for whom the sample sizes permit such comparisons), have uniformly lower participation rates than those from two-parent families for any given level

---

[14]This is seen by comparing the coefficient on "parents' educ DK" with "years of par educ" evaluated at any given number of years.

Table 6: Predicted Participation Rates by Family Type

Parent Education	Two-Parent Families		Single Mother Families	
	Direct Effect Model	Total Effect Model	Direct Effect Model	Total Effect Model
A) Any Postsecondary				
Male				
Don't know	0.618	0.500	0.527	0.341
No high school	0.668	0.569	0.610	0.483
High school	0.760	0.713	0.672	0.599
College	0.812	0.795	0.711	0.672
University	0.857	0.860	0.747	0.739
Female				
Don't know	0.781	0.718	0.739	0.627
No high school	0.704	0.672	0.737	0.652
High school	0.786	0.793	0.757	0.733
College	0.832	0.857	0.770	0.782
University	0.871	0.906	0.783	0.825
B) University				
Male				
Don't know	0.100	0.104	0.071	0.041
No high school	0.167	0.146	0.169	0.141
High school	0.271	0.286	0.251	0.245
College	0.354	0.405	0.315	0.333
University	0.444	0.534	0.386	0.431
Female				
Don't know	0.222	0.214	0.149	0.141
No high school	0.159	0.186	0.124	0.174
High school	0.269	0.365	0.216	0.291
College	0.360	0.507	0.295	0.384
University	0.459	0.649	0.385	0.485

Note: Aside from the regressors that define each cell, the predictions are with all indicator
variables set to zero (i.e., the prediction is for someone in all the omitted groups).

of parental education. Those who lived under other arrangements — alone, or with others — for whom parental education is not measured, fared worst of all (detailed calculations not shown).

Geography: Province and Urban-Rural Residence. While relatively few of the provincial coefficients are statistically significantly different from Ontario (the omitted category), in the any postsecondary regressions, individuals from New Brunswick and Manitoba have lower rates of attendance than Ontario. This pattern, however, disappears for the university models, indicating that the differences occur at the college level. Nova Scotia clearly focuses on university education and has the highest rate of university participation in the country for both sexes. In contrast, the coefficients for Quebec are negative except for the female any post-secondary regression, which reflects at least in part the CEGEP system, where "college" includes the equivalent of the final year(s) of high school. Quebec appears to have one of the lowest rates of university participation.[15]

Living in a rural area has a uniformly negative impact, although the effect is statistically insignificant for any postsecondary, it is quite sizeable and statistically significant for university attendance among both males and females. This is consistent with the descriptive statistics and suggests that access to community college is easier for those living in rural areas than is access to university.

Ethnicity and Language. Most of the minority language variables are not statistically significant, indicating that rates of postsecondary participation are not substantially different for English-speakers in Quebec, French-speakers outside Quebec, or those who speak a third language in any province (in comparison to the majority language speaker in each case — francophones in Quebec, anglophones elsewhere). The one exception is francophone females outside Quebec, who have an estimated 17% *higher* — not lower — rate of any postsecondary education than others. The absence of minority language effects presumably attests to a combination of government and institutional policies which attempt to provide individuals with opportunities for pursuing higher education in the language of their choice (a system that is perhaps especially developed in the case of anglophones in Quebec and francophones in New Brunswick), along with minorities' ability to adapt to local circumstances or any particular motivation or other unobserved characteristics they might possess. The absence of a third-language effect is also interesting in this respect.

Ethnic origin yields a number of quite strong findings. After controlling for other factors, individuals of Asian and South/East European ethnicity are much more likely to pursue postsecondary studies than others. For Asians, this trend is especially strong among males, particularly in the university models, where, holding other factors constant, they have a remarkable 27 percentage point higher rate of participation than those of the baseline (omitted) North and West European heritage.

---

[15]Joint statistical tests (F-tests) of the province of residence coefficients showed the group to be strongly statistically significant for each sex.

Ross Finnie, Eric Lascelles and Arthur Sweetman

For South and East Europeans, the effect is also generally strong and positive, and equally so for both genders, leaving this group with the highest participation rates among females. Those with mixed origins also tend to have relatively higher participation rates, while the pattern for those with other origins is mixed. Native (First Nation) Canadians have lower participation rates only in the female university model, but we will see below that the total effects are different and that the indirect effects play an especially important role for this group.[16]

The Intermediate Variables. The intermediate variables generally take the expected signs. For example, failing a grade in elementary school is strongly negative — even after taking high-school grades and other factors into account, suggesting a long-lasting correlation. A higher grade point average has the expected strong positive effects, with the importance of having an 'A' average (relative to the omitted 'B' comparison category) being especially strong for university. Interestingly, regularly skipping classes in high school does not appear to have any effect on postsecondary or university enrolment — again, once grades and other factors are taken into account. Also, working more than 20 hours per week while in high school ("Long work") reduces the likelihood of any postsecondary and university attendance by about 5% and over 10%, respectively. The highest rates are for those who work a little, or not at all in the case of the male university model.

Interestingly, once grades are controlled for, having difficulty in math, science, or the primary language of instruction (English or French) in high school does not appear to significantly affect postsecondary participation. Enjoying high school generally has a positive effect, but is only statistically significant for the any postsecondary model. A surprising, and almost paradoxical, finding is that respondents who find high-school classes interesting generally have the same, or lower in one model, likelihood of going on than those who do not in this regression context. Similarly, strong class participation has a statistically significantly positive effect only for

---

[16]For an intergenerational analysis of educational attainment by ethnic group see Dicks and Sweetman (1999). Also, joint statistical (F-tests) of the ethnicity and language variables showed the ethnic ones to be strongly significant, but the language set was not so except for the females any postsecondary regression. Language does not appear to be an important indicator of postsecondary attendance in general.

university. Also, not getting along with teachers mostly reduces the likelihood of going on, especially in the any postsecondary models.

Parents' opinions of the importance of high school have the intuitively expected effects (where significant), but should be interpreted with caution, since almost all respondents placed their parents in the "high importance" category. Perhaps more interesting is that those whose friends attached only a medium importance to high school (as opposed to high) are significantly less likely to go on. Peer group effects seem to matter, although these results might also reflect self-sorting. Being limited in activity also has negative effects, but significantly so only for females.

The Total Effect Models and the Implied Indirect Effects

We turn now to the total effect models, based on equation (8) above, and the implied indirect effects from equation (10) or (11) (the difference between the total and the direct effects), as well as the resulting percentage of the total effect of each variable that is indirect. For parental education, strong as the direct effects were seen to be, the total effects are generally about 50% larger. Each additional year of parental education (taking the two-parent case read directly from the relevant variable as an example) is worth a 4 or 3.1 percentage point increase in the probability of any post-secondary attendance (males and females, respectively), and 5.4 or 6.5 percentage points for university participation. Otherwise put, close to half (37 to 43%) of the effects of parental education operate indirectly through the intermediate variables included in the models, the rest being the direct effects that remain once these other factors are controlled for.

The cumulative effects of parental education, as well as the differences in participation rates between single-mother and two-parent families, are best seen in Table 6 — which shows fitted participation rates at various levels of parental education. Here we see that the family effects are also stronger in the total effects model than the direct effects model. For girls, the likelihood of university access is up to 40% higher in a two-parent family, while the direct effect model shows at most a 25% difference. And like the direct effect models, the parental education-participation relationship appears to be somewhat flatter for the single-mother and single-father family types than two-parent families, although the relevant interactions are once more non-significant in most cases.

The provincial coefficients are largely of the same sign and otherwise of the same pattern as in the direct models, although the majority of

Ross Finnie, Eric Lascelles and Arthur Sweetman

individual coefficients are again not statistically significant. In the cases where the coefficient estimates are small, large "percentage indirect" effects can result simply because the coefficients are effectively bouncing around small, imprecisely estimated numbers. (A negative number for the percentage of the total effect that is indirect means that the latter is greater than the former — which occurs where the indirect and direct effects go in opposing directions.) It is thus worth focusing here, as elsewhere, exclusively on the statistically significant effects.

Limiting ourselves to the provinces where the direct and total effects are both statistically significant, the percentage of the effect that is indirect can be seen to range up to 48% of the total. Thus, most provinces associated with intermediate student characteristics and outcomes favourable to going on to postsecondary education also appear to have an additional direct effect on that dynamic (i.e., students in a given province are more likely to go on not only because of their measured characteristics, but for other reasons beyond those characteristics). One possibility is that provinces that are more (or less) "pro-education" tend to be so at both the public and postsecondary levels and supply more (or fewer) postsecondary opportunities, that is, more (or fewer) places at colleges or universities. Another possibility is that the province variables are capturing unobserved heterogeneity — of the underlying populations, of labour market opportunities, or of other factors that affect postsecondary education participation rates at all levels.

The minority language effects are largely the same as in the direct models. Francophone women outside Quebec continue to be seen to enrol in any postsecondary education at greater rates than their anglophone co-residents. A new finding is that the indirect effects give francophone men an advantage in terms of university attendance, but this is largely offset by the direct effects seen earlier.

Turning to the ethnic variables, in most of the statistically significant cases, the total effects are greater than the direct effects seen previously, indicating that the direct effects alone underestimate the total influence of ethnicity, and that a substantial component of these effects comes through the intermediate variables (i.e., higher grades and so on). Asian men are again the most dramatic example. They are 23% more likely to engage in any postsecondary schooling, and a rather astounding 44% more likely to go to university than the omitted European group (and are also ahead of all others) for a given set of background characteristics. The indirect shares of these effects are 44 and 34%, respectively. Asian women have much smaller advantages. Those from Southern and Eastern European have the next greatest general advantage, and in this case for men and women alike. Again the total effects are greater than the direct effects, indicating that a substantial portion of their overall higher rates (13–38% after holding other factors constant) operates through the intermediate variables included in the models. The other ethnicity effects are generally smaller and more mixed.

For Native Canadians, the indirect effects are everywhere negative, statistically significant and sometimes quite large, implying that Native Canadians would have lower postsecondary attendance rates than those observed if these effects were all that mattered. Although Native Canadians finish high school with significant disadvantages in terms of their grades and other characteristics, these are largely overcome when postsecondary participation is finally determined (i.e., after taking the direct effects into account), except in the case of any postsecondary education for females. This said, all of these models control for some of the factors that presumably drive Native Canadians to lower participation rates, such as lower parental education levels and living in rural areas, so their overall (not regression adjusted) participation rates remain lower than other groups' (see Table 1). This exercise helps disentangle the particular sources of those overall lower rates suggesting that the gap can be attributed to observable characteristics — and thus points to where policy might be brought to bear to equalize their postsecondary opportunities.

The disadvantages for male rural dwellers in terms of university attendance are maintained in the total effects model, and even slightly stronger than in the direct model, 16% of the total effect being indirect. The female disadvantage, on the other hand, becomes insignificant in the total effect models, as the positive indirect effects offset the negative direct effects (each significant on its own). In other words, the total effect models miss the fact that females who live in rural areas tend to have high-school outcomes and related attributes which should predispose them towards going on to university (if only slightly), while they then actually attend at lower rates than these characteristics would suggest. Whether the latter effect is due to the distance from institutions and related cost factors, attitudes towards university, or other factors cannot, however, be determined from this data.

It is worth drawing attention to the nature of these results: the coefficients reflect differences in participation rates *holding other factors constant*. The effects of Native ethnicity are, for example, seen to be not particularly strong in the direct effects models, and it is only the estimation of the indirect effects where it is found to have more influence. But even here, we control for parental education and place of residence, and these are

Ross Finnie, Eric Lascelles and Arthur Sweetman

clearly factors that work against Native Canadians — as evidenced in their overall low participation rates. This is, of course, what a regression model does, and this property in no way undermines the use of this approach for sorting out the various factors that affect postsecondary participation. It only emphasizes the need to interpret the results appropriately. Comparing direct and total effects — and in turn comparing the findings with the raw overall participation rates — helps us do this.

It is also important to recognize that some of these variables need to be interpreted with care, especially the intermediate ones. One set, including those representing grades and the other measures of performance, are fairly objective and thus relatively clear in meaning. But the attitudinal and behavioural measures are probably more prone to measurement error. And throughout, almost any of the variables included in the models may be correlated with unobserved factors, including "ability", motivation, and other individual, family, and environmental influences.

Alternative Specifications

Table 7 presents the key parental education and family-type variables for the specification where the former is represented in a series of dummy variables representing the categories available in the raw data: less than high school completed, high school completed (the omitted category), some or completed college, and some or completed university.[17] The models also include the other variables shown in the linear parental education models, but these are not shown because their results do not change to any significant degree.

The parental education variables generally take on the expected sets of coefficients in both the direct and indirect models, and in most cases each higher level of parental education corresponds to a higher level of post-secondary attendance. The effects are especially strong for the university attendance model where, for example, the likelihood of participating is 32

---

[17]These categories still pertain to the level of the most highly educated parent, but the findings are again similar (although a bit stronger) when the analysis is restricted to situations where both parents have the indicated level of schooling (results not shown).

Table 7: Regression Results — Dummy Variable Specification

Variable	Direct Effect Coef.	Std. Err.	Total Effect Coef.	Std. Err	Indirect Effect Coef.	Std. Err.	% Indirect
A) Any Postsecondary -- Male							
Parent educ DK	-0.097	[0.060]	-0.179 ***	[0.065]	-0.082 **	[0.035]	46%
Parent educ no HS	-0.009	[0.043]	-0.065	[0.045]	-0.057 ***	[0.020]	87%
Parent educ college	0.066 *	[0.039]	0.079* *	[0.044]	0.013	[0.020]	17%
Parent educ uni	0.125 ***	[0.034]	0.194 ***	[0.037]	0.069 ***	[0.018]	36%
Par DK & live father	0.165	[0.200]	0.190	[0.215]	0.025	[0.090]	13%
Par no HS & live father	-0.268	[0.164]	-0.235	[0.189]	0.033	[0.077]	-14%
Par coll & live father	-0.095	[0.272]	-0.195	[0.273]	-0.100	[0.100]	51%
Par uni & live father	-0.355 *	[0.193]	-0.373 *	[0.206]	-0.018	[0.088]	5%
Par DK & live mother	-0.033	[0.139]	-0.085	[0.147]	-0.053	[0.071]	62%
Par no HS & live mother	-0.016	[0.112]	-0.014	[0.125]	0.002	[0.056]	-12%
Par coll & live mother	-0.104	[0.131]	-0.175	[0.151]	-0.071	[0.085]	40%
Par uni & live mother	-0.040	[0.124]	-0.030	[0.141]	0.010	[0.057]	-34%
Live father	0.179	[0.114]	0.096	[0.125]	-0.083	[0.052]	-86%
Live mother	-0.050	[0.081]	-0.076	[0.083]	-0.025	[0.034]	34%
Live other	-0.138 **	[0.069]	-0.228 ***	[0.076]	-0.090 ***	[0.035]	40%
R^2	0.259		0.111		N/A		
B) Any Postsecondary -- Female							
Parent educ DK	0.023	[0.071]	-0.039	[0.074]	-0.062 **	[0.026]	157%
Parent educ no HS	-0.004	[0.040]	-0.053	[0.043]	-0.050 ***	[0.015]	93%
Parent educ college	0.108 ***	[0.036]	0.139 ***	[0.037]	0.031 **	[0.014]	22%
Parent educ uni	0.090 ***	[0.034]	0.136 ***	[0.034]	0.046 ***	[0.015]	33%
Par DK & live father	-0.211	[0.227]	-0.411	[0.339]	-0.200	[0.156]	49%
Par no HS & live father	-0.438 ***	[0.158]	-0.425 **	[0.179]	0.013	[0.083]	-3%
Par coll & live father	-0.058	[0.100]	-0.113	[0.097]	-0.055	[0.085]	48%
Par uni & live father	-0.148 *	[0.078]	-0.133	[0.084]	0.015	[0.061]	-11%
Par DK & live mother	0.042	[0.166]	0.000	[0.177]	-0.042	[0.063]	-14350%
Par no HS & live mother	0.036	[0.099]	0.026	[0.104]	-0.010	[0.043]	-39%
Par coll & live mother	0.153 *	[0.093]	0.119	[0.093]	-0.034	[0.046]	-29%
Par uni & live mother	-0.057	[0.119]	-0.082	[0.136]	-0.025	[0.045]	31%
Live father	0.219 ***	[0.066]	0.240 ***	[0.077]	0.021	[0.044]	9%
Live mother	-0.062	[0.075]	-0.078	[0.080]	-0.016	[0.031]	21%
Live other	-0.140 **	[0.059]	-0.205 ***	[0.061]	-0.065 **	[0.027]	32%
R^2	0.220		0.117		N/A		
C) University -- Male							
Parent educ DK	-0.110 **	[0.045]	-0.152 ***	[0.043]	-0.042	[0.028]	28%
Parent educ no HS	-0.012	[0.036]	-0.068 *	[0.038]	-0.056 ***	[0.019]	82%
Parent educ college	0.020	[0.040]	0.041	[0.044]	0.021	[0.019]	51%
Parent educ uni	0.220 ***	[0.037]	0.316 ***	[0.042]	0.097 ***	[0.021]	31%
Par DK & live father	-0.025	[0.176]	-0.053	[0.207]	-0.028	[0.082]	53%
Par no HS & live father	-0.145	[0.151]	-0.083	[0.164]	0.063	[0.062]	-76%
Par coll & live father	-0.227	[0.154]	-0.256 *	[0.148]	-0.029	[0.099]	11%
Par uni & live father	-0.426 ***	[0.158]	-0.453 ***	[0.162]	-0.026	[0.070]	6%
Par DK & live mother	0.096	[0.092]	-0.004	[0.082]	-0.100	[0.069]	2456%
Par no HS & live mother	0.012	[0.091]	0.066	[0.097]	0.055	[0.053]	82%
Par coll & live mother	0.135	[0.117]	0.059	[0.128]	-0.076	[0.073]	-130%
Par uni & live mother	-0.070	[0.126]	-0.069	[0.131]	0.000	[0.055]	0%
Live father	0.101	[0.132]	0.006	[0.141]	-0.095 **	[0.048]	-1629%
Live mother	-0.019	[0.064]	-0.062	[0.063]	-0.042	[0.033]	68%
Live other	-0.028	[0.048]	-0.117 **	[0.050]	-0.089 **	[0.035]	76%
R^2	0.328		0.168		N/A		

Ross Finnie, Eric Lascelles and Arthur Sweetman

Table 7 *(continued)*

D) University -- Female

Parent educ DK	0.026	[0.063]	-0.099	[0.071]	-0.125 ***	[0.035]	126%
Parent educ no HS	-0.015	[0.043]	-0.081 *	[0.046]	-0.066 ***	[0.018]	82%
Parent educ college	0.101 **	[0.047]	0.147 ***	[0.051]	0.046 **	[0.019]	31%
Parent educ uni	0.244 ***	[0.040]	0.345 ***	[0.044]	0.101 ***	[0.020]	29%
Par DK & live father	-0.009	[0.275]	-0.171	[0.275]	-0.162	[0.152]	95%
Par no HS & live father	0.252	[0.317]	0.234	[0.317]	-0.018	[0.099]	-8%
Par coll & live father	-0.053	[0.281]	-0.093	[0.333]	-0.040	[0.125]	43%
Par uni & live father	-0.091	[0.276]	-0.011	[0.306]	0.079	[0.089]	-691%
Par DK & live mother	-0.153	[0.137]	-0.142	[0.137]	0.012	[0.078]	-8%
Par no HS & live mother	-0.131	[0.104]	-0.152	[0.108]	-0.021	[0.059]	14%
Par coll & live mother	-0.139	[0.120]	-0.208	[0.136]	-0.069	[0.064]	33%
Par uni & live mother	-0.166	[0.130]	-0.276 *	[0.148]	-0.110 *	[0.061]	40%
Live father	-0.012	[0.241]	-0.031	[0.258]	-0.019	[0.062]	60%
Live mother	0.059	[0.073]	0.065	[0.088]	0.006	[0.041]	10%
Live other	-0.037	[0.053]	-0.116 **	[0.053]	-0.079 ***	[0.028]	68%
R^2	0.297		0.149		N/A		

Notes: Robust standard errors in brackets: * 10% significance; ** 5% significance;
** 1% significance.
Other regressors are as in the comparable regressions in Tables 3 through 6.
N(female)=2998; N(male)=2671.

and 35% higher for those with university-educated parents as opposed to high school in the total effect models (males and females respectively), and 22 and 24% higher in the indirect models. The size of the indirect effect and the percentage of the total effect that is indirect naturally varies, but is generally substantial. For the cases where both the direct and total effects are statistically significant, the indirect effect comprises 17 to 31% of the total effect.

Another additional finding centres on the relative importance of father's versus mother's education on postsecondary attainment, as seen in Table 8. Including each of these shows that father's education has a far greater influence upon the attainment of male respondents than does mother's education, while the reverse is true for female respondents, although to a slightly lesser extent. This pattern is particularly strong in the university models. Given the nature of the data, this effect is only verified for two-parent families, since we only observe the education of parents residing with the youth.

Table 8: Regression Results — Father-Mother Specification

Variable	Direct Effect Coef.	Std. Err.	Total Effect Coef.	Std. Err	Indirect Effect Coef.	Std. Err.	% Indirect
A) Any Postsecondary -- Male							
Fath educ DK	-0.067	[0.064]	-0.123 *	[0.068]	-0.057 *	[0.031]	46%
Fath educ no HS	-0.015	[0.041]	-0.062	[0.043]	-0.047 **	[0.018]	76%
Fath educ coll	0.093 **	[0.043]	0.113 **	[0.046]	0.020	[0.019]	18%
Fath educ uni	0.140 ***	[0.040]	0.195 ***	[0.045]	0.056 **	[0.022]	29%
Moth educ DK	0.003	[0.059]	-0.032	[0.059]	-0.035	[0.029]	109%
Moth educ no HS	0.028	[0.037]	-0.001	[0.040]	-0.029	[0.018]	2038%
Moth educ coll	0.002	[0.038]	0.002	[0.046]	0.000	[0.022]	5%
Moth educ uni	0.029	[0.040]	0.056	[0.043]	0.027	[0.021]	48%
R^2	0.245		0.111		N/A		
B) Any Postsecondary -- Female							
Fath educ DK	0.016	[0.062]	-0.042	[0.060]	-0.058 **	[0.028]	138%
Fath educ no HS	0.030	[0.037]	0.010	[0.039]	-0.021	[0.015]	-215%
Fath educ coll	0.060	[0.037]	0.077 *	[0.042]	0.017	[0.017]	22%
Fath educ uni	0.049	[0.037]	0.061	[0.040]	0.012	[0.018]	20%
Moth educ DK	0.041	[0.059]	0.022	[0.060]	-0.020	[0.027]	-91%
Moth educ no HS	-0.023	[0.036]	-0.065 *	[0.038]	-0.043 **	[0.017]	65%
Moth educ coll	0.063 *	[0.034]	0.090 **	[0.038]	0.027	[0.017]	30%
Moth educ uni	0.082 **	[0.035]	0.119 ***	[0.037]	0.037 **	[0.017]	31%
R^2	0.195		0.082		N/A		
C) University -- Male							
Fath educ DK	-0.162 ***	[0.052]	-0.191 ***	[0.055]	-0.029	[0.030]	15%
Fath educ no HS	-0.087 **	[0.036]	-0.120 ***	[0.039]	-0.033 *	[0.019]	28%
Fath educ coll	-0.026	[0.050]	-0.003	[0.052]	0.024	[0.022]	-806%
Fath educ uni	0.200 ***	[0.047]	0.290 ***	[0.054]	0.090 ***	[0.026]	31%
Moth educ DK	0.025	[0.053]	-0.005	[0.055]	-0.029	[0.029]	643%
Moth educ no HS	0.024	[0.037]	-0.014	[0.039]	-0.037 **	[0.018]	274%
Moth educ coll	0.011	[0.046]	0.032	[0.052]	0.021	[0.024]	65%
Moth educ uni	0.086 *	[0.045]	0.121 **	[0.053]	0.036	[0.024]	29%
R^2	0.351		0.206		N/A		
D) University -- Female							
Fath educ DK	-0.052	[0.065]	-0.145**	[0.066]	-0.093 **	[0.036]	64%
Fath educ no HS	-0.019	[0.043]	-0.037	[0.047]	-0.018	[0.020]	49%
Fath educ coll	0.058	[0.050]	0.095*	[0.056]	0.038	[0.025]	40%
Fath educ uni	0.131 ***	[0.046]	0.197***	[0.051]	0.066 ***	[0.025]	33%
Moth educ DK	0.047	[0.070]	0.014	[0.075]	-0.034	[0.035]	-251%
Moth educ no HS	0.015	[0.038]	-0.050	[0.041]	-0.066 ***	[0.019]	130%
Moth educ coll	0.089 *	[0.047]	0.122**	[0.052]	0.032	[0.024]	27%
Moth educ uni	0.218 ***	[0.047]	0.279***	[0.052]	0.061 **	[0.025]	22%
R^2	0.317		0.167		N/A		

Notes: Robust standard errors in brackets: * 10% significance; ** 5% significance;
*** 1% significance.
Other regressors are as in the comparable regressions in Tables 3 through 6.
N(female)=2036; N(male)=2075.

Ross Finnie, Eric Lascelles and Arthur Sweetman

Conclusion

Main Findings

This paper has examined postsecondary participation in Canada using Statistics Canada's School Leavers and Follow-Up Surveys. Using a block recursive technique, we identify the direct and indirect effects of a number of family background characteristics, as well as the effects of a set of intermediate variables representing high-school outcomes and related attitudes and behaviour which are interesting on their own, as well as representing paths through which the background variables operate to affect participation. Two measures of postsecondary access are used: any postsecondary, including community colleges and trade-vocational schools, right up to and including university, and university (alone). The analysis is broken down by sex.

The results point to the many and varied factors which affect postsecondary participation and the value of using detailed regression models to identify these influences. The strength of the family background effects even after a wide array of other factors, including elementary and high-school academic performance and related measures, have been controlled for are particularly interesting. Family background appears to have an enduring effect on the determination of who goes on to postsecondary participation, even among what appear to be equally qualified, and perhaps even equally motivated young people.

Parental education has uniformly strong direct and indirect effects on access. Each additional year of parental education increases the likelihood of university attendance (where the effects are strongest) as much as about five percentage points. The relative university attendance rates for those whose parents have a high-school diploma and those with at least some university education are 29 versus 53% in the case of men, and 37 versus 65% for women (holding other factors constant). Parental education has another interesting property: father's education seems to have a much stronger effect on sons than daughters, while mother's education has a much greater influence over daughters than sons. Between 37 and 44% of these effects are indirect, the rest direct (i.e., they remain after controlling for intermediate outcomes). By family type, those from two-parent families are approximately 25% more likely to go on to higher schooling than those from single-mother families according to the direct effects model, and at rates of up to 40% greater according to the total effects model.

Participation rates vary by province to some degree, and in most cases the direct and indirect effects work in the same direction. Those from provinces other than Ontario tend to have lower rates of any postsecondary participation (holding other factors constant — including the family background measures), but higher rates of university education. Living in a rural area during high school decreases the likelihood of postsecondary attendance, but the effects are statistically significant only in the university models. In these latter cases, for males, the direct and indirect effects work in the same direction, while for females, interestingly, the indirect effects actually favour access while the direct effects are negative, the net negative influence being not statistically different from zero.

Speaking a minority language (English in Quebec, French outside Quebec, or any other language in any province) does not seem to have a statistically significantly effect on access, except for francophone females outside Quebec in the any postsecondary (but not university) models, who attend at a higher rate than their anglophone neighbours. Asian ethnicity has a very positive effect upon attendance, particularly for men, and especially in the university models. In most, but not all cases, the direct and indirect effects work in the same direction: ethnicity is thus associated with various high-school and related outcomes as well as the tendency to go on to further studies conditional on a given set of attributes (background and intermediates). Postsecondary participation rates are uniformly the lowest for Native (First Nation) Canadians, but the effects are almost entirely indirect, operating through high-school grades and related outcomes (i.e., Native ethnicity has a negative effect on these), as well as through the levels of the background variables (e.g., lower levels of parental education). In short, our approach shows that the negative effect of native ethnicity is played out early on, during the high-school years (when the intermediate variables are formed) or before, rather than at the point of entry into postsecondary schooling.

Turning to the intermediate variables, which are presented in Appendix 1, the results show that working a moderate number of hours at an outside job while in high school is associated with higher levels of attendance in the any postsecondary models and also in the university models for girls, but working too many hours uniformly decreases the likelihood of participation by either measures. High-school academic performance, captured by the individual's grade average, has a strong, positive influence in both the any postsecondary and university models, while failing a grade in elementary school is an additional predictor, early and enduring, in the any postsecondary models. Participating in class and school activities also generally have positive effects, as expected.

Although gender differences are not the focus of this paper, it is worth noting that the descriptive statistics indicate that boys are seriously worse off than girls in terms of the intermediate variables. They fail more often, have lower high-school grades, enjoy school less and find it less interesting, and get along with teachers less. Given all this, it is not surprising they have statistically lower rates of postsecondary and university attendance.

Policy Implications

These findings have a number of potentially important policy implications. First, the fact that family background has an important (total) impact on postsecondary participation points to an associated set of fundamental inequalities of opportunity to be addressed — however that might best be done.

Second, the finding that over half of the family background effects remain even after the very broad set of control variables representing individuals' high-school outcomes, and related attributes and attitudes, are included points to a role for policy measures to further expand post-secondary opportunities for those from less privileged social backgrounds even at the point of finishing high school. It is interesting to contrast this finding with that of Carneiro and Heckman (2002) for the United States, who argue that family background, as captured by family income, no longer affects university attendance once measured student ability is controlled for. Policy measures might include initiatives as simple as ensuring that students have a good understanding of the benefits (and costs) of post-secondary education so that they make the career choices that are best for them in the long run — those from less privileged backgrounds as much as others.[18] It would also be important to ensure that student financial aid is

---

[18]Junor and Usher (2002) discuss findings which show that youths from low-income families tend to underestimate the benefits and overestimate the costs of postsecondary education relative to those from higher income families, while Betts (1996) surveys first-year US university students and finds that they know remarkably little about the educational requirements of the jobs they aspire to.

doing its job of ensuring that cost is not a constraint to postsecondary participation.[19]

Third, the results point to important inequalities being generated during high school and even before this. And it can be imagined that having an even larger and better set of intermediate measures would likely identify other/additional indirect routes by which family characteristics affect postsecondary participation. Such inequalities could be addressed by policy measures such as providing tutoring programs and other "catch-up" initiatives, introducing a greater array of after-school activities open to all, giving better information regarding the benefits of higher education from a young age, and so on.

One potentially valuable example of such a program is discussed by Hô and Legault (2002), who describe an undertaking whereby the Quebec government provides greater resources to schools in low socio-economic status neighbourhoods in an effort to improve their educational outcomes. These types of early interventions are clearly required if equality of access is to be achieved. The US literature on their long-standing Head Start program points to other sorts of interventions that can help equalize life chances — which heavily depend on postsecondary education.[20] In unravelling to some degree the full set of relationships that determine postsecondary participation, perhaps the most important overall policy implication of the results reported here is the need to shift at least some of the policy emphasis towards "starting early" if there is to be greater equality of access to postsecondary education in Canada.

Finally, although not the focus of this paper, one ancillary observation is that boys lag behind girls in high-school outcomes — and postsecondary access. Perhaps it is also time to direct more attention to these issues, including the underlying causes and effects and related policy implications.

---

[19]See Hemingway (2003) for suggestions of where aid is currently insufficient.

[20]See Currie (2001) for a review of the effects of early intervention programs in the United States.

Ross Finnie, Eric Lascelles and Arthur Sweetman

Appendix 1: The Intermediate Variable Models

Given the large number of intermediate equations (one per intermediate variable) and regressors, only a few selected results are presented in Table A1. These are examples of the relationship between a subset of the family background factors and three intermediate variables — they represent the indirect paths by which family background can affect postsecondary participation.[21] The results shown capture the effects of parental education and family type on the probability of having failed a grade in elementary school, of obtaining an 'A' average in high school, and of working long hours.

Parental education has a strong positive effect on the likelihood that the respondent had an 'A' average and (especially for males) a negative effect upon the likelihood of failing a grade in elementary school. It does not have as strong an effect on working long hours, but family structure is a better predictor of this. Each additional year of parental education increases the likelihood of an 'A' average for both males and females by approximately 4%.[22] Since obtaining an 'A' average in high school increases the likelihood of university attendance by almost 20% (as will be seen below), each year of parental education has, in addition to its direct effects, an indirect effect — through its influence on the individual's probability of getting an 'A' average — of almost 1% on the likelihood of university attendance. In contrast, failing a grade also has a strong (negative) effect on postsecondary participation, thus comprising another path by which parental education affects the likelihood of going to college or university.

The cumulative indirect influence of the full set of background variables on each intermediate outcome results in a substantial indirect effect of family background on postsecondary access. This is, however, best seen in the comparison of the direct and indirect effect models.

---

[21]No distinction needs to be made between the two definitions of post-secondary access here because these variables do not enter the intermediate regressions.

[22]The proper interpretation of the various combinations of parental education and family-type variables (including interactions) are explained below, but for the purposes here, we can focus on the general "years of parental education variable", which has a straightforward interpretation for two-parent families.

Table A1: Selected Intermediate Regressions

Background Variables	Selected Intermediate Dependent Variables					
	Failed Elem Grade		"A" Average		Long Working Hours	
	Coef.	Std. Err	Coef.	Std. Err	Coef.	Std. Err
A) MALE						
Years of par educ	-0.022 ***	[0.006]	0.043 ***	[0.006]	-0.001	[0.006]
Par educ DK	-0.226 **	[0.090]	0.397 ***	[0.078]	-0.064	[0.080]
Yrs par educ & live fath	0.043 **	[0.017]	-0.040 ***	[0.008]	-0.040 *	[0.021]
Yrs par educ & live moth	-0.012	[0.016]	-0.046 ***	[0.014]	0.018	[0.013]
Par educ DK & live fath	0.749 **	[0.297]	-0.392 ***	[0.110]	-0.190	[0.341]
Par educ DK & live moth	0.308	[0.246]	-0.480 **	[0.194]	0.658 ***	[0.216]
Live father	-0.478 **	[0.189]	0.323 ***	[0.101]	0.494 *	[0.284]
Live mother	0.200	[0.209]	0.489 ***	[0.180]	-0.266 *	[0.161]
Live other	-0.311 ***	[0.091]	0.410 ***	[0.078]	0.226 **	[0.099]
R-squared	0.086		0.136		0.077	
B) FEMALE						
Years of par educ	-0.010 ***	[0.003]	0.045 ***	[0.006]	-0.001	[0.003]
Par educ DK	0.081	[0.093]	0.305 ***	[0.080]	0.249 ***	[0.084]
Yrs par educ & live fath	-0.020	[0.017]	-0.021	[0.047]	0.001	[0.009]
Yrs par educ & live moth	0.006	[0.008]	-0.020	[0.019]	0.019	[0.012]
Par educ DK & live fath	-0.149	[0.373]	-0.514	[0.602]	-0.285 *	[0.151]
Par educ DK & live moth	-0.200	[0.132]	-0.370	[0.233]	0.129	[0.206]
Live father	0.245	[0.253]	0.428	[0.598]	-0.105	[0.125]
Live mother	0.187	[0.102]	0.309	[0.231]	-0.310	[0.143]
Live other	-0.094 *	[0.051]	0.570 ***	[0.091]	0.170 **	[0.069]
R-squared	0.068		0.113		0.100	

Notes: Robust standard errors in brackets: * 10% significance; ** 5% significance; *** 1% significance.
The regressions contain the full set of background variables seen in Table 1.
N(female)=2998; N(male)=2671.

Appendix 2: Key Variable Definitions

For the dummy and father-mother specifications, parental education is categorized as No HS, HS, College, University, or Don't Know. For the linear specification, we transform known responses onto a linear scale using the number of years that each level of education generally requires. The No HS variable is broken down into two parts, with Less than Grade 9 given a value of 8, while HS Incomplete = 10. The rest of the variables proceed logically, with HS = 12, College = 14, and University = 16.

A set of family-type dummy variables is created to represent possible family types while the respondent was in high school. The possible choices are Live 2 Parents, Live Mother, Live Father, and Live Other. Parental education and family type are interacted in a variety of manners, depending on the specification selected. In each instance, every parental education variable is interacted with every dummy variable. For the father-mother specification, no interaction is necessary since that specification is restricted to 2 Parent families only.

Provincial variables are included, representing the province of high school residence. This acts as a proxy for where the student grew up and was educated. Similarly, an urban/rural designation is created, representing the respondent's residence while in high school.

The language spoken in the home of the respondent ("first language") is not included as a variable. Instead, we create a set of minority language dummy variables. Specifically, English-speakers in Quebec are assigned one dummy variable (English in Quebec); French-speakers outside Quebec are assigned another (French outside Quebec); and respondents with another first language are placed in a third minority language dummy variable (Other Lang.). This leaves the province variables to represent those of the majority language group in each province while these minority language indicators allow language effects to vary by region, something that more conventional specifications do not permit.

The ethnicity of each respondent is captured by distilling the detailed ethnicity categories in the SLS/SLFS into eight dummy variables representing various world regions. These are North & West Europe, South & East Europe, Canadian, Asian, Native, Other, Mixed, and Unknown. We assign individuals to a particular ethnic category unless they indicate multiple backgrounds overlapping more than one of our categories. Such persons were placed into the catch-all Mixed category. There are some exceptions to this rule. Specifically, anyone claiming Native origin, regardless of other ethnic background, is placed solely in the Native category.

Conversely, the Canadian ethnicity of any respondent is ignored unless it is the only category they chose, in which case the person is given that classification. Those who indicated Other in the SLS/SLFS are placed into our Other category, except in a few special cases.[23] Those who selected Unknown in the survey are placed into the Unknown category in our study.

The high-school academic success of students is reported using dummy variables representing the traditional range of letter-grades. One adjustment has been made, namely combining 'D' and 'F' averages into a single variable. The sample size of these two variables on their own was quite small, and the effects were similar.

The perceived high-school success of respondents in math, science, and their primary language is broken into three sets of dummy variables. Each set contains the possible responses of "difficulty", "no difficulty", or "not applicable".

The number of hours performed each week at a job during the school year is captured using four dummy variables.[24] These categories are No Work, Short Work (less than ten hours), Med. Work (10 to 19 hours), and Long Work (20+ hours).

Further variables used in this study required no special modification.

---

[23]Individuals choosing an ethnicity of Other in the SLS/SLFS are then further grouped by that survey into a number of subcategories consisting of less represented areas of the world. Some of these areas match up well with the ethnic categories we created. Respondents from such areas are shifted out of Other and added to the appropriate ethnic category.

[24]Hours of Work could not be left in its original linear form because estimation indicated that a lower number of working hours was beneficial with regard to the likelihood of postsecondary attendance, whereas a high number of hours can be quite detrimental. The concave shape of this relationship does not lend itself to linear representation.

References

Betts, J.R. 1996. "What Do Students Know about Wages? Evidence from a Survey of Undergraduates", *Journal of Human Resources* 31(1), 27-56.

Bouchard, B. and J. Zhao. 2000. "University Education: Recent Trends in Participation, Accessibility and Returns", *Education Quarterly Review* 6(4), 24-32.

Bushnik, T. 2003. "Learning, Earning and Leaving: The Relationship between Working While in High School and Dropping Out". Working Paper. Ottawa: Statistics Canada.

Butlin, G. 1999. "Determinants of Post-Secondary Participation", *Education Quarterly Review* 5(3), 9-35.

Cameron, S.V. and C. Taber. 2004. "Estimation of Educational Borrowing Constraints Using Returns to Schooling", *Journal of Political Economy* 112(1), 132-182.

Carneiro, P. and J. Heckman. 2002. "The Evidence on Credit Constraints in Post-Secondary Schooling", *Economic Journal* 112, 705-735.

Christofides, L.N., J. Cirello and M. Hoy. 2001. "Family Income and Postsecondary Education in Canada", *The Canadian Journal of Higher Education* 31(1), 177-208.

Coleman, J.S. 1966. *Equality of Educational Opportunity*. Washington, DC: National Center for Educational Statistics.

Corak, M., G. Lipps and J. Zhao. 2003. *Family Income and Participation in Postsecondary Education*. Analytical Studies Research Paper Series No. 210. Ottawa: Statistics Canada.

Currie, J. 2001. "Early Childhood Intervention Programs: What Do We Know?" *Journal of Economic Perspectives* 15(2), 213-238.

De Broucker, P. and L. Lavallée. 1998a. "Getting Ahead in Life: Does Your Parents' Education Count?", *Education Quarterly Review* 5(1), 22-28.

_____. 1998b. "Intergenerational Aspects of Education and Literacy Skills Acquisition", in M. Corak (ed.), *Labour Markets, Social Institutions, and the Future of Canada's Children*. Ottawa: Statistics Canada.

Dicks, G. and A. Sweetman. 1999. "Education and Ethnicity in Canada: An Intergenerational Perspective", *Journal of Human Resources* 34(4), 668-696.

Dynarski, S. 2002. "The Behavioural and Distributional Implications of Aid for College", *The American Economic Review* 92(2) (May), 279-285.

Finnie, R. and C. Laporte. 2004. *Access to Post-Secondary Education: Evidence From the Post-Secondary Education Participation Survey*. Analytical Studies Research Paper. Ottawa: Statistics Canada. Forthcoming.

Finnie, R., C. Laporte and E. Lascelles. 2004. *Family Background and Access to Post-Secondary Education: What Happened in the 1990s?* Analytical Studies Research Paper. Ottawa: Statistics Canada. Forthcoming.

Foley, K. 2001. *Why Stop After High School? A Descriptive Analysis of the Most Important Reasons that High School Graduates Do Not Continue to PSE*. Montreal: Canada Millennium Scholarship Foundation.

Frenette, M. 2002. *Too Far to Go On? Distance to School and University Participation*. Analytical Studies Research Paper Series No. 191. Ottawa: Statistics Canada.

_____. 2003. *Access to College and University: Does Distance Matter?* Analytical Studies Research Paper Series No. 201. Ottawa: Statistics Canada.

Greene, W.H. 2003. *Econometric Analysis*, 5th edition. Upper Saddle River, NJ: Prentice Hall.

Haveman, R. and B. Wolfe. 1995. "The Determinants of Children's Attainments: A Review of Methods and Findings", *Journal of Economic Literature* 34, 1829-1878.

Heller, D. 1997. "Student Price Response in Higher Education: An Update to Leslie and Brinkman", *Journal of Higher Education* 68(6), 624-659.

Hemingway, F. 2003. *Assessing Canada's Student Aid Need Assessment Policies*. Montreal: Canada Millennium Scholarships Foundation.

Hô, V.H.G. and G. Legault. 2002. "Les indicies socio-economiques, outil de politique de l'éducation au Québec", in P. de Broucker and A. Sweetman (eds.), *Towards Evidence-based Policy for Canadian Education/Vers des politiques canadiennes d'éducation fondées sur la recherché*. Kingston: John Deutsch Institute, Queen's University, 189-204.

Junor, S. and A. Usher. 2002. *The Price of Knowledge: Access and Student Finance in Canada*. Montreal: Canada Millennium Scholarship Foundation.

Kane, T.J. 2001. "College-Going and Inequality: A Literature Review". Paper prepared for the Thomas Sage Foundation.

Knighton, T. and S. Mirza. 2002. "Postsecondary Participation: The Effects of Parents' Education and Household Income", *Education Quarterly Review* 8(3), 25-32.

Looker, D.E. 2001. *Why Don't They Go On? Factors Affecting the Decisions of Canadian Youth not to Pursue Post-secondary Education*. Montreal: Canada Millennium Scholarship Foundation.

Ma, X. and D. Klinger. 2000. "Hierachical Linear Modelling of Student and School Effects on Academic Achievement", *Canadian Journal of Education* 25(1), 41-55.

Moffitt, R.A. 1999. "New Developments in Econometric Methods for Labor Market Analysis", in O. Ashenfelter and D. Card (eds.), *Handbook of Labor Economics*. Amsterdam: Elsevier, 1367-1397.

Ruhm, C.J. 1997. "Is High School Employment Consumption or Investment?" *Journal of Labor Economics* 15(4), 735-776.

Willms, J.D. 1999. "Quality and Inequality in Children's Literacy: The Effects of Families, Schools, and Communities", in D. Keating and C. Hertzman (eds.), *Developmental Health and the Wealth of Nations: Social, Biological, and Educational Dynamics*. New York: Guilford Press, 72-93.

Zhao, J. and P. de Broucker. 2001. "Participation in Postsecondary Education and Family Income", *The Daily*. Ottawa: Statistics Canada, December 7.

_____. 2002. "Participation in Postsecondary Education and Family Income", *The Daily*. Ottawa: Statistics Canada, January 9.

Do the *Maclean's* Rankings Affect University Choice?: Evidence for Ontario

Richard E. Mueller and Duane W. Rockerbie

Introduction

Since 1991, *Maclean's* magazine has provided its annual rankings of Canadian universities in one of its November issues. Universities are assigned one of three categories: medical/doctoral, comprehensive or primarily undergraduate. These rankings are computed in a number of straightforward steps. First, *Maclean's* performs a detailed survey of every university in Canada, asking each university to provide statistical variables that, in some way, reflect their quality of education. The major fields of interest are: characteristics of the student body, class sizes, characteristics of instructors, faculty awards and grants, student scholarships and bursaries, operating budgets, library acquisitions, and alumni support. Participation in the survey is voluntary and indeed some universities choose not to participate in various years. All variables are purported to help

We would like to thank B. Curtis Eaton, Steve Easton, and seminar participants at the 36th annual meeting of the Canadian Economics Association, Calgary, AB, May 30 – June 2, 2002 and at the Higher Education in Canada conference held at the John Deutsch Institute for the Study of Economic Policy, Queen's University, February 13–14, 2004 for useful comments.

students and their parents select the appropriate university to attend in order to attain a degree.

The focus of this paper is not on the statistical properties and overall reliability of the *Maclean's* rankings. Rather we take the rankings for what they are intended to be: a sort of *Consumer Reports* for prospective students and parents. None of the shortcomings of the rankings will affect student and parent choices if they are too difficult to understand or just not relevant to what is deemed important by students and parents. Despite all of its shortcomings, the *Maclean's* rankings have two desirable properties: they are easy to read and they are readily available. There is no other means of national comparison. Their credibility is ultimately determined by the students who use them and their parents, who often pay the bill. We wish to determine if the *Maclean's* rankings influence students' choices of university within a theoretical framework that recognizes the disequilibrium nature of Canada's public education system.

The *Maclean's* Rankings

The *Maclean's* rankings are computed from a fairly simple system of descriptive variables and assumed weights. A full list of the variables collected and the weights assigned to each category is given in Table 1. Weights are assigned to the university ranking of each statistical variable to reflect their perceived importance in making up the final ranking. The weights are identical across universities but were altered in 1992, with some revisions in 1994 and only minor changes in the weightings since. In the 2001 survey, for example, characteristics of the study body received the highest weighting (0.21 or 0.22 depending on the type of university). The reputation of the university received the next highest weighting (0.20) followed by class sizes (0.17 or 0.18), faculty quality (0.17), and measures of finances and library quality (both at 0.12). A ranking is assigned to each of these characteristics based on the relative position of the university in comparison to all other universities in the same category. Multiplying the value of each ranking by its weight and then summing across all performance categories gives a final score for each university.

The rankings divide Canadian universities into three broad groups: *Medical/Doctoral* are the large research universities with major PhD programs and medical schools; *Comprehensive* universities tend to be smaller institutions that offer a wide range of programs, including

Richard E. Mueller and Duane W. Rockerbie

Table 1: The *Maclean's* Ranking Methodology, 1991–2001

Category/Subcategory (description)	Year										
	1991	1992[a]	1993	1994	1995	1996	1997	1998	1999	2000	2001
						Weighting (%)					
Student Body	15	20	20	21-22	21-22	21-22	21-22	21-22	21-22	21-22	21-22
Average entering high-school grade	4.5	12	12	12	12	12	12	12	12	12	11
Proportion with 75% entering grade or higher			3	3	3	3	3	3	3	3	3
Proportion of 2nd year students who graduate on time			2	2	2	2	2	2	2	2	2
Out-of-province (proportion of first year students)			1	1	1	1	1	1	1	1	1.5
International students (proportion of graduate students)			1	1[b]	1[b]	1[b]	1[b]	1[b]	1[b]	1[b]	1[b]
International students (proportion of first year students)											0.5
Student awards over previous five years			1	3	3	3	3	3	3	3	3
Acceptance rate	10.5										
Classes	18	18	18	17-18	17-18	17-18	17-18	17-18	17-18	17-18	17-18
Median class size (1st year)			3								
Class sizes: 1st and 2nd year level			6.5	7-7.5[c]	7-7.5[c]	7-7.5[c]	7-7.5[c]	7-7.5[c]	7-7.5[c]	7-7.5[c]	7-7.5[c]
Class sizes: 3rd and 4th year level			6.5	7-7.5[c]	7-7.5[c]	7-7.5[c]	7-7.5[c]	7-7.5[c]	7-7.5[c]	7-7.5[c]	7-7.5[c]
Classes taught by tenured/tenure-track faculty (%)			3	3	3	3	3	3	3	3	3
Faculty	30	20	20	17	17	17	17	17	17	17	17
Faculty with PhD (%)			3	3	3	3	3	3	3	3	3
Awards per full-time faculty (national awards)	7.5		6	3	3	3	3	3	3	3	3
Humanities grants (# and $ value)			5.5	5.5	5.5	5.5	5.5	5.5	5.5	5.5	5.5
Medical/science grants (# and $ value)			5.5	5.5	5.5	5.5	5.5	5.5	5.5	5.5	5.5
Student-professor ratio	10.5										
1st year courses taught by established professors (%)	6										
PhDs in arts and science faculties (%)	6										

Table 1 (continued)

Finances	30	10	10	12	12	12	12	12	12	12	12	12
Operating budget per student	21		3.3	3.3	3.3	3.3	3.3	3.3	3.3	3.3	3.3	3.3
Scholarships & bursaries (% of budget)			3.3	4.3	4.3	4.3	4.3	4.3	4.3	4.3	4.3	4.3
Student services (% of budget)			3.3	4.3	4.3	4.3	4.3	4.3	4.3	4.3	4.3	4.3
Scholarships/bursaries per undergraduate student ($)	3											
Residential beds per undergraduate student	3											
Spending per student on non-academic services	3											
Library	12	12	12	12	12	12	12	12	12	12	12	12
Holdings per student (number of volumes)	4		4	3-4[d]	3-4[d]	3-4[d]	3-4[d]	3-4[d]	3-4[d]	3-4[d]	3-4[d]	3-4[d]
Acquisitions (percentage of library budget)	4		4	4	4	4	4	4	4	4	4	4
Expenses (percentage of operating expenditures)	4		4	4	4	4	4	4	4	4	4	4
Total holdings (volumes)				1[e]	1[e]	1[e]	1[e]	1[e]	1[e]	1[e]	1[e]	1[e]
Reputation	25	20	20	20	20	20	20	20	20	20	20	20
Alumni support (% alumni donating over five years)	5		5	5	5	5	5	5	5	5	5	5
Reputational survey (of university administrators, etc.)	20		15	15	15	15	15	15	15	15	15	15
Percentage of out-of-province and foreign students	5											
Total	100	100	100	100	100	100	100	100	100	100	100	100

Notes: [a] Weights for subcategories were not included in 1992.
[b] For medical/doctoral and comprehensive institutions only.
[c] 7.5% for primarily undergraduate, and 7% for the other two categories.
[d] 4% for medical/doctoral and 3% for the other two categories.
[e] For medical/doctoral category only.

professional schools, at both the undergraduate and graduate levels; and, *Primarily Undergraduate* schools have few graduate programs and focus on undergraduate education. Each university that participates in the rankings is placed within one of the groups and then ranked against other universities in the group (i.e., its peer institutions). Each institution has remained within one of these three groups over the life of the rankings.

The *Maclean's* ranking system has come under severe criticism, mainly from academic sources. These criticisms are summarized by Page (1995, 1996, 1999), and include:

- Differences in ranks cannot be easily interpreted. The difference between the top-ranked school and the second-ranked school may be very small, but the ranking will not reflect this.
- Spearman rank-order correlations consistently show that the rankings for the six broad categories are only weakly correlated. Given that the variables are defined so that an increase in any of them should be an increase in perceived quality, the lack of correlation is perplexing.
- Many of the categorical index numbers are only weakly correlated with the final rankings.
- The mean values of the categorical index numbers are uncorrelated with the final rankings.
- The rank scores of the categorical index numbers are not significantly different between the top half and bottom half universities (on final rankings) for a majority of the categories.

Inconsistencies also appear in the text that accompanies the rankings. Occasionally a university will score highly on many of the categorical rankings, but not deserve mention in the text. Also the use of terms, such as "leaders of tomorrow", may be unqualified metaphors given the type of data collected.

We acknowledge that the annual *Maclean's* rankings have significant statistical flaws and that they may not accurately reflect the quality of any Canadian university. The educational experience of any student is a complex interaction of the resources a university can provide and the effort a student is willing to give. Any ranking system cannot account for the latter. Nevertheless students and parents may believe that a higher ranking in the annual *Maclean's* survey gives the student a higher probability of success for a given amount of anticipated student effort. We wish to test this assertion.

Setup of the Model

In Canada, universities are publicly funded and typically ration the number of newly admitted students according to some measure of quality, such as grade point average (GPA).[1] This is a necessary consequence of the inability of Canadian universities to adjust tuition fees to their market clearing rates due to legislated tuition ceilings.[2]

Empirical evidence for the province of Ontario (Table 2) shows that the number of new applicants far exceeds the available supply of new seats. Using the ratio of total applications to total acceptances, demand exceeded supply by between 3.98 (Lakehead University) and 6.85 (Ryerson) times over the period 1991–2000. We do not know if this is typical of all Canadian universities due to a lack of detailed data for many institutions. We also do not know how many students applied to each university who had little intention of actually attending if accepted. Perhaps they apply to more than one university so they can rank their choices if accepted.[3] Nevertheless the data is suggestive that excess demands can and do occur.

The disequilibrium model developed in this paper assumes that the market for new university admissions is not cleared by the price of tuition. Other studies of higher education demand typically assume that the supply of seats for newly admitted students is infinitely elastic at the market price of tuition. This allows the aggregate education demand function to be

---

[1]In fact, Canadian universities currently ration available slots almost exclusively on the basis of high-school grades. A recent article in the *National Post* (Sokoloff, 2002), for example, notes that "admissions decisions in Canadian universities have been made by a computer rather than a person, based on information supplied on standardized applications forms and a high school transcript". The same article, however, notes that other criteria along the lines of the American model (e.g., SAT scores, extra-curricular activities, etc.) are beginning to be used in admissions decisions in light of the increased competition for slots, especially at high-profile programs at prestigious universities.

[2]Alberta universities, for example, are not allowed to charge tuition fees in excess of 30% of total operating revenues. In Quebec, tuition fees have been frozen for a number of years. Other provinces use similar legislation under their Universities Acts.

[3]Ontario universities and BC universities use a standardized application form that allows students to choose more than one university.

Table 2: Ratio of Total Applications to Total Registrations, Secondary School Students, Ontario Universities, 1991–2000

	1991	1992	1993	1994	1995	1996	1997	1998	1999	2000	Average 1991-2000
Brock	5.75	5.07	5.12	4.69	4.22	4.55	4.53	4.19	4.46	6.06	4.86
Carleton	3.41	3.32	3.22	3.67	4.45	4.19	3.99	4.51	4.77	5.25	4.08
Guelph	5.74	5.54	5.57	4.93	5.01	3.84	4.64	4.64	5.11	5.04	5.01
Lakehead	3.92	3.77	3.97	4.02	4.11	3.66	3.38	3.73	4.60	4.67	3.98
Laurentian	3.31	3.59	3.93	3.88	3.85	3.79	3.62	4.06	4.86	5.03	3.99
McMaster	4.43	5.68	4.74	5.86	4.89	4.72	4.93	5.39	6.42	5.71	5.28
Nipissing			2.61	4.20	3.80	4.38	3.88	3.51	4.82	4.93	4.02
Ottawa	4.21	4.60	4.57	4.89	4.49	4.31	4.61	4.23	4.71	5.41	4.60
Queen's	4.87	5.05	4.77	4.14	4.76	4.66	4.44	5.26	5.97	6.44	5.04
Ryerson	5.91	5.55	5.76	8.05	7.38	6.22	6.26	7.26	7.90	8.18	6.85
Toronto	3.49	4.18	4.06	3.88	3.09	3.45	3.76	3.93	4.82	5.47	4.01
Trent	5.70	5.66	6.00	5.37	4.26	4.48	4.13	4.51	4.24	5.14	4.95
Waterloo	4.09	4.71	4.83	4.26	3.72	3.99	3.34	4.56	4.53	5.28	4.33
Western Ontario	4.36	4.46	3.92	4.12	4.33	4.31	3.87	4.88	5.26	5.82	4.53
Windsor	4.15	3.81	4.15	3.65	3.98	3.94	4.00	3.91	4.99	4.58	4.11
Wilfrid Laurier	6.40	5.57	6.13	5.08	4.78	4.11	4.42	3.83	4.73	5.12	5.02
York	3.61	3.63	4.44	3.64	3.84	3.90	3.72	4.50	4.87	5.26	4.14
Average	4.59	4.64	4.58	4.61	4.41	4.26	4.21	4.52	5.12	5.49	4.64

Note: Nipissing did not become an independent university until 1993.

Source: Council of Ontario Universities.

estimated using least squares. Recent examples of this approach are Paulsen and Pogue (1988), King (1993), Duschesne and Nonneman (1998), and Ehrenberg and Monks (1999). An alternative approach to estimating education demand is to use survey data to isolate determinants of institutional choice by individual students. Typically multinomial logit functions are estimated where students face a choice to enrol or not to enrol. Once enrolled, the student may also choose the particular institution and the type of program to study. Endogeneity of enrolment demand with supply is not treated in this literature. Surveys can be found in Ordovensky (1995) and Corman and Davidson (1984).

Estimating an equilbrium model that is actually in disequlibrium produces biased parameter estimates.[4] That is not to say that previous studies for other countries have produced biased results, only that an equilibrium approach would not seem to be appropriate for Canadian universities. To motivate the form of our model, we will assume that there is always an excess demand for slots at current tuition levels. This allows us to restrict the focus to the portion of the typical demand-supply diagram that is below the market-clearing price. Determining expected signs for the parameter estimates then becomes possible. Figure 1 helps to clarify the exposition of our approach.

Previous studies have assumed that the tuition fee is exogenous to changes in demand and supply. We concur with this assumption as a characterization of the short run. Institutional rigidities prevent tuition fees rising to clear the new admissions market. Tuition fees, however, do increase over time in Canada, but with considerable lags to excess demands, so that in the short run tuition fees are treated as rigid in response to the quantity of new applications. What does clear the market is student quality as measured by grade point average. The term GPA* is the minimum entry grade point average for applying high-school students. Raising GPA* shifts the demand for new admissions to the left in Figure 1 so that an equilibrium is obtained *ex post* at Q_s. Hence an *ex ante* excess demand becomes an *ex post* equilibrium at tuition fee P by raising GPA*.

---

[4]Paulsen and Pogue (1988) discuss this issue but ultimately assume an infinitely elastic supply curve of slots.

Figure 1: The Excess Demand for New Admissions

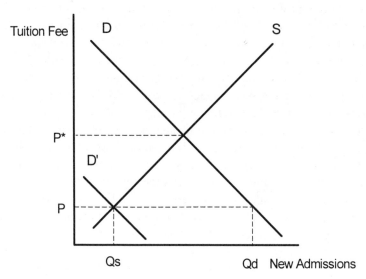

Obviously the value of GPA* differs for every Canadian university[5] and can change from one year to the next. Unfortunately, GPA* is not reported in easily obtainable university statistics, so we approximate it using the average GPA for all newly entering students.[6]

We assume that high-school graduates cannot observe the value of GPA* for any university before making their choice of where to apply. That

---

[5]We do not consider enrolment choices at colleges and trade schools. Ordovensky (1995) found that a high GPA out of high school had the greatest effect on university enrolment, followed by colleges, then trade schools, using data for the United States.

[6]This requires the assumption that the average entry level GPA moves roughly in concert with GPA*. A uniform distribution of entry level GPAs would ensure this is true; however, this is probably not the case. A casual perusal of various university Web sites failed to yield detailed information on average high-school grades required for admission. From the universities' point of view, publishing entry requirements *ex post* may ultimately limit the number of registrants in the new academic year. Universities routinely accept the best applicants in the first round of the admissions process, before "lowering the bar" during subsequent admissions rounds.

is, we believe the *ex ante* application demand curve in Figure 1 is where it is based on observable values of the exogenous variables, but not GPA*. This assumption implies that students do not ration themselves, that is, decide not to apply to a university since they know their GPA won't make the cut. In that case, excess demand does not exist if GPA* is the only factor for admission. Certainly universities compute forecasts of demand and enrolments for the next academic year; however, we assume these forecasts are used for formulating budgets and ensuring that enough resources are available to accommodate the new enrolment. The exact value of GPA* is not computed until all applications are received. This treats GPA* as an *ex post* rationing device rather than treating it is as a device for potential applicants to ration themselves.

It may be the case that some universities establish minimum GPA's for students to apply, announce GPA*, and still receive more applications than available spots. The university might then ration the number of applications using other measures of quality, such as awards, special high-school programs, letters of recommendation, etc. A number of Canadian universities state the minimum GPA (or sometimes a range) to apply on their application packages, usually with the caveat that meeting the minimum GPA does not guarantee admission. Our model is also consistent with this rationing approach as long as the non-GPA measures of quality are strongly correlated with the student GPAs. Since we use the average GPA of admitted students, and not the actual cut-off GPA, it would make sense that our GPA measure will increase as universities revert to other quality measures that are correlated with GPA.

The rationing model can be more clearly explained using Figure 2 which plots the value of GPA* for any given level of *ex ante* excess demand for student slots. The line is a schedule representing all rationing equilibria where *ex post* demand and supply are equated in Figure 1. It is drawn as linear for convenience.[7] The intercept with the vertical axis gives the minimum grade point average for entry if there is no excess demand for student slots. We assume that this does not change so that a university will enforce a minimum quality standard that is specific to that university,

---

[7]The rationing equilibria schedule is essentially an excess demand curve that is inverted with the implicit price, GPA*, on the vertical axis.

Richard E. Mueller and Duane W. Rockerbie

Figure 2: The Schedule of Rationing Equilibria

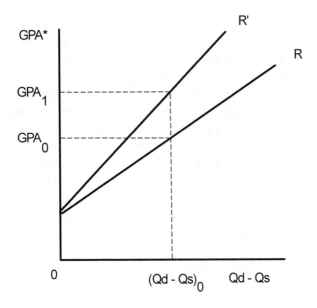

regardless of shifts in application demand or slot supply.[8] In this case, changes in any of the exogenous variables, except tuition fees, in the demand or supply functions serve to pivot the equilibria schedule around the intercept. For instance, an increase in the *Maclean's* ranking for university i may pivot the schedule upwards from R to R' as the demand for student slots, as given by new applications, shifts to the right in Figure 1. For a given initial excess demand and GPA*, an increase in the ranking requires a greater rationing GPA (GPA_1) just to maintain the initial excess demand. An increase in tuition fees for university i, holding the demand and supply curves constant in Figure 1, would reduce the excess demand

---

[8]Without this assumption, it is impossible to predict what will happen to GPA* given a shift in demand or supply that results in a new long-run equilibrium tuition fee. Consider a shift in application demand in Figure 1. The long-run tuition fee will increase as will student slots. If the supply curve is elastic, then the long-run GPA* may increase since tuition fees will not rise by very much. The opposite is true if the supply curve is inelastic. We assume GPA* does not change. The intercept can also represent the minimum GPA to apply if other quality measures are used.

for student slots and result in a movement down schedule R towards the intercept.[9]

In the short run, each university adjusts GPA* to alleviate excess demand for student slots. In the long run, a university has some ability to raise its tuition fees and reduce the pressure on GPA* as the excess demand is reduced. Holding everything else constant, reaching an equilibrium price at P* in Figure 1 is a desirable property to ensure stability of the model. The speed at which tuition fees can be raised is governed by institutional rigidities, such as operating budgets and provincial regulations, and the desire to raise fees. There should exist a trade-off between higher tuition fees and easing the GPA requirement in the long run. A logical extension of the method developed in this paper would be to estimate this long-run trade-off in order to determine just what P* is and how long it takes to reach it. A functional form would need to be derived from a constrained utility maximization model of a representative university. Ideally this functional form would represent the marginal rate of substitution between the two market-clearing devices and would provide a theoretical argument for the slope of the short-run and long-run response functions to excess demand. We choose not to model the long-run trade-off between tuition fees and GPA* since our main concern for the present is the effect of the *Maclean's* rankings on university applications in the short run. We simply estimate the slope of the short-run rationing schedule in Figure 2 and provide some insights on its magnitude. The steeper the slope of the rationing equilibria schedule, the greater the student quality for a given level of excess demand.

The theoretical development above suggests that we should estimate the schedule R in Figure 2. The estimation is complicated by the fact that a change in one of the exogenous variables, except the tuition fee, changes the slope of schedule R. An interaction model is necessary and is assumed to take the form

---

[9]To illustrate this concept, consider an increase in tuition fees holding everything else constant. This change can only occur if there is an upward movement in tuition towards the long-run equilibrium tuition for demand and supply fixed curves (i.e., P* in Figure 1). The result is less pressure on the rationing GPA. Since tuition is not a factor in the short-run excess demand function we use, an increase in tuition fees moves the rationing equilibrium down schedule R in Figure 2.

$$GPA_{it}^* = a + \beta_1(Q_{dit} - Q_{sit}) + \widetilde{\beta}(Q_{dit} - Q_{sit})X_{it} + e_{it}, \qquad (1)$$

where i denotes the university and t denotes the time period. The minimum entry GPA serves as the implicit price in the short run, given the tuition fee charged by each university. The excess number of new applications, $Q_{dit} - Q_{sit}$, is endogenous and hence an instrumental variable will be constructed in its place. The matrix X_{it} contains a set of independent variables that shift the demand curve for new applications and the supply curve of new spots in Figure 1. These will be discussed in detail in the next section.[10] The vector $\widetilde{\beta}$ contains coefficients for each of the interaction terms that are shifts in the slope of the equilibria schedule.

Independent Variables

Independent variables affecting new admissions demand and slot supply must be chosen for the vector X to estimate equation (1), some of which will be identical across all universities, while the remainder will be specific to each institution.[11] Generally the demand for higher education can be thought of as the demand for a good that yields consumption and accumulates human capital.[12] The consumption component can be modelled using

---

[10]The tuition fee (P) is not included in the vector X. It is determined by the interaction of demand and supply for spots in an equilibrium model. In the case of unobservable excess demand or supply, P would be part of an econometric specification to predict excess demand or supply. Since our measure of excess demand or supply is observable, P is whatever it is at those levels but is not needed in the estimation of (1) given our IV estimate of excess demand. P falls out when we take $Q_{dit} - Q_{sit}$.

[11]These variables are outlined in Table 4.

[12]An alternative to the human capital approach to education demand is the signaling approach. Rather than gaining human capital from education, graduates acquire a signal as to their inherent productivity that potential employers utilize. Spence (1973) states the basic argument. Bedard (2001) suggests that reducing the availability of higher education (by greater rationing in our model) increases the value of the high-school graduate designation and should reduce dropout rates in high school. We do not consider these effects on the number of applications.

Do the Maclean's Rankings Affect University Choice?

a permanent income consumption model that relies on the distinction between temporary and permanent changes in disposable income. A change in consumption spending is determined by the equation below.

$$\Delta C_t = R_t Y_t + \frac{\Delta A_t}{L} \tag{2}$$

In (2), R is a real interest rate, Y is disposable income, A is the consumer's stock of assets and L is the number of periods left to live. Temporary increases in income cause only small increases in consumption spending since the temporary increase is spread over the consumer's lifetime. The theory posits that the consumer will spend the interest earned on purchasing assets plus a fraction of the stock of assets purchased from temporary increases in income. Permanent increases in income carry a marginal propensity to consume close to one if there is no bequest motive. This approach suggests that the consumer's current and expected future stock of assets and the real interest rate are important determinants of consumption spending. There are two reasons why this approach does not lend itself well to this paper. First, obtaining data on the stock of assets for Canada is both difficult and unreliable. Empirical estimates of the total stock of assets typically include the physical capital stock, human capital, the market value of government securities, real high-powered money, and an adjustment for the consumption of durable goods (Rockerbie, 1997). Second, most newly admitted university students do not have a substantial stock of assets from which to consume. They may be consuming from their expected stock of assets over their lifetime, which is unobservable and may not be related to their current stock of assets. We choose not to include a measure of the stock of assets. The real interest rate (R) can be used as a discount rate for the future stock of assets and will be retained in the estimation.[13] Otherwise, new admissions are modelled simply as a function of real disposable income per capita (Y). The shortcoming of this method is that the marginal propensity to consume will be some value between the short-run and long-run marginal propensities to consume, however we use this specification since an accurate estimate of the marginal propensity to consume is not the main focus of this paper.

---

[13]Although we acknowledge that the effect of the real interest rate on consumption is ambiguous since it depends on the magnitudes of the substitution and wealth effects.

We use the provincial unemployment rate for 18 to 24-year-olds (URATE) to capture the opportunity cost (foregone income) of attending university. A measure of disposable income per capita among this age group would be preferable, but is not available. If wages move inversely with the unemployment rate, an increase in the unemployment should increase the excess demand for admissions. The population of 18 to 24-year-old Ontario high-school graduates (POP) is included as an independent variable to account for the scale of demand.[14]

The full price for tuition is often less for some students due to the provision of scholarships and bursaries. We use the average real scholarship and bursary awards per full-time student (S) to control for subsidies to tuition fees. This is computed for university i at time t using the figures reported by *Maclean's*.

$$S_{it} = \frac{\$Awards}{\$Operating\ Budget} \bullet \frac{\$Operating\ Budget}{Full\ time\ students} \tag{3}$$

The *Maclean's* university ranking for each university (RANK) enters as an independent variable in the demand specification to capture the quality of each institution, at least in the minds of those who use the rankings to choose a university. *Maclean's* segments universities into three broad categories: primarily undergraduate, comprehensive (COMP), and medical/doctoral (MD). We assign dummy variables for COMP and MD. We only use the rankings for Ontario universities. This introduces a potential source of bias since students may choose to attend a university outside Ontario due to a change in the rankings outside Ontario, without any change in the rankings within Ontario. To control for this potential bias, we include the median ranking of non-Ontario universities (ORANK) lagged by one year as an independent variable.

The demand for new admissions in equation (1) is summarized as

$$GPA_{it}^* = f(Q_{dit}, P_{it}, Y_t, POP_t, R_t, S_{it}, URATE_t, RANK_{it-1}, ORANK_{it-1}). \tag{4}$$

---

[14]We could only obtain sporadic data for the number of high-school graduates by gender. A complete series of total graduates is available from the Statistics Canada publication *Education in Canada*, but is not reported by gender. Our series correlated reasonably well with the observations for male and female high-school graduates that we could obtain (0.697 for males and 0.772 for females).

We have no theory to guide the choice of the independent variables in an enrolment supply equation in Figure 1. It would make sense that the number of new admission slots depends strongly on the ability of a university to finance those new slots out of its operating budget. With tuition fees making up a small proportion of total operating budgets, universities in Canada rely on provincial funding (and some private funding) to operate. This constrains the ability of these institutions to offer new admissions slots. We use the real net operating budget (NOB) which equals the real total operating budget less real total tuition revenue, as a measure of this budget constraint and treat it as exogenous.

Universities that draw students from large urban centres may feel the need to supply more new enrolment slots so that the rationing GPA is not too high. They may feel pressure to do this despite a constant budget per full-time student. This effect could be captured by including the population of potential students within the appropriate age group who are within some critical distance of the university. For example, Frenette (2002) has shown that the probability of attending university decreases with the distance from home to the nearest university campus. The question is what distance should be used? Some universities are located within large urban centres and in that case the distance measure would be the city radius. Other universities are quite large but are not located in large urban centres (Queen's University or the University of Western Ontario are examples). Casual empirical evidence suggests that the bulk of full-time students attending a university originate from the province in which the university is located. Queen's University, for example, averaged approximately 87% for the period 1976–99 and all other Ontario universities average approximately 95%.[15] We feel these statistics, along with the geographic proximity of most Ontario universities to urban centres, justify using the Ontario 18 to 24-year-old high-school graduate population (POP).

The supply of new spots for students is summarized by

$$GPA_{it}^* = f(Q_{sit}, P_{it}, NOB_{it}, POP_t) \tag{5}$$

---

[15]Source: http://www.queensu.ca/irp/pdfiles/fallheadcounts/pi2001.pdf.

Data

The main data source used in the subsequent estimation is the *Maclean's* magazine annual ranking of Canadian universities. This special edition of Canada's main news magazine has been published each November since 1991. The final rankings for all Ontario universities, as well as the total number of institutions ranked each year across Canada are presented in Table 3.

Unlike the better known college rankings from *U.S. News & World Report* in the United States, the methodology used to compile the rankings has changed very little since they began over a decade ago.[16] This provides us a consistent dataset over a ten-year period (1992–2001). Furthermore, the weighting of each subcategory differs only slightly between groups (e.g., the total number of volumes in the university library is included as a criteria for medical/doctoral institutions, but not for the other two groups). Thus, although the rankings are within one group, prospective students can still make comparisons between groups. In addition to the rankings and sub-rankings, since 1994 *Maclean's* has included the raw data used to compute the rankings. For example, data on average entering high-school grades is given for each university, and these figures are used to compute the sub-ranking for student body quality. This raw data (not reported here) will be used in our empirical estimation.

A secondary source of data was provided by the Council of Ontario Universities (COU).[17] A unique feature of applying for university in Ontario is the application form. Up until 1998, students could apply to as many as three Ontario universities using one application (since 1998 this number is unlimited).[18] Students rank order their preferences on this application form. The applications are then processed by the COU and forwarded to individual universities for final admissions decisions.

---

[16]The ranking methodology did change somewhat in 1992, but has remained essentially the same since. See Table 1 for details.

[17]Thanks to Judith Pearse of the Council of Ontario Universities for providing us with this data.

[18]Only the number of applications from students who rank a university in the top three positions is used from 1998 onward to ensure conformity with the data prior to 1998.

Table 3: *Maclean's* Rankings of Ontario Universities, 1991–2001

Group/University	Year										
	1991	1992	1993	1994	1995	1996	1997	1998	1999	2000	2001
Medical/Doctoral											
McMaster	4	4	5	5	5	5	5	6	6	7	8
Ottawa	9	8	9	11	9	10	11	11	12	9	10
Queen's	2	3	2	2	2	2	2	2	2	3	3
Toronto	3	2	3	1	1	1	1	1	1	1	1
Western	10	10	11	8	7	6	9	5	5	5	6
Total number of institutions ranked	15	15	15	11	11	13	15	15	15	15	15
Comprehensive											
Carleton[1]	11	6	9		8	9	7	7	7	8	8
Guelph	1	3	4	4	4	4	2	2	1	2	3
Waterloo	4	1	2	1	3	2	4	3	2	3	1
Windsor	9	11	10	7	7	7	8	8	8	7	9
York	3	5	5	5	5	5	5	5	5	5	6
Total number of institutions ranked	12	11	13	7	9	11	13	12	12	11	11
Primarily Undergraduate											
Brock	14	11	13	11	13	14	14	17	19	15	12
Lakehead	13	12	18	14	16	17	15	18	20	21	13
Laurentian	16	16	19	15	18	18	17	16	15	17	18
Nippising[2]			22	15	15	16	20	21	18	14	17
Ryerson[3]			21	18	17	19	19	19	17	19	19
Trent	6	2	2	2	2	3	3	4	3	4	3
Wilfrid Laurier	12	4	6	5	4	4	5	5	5	5	7
Total number of institutions ranked	18	18	23	18	19	19	23	21	21	21	21

Notes: [1] Carleton did not take part in the rankings in 1994.
[2] Nippising became independent of Laurentian only in 1993.
[3] Ryerson did not take part in the rankings until 1993.

Richard E. Mueller and Duane W. Rockerbie

Universities then attempt to admit students to their highest preference ranking using some sort of rationing device, normally high-school grades, until all positions are filled. This means that all Ontario universities subscribe to the same initial application process and might coordinate their admission strategies. This data allows us to determine: (i) the total number of applications for each institution from both secondary school and non-secondary school applicants, (ii) the rank ordering of these applications, and (iii) the number of students who registered at each institution. Furthermore, this data is disaggregated by gender. The admission process, coupled with the fact that almost all applicants are Ontario residents, results in a very homogeneous sample. Reliable applications and admissions data from other provinces are not as readily available. Furthermore, given the rather collusive nature of the process in Ontario, including data from other provinces could introduce undesirable distortions in the data.

The most recent data we utilize from the COU is for 2000, whereas the *Maclean's* data is useful only since 1994 (the year in which the disaggregated data behind the rankings began to be published). Thus, we have seven years of data on 16 Ontario universities (i.e., 112 observations). However, Carleton University did not participate in the rankings in 1994. This resulted in two observations being dropped from the sample.[19] Our final dataset contains 110 observations. We also limit our sample to students who are applying to university directly from high school. A key variable in our analysis is average entering high-school grade (GPA*), found in the *Maclean's* data since 1994. The COU collects data on secondary school students and others (which include foreign students, transfers from colleges, etc.). However, since students in the other category may be admitted using criteria other than high-school grades, inclusion of these individuals would likely bias our results. Thus, for compatibility between the two data sources, we limit the subsequent analysis to entering secondary school students.

---

[19]Since the raw data for 1994 is not available for Carleton, this observation had to be dropped. The 1995 observation was also excluded since decisions in that year are assumed to be based on the lagged ranking, which obviously does not exist. Queen's University was also dropped from the sample (for reasons explained below).

Estimation

The demand for new applications in equation (1) was estimated by first pooling the observations for all 17 Ontario universities so the time-series observations for university i are followed by the time-series observations for university $i+1$ in a "stacked" vector. It is then customary to include fixed effects parameters, a dummy variable for 15 of the 16 universities, to account for differences in mean GPA*s. We found that the inclusion of the fixed effects parameters accounted for such a large proportion of the variation in GPA* that there was little variation left to explain the independent variables in (1). Hence we chose an alternative strategy of assigning a dummy variable for medical/doctoral schools (MD) and a dummy variable for comprehensive schools (COMP). We believe this may more accurately reflect the choices that students make between the category a particular university falls in, rather than treating each university as a unique category (i.e., a fixed effect). The dummy variables can act to vertically shift the equilibria schedule in Figure 2, or shift its slope, or both. Hence we include the interaction dummy terms as well as the usual intercept dummy terms. Table 4 contains a list of all variables used in estimation, their acronyms, and a brief description of each.

Least squares was used to estimate the pooled equation (1) utilizing White's (1980) heteroskedasticity consistent covariance matrix estimator to provide efficient estimates. An instrumental variable for excess demand (EXD = $Q_{dit} - Q_{sit}$) was constructed using real tuition (P) as well as all of the exogenous variables in the X matrix (i.e., the lagged ranking (RANK), the median rank of non-Ontario universities in the same category (ORANK), Ontario population of high-school graduates 18–24 years old by sex (POP), real disposable income per capita in Ontario (Y), Ontario annual unemployment rate of 17 to 19-year-olds by sex (URATE), real scholarships per student (S), a real interest rate (R) and dummies for comprehensive (COMP) and medical/doctoral (MD) universities), as well as net real operating budget (NOB). The predicted values of excess demand (PXD) were then used to estimate equation (1), along with interaction terms to account for changes in the slope of the R function in Figure 2, and the variables MD and COMP to account for qualitative differences in university types. These results are presented in Table 5 for males and females.

Table 4: Variable Names, Acronyms, and Descriptions

Variable Name	Acronym	Description
Average high school entering grade	GPA	Average high-school grade of students entering from high school
Real tuition	P	Tuition deflated by the Ontario CPI (1992=100)
Lagged *Maclean's* ranking	RANK	*Maclean's* ranking by category lagged one year
Lagged *Maclean's* outside ranking	ORANK	Median *Maclean's* ranking for non-Ontario universities lagged one year
Population	POP	Ontario population of 18 to 24-year-old high-school graduates (gender specific in thousands)
Real interest rate	R	90-day t-bill rate minus % change in CPI
Real disposable income	Y	Real disposable income per capita
Unemployment rate	URATE	Provincial annual unemployment rate of 17 to 19-year-olds (gender specific)
Real scholarships per student	S	Value of Scholarships per student deflated by the CPI (1992=100) in thousands
Medical/doctoral	MD	Medical/doctoral institutions in the *Maclean's* rankings
Comprehensive	COMP	Comprehensive institutions in the *Maclean's* rankings
Net real operating budget	NOB	Operating budget less total tuition revenue deflated by the CPI (1992=100) in millions
Secondary school applications (Q_d)	APP	Adjusted total number of applications from high-school students (see text for details)
Secondary school registrations (Q_s)	REG	Total number of registrants from high school
Excess demand	EXD	Total applications less total registrations (APP - REG)/1000
Predicted excess demand	PXD	Predicted excess demand from 1st stage regression

Table 5: Estimation of Average Entering Grades, Males and Females
(heteroskedasticity corrected z statistics are in parentheses)

	Males		Females	
	(1)	(2)	(3)	(4)
Predicted excess demand (PXD)	2.427	2.736	1.273	0.582
	(0.57)	(0.65)	(0.33)	(0.35)
Ranking lagged interaction (PXD*RANK)	-0.172 *	-0.172 *	-0.134 *	-0.133 *
	(10.34)	(10.34)	(9.52)	(9.66)
Outside ranking lagged interaction (PXD*ORANK)	-0.065	-.060	-0.047	-0.040
	(1.81)	(1.78)	(1.61)	(1.55)
Population interaction (PXD*POP)	0.003		0.010	0.014
	(0.44)		(0.77)	(1.47)
Unemployment rate interaction (PXD*URATE)	0.079	0.08	0.069	0.056
	(1.31)	(1.33)	(1.51)	(1.46)
Real scholarships interaction (PXD*S)	0.831	0.809	1.173 **	1.342 *
	(1.47)	(1.45)	(2.06)	(2.75)
Net operating budget interaction (PXD*NOB)	-0.007 *	-0.006 *	-0.006 *	-0.007 *
	(3.14)	(3.13)	(3.41)	(4.09)
Real interst rate interaction (PXD*R)	0.058 **	0.059 **	0.091 *	0.088 **
	(2.20)	(2.25)	(2.75)	(2.69)
Real disposable income per capita interaction (PXD*Y)	0.249	0.289	0.121	
	(1.21)	(1.54)	(0.53)	
Medical/doctoral interaction (PXD*MD)	-1.825 *	-1.811 *	-1.519 *	-1.446 *
	(3.13)	(3.11)	(2.99)	(2.98)
Comprehensive interaction (PXD*COMP)	-1.717 *	-1.706 *	-1.330 *	-1.261 *
	(4.04)	(4.02)	(3.45)	(3.55)
Comprehensive (COMP)	2.559 **	2.571 **	2.500 **	2.311 **
	(2.19)	(2.20)	(2.14)	(2.10)
Medical/doctoral (MD)	5.671 *	5.645 *	5.285 *	4.879 *
	(2.66)	(2.65)	(2.45)	(2.41)
Constant	74.339 *	74.345 *	73.823 *	73.769 *
	(130.45)	(130.18)	(140.24)	(140.14)
Observations	110	110	110	110
R^2	0.79	0.79	0.81	0.81

Note: * and ** denote significance at the 1 and 5% levels, respectively.

The first column of Table 5 provides the results for male applicants using the overall *Maclean's* ranking for all 16 Ontario universities.[20] The estimated coefficient for each interaction term gives the shift in the slope of the rationing schedule for a one unit change. Thus the coefficient for PXD*RANK indicates that an improvement in the ranking of one position (a decrease in RANK) increases the slope of the rationing schedule by 0.172. All the coefficients in column (1) appear to have the predicted sign. The interaction variable PXD*NOB is the only supply variable in the regression and carries a negative sign (an increase in operating budget increases the supply of slots and reduces the slope of the rationing schedule). For males, statistically significant coefficients include RANK, NOB and R. The constant provides an estimate of the average GPA for those admitted to primarily undergraduate universities when excess demand is zero (the intercept of the rationing schedule in Figure 2), while the COMP and MD coefficients estimate how much higher average GPA is for comprehensive and medical/doctoral universities when excess demand is zero. These estimates are 74.3%, 76.9% and 80% for primarily undergraduate, comprehensive and medical/doctoral schools respectively.

Column (2) of Table 5 provides coefficient estimates of equation (1) when interaction variables with z-statistics of less than one were dropped from the regression. The results are no different from column (1) with all independent variables included.

Columns (3) and (4) continue the same regression procedures for female applicants. The results are basically the same as the regressions for male applicants except that real scholarships (S) significantly affect female excess demand. Curiously, almost all of the coefficients are smaller than their male counterparts.[21] This suggests that female applicants are not as sensitive as males to changes in the independent variables in the demand

---

[20]Due to parameter instability, Queen's University was excluded from the sample. The sample data suggests that high-school students who are admitted to Queen's have the highest GPAs in Ontario. Yet the excess demand for slots is very small relative to other universities, resulting in a negative slope for the rationing schedule for medical/doctoral schools. Grades needed for admission for high-school students for the 2002–2003 academic year are listed as 82% in Arts, 85% in Sciences, and 87% in Commerce on the Queen's University Web page. It would appear that Queen's does a good job of rationing potential applicants before they even apply.

[21]Although probably not significantly so.

specification in (4), since the rationing GPA* does not increase to as great a degree as for male applicants.

The partial derivatives (slope of the rationing schedule) for the regressions of equation (1) are presented in Table 6. Each derivative is evaluated at the sample mean for the particular right-hand-side variable. Thus the derivative for the slope of the rationing schedule for medical/doctoral universities is computed as ($\beta_k \in \tilde{\beta}$ for $k > 1$):

$$\frac{\partial GPA}{\partial EXD} = \hat{\beta_1} + \hat{\beta_2}\overline{RANK} + \hat{\beta_3}\overline{URATE} + \hat{\beta_4}\overline{S} + \hat{\beta_5}\overline{NOB}$$
$$+ \hat{\beta_6}\overline{R} + \hat{\beta_7}\overline{Y} + \hat{\beta_8}\overline{ORANK} + \hat{\beta_9} \tag{6}$$

while the derivative for the change in the slope of a one-unit improvement in the *Maclean's* ranking is computed as

$$\frac{\partial GPA}{\partial RANK} = \hat{\beta_2}\overline{PXD} \tag{7}$$

The top half of Table 6 reports the sample means used to compute the partial derivatives. The bottom half of Table 6 reports the estimated partial derivatives, first when all the independent variables are included in the regressions, and second when highly insignificant independent variables are excluded from the regressions.[22] Recall from Table 5 that medical/doctoral schools had the highest average entrance standard based on the constant term, followed by comprehensive schools and primarily undergraduate schools. The results in Table 6 suggest that primarily undergraduate schools have the highest GPA rationing standards *on the margin*, followed by comprehensive schools and medical/doctoral schools (1.4744, 1.03, and 0.3434 for females). All three derivatives are statistically significant at the 99% confidence level.[23] Perhaps comprehensive and medical/doctoral schools consider other quality measures that are not as highly correlated

---

[22]An independent variable was dropped from a regression if the absolute value of its t-statistics was less than one.

[23]The null hypothesis that all the population coefficients for the relevant interaction variables are equal to zero was tested using a standard Wald test.

Richard E. Mueller and Duane W. Rockerbie

Table 6: Sample Means and Partial Derivatives by University Type
(partial derivatives calculated at university-type means)

	Medical/ Doctoral	Compre- hensive	Primarily Undergraduate
		Means	
Excess demand, thousands, males (EXDM)	5.563	4.083	1.892
Excess demand, thousands, females (EXDF)	6.360	4.539	2.169
Ranking lagged (RANK)	6.071	5.0606	13.204
Outside Ontario ranking lagged (ORANK)	8.429	7.212	9.214
Population of high-school graduates, males (POPM)	149.514	149.846	149.514
Population of high-school graduates, females (POPF)	126.043	126.140	126.043
Unemployment rate, males (URATEM)	18.87	18.86	18.87
Unemployment rate, females (URATEF)	15.81	15.85	15.81
Real scholarships, $ thousands (S)	0.4117	0.2481	0.1701
Net real operating budget, $ millions (NOB)	141.46	91.27	24.33
Real interest rate (R)	3.39	3.22	3.39
Real disposable income per capita, $ thousands (Y)	18.60	18.61	18.60
Grade point average (GPA)	82.28	80.68	76.89
		Partial Derivatives	
		Males (all variables included)	
$\delta GPA/\delta EXD$	0.3867 *	0.9343 *	1.4942 *
$\delta GPA/\delta RANK$	-0.9594 *	-0.7042 *	-0.3263 *
		Males (only significant variables included in second-stage regression)	
$\delta GPA/\delta EXD$	0.3905 *	0.9296 *	1.4902 *
$\delta GPA/\delta RANK$	-0.9586 *	-0.7036 *	-0.3260 *
		Females (all variables included)	
$\delta GPA/\delta EXD$	0.2932 *	0.9710 *	1.4429 *
$\delta GPA/\delta RANK$	-0.8530 *	-0.6087 *	-0.2909 *
		Females (only significant variables included in second-stage regression)	
$\delta GPA/\delta EXD$	0.3434 *	1.0300 *	1.4744 *
$\delta GPA/\delta RANK$	-0.8458 *	-0.6036 *	-0.2884 *

Notes: (1) These figures give the effects of a 1,000 person increase in excess demand or a one-position decline in the rankings on the average high school entering grade in percentage points.

(2) These are calculated using the mean values above and the coefficient estimates from Table 5.

(3) * denotes significance at the 1% level.

Do the Maclean's Rankings Affect University Choice?   363

with average GPA than primarily undergraduate schools since they have higher quality applicants on the average. Figure 3 plots the fitted values for all three rationing schedules when the values from columns (2) and (4) of Table 5 are used. The heavier lines represent female applicants and the lighter lines represent male applicants (the lines for primarily under-graduate schools are too close to make a distinction). The effect of the *Maclean's* ranking on mean grade point average is quite clear from Table 6: an improvement in the ranking increases the mean grade point average and thus improves the average quality of admitted students. This is the result of an increase in excess demand. Students appear to consider the rankings carefully when deciding where to apply. The effect is the strongest for medical/doctoral schools where a one position improvement in the ranking increases the mean GPA of those admitted by 0.96 percentage points for males and 0.85 percentage points for females. The effect of the

Figure 3: Fitted Values for Rationing Schedules

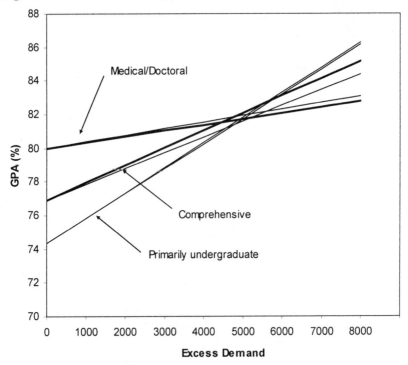

Richard E. Mueller and Duane W. Rockerbie

ranking is reduced as we move to comprehensive schools (0.70 percentage points for males and 0.60 percentage points for females), then primarily under-graduate schools (0.33 percentage points for males and 0.29 percentage points for females). An increase in the ranking pivots the rationing schedule upward for all university types, resulting in more stringent entrance requirements and a higher mean GPA for the first-year class.[24]

Conclusions

Determining whether *Maclean's* annual rankings of universities have any significant effect on enrolment and entrance standards is complicated by the fact that all Canadian universities operate at a disequilibrium. Institutional rigidities prevent tuition fees from rising to equate demand and supply for new student slots. Thus universities must resort to rationing the number of applying students to meet the number of new slots. This can take two different forms. Some universities appear to set minimum GPA requirements that are below the average GPA of most applicants in order to enforce a minimal standard. They then ration students by highest GPA until the available slots are filled. Other universities announce rigid GPA minimums that are more realistic (higher), then ration students using other quality measures, such as scholarships, awards, special high-school programs, letters of recommendation, etc. We argue that as long as the average GPA of newly admitted students is strongly correlated with these other quality measures, the two rationing methods can be treated the same.

We estimate an interaction model that estimates the rationing equilibria when application demand exceeds slot supply, using data for 16 Ontario

---

[24]The effect of an improvement in the ranking on excess demand can be computed by inverting (1) and taking the derivative. This gives $\partial EXD / \partial RANK = -\beta_2 (GPA_{it} - \alpha) / (\beta_1 + \widetilde{\beta} X_{it})^2$ where the sample means and the coefficients (with t-statistics greater than one in absolute value) from Table 5 are used to evaluate the derivative (β_1 is the coefficient for PXD and β_2 is the coefficient for PXD*RANK). The marginal effect of the ranking on the excess demands for medical/doctoral, comprehensive, and primarily undergraduate universities are 66.1, 92.0, and 11.9 applications respectively for males, and 46.4, 61.5, and 10.0 applications for females.

universities over the sample period 1994–2000. The model fits well and the results are very clear. Generally, greater excess demand increases entrance standards and thus the average GPA of successful applicants. The results also suggest that, although primarily undergraduate universities have the lowest admission standards when there is no excess demand, they are more stringent on the margin, that is, when excess demand for slots increases. This could be due to comprehensive and medical/doctoral schools adopting alternative quality measures that are not as strongly correlated with a student's GPA.

The *Maclean's* rankings appear to have a strong effect on where students choose to apply to (and end up). The effect was most notable for medical/doctoral universities, followed by comprehensive, and then primarily undergraduate universities. An improvement in ranking, even by just one position, can significantly increase the number of applicants. This may be a desirable result for a university if it has the resources to accommodate at least some of those applicants. Alternatively, a university can improve the quality of its newly admitted students by moving up in the rankings if new slots are not available. Universities, at least those in Ontario, would be well advised to take the *Maclean's* rankings seriously or either risk losing students to those that do or risk lowering their average quality of students. Despite their many statistical shortcomings and claims of irrelevance by university administrators and faculty, students and parents do appear to use the rankings when facing the very important choice of where to obtain a degree.

References

Bedard, K. 2001. "Human Capital versus Signaling Models: University Access and High School Dropouts", *Journal of Political Economy* 109(4), 749-775.

Corman, H. and P. Davidson. 1984. "Economic Aspects of Postsecondary Schooling Decisions", *Economics of Education Review* 3, 131-139.

Duschesne, I. and W. Nonneman. 1998. "The Demand for Higher Education in Belgium", *Economics of Education Review* 17(2), 211-218.

Ehrenberg, R. and J. Monks. 1999. "U.S News & World Report College Rankings: Why Do They Matter?" *Change* (Nov/Dec).

Frenette, M. 2002. *Too Far To Go On? Distance to School and University Participation*. Business and Labour Market Analysis Division Research Paper No. 191. Ottawa: Statistics Canada.

King, J. 1993. "The Demand for Higher Education in Puerto Rico", *Economics of Education Review* 12(3), 257-265.

Ordovensky, J. 1995. "Effects of Institutional Attributes on Enrollment Choice: Implications for Postsecondary Vocational Education", *Economics of Education Review* 14(4), 335-350.

Page, S. 1995. "Rankings of Canadian Universities: Pitfalls in Interpretation", *The Canadian Journal of Higher Education* 25(2), 17-28.

_____. 1996. "Rankings of Canadian Universities, 1995: More Problems in Interpretation", *The Canadian Journal of Higher Education* 26(2), 47-58.

_____. 1999. "Rankings of Canadian Universities and Help to Students", *Guidance and Counselling* 14(3), 11-13.

Paulsen, M. and T. Pogue. 1988. "Higher Education Enrollment: The Interaction of Labor Market Conditions, Curriculum, and Selectivity", *Economics of Education Review* 7(3), 275-290.

Rockerbie, D. 1997. "Are Consumers Ricardian when Some are Liquidity Constrained? Evidence for the United States", *Applied Economics* 29(6), 821-827.

Sokoloff, H. 2002. "High Grades are no Longer Enough", *National Post*, May 4.

Spence, M. 1973. "Job Market Signalling", *Quarterly Journal of Economics* 87(3), 355-374.

White, H. 1980. "A Heteroskedasticity-Consistent Covariance Matrix Estimator and a Direct Test for Heteroskedasticity", *Econometrica* 48(4), 817-838.

Rising Tuition and Supply Constraints: Explaining Canada-US Differences in University Enrolment Rates

Nicole M. Fortin

Introduction

Talks of a New Economy and population aging have fuelled concerns about impeding shortages of highly skilled workers. While the 1980s have seen dramatic increases in enrolment rates at higher education institutions in both Canada and the United States, in the 1990s enrolment rates levelled off in Canada. Total enrolment at Canadian universities increased at an annual rate of 4.1% between 1973 and 1990, but registered almost no growth in the 1990s.[1] In the United States, total enrolment at all universities

I would like to thank Charles Beach, David Card and Thomas Lemieux for comments on this manuscript. I am indebted to Miles Corak for graciously sharing his data on provincial tuition rates and to Herb O'Heron for helpfully providing data on provincial enrolments. Financial support was provided by SSHRC Grants INE #512-2002-1005.

[1]According to Statistics Canada numbers obtained from the Association of Universities and Colleges of Canada (AUCC), total enrolment went from 495,000 in 1973 to 841,000 in 1990, but finished off at 843,000 in 1999. Total enrolment is the simple sum of full-time and part-time fall enrolment.

and four-year colleges (private and public) increased at an annual rate of 1.8% between 1973 and 1990, and continued to increase at an annual 0.8% rate during the 1990s.[2] The annual rate of increase of 1.7% at US four-year public institutions was initially similar, but in the 1990s, the annual rate of increase of 0.2% was comparable to Canada's rate.[3]

The past 25 years have also seen spectacular increases in tuition levels at institutions of higher education in both countries. In 1973, the average real Canadian tuition (in 1999 CDN$) was around $2,300, in 1999 it had climbed to $3,100.[4] In the United States, over the same period, average real tuition (in 1999 US$) at public institutions went from $2,100 to $3,700.[5] Can these significant rises in tuition levels be implicated in the slowdown of enrolment rates? Or alternatively, can this slowdown be traced back to the dramatic changes in cohort size and direct government funding over that period? This paper addresses this puzzle by evaluating the impact of demographic changes and higher education policies on enrolment rates. The analysis is set at the provincial/state level where policymakers determine the level of higher education funding, as well as tuition and capacity levels at public universities and colleges.

In Canada, constitutional responsibility with education rests with the provinces and provincial funding is the main source of general operating support for postsecondary institutions. In 1973, provincial funding constituted 72% of educational expenditures of universities; in 1999 it was down to 57%.[6] The provinces rely on federal transfers to provide that

---

[2]Total fall enrolment at all four-year institutions of higher education went from 6,590,000 in 1973 to 8,580,000 in 1990, and ended up at 9,200,000 in 1999. These numbers are extracted from Table 197 of National Center for Education Statistics (2003).

[3]Total enrolment at four-year public institutions of higher education went from 4,530,000 in 1973 to 5,850,000 in 1990, and totaled 5,970,000 in 1999.

[4]These figures from Corak, Lipps and Zhao (2003) are for Arts programs.

[5]Average tuition levels are derived using data from Raudenbush (2002). See the Appendix for details.

[6]To enhance comparability with US data, educational expenditures of universities are computed as total expenditures [CANSIM II series V1992346] minus capital expenditures [series V1992357]. See the data Appendix and Table A1.

funding and the steep decline in provincial support in the 1990s can be, in part, traced back to the federal deficit fighting over that period (Cameron, 2005). As shown below, there are nevertheless substantial differences across provinces in the growth of provincial funding per college-age person. Direct federal incursions into this area of provincial jurisdiction take the form of research grants and student aid. Excluding student aid, direct federal funding has been the subject of substantially fewer fluctuations over time. These federal expenditures amounted to 15% of educational expenditures in 1973 and 12% in 1999, noting that the impact of more recent federal initiatives such as the Canada Foundation for Innovation and the Canada Research Chairs mostly fall after the period of study (see Snowdon, 2005).[7]

In the United States, states and local governments have also historically invested heavily in university/college education through direct and indirect subsidies, but that support has been eroded with each recession, especially with the recession of the early 1990s. The state appropriations constituted about 59% of general education revenues of public higher education institutions in 1973; by 1999, however, state appropriations were down to roughly 46%.[8] The share of federal appropriations, grants, and contracts in the general education revenues of postsecondary public institutions is also sizeable, but as in Canada it has been more stable over time. It went from 16% in 1981 to 14% in 1999.

Empirical studies of the political economy of public education across jurisdictions have found that higher public spending on postsecondary education are related to equal opportunities objectives, such wealth or income level and distribution (Humphreys, 2000), social homogeneity (Quigley and Rubinfeld, 1993; Poterba, 1996 for K–12 education) and lower support for private higher education (Goldin and Katz, 1999). In the United States, the levels of state appropriations have also been found to be

---

[7]See Table A1.

[8]These numbers are for all public institutions of higher education, including two-year colleges, but excluding vocational and trade colleges. Note, however, that the share of educational expenditures going to universities and four-year colleges has been remarkably constant at 79% of the expenditures of all public institutions over the entire period. The percentage distribution of general education revenues of higher education per FTE student are reported separately for universities, four-year colleges and two-year colleges in Table 39-1 of National Center for Education Statistics (1999a).

determined by legislative choices (Koshal and Koshal, 2000) and by the lobbying activities of public institutions and their governing bodies (Lowry, 2001b; Hearn, Griswold and Marine, 1996). Other factors, such as the importance of research-intensive industries (Goldin and Katz, 1999), were also found to be significant. Here, provincial/state appropriations are taken to be a reduced form estimate of these factors.

Faced with dwindling government support, higher education institutions had to increase their tuition revenues.[9] In Canada, the share of educational expenditures coming from tuition and fees went from a low of 10% in 1980 to a high of 21% in 1999. In the United Stated, tuition fees as a share of general education expenditures were at a low of 16% in 1980, but up to 24% in 1999. However, as shown below, the size and timing of the increases in tuition did vary considerably across provinces and states. The combination of often-times abruptly varying provincial/state tuition levels and provincial/state funding creates a potentially attractive source of the identification of the impact of these policies.

A primary finding of the paper is an estimated elasticity of student demand with respect to tuition fees of -0.15, which is surprisingly similar in Canada and the United States. When controlling for supply factors such as provincial/state funding, provincial/state trends, and demographics, the elasticity of enrolment rates with respect to tuition ranges from -0.09 to -0.14, over the 1973–99 period. Thus at worst, the near doubling (a 100% increase) of tuition fees between 1989/90 and 1990/91 experienced by Quebec students (Corak, Lipps and Zhao, 2003) would have reduced the enrolment rate from 23.3 to 20.3%, in the absence of the countervailing effects of increases in provincial funding and decreases in college-age population. It actually increased to 24.8%.

Another major finding is the substantial role played by the supply of university/college seats in determining enrolment rates, in particular in the 1970s when real tuition plummeted and in the 1990s when provincial/state appropriations per college-age person faltered. Over the entire period, the elasticity of student supply with respect to provincial/state funding is generally larger in Canada (0.33) than in the United States (0.11). When

---

[9]Lowry (2001a), who uses NCES data from individual campuses for 1994–95, finds that higher tuition revenues are associated with lower state government funding, but are higher in states where public universities have more financial autonomy. Fortin (2004) finds a similar negative relationship between tuition and state appropriations using pooled cross-sections of states from 1973 to 1993.

controlling for changes in tuition fees and demographics, the elasticity of enrolment rates with respect to provincial/state funding is somewhat reduced, ranging from 0.29 to 0.07 over the 1973–99 period. That is, the 13% decline in provincial funding, from 1992 to 1996 in Canada, would have led to a 0.8 percentage point decline in enrolment rates in the absence of other countervailing trends.[10] Enrolment rates actually went from 23.8 to 23.5%, thus the negative impact of the decline in provincial funding substantially wiped out the secular upward trends in enrolment rates.

The remainder of the paper is organized as follows. The next section sets out the economic framework of enrolment supply and demand used to analyze the potential impact of higher education polices on enrolment rates. The third section presents the broad aggregate and provincial/state trends in the key variables of interest. The empirical results are presented in the fourth section. A policy analysis of the findings concludes.

Enrolments in a Supply and Demand Framework

In a higher education economic framework, the observed enrolment rates can be seen as outcomes of a supply and demand model, where prospective students demand university/college seats and public institutions supply those seats with tuition fees serving as the intermediating price. Enrolment supply is positively related to tuition fees, which have the potential to increase the revenues of higher education institutions. Enrolment demand is negatively related to tuition fees, which increase the cost of attending university or college. However, as pointed out by Clotfelter (1999), a singular feature of the higher education market is the presence of non-price rationing: excess demand for college seats is a necessary condition for selectivity in admissions. In turn, selectivity in admissions is the mechanism used by institutions to set a lower bound on the quality of applicants. Institutions can in theory use a combination of these two instruments — price and grades — to equilibrate supply and demand.

In practice, different countries have favoured more or less rigid institutional frameworks. In France, admission in the elite "Grandes Écoles" is restricted to very high aptitude students on the basis of an

---

[10]This calculation uses the more precise estimate of 0.25 of column (5), Table 1.

admission test that often requires attendance in preparatory schools, but tuition is very low (€380). There is virtually universal and free access (on average €200 at LaSorbonne) to universities thought to be of lower quality.[11] The United States enjoys a mixed system of private and public institutions. Admission to the American elite private institutions is restricted by very high tuition (US$20,015 in 2003–04) and/or very high grades.[12] Public institutions use a combination of price and grades with public research universities requiring moderate tuition (US$4,793 in 2003–04) and restricting access on the basis of aptitude, while public community and technical colleges have very low tuition (US$2,142) and unrestricted admission.[13]

As often thought, the Canadian higher education system can be placed at some intermediate point between the French and American systems: it attempts to emphasize wider access while being somewhat preoccupied with quality. Skolnik and Jones (1992) argue that Canadian universities are not hierarchically differentiated. Yet, while there are no elite private institutions in Canada, the three best public research universities (University of Toronto, University of British Columbia and McGill) rank 18th, 28th and 50th in North America, respectively.[14] Like in the United States, Canadian public institutions have less latitude in setting tuition fees than private institutions. Until the mid-1990s tuition was set at the provincial level with institutions having very few options to ask for

---

[11]In the academic ranking of world universities (ed.sjtu.edu.cn/ranking. htm), the highest ranking French university, Université Paris VI is ranked 65th, while the top ranking Canadian university, the University of Toronto, is ranked 23rd.

[12]At some elite universities/four-year colleges, as much as 40% of students are admitted on a needs-blind basis with an average of US$18,000 in scholarships. Yet because of its high cost, needs-blind admission for high aptitude students at elite universities has been curtailed following the 1991 law suit (Salop and White, 1991).

[13]Card and Krueger (2003) report admission rates of 40% at UC-Berkeley and 85% at UC-Santa Cruz.

[14]The few Canadian private institutions (such as Alberta's King's College) are religiously-based, not-for-profit, and focused on undergraduate education. These rankings (ed.sjtu.edu.cn/ranking.htm) emphasize health and science.

differential tuition.[15] In the mid-1990s, however, institutions in Ontario began asking close to market price for professional programs.

In theory, institutions can compete for the best students by using combinations of price and grades — or price discrimination — almost on a per student basis with "merit" based scholarships. In Canada, institutional outlays to student support went from 7.5% in 1980 to 10.4 in 1999. Meanwhile in the United States, public institutional outlays to student scholarships and fellowships increased from 3% to 6%. Yet much of the competition among institutions may take other forms, including the influential Canadian *Macleans's* and *U.S. News and World Report* rankings of universities and colleges (Mueller and Rockerbie, 2002; Monks and Ehrenberg, 1999).

Governments, on the other hand, are concerned with equality of opportunity objectives. In the 1970s in particular, many jurisdictions kept hikes in tuition fees well below the inflation rate. At times, they have even frozen nominal tuition fees. Governments also offer means-tested scholarships and loans, making the net cost of attending universities less than posted tuition for many students. While Clotfelter (1999) finds some evidence of increasing inequality in the link between socio-economic status and college attendance, this troublesome trend is sharpest among private universities. In Canada, Corak, Lipps and Zhao (2003) find no evidence of an increase in the link between parental income and participation in post-secondary education.[16] Recent research (Kane, 2003) has also focused on financial aid as a way to alleviate the potential inequality increasing effect of rising tuition.

Here, the intricacies of asking "who" gets a university education are pushed into the background. Rather, I ask "how many" can get a university education given jurisdiction-specific higher education policies and underlying demographics, thus abstracting from the issue of non-price rationing. While this is clearly a step back from the current American research in higher education (Hoxby, 2004) where the issues of college choices are paramount, it is more appropriate for the Canadian context and

---

[15]Corak, Lipps and Zhao (2003) report specific differences by institutions and fields of study in differential tuition increases.

[16]The importance of that link is also evaluated in Christofides, Cirello and Hoy (2001), Knighton and Mirza (2002), Coelli (2004) among others.

may actually be very relevant to American public institutions that are still attended by the majority of postsecondary students.

In economics, the postsecondary enrolment decisions of high-school graduates are seen as solutions to a simplified version of the human capital investment model. After completing high school, individuals are faced with the decision of whether or not to get a university degree by maximizing the discounted present value of lifetime earnings, net of education costs.[17] Assuming that the marginal cost of attending university rises faster than the marginal benefit, the discounted lifetime earnings function is concave and the solution to this maximization problem equates the marginal costs of a university education to the marginal benefits. Individual heterogeneity in the decision to attend university or not will arise from differences in the marginal benefits of obtaining a university degree or differences in the marginal costs of obtaining a university degree. Aggregating across individuals in any given jurisdiction will imply that jurisdictional differences in educational attainment will arise from differences in the returns to a university/college education and in the marginal costs of that education. Thus, enrolment rates should be higher in jurisdictions with higher returns to a university degree and lower net costs of attendance, and conversely.

Yet precise information about the marginal benefits and the marginal costs of a university education may not be precisely known or correctly estimated by prospective students. In evaluating the marginal benefits, do prospective students use the national university/college premium or rather the provinces/state-specific values? Do they use a contemporaneous, past, or discounted expected present value of that premium? In evaluating the marginal costs, prospective students may not be fully aware of the parameters of the financial assistance available to them and may make irrational decisions (Avery and Hoxby, 2004). Because of these informational difficulties, it is reasonable to believe that the very concrete level of tuition fees may have an unduly important effect on those decisions.

On the enrolment supply side, the ability of public institutions of higher education to supply university/college seats greatly depends on the level of provincial/state funding, which constitute their most important single revenue source. There are many quasi-fixed costs associated with the

---

[17]This formulation is appropriate if people can borrow and lend at a fixed interest rate, and if they are indifferent between attending school and working. More generally, differences in aptitudes and tastes for schooling relative to work may lead to differences in the optimal level of schooling across individuals.

Nicole M. Fortin

expansion of college seats. At the extensive margin, increasing the number of college seats by increasing the number of institutions entails expansions in physical buildings which are not easily scaled down.[18] Card and Lemieux (2001) argue that the partial adjustment of the higher education system to the temporary bulge in enrolment caused by the baby boom may have been a rational response. At the intensive margin, increasing the number of seats at existing institutions may imply the hiring of tenured or tenured-track faculty whose numbers are also not easily brought down. Bound and Turner (2002) argue that institutions face a quality-quantity trade-off in expanding the number of college seats. When financial resources do not fully adjust to changes in the college-age population, limiting the expansion of college seats preserves institutional quality. Either argument has become known as the "cohort crowding" hypothesis, which implies a negative impact of cohort size on enrolment rates. However, the 1980s onwards were characterized by the baby-bust cohort becoming of college-age, thus one should expect enrolment rates going up as a "cohort hollowing" effect. Thus the more important determinants of enrolment supply will be the logarithm of the number of college persons and the logarithm of provincial/state appropriations per college-age person, since the appropriate per capita basis in this context is per college-age person.

Given the above considerations, it is reasonable to think that tuition levels seldom play the equilibrating role that prices ought to play in a supply and demand system. Thus the higher education system is often in a state of dis-equilibrium, where the enrolment rate is determined by the short side of the market. If tuition is too low, the short side of the market will be the supply side and the provincial/state appropriations will determine the enrolment rates. If tuition is too high, the short side of the market will be the demand side and the tuition levels will determine the enrolment rates. Another complication arises from the fact that at times, tuition levels are exogenously determined by policymakers, when tuition levels are frozen in nominal terms, for example (as in Quebec in the early 1980s). At other times, tuition levels and provincial/state funding are negatively correlated. It is also possible for tuitions to be high while low provincial/state funding

---

[18]The option of leasing regular office space is one that maintains higher flexibility, yet some physical demands (labs, amphitheatre, etc.) of instruction rarely make this choice a long-term one.

determines enrolment rates. A reduced form equation of enrolment rates that focuses on higher education policies will be of the form[19]

$$E_{jt} = \beta_0 + \beta_1 Tui_{jt} + \beta_2 App_{jt} + \beta_3 Col_{jt} + \in_{jt} \qquad (1)$$

where E_{jt} represents the logarithm of the ratio of FTE fall enrolments in public universities and four-year colleges divided by the number of persons aged 18 to 24 in jurisdiction j at time t, Tui_{jt} represents the logarithm of average tuition, App_{jt} represents the logarithm of per college-age person provincial/state appropriations, Col_{jt} the logarithm of the number of persons aged 18 to 24. The jurisdiction-time specific errors are further modelled as $\in_{jt} = \beta_j J_j + \beta_t P_t + \varepsilon_{jt}$, where J_j are jurisdiction-specific dummies, and P_t time period dummies.

Other authors (Quigley and Rubinfeld, 1993; Berger and Kostal, 2002; among others) have attempted to estimate separate more structural models of enrolment demand and supply. The difficulties are of finding appropriate instruments to identify either curve. Quigley and Rubinfeld (1993), for example, acknowledge that the negative sign on tuition in their legislative supply equation may be the result of an identification problem. My goal here is a more modest assessment of the relative role of demographics, government cut-backs, and tuition on enrolment rates.

Canada-US Differences in Higher Education and Population Trends

The most important changes of the latter part of the twentieth century with respect to potential determinants of educational attainment have been demographic changes. Both Canada and the United States experienced sizeable baby booms in the 1950s and 1960s, so that 20 years or so after, the college-age population as a fraction of the total population was at an all time high in the early 1980s. Figure 1 presents a dramatic illustration of

---

[19]There are substantial difficulties in estimating formal dis-equilibrium models with controlled prices, such as establishing which regime prevails in each jurisdiction at each time period. The approach here is closer in spirit to the one suggested by Hendry and Spanos (1980) which concentrates on market pressures.

Nicole M. Fortin

Figure 1: Trends in College Population and University Enrolment

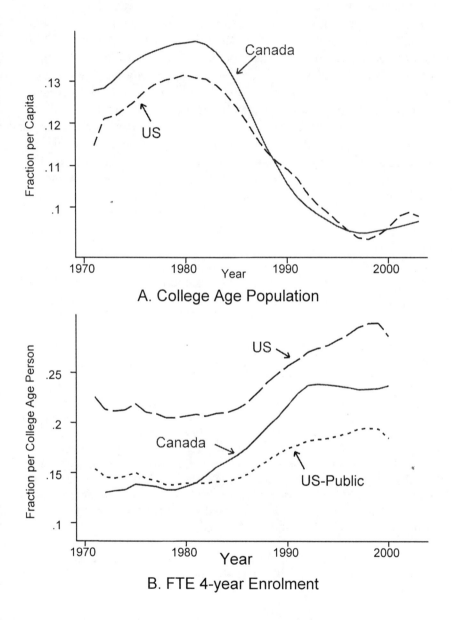

A. College Age Population

B. FTE 4-year Enrolment

the changes in the college-age population (individuals aged 18 to 24) and in university/college enrolment per college-age person.[20] The baby boom and the baby bust are clearly shown in panel A. In 1980, the college-age population represented at least 13% of the total population, by 1999 that percentage was less than 10%.[21] Panel A also shows that the decline of the college-age population was more pronounced in Canada than in the United States. Basically, the baby bust created an opportunity that I will argue is modulated by higher education policies, for enrolment rates to climb as more college seats per college-age person became available.

Panel B focuses on fall FTE enrolment at Canadian universities and at American universities and four-year colleges per college-age person.[22] For the United States, the enrolment rates computed at the ratio of FTE enrolment to the college-age population are given for both private and public institutions and for public institutions alone. The cross-country comparison shows differences in the magnitude and the timing of the rise in enrolment rates in response to roughly similar population trends. In the United States, enrolment rates were roughly stagnant at around 20% from the early 1970s to the early 1980s. But starting in 1984, US enrolment rates at both public and private institutions began climbing to reach a high of 30% in 1999. The climb at public institutions alone is a lot less pro-

------

[20]It is typical in education research to think of individuals aged 18 to 24 as representative of the college-age population. According to the National Center for Education Statistics (1999c) (Table 13) 18 to 22-year-olds constituted only 54% of all undergraduate enrolments in the fall of 1997. By including the 22 to 24-year-olds, 70% of potential enrollees are captured. In Canada, it is somewhat inaccurate to include 18-year-olds from Ontario in the college-age population since in the period under study, high school included grade 13. However, according to Statistics Canada (2003), 18 to 24-year-olds constituted 80% of university enrollees in 2001, down from 82% in 1991. See the data Appendix for more detail.

[21]If the average life span was 70 years and the population was uniformly distributed across age groups, there would be 10% of individuals in each seven-year age group.

[22]Full-time equivalent (FTE) enrolment is either provided by the institutions in the United States or computed as the sum of full-time fall enrolment plus one-third of part-time fall enrolment.

Nicole M. Fortin

nounced, moving from 14% in 1984 to 19% in 1999.[23] Canadian enrolment rates began to climb earlier and more abruptly, going from 14% in 1981 to 24% in 1992, but remaining around that number for the rest of the 1990s.

Figure 2 displays similar numbers as per college-age person growth indexes (1980=100). The indexes of enrolment rates at Canadian universities and US public four-year institutions are coupled with corresponding indexes for real financial and higher education policy variables. In panel A, the dramatic cross-country differences in the growth of public enrolment curiously contrast similar trends in the growth of expenditures. In the 1980s, the per college-age person real educational expenditures of public institutions experienced sizeable annual growth rates in both countries. However, in the 1990s that growth stalled in Canada, and so did the growth in the enrolment rate. In the 1980s, while in Canada the growth of public expenditures per college-age person roughly matched the growth in enrolment rates, in the United States it seriously outpaced that of enrolment rates. It is beyond the scope of this paper to fully explain these differences. Ehrenberg (2004) cites as a key factor in the stupendous growth in US higher education expenditures the increasing institutional costs of scientific research, fuelled by major advances in genomics, advanced material, and information technology, among others. Another clue is the relatively constant or even declining student-faculty ratio in the United States versus an increasing ratio in Canada in the 1990s. In Canada, the FTE-students to FTE-faculty ratio went from 16.6 in 1991 to 19.4 in 1999, while over the same period, the American ratio went from 17.6 to 15.8.[24]

Panel B of Figure 2 plots the growth indexes of the two main revenue sources of public institutions of higher education: tuition fees and provincial/state funding. In the 1970s in both countries, tuition increases did not match the inflation rates of the period, so the growth in real average tuition exhibits a negative trend. In Canada that negative trend is particularly severe: real average tuition declined by more than 60% from

---

[23]The difference in total and public enrolment rates in the United States reflects the fact that about one-third of university and four-year college students are enrolled at private institutions.

[24]The Canadian numbers are from the Canadian Association of University Teachers (2003), they may not be fully comparable to the US numbers since the CAUT considers that 3.5 part-time students is equivalent to one full-time student. The US numbers are from Table 223 of the National Center for Education Statistics (2003) and include all public institutions.

Figure 2: Per College-Age Person Growth Indexes

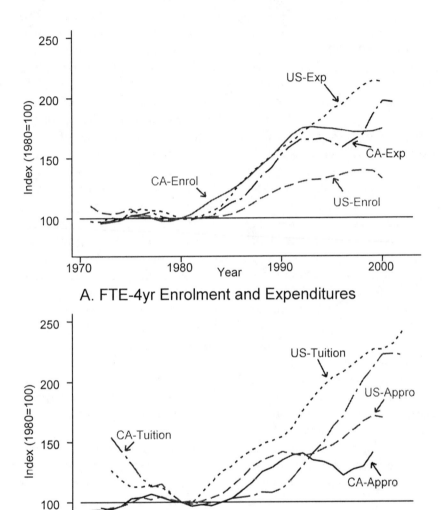

A. FTE-4yr Enrolment and Expenditures

B. Average Tuition and Prov/State Appropriations

Nicole M. Fortin

1973 to 1982. In the United States, that negative trend in real tuition levels halted with the recession of the early 1980s. By contrast, during the 1970s, provincial/state funding generally kept up with inflation.

After the recession of the early 1980s, there were startling changes in these trends. In the United States, the downward trend in real average tuition was reversed and replaced by steady increases in real tuition, averaging 5.6% a year. In Canada, the downward trend also stopped, but the following increases in real tuition averaged less than 1% a year. In the 1980s, there were quite impressive annual increases in per college-age person provincial/state funding of 3.2 and 4.2% in Canada and the United States, respectively, about 1% of which came from the decrease in the college-age population.[25] In terms of increases in the revenues of higher education institutions, the 1980s was certainly the most favourable decade in the period under study.

The 1990s signaled yet another turn of events in higher education policies. As pointed out by Humphreys (2000), US state appropriations are cyclical, and they began another downturn with the recession of the early 1990s. Given that tuition revenues and state appropriations are the two most important sources of revenues of American higher education institutions, whenever the growth of public educational expenditures is non-negative, a decline in either revenue sources has eventually to be compensated by an increase in the other. In many US states, there is thus a negative relationship between tuition levels and state appropriations, as pointed out by many authors (Berger and Kostal, 2002; Lowry, 2001a; Koshal and Koshal, 2000; Fortin, 2004). Not surprisingly, the pace of increases in real tuition fees in the United States also picked up, increasing at a rate of 8% a year.

In Canada, the link between these two revenue sources is not as strong perhaps because provinces have the ability to run budget deficits and because tuition revenues made up a relatively smaller share of educational revenues until 1995 when they became more important than federal appropriations (see Table A1). Nevertheless, after years of near stagnation, real tuition began to rise in the 1990s in Canada at the accelerated pace of 11% per year, almost getting close to US levels in 2000. Thus, to the extent that the hypothesized negative role of tuition on enrolment demand and

---

[25]For the period 1983 to 1992, the annual rate of increase of provincial funding is similar to that of the United States for the 1980s.

positive role of government funding on enrolment supply are supported empirically, which I will verify in the next section, the 1990s would appear to be the decade least favourable to increases in enrolment rates in both countries, but in Canada in particular.

The broad aggregate cross-country trends in demographics and higher education variables depicted in Figures 1 and 2 mask important jurisdictional differences which will prove sufficient to allow the identification of the effects sought. I now turn to a brief description of some of these jurisdictional differences in college-age population and enrolment rates depicted in Figures 3a, b and c and in higher education policies displayed in Figures 4a, b and c.

Figure 3a shows the growth indexes (1980=100) of college-age population and FTE enrolment rates for each of the ten Canadian provinces. As could be inferred from Figure 1, there are many provinces (about seven) which experienced spectacular growth in university enrolment rates in the 1980s in particular. But there are also some provinces (Ontario, Manitoba, and British Columbia) where the baby bust of the 1990s was less pronounced and where increases in enrolment rates were less spectacular, actually closer to American enrolment rates.

Figures 3b and 3c display the growth indexes (1980=100) of college-age population and FTE enrolment rates at public universities and four-year colleges for the 50 US states.[26] Again there is a lot of diversity across the US states in patterns of college-age population growth. In the 1990s, the college-age population actually increased in Arizona, Nevada, and Utah, was stable in many other states (such as Alabama, Arkansas, California, Florida, Georgia, Texas), but declined in most other states. The figures also show different growth patterns in public enrolment rates across the states. While most states experienced growth in public enrolment rates in the 1990s, there are some states where there was very little growth, such as Arizona, California, Hawaii, and Washington.

Figures 3a, b and c highlight the potential impact of cohort size on enrolment rates. Clearly in jurisdictions where the baby bust was compensated by the in-migration of college-age persons, the growth in enrolment rates was stunted. In a state like Wyoming where there are no private institutions, the growth of enrolment rates seems to mirror the growth of the college-age population signaling substantial "cohort crowding", where

---

[26]Note for graphical illustration, the growth indexes are capped at 275. This explains the flat line in the 1990s for enrolment rates in Alaska.

Nicole M. Fortin

Figure 3a: College-Age Population (solid line) and Enrolment Rates (plus line)

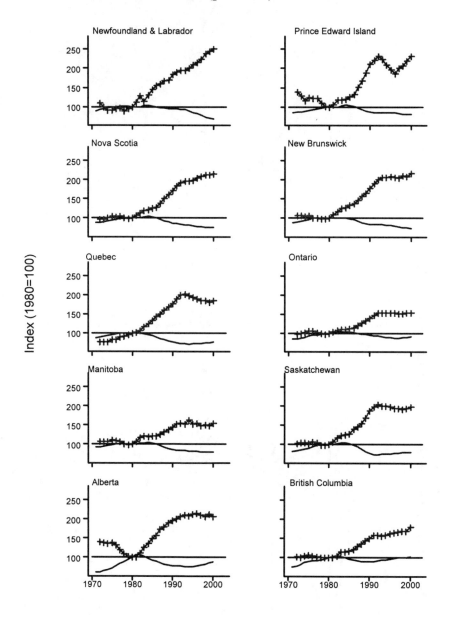

Figure 3b: College-Age Population (solid line) and Public Enrolment Rates (plus line)

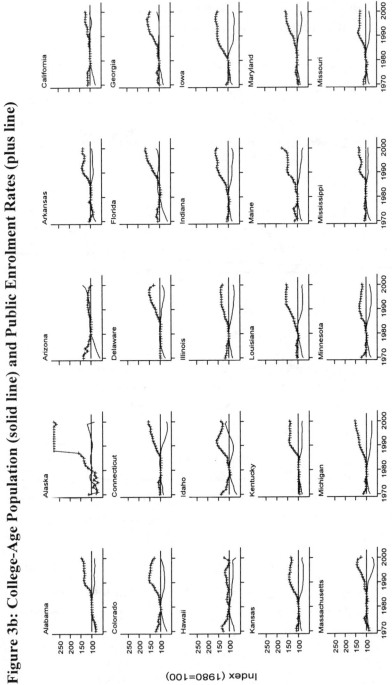

Index (1980=100)

Figure 3c: College-Age Population (solid line) and Public Enrolment Rates (plus line)

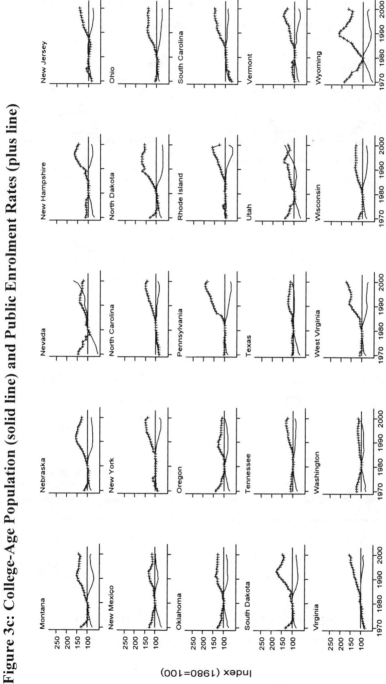

Index (1980=100)

Figure 4a: Provincial Funding Per College-Age Person (solid line) and Average Tuition (plus line)

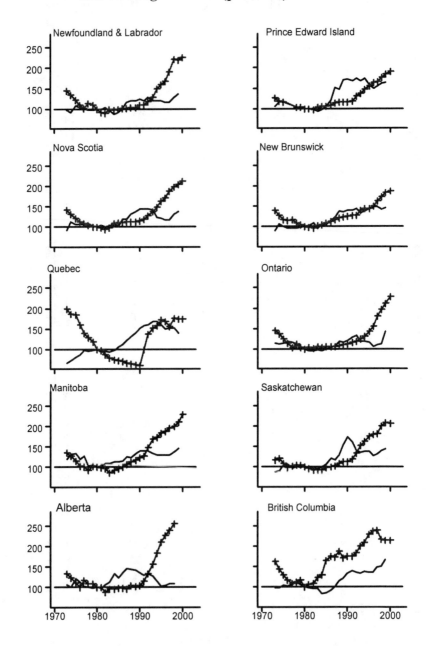

Nicole M. Fortin

Figure 4b: State Appropriations Per College-Age Person (solid line) and Average Tuition (plus line)

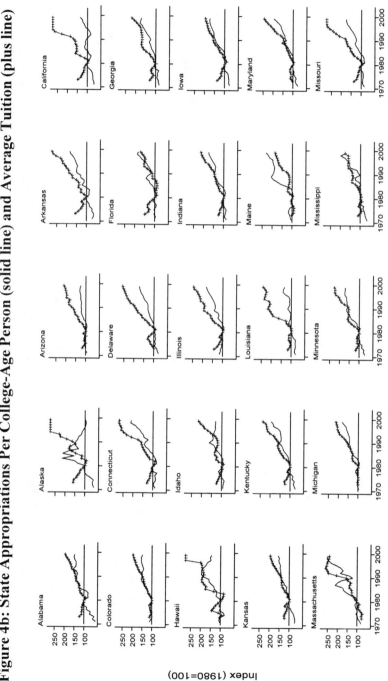

Figure 4c: State Appropriations Per College-Age Person (solid line) and Average Tuition (plus line)

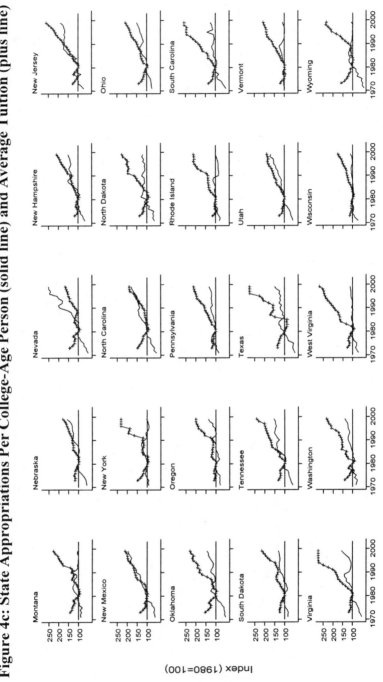

Nicole M. Fortin

increases (decreases) in the college-age population entail decreases (increases) in the enrolment rate. The country-specific magnitude of this effect will actually be evaluated below.

Figures 4a, b and c display the growth paths of average tuition and provincial/state appropriations per college-age person by jurisdiction.[27] Figure 4a displays these growth rates for the Canadian provinces. The general pattern of average real tuition growth for Canada (Figure 2) was U-shaped with average tuition beginning to show significant increases only in the 1990s, while the US pattern was more V-shaped with significant increases beginning in the 1980s. The "by-province" graph shows that two provinces depart from the general Canadian pattern: Quebec, where real average tuition continued to decline until 1990 and British Columbia, which saw some sizeable increases in the mid-1980s.

There are also important interprovincial differences in the timing and growth of provincial funding per college-age person. Some provinces (PEI, Quebec, Saskatchewan, Alberta, and BC) show spurts of growth in provincial funding in the mid-1980s and/or in the early 1990s, while others do not. Despite the 1996 reductions in federal block grants through the combination of health-care and education transfers into the Canada Health and Social Transfer (CHST), there were substantial differences in the decline in provincial appropriations in the late 1990s, with some provinces (NFLD, NB, Manitoba, BC) showing fewer cut-backs than others.[28]

Similarly for the United States, the aggregate pattern of growth of real average tuition and state appropriations per college-age person mask important differences across states as shown in Figures 4b and 4c. In most states, the 1970s was a period of declining real tuition which arrested in the early 1980s. The tuition readjustments varied considerably by state. Some states (such as California, Hawaii, and West Virginia) imposed sharp tuition increases right away to bring tuition up to the real mid-1970s levels. Some states imposed gradual and moderate increases, while others saw steeply increasing tuition levels. New York, North Carolina, Nevada, and Wyoming are states that exhibit patterns of tuition increases similar to the Canadian pattern where increases in tuition are delayed until the 1990s.

---

[27]Note that for the purpose of graphical exposition the tuition growth indexes are capped at 275.

[28]Prior to 1996, the federal government provided funding for education in terms of cash transfers and tax points to the provinces through its Established Programs Financing transfer (EPF).

The patterns of growth in state appropriations per college-age person also show substantial differentiation across states. There are some states where state appropriations per college-age person show a roughly steady growth (Arizona, Delaware, New Mexico, and Utah) or stagnation (West Virginia, Wisconsin). But for most states, there are many spurts of growth in state appropriations per college-age person as well as discontinuous declines. There are sufficient variations across jurisdictions to allow for the identification of the effects of tuition levels and provincial/state funding on enrolment rates.

The Impact of Demographics and Higher Education Policies on Enrolment Rates

I now turn to the formal analysis of the impact of demographics and higher education policies on enrolment rates. The estimated coefficients from equation 1, along with the robust standard errors (in parentheses), are reported in Table 1, panel A for Canada and panel B the United States. The logarithm of the jurisdiction-specific ratio of FTE four-year enrolment divided by college-age population is the dependent variable and the regressions are estimated by weighted least squares, where the weights are the provincial/state total population estimates. Year and jurisdiction dummies are included in all regressions to control for time and jurisdiction-specific effects. In columns (5) and (6), jurisdictional linear trends and quadratic trends are also included, these may capture jurisdiction-specific labour market trends, for example. The results are generally found to be robust to the introduction of these trends.

Column (1) shows the dramatic negative impact of log college-age population on log enrolment rates. In Canada, the estimated effect of −1.04 (0.10) indicates perfect crowding: a 1% increase (decrease) in the college-age population entails a 1% decrease (increase) in the enrolment rate. While 11 of the 93 universities associated with the AUCC were founded after 1973, these were generally smaller institutions. Thus virtually all increases in college seats had to come at the intensive margin, that is, at the expense of quality, as the increase in faculty-student ratio reported

Table 1: Impact of Higher Education Policies on University/Four-Year College Enrolment Rates

Time Period :	(1)	(2)	(3)	(4)	(5)	(6)	(7)	(8)	(9)
				1973–1999			1973–1980	1981–1990	1991–1999
A: CANADA									
Dependent variable:			Provincial Log Enrolment Rates						
Log college age	−1.037	−0.929	−0.743	−0.767	−0.909	−0.783	−0.843	−1.034	−0.255
population	(0.105)	(0.090)	(0.064)	(0.070)	(0.070)	(0.066)	(0.077)	(0.110)	(0.104)
Log average		−0.148		−0.087	−0.141	−0.067	−0.336	−0.057	0.043
provincial tuition		(0.029)		(0.019)	(0.018)	(0.034)	(0.051)	(0.029)	(0.047)
Log provinial funding			0.334	0.293	0.253	0.205	0.292	0.132	0.199
per college-age person			(0.039)	(0.035)	(0.028)	(0.034)	(0.054)	(0.059)	(0.056)
R-squared	0.96	0.97	0.97	0.98	0.99	0.99	0.99	0.98	0.98
No. observations	270	270	270	270	270	270	80	100	90
B: UNITED STATES									
Dependent Variable:			State Four-Year Public Log Enrolment Rates						
Log college age	−0.522	−0.541	−0.488	−0.517	−0.525	−0.526	−0.672	−0.752	−0.65
population	(0.037)	(0.031)	(0.038)	(0.034)	(0.035)	(0.036)	(0.096)	(0.067)	(0.052)
Log average		−0.152		−0.134	−0.132	−0.132	0.063	−0.127	−0.076
public tuition		(0.018)		(0.019)	(0.020)	(0.022)	(0.037)	(0.023)	(0.021)
Log state appropriation			0.114	0.073	0.081	0.080	0.166	−0.004	0.137
per college-age person			(0.022)	(0.022)	(0.024)	(0.024)	(0.029)	(0.032)	(0.021)
R-squared	0.95	0.95	0.95	0.95	0.96	0.96	0.98	0.98	0.99
No. observations	1350	1350	1350	1350	1350	1350	400	500	450
Year dummies	Yes	Yes	Yes	Yes	Yes	Yes	Yes	Yes	Yes
Prov/state dummies	Yes	Yes	Yes	Yes	Yes	Yes	Yes	Yes	Yes
Prov/state trends	No	No	No	No	Yes	Yes	No	No	No
Prov/state quadratic trends	No	No	No	No	No	Yes	No	No	No

Note: Robust standard errors are in parentheses. Models are estimates by weighted least squares, where the weights are the provincial/state population estimates.

previously indicates.[29] In the United States, increases in the number of public four-year degree-granting institutions were comparable, going from 537 to 613 institutions from 1975 to 1999.[30] But the capacity of the higher education system was substantially aided by the presence of 1,730 private four-year institutions in 1999.[31] It is not surprising that for the United States, the estimated effect of log college-age population is substantially lower at –0.52 (0.04). This estimate is very close to results of about –0.41 (0.04) found by Bound and Turner (2002), who present results using the logarithm of total FTE enrolment as the dependent variable for the 1967–97 period.

In column (2), the logarithm of real average tuition is added to the explanatory variables. This yields an elasticity of –0.15 (0.3 – 0.2) of enrolment rates with respect to tuition, that is amazingly identical in both countries. The impact of tuition on college enrolment rates is most often reported in terms of the impact of a $1,000 change in direct costs on student demand. Leslie and Brinkman (1987) perform a meta-analysis of 25 US student demand studies who seek to evaluate the impact of student responses to tuition using 1960s and 1970s data. The meta-analysis attempts to harmonize the results of studies using national, state, individual, district, and institutional samples that are based on experiments, hypo-thetical situations, cross-sectional and time-series designs, etc. The results of most studies are found to lie in the very close range of –0.03 to –0.05 percentage point decline in the participation rates among 18 to 24-year-olds to a $1,000 tuition increase.[32] Kane (2003) brings this meta-analysis up to date by including the results of more recent studies that use state-time

---

[29]In fact, most Canadian universities (58) were founded before 1960. There is no formal university accreditation system in Canada. But membership in the AUCC coupled with provincial government charters is generally deemed equiv-alent. Note that there are 129 universities listed on www.schoolfinder.com.

[30]See Table 245 of National Center for Education Statistics (2001).

[31]As noted earlier, about one-third of students attending four-year institu-tions are enrolled in private institutions.

[32]The results are reported as a 0.5 to 0.8 percentage point decline in the participation among 18 to 24-year-olds to a $1,000 tuition increase in 1982–83 dollars when tuition averaged $3,420. The conversion above uses a 177.1 value for the CPI in 2001.

differences in public tuition levels or evaluate the impact of changes in financial aid. As with the previous studies, the later ones assume that the supply of college seats is perfectly elastic and find similar estimates of –0.04 (0.01). Given an average tuition of $4,000 in 2001, a $1,000 increase corresponds to a 25% increase. With an elasticity of –0.15, this increase would lead to –0.0375 (–0.15*0.25) decline in enrolment rates consistent with the more recent US findings. It is interesting that despite substantial differences in the financing of higher education institutions in Canada and in the United States, the negative impact of tuition on enrolment rates in Canada is similar to that of the United States.

The estimates of the tuition effects are very robust to the introduction of supply effects (government funding), jurisdiction-specific linear and quadratic trends in the United States, less so in Canada, but the number of observations there is five times smaller. In Canada, the estimates of column (5) that control for supply effects and provincial linear trends are more precisely estimated. Both Kane (1994) and Card and Lemieux (2001) had difficulty finding significant negative tuition effects in the presence of state-fixed effects using Current Population Survey data. As pointed out by Kane (2003), one problem, as with Canadian labour force survey data, is that many students are assigned to the state or province of residence of their parents rather than to their jurisdiction of college attendance.

In column (3), the logarithm of real state appropriations per college-age person replaces tuition and yields an estimated elasticity of enrolment supply with respect to provincial/state funding ranging from 0.114 (0.022) to 0.334 (0.039) for the United States and Canada, respectively. Given that the share of provincial funding out of the educational expenditures of higher education institutions is somewhat larger than the share of US state appropriations, this result is not surprising. These results indicate that in Canada the positive impact of provincial appropriations is more important than the negative impact of tuition over the entire period.

This inference is further confirmed in column (4) which includes both log average tuition and log provincial/state appropriations per college-age person as regressors. Whereas introducing the main determinant of enrolment demand — tuition — substantially weakens the positive impact of state appropriations per college-age person on enrolment rates in the United States, this reducing effect is much smaller in Canada. This is consistent with a larger impact of provincial funding in Canada. Using the more precise Canadian estimates (column (5)), the elasticity of enrolment rates with respect to tuition fees of about –0.13 to –0.14 is found to be similar in both countries. For the United States, it is remarkably robust to the introduction of state linear and quadratic trends.

As pointed out in the descriptive analysis of the previous section, the three decades of the 1970s, 1980s, and 1990s can be characterized as different regimes in terms of trends in higher education policies. Columns (7), (8), and (9) report estimates for the three decades separately. For Canada, the 1970s were characterized by steep declines in tuition and slow increases in provincial funding; the 1980s were characterized by relatively stable tuition levels and moderately rising provincial funding; the 1990s saw tuition escalate very steeply while provincial funding barely increased. The analysis shows that both tuition and provincial appropriations had significant impacts on enrolment rates in the 1970s and in the 1980s. In the 1990s, the college-age population stabilized and there were severe provincial funding cutbacks, then only provincial funding is significant consistent with the enrolment supply side of the market becoming binding. The wrong sign of tuition is investigated below in the context of rising institutional student support and direct federal funding.

In the United States, real tuition also declined in the 1970s but not as steeply as in Canada, state appropriations showed slow increases. The 1980s were characterized by rising tuition and substantial growth in state appropriations; in the 1990s, tuition escalated even more rapidly while increases in state funding slowed. The results from columns (7), (8), and (9) for the United States show that in the 1970s only state appropriations have a significant impact on enrolment, in the 1980s only tuition has a significant impact, and in the 1990s both appropriations and tuition have significant effects.

The non-significance of either tuition or jurisdictional funding can be attributed either to insufficient interjurisdictional variations to allow identification or to enrolments being determined by the short side of the market. Since there is actually more variation in state appropriations in the 1980s than in the 1970s, the first hypothesis can be ruled out. Rather, the results are consistent with enrolment supply being the short side of the market in the 1970s when the college-age population was increasing and enrolment demand becoming the short side of the market in the 1980s when the college-age population was decreasing. In the 1990s, there was a more substantial echo of the baby-boom generation becoming of college age in the United States than in Canada, thus the more significant role of cohort size is not surprising. Some "wrong" signs on tuition levels (column 7, panel B; column 9, panel A) and on state appropriations (column 8, panel

B) could signal some endogeneity problems, but these effects are never significant.

A response of governments and institutions to the skyrocketing tuitions of the 1990s has been a substantial increase in student aid. One way for institutions to increase tuition while mitigating its adverse impact on lower income students is to give back some portion (as much as one-third) of the increase in tuition revenues to students in the form of scholarships. As indicated earlier, these outlays as a share of the expenditures of higher education institutions have indeed been increasing over time in Canada and the United States (see Table A1). One obvious problem with this strategy is that it also mitigates the impact of rising tuition on the ability of institutions to supply more college seats.

Table 2 assesses the impact of institutional outlays going to student support and of direct federal funding on enrolment rates in Canada.[33] Column (1) shows that for the entire period, student support has a positive and significant impact on enrolment rates equal to more than half the negative effect of tuition. However, comparing the estimates of column (1), Table 2 to those of column (4), panel A, Table 1 shows that adding student support reduces the positive effect of provincial funding on enrolment rates but leaves the negative effect of tuition basically unchanged. Column (2) adds the logarithm of direct federal funding as another explanatory variable (see Table A1). The effect of direct federal funding is positive and significant, and of about the same order of magnitude as the effect of tuition. Interestingly it does not seem to crowd out the total effect of provincial funding and institutional student support.

---

[33]A more complete analysis of the impact of student aid would include the impact of loans and grants from the Canada Student Loans and Canada Study Grants programs, as well as from the various provincial programs, the Newfoundland/Labrador Provincial Student Loan Program, the Prince Edward Island Student Loan Program, the Nova Scotia Student Assistance Program, the New Brunswick Financial Loans, the Quebec Student Assistance Program (Aide financière aux études), the Ontario Student Assistance Program (OSAP), the Manitoba Student Financial Assistance Program (MSFAP), the Saskatchewan Student Loans Program, the Alberta Student Loan Program, and the British Columbia Student Assistance Program (BCSAP). Some of the provincial programs do include grants. Yet, the analysis of the impact of loans requires the use of an intertemporal framework and is beyond the scope of the present study.

Table 2: Impact of Institutional Outlays on Student Support and Federal Funding on University Enrolment Rates in Canada

	(1) 1973–1999	(2) 1973–1999	(3) 1973–1980	(4) 1981–1990	(5) 1991–1999	(6) 1991–1999
Time Period						
Econometric Specification	OLS	OLS	OLS	OLS	OLS	IV
Dependent variable:	Provincial Log Enrolment Rates					
Log college age population	-0.706 (0.063)	-0.581 (0.070)	-0.746 (0.090)	-0.890 (0.110)	-0.268 (0.120)	-0.369 (0.134)
Log average provincial tuition	-0.094 (0.018)	-0.109 (0.017)	-0.316 (0.055)	-0.089 (0.027)	0.040 (0.056)	-0.108 (0.078)
Log provinial funding per college-age person	0.253 (0.041)	0.277 (0.039)	0.271 (0.053)	0.007 (0.032)	0.163 (0.070)	0.213 (0.062)
Log direct federal per college-age person		0.089 (0.029)	0.044 (0.027)	0.053 (0.030)	-0.085 (0.041)	
Log institutional outlays on student support per college-age person	0.039 (0.019)	0.022 (0.019)	0.045 (0.027)	0.067 (0.019)	-0.025 (0.027)	
R-squared	0.98	0.98	0.99	0.98	0.99	0.98
No. observations	270	270	80	100	90	90
First-stage estimates of the instruments:						
Determinants of log average tuition						
Log direct federal per college-age person						0.428 (0.140)
Log institutional outlays on student support per college-age person						0.166 (0.077)
Overid test (p-value)						0.941
Year dummies	Yes	Yes	Yes	Yes	Yes	Yes
Provincial dummies	Yes	Yes	Yes	Yes	Yes	Yes

Note: Robust standard errors are in parentheses. Models are estimates by weighted least squares, where the weights are the provincial population estimates.

Nicole M. Fortin

Column (3), (4), and (5) investigate differential impacts across the three decades under study. The inference for the 1970s and 1980s is similar to that of Table 1. For the 1990s, the effect of student support and federal funding turns negative, although it is not significant. This signals an endogeneity problem coming from the link between rising tuition and rising student support that can be corrected with an instrumental strategy reported in column (6). The effect of tuition then becomes negative and is of the same order of magnitude as in column (1)/(2). It remains insignificant, confirming that enrolment supply is the short side of the market over the 1990s. However, it shows some possible crowding out of institutional student support and federal funding, these sources of funding seem to merely compensate the increases in tuition rather than help generate new college seats.

Overall, the analysis shows that the impact of higher education policies on enrolment rates has to be understood in the context of underlying demographics. Similarly, the impact of rising tuition has to be understood in the context of the overall funding of higher education institutions and their ability to increase the number of college seats while maintaining the quality of instruction. The impact of financial aid on enrolment rates needs to be assessed, bearing in mind the possibility that it could be offset by other government cutbacks.

Conclusion

This paper studies the impact of jurisdiction-specific higher education policies on enrolment rates in Canada and in the United States over the last three decades of the twentieth century. Looking back at the mistakes of the past may enable us to formulate more adequate policies for the future. In that context, the present study reveals that the declining real tuitions of the 1970s were probably unfortunate for institutions of higher education. In the 1970s, the college-age population was increasing so that increases in the number of college seats were necessary to augment enrolment rates. Instead, declining real tuition seriously impaired the ability of higher education systems in both countries to expand and enrolment rates were largely stagnant.[34] Issues associated with money illusion (Shafir, Diamond and Tversky, 1997) may explain why policymakers and their constituents fail to realize that, in the presence of double digit inflation, stable nominal tuition levels meant steeply declining real tuition. Allan W. Ostar, the executive director of the American Association of State Colleges and Universities in the 1970s is cited (Russell, 1998) as saying: "Low tuition higher education ... is the envy and wonder of the world .... It has contributed enormously to our progress and well-being as a nation."

In the 1980s, the college-age population was declining and higher education expenditures began to rise sharply.[35] The response of many US states was a substantial rise in tuition levels, which had been eroded by the high inflation of the late 1970s. By contrast, most Canadian provinces refrained from imposing tuition hikes until the 1990s, despite some calls to the contrary (Gerson, 1985). As a consequence, the Canadian enrolment rate rose sharply and early in the 1980s, while increases in American public enrolment rates were delayed and more modest. Given the downward trend in demographics, it can be argued that tuition increases were detrimental to increases in enrolment rates. Yet Canada may have done too much of a good thing.

At the beginning of the 1990s, the comparatively low Canadian tuition levels were no longer sustainable. As provincial appropriations began to plummet, sharp increases in tuition followed. Since the 1990s witnessed the bottom of the baby bust reaching college-age, the increases in tuition, which were partly compensated by increases in institutional financial aid, did not have as detrimental an impact on enrolment rates as did government cutbacks. The results above show that in the 1990s enrolment (institutional) supply was constraining enrolment rates in Canada. Only three universities were founded in the 1990s and the student-faculty ratio increased

---

[34]Quebec is one jurisdiction that expanded its higher education system by introducing the Université du Québec system in 1969–70 despite declining real tuition. There the enrolment rates increased over the 1970s.

[35]Cited factors (Russell, 1998) responsible for the increase were the doubling of purchases regularly utilized by campuses, including energy costs. In the United States, the negative trend in the growth of real average salary of faculty has been credited for the relative flat growth in public educational expenditures until 1984 (Froomkin, 1990).

substantially in most provinces.[36] By contrast, in the United States state appropriations began to pick up in the mid-1990s. Over the 1990s, 216 four-year higher education degree-granting institutions were added (admittedly only 14 public) and the student-faculty ratio declined.[37]

Table 3 shows the impact on university enrolments of some alternative higher education policies for Canada as a whole, and for its three largest provinces: Quebec, Ontario, and British Columbia. In the first panel, the table reports descriptive statistics on the number of FTE university enrollees, the size of the college-age population, the resulting university enrolment rates, the average provincial tuition for arts programs and the provincial funding per college-age person. The provincial funding per college-age person is presented as the appropriate per capita measure of the potential impact of funding, that is the correct way to control for the different sizes of the provinces.[38] Average annual growth rates are indicated in parentheses below the numbers. For example, for Canada as a whole, the number of university enrollees increased by 3.7% a year from 1980 to 1990, and by just 0.5% from 1990 to 1999.

In the second panel of Table 3, simulated university enrolments are computed under alternative policies using the estimated elasticities of column (5) Table 1, which are the most precisely estimated. There an increase of 1% in tuition yields a 0.14% decrease in enrolment rates and a decrease of 1% in provincial funding yields a 0.25% decrease in enrolment rates. The fact that the negative impact of decreasing provincial funding is almost twice as large as the negative impact of rising tuition has to be understood in the context of the excess demand for university seats.[39]

---

[36]These institutions (University of Northern British Columbia, Royal Roads University, and Nipissing College) were of small size. Student-faculty ratio was more stable in Newfoundland, Prince Edward Island, Nova Scotia, and Manitoba (Canadian Association of University Teachers, 2003).

[37]See Table 245, National Center for Education Statistics (2001).

[38]Provincial funding per capita would be the correct measure for an analysis of the willingness to pay, while the per college-age person measure is more appropriate to the ability to consume.

[39]The estimates of column (6) Table 2 indicate a 2:1 ratio for the 1990s per se, but are less precisely estimated.

Table 3: Simulated Impacts of Changes in Higher Education Policies on University Enrolment in Canada

	(1)	(2)	(3)	(4)	(5)	(6)	(7)	(8)
	Canada		Quebec		Ontario		BC	
Academic Years Ending	1990	1999	1990	1999	1990	1999	1990	1999
FTE university enrollees	635	674	165	168	252	262	49	62
(in 1,000s)	(3.7)	(0.5)	(3.4)	(0.2)	(3.3)	(0.4)	(3.3)	(2.5)
College-age population	2,928	2,876	708	702	1,122	1,055	326	368
(in 1,000s)	(−1.4)	(−0.2)	(−2.4)	(−0.1)	(−0.4)	(−0.5)	(−1.1)	(−1.2)
University enrolment rates	21.7	23.4	23.3	24	22.4	24.9	14.9	16.9
	(6.0)	(0.7)	(7.7)	(0.2)	(3.9)	(1.0)	(4.9)	(1.2)
Average provincial tuition	1,600	3,100	600	1,700	1,900	3,600	2,000	2,500
(in 1999 CDN$)	(−0.7)	(−8.4)	(−4.0)	(−16.5)	(−2.7)	(−8.1)	(−6.7)	(−2.3)
Provincial funding	2,595	2,719	3,108	2,834	2,289	2,733	2,212	2,760
per college-age person								
(in 1999 CDN$)	(3.5)	(0.5)	(13.2)	(−0.8)	(2.0)	(1.7)	(3.4)	(2.2)
	Simulated Enrolments under Alternative Higher Education Policies							
Annual average real change over the 1990s								
A: Tuition increase at 4%/year		710		195		276		61
B: Tuition increase at 2%/year		727		199		282		62
C: Provincial funding increase at 1%/year		681		175		258		61
D: Provincial funding increase at 2%/year		696		179		264		62
E: Tuition increase at 2%/year and provincial funding increase at 2%/year		751		209		283		62

Note: Average yearly growth rates over the previous ten years are shown in parentheses. The simulated enrolment uses elasticities of enrolment rates with respect to tuition of −0.14 and with respect to provincial funding of 0.25, as estimated in column (5) of Table 1.

Nicole M. Fortin

Policy A cuts by half the yearly Canadian average increase in tuition over the 1990s, policy B reduces it to a fourth. Policy C doubles the yearly Canadian average increase in provincial funding over the 1990s, policy D increases it four-fold. Policy E is essentially the British Columbian policy: it includes yearly increases of 2% in both tuition and provincial funding. The simulation shows that, for Canada as a whole, this latter policy would have resulted in 75,000 more university students in 1999 and raised the university enrolment rate from 23 to 26%.

At the dawn of the twenty-first century, there is much worry about the future of higher education in both countries (Ehrenberg, 2005; Laidler, 2002). Population projections of the Canadian college-age population show increases up to around 2012 (Statistics Canada, 2003). The modest but sustained growth, coupled with a higher propensity to attend university as a result of parents' higher educational attainment, signals a continued excess demand for college seats. Thus, enrolment demand should not be expected to become the constraining side of the market until 2025. Tuition increases are unlikely to be the factor adversely affecting the supply of skills, although they could undermine equality-of-opportunities objectives. Note that these objectives are also undermined when a restricted supply of university/college seats implies that institutions increasingly ration seats using grades, themselves linked to socio-economic status.

Arguments that support continued tuition increases point to the persistently favourable labour market outcomes of university/college graduates. In the United States, increases in the college/high-school wage premium had slowed down in the 1990s. In Fortin (2004), I link this deceleration to the increase in enrolment rates associated with the relatively favourable higher education policies of the 1980s.[40] These increases in enrolment rates translated into increases in the relative supply of college graduates in the 1990s, which exerted downward pressure on the premium. A similar inference likely holds for Canada where the near stagnant university/high-school premium of the 1990s (Burbidge, Magee and Robb, 2002) was replaced by a climbing premium in the 2000s (Boudarbat, Lemieux and Riddell, 2003). As pointed out by Freeman and Needels (1993), the steeply increasing enrolments of the 1980s, which here are traced back to the relatively flat increases in tuition over that period, suppressed the growth of the university premium in the 1990s. By contrast,

---

[40] I study the college/high-school wage premium among young workers ten years away from entering college.

the skyrocketing tuition fees and severe government cutbacks implied stagnant enrolment rates over the 1990s. Thus, the relatively stable university premium of the 1990s gave way to a rising premium in the 2000s.

Even if Canadian tuition fees reach American levels, the ability of Canadian universities/colleges to supply college seats will become the key issue and issues of direct funding will rise to the top of the agenda. Yet it is difficult to see how the fiscal position of the provinces (and of the states, for that matter) could allow them to restore funding (as say a share of total educational expenditures) to the level of the 1980s. Federal incursions in higher education have continued to favour research infrastructure grants (Canadian Foundation for Innovation) and student financial aid (Millennium Scholarships), but also included funds towards the indirect costs of research and the hiring of faculty (Canada Research Chairs). Much future research is needed to assess the impact of these recent funding initiatives on enrolment rates in a supply and demand framework.[41] The fungibility of diverse sources of funding and the extent to which the impact of financial aid is mitigated when that aid crowds out other forms of funding, are not well understood.

However, it is difficult to see how these sources of funding could lead to an expansion in the number of institutions that require basic infrastructure funding. Private sources of funding, while is a subject of concern, are another inescapable avenue to consider. Another controversial idea calls for increases in the hierarchical differentiation of Canadian institutions as a way to preserve quality, at least in some parts of the higher education system. In the United States where hierarchical differentiation is a desired outcome, a sizeable share of college seats is supplied by private institutions so that overall institutional supply is less constrained. Rather, skyrocketing tuition levels and financial aid are the subject of much research in higher education.

---

[41]Most of the research on the recent innovations focuses on enrolment demand rather than on enrolment supply (e.g., Junor and Usher, 2002).

Nicole M. Fortin

Data Appendix

Canadian Data

Education Data

Most educational data series used in the paper are extracted from the CANSIM II database which compiles data from Statistics Canada's "Survey of Federal Government Expenditures in Support of Education" (Statistics Canada, 2002). The expenditures data is extracted from the CANSIM II, Table 4780008 — Total Expenditures on University Education by Type of Expenditures. The table provides data for Canada as a whole and separately by provinces and territories. To enhance comparability with US data, educational expenditures of Canadian universities are computed as total expenditures minus capital expenditures. The Canadian educational expenditures thus comprise expenditures on instruction, libraries, administration, plant maintenance, student services, sponsored research, student support, departmental and other expenditures.

The sources of funding are extracted from Table 4780001 — Total Expenditures on Education, by Direct Source of Funds and Type of Education. For example, for Canada as a whole, direct federal funds are from series V1996809, provincial funds are from series V1996815, student fees from series V1996833.

The full-time and part-time enrolment figures were made available by the Association of Universities and Colleges of Canada (AUCC). Full-time equivalent enrolment (FTE) is computed as the sum of full-time fall enrolment plus one-third of part-time fall enrolment for comparability with the US data. In Canada, the ratio of 3.5 part-time students for one full-time student has also been used.

The source for the tuition data is Statistics Canada's "Tuition Fees and Living Accommodations at Canadian Universities Survey". From 1979 to 2002, detailed information on tuition fees are available from this source for a host of disciplines for each degree-granting institution in Canada.

The Consumer Price Index used comes from CANSIM II Table 3260002, series V737344 (CPI, Canada, All-items). Note the related provincial price indexes are for time-series use and not appropriate for interprovincial comparisons: they are all equal to 100 in 1992.

Population Data

The population data is extracted from the CANSIM II Table 051-0001 — Estimates of population, by group and sex, Canada, provinces and territories, annual. Preliminary, updated and final postcensal estimates are based on the most recent census adjusted for net census under coverage and estimates of the components of demographic change since the last Census. Intercensal estimates are based on postcensal estimates and data from the most recent Census counts adjusted for net undercount preceding and following the year in question.

American Data

Education Data

The information on enrolment and expenditures is drawn from various reports, as indicated in the text, of the National Center for Education Statistics. A number of state-level tabulations are performed by the NCES and are available through online publications at nces.ed.gov.

The enrolment data used is the full-time equivalent fall enrolment in four-year institutions of higher education in a given state from Tables 58 and 60 of National Center for Education Statistics (1998b), updated to 1999 with Table 201 of National Center for Education Statistics (2003). The enrolment data is available separately for public and private institutions.

The US expenditures data is restricted to educational and general expenditures. They comprise expenditures on administration and general expense, instruction and departmental research, organized research, plant operation and maintenance, organized activities related to instructional departments, extension and public service, scholarships and fellowships, and others. But they exclude expenditures by university hospitals, dormitories, food-service operations, bookstores, and other independent operations. The expenditures information is extracted from Tables 350 and 351 of National Center for Education Statistics (2003) with earlier data from Table 88 of National Center for Education Statistics (1999b).

Detailed state-appropriations data is available in a series of "Appropriations of State Tax Funds for Operating Expenses" reports by M.M. Chambers, sometimes called the "Chambers Reports" available from

1961 onwards. The reports are posted on the Grapevine Web site: www.coe.ilstu.edu/grapevine/Welcome.htm. Details of the amounts included in the appropriations for each of the 50 states are available in those reports. However, I use the state summary tables that should be viewed as approximations of the amounts that are destined to four-year public institutions of higher education.

Prior to 1986, tuition data is not available from the NCES. However, the Washington State Higher Education Coordination Board (Raudenbush, 2002) has compiled historically consistent data, from 1972–73 onwards, on tuition and fee rates at public institutions using surveys of state agencies or individual institutions. The data is available separately for residents and non-residents and for universities, colleges and state universities and community colleges. Where applicable, an average of the tuition at universities and at colleges and state universities is constructed for residents and non-residents separately. Then a weighted average of the tuition for residents and non-residents is constructed using the 1996 proportion of residents versus non-residents tuition available from the Table 7 of National Center for Education Statistics (1998a).

Population Data

The national estimates of the United States resident population were downloaded from the Web site of US Census Bureau: www.census.gov/population/www/estimates. The estimates include persons resident in the 50 states. The criteria for residence defines a resident of a specified area as a person "usually resident" in that area. College students living away from home while attending college are counted where they are living at college. College students living at their parental home while attending college are counted at their parental home. Details on the sources and methods for obtaining the postcensal estimates are available from the Web site.

The population estimates by states were downloaded from the Web site of the US Census Bureau: www.census.gov/population/www/estimates/statepop.html. The Population Estimates Program produces estimates of the total resident population, as well as estimates by age and sex for states for each year (as of July 1). The data used was compiled from the "Single Years of Age by Sex" for the 1990s and 1980s, and from the "Selected Age Groups" for the 1970s.

Table A1: Educational Expenditures (in millions of current CDN$) of Canadian Universities by Source of Funds and Purpose

	(1)	(2)	(3)	(4)	(5)	(6)	(7)	(8)	(9)
Academic Year Ending	Total	Federal Funds	% of Total	Provincial Funds	% of Total	Student Fees	% of Total	Expenditures on Student Support	% of Total
1973	1,866	275	14.7	1,346	72.1	238	12.8	184	9.9
1974	2,184	305	14.0	1,583	72.5	253	11.6	198	9.0
1975	2,551	332	13.0	1,931	75.7	273	10.7	231	9.1
1976	2,832	360	12.7	2,148	75.9	291	10.3	233	8.2
1977	3,175	395	12.4	2,417	76.1	328	10.3	255	8.0
1978	3,402	416	12.2	2,612	76.8	340	10.0	271	8.0
1979	3,700	429	11.6	2,826	76.4	358	9.7	278	7.5
1980	4,145	491	11.8	3,111	75.1	401	9.7	315	7.6
1981	4,676	618	13.2	3,431	73.4	469	10.0	351	7.5
1982	5,312	735	13.8	3,885	73.1	561	10.6	394	7.4
1983	5,641	856	15.2	4,067	72.1	623	11.1	434	7.7
1984	6,149	944	15.4	4,296	69.9	678	11.0	527	8.6
1985	6,561	1,035	15.8	4,509	68.7	730	11.1	560	8.5
1986	6,818	1,039	15.2	4,856	71.2	767	11.2	605	8.9
1987	7,424	1,156	15.6	5,206	70.1	830	11.2	707	9.5
1988	8,093	1,367	16.9	5,649	69.8	911	11.3	806	10.0
1989	8,783	1,480	16.8	5,986	68.2	1,012	11.5	843	9.6

continued

Nicole M. Fortin

Table A1 (continued)

1990	9,695	1,685	17.4	6,407	66.1	1,179	12.2	957	9.9
1991	10,503	1,716	16.3	6,843	65.2	1,381	13.1	949	9.0
1992	10,900	1,764	16.2	6,943	63.7	1,563	14.3	1,221	11.2
1993	10,972	1,799	16.4	6,741	61.4	1,699	15.5	1,124	10.2
1994	11,059	1,875	17.0	6,674	60.3	1,825	16.5	1,099	9.9
1995	11,001	1,677	15.2	6,589	59.9	1,942	17.7	1,071	9.7
1996	10,891	1,500	13.8	6,297	57.8	2,127	19.5	1,067	9.8
1997	11,527	1,441	12.5	6,694	58.1	2,353	20.4	1,329	11.5
1998	12,092	1,639	13.6	6,931	57.3	2,562	21.2	1,263	10.4
1999	13,718	1,960	14.3	7,818	57.0	2,874	21.0	1,433	10.4

Note: Numbers are from Statistics Canada's "Survey of Federal Government Expenditures in Support of Education" extracted from the CANSIM II Table 478001 — Total Expenditures on Education, by Direct Source of Funds and Type of Education and Table 478008 Total Expenditures on University Education by Type of Expenditures. Column (1) is Total expenditures [series V1992346] minus capital expenditures [series V1992357]. Direct federal funds in column (2) are from series V1996809, provincial funds are from series V1996833 and expenditures on student support are from series V1996815, student fees from series V1992358.

References

Avery, C. and C.M. Hoxby. 2004. "Do and Should Financial Aid Packages Affect Students' College Choices?" in C.M. Hoxby (ed.), *College Choices: The Economics of Where to Go, When to Go, and How to Pay for It*. Chicago: University of Chicago Press and NBER.

Berger, M.C. and T. Kostal. 2002. "Financial Resources, Regulation, and Enrollments in US Public Higher Education", *Economics of Education Review* 21(2), 101-110.

Boudarbat, B., T. Lemieux and W.C. Riddell. 2003. "Recent Trends in Wage Inequality and the Wage Structure in Canada". INE-TARGET Working Paper No. 6. Vancouver: University of British Columbia.

Bound, J. and S. Turner. 2002. "Cohort Crowding: Why Does Cohort Size Affect Collegiate Attainment?" University of Michigan. Unpublished paper.

Burbidge, J.B., L. Magee and A.L. Robb. 2002. "The Education Premium in Canada and the United States", *Canadian Public Policy/Analyse de Politiques* 28(1), 203-217.

Cameron, D.M. 2005. "Collaborative Federalism and Post-Secondary Education: Be Careful What You Wish For", in this volume.

Canadian Association of University Teachers (CAUT). 2003. "CAUT Almanac of Post-Secondary Education in Canada". Technical Report. Ottawa: CAUT.

Card, D. and A.B. Krueger. 2003. "Would the Elimination of Affirmative Action Affect Highly Qualified Minority Applications? Evidence from California and Texas". University of California at Berkeley. Unpublished paper.

Card, D.E. and T. Lemieux. 2001. "Dropout and Enrollment Trends in the Postwar Period: What Went Wrong in the 1970s?" in J. Gruber (ed.), *Risky Behavior Among Youths*. Chicago: University of Chicago Press, 439-482.

Christofides, L.N., J. Cirello and M. Hoy. 2001. "Tuition Increases and Inequality in Post-Secondary Education Attendance", *Canadian Journal of Higher Education* 31, 177-208.

Clotfelter, C.T. 1999. "The Familiar but Curious Economics of Higher Education: Introduction to a Symposium", *Journal of Economic Perspectives* 13 (Winter), 3-12.

Coelli, M. 2004. "Tuition Increases and Inequality in Post-secondary Education Attendance". University of British Columbia. Unpublished paper.

Corak, M., G. Lipps and J. Zhao. 2003. "Family Income and Participation in Post-secondary Education". Analytical Studies Branch Research Paper Series No. 210. Ottawa: Statistics Canada.

Ehrenberg, R.G. 2005. "Key Issues Currently Facing American Higher Education", in this volume.

Fortin, N.M. 2004. "Decelerating Wage Inequality and Higher Education: Cross-State Evidence from the 1990s". (Earlier version as INE-TARGET Working Paper No. 2.) Vancouver: University of British Columbia.

Freeman, R. and K. Needels. 1993. "Skill Differentials in Canada in an Era of Rising Labor Market Inequality", in D. Card and R. Freeman (eds.), *Small Differences that Matter: Labor Markets and Income Maintenance in Canada and the United States*. Chicago: University of Chicago Press and NBER.

Froomkin, J. 1990. "The Impact of Changing Levels of Financial Resources on the Structure of Colleges and Universities", in S.A. Hoenack and E.L. Collins (eds.), *The Economics of American Universities*. Albany, NY: State University of New York, 189-214.

Gerson, M. 1985. "Higher Tuition, Lower Enrollments Urged for Ontario's Universities", *The Chronicle of Higher Education* 29 (January), 35-36.

Goldin, C. and L.F. Katz. 1999. "The Shaping of Higher Education: The Formative Years in the United States, 1980 to 1940", *Journal of Economic Perspectives* 13 (Winter), 37-62.

Hearn, J.C., C.P. Griswold and G.M. Marine. 1996. "Region, Resources, and Reason: A Contextual Analysis of State Tuition and Student Aid Policies", *Research in Higher Education* 37, 241-278.

Hendry, D.F. and A. Spanos. 1980. "Disequilibrium and Latent Variables". London: London School of Economics. Unpublished paper.

Hoxby, C.M. 2004. "It is not just About Attending College Anymore", in C.M. Hoxby (ed.), *College Choices: The Economics of Where to Go, When to Go, and How to Pay for It*. Chicago: University of Chicago Press and NBER.

Humphreys, B.R. 2000. "Do Business Cycles Affect State Appropriations to Higher Education?" *Southern Economic Journal* 67, 398–413.

Junor, S. and A. Usher. 2002. *The Price of Knowledge: Access and Student Finance in Canada*. Montreal: The Canada Millennium Scholarship Foundation.

Kane, T.J. 1994. "College Entry by Blacks Since 1970: The Role of College Costs, Family Background, and the Returns to Education", *Journal of Political Economy* 102 (October), 878-911.

_____. 2003. "A Quasi-Experimental Estimate of the Impact of Financial Aid on College-Going". NBER Working Paper No. 9703. Cambridge, MA: National Bureau of Economic Research.

Knighton, T. and S. Mirza. 2002. "Postsecondary Participation: The Effects of Parent's Education and Household Income", *Education Quarterly Review* 8 (August), 25-31.

Koshal, R.K. and M. Koshal. 2000. "State Appropriations and Higher Education Tuition: What is the Relationship?" *Education Economics* 8, 81-89.

Laidler, D. 2002. "Renovating the Ivory Tower: An Introductory Essay", in D. Laidler (ed.), *Renovating the Ivory Tower: Canadian Universities and the Knowledge Economy*. C.D. Howe Policy Paper No. 37. Ottawa: Renouf Publishing, 201-222.

Leslie, L.L. and P.T. Brinkman. 1987. "Student Price Response in Higher Education: The Student Demand Studies", *Journal of Higher Education* 58 (March-April), 181-204.

Lowry, R.C. 2001a. "The Effects of State Political Interests and Campus Outputs on Public University Revenues", *Economics of Education Review* 20(2), 105-119.

_____. 2001b. "Governmental Structure, Trustee Selection, and Public University Prices and Spending: Multiple Means to Similar Ends", *American Journal of Political Science* 45 (October), 845-861.

Monks, J. and R.G. Ehrenberg. 1999. "The Impact of U.S. News & World Report College Rankings on Admission Outcomes and Price Decisions at Selective Private Institutions". NBER Working Paper No. 7227. Cambridge, MA: National Bureau of Economic Research.

Mueller, R.E. and D.E. Rockerbie. 2002. "Do the Maclean's Rankings Affect University Choice? Evidence from Ontario". University of Lethbridge. Unpublished paper.

National Center for Education Statistics. 1998a. "Residence and Migration of First-time Freshmen Enrolled in Degree Granting Institutions: Fall 1996", NCES No. 98-227, by T. Snyder, L. Hoffman and C. Geddess. Washington, DC: US Department of Education.

_____. 1998b. "State Comparisons of Education Statistics: 1969-70 to 1996-97", NCES No. 98-018, by T. Snyder, L. Hoffman and C. Geddess. Washington, DC: US Department of Education.

_____. 1999a. "The Condition of Education – 1999", NCES No. 99-022. Washington, DC: US Department of Education.

_____. 1999b. "Digest of Education Statistics 1998", NCES No. 99-036. Washington, DC: US Department of Education.

_____. 1999c. "Fall Enrollment in Postsecondary Institutions, 1997", NCES No. 99-162, by S. Barbett. Washington, DC: US Department of Education.

_____. 2001. "Digest of Education Statistics 2000", NCES No. 2001-034, by T. Snyder and C.M. Hoffman. Washington, DC: US Department of Education.

_____. 2003. "Digest of Education Statistics 2002", NCES No. 2003-060, by T. Snyder and C.M. Hoffman. Washington, DC: US Department of Education.

Poterba, J.M. 1996. "Demographic Structure and the Political Economy of Public Education", NBER Working Paper No. 5677. Cambridge, MA: National Bureau of Economic Research.

Quigley, J.M. and D.L. Rubinfeld. 1993. "Public Choices in Public Higher Education", in C.T. Clotfelter and M. Rothschild (eds.), *Studies of Supply and Demand in Higher Education*. Chicago: University of Chicago Press, 243-283.

Raudenbush, K. 2002. "Tuition and Fee Rates – A National Comparison", Technical Report. Washington, DC: Washington Higher Education Coordinating Board.

Russell, H.J. 1998. "Explaining Trends in Interstate Higher Education Finance: 1977 to 1996". Eric Collection of Association for the Study of Higher Education conference papers, Murray State University, November.

Salop, S.C. and L.J. White. 1991. "Policy Watch: Antitrust Goes to College", *Journal of Economic Perspectives* 5 (Summer), 193-202.

Shafir, E., P. Diamond and A. Tversky. 1997. "Money Illusion", *Quarterly Journal of Economics* 112(2), 341-374.

Skolnik, M.L. and G.A. Jones. 1992. "A Comparative Analysis of Arrangements for State Coordination of Higher Education in Canada and the United States", *Journal of Higher Education* 63 (March-April), 121-142.

Snowdon, K. 2005. "'Muddy Data': University Financing in Canada", in this volume.

Statistics Canada. 2002. "Federal Government Expenditures in Support of Education: Guidelines". STC/ECT No. 175-60251. Ottawa: Centre for Education Statistics.

_____. 2003. "Education Indicators in Canada". Report of the Pan-Canadian Education Indicators Program 2003. Ottawa: Centre for Education Statistics.

Section V

Student Financing and Postsecondary Education

Recent Changes in Effective Tax Rates on PSE Level Human Capital in Canada

Kirk A. Collins and James B. Davies

Introduction

There has been considerable interest in recent years in the tax treatment of education and training. Boskin (1975) analyzed and described the different incentive effects of the tax system on human capital. Since then these effects and their welfare consequences have been studied in a general equilibrium context by Davies and Whalley (1991), Dupor *et al.* (1996), Perroni (1995), and Heckman, Lochner and Taber (1999). Some features of the tax system, for example, progressivity, tend to discourage human capital formation, while others — deductions or credits — have the opposite effect. In order to know the net impact, one needs estimates of the effective tax rate (ETR) on human capital. The ETR is the difference between gross and after-tax rates of return to human capital. It takes into account support students receive via the tax system while in school, tax support parents may receive in saving for the kids' education, and taxation of income flows over the lifetime after graduation.

As in the case of any other investment, when investing in human capital there is an initial net outflow (e.g., cost of a university education) and later a series of net inflows (e.g., the increase in income received over the life cycle as a result of going to university). While it is nice to have a high before-tax rate of return, the bottom line is the after-tax return. The ETR is a tool that allows us to say just how much the tax system reduces this return. The ETR on human capital reflects the propensity of the tax authority to garnish the (future) wages of those investing in human capital. The higher the ETR, the more the tax system "penalizes" the individual for investing. The purpose of this paper is to explore the size of this penalty and how it may affect human capital investment in Canada.

While many studies of the rate of return to human capital investment have been performed that could have identified the ETR, in practice this has not generally been done. (See e.g., Stager, 1996; Vaillancourt, 1995, 1997; Vaillancourt and Bourdeau-Primeau, 2002; Rathje and Emery, 2002.) Published results of these studies tend to compare the *public* rate of return on human capital investment and the after-tax rate of return to the individual. The difference between these two rates is an indicator of the total impact of taxes and expenditures, but it does not identify their separate effects. Given that significant changes in the tax treatment of education and in tax rates have taken place in Canada in recent years separating these impacts is of interest.

In previous work (Collins and Davies, 2003, 2004) we set out the idea of the human capital ETR and provided some analysis of its theoretical properties. Mintz (2001) reports the results of related work. Collins and Davies (2003) did a Canada-US comparison, using 1998 Survey of Consumer Finance (SCF) earnings data for Canada and March 1998 Current Population Survey (CPS) data for the United States. Results showed that ETRs on university level human capital were about twice as high in Canada as in the United States. We used 1995 SCF data to estimate ETRs at the university level under the 1998 tax system (Collins and Davies, 2004). We found that these were sizeable although not as large as marginal ETRs found for physical capital by previous authors. They varied considerably across individuals. On average they were greater for males than for females, and increased with income. The ETRs were lower for individuals who took out student loans, and for those who took advantage of Registered Education Savings Plans (RESPs). There were also differences in ETRs created by a number of other tax features. The conclusion was that Canada had far from uniform tax treatment of human capital.

This paper examines the impact of the changes in the tax system since 1998 on first-degree university level human capital ETRs in Canada. We model the impacts of both personal income tax and the two major payroll taxes, Canada Pension Plan (CPP) and Employment Insurance (EI). As in our previous work we use the Ontario system to represent provincial taxes. Our results take the form of a comparison of 1998 and 2003. In both cases we use the 1998 SCF as our source of earnings data, allowing us to concentrate on the impacts of changes in taxation.

There have been important changes in the tax system affecting human capital since 1998. One is that students' tax credits have become more generous. The education amount was $200 in 1998, but rose to $400 federally for the 2003 tax year. Another is that the federal personal income tax (PIT) rate schedule has changed considerably. In 1998 we still had three tax brackets, with marginal tax rates (MTRs) of 17, 26, and 29%. The 2001 tax year saw this replaced by four tax brackets with rates of 16, 22, 26, and 29% and less steep progression over a broad middle-income range. All surtaxes had also been eliminated by 2003. The result of these changes was that both PIT progressivity and average tax rates had fallen significantly, both of which tend to reduce human capital ETRs, as we shall see.

In addition to studying ETRs, we (Collins and Davies, 2004) compute effective subsidy rates (ESRs). ESRs reflect the subsidy per full-time equivalent student that results from governments' direct grants to universities and subsidized student loans. The values of the ESRs will differ depending upon a number of factors. For instance, fields of study are treated differently in provincial funding formulas. The physical sciences, engineering, and medicine are more heavily subsidized, due to their need for laboratories, special equipment, etc., than the humanities or social sciences and, therefore, have much higher ESRs.[1] Interestingly, ESRs are also higher for women than for men — because equal subsidies are relatively more important for females due to their lower earnings. We find that, on average, for both genders combined, ESRs were larger than ETRs (Collins and Davies, 2004). For females they were more than twice as great. Since 1998, tuition and ancillary fees have risen considerably at most Canadian universities and operating grants from (mainly provincial) governments have declined in relative terms as a source of university finance. This means that ESRs have likely been declining. Unfortunately, we were not able to obtain the data necessary to update our 1998 ESR estimates to 2003, so that we cannot currently say whether ESRs or ETRs have fallen more in the last few years.

The remainder of the paper is organized as follows. The next section lays out the concept of the human capital ETR, and discusses some of its

---

[1]See Collins (2004) for an illustration of how the different fields are treated in the funding formulas. Vaillancourt (1997) also has estimates of net subsidy rates by field of study.

properties and behaviour. The third section then describes the relevant features of the Canadian tax system and how it changed from 1998 to 2003. Our results are presented in the following section, and the final section holds our conclusions.

Concepts and Methods

The ETR Concept

Computing the effective tax rate on human capital requires a comparison of before- and after-tax rates of return to human capital. Estimates depend on individual circumstances and require a comparison of the taxes that would be paid in the absence of taking a degree versus those paid if extra schooling is obtained. The most meaningful calculation compares the before- and after-tax rates of return to participation in a complete education program, whether it be a community college, undergraduate university study, MA or PhD work.[2] These tax rates are similar to the commonly computed EMTRs on physical capital in that they measure the effective tax rate on the last meaningful unit of education, but since these units are not small, in our work we examine *effective tax rates* (ETRs) rather than EMTRs.

The ETR for human capital is defined as the gap between gross- and net-of-tax rates of return to a whole program of study, r_g and r_n, respectively:

$$ETR = \frac{r_g - r_n}{r_g} = 1 - \frac{r_n}{r_g} \tag{1}$$

---

[2]The situation for on-the-job training (OJT) is different. (This is one of the reasons that we do not deal with OJT in this paper. It would require a separate study.) One can imagine OJT being provided in quite small units, and the sensitivity of results to the size of the investment becomes less of a problem. This is because the relevant tax on the employer's side, that is, the corporate tax, is levied at a flat rate, and provided investments are not too large individuals' marginal tax rates will also not be strongly affected by OJT.

Kirk A. Collins and James B. Davies

This definition, which is built on the use of internal rates of return, follows the methodology applied in computing ETRs on personal financial assets by Davies and Glenday (1990).[3]

Suppose that an individual aged t is planning to engage in a program of education that will take m years of study. We will assume that after this program is completed the individual will stay in the labour force until age T. Students may continue to earn while going to school. Their wage rates can vary over time, perhaps increasing while they are still in school, and likely rising in real terms over much of the lifetime after graduation. Actual earnings before-tax are given by E_t, which is the product of the wage rate and hours worked. Earnings before-tax in the absence of the educational program would have been E_t^*, where we assume that $E_t^* < E_t$ in the $T - m$ years after graduation. Forgone earnings costs of education, FE_t, are thus $E_t^* - E_t$ in the first m years. In addition to these costs, there are private direct costs of education, C_t. After-tax variables will be denoted E_t^a, E_t^{a*}, FE_t^a, and C_t^a. Initially we will assume that human capital investments are self-financed, that is that student loans are absent.

Rates of return on the investment described are calculated as internal rates of return. For example, we can compute the gross private rate of return, r_g, from:

$$\sum_{t=1}^{T} \frac{E_t - C_t}{(1 + r_g)^{t-1}} = \sum_{t=1}^{T} \frac{E_t^*}{(1 + r_g)^{t-1}}. \tag{2}$$

By replacing E_t, E_t^*, and C_t with the after-tax variables E_t^a, E_t^{a*}, and C_t^a, we could compute the net after-tax rate of return, r_n, using this same equation.[4] Note that in the case of a flat tax with tuition and other direct

---

[3]An alternative is to define the ETR as the ratio of the present value of net taxes on labour income over the lifetime to the present value of lifetime earnings. (See Mintz, 2001.) While the two approaches will often produce similar results, this is not always the case. We prefer the approach followed here in part because it does not require any assumption to be made about individuals' discount rates.

[4]Note that as in all such studies we are, in fact, computing rates of return to a lifetime investment program that merely *begins* with university attendance. According to human capital theory, earnings rise over most of the working lifetime due to continued human capital accumulation, for example, via on-the-job training,

costs of education deductible $r_n = r_g$, and ETR = 0. This is because with such a tax levied at the rate, say, τ, we have $E_t^a = (1 - \tau)E_t$, $E_t^{a^*} = (1 - \tau)E_t^*$, and $C_t^a = (1 - \tau)C_t$, . That is, the three variables have the same relative values after- as before-tax. This type of tax system may be referred to as *neutral* with respect to human capital.[5] It imposes a zero ETR because the forgone earnings and direct costs of education are implicitly subsidized at the same rate, τ, at which the gains from education are taxed.

Note that the term "neutrality" has a special, and limited, meaning here. It is simply a benchmark. There is no implication that a zero ETR on human capital is the optimal rate. Externalities of human capital, or capital market imperfections that make it difficult for students to finance their studies, could call for a negative ETR.[6] Absent such factors, a non-zero ETR could be needed in the second-best solution if there were a positive EMTR on physical capital. In that case, while a low ETR would avoid depressing investment it would also tilt the playing field away from physical capital investment, causing a distortion in the composition of investment. Clearly,

---

after graduation. The returns to such postschool investments are implicitly included in the rates of return calculated here.

[5]Note that "neutral" is used here in a special sense. We do not imply, e.g., that a tax system that is neutral with respect to human capital is non-distortionary in its treatment of human vs. physical capital. That depends on the effective tax rate on physical capital, and also on whether there are any relevant non-tax distortions (e.g., capital market imperfections).

[6]See Davies (2002) for a review of the empirical evidence on the size of human capital externalities. The evidence is mixed, with some recent studies, such as Heckman and Klenow (1997) and Acemoglu and Angrist (2001) arguing that human capital externalities that had previously been claimed to be large may in fact be weak or non existent. Doubt has also been cast on the importance of borrowing problems. See e.g., Shea, 2000; and Cameron and Taber, 2000. Note also that Corak, Lipps and Zhao (2003) find university participation rates of students from low income families rose substantially in Canada from 1979 to 1997, despite rising tuition fees. (This aspect of the Corak *et al.* results was reported by Caroline Alphonso in "Fee Hikes Not Forcing Students Away", *Globe and Mail*, Saturday, Oct. 2, 2003, p. A3.) Rathje and Emery (2002) provide estimates of how large the externalities from human capital would have to be to raise social rates of return on university programs with lower market rates of return to an adequate benchmark level.

Kirk A. Collins and James B. Davies

optimal design of the tax treatment of human capital is contingent on any constraints (political or otherwise) on the tax treatment of physical capital.

By replacing private costs with public costs, C_t^p, we can use (2) to compute the public rate of return, r_p. Given r_p we can define the effective subsidy rate (ESR) on human capital:

$$ESR = \frac{r_g - r_p}{r_g}. \tag{3}$$

Whether the tax and expenditure systems combined have an incentive or disincentive effect on human capital investment can be investigated by computing the *net* effective tax rate on human capital, ETR − ESR.

We (2004) investigate the theoretical behaviour of ETRs in a simple environment where there are just two periods: the schooling period and the working period. We define τ_s as the average tax rate that would have applied to forgone earnings during the schooling period if the person had *not* gone to university, and τ_w as the average tax rate over the working lifetime on the incremental earnings due to taking the university route. The most important results can then be summarized as follows:

Zero Direct Costs, No Student Loans: When C = 0 and there are no student loans we have:

$$ETR\big|_{C=0} = \frac{r_g - r_n}{r_g} = \frac{\tau_w - \tau_s}{1 - \tau_s} \tag{4}$$

Result 1. The ETR > 0, = 0, or < 0 according to whether $\tau_w > \tau_s$, $\tau_w = \tau_s$ or $\tau_w < \tau_s$. The ETR rises with τ_w and falls with τ_s.

Result 2. If $\tau_w > \tau_s$, equal absolute or equal proportional increases in taus and tauw increase the ETR.

The first of these results indicates that a progressive tax system will have ETR > 0. Also, the ETR will tend to rise with increasing progressivity, which will increase the gap between τ_w and τ_s. The second result has the interesting implication that taxes that are close to a blow-up of the basic tax system, like provincial PIT in Canada outside Quebec prior to the change in the tax collection agreements in 2001, raise the ETR. Moreover, even adding a *flat* provincial income tax to the federal PIT as in Alberta, which would raise τ_w and τ_s by the same absolute amount, raises the ETR. Further, in a lifetime context one could think of general sales taxes, like provincial sales taxes or the goods and services tax (GST) as approximately equivalent to flat wage taxes. Bringing them into the analysis (which we do not do in the calculations reported in this paper) would again raise the ETR.[7]

Positive Direct Costs, Student Loans: **Result 3.** If C is deductible at a rate less than τ_w, the ETR > 0 if $\tau_w > \tau_s$.

Result 4. Increases in credits or deductions for C or in interest deductibility on student loans reduce the ETR.

Result 5. A rise in tuition or other direct costs raises the ETR.

These results are also relevant in Canada. First, federal PIT gives a tuition credit at the basic federal tax rate of 16%. While the education amount, of $400 per month, also deductible at a 16% rate, adds to this tax assistance, as long as it is not exceeded by non-tuition direct costs we still have that the overall deduction rate on C is not greater than 0.16. Since most university graduates will penetrate tax brackets with higher MTRs over their working lives, they have $\tau_w > 0.16$. Hence by Result 3, progressivity of the tax system still gives us ETR > 0 even with tax assistance for education expenses.

Result 4 is interesting since interest deductibility on student loans was zero before 1998, when it was made deductible at the base federal PIT rate. Also, the deductibility of C has been increasing via the rising education amount. This greater tax assistance for students reduces ETRs. On the other hand, Result 5 says that the increasing out-of-pocket costs of education we have seen in recent years have likely increased ETRs. This indicates that whether ETRs have been rising or falling is a question that can only be resolved by looking at the data. It also illustrates the interesting point that changes in parameters *outside* the tax system can affect the strength of tax disincentives for human capital accumulation.

---

[7]Since Alberta, alone among the provinces, does not have a provincial sales tax, and since its flat PIT, while raising the ETR above the purely federal level does so less than would a more progressive provincial income tax, it stands out as the province that adds the least to the tax disincentive to invest in human capital in Canada.

Estimation Methods

Rates of return on human capital could be estimated with some precision if we had panel data on education and earnings over complete lifetimes. If, in addition, we had full information about taxes paid, these rates of return could be computed on a before- and after-tax basis. In fact, while some panel data is available, it covers much less than a full lifetime. Also, we are not really so interested in the *ex post* differences in before- and after-tax returns earned by cohorts born long ago. A more likely goal, and the one we try to achieve in this paper, is to try to summarize the incentive or disincentive effects for human capital provided by the tax system that is in force at a particular moment in time. This suggests calculating the after-tax rate of return assuming that the current tax structure stays in place over the long run. This is in a similar spirit to the common practice of estimating human capital rates of return using cross-section earnings data (which we of course also follow).[8]

Our attention in the calculations reported in the fourth section is focused on ETRs for people at particular quantiles of the earnings distribution, especially the median. We believe this has more value than computing rates of return and ETRs using average earnings. Since the skewness of the earnings distribution changes over the lifetime, average earnings do not correspond to the earnings of a person at a constant percentile of the distribution over the lifetime. Also, the rate of return computed using average earnings does not equal the average rate of return. The latter could be estimated by averaging the rates of return for people at all quantiles, which would in general produce a different result.

---

[8]It might be suggested that one should attempt to incorporate secular changes that could reasonably be anticipated by individuals. Thirty years ago this would have included secular wage growth. However, over the last two decades in Canada the rate of growth of real wages has been very low, and sometimes negative, so that a constant rising path of wages can hardly be confidently anticipated. In the same vein, it is very difficult to predict what will happen to the tax system in the future. One might suppose that tax rates will have to rise to finance the health-care and pension costs of an aging population, for example. But if we look at recent history in Canada, despite our new-found high sense of fiscal responsibility the trend is actually towards lower tax rates. So it is very difficult to know what even a very well-informed taxpayer would expect about the future evolution of the tax system.

Treatment of Human Capital under the Canadian Tax System

The calculations in the next section incorporate the effects of both the personal income tax system (federal and provincial) and payroll taxes, as they applied in the 1998 and 2003 tax years. As we describe below, federal budgets in the period 1996–98 ushered in a number of changes that provided more tax support for students and for parents saving for their children's education.[9] These were all operative by the 1998 tax year. The last five years have seen further increases in the tax support for students. But, more importantly for human capital ETRs, they have seen a significant reduction in the progressivity of the tax system.

The Personal Income Tax (PIT) System in 1998

As shown in Table 1, in 1998 basic federal marginal rates of 17%, 26%, and 29% were levied on taxable income in the ranges 0–$29,590, $29,591 –$59,180, and $59,181+. (These rates and brackets were in force from 1993 to 1999.) Adding in surtaxes and provincial income tax, the full marginal rates in the three brackets came to about 26, 40, and 46% (Canadian Tax Foundation, 1999, Table 3.5). Important deductions made in arriving at taxable income included those for Registered Retirement Savings Plan (RRSP) and Registered Pension Plan (RPP) contributions and child-care expenses. Rather than providing personal allowances or exemptions as in most other countries, a system of personal credits was applied. These gave all taxpayers the same relief as if they had received personal deductions but were in the 17% marginal tax bracket. On that basis, the credits given were equivalent to deductions of $6,456 for the taxpayer and $5,380 for a dependent spouse or child over 18.

Refundable tax credits for children under 18 were provided via the Canada Child Tax Benefit (CCTB) and the National Child Benefit Supplement (NCBS). The latter was clawed back on family net incomes above $25,921 and $20,921 respectively. These programs have little impact

---

[9]In a more comprehensive investigation some other taxes would also be taken into account. In the previous section we remarked on the impact of sales taxes. In addition, corporate income taxes have impacts on human capital formed via on-the-job training. See Collins and Davies (2004).

Table 1: Tax Features, 1998 and 2003

1. Federal Personal Income Tax

1998		2003	
Taxable Income	Marginal Tax Rates	Taxable Income	Marginal Tax Rates
0 – $29,590	17%	0 – $32,183	16%
29,591 – 59,180	26	32,184 – 64,368	22
59,181+	29	64,369 – 104,648	26
		104,649+	29

Basic Fed. Tax	Surtax
0 – $12,500	3%
$12,501+	8

Basic Personal Amount: $6,456		Basic Personal Amount: $7,756	
Education Amounts:	FT 200 per mo.	Education Amounts:	FT 400 per mo.
	PT 60 per mo.		PT 120 per mo.

2. Combined Federal and Provincial Marginal PIT Rates, Including Federal Surtaxes (Canadian Tax Foundation Estimates)

1998		2002	
Taxable Income	Marginal Tax Rates	Taxable Income	Marginal Tax Rates
0 – $29,590	26%	0 – $31,677	24.3%
29,591 – 59,180	40	31,678 – 63,354	33.4
59,181+	46	63,355 – 103,000	39.5
		103,001+	44.1

3. Ontario Personal Income Tax

1998		2003	
Taxable Income	Marginal Tax Rates	Taxable Income	Marginal Tax Rates
0 – $29,590	7.27%	0 – $32,435	6.05%
29,591 – 59,180	11.12	32,436 – 64,871	9.15
59,181+	12.40	64,872+	11.16

Basic Prov. Tax	Surtax	Basic Prov. Tax	Surtax
$4,057 – 5,217	20%	$3,747 – $4,727	20%
$5,218+	53	$4,728+	56

4. Payroll Taxes

		1998	2003
CPP:	Ceiling	$36,900	$39,900
	Basic Exemption	$3,500	$3,500
	Employee Cont'n. Rate	3.2%	4.95%
EI:	Ceiling	$39,000	$39,000
	Employee Cont'n. Rate	2.7%	2.1%

on costs of education, since relatively few students have children, but they increase marginal tax rates for many graduates, and therefore drive up the ETR on human capital somewhat.[10]

The tax relief on tuition and other direct expenses provided by the PIT comes in the form of various credits, not as a deduction. In 1998 a credit was given for 17% of tuition and additional mandatory fees paid to approved postsecondary institutions. A further credit equal to 17% of the "education amount" was provided. The education amount was $80 per month prior to 1996, but was raised in steps to $200 per month by 1998. Since most students have low incomes, these credits would in many cases not be very valuable if they were only available to reduce the student's own tax liability. Their value is enhanced by the fact that any unused portion can be transferred to a spouse, parent or grandparent.[11] Also, in 1997 a carryforward provision for unused education credits was introduced that would allow students to obtain tax relief themselves in later years. These measures ensured that by 1998 the effective implicit federal subsidy on direct costs of education via PIT was close to being uniform at a 17% rate. Adding in provincial tax, the average rate of relief was about 26%.

Note that the "education amount" credits are not related to actual expenditures, but are simply paid as a lump sum. They are thus similar to a system of student grants. This form of assistance would not have a tax-side rationale under a flat tax, but with progressivity might be advocated as a rough offset to the effect of graduated marginal tax rates on human capital ETRs.

The PIT system also provides assistance for education and training via registered savings plans. First, Canadians are able to withdraw funds from their RRSPs without penalty two years after contributions are made. This means that, assuming contribution limits are not binding, parents could save

---

[10]The NCBS was clawed back at rates ranging from 12.1% for one-child families to 26.8% for a family with three or more children. This means that the credit was already clawed back completely for most families at net income of $25,921, where the CCTB clawback kicked in at rates from 2.5% to 5.0%. The latter relatively low rates mean that the CCTB clawback range is very wide. The clawback affects families with incomes up to $67,000 - $75,000. However, since the CCTB clawback rates are relatively low, their impact on human capital ETRs would be fairly small.

[11]That is, up to a limit of $5,000 minus the part of the credit used by the student to reduce his/her tax liability to zero.

Kirk A. Collins and James B. Davies

for their children's postsecondary education via their RRSPs. While this avenue is no doubt sometimes chosen, it is not as attractive as it might be since RRSP contribution limits have been held at relatively low levels.[12] Also, withdrawals are taxed. Parents will typically be in their peak earning years when their kids go to college, and will therefore face high tax rates on withdrawals. This will also make the RRSP saving route less attractive.

Parents are encouraged to save for their kids' education via Registered Education Saving Plans (RESPs). In contrast to an RRSP, contributions to an RESP are not tax deductible. However, income earned within the plan is tax free, and if the proceeds are spent on the child's education withdrawals of accrued income enter the child's income for tax purposes. Given that postsecondary students are generally in low tax brackets, the result is that the net of tax rate of return on RESP saving generally exceeds that on non-sheltered saving.[13] While RESPs provide a higher rate of return than on non-sheltered saving, in the pre-1998 regime they were not sufficiently attractive to induce much use. This may have been due to the opportunities for fully sheltered saving (e.g., via RRSPs) or because a higher rate of return could be achieved by paying down mortgages and consumer debt.[14]

The 1996, 1997, and (especially) 1998 federal budgets introduced a number of changes intended to reduce burdens on postsecondary students and to stimulate education and training in Canada. The following were the principal changes:

---

[12]The current contribution limit for RRSPs plus Registered Pension Plans is the lesser of $13,500 or 18% of earnings per year. The dollar limit is slated to rise to $14,500 in 2004 and to $15,500 in 2005, after which it will be indexed to the average industrial wage. These levels represent a significant retreat, however, from those promised by earlier federal budgets. The 1984 and 1985 budgets promised a limit of $15,500 by 1990, with subsequent indexation.

[13]Since withdrawals are generally taxed at a low rate, RESPs approximate Roth IRA plans in the United States, which have non-deductible contributions and tax-free withdrawals. Greater use of this type of sheltered saving has been urged for Canada by, e.g., Kesselman and Poschmann (2001).

[14]In Canada, interest on mortgages and consumer debt is not tax deductible. This makes paying down these forms of debt a popular form of saving for those in the age range of about 25–45.

- The 1996 and 1997 budgets announced that the education amount would be raised from its original $80 per month to $150 per month in 1997 and $200 per month in 1998.
- The education amount was extended to part-time postsecondary students in the 1998 budget, at $60 per month. Part-time students also became eligible to claim the child-care expense deduction (CCED) for the first time, up to $2,200 per year.
- Canada Study Grants (CSGs) of up to $3,000 per year were created in the 1998 budget for both full- and part-time students in financial need who had children or other dependents.
- Interest on student loans became eligible for a tax credit at the 17% rate in the 1998 budget.
- Tax-free withdrawals of up to $10,000 per year ($20,000 in total) from RRSPs were introduced in the 1998 budget to finance full-time training or education (or part-time for disabled people). These withdrawals must be repaid within ten years.
- The 1996 and 1997 budgets raised the annual contribution limits on RESPs from $1,500 to $4,000 per student, and also increased the lifetime limit on contributions from $31,500 to $42,000. The 1998 budget introduced Canada Education Saving Grants (CESGs) equal to 20% of RESP contributions up to a limit of a $400 annual grant per student. CESG amounts become part of the RESP. The 1998 budget also made it possible to transfer an RESP balance to an RRSP if the student did not go on to qualifying study after leaving high school.

All of these provisions acted to increase the net-of-tax expected return to planned or actual human capital investment for some taxpayers.[15] Note, however, that the incidence of the increased returns varies greatly. Increased education amounts raise r_n for almost all students. On the other hand, interest credits only benefit those with student loans, and the RESP/RRSP provisions have similarly limited incidence. Note also that the value of the RESP/RRSP measures will vary substantially even among those who make use of these savings plans. CESGs are proportional to RESP contributions; the benefit of RESP saving depends on how attractive

---

[15]The RESP and RRSP provisions might be seen as raising the rate of return to financial assets. However, the benefits in question are only realized as a result of planned or actual human capital investment. They are therefore regarded here as increasing the net expected return on *human* capital.

Kirk A. Collins and James B. Davies

is the after-tax rate of return on the next-best saving vehicle; the value of the option to rollover unused RESP funds into an RRSP depends on how likely it is that education plans will fall through; and the benefit of being able to take money out of an RRSP temporarily to finance education depends on the size of the tax rate thereby avoided.

Personal Income Tax Changes since 1998

Since 1998 the most important PIT changes affecting human capital have been (i) a doubling of the education amounts in the 2001 tax year (to $400 and $120 per month for full-time and part-time students respectively), (ii) reductions in federal tax rates and changes in the rate structure, (iii) the freeing-up of provincial PIT rate structures, and (iv) re-indexation of brackets, credits, and deductions announced in the February 2000 budget.

Changes in rate structure over the last five years have taken us from a sharply graduated three-bracket structure to more gradual progressivity. For the 2003 tax year, as shown in Table 1, federal rates apply at the rates of 16, 22, 26, and 29% on taxable income in the ranges 0 – $30,183; $32,184 – $64,368; $64,369 – $104,648; and $104,649+. All federal surtaxes have now been removed. Including a representative nominal provincial tax, Canadian Tax Foundation (2003, Table 3.5) estimates that full marginal rates in the four brackets were 24%, 33%, 40%, and 44% in 2002. (Results for 2003 are not yet available.) The comparison with the much more progressive 1998 structure shown in Table 1 is striking. This reduced progressivity has reduced human capital ETRs in Canada considerably, as discussed in the next section.

Re-indexation of the tax system has already had a non-trivial effect on the PIT structure. From 2001 to 2003 it resulted in a 4.6% upward shift in brackets, credits, and deductions. Thus, for example, the threshold for entering the 26% federal marginal tax bracket rose from $61,510 to $64,369. Such changes ensure that, holding the real earnings structure constant, average personal tax rates before and after university graduation will not change due to inflation, preventing any tendency for the ETR on human capital to rise or fall as a result of the "bracket creep" that would otherwise be present.[16]

Prior to the 2001 tax year all nine provinces that were signatories to the federal-provincial tax collection agreements were bound to levy their basic PIT as a flat percentage of the basic federal tax. (Quebec levied and collected its own separate PIT.) Under this arrangement, federal surtaxes did not affect provincial PIT, and the provinces were free to enact their own surtaxes and credits in addition to those provided by Ottawa. While in the 1970s and 1980s provincial PIT payments could broadly be thought of as proportional to federal, by 1998 this approximation was becoming strained. Some provinces, notably Ontario, levied sizable surtaxes, and a wide range of provincial credits were provided, for example, provincial political contributions, qualifying investments, property and sales taxes, and dependent children. Finally, the Quebec rate structure was somewhat less progressive than the federal structure, featuring marginal rates of 17%, 21.25%, and 24.5% on taxable incomes of 0 – $26,000; $26,001 – $52,000; and $52,000+ in 2001, for example.

Beginning in 2001 provinces covered by the tax-collection agreements were free to levy tax as a function of federal taxable income rather than basic federal tax. This has already led to significant differences in rate structure across the provinces, and divergence from the federal structure. While as of 2002 six provinces still kept the three-bracket structure, New Brunswick followed the federal lead to create a new $103,000+ bracket. Alberta had introduced a flat tax at a 10% rate. British Columbia had five brackets, with the top one beginning at $86,785.

Table 1 provides detail on the Ontario PIT system, which is used in the calculations reported in the next section, but also reports the Canadian Tax Foundation's estimates for full marginal tax rates in 2002 (the latest available), including federal surtaxes as well as a stylized representative provincial PIT. The CTF figures echo both the reduced tax rates seen at the federal level and reduced progressivity. *Both* of these factors should act to reduce human capital ETRs, as discussed in the previous section.

---

[16]In the long run "bracket creep" pushes everyone into the top bracket, giving essentially a flat tax structure with a low ETR. However, in the short run the increase in tax rates that would be paid during the university years by students if they stopped their schooling after high school may be larger than the increase in tax rates over the working lifetime, giving the opposite effect.

Kirk A. Collins and James B. Davies

In terms of the overall PIT rate structure, note from the CTF estimates that the bottom MTR declined from 26% in 1998 to 24% in 2003, and the top rate fell from 46 to 44%. In between, for incomes in about the $30,000 – $100,000 range, the total MTR declined by about 6.5 percentage points. Thus, the decline in progressivity centred on a broad middle-income range, where it should have a large effect on tax rates faced by most university graduates.[17]

The Ontario system shows reduced nominal MTRs in each tax bracket over the period 1998–2003, but a reduction in surtax thresholds and an increase in the top surtax rate. Thus, changes in the Ontario system increased progressivity somewhat.[18] Reduced rates tend to lower ETRs, while increased progressivity does the opposite. The net impact of the Ontario changes is therefore not clear. One thing that is clear, however, is that ETRs would be lower in Ontario in 2003 if its conservative government had opted for a flat provincial income tax along with Alberta's when it got the opportunity.

Payroll Taxes

In 1998 employees and employers each paid Canada Pension Plan contributions at a rate of 3.2% on earnings between the basic exemption of $3,500 and ceiling of $36,900. Employment insurance contributions were paid at a rate of 2.7% by the employee and 3.78% by the employer, on earnings up to $39,000. As of 2003 the weight of CPP contributions had increased considerably, with the basic exemption unchanged, a higher earnings ceiling at $39,900, and an employee contribution rate of 4.95%. On the other hand, the EI earnings ceiling was unchanged and the contribution rate had gone down to 2.1%. Adding together the two payroll taxes, the total

---

[17]An appropriate measure of local progressivity is the ratio of the MTR to the average tax rate: MTR/ATR. This ratio declined between 1998 and 2003 in the middle-income range, but rose in the $103,000+ top bracket. Thus, while for the bulk of the distribution it is correct to say that progressivity declined over these five years, for the top few percentiles of taxpayers the opposite is true.

[18]Levying fat surtaxes on high-income people, and increasing progressivity over time is a curious tack for a radical conservative government like that in power in Ontario during this period. The contrast with the flat tax adopted by Alberta's conservative government is striking.

employee contribution rate where both contributions are payable rose from 5.9% in 1998 to 7.05% in 2003.

In the overall scheme of things both CPP and EI are regressive. They increase average tax rates on forgone earnings of university students significantly, but have a weaker impact on the earnings gain achieved by graduates, most of whom will have earnings above the CPP and EI earnings ceilings over much of their working lives. These impacts *reduce* ETRs. The rising trend of payroll taxes in Canada hence should strengthen the trend for human capital ETRs to decline. This effect will be largest for those workers with incomes above the EI and CPP contribution ceilings for the longest portion of their working lives. For less successful university graduates, the effect will be weaker or could even be reversed. If one spent one's entire working life below the CPP and EI earnings ceilings, CPP + EI contributions would have the same effect as a flat tax. For these people, Result 2 discussed in the previous section applies, and CPP/EI would increase the ETR.

It could be objected that CPP and EI contributions are not taxes, but benefit-related charges. In principle, we should take the expected benefits into account in our equation (2), allowing them to affect the calculation of before- and after-tax rates of return on human capital. In practice, both the take-up rate of EI for university graduates and the discounted value of CPP pension benefits are low, so that this would have little effect on our calculations.

Effective Tax Rates on Undergraduate University Education in Canada

Data and Assumptions

In order to gauge the size of ETRs in Canada we compute representative values of the net- and gross-of-tax rates of return, r_n and r_g. To do this we use Statistics Canada's 1998 Survey of Consumer Finance (SCF) to model actual and potential earnings, E_t and E_t^*, before- and after-tax. As explained earlier, and in keeping with previous studies, we perform our calculations as if the 1998 cross-section were a snapshot from an economy in steady state. From this dataset we took median earnings, and other quantiles, of full-time male and female workers conditioned on the highest completed level of schooling being high school or a bachelor's degree, as the basis for E_t^* and E_t respectively. We have used median rather than mean earnings since we wish to investigate rates of return and ETRs for an "average" student. Since earnings are positively skewed the mean is above the median and is not representative for the typical student.

To adjust earnings to 2003, we first scaled up earnings by the percentage difference between mean full-time earnings of males and females in the 2001 SLID and 1998 SCF (8.44% and 4.89% for females and males respectively). We then scaled up further by 2.73%, the increase in the average weekly earnings of full-time workers between 2001 and 2003. (Figures on average weekly earnings by sex do not appear to be available.) This gave total increases of 11.17% and 7.62% for females and males respectively from 1998 to 2003. For both genders note that there is an implied decline in real earnings, as the consumer price index (CPI) rose 13.4% from 1997 to 2003.

The estimation of E_t, E_t^*, and their differential is clearly critical. This requires specification of a counterfactual scenario. How much would the university graduate have earned if he/she had stopped formal education after high school? Our counterfactual says they would have received the amount earned by high school graduates of the same age and gender and at the same quantile among high-school grads.[19] Some authors have argued that university graduates have greater ability and that a differential (typically 10 or 15%) therefore needs to be applied to the earnings of high-school graduates when forming the counterfactual. (See, e.g., Stager, 1996.) We take a comparative advantage view, in which it is not necessarily clear that the median university graduate would have earned more than the

---

[19]An alternative to our approach would be to estimate earnings functions and hold more variables constant in forming the counterfactual. We hold constant age, gender, hours of work, and education-specific earnings percentile. A regression approach would allow additional variables, such as region, industry, occupation, marital status, and so on to be held constant. We do not believe that is a superior approach, however, since we are interested in the total return to deciding to be a university graduate. This includes earnings gains that come from moving to the regions, industries or occupations where jobs for university graduates are concentrated.

median high school graduate if his/her education had been terminated after high school.[20] We therefore do not apply an ability differential.

We have specified costs and tax features, as far as possible to be those prevailing in the academic years 1998–99 and 2003–04 respectively. In 1998–99 undergraduate tuition fees averaged $3,253, and additional fees of $342, according to Statistics Canada. Other direct expenses (books, supplies, and return transportation to the educational institution) were assumed to be $1,000 per year. Thus we estimate total direct expenses to have averaged $4,595. In 2003–04 tuition had risen to $4,025, and additional fees had shot ahead to $623. If other direct expenses had kept pace with inflation they would be $1,122 in 2003, giving total direct expenses of $5,770.

The calculations we report below are for full-time students.[21] Full-time students are assumed to work the equivalent of four months per year, during which they would earn the same amount as a high-school graduate. As in previous studies, we reduce these earnings somewhat (by 20%) to allow for unemployment and job search.[22]

In modelling the taxes paid by workers after graduation we have assumed that they do not claim a credit for a dependent spouse. We also ignore the tax consequences of having children. The incidence of dependent spouses has been declining rapidly in recent years, and we expect will be very low over the lifetimes of recent graduates. Ignoring children leads to an overstatement of tax burdens over the working lifetime, but only a small

---

[20]Studies have shown that skill levels among university graduates are not equivalent and that many have ended up taking jobs that were predominantly held by high-school graduates previously. (See, e.g., Pryor and Schaffer, 1997.) Therefore, to assume a positive ability differential could be somewhat misleading.

[21]Collins and Davies (2004) report results for part-time students as well, showing that their ETRs are somewhat above those of full-time students. For example, in the base case full-time males had an ETR of 0.193, while the ETR for part-time males was 0.215. The figures for females were 0.119 and 0.133 respectively. ETRs for those who attend part-time are lower because they spend more time working while going to school, leading to a higher marginal tax rate (i.e., a higher implicit subsidy) on their forgone earnings.

[22]Morisette (1998, p. 32) reports that the unemployment rate for all men aged 17 to 24 in 1996 was 14.8%. In addition, 5.3% had involuntary part-time employment, for a total of 20.1% who did not have full-time employment.

Kirk A. Collins and James B. Davies

error in the calculation of the taxes paid on the incremental earnings due to education.

While we, of course, take account of "personal amount" credits, we make no allowance in our main results for deductions from income after graduation. The principal deduction that could potentially be modelled is that for RRSP/RPP contributions. However, this would be misleading since our calculations only consider earnings over the working lifetime. If we took the tax relief on RRSP/RPP contributions into account we would have to also model the tax paid on withdrawals. Ignoring both contributions and withdrawals should be approximately offsetting.

Results

Results from our base case are shown in Table 2. This case assumes a single student with no dependents who finances his/her education without the help of a student loan or an RESP. The estimated rates of return are lower than those found by Stager (1996) and Vaillancourt and Bourdeau-Primeau (2002) using 1991 and 1991 and 1995 Census data respectively. Whereas we find the net-of-tax private rate of return was 8.9% for male students in 1998 for example, and 12.5% for female, Vaillancourt and Bourdeau-Primeau found figures of 16 and 19% in 1991, and 17 and 20% in 1995. Stager obtained private rates of return of 13.8% for men and 17.6% for women in 1991. Rathje and Emery (2002) also found lower rates of return than Vaillancourt and Bourdeau-Primeau and Stager, believing a principal reason was the use of more recent, and higher, tuition fees — from the 1998–99 school year.[23] We also use more recent fees in our 2003 calculations bringing them right up to 2003–04. In addition, we differ from Vaillancourt and Bourdeau-Primeau, and Stager by using 1998 SCF rather

---

[23]Rathje and Emery give rates of return by area of study, and do not report average rates of return across those areas. A simple average of their rates of return in the core areas of the humanities, science, and social science is 5.3% for males and 25.2% for females.

Table 2: Rates of Return and Effective Tax Rates for First University Degree Graduates: 1998 and 2003 Tax System, No Student Loans, No Dependents (Base Case)

	IRR (%) Net-of-Tax (1)	IRR (%) Gross-of-Tax (2)	ETR [(2) – (1)] / (2)
Males			
1998	8.87	10.94	0.189
2003	9.22	10.60	0.130
Females			
1998	12.52	14.01	0.106
2003	12.64	13.68	0.076

Notes: IRR = internal rate of return; ETR = effective tax rate.
Source: Authors' calculations using the 1998 SCF and 1998 and 2003 tax systems.

than 1991 or 1996 Census data, excluding the self-employed, and by using median rather than mean earnings.[24]

A notable feature of these results is that, as in previous studies, the rate of return is considerably higher for females than for males. The reason is that the earnings of women with a university degree are much closer to those of their male counterparts than is the case for workers with only high school.

Table 2 shows a relatively small difference between gross and net private rates of return for university graduates. The proportional difference is, of course, the effective tax rate. At 18.9% and 10.6% for male and female students respectively in 1998, the ETRs indicate that, in the no-loan, no-RESP case, human capital investment is not taxed as heavily as

---

[24]The use of medians tends to give lower estimated rates of return because the gap between median and mean earnings rises, both absolutely and proportionally, over the lifetime. Thus our estimates of forgone earnings are closer to those of Vaillancourt and Bourdeau-Primeau and Stager than our estimates of the earnings gain accruing over the working lifetime.

Kirk A. Collins and James B. Davies

McKenzie, Mansour and Brule (1998) find physical capital is taxed. The difference in ETRs for men and women reflects the impact of progressivity. Male university graduates still earn more than women and their earnings increments due to education are therefore taxed more heavily on average.

The most interesting result in Table 2 is the large drop in ETRs from 1998 to 2003. For males there is a decline from 18.9% to 13.0%, and for females there is a drop from 10.6% to 7.6%. As we show later, these declines are largely the result of the flattening of the federal rate structure that took place in 2001. They also owe something to the reduction in overall PIT rates and to the *increase* in CPP and EI contributions. (See the discussion of how these effects operate in the previous section.)

Turning to Table 3, for 1998 we see the effects not only of taxes, but also of subsidies to universities. The second column shows, again, the gross-of-tax private rate of return, which does not take subsidies into account. The first column of figures is the direct costs of university education which are funded by government and do not enter the private calculation.[25] An effective subsidy rate (ESR) can be calculated as the proportional difference between these rates of return. We find that the subsidy rates obtained are greater than the effective tax rates for 1998 shown in Table 2 for both males and females. We thus find a negative net effective tax rate, ETR − ESR, as shown in the last column of the table. This would imply that overall the public sector *encourages* human capital investment — a conclusion that is in line with the results of earlier studies and that would be strengthened by taking into account student loans, bursary programs, and the Canada Millennium Scholarships.

---

[25]In estimating direct costs one must keep in mind that part of universities' costs that are incurred for graduate education, research, and other non-instructional purposes. No estimates are available that separate these functions from under-graduate education. Tenure-track university professors are typically expected to devote 40–50% of their time to teaching, including graduate teaching. We think a reasonable guess is that about 30% of operating costs are incurred for under-graduate education. Estimates are also not available for capital costs (interest, depreciation, etc.) on a national basis, but Stager (1996) estimates that capital costs are about 60% of operating costs. On this basis we have a figure of 50% ($\cong$ 1.6 X 30%) of operating costs as an estimate of total direct costs of undergraduate university education.

Table 3: Base-Case Rates of Return, Effective Subsidy Rates, and Tax Minus Subsidy Rate

	IRR (%) Public (1)	IRR (%) Gross-of-Tax Private (2)	ESR [(2) – (1)] / (2)	ETR – ESR
Males				
1998	7.77	10.94	0.290	–0.101
2003	8.57	10.60	n.a.	n.a.
Females				
1998	11.05	14.01	0.211	–0.105
2003	11.19	13.68	n.a.	n.a.

The most recent available national data for university finances is for 2001. Since changes have been occuring fairly rapidly in university budgets over the last few years, we do not think it is safe to apply 2001 patterns to 2003 in order to estimate the ESR. Still, it is clear that the ESR must have been declining, since tuition fees have been rising quite sharply. Casual empiricism suggests that the drop in the ESR is likely of the same order of magnitude as the decline in the ETR.

Next we study the effects of Canada Education Savings Grants (CESGs).[26] CESGs add 20% to RESP contributions annually, up to a grant limit of $400 per child. Net-of-tax rates of return rise and effective tax rates decline. In the case of full-time male university students, Table 4 indicates that the 1998 ETR drops from 18.9% to 15.2% when parents make annual contributions of just $650 over a 15-year period. If annual contributions of $2,000 are made, the ETRs fall much further — to just 6.5% for males and

---

[26]We do not attempt to estimate the impact of RESPs per se on the ETRs since the effects vary greatly across taxpayers depending on their use of RESPs versus other saving vehicles. Also, prior to the introduction of CESGs. RESPs were not very popular. Thus we believe the most important effect to study is that of CESGs.

Table 4: Rates of Return and Effective Tax Rates with CESGs, 1998 and 2003 Tax System, No Student Loans, No Dependents

Sex	Yearly Contribution ($)	IRR (%) Net-of-Tax (1)	IRR (%) Gross-of-Tax (2)	ETR [(2) – (1)] / (2)	ESR*	ETR – ESR
Male						
1998	650	9.27	10.94	0.152	0.290	−0.137
2003	650	9.50	10.74	0.116	n.a.	n.a.
Female						
1998	650	13.90	14.01	0.008	0.211	−0.203
2003	650	13.01	13.83	0.060	n.a.	n.a.
Male						
1998	2000	10.23	10.94	0.065	0.290	−0.224
2003	2000	10.00	10.74	0.070	n.a.	n.a.
Female						
1998	2000	15.44	14.01	−0.102	0.211	−0.313
2003	2000	13.66	13.83	0.012	n.a.	n.a.

Notes: 1. CESG = Canada Educational Study Grant. CESG benefits incorporated here are based on an example provided by Department of Finance (1998, p. 35). Contributions are made over a 15-year period and earn a 5% rate of return.
2. * ESR = [(2) – Appropriate entry from col. 1 of Table 1.2] / (2).
Source: See Table 2.

−10.2% for females. We (2004) found that the effects for part-time students were also large. Table 4 shows smaller absolute reductions due to CESGs in the ETR in 2003 than in 1998 (for males, 6.0 vs. 12.4% points; for women 6.4 vs. 20.8% points). This is due to the fact that the maximum benefit from CESGs was not increased between 1998 and 2003.

Table 5 replicates the base case of Table 2 for graduates at the 25th and 75th percentile of the earnings distribution, rather than at the median. We see that for both sexes there is a drop in the ETR (but an increase in rates of return) of going to the 25th percentile case from the median; and there is an increase in the ETR going to the 75th percentile. In 1998 females' ETRs

Table 5: Rates of Return and Effective Tax Rates for 25th and 75th Quantiles, 1998 and 2003 Tax System, No Student Loans, No Dependents

Sex	Quantile	IRR (%) Net-of-Tax (1)	IRR (%) Gross-of-Tax (2)	ETR [(2) – (1)] / (2)
Male				
1998	25th	10.28	11.71	0.122
2003	25th	10.36	11.29	0.082
Female				
1998	25th	14.56	15.81	0.079
2003	25th	14.46	15.31	0.056
Male				
1998	75th	6.50	8.49	0.234
2003	75th	6.93	8.30	0.165
Female				
1998	75th	9.86	11.99	0.178
2003	75th	10.31	11.77	0.124

Source: See Table 2.

were 7.9, 10.6 and 17.8% at the 25th percentile, median, and 75th percentile respectively. The figures for men were 12.2, 18.9, and 23.4% respectively. In 2003, the range of values is 5.6, 7.6, and 12.4% for women and 8.2, 13.0 and 16.5% for men. These results again echo the progressivity of the tax system. As we move to higher percentiles we encounter people who not only have higher, but more peaked age-earnings profiles over the lifetime. They will see a much larger portion of their lifetime earnings taxed at high marginal rates than those earning at low quantiles of the distribution, and will accordingly suffer more from the negative effect of income tax progressivity on their net rate of return on human capital.

In order to get a complete assessment of the incentive effect on human capital formation one must of course deduct the ESR from the ETR. Looking back at Table 3 we see that if the graduates at the 75th percentile in 1998 had the same ESRs as median workers, the ETR – ESR figures would be –5.6% and –3.3% for males and females respectively. However, the assumption that the ESRs at higher percentiles are the same as at the median may be incorrect. The highest paid graduates are those in professional programs like engineering and medicine, which in 1998 were still more heavily subsidized than general arts and science programs. Vaillancourt (1997) finds that the difference is sufficient that the net subsidy rates (i.e., ESR − ETR) in 1990 were highest in science, engineering and medicine and lowest in the humanities and social science.[27]

Finally, in order to get a better idea of what is causing the substantial decline in ETRs, we decompose the effects. Table 6 reports the results. We start from the 1998 results and change individual tax aspects, and tuition fees, in turn. The increase in tuition fees reduces both before- and after-tax rates of return to education, but does so close to equi-proportionally, so there is no change in the ETR for males, and a very slight decline for women. The change in CPP/EI rates, first, increases after-tax rates of return for both men and women, and as expected reduces their ETRs slightly — from 18.9% for men to 18.3% and from 10.6% for women to 9.1%. The increase in tuition and education amount credits also raises ETRs a little. These changes by themselves would reduce the male ETR to 17.7% and the female to 9.3%. In contrast to these small effects, the change to the 2003 tax-rate structure has a dramatic impact. It cuts the male ETR down to 9.6%, and reduces the female ETR to just 3.7%. Clearly, it is the flattening of the PIT tax structure over the period 1998–2003 that has had the biggest impact on human capital ETRs.

Conclusion

In past work we have argued that effective tax rates are a useful device for summing up the effects of the tax system on the incentive to invest in human capital, and have illustrated the approach for undergraduate university level education in Canada. Here we have continued that work, examining two broad features of ETRs in 1998 and 2003 — how high they are for the median person, and how they vary across individuals.

---

[27]The net subsidy rates implied by Vaillancourt's 1990 results for males are 17.6% in medicine, 10.6% in engineering, 6.0% in natural science, 2.2% in social science, and 0.6% in humanities. These figures represent the difference between private and public rates of return in Panel B of Vaillancourt's Table 3, p. 6.

Table 6: Decomposing IRR and ETR Changes from 1998 to 2003 by Changing Tax Aspects and Tuition One at a Time

		IRR (%) Net-of-Tax (1)	IRR (%) Gross-of-Tax (2)	ETR [(2) – (1)] / 2
Case	**Males**			
	1998	8.87	10.94	0.189
1.	2003 CPP/EI	8.94	10.94	0.183
2.	2003 Tax rates	9.89	10.94	0.096
3.	2003 Credits	9.01	10.94	0.177
4.	2003 Tuition	8.50	10.50	0.189
	2003	9.22	10.60	0.130
	Females			
	1998	12.52	14.01	0.106
1.	2003 CPP/EI	12.74	14.01	0.091
2.	2003 Tax rates	13.50	14.01	0.037
3.	2003 Credits	12.71	14.01	0.093
4.	2003 Tuition	12.02	13.43	0.105
	2003	12.64	13.68	0.076

Our main finding has been that ETRs fell between 1998 and 2003. In our base case there was a decline from 10.6% to 7.6% for females and a drop from 18.9% to 13.0% for males. These declines are partly the result of the drop in personal income tax rates over this period, but they are mainly due to the decline in progressivity of the PIT system in a broad middle-income range. Increases in CPP and EI contribution rates, which are regressive, have also helped to reduce ETRs a little by eroding overall tax progressivity. Finally, increased tuition and education amount tax credits have reduced ETRs somewhat.

It seems of some interest to us that the main reduction in tax disincentives for human capital accumulation in the last five years has not come from the measures explicitly aimed at this goal, such as the doubling of the monthly education amount credit from $200 to $400 for full-time university students, but from quite a different source. While it is possible

Kirk A. Collins and James B. Davies

that reducing tax disincentives to education was a motive for the flattening of the federal PIT rate structure, that was not one of the reasons for the change that the government highlighted. This echoes our earlier result, in Collins and Davies (2004), that the targeted measure of making interest on student loans deductible, introduced in 1998, had a very small quantitative effect on human capital ETRs.

We have also seen that, as of 1998, effective subsidy rates, ESRs, were larger than ETRs and resulted in a negative net "tax" rate, ETR – ESR, on human capital. In the last five years we know that ESRs have decreased, offsetting to some degree the decline in ETRs that has occurred. We do not have good enough information on university finances for 2003 yet to be able to judge reliably whether ETR – ESR rose or fell over the last five years. However, our intuition suggests that the decline in ESRs has likely been of a similar size to the reduction in ETRs. Thus the good that has come from the flattening of the PIT rate structure has probably been undone by the falling government support for university operating budgets. This creates a policy dilemma for governments that want to avoid discouraging university enrolment in the future. As explained by Boothe and Carson (2003), provincial budgets are under extraodinary, relentless, and ever worsening pressure from health-care spending. This is reducing the amount available for spending in all other areas. Since universities have private as well as public sources of funding they are especially vulnerable targets for provincial spending reductions. The prognosis therefore seems to be that ESRs are likely to continue declining in Canada, unless initiatives such as the first-year university grants announced in the recent federal Throne Speech prove strong enough to counter the trend.

There has recently been considerable controversy over Registered Education Savings Plans, and the 20% subsidy to the first $2,000 of saving per beneficiary per year that are provided through them. Studies by Kesselman and Poschmann (2001) and Milligan (2002) have shown that the benefits are concentrated among high-income groups. At the same time, the recent survey work reported by Corak, Lipps and Zhao (2003) has shown that while the university participation rates of students from both low- and high-income families have trended upward over the last 20 years, there has been a decline in the last ten years for the hard-pressed middle group. This group includes many families in which students cannot qualify for student loans because they fail the means test. These families apparently get little benefit from RESPs or CESGs since they have little discretionary income to allocate to education saving.

Our results show that CESGs have a very dramatic impact on the tax disincentive effect of going to university. When maximum CESGs are received for 15 years, for example, the ETR for a median female earner in our base case was reduced from 7.6% to 1.2% and from 13.0% to 7.0% for males. It can be asked whether it is appropriate to put such a powerful instrument in the hands of high-income families without providing comparable assistance to lower-income families.

There would seem to be one possible argument *in favour of* CESGs that emerges from our work. In addition to looking at the situation of the median earner we have examined results for people consistently at the 25th and 75th percentiles of the earnings distribution over their lifetimes. It turns out that the ETR at the 75th percentile is about twice as large as at the 25th percentile for males, and slightly greater than that for females. This is a result of tax progressivity. Even larger differentials can be expected as one goes further into the extremes of the earnings distribution. If it was the case that high earning students always came from high-income families then CESGs could be seen as a "magic bullet" — a targetted tax break designed to offset the extraordinary tax disincentives to human capital accumulation for high earners.

While CESGs may help to overcome high ETRs for some high earners, the bullet is blunt rather than magic. Corak and Heisz (1999) have found, using longitudinal Canadian tax data, that the intergenerational correlation of income in Canada between fathers and sons is actually quite low — about 0.2. This implies that there are more high earners from middle or low-income backgrounds than from high-income families. CESGs help some people faced with high ETRs but probably only a small minority.

A related argument that could be made in favour of CESGs is that low- and middle-income families could save for their children's university education via RRSPs. They could do this without reducing their retirement savings, given that they are likely not at their RRSP contribution limits. High-income families, on the other hand, are likely to be at those limits and able to save only a fraction of the amount they would like to save for retirement in this sheltered form. Hence, it would be much less advantageous for them to take funds out of RRSPs to fund their children's education. This argument works better than arguing on the basis of children's earning potential, since it is based on the income status of the parent not that of the child (which is only weakly related to parental income).

Finally, we would comment that the strong ETR gradient as one goes up students' earnings scale should be a serious concern for policymakers who care about the efficiency, and not only the equity, of university education in Canada. Investing more in high-quality university education, and directing students to areas where there is strong demand for graduates, have been seen as key factors in achieving a higher rate of productivity growth in numerous official and other reports and studies. This thrust is also part of the federal government's official innovation policy, and is reflected in major federal programs like the Canada Millennium Scholarships, the Canada Fund for Innovation (CFI), and Canada Research Chairs (CRCs). If the tax system is discouraging the "best and brightest" from investing in university education then it may be having a counter-productive effect on human capital accumulation.

Concerns over high ETRs on high ability students also need to be seen against the backdrop of the expenditure side of government operations. Provincial grants are declining as a funding source for universities, and the burden of funding is being thrown increasingly onto tuition fees. This means that ESRs are almost certainly going down. Further, they are likely declining the most in those areas that produce disproportionate numbers of high earners. In Ontario and some of the other provinces, while tuition fees are still regulated for general arts and science programs, they have been completely deregulated in some high demand areas, like business admin-istration and medicine. Tuition fees have also been allowed to rise more quickly in other cases (engineering and computer science, for example), than they have in arts and science. We believe it is likely that the net tax rate on human capital investment, ETR – ESR, has been rising in areas like business, engineering, and computer science — certainly relative to general university programs, but perhaps also in absolute terms.

Appendix

Basic Data

1. Our estimates of tuition and additional expenses are based on Statistics Canada data for 200X-Y. See http://www.statcan.ca/Daily/English/970825/ d970825.htm#art2. An average was taken over arts degrees across the country.

2. Data on "other expenses" was taken from a variety of sources — Statistics Canada databases, university Web sites, and university calendars. "Other expenses" refers to items that are only required for schooling (e.g., books and supplies).

3. The earnings data comes from Statistics Canada's 1998 Survey of Consumer Finance microdata tape.

4. Part-time earnings for full-time students are assumed to be summer earnings and therefore comprise a maximum of four months of earnings potential. To account for unemployment and job search the value is reduced by 20%.

Public Rates of Return

1. Data on government spending and enrolment for male and female, full-time and part-time students was obtained from the Statistics Canada Web site.

2. Current and capital expenditures on undergraduate instruction are assumed to equal one-half of operating expenditures. The justification for this assumption is given in the text of the paper.

3. Public expenditures per student are calculated as in Vaillancourt (1995). Operating expenditure on universities is divided by full-time equivalent (FTE) enrolment, where a part-time student counts as one-third of a full-time student.

Tax Features

Tax Credits

In addition to basic personal amounts, students are eligible for non-refundable credits on tuition and certain additional fees. They may also be eligible for non-refundable credits in the form of the education amount, and on interest paid on student loans. As outlined in the paper, the federal education amount for full-time students was $200 per month in 1998 and $400 per month in 2003. Part-time students were first allowed to claim an education amount of $60 per month at the federal level in 1998; in 2003 this had risen to $120. In 1998 students received the same education amounts at the federal and Ontario levels. In 2003 the Ontario amount for part-time students was $126 per month, and the full-time amount was $421. The taxpayer earned a net credit applicable to federal tax equal to 17% of the amount claimed in 1998 and 16% in 2003. There is a further credit against provincial tax. The sum of these equalled 25% in Ontario in 1998 and 22.05% in 2003.

Registered Education Savings Plans (RESPs) and Canada Education Savings Grants (CESGs)

1. In both 1998 and 2003 the federal government allowed taxpayers to contribute up to $4,000 per child to an RESP.

2. Since January 1, 1998 the federal government has been providing a CESG, equal to 20% of the first $2,000 of RESP contributions per child. We assume alternative RESP contribution values of $650/year and $2,000+/year in calculating the amount of CESG awarded.

3. The calculation for the CESG amount is based on an example in the 1998 federal budget documents, which assumed a 5% rate of return and a contribution rate of $650/year. For a contribution rate of $2,000/year the CESG amount increases proportionally.

References

Acemoglu, D.J. and J. Angrist. 2001. "How Large are the Social Returns to Education? Evidence from Compulsory Schooling Laws", *NBER Macroeconomics Annual* 15, 9-58.

Boothe, P. and M. Carson. 2003. *What Happened to Health Care Reform?* Commentary No. 193. Toronto: C.D. Howe Institute.

Boskin, M.J. 1975. "Notes on the Tax Treatment of Human Capital", in *Conference on Tax Research*, Office of Tax Analysis. Washington, DC: Department of the Treasury.

Cameron, S. and C. Taber. 2000. "Borrowing Constraints and the Returns to Schooling". NBER Working Paper No. 7761. Cambridge, MA: National Bureau of Economic Research.

Canada. Department of Finance. 1998. *The Canadian Opportunities Strategy*. February 1998 budget paper. Ottawa: Supply and Services Canada.

Canadian Tax Foundation. 1999. *Finances of the Nation 1998*. Toronto: The Foundation.

_____. 2003. *Finances of the Nation 2002*. Toronto: The Foundation.

Collins, K.A. 2004. "Taxation, Human Capital, and Tuition Fee Deregulation: A Study of Canadian Universities". University of Western Ontario. Unpublished paper.

Collins, K.A. and J.B. Davies. 2003. "Tax Treatment of Human Capital in Canada and the United States: An Overview and Examination of the Case of University Graduates", in R.G. Harris (ed.), *North American Linkages: Opportunities and Challenges for Canada*. Calgary: University of Calgary Press, 449-486.

_____. 2004. "Measuring Effective Tax Rates on Human Capital: Methodology and an Application to Canada", in P.B. Sørensen (ed.), *Measuring the Tax Burden on Capital and Labor*. Cambridge, MA: MIT Press.

Corak, M. and A. Heisz. 1999. "The Intergenerational Earnings and Income Mobility of Canadian Men: Evidence from Longitudinal Income Tax Data", *Journal of Human Resources* 34(3), 504-533.

Corak, M., G. Lipps and J. Zhao. 2003. *Family Income and Participation in Post-Secondary Education*. Analytical Studies Branch Research Paper Series, Catalogue No. 11F0019MIE - No. 210. Ottawa: Statistics Canada.

Davies, J.B. 2002. "Empirical Evidence on Human Capital Externalities". University of Western Ontario. Unpublished paper.

Davies, J.B. and G. Glenday. 1990. "Accrual Equivalent Marginal Tax Rates for Personal Financial Assets", *Canadian Journal of Economics* 23, 189-209.

Davies, J.B. and J. Whalley. 1991. "Taxes and Capital Formation: How Important is Human Capital?" in D. Bernheim and J. Shoven (eds.), *National Saving and Economic Performance*. Chicago: University of Chicago Press.

Dupor, B., L. Lochner, C. Taber and M.B. Wittekind. 1996. "Some Effects of Taxes on Schooling and Training", *American Economic Review* 86, 340-346.

Heckman J.J. and P.J. Klenow. 1997. "Human Capital Policy". University of Chicago. Unpublished paper.

Heckman, J.J., L. Lochner and C. Taber. 1999. "General Equilibrium Cost-Benefit Analysis of Education and Tax Policies", in G. Ranis and L.K. Raut (eds.), *Trade, Growth and Development: Essays in Honor of Prof. T.N. Srinivasan,* Contributions to Economic Analysis, Vol. 242. Amsterdam, New York and Oxford: Elsevier Science, North-Holland, 291-349.

Kesselman, J. and F. Poschmann. 2001. *A New Option for Retirement Saving — Tax-Prepaid Savings Plans.* Commentary No. 149. Toronto: C.D. Howe Institute.

McKenzie, K.J., M. Mansour and A. Brule. 1998. "The Calculation of Marginal Effective Tax Rates". Working Paper 97-15, Technical Committee on Business Taxation. Ottawa: Department of Finance.

Milligan, K. 2002. *Tax Preferences for Education Saving: Are RESPs Effective?* Commentary No. 174. Toronto: C.D. Howe Institute.

Mintz, J.M. 2001. *Most Favored Nation: Building a Framework for Smart Economic Policy.* Policy Studies No. 36. Toronto: C.D. Howe Institute.

Morisette, R. 1998. "The Declining Labour Market Status of Young Men", in Statistics Canada Publication No. 89-553-XPB. *Labour Markets, Social Institutions, and the Future of Canada's Children.* Ottawa: Statistics Canada.

Perroni, C. 1995. "Assessing the Dynamic Efficiency Gains of Tax Reform When Human Capital is Endogenous", *International Economic Review* 36, 907-925.

Pryor, F.L. and D. Schaffer. 1997. "Wages and the University Educated: A Paradox Resolved", *Monthly Labor Review* 120(7), 3-14.

Rathje, K.A. and J.C.H. Emery. 2002. "Returns to University Education in Canada Using New Estimates of Program Costs", in D. Laidler (ed.), *Renovating the Ivory Tower: Canadian Universities and the Knowledge Economy.* Toronto: C.D. Howe Institute, 241-264.

Shea, J. 2000. "Does Parents' Money Matter?" *Journal of Public Economics* 77, 155-184.

Stager, D.A.A. 1996. "Returns to Investment in Ontario University Education, 1960-1990, and Implications for Tuition Fee Policy", *Canadian Journal of Higher Education* 26(2), 1-22.

Vaillancourt, F. 1995. "The Private and Total Returns to Education in Canada, 1985", *Canadian Journal of Economics* 28(3), 532-554.

_____. 1997. "The Private and Total Returns to Education in Canada, 1990: A Note". Centre de recherche et développement en économique, Université de Montréal. Unpublished paper.

Vaillancourt, F. and S. Bourdeau-Primeau. 2002. "The Returns to University Education in Canada, 1990 and 1995", in D. Laidler (ed.), *Renovating the Ivory Tower: Canadian Universities and the Knowledge Economy.* Toronto: C.D. Howe Institute, 215-240.

Comments

John B. Burbidge

Introduction

Governments around the world act to alter private incentives to invest in human capital. It is therefore natural that a conference on postsecondary education would explore the impact of various government policies, including tax policy, on an individual's education decisions. Thus one would expect to find a session like this one in any country in which this sort of conference happened to occur. What may have been less obvious to the non-economists is the quality of the two papers in this session. Both papers are world class — outstanding contributions not only to the literature on Canada's tax system but, *mutatis mutandis*, models of how one ought to think about the effects of the tax system on human capital decisions in any country. Given the quality of the research produced by Kirk Collins, Jim Davies, and Kevin Milligan one could have argued that the best option for a discussant would have been to say very little and to have encouraged the authors involved to comment on each other's research. In the event, I was not that well behaved. But my comments are intended to complement, rather than to quarrel with, these papers.

I thank Robin Boadway and Arthur Sweetman for helpful comments and SSHRC for financial support.

Kirk and Jim emphasize that their paper is not about distortions to the margin between human and physical capital but rather about the effects of the tax system on education decisions, in particular, the decision of whether or not to attend university. And Kevin is concerned primarily with distributional issues, in particular, whether or not Registered Education Savings Plans (RESPs) achieve the redistributional goals listed in their mission statement. I cannot speak for other readers, but having read both papers over a couple of times I felt the need for one of Robert Solow's "cheap vehicles" — a simple theoretical framework that could serve as some sort of benchmark of how human capital might be treated in an efficient tax system. This is where I will begin. I then turn to some empirical issues in each paper.

A Theoretical Framework

Cheap vehicles are bundled with strong assumptions. I shall assume that individuals do not have a labour-leisure choice — acceptance of a job means accepting fixed hours of work per week and a retirement date — so earnings in each time period are an endowment. In a simple life-cycle framework, which abstracts from inheritances and bequests, a proportional tax on earnings and a proportional tax on consumption are effectively taxes on endowments and therefore do not cause any deadweight loss. An income tax, however, which taxes interest income as well as wage earnings, alters the after-tax return on saving or lending, twists the individual's budget constraint and therefore leads to lower individual well-being for given tax revenue than either a wage or a consumption tax.

Add a schooling decision to this framework. Suppose it is true that a university education is entirely a private good, education has no effects on preferences, and the costs of education are either forgone earnings or direct costs of schooling. Absent any government intervention and with perfect capital markets (assumed above), each person would choose the level of schooling to equate the marginal costs of schooling to the marginal benefits of schooling. Given my assumptions this choice would be socially efficient. Now reintroduce a tax system. A proportional tax on earnings or consumption is still efficient because either one scales both the benefits and costs of going to school by the same proportion and does not distort the (efficient) level of schooling. The interest tax component of the income tax, however, is now inefficient for two reasons. Not only does it distort the saving decision, but by lowering the after-tax rate of return it raises the present value of the marginal benefits of attending school without raising marginal cost and thus induces a schooling level that is too high (see Heckman, 1976; and Driffill and Rosen, 1983).

Governments are, of course, aware that income taxes distort saving and human capital decisions and have created vehicles to reduce these distortions (as well as achieve other objectives). This brings us to the two papers in this session. There are two main ways to avoid the distortions caused by the taxation of interest income: tax deferral and tax pre-payment. Vehicles like Registered Retirement Savings Plans (RRSPs) defer taxes; contributions are deductible, interest on principal accumulates tax free, and then income taxes are paid on principal and interest when funds are withdrawn. RESPs are akin to a tax-pre-payment instrument: contributions are paid out of after-tax income and inside the RESP, funds grow at the pre-tax interest rate. But, as Kevin observes while the principal is not taxed on withdrawal, accumulated interest may be taxed and the 20% subsidy for contributions may not offset this tax. So on efficiency grounds it is difficult to see why a government would create RESPs when RRSPs already exist.

Can RRSPs make a non-linear income-tax system function as a proportional consumption tax? Elsewhere I have argued that in a world without a schooling decision, if agents act to minimize the present value of taxes paid over the lifetime, the intuition of the tax deferral system outlined above works and the answer is "yes" (see Burbidge, 2004). Adding a schooling decision to this model, I show in the Appendix that if it is optimal for the individual to contribute to an RRSP account during the schooling period then the non-linear income-tax system will not distort the human capital decision, that is, each person will choose the same level of human capital with the income tax and RRSP system in place as they would have chosen had there been no income tax. Alternatively, I show that if it is optimal not to contribute to RRSPs during the schooling period then the level of schooling chosen may be below the efficient level. The reason is that in a non-linear tax system, if optimal RRSP contributions equal zero, the person may face a higher marginal tax rate in the post-education period than in the schooling period. This lowers the marginal benefits of human capital acquisition relative to the marginal costs and induces too little schooling. In these circumstances there may be a case for government subsidization of university education.

Accordingly, when Kirk and Jim find that effective tax rates (ETRs) on human capital declined between 1998 and 2003 it may be that neither the 1998 nor the 2003 tax systems distorted the human capital decision. Those deciding in 1998 whether or not to attend university may have used the

1998 tax system, including the associated RRSP system, to forecast what the tax system would be over their lifetimes. If they obeyed the assumptions of the model described above and they used RRSPs during their schooling years the 1998 tax system may not have distorted their university attendance decision. The same may be true of those making a similar decision in 2003 with the 2003 tax system in mind. On the other hand, if those attending university did not use RRSPs then either or both tax systems may have induced a less than efficient level of participation in university education. It is important to realize that changes in the tax system before or during someone's university career can distort the university decision; changes in the tax system after one has finished education amount to increases or decreases in taxes on rents to human capital that already exist.

This discussion raises the issue of how a student forecasts earnings and taxes with and without a university education. The individual should be trying to guess what the earnings level would be with each education level and what taxes would be payable under each alternative. This is, of course, a difficult forecasting exercise. Does one use current cross-sectional earnings? Does one attempt to forecast expected earnings for one's cohort based on the experience of recent cohorts? These sorts of questions lead us into a discussion of age, year, and cohort effects in earnings data, a subject to which I turn in the next section. Before doing so, however, I should repeat that my "cheap" theoretical model may be interpreted as complementing Kevin's attack on RESPs. Not only may the real effects of this program conflict with its stated redistributional objectives, the RESP system may distort what would otherwise be a relatively efficient personal-income-tax-RRSP system.

Some Empirical Issues

The problem of identifying (the linear component of) age, year, and cohort effects in earnings (or other) data is well known. Age is identically equal to observation year minus birth year. Burbidge, Magee and Robb (2000) explore the sensitivity of median earnings forecasts to assumptions about the relative importance of year and cohort effects. If the economy were in stationary state, all cross-sectional real age-earnings profiles, conditional on education level, would coincide with each other. It would be straightforward to predict what earnings would be for any earnings quantile and education level. Figure 1 graphs smoothed real median earnings for

Figure 1: Median Earnings for Non-University Grads: Canadian Males Aged 25–60

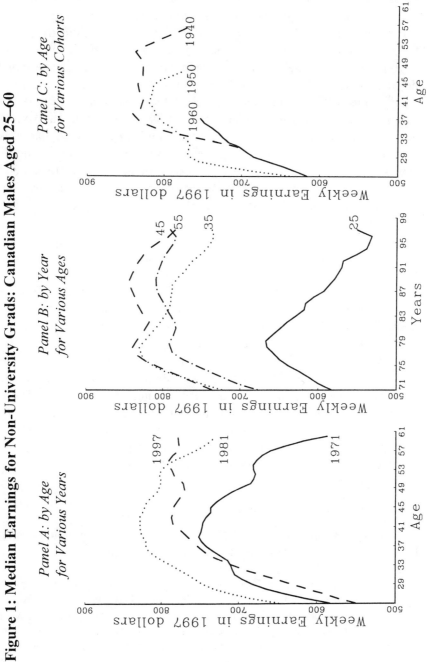

Panel A: by Age
for Various Years

Panel B: by Year
for Various Ages

Panel C: by Age
for Various Cohorts

Canadian males aged 25 to 60 without a university degree. Inspection of panels A and B reveals that cross-sectional, real-age earnings profiles shifted substantially over the 1971 to 1997 data period, tending to rise for the first ten years and then to decline between 1981 and 1997, particularly at younger ages.[1] Panel C graphs the available segments of age-earnings profiles for the 1940, 1950, and 1960 cohorts. Although the 1940 and 1950 profiles intersect each other there is a clear downward trend in cohort real earnings over time. Figure 2 contains the graphs for males with a university degree. Again panels A and B point to an upward trend in real earnings over the 1970s and to a downward trend at all ages since 1981. Panel C shows that successive cohorts of university graduates have had to contend with lower real earnings. It is difficult to be sure but it would appear that year effects dominate the data for the 1970s and cohort effects have been more important since 1981.

The real earnings of the 1940, 1950, and 1960 cohorts are listed in Table 1 together with the university to non-university earnings ratios. Looking across the cohorts the earnings ratios are most different at younger ages and tend to converge at older ages. Since calculations of ETRs are probably more sensitive to earnings differences at younger ages I would think ETR calculations could be affected by the different patterns across the cohorts. One way to proceed would be to follow Burbidge *et al.* by generating two predictions of (median) real earnings, one for university and another for high school. The first could attribute recent changes to cohort effects and the second could attribute recent changes to year effects. These alternatives should provide some indication of the sensitivity of ETRs to the assumptions required to make earnings projections. In addition, one should be able to calculate a standard error for any particular ETR. Both of these would enable researchers to compare the sensitivity of the ETRs to the tax system and the earnings projections.[2]

---

[1]Figure 1 updates Figure 9.3 in Burbidge, Magee and Robb (2000, p. 197). Please see this paper for details on data selection and smoothing.

[2]I am indebted to Jim Davies for drawing my attention to the recent paper by Heckman, Lochner and Todd (2003) who have this to say: "collections of micro data over many years have made cohort analyses possible, and these analyses reveal that wage patterns have changed dramatically across cohorts and that cross-sections no longer approximate cohort or life cycle change ... the rates of return to schooling estimated from cross-sections of workers ... are likely to differ from the rates of return faced by cohorts making their schooling decisions".

Figure 2: Median Earnings for University Grads: Canadian Males Aged 25–60

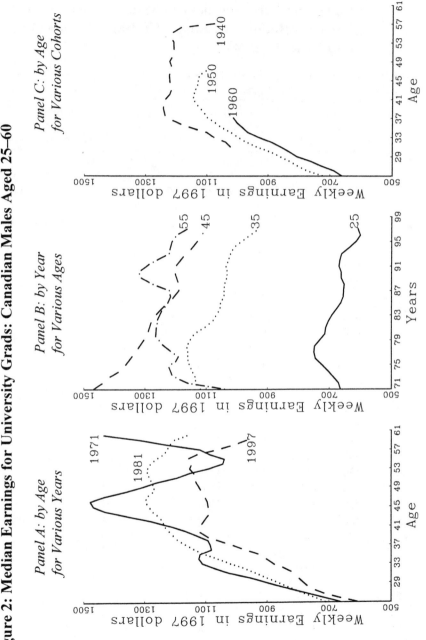

Table 1: Median Weekly Earnings by Age, Cohort, and Education Level and the University to Non-University Earnings Ratios: Canadian SCF Data for Full-Time, Full-Year, Male Workers

| | Cohorts | | | | | | UN/NON-UN RATIO | | |
| | 1940 | | 1950 | | 1960 | | | | |
AGE	NON-UN	UN	NON-UN	UN	NON-UN	UN	1940	1950	1960
25			639	725	616	663		1.14	1.08
26			685	775	631	687		1.13	1.09
27			723	804	647	727		1.11	1.12
28			756	832	666	764		1.10	1.15
29			767	863	684	808		1.13	1.18
30			771	895	694	833		1.16	1.20
31	705	1024	766	940	703	860	1.45	1.23	1.23
32	730	1040	768	973	717	891	1.43	1.27	1.24
33	760	1078	775	1000	724	932	1.42	1.29	1.29
34	792	1101	784	1022	730	966	1.39	1.31	1.32
35	813	1155	790	1054	738	984	1.42	1.33	1.33
36	828	1200	801	1075	748	1003	1.45	1.34	1.34
37	838	1232	807	1099	753	1014	1.47	1.36	1.35
38	841	1242	812	1109			1.48	1.37	
39	832	1242	813	1122			1.49	1.38	
40	826	1242	820	1136			1.50	1.39	
41	828	1235	819	1145			1.49	1.40	
42	829	1222	817	1143			1.47	1.40	
43	835	1217	816	1138			1.46	1.40	
44	835	1219	814	1131			1.46	1.39	
45	834	1224	806	1130			1.47	1.40	
46	828	1224	791	1126			1.48	1.42	
47	828	1221	776	1103			1.48	1.42	
48	828	1218					1.47		
49	828	1223					1.48		
50	833	1214					1.46		
51	838	1216					1.45		
52	828	1204					1.46		
53	814	1210					1.49		
54	800	1220					1.52		
55	786	1213					1.54		
56	772	1188					1.54		
57	778	1064					1.37		

John B. Burbidge

I suspect that cohort effects may also be important in Kevin's work on RESPs. Even though RRSPs were introduced in 1957 they were not used much until the 1970s and there are certainly big differences across cohorts in RRSP holdings. The same may be true of RESPs. It may take some time for people to react to the changes made to RESPs in 1998 and those using RESPs in the 1999 Survey of Financial Security might differ from those using RESPs in a more recent SFS. It would also be useful to control for three marital statuses: married or common law, single never married, and the rest. I think the last two categories might exhibit very different RESP-holding behaviours.

Appendix

This appendix extends the two-period life-cycle model in Burbidge (2004) to consider human capital accumulation.

I use this notation.

$s \equiv$ time in period 1 spent in school, $0 \le s \le 1$

$f(s) \equiv$ direct costs of going to school; $f'(s) > 0, f''(s) > 0$

$e_1 \equiv$ real earnings in period 1 if person works full time

$e_2(s) \equiv$ real earnings in period 2, $e_2'(s) > 0, e_2''(s) < 0$

$c_i \equiv$ real consumption in period i

$x_1 \equiv$ RRSP contribution in period 1

$y_i \equiv$ taxable income in period i

$w_i \equiv$ wealth held outside RRSPs at the beginning of period i

$r \equiv$ pre-tax real interest rate, inside or outside RRSPs

$\tau(y_i) \equiv$ income tax function for any period

$t^c \equiv$ proportional consumption tax rate

I assume that the income-tax function is differentiable, increasing and strictly convex. In addition, I presume all marginal tax rates lie between zero and unity.

The consumer faces the following constraints.

$$y_1 = e_1(1-s) - f(s) - x_1, \; x_1 \geq 0$$

$$y_2 = e_2(s) + (1+r)x_1 + rI(w_2)w_2$$

$$I(w_2) = \begin{cases} 0, \; w_2 \leq 0 \\ 1, \; w_2 > 0 \end{cases}$$

$$w_1 = 0 \tag{1}$$

$$w_2 = e_1(1-s) - f(s) - x_1 - \tau(y_1) - (1+t^c)c_1$$

$$w_3 = 0 \; or$$

$$(1+t^c)\left(c_1 + \frac{c_2}{1+r}\right) = e_1(1-s) - f(s) - \tau(y_1) + \frac{e_2(s) - \tau(y_2)}{1+r}$$

The last equation is the individual's budget constraint. In a life-cycle model without gifts or bequests the present value of consumption must equal the present value of earnings, less direct schooling costs and the present value of income taxes paid. I assume that if wealth held outside RRSPs is positive the interest income on this wealth is taxable. It may be optimal for the individual to borrow to make a larger contribution to the RRSP than would be possible otherwise. Thus w_2 could be negative. As written, the income-tax system is like that in Canada after 1982 where $I(w_2) = 1$ only when $w_2 > 0$.

In this setting, a consumption tax induces a parallel inward shift of the consumer's budget and is equivalent to a lump-sum tax. Working out the effects of the income tax is a little more difficult. To reduce notational clutter set $t^c = 0$.

The consumer's problem is to choose c_1, c_2, s and x_1 to maximize utility $u(c_1, c_2)$ subject to the constraints listed above. Using (1) write

$$c_1 = e_1(1-s) - f(s) - x_1 - w_2 - \tau(y_1)$$

$$c_2 = e_2(s) + (1+r)x_1 + (1+r)w_2 - \tau(y_2), \tag{2}$$

so the consumer's problem can be rewritten as:

$$\underset{0 \le s \le 1,\, x_1 \ge 0,\, w_2}{Max} \quad u\begin{pmatrix} e_1(1-s) - f(s) - x_1 - w_2 - \tau(y_2), \\ e_2(s) + (1+r)x_1 + (1+r)w_2 - \tau(y_2) \end{pmatrix} \quad (3)$$

Assuming an interior solution for s, the Kuhn-Tucker conditions are

$$-(e_1 + f'(s))(1 - \tau'(y_1))u_1 + e_2'(s)(1 - \tau'(y_2))u_2 = 0 \qquad (4)$$

$$x_1 \left[\underbrace{\tau'(y_1) - 1)u_1 + (1+r)(1 - \tau'(y_2))u_2}_{\le 0} \right] = 0 \qquad (5)$$

and

$$-u_1 + (1 + r(1 - I\tau'(y_2)))u_2 = 0. \qquad (6)$$

Optimal behaviour depends on the shape of the tax function, the person's preferences for current and future consumption and the pattern of earnings. In Burbidge (2004) I argue it is plausible that in an optimal plan $w_2 \le 0$, and thus $I = 0$. Then (6) implies

$$u_2 = \frac{u_1}{1+r}.$$

Substituting this equation into (4) and (5) obtain

$$(e_1 + f'(s))(1 - \tau'(y_1)) = \frac{e_2'(s)}{1+r}(1 - \tau'(y_2)) \qquad (7)$$

and

$$x_1 \left[\underbrace{\tau'(y_1) - 1) + (1 - \tau'(y_2))}_{\le 0} \right] = 0. \qquad (8)$$

If $x_1 > 0$, then (7) and (8) imply

$$y_1 = y_2 \ and$$
$$e_1 + f'(s) = \frac{e_2'(s)}{1+r} \ .$$

The latter equation is the condition for the efficient level of human capital. If $x_1 > 0$, then it's possible that

$$1 - \tau'(y_2) < 1 - \tau'(y_1) \ and$$
$$e_1 + f'(s) < \frac{e_2'(s)}{1+r} \ ,$$

so too little human capital is accumulated.

References

Burbidge, J.B. 2004. "Tax Deferred Savings Plans and Interest Deductibility", *Canadian Journal of Economics* 37(3).

Burbidge, J.B., L. Magee and A.L. Robb. 2000. "Cohort, Year and Age Effects in Canadian Wage Data", in F.T. Denton, D. Fretz and B.G. Spencer (eds.), *Independence and Economic Security in Old Age.* Vancouver, BC: UBC Press, 183-214.

Driffill, E.J. and H.S. Rosen. 1983. "Taxation and Excess Burden: A Life-Cycle Approach", *International Economic Review* 24, 671-683.

Heckman, J.J. 1976. "A Life Cycle Model of Earnings, Learning and Consumption", *Journal of Political Economy* 84 (August), S11-S44.

Heckman, J.J., L.J. Lochner and P.E. Todd. 2003. "Fifty Years of Mincer Earnings Regressions". Unpublished paper.

Who Uses RESPs and Why

Kevin Milligan

Introduction

One of the primary justifications for government participation in the financing of postsecondary education is to correct for imperfections in the credit market. If individuals cannot access credit, they may underinvest in the acquisition of education. A government intervention that improves credit access for constrained students carries the potential to ameliorate the imperfection and result in efficient education choices. Governments around the world subsidize student loans and tuition, perhaps with this motivation in mind.

In addition to subsidizing student loans, the Canadian federal government also provides special tax treatment of savings through Registered Education Savings Plans (RESPs) and the accompanying Canada Education Savings Grants (CESGs). If household savings rise as a result of these tax measures, then dependence on credit markets is decreased. Through this

Research funding provided by SSHRC. I thank the NBER for hosting me while this paper was written. I thank Alfred Kong for excellent research assistance, and Catherine Deri and Sonia Laszlo for providing helpful comments on an earlier draft. Helpful comments were also received from the discussant John Burbidge and other participants at the John Deutsch Institute conference on higher education held at Queen's University in February 2004.

mechanism, tax preferences for savings could assist in improving access to postsecondary education in Canada.

Improving access appears to be the objective of RESPs and CESGs. These measures were included as components of the "Canadian Opportunities Strategy", announced in the 1998 federal budget. The goal of the strategy was clearly laid out:

> The *Canadian Opportunities Strategy* will help ensure that all Canadians — especially those with low and middle incomes — have an equal opportunity to participate in the changing economy. It will do so by reducing financial barriers and other obstacles that stand in the way of acquiring skills and knowledge. (Canada. Department of Finance, 1998, p. 7)

The particular aims of the RESP and CESG components of the Canadian Opportunities Strategy, are to "encourage families to save early for their children's education" (ibid., p. 35). Funds contributed to RESPs may represent net additions to household savings, or the contributions may simply be reallocations of assets from other accounts; funds that would have been saved even in the absence of the RESP and CESG measures.[1] No matter which case holds, however, families who participate in RESPs and CESGs are likely made better off through their participation. They may be better off because they save more, or they may be better off because they can replace their own savings with the government transfers. Either way, if the families who participate are families who would have financial difficulty accessing credit, then the RESPs and CESG tax measures will contribute to the stated objective of the Canadian Opportunities Strategy.

The goal of this paper is to empirically examine RESP participation to assess who uses RESPs and CESGs and to begin an examination of why those families do so. In the empirical work that follows, I show that participation in RESPs is heavily concentrated among high-income, high-wealth, and high-education families. The analysis suggests that the most important barriers to participation among low-income families may be the smaller probability of postsecondary attendance and the fixed costs of account initiation.

---

[1] Recent evidence in Ma (2003) suggests that contributions to education savings plans in the United States (so-called "529 plans") have increased household savings. The broader literature on tax incentives and savings, as surveyed in Bernheim (2002), is inconclusive on this question.

The Speech from the Throne on February 2, 2004 included an admission that "participation by lower income families — often those who could most benefit — has been disappointingly low". It is expected that the federal government will soon present new proposals for the RESP and CESG programs. While this paper will not analyze any new proposals directly, I aim to contribute to the understanding of what motivates contributions to the programs. An understanding of how these decisions are made is an important building block for any policy reform.

In the rest of the paper I first describe and assess the tax treatment of RESPs. This is followed by the presentation of aggregate statistics on RESP participation and contributions. Next, I provide empirical evidence of the patterns of RESP participation using a microdata sample. I then lay out several explanations for the striking lack of participation among low-income families, and present an empirical examination of some of the possibilities. Finally, I conclude with an analysis of the RESP and CESG tax measures and discuss some possibilities for reform.

The Tax Treatment of RESPs

The federal government introduced RESPs in 1974, but it was not until reforms in 1997 and 1998 that participation became more widespread. The discussion below is drawn from Canada Customs and Revenue Agency (2002) and Donnelly, Welch and Young (1999).

Contributions to RESP accounts come out of after-tax income — no deduction is allowed. Income earned on funds inside the RESP is exempt from annual taxation. This is potentially of great benefit because funds accrue more quickly when returns are not taxed annually. Finally, some withdrawals from the RESP are taxed. Taken together, the tax treatment is comparable to, although less favourable than, Tax-Prepaid Savings Plans (as proposed by Kesselman and Poschmann, 2001), or Roth Individual Retirement Accounts in the United States. I discuss in greater detail the treatment of contributions and withdrawals in turn.

A specific beneficiary is nominally attached to contributions. The contributors (called "subscribers" in the legislation) need not be related to the beneficiary. However, a family plan can designate several beneficiaries, related to the subscriber by blood or adoption. The funds in the family plan can then be withdrawn by any of the joint beneficiaries. There are no age limits to beneficiaries, but accounts must be closed 26 years after being opened. In a given year, total contributions across subscribers are limited to $4,000 per beneficiary, with a further constraint of $42,000 over a lifetime. There are no foreign investment restrictions for funds held in RESPs, as there are with Registered Retirement Savings Plans (RRSPs).

The federal government has paid Canada Education Savings Grants into RESP accounts since 1998. The grant is paid as a match of 20 cents on the dollar for contributions up to $2,000, making a maximal grant equal to $400. CESGs are only paid to beneficiaries aged 17 and under, and are exempt from taxation when granted. If the beneficiary (or, in the case of a family plan, the beneficiaries) do not attend postsecondary education, then the original CESG principal must be returned to the government.

Withdrawals of the original principal contributed to the RESP account are treated differently from withdrawals of the accumulated income. The original principal can be withdrawn at any time without tax consequence. In contrast, the accumulated income earned on the principal (and the CESG amounts) is taxable on withdrawal, with the tax treatment taking one of two forms depending on the postsecondary student status of the beneficiary.

If the beneficiary is enrolled full-time in a qualifying postsecondary program, then a withdrawal called an Educational Assistance Payment is permitted. Educational assistance payments are treated as taxable income for the beneficiary in the year of withdrawal. This taxation of withdrawals is mitigated somewhat by the generous non-refundable credits claimed by students.[2] However, the taxation of accrued income makes the RESP a less attractive proposition than other tax-preferred accounts (such as Tax-Prepaid Savings Plans) which do not tax accrued income at all.

The second type of withdrawal is called an accumulated income payment. If the beneficiary does not attend postsecondary education by the age of 21, or if the beneficiary dies, then funds may be withdrawn from the RESP through an accumulated income payment.[3] These payments are included in the subscriber's taxable income in the year of withdrawal. Moreover, the accumulated income payment is subject to an additional surtax of 20% (12% in Quebec). Both the income tax and the surtax on the payment can be avoided, however, by rolling the payment directly into the

---

[2]A typical full-time student in 2004 might claim $400 per month for the education credit, $4,025 for the tuition credit, and $8,012 for the basic personal amount, totalling $16,837 per year.

[3]The RESP must have been in existence for ten years and the recipient of the accumulated income payment must be a permanent resident of Canada.

subscriber's RRSP account. The rollover requires adequate RRSP contribution room and is subject to a lifetime maximum of $50,000.

The basic economic effect of the RESP is the possibility of tax-exempt accrual of investment income. Given the complexity of the RESP rules, the tax-exempt accrual is achieved in a very expensive way for society, as resources are diverted to pay for the administration of the accounts in government, accounting firms, and financial institutions. As a counter-example, taxpayers in the United Kingdom may contribute up to £7,000 per annum to an individual savings account out of after tax-income (Adam and Shaw, 2003). Income on the contributions is simply exempted from tax and one is not even required to report to the tax authorities that one holds an account (United Kingdom, 2002, p. 11). The administrative burden of individual savings accounts seems smaller than that imposed on society by RESPs.

Aggregate RESP Statistics

To begin the empirical analysis, I draw together aggregate statistics on RESP contributions and CESG payments from various government publications. The primary source is the *Estimates* published annually by the Treasury Board of Canada. I use the retrospective *Department Performance Reports* for Human Resources Development Canada (HRDC), published as Part III of the *Estimates*.[4] In addition, HRDC publishes administrative data on RESPs in the *CESG Quarterly Statistical Review*. Finally, I take data from the *Tax Expenditures* publication produced by the Department of Finance.

The statistics are reported in Table 1. The columns of the table indicate the fiscal year of the data.[5] The first row displays the annual expenditures on CESGs to families, not including administrative costs. The program started in 1998–99, paying out $267.3 million dollars. Since CESGs can be

---

[4]The data on CESGs in the Departmental Performance Reports is the same as reported in the official Public Accounts of Canada.

[5]Fiscal years run from April 1 to March 31. The tax-expenditure data in the fourth row is on a calendar year basis. The data for tax expenditures is therefore aligned with the first year of the fiscal year: 1997–98 contains the 1997 data, 1998–99 contains the 1998 data, and so on.

Table 1: Aggregate Statistics on Registered Education Savings Plans and Canada Education Savings Grants

	1997–98	1998–99	1999–2000	2000–01	2001–02	2002–03
CESG expenditures[a]	–	267.3	334.1	433.5	334.2	342.9
Percentage of children with RESPs[b]	4.7	10.0	15.0	20.0	23.0	26.0
Total amount held in RESPs[c]	2,398	3,920	5,414	7,153	9,000	–
Estimated Tax Expenditure for RESP[d]	32	30	40	80	78	105

Notes: Data in rows 1, 2, and 4 are in millions of current dollars.
Sources: [a] Annual Department Performance Reports for HRDC, various years (*Estimates*, Part III, Treasury Board of Canada).
[b] Annual Department Performance Reports for HRDC, various years (*Estimates*, Part III, Treasury Board of Canada).
[c] Canada Education Savings Grants Quarterly Statistical Review, April 2002. Data for 2001–02 comes from Department Performance Reports for HRDC (*Estimates*, Part III, Treasury Board of Canada).
[d] *Tax Expenditures and Evaluations 2002* (Department of Finance, 2002). The tax expenditure data is on a calendar year basis, not fiscal year.

claimed retrospectively back to 1998, some of the increase in the subsequent two years may reflect claims for "unused grants from 1998–99. By 2002–03, the expenditure settled at $342.9 million.

The scale of these expenditures relative to other federal interventions in postsecondary education is impressively large. The federal government expects to spend $406.5 million on student loans in 2003–04, and $240 million on the Canada Research Chairs program. Spending on either of these programs could be approximately doubled if the amount of money spent on the CESG were to be allocated in those directions. The $433.5 million spent on CESGs in 2000–01 would have been sufficient to send a cheque of $830.62 to each of the 521,900 full-time undergraduate students enrolled in that year.[6] These examples provide the context of the fiscal commitment to the CESG.

The second row reports the estimated percentage of children aged 0 to 17 who were beneficiaries of an RESP in each year. From 4.7% in 1997–98 before the reform, the participation rate has grown steadily to 26.0% by 2002–03.

In the third row, I provide the estimated stock of RESP holdings for each year. Until 2001–02, the data came from HRDC directly (Canada. HRDC, 2002), while the 2001–02 data is from a report in Treasury Board of Canada (2003). In 1997–98, $2.4 billion was held in RESPs. The amount grew by less than $2 billion per year, up to an estimated $9 billion in 2001–02. In 2002, the total stock of household assets stood at $4.37 trillion, meaning that RESPs represented about 0.21% of household assets.[7] RRSP assets in 2001 totalled $292.5 billion, more than 32 times the RESP total for that year.[8] Data on annual RESP contributions is not publicly available, but the 2003 *Report on Planning on Priorities* estimates contributions of $2.1 billion in 2002–03. This is equal to 7.8% of the $27.1 billion contributed to RRSPs in 2002.[9]

---

[6]Data on enrolment is taken from Statistics Canada's *The Daily* for April 17, 2003.

[7]Total assets data comes from CANSIM vector V33462.

[8]Data on RRSP assets is taken from Statistics Canada's *The Daily* for November 17, 2003.

[9]Data on RRSP contributions is taken from Statistics Canada's *The Daily* for October 23, 2003.

The final row of the table provides the estimated tax expenditures for the forgone tax revenue on RESP income. Since the tax expenditure calculations assume that all income would be completely taxed in the absence of RESPs, these estimates represent an upper bound to the revenue cost of RESPs. In 2002–03, the estimate is $105 million. Compared to the cost of the CESG, the forgone tax revenue on accumulating income appears relatively small. However, as the stock of savings in RESPs grows in the future with the maturing of the program, this tax expenditure will grow.

Who Uses RESPs? An Empirical Examination of Incidence

The aggregate statistics in the previous section provided information on some of the overall trends in the RESP and CESG programs. In order to go deeper into the numbers, I turn to an analysis of microdata from 1999. I draw the sample for analysis from the master files of the 1999 Survey of Financial Security.[10] The survey combines information on wealth, labour market activity, demographics, and attitudes about household finances. In particular, the master files have the advantage that RESP holdings are broken out separately from other assets. The family is the unit of observation in the Survey of Financial Security, meaning that RESP holdings, along with the other wealth measures, are recorded on a family basis.[11]

The analysis below breaks down RESP participation against various demographic measures. With this analysis, I can compare the incidence of RESP use against the goals set out in the *Canadian Opportunities Strategy*. Assessing the causal importance of the different factors will be the focus of the later section, where I pursue a multivariate analysis.

---

[10]More information on the Survey of Financial Security is available in Statistics Canada (2001).

[11]More precisely, I use the Census Family as the unit of observation. A Census Family is comprised of parent(s) with their children, childless couples, or grandparents living with their grandchildren. I also include single individuals.

The Evidence

Table 2 displays several statistics about RESP account balances, as observed in the survey in 1999. Overall, 5.8% of families held an RESP. Among those who hold an RESP, the mean balance in the account was $7,105. The distribution of assets is highly skewed across families, with the median balance at less than half the value of the mean. A large proportion of the families in the sample, however, do not have children living in the home. The next rows in the table break down the sample into families who have no children and those who have one or more children. Although anyone can make contributions to an RESP in the name of a beneficiary, the participation rate for families without children in the home is slightly less than 1%; less than one-sixteenth of the rate for families with children.

The mean account balance for those without children is $13,542 — more than twice the level of those with children. This disparity is much smaller at the median, suggesting the difference at the mean is driven mostly by large balances at the high end of the distribution.

The next table reports statistics on RESPs broken down across demographic and economic categories. For this analysis, I discard the families with no children and focus on those with one or more children. Both the participation rate and the mean conditional on participation are shown, along with the breakdown of the distribution of families across the categories.

The first set of results in Table 3 considers marital status, followed by children. Approximately 83% of the sample has two parents in the family. Participation and the average RESP balance for married families are both about twice the corresponding figures for single families. Comparing across families with different numbers of children, participation rates are similar. The mean account balance increases monotonically with the number of children, suggesting that families may be opening accounts for each of their children.

The next two categories look at the age of the youngest and the age of the oldest child in the family. In a mature RESP system, one might expect that the proportion of children with an account would be higher for older children, as parents who only contribute sporadically would have more chances to contribute. However, since the RESP rules were liberalized only in 1998, the breakdown by child age effectively records the pattern for a newly introduced program. For either age measure, the participation rate in the 15 to 17 category is about half the participation rate in the zero to four

Table 2: RESP Participation and Account Balance for All Families

	Observations	Proportion Positive	Mean	Std Dev	25th	Median	75th
				Conditional on Positive			
RESP account balance	15933	0.058	7105	17793	1700	3500	6800
Number of children	1.000						
zero	0.681	0.010	13542	39310	2000	4200	10000
positive number of children	0.319	0.160	6277	12343	1600	3200	6000

Notes: All values reported in 1999 Canadian dollars. Sample weights used in calculations. Data is taken from the Survey of Financial Security, using all 15,933 observations.

Kevin Milligan

Table 3: RESP Participation and Account Balance for Families with Children

	Distribution	Proportion Positive	Conditional Mean
Marital status	1.000		
Married/common-law	0.832	0.178	6,480
Single	0.168	0.068	3,663
Number of children	1.000		
1	0.425	0.138	4,986
2	0.406	0.185	6,448
3 or more	0.169	0.155	8,685
Age of youngest child	1.000		
Age 0–4	0.362	0.190	3,675
Age 5–9	0.248	0.167	8,726
Age 10–14	0.245	0.149	7,830
Age 15–17	0.145	0.090	7,857
Age of oldest child	1.000		
Age 0–4	0.196	0.205	2,648
Age 5–9	0.230	0.180	7,806
Age 10–14	0.296	0.161	6,230
Age 15–17	0.277	0.110	9,065
Income quintiles	1.000		
1 (low)	0.200	0.080	6,920
2	0.200	0.140	4,225
3	0.200	0.125	5,640
4	0.200	0.176	5,133
5 (high)	0.200	0.279	8,131

Table 3 *(continued)*

	Distribution	*Proportion Positive*	*Conditional Mean*
Wealth quintiles	1.000		
1 (low)	0.200	0.051	2,118
2	0.200	0.131	3,197
3	0.200	0.174	3,801
4	0.200	0.164	6,724
5 (high)	02.00	0.280	9,755
Older parent's education	1.000		
Less than high school	0.179	0.068	3,990
High school graduate	0.203	0.132	5,538
Some postsecondary	0.414	0.165	6,716
University degree	0.204	0.259	6,614
Immigrant status	1.000		
Born in Canada	0.736	0.138	6,614
Born outside Canada	0.264	0.222	5,696
Age of older parent	1.000		
Less than 25	0.021	0.068	3,084
25–29	0.070	0.116	1,719
30–34	0.149	0.177	3,072
35–39	0.233	0.160	5,842
40–44	0.234	0.158	6,540
45–49	0.160	0.180	9,066
50–54	0.085	0.179	9,695
55 and over	0.049	0.117	6,257

Table 3 *(continued)*

	Distribution	*Proportion Positive*	*Conditional Mean*
Province	1.000		
Newfoundland	0.019	0.149	6,119
Prince Edward Island	0.005	0.173	2,758
Nova Scotia	0.032	0.170	6,630
New Brunswick	0.025	0.146	6,058
Quebec	0.245	0.110	4,309
Ontario	0.377	0.183	6,542
Manitoba	0.037	0.158	6,932
Saskatchewan	0.033	0.217	7,137
Alberta	0.103	0.153	9,107
British Columbia	0.126	0.180	5,519
Urban area size	1.000		
Rural	0.187	0.166	5,731
0 to 29,999	0.164	0.121	7,130
30,000 to 99,999	0.101	0.151	4,827
100,000 to 499,999	0.102	0.163	9,275
500,000 and up	0.445	0.173	5,916

Notes: All values reported in 1999 Canadian dollars. Sample weights used in calculations.
Data taken from the 1999 Survey of Financial Security, based on the 5,394 families with children.

age group. Why is there such a strong difference? One possibility is that the fixed costs of setting up an account (the time and effort taken) are perceived to be greater than the benefit over the shorter time horizon for older children.

To examine the effect of income, I break the sample into quintiles by family pre-tax income. The participation rate in the lowest income quintile is 0.08, rising by a factor of more than three to 0.279 for the highest quintile. Only 27.5% of RESP participants are in the bottom two income quintiles. In the same manner, RESP statistics across quintiles formed on total net wealth are presented next. The participation rates across wealth quintiles are even more skewed towards the high end, with only 5% participation in the lowest wealth quintile.

For education, I break down the sample into four categories by the education level of the older parent. The participation rate among those with less than high school is only 0.068, while those with university degrees have participation rates four times higher at 0.259. Since education, income, and other factors are strongly correlated with each other, a multivariate analysis is necessary to address any causal inferences.

In the sample, 26.4% of families have one parent born outside Canada. Interestingly, the participation rate among these families is 62% higher, at 0.222. Again, this could be a result of other demographic and economic variables that differ across immigrant and non-immigrant families, so the multivariate analysis later is necessary to make stronger inferences.

For the age of the older parent, participation rates are fairly flat after 30 years of age, although the mean account balance grows strongly with age. Families at middle ages have higher income and wealth levels, which might explain their higher participation. Finally, the breakdown by geography is presented. The province with the highest participation rate is Saskatchewan, at 21.7% of families with children. In contrast, only 11% of Quebec families hold an RESP account. Looking at the population of the area of residence, the lowest participation rate is found in small urban centres, with less than 30 thousand in population.

Assessing the Evidence

The evidence presented in this section indicates clearly that the RESP program is used mostly by high-income, high-wealth, and high-parental education households. Since the Canada Education Savings Grants are paid to RESP participants, it can also be concluded that the distributional impact of the CESG is skewed towards higher income Canadians. How does this finding compare to the objectives of the program?

The goal of the *Canadian Opportunities Strategy* is to focus govern-ment assistance on those with "low and middle incomes". It is clear that this stated goal is not being met with the RESP and the CESG programs. Beyond the originally stated goal, the economic justification for the pro-gram relies on difficulties with access to credit markets. High-income and high-wealth households are not likely to be credit constrained, suggesting that the credit constraint economic rationale for the program is also dubious. Taken together, this evidence finds no justification for the RESP and CESG tax measures as a useful tool for government intervention in postsecondary education.

Discussion: Why Don't Low-Income Households Use RESPs?

The statistical analysis strongly suggests that low-income households do not contribute to RESPs. While this finding is relevant to the evaluation of the current structure of the program, a deeper analysis of *why* low-income households do not use RESPs may prove helpful for any changes to the RESP program, or for understanding other savings incentive measures. In this section, I put forward five explanations that may underlie the low participation of low-income households.

Children from Low-Income Families are Less Likely to Attend

One reason for lower participation is the smaller likelihood of post-secondary attendance for children from low-income households. Because non-attendance leads to tax penalties on withdrawals from RESPs, families who do not expect their children to attend are not likely to contribute to RESPs. Junor and Usher document (2002, p. 48) that university participation among 18 to 21 year olds is 39% in the highest family income quartile, more than double the 19% rate for the lowest quartile.[12] Participation in any postsecondary program (including community colleges) does not differ as much between the quartiles, at 70% for the highest and 56% for the lowest. Although RESP funds can be used for any type of postsecondary education, the costs of attending college might be lower than university. So, it is not clear which is the better measure. In either case, differential attendance can explain some of the gap in RESP participation.

---

[12]The data is drawn from the Survey of Labour and Income Dynamics. The calculations are made by taking a sample of 16-year-olds between 1993 and 1996 and observing whether they attend any postsecondary education by 1998.

Moving beyond observed behaviour, the 2002 Survey of Approaches to Education Planning reports on the expectations of parents for their children's education attainment. In Figure 1, I graph the proportion of families in different income groups reporting that they expect their child to attend university, or any postsecondary education.[13] Among families with income less than $30,000, 49.6% expect their child to go to university, and 75.3% expect attendance at some form of postsecondary institution. In contrast, the comparable numbers for families with incomes of $80,000 or more expect university in 66.0% of the cases, and any postsecondary in 90.2%. These patterns of expectation line up with the observed patterns of RESP participation, suggesting that expectations may matter for the participation decision.

Low-Income Households Face Information Barriers

Savings behaviour is closely connected to attitudes and information about household finances. Becker and Mulligan (1997) develop a theoretical framework in which households must expend effort to learn how to think about future expenditures. Someone from a propitious upbringing might learn these things from his or her parents or peers, while those from less fortunate backgrounds may never have learned. In the model, knowledge about why and how to save is a key determinant of savings rates.

There is strong evidence in favour of this type of model for savings. Ameriks, Caplin and Leahy (2003) provide evidence that financial planning is a key determinant of wealth accumulation — those who have a "propensity to plan" save much more than those who don't. Bernheim, Garrett and Maki (2001) and Bernheim and Garrett (2003) show that financial education is strongly related to attitudes about savings, and also subsequent savings behaviour.[14]

---

[13]The statistics come from special tabulations on the data performed by Statistics Canada.

[14]These papers use a non-experimental causal framework which allows for inferences about financial education even in the presence of unobserved differences in the propensity to save.

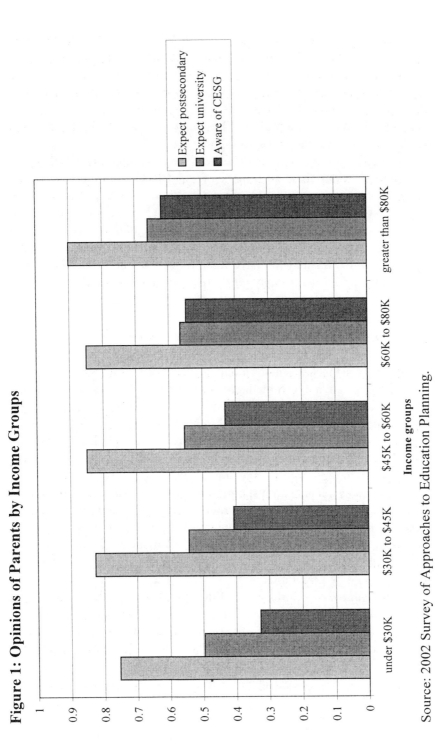

Figure 1: Opinions of Parents by Income Groups

- Expect postsecondary
- Expect university
- Aware of CESG

Income groups

Source: 2002 Survey of Approaches to Education Planning.

In this type of framework, opening an RESP account is costly. The state of a family's knowledge about saving determines the expenditure of psychic and real effort necessary to open an RESP account. These psychic costs represent part of the fixed cost of opening an RESP account, and therefore a potential barrier to participation by low-income households. While the financial benefit of the CESG may help on this front, it may not be enough to counteract the entire fixed cost.

The 2002 Survey of Approaches to Education Planning asked survey respondents about their awareness of the CESG. In Figure 1, CESG awareness by income group is graphed. While 32.7% of families with income less than $30,000 were aware of the CESG, the comparable number for those with family incomes greater than $80,000 was 61.9%. This finding is suggestive, but not conclusive. Parents who were simply not interested in RESPs may not have cared to learn about the CESG; awareness with program details may *follow* the decision to participate.

Less Complicated Alternatives are Available

Another reason that households might not participate in RESPs is that many alternative tax advantaged methods of saving for education are available. While trust accounts or RRSPs are not likely to be disproportionately used by low-income households, saving through housing equity (by paying off mortgage debt) is an opportunity that low-income households may pursue. By making heavier mortgage payments early in life, a family can "free up" resources at middle age to pay for education expenses. This strategy implicitly takes advantage of the pre-tax rate of return on investments in housing equity; a family could follow this strategy without being acutely aware of it. Given that a low-income family setting up an RESP may take on greater tax risks (from non-attendance) and greater fixed costs (psychic or real) than a high-income family, following the easier housing equity strategy might be preferable.

In the Survey of Approaches to Education Planning, those who do not participate in RESPs are asked why they do not participate. The modal response (31.7%) was lack of awareness, but the second largest response was the relative difficulty of saving through an RESP. However, this response did not vary enough across income groups to provide an explanation for the low participation of low-income Canadians in RESPs.

Financial Aid Rules

A further possibility is that withdrawals from RESPs will diminish financial aid, scholarship, or bursaries that are distributed according to financial need. For the United States, Feldstein (1995) and Dick, Edlin and Emch (2003) calculate that the implicit tax on savings incorporated into college scholarship rules has a large impact on the return to saving and on the accumulated assets of families with college-bound students.[15] The treatment of RESP income could have a similar impact on Canadian families. For example, in British Columbia, the provincial student loan eligibility formula "taxes" RESP withdrawals by decreasing the loan amount dollar for dollar with RESP income. Given the implicit tax rates on accumulated RESP funds, families who will be eligible for financial aid may choose not to save through RESPs, although they may still save in other forms.

Low-Income Families Can't Afford to Save

In a standard economic model of consumption, even a very low-income household still saves a portion of its income to prepare for future spending needs. A family chooses to allocate its available resources over different periods of consumption by means of saving. In such a basic model, the argument that a family cannot "afford" to save makes no sense. However, in the presence of fixed costs in opening an account, a family that would save only a small amount through RESPs might find that the benefits do not exceed the fixed costs. Under this scenario, low-income families would not save through RESPs.

These five explanations contain several common elements, including the possibility that information problems and fixed costs inhibit RESP participation. I now turn to a multivariate analysis of the Survey of Financial Security data to seek evidence on these explanations.

---

[15]Recent evidence by Long (2005) shows that previous results are sensitive to modelling assumptions, however.

Multivariate Evidence

By examining RESP participation and account balances in a multivariate framework, I can potentially find evidence in favour or against some of the different hypotheses outlined in the previous section. For the participation decision, I analyze the data using a probit model, which accounts for the binary nature of the dependent variable. For the level of the account balance, I estimate a Tobit model, which accounts for the censoring of the dependent variable at zero.[16]

The treatment of wealth in the regression requires some thought. If RESP contributions represent savings that would not have occurred in the absence of the incentive, then making RESP contributions increases a family's measured wealth. In this case, including wealth measures as explanatory variables on the right-hand side of the regression introduces an endogenous variable, as movements in the dependent variable may influence the wealth position of the family. On the other hand, if RESP account balances represent savings that would have occurred even in the absence of the incentives, then including wealth measures on the right-hand side of the model introduces no endogeneity problem. As I do not wish to take a stand on this issue for the purposes of this paper, I report estimates with and without wealth quintile controls.

The results appear in Table 4. The first column displays the probit estimates of participation. I report the incremental probabilities for each independent variable, derived from the regression coefficients.[17] The interpretation of the magnitudes of the estimates is made relative to the excluded category in each case. I indicate the statistical significance of each estimate with asterisks.

The first estimate suggests that being married instead of single (the excluded category) increases the probability of participating by five percentage points. Given that the average participation rate is 16%, a five percentage point increase is relatively large. This result is conditional on

---

[16]Since families cannot hold negative balances in RESP accounts, no family will be observed in the data with less than zero dollars in their RESP account.

[17]The incremental probabilities predict the change in the probability of participation when the variable of interest moves from zero to one, evaluated at the mean level of the other independent variables.

Kevin Milligan

Table 4: Regression Results for RESP Participation and Account Balance

	With no Wealth Controls		With Wealth Controls	
	Probit Has an RESP	Tobit RESP Balance	Probit Has an RESP	Tobit RESP Balance
Psuedo R-squared	0.0908	0.0226	0.0923	0.0274
Mean of dep. variable	0.160	6,277	0.160	6,277
Married or common-law	0.050 (0.016) ***	6,475 (1,285) ***	0.033 (0.016) *	4,879 (1,277) ***
Two children	0.042 (0.016) ***	2,201 (890) **	0.035 (0.016) **	1,657 (884) *
Three or more children	0.024 (0.025)	1,643 (1,346)	0.015 (0.024)	1,028 (1,339)
Youngest age 5–9	0.003 (0.019)	2,018 (1,176) *	-0.008 (0.018)	1,106 (1,171)
Youngest age 10–14	-0.002 (0.026)	2,077 (1,649)	-0.016 (0.024)	853 (1,648)
Youngest age 15–17	-0.020 (0.036)	-166 (2,375)	-0.036 (0.032)	-1,562 (2,370)
Oldest age 5–9	-0.039 (0.020) *	-1,954 (1,280)	-0.034 (0.020)	-1,557 (1,266)
Oldest age 10–14	-0.059 (0.025) **	-4,599 (1,731) ***	-0.052 (0.025) **	-4,052 (1,722) **
Oldest age 15–17	-0.113 (0.026) ***	-8,440 (2,174) ***	-0.105 (0.026) ***	-7,801 (2,170) ***
2nd income quintile	0.001 (0.029)	-587 (1,683)	-0.017 (0.027)	-1,763 (1,711)
3rd income quintile	0.045 (0.031)	1,929 (1,546)	0.006 (0.028)	-498 (1,598)
4th income quintile	0.043 (0.030)	2,314 (1,538)	-0.013 (0.027)	-1,533 (1,606)
Highest income quintile	0.137 (0.036) ***	6,682 (1,557) ***	0.044 (0.033)	1,037 (1,640)
2nd wealth quintile	--	--	0.134 (0.030) ***	8,468 (1,446) ***
3rd wealth quintile	--	--	0.145 (0.031) ***	9,354 (1,495) ***
4th wealth quintile	--	--	0.196 (0.036) ***	12,646 (1,570) ***
Highest wealth quintile	--		0.313 (0.047) ***	16,812 (1,682) ***

Table 4 *(continued)*

	(1)			(2)			(3)			(4)		
High-school graduate	0.049	(0.025)	**	3,778	(1,264)	***	0.039	(0.025)	*	2,985	(1,255)	**
Some postsecondary	0.058	(0.019)	***	5,194	(1,064)	***	0.047	(0.019)	**	4,310	(1,059)	***
University degree	0.124	(0.027)	***	7,719	(1,171)	***	0.094	(0.026)	***	5,898	(1,170)	***
Immigrant	0.079	(0.017)	***	3,761	(828)	***	0.087	(0.017)	***	4,352	(820)	***
Older spouse 25–29	-0.001	(0.048)		1,899	(3,498)		-0.013	(0.042)		965	(3,511)	
Older spouse 30–34	0.042	(0.053)		4,889	(3,313)		0.007	(0.044)		2,334	(3,356)	
Older spouse 35–39	0.032	(0.051)		4,857	(3,330)		-0.011	(0.042)		1,500	(3,379)	
Older spouse 40–44	0.047	(0.054)		6,072	(3,368)	*	-0.003	(0.045)		2,286	(3,412)	
Older spouse 45–49	0.079	(0.061)		8,284	(3,427)	**	0.010	(0.048)		3,444	(3,476)	
Older spouse 50–54	0.093	(0.069)		9,419	(3,546)	***	0.009	(0.051)		3,765	(3,600)	
Older spouse 55 and over	0.024	(0.060)		4,535	(3,728)		-0.044	(0.039)		-1,377	(3,781)	
Prince Edward Island	-0.002	(0.043)		-9,125	(5,277)	*	-0.012	(0.039)		-9,627	(5,192)	*
Nova Scotia	0.003	(0.031)		6,193	(3,083)	**	-0.005	(0.029)		5,288	(3,047)	*
New Brunswick	-0.022	(0.030)		4,394	(3,307)		-0.027	(0.027)		3,744	(3,272)	
Quebec	-0.071	(0.023)	***	10,331	(2,636)	***	-0.074	(0.022)	***	9,527	(2,599)	***
Ontario	-0.037	(0.025)		12,859	(2,590)	***	-0.044	(0.024)	*	11,748	(2,554)	***
Manitoba	-0.033	(0.026)		2,786	(3,044)		-0.041	(0.024)		1,789	(3,009)	
Saskatchewan	0.044	(0.035)		7,574	(2,994)	**	0.016	(0.031)		5,495	(2,956)	*
Alberta	-0.048	(0.022)	*	7,107	(2,723)	***	-0.058	(0.020)	**	5,918	(2,689)	**
British Columbia	-0.034	(0.024)		8,417	(2,682)	***	-0.042	(0.022)	*	7,274	(2,648)	***
Urban size <30K	-0.037	(0.018)	*	-1,746	(1,193)		-0.029	(0.018)		-1,113	(1,177)	
Urban size 30K to 100K	-0.021	(0.022)		-202	(1,366)		-0.012	(0.022)		361	(1,352)	
Urban size 100K to 500K	-0.039	(0.019)	*	-249	(1,327)		-0.027	(0.020)		805	(1,314)	
Urban size 500K+	-0.023	(0.019)		44	(998)		-0.014	(0.018)		615	(991)	

Note: Reported are regression coefficients and standard errors from regressions on 5,393 observations from the Survey of Financial Security. Three asterisks indicate statistical significance at the 1% level, two asterisks for the 5% level, and one asterisk for the 10% level.

the level of income and education in the household, so it picks up the unobserved difference in the propensity to contribute between single and married households.

The age of the youngest child is a fairly weak predictor of participation. The estimated magnitudes are small and statistically indistinguishable from zero. In contrast, the age of the oldest child has a strong effect on participation. If the oldest child is in the 15 to 17 age range, the probability of the family participating decreases 11.3% relative to a family with the oldest child aged 0–4, holding all other factors constant. As discussed earlier, because the survey followed closely after the expansion of the program in 1998, these estimated coefficients do not reflect what might appear in the longer run. The lower participation among families with older children provides some evidence in favour of the hypothesis that fixed costs present a barrier to RESP participation. Families with older children may not have seen it as worth their time and effort to open an account for children who had a short time horizon before entering postsecondary education.

The next two sets of results examine income and education. The income estimates suggest that there is little difference among the participation rates of the first four quintiles, as the estimates are not statistically different from the excluded lowest income quintile. For families in the highest income quintile, however, there is a large and statistically significant effect of 13.7 percentage points relative to the low-income quintile. For education, the largest effect is found for university graduates, who have a 12.4 percentage point higher chance of participating than those without a high-school education. These results suggest that both education and income exert independent and positive influence on RESP participation. Underlying these effects may be differing educational attainment expectations, or different levels of awareness about RESPs.

Immigrant families are estimated to have a participation rate 7.9% higher than observationally equivalent non-immigrant families. This result is economically and statistically large. If one posits that immigrant families have less access and experience with Canadian institutions, then this finding is evidence against information being a barrier to RESP participation.[18]

---

[18]In the Survey of Approaches to Education Planning, immigrant families have approximately the same awareness of the CESG, 49.78% compared to 47.2% for the Canadian born. Regressions including variables indicating the decade of immigration do not show statistically different effects for recent versus older immigrants.

In contrast, this finding may result from the flow of information through immigrant networks.[19] If information flows more quickly in such networks, then immigrants may have more information than the native born. Either way, this finding demonstrates that any "information barrier" to RESP participation is far from insuperable.

Differing education attainment expectations for immigrant and non-immigrant families might also explain this finding. In the 2002 Survey of Approaches to Education Planning, 74.9% of immigrant children are expected by their parents to attend university in the future, while only 52.2% of Canadian-born parents have this expectation.[20] This evidence does not support the importance of information barriers to RESP participation, but instead suggests that differential expectations may be a stronger explanation.

The age variables display an increasing pattern of coefficients for older parental age groups. However, none of the estimates is statistically significantly different from zero, ruling out a statistically strong difference from the behaviour of parents under age 25 (the excluded category). The provincial estimates look very similar to the univariate analysis. Saskatchewan residents are predicted to have a 4.4 percentage point higher probability of participation than Newfoundland residents, although the result is not statistically significant. On the other side, Quebec residents are a statistically significant 7.1 percentage points less likely to contribute than Newfoundland residents. For urban area size, the point estimates for the four urban categories are all negative, suggesting that those residing in rural areas are more likely to contribute than observationally equivalent urban dwellers.

Overall, the participation evidence suggests that families with married parents, more and younger children, higher income, more education, and who are immigrants are more likely to contribute to RESPs. Although these types of families are more likely to contribute, it is possible that the size of their contributions is smaller than other families. To investigate this possibility, I pursue an analysis using the level of the RESP account balance as the dependent variable.

---

[19]See Deri (2003) for a description and evidence on immigrant network effects in Canada.

[20]The expectation variable is available only for children age 13 to 18. A similar difference can be found looking at parents' "hope" of attendance, or at post-secondary education rather than just university.

The second column of Table 4 reports the coefficients for the Tobit equation explaining the observed RESP account balance for each family. Most of the coefficients share similar patterns with the probit equation in the first column, with some exceptions. In particular, the provincial dummy variables display a very different pattern. Relative to the excluded Newfoundland variable, residents of Ontario are predicted to have $12,859 more in their RESP account, even though they are predicted to be less likely to have an account. This may reflect differences in financial wealth across the provinces, which is not included as a control in this specification.

The third and fourth columns of the table report the probit and Tobit results for models including the possibly endogenous wealth quintile of the household. These variables are strongly significant and in many cases substantially change the estimates for the other factors, reflecting the correlation of wealth with the other factors.

With the wealth quintiles included, the explanatory power of being in the high-income quintile decreases sharply. The magnitude of the estimate falls by more than half, and is no longer statistically distinguishable from zero. This suggests that the availability of stocks of wealth rather than flows of income drives RESP participation. It is not lack of income which inhibits participation, but lack of wealth. This raises doubts about the explanation that non-participators "can't afford to save" because they must spend income on immediate needs. Instead, it suggests that households who already had stocks of wealth are most able to set up an account, perhaps by transferring assets from non-RESP accounts.

The gradient of participation with education persists with the inclusion of wealth quintiles, but the gradient with age does not. So, even with the same levels of wealth and income, a family with a university educated older parent is 9.4 percentage points more likely to have an RESP account. Again, this may reflect either higher financial sophistication or higher educational expectations for their children. For age, however, none of the coefficients is statistically significant, suggesting that the positive age gradient observed in the first two columns was solely driven by the fact that older families have more wealth.

The regression analysis has raised three key pieces of evidence that help to untangle the puzzle of low RESP participation among low-income families. First, the low participation of families with older children suggests that the fixed cost of opening an account is important. Second, immigrants are more likely to contribute than native-born Canadians, indicating information barriers to participation may not be as important as educational expectations. Finally, in the specifications including both income and wealth quintiles, I find that wealth explains RESP behaviour much better than income, suggesting that the pre-existence of other forms of savings is more important for RESP participation than having a higher flow of income.

Conclusion

In this paper, I present empirical evidence that RESP and CESG participation is concentrated among high-income, high parental education households. I suggest several possible explanations for lower participation among low-income households, and present some evidence that sheds light on the relative importance of the different explanations. The evidence suggests that differing educational expectations and the presence of fixed costs may best explain the gap in participation between high- and low-income families.

Any design for the tax and transfer system must strike a balance between redistributive and efficiency enhancing measures. However, for the tax system to find such a balance it is necessary for those measures *intended* to be redistributive to *actually* be redistributive. The distributional incidence of RESPs and CESGs is directly at odds with the stated goal of the *Canadian Opportunities Strategy* to direct government assistance to low- and middle-income Canadians. It also conflicts with the economic justification of ameliorating credit access problems. Consequently, it seems hard to justify these tax measures within the context of the stated objectives of improving access to postsecondary education.

Beyond the stated redistributive goal, do RESPs and CESGs have a role in the tax system? By providing tax-free accrual of income on investments, RESPs help to move the income tax system towards a consumption tax base, which may improve economic efficiency. However, Milligan (2002) argues that RESPs provide the tax-free accrual in a needlessly complicated way. Simpler tax measures, such as an expanded RRSP program or the Tax-Prepaid Savings Account, could achieve the same result more effectively.

CESGs might play an important role by providing an additional incentive to overcome the psychic costs and information barriers that limit the participation of low-income families in the financial system. After having opened an RESP account, however, the benefit of the incentive would be exhausted as the family has already learned why and how to save.

A reform that targeted the grant benefit to the opening of an account might better achieve the goal of overcoming the fixed costs, but without the distributional consequence of a long stream of payments to high-income families.

Finally, the CESG and the RESP provide tax relief to families with children, which some may find desirable. However, by tying the subsidy to education and providing it through a complicated tax measure, the subsidy becomes too narrowly targeted and expensive to administer. Other policy tools such as enhancements of the National Child Benefit, the introduction of a dependent credit or deduction, or the lowering of general tax rates would achieve this goal more simply and effectively.

In the context of wholesale reform of federal involvement in post-secondary education finance, a retrenchment of the CESG would provide funds that could be used in other ways. For example, proposals to reform the federal student loans program, such as that proposed by Finnie, Usher and Vossensteyn (2005), may require additional resources. The evidence presented in this paper suggests that such reallocations should form a key component of any reform that aims to increase postsecondary participation among low-income families.

References

Adam, S. and J. Shaw. 2003. *A Survey of the U.K. Tax System.* Briefing Note No. 9. London: Institute for Fiscal Studies.

Ameriks, J., A. Caplin and J. Leahy. 2003. "Wealth Accumulation and the Propensity to Plan", *Quarterly Journal of Economics* 118(3), 1007-1047.

Becker, G.S. and C.B. Mulligan. 1997. "The Endogenous Determination of Time Preference", *Quarterly Journal of Economics* 112(3), 729-758.

Bernheim, B.D. 2002. "Taxation and Saving", in A.J. Auerbach and M. Feldstein (eds.), *Handbook of Public Economics* Vol. 3. Amsterdam: Elsevier Science.

Bernheim, B.D. and D.M. Garrett. 2003. "The Effects of Financial Education in the Workplace: Evidence from a Survey of Households", *Journal of Public Economics* 87(7-8), 1487-1519.

Bernheim, B.D., D.M. Garrett and D.M. Maki. 2001. "Education and Saving: The Long-Term Effects of High School Financial Curriculum Mandates", *Journal of Public Economics* 80(3), 435-465.

Canada. Department of Finance. 1998. *The Canadian Opportunities Strategy.* Budget paper. Ottawa: Supply and Services Canada.

_____. 2002. *Tax Expenditures and Evaluations*. At http://www.fin.gc.ca/purl/taxexp-e.html.

Canada. Human Resources Development Canada (HRDC). 2002. "Canada Education Savings Grant Quarterly Statistical Review: April 2002", Knowledge Management and Analysis. Ottawa: HRDC.

Canada. Treasury Board. various years. *Estimates*. At http://www.tbs-sct.gc.ca/tb/estimate/EstimE.html.

Canada Customs and Revenue Agency. 2002. *Registered Education Savings Plans*. Publication No. RC4092-02. Ottawa: Supply and Services Canada.

Deri, C. 2003. "Social Networks and Health Service Utilization in Canada". Ottawa: University of Ottawa. Unpublished paper.

Dick, A.W., A.S. Edlin and E.R. Emch. 2003. "The Savings Impact of College Financial Aid", *Contributions to Economic Analysis and Policy* 2(1). At http://www.bepress.com/bejeap/contributions/vol2/iss1/art8.

Donnelly, M., R. Welch and A. Young. 1999. "Registered Education Savings Plans: A Tax Incentive Response to Higher Education Access", *Canadian Tax Journal* 47(1), 81-109.

Feldstein, M. 1995. "College Scholarship Rules and Private Saving", *American Economic Review* 85(3), 552-566.

Finnie, R., A. Usher and H. Vossensteyn. 2005. "A New Architecture for the Student Financial Aid System", in this volume.

Junor, S. and A. Usher. 2002. *The Price of Knowledge: Access and Student Finance in Canada*. Montreal: Canada Millennium Scholarship Foundation.

Kesselman, J.R. and F. Poschmann. 2001. "Expanding the Recognition of Personal Savings in the Canadian Tax System", *Canadian Tax Journal* 49(1), 40-101.

Long, M.C. 2005. "The Impact of Asset-tested College Financial Aid on Household Savings", *Journal of Public Economics*. Forthcoming.

Ma, J. 2003. "Education Saving Incentives and Household Saving: Evidence from the 2000 TIAA-CREF Survey of Participant Finances". NBER Working Paper No. 9505. Cambridge, MA: National Bureau of Economic Research.

Milligan, K. 2002. *Tax Preferences for Education Saving: Are RESPs Effective?* Commentary No. 174. Toronto: C.D. Howe Institute.

Statistics Canada. 2001. "The Assets and Debts of Canadians: An Overview of the Results of the Survey of Financial Security". Catalogue No. 13-595-XIE. Ottawa: Statistics Canada.

United Kingdom. 2002. "ISAs, PEPs, and TESSAs", Personal Taxpayers Series IR2008, Department of Inland Revenue. At http://www.inlandrevenue.gov.uk/pdfs/ir2008.htm.

Meeting the Need: A New Architecture for Canada's Student Financial Aid System

Ross Finnie, Alex Usher and Hans Vossensteyn

Introduction

Canada's student financial aid system should have a relatively simple primary function: to ensure that every qualified individual has the financial means to pursue postsecondary studies without suffering undue hardship. Otherwise put, cost should not be a barrier to going to college or university.

Beyond this broad objective, more specific aspects of the definition of "access" arise. We choose to view the concept as including: that individuals are able to enrol in their programs of choice (provided, of course, they qualify); that they have the opportunity of attending the institutions they prefer, including, importantly, going out of town (again assuming they meet the relevant entry standards); that they need not work at outside jobs during school to the degree that it adversely affects their studies; and that paying for the schooling does not put unreasonable demands on family resources or lead to the accumulation of excessive debt burdens in the postschooling period.

The authors are grateful for comments received from Sean Junor and other participants at the "Higher Education in Canada" conference held at Queen's University, February 13–14, 2004 organized by the John Deutsch Institute.

This may sound simple, or even obvious. And one might reasonably expect, given the plethora of student aid-related programs currently in existence, that the current system was doing its job of removing financial barriers to postsecondary education. After all, we have the Canada Student Loans Program and its provincial counter-parts, the Canada Millennium Scholarship Foundation, myriad grant programs at both the federal and provincial levels, debt-remission programs, programs that help individuals facing difficulties with their student loans in the postschooling period, education-related tax credits, Canadian Education Savings Grants, Registered Education Savings Plans, all kinds of institutional-level support, and more — all of which cost almost $5 billion each year.[1]

Unfortunately, these are not doing the job, or at least not the full job, of guaranteeing access in the manner intended. They do not supply enough money to some who need it, while providing support to others who do not. We should be doing better.

What is needed is a "New Architecture" for student financial assistance in this country. We propose replacing the current hodgepodge of programs with a single program that effectively and efficiently delivers support to those who need it without squandering scarce dollars on those who do not. The good news is that this system could be developed without inventing a whole new set of structures and procedures from the ground up — a disruption that would carry its own set of special challenges and costs. The better news is that we could implement such a system without spending any new public money. This is one policy area where the solution depends not so much on new and more financing, but on doing better with the existing resources.

Not only is reform of the student financial aid system possible, it is important, since providing every Canadian with the chance to pursue post-secondary studies is both a basic issue of fairness or social justice, and essential to ensuring that we have the skilled labour force needed in the emerging knowledge-based economy in the years and decades to come.[2]

---

[1] See Finnie, Schwartz and Lascelles (2003) for a description of the current system of student financial aid and associated levels of government spending. See also Junor and Usher (2002), and AUCC (2002).

[2] See Human Resources Development Canada (2002) for the federal government's discussion of this point.

Ross Finnie, Alex Usher and Hans Vossensteyn

The student financial aid issue is a case where doing the right thing also makes good economic sense — a potent context for policy discussions.

In this paper, we begin by describing the existing student financial aid system and its main shortcomings. We then place the issue in an international perspective by reviewing the various approaches to providing student assistance in existence around the world and situating the Canadian system in that context. This leads us to a description of the New Architecture that we propose, including not only the key elements of the plan, but also consideration of some of the associated design and implementation challenges. The concluding section summarizes the major points of the paper and identifies the policy debates that might be expected should Canada begin to move towards such a system.

The Existing System

Before describing our proposed New Architecture for student financial aid in Canada, we offer an outline sketch of the current system and some of its principal shortcomings.

A Sketch of the Current Canadian System

The Canadian system of student assistance, which is an area of joint policy responsibility between the federal and provincial governments, is dauntingly complex.[3] There are loan programs at the federal and provincial levels, provincial need-based grant and debt-remission programs, other grants for particular demographic groups and those in certain disciplines (e.g., Aboriginals, female graduate students in the sciences), still more grants and tax credits for families who save for their children's education, other tax credits to help defray direct expenses (tuition fees and the standard education credit) and the interest paid on student loans, various forms of institutional-based aid, privately funded bursaries, and more. The major components of this system will now be described in turn.

---

[3]See Finnie, Schwartz and Lascelles (2003) and Junor and Usher (2002) for descriptions of the existing Canadian student financial assistance system and estimates of spending on the different forms of aid.

Student loans and need-based grants. We pay the greatest attention to the major loan and grant programs, since our New Architecture essentially builds upon these while eliminating most other major sources of aid. These alone, however, comprise a complex system. As one recent publication noted:

> it has two national loan programs (one for full-time students and one for part-time students). It has three quite separate methods of providing assistance to students (need-based, income-based, and universal grants). It has five national grant programs, seven provincial/territorial (P/T) loan remission programs, eight P/T grant programs, 12 P/T loan programs, 13 P/T student assistance programs, 15 major providers of public student assistance, over 40 different student assistance limits (depending on a student's province, marital status, dependents, and level of study), more than 100 different loan/grant combinations within these aid limits, and hundreds of thousands of possible aid configurations once assessed need is taken into account. (Junor and Usher, 2002, p. 115)

But despite the complexity and variation that exists across the country, most student loan and associated need-based grant systems follow a single paradigm. We now describe that system.

Close to 99% of all need-based loan and grant assistance goes to *full-time* students (defined as at least 60% of a full course load). A similar percentage of aid is given on the basis of "need" as opposed to personal or family income, where need is defined as the difference between "costs" and "resources", though the manner in which these are assessed differs slightly from province to province.

In general, accepted costs include the following items:
- tuition and mandatory fees,
- books, equipment (up to $3,000 max),
- housing costs (based on province of residence and at home/away from home status),
- travel costs (if living away from home), and
- other living expenses.

While the resources considered to be available to the student are based on the following:
- an assumed parental contribution calculated as a percentage of family income (if the individual is considered "dependent") or a percentage of spousal income if married,

- minimum contributions from the student's summer income plus 80% of in-school earnings over $1,500, and
- adjustments for scholarships received, liquid student assets, savings (partial exemption for RRSP savings), and equity held in a motor vehicle ($5,000 exemption).

The principal contributions on the part of parents and students are deemed, or estimated, and therefore do not necessarily represent actual amounts. The true parental contribution may, for example, range from zero to much more than the indicated amounts, while students might earn and save more or less what the standard formulas assume. While such an approach means that the different circumstances faced by individual students are not taken into account beyond the related formulas, it represents a relatively efficient and non-intrusive means of calculating students' needs and is similar to formulas used in other countries.

The first dollars of need, costs minus resources, are always met by loans. Only if the loan attains a certain level does a student become eligible for grants. The exact level at which loans turn into grants differs by province (see Appendix for these and other details regarding the country's need-based grant and loan programs) but in much of the country it is in excess of $7,000 per year. In a number of provinces (British Columbia, Quebec, Alberta, and Ontario) some or all grants are provided "up front"; that is to say, at the same time that loan assistance is distributed in September and January. In other cases (Alberta, Saskatchewan, Manitoba, Ontario, and the four Atlantic provinces) grants are provided as "loan remission" after a student has successfully completed a year of studies (see Appendix for details). Loan assistance is always portable across provincial boundaries. In most but not all cases, grant assistance is portable as well.

Although the student assistance system *calculates* need for all students, it does not necessarily *meet* that need. In most provinces, the maximum assistance available for a single student with no dependents is $275 per week, or $9,350 for a standard 34-week school year. For students with children, the amount ranges from $315/week ($10,710/year) to $500/week ($17,000/year). Quebec has much higher assistance limits, but also a stricter need-assessment system, which makes it more difficult to receive greater amounts of support. Remarkably, these maxima, with small exceptions, have remained unchanged since 1994, although in its February 2004 Speech from the Throne the federal government outlined a plan to increase these limits and allow students to borrow greater amounts.

While a student remains enrolled on a full-time basis, governments pay the interest on the student loan. At the end of studies, interest begins to accumulate on the loan, but students are not required to make payments during an initial six-month "grace period" (although interest accumulates). After the six months are up, students must begin paying back their loans at a steady rate.

Since the beginning of the 1990s, there have been four different regimes under which student loans were issued and paid back. Before 1995, private financial institutions issued loans, although government loan programs determined eligibility, and institutions could not refuse to issue a loan that had been approved. Governments, both federal and provincial, guaranteed these loans by committing themselves to buying defaulted loans at full value (including outstanding interest) from the lending institution. From 1995 to 2000, instead of acting as guarantor, the government paid lenders a 5% "risk premium" on all loans going into repayment in a given year. In return, the banks assumed virtually full responsibility for collection. When the 1995–2000 agreement ended, an interim arrangement was put into place whereby the government became the lender (although it continued to issue loans through private institutions) and assumed full responsibility for all new loans issued. Since 2001, the government has issued student loans directly and assigned their management and collection to private companies brought into existence for this purpose.

Interest relief (IR) provides assistance for students in repayment with very high debt-to-income ratios. More recently, the very few students whose debt-to-income ratios are persistently high over a period of three years or more have been eligible for debt reduction in repayment (DRR), which reduces the principal owed. This program has had miniscule participation rates to date.

Nine provinces and one territory participate in the Canada Student Loans Program. In these provinces, need is met — in theory at least — on a 60/40 basis; that is to say, the Government of Canada provides assistance equal to 60% of need up to a maximum of $165/week while the provinces pay the remaining 40%. Given that many provinces also provide assistance over $275/week to students with dependents, and that provinces are typically larger per capita providers of grant assistance, the actual distribution of overall student assistance costs is actually closer to 40/60.

Quebec, the Northwest Territories, and Nunavut have chosen to opt out of the Canada Student Loans Program. They have their own loan systems, to which the Government of Canada contributes through a system of alternative payments that are built into the national student loans legislation.

Overall, the Canadian student loan system reaches about 450,000 university and college students each year, and about 40% of all post-secondary graduates borrow from government programs at some point during their schooling (Finnie, 2001). Estimates of spending on student loans and need-based grants vary because of the lack of a standard methodology for measuring expenditures, but are likely in the range of $2.3–2.4 billion. As a result, students receive a total of approximately $3 billion each year in loans and $1–2 billion in grants, depending on what exactly is counted, and how. Slightly under half of the total grant money comes in the form of back-end "remission" (a sort of delayed grant).

Tax credit and savings programs. Canada has used tax expenditures to subsidize students for over 40 years. Tax expenditures can be viewed as direct spending programs delivered through the tax system, and those related to postsecondary education are in this sense little different than traditional direct student aid programs.

Tuition fees and a monthly "education amount" were originally tax *deductions*. But since these deductions provided more benefit to those with higher incomes (who have higher marginal tax rates), they were — like numerous other tax deductions — turned into the somewhat less regressive tax *credits* in the 1987 Tax Reform. At present, all tuition and compulsory fees (save student association fees) are eligible for the tuition tax credit, while the value of the monthly "education amount" tax credit was raised from $200 to $400 per month ($200 per month for part-time students) in 1991.[4] Students can use these credits in one of three ways. They may use them to reduce their own current tax liability; they may transfer them to a parent, guardian, spouse, or grandparent to reduce *their* current tax liability; or they may "carry forward" the value of any unused credits to reduce their tax liability in future years.

In addition to these credits, there are a number of smaller tax expenditures, including: (i) *Deduction for Moving to Study:* Students who move to study may deduct any expenses related to the move; (ii) *Deduction for Scholarship Income:* The first $3,000 of income from scholarships in any year is tax-free (in Quebec, all scholarship income is tax-free); and (iii) *Student Loan Interest Tax Credit:* A tax credit is given equal to the value

---

[4]Individuals are able to deduct a certain percentage of actual tuition fees (currently 16% or 17% of the standard education-deduction amount) from their tax payable.

of interest paid on a student loan during a calendar year. This may be used immediately to reduce tax payable or carried-forward for up to five years.

These tax expenditures originate in the federal income tax code. But because provincial taxes are linked directly to federal taxes, tax expenditures at the federal level also result in provincial tax expenditures. Quebec, having its own tax system, also has its own set of tax expenditures, and certain other provinces have their own education-related tax provisions in addition to those that derive from the federal system. For example, Ontario has tax credits related to the hiring of co-op students, while Saskatchewan has a special one-time, non-refundable tax credit of $350 program to encourage recent graduates to stay in the province after graduation.

In addition to these forms of tax-based assistance, which are intended to offset education-related expenses directly, other tax-based measures have been put in place to encourage savings. Since 1972, the Canadian tax code has given special status to Registered Education Savings Plans (RESPs). RESPs are savings accounts that permit tax-deferred growth (growth in the fund is left untaxed until income is withdrawn, at which time it becomes taxable in the hands of the beneficiary). Up to $4,000 per year may be contributed to an RESP. These vehicles are much more often used by upper-income families who have the means to save and would probably do so anyway, or otherwise find the means of financing their children's educations, rather than by lower-income families who are in greater need of assistance (Milligan, 2002).

In 1998, the Government of Canada created the Canada Education Savings Grant (CESG) in an attempt to encourage more Canadian families to save for their children's education. Under this plan, the government "tops up" every dollar contributed to an RESP by donating 20 cents of its own, up to a maximum of $400 per year. Data from the most recent Survey of Approaches to Educational Planning (Shipley, Ouellette and Cartwright, 2003) indicates that educational savings are expanding quickly, although other sources point out that the majority of this program's money has gone to upper-income families (Milligan, 2002; Usher, 2004).

In total, education-related tax expenditures in Canada currently amount to approximately $1.7 billion per year, of which approximately two-thirds comes from Ottawa. In addition, annual CESG expenditures (which come exclusively from the federal government) now total close to $400 million.

Summing up the current system. The Canadian student financial aid system thus provides a substantial amount of support to students and their families in myriad ways. Especially in the case of loans and grants, much of this money is targeted to those who need it. However, due to the different eligibility criteria, some of this assistance also ends up with students who may not be so needy, while the other forms of aid — tax credits and certain other grants in particular — are even worse in this respect. We now turn to discuss the major flaws of this system in terms of delivering adequate amounts of aid where it is needed.

Major Flaws of the Current System

While this student financial aid system has some very sound elements and increases many Canadians' access to postsecondary education and improves the terms under which they are able to study and how they finance that schooling, it also has some major flaws. These include the following.

Tax credits represent a relatively large share of student aid, but are poorly targeted. Canadian governments collectively spend almost 40% of all their student financial aid dollars in the form of education-related tax credits, but these tax credits are distributed almost entirely without reference to need. Much of the money goes towards students from higher-income families — or their parents (or even grandparents) — who do not really need the assistance to ensure their access to postsecondary studies, while lower-income families are unable to benefit at all because they do not have the tax obligations required to take advantage of the benefits, or at best receive no more assistance than higher-income families.[5]

In addition, it is likely that many individuals are not fully aware of these credits or their value, while the benefits are not received until after individuals (students or those to whom they pass their credits along) receive their tax refunds, typically after the school year to which the benefits are meant to apply. Spending on tax credits would thus be better directed towards programs that are specifically designed to help students from low-income families who really need the assistance.

---

[5]It could be argued that the small amounts spent on tax credits on student loans in repayment are at least partially based on need (i.e., the individual once qualified for a student loan and continues to make payments on that debt), but even here the targeting is not very precise, since higher-income individuals are eligible for the credits as much as those with lower earnings.

A too-large "independent" class. Other forms of Canadian student assistance — grants, loans, loan remission, etc. — are designed to be need-based. In theory, this means that more assistance should flow to students from lower-income backgrounds. In practice, however, because the assistance provided to "independent" students is actually greater in total dollar terms than the amount that goes to individuals who depend on their parents, and because students are too often considered "independent" of their parents, much of Canada's need-based assistance goes to students from wealthier families.

Across the country, students are considered independent if they are (or have been) married, have a child (in Quebec: 20 weeks or more into a pregnancy), have been available to the labour force on a full-time basis for two years, or have been out of secondary school for more than four years (in Ontario: five years; in Quebec: 90 credits or more completed at the undergraduate level). The last criterion is especially problematic because it makes individuals who have taken their time getting into or through post-secondary programs (including those who choose to travel or take a bit of time off from school) independent towards the end of their studies.

There is no question that treating students as independent and making them eligible for financial assistance without regard to their family's income is appropriate in some cases. But the current rules and practices are not restrictive enough, and need to be reformed so that at least some of the money now spent on students from higher-income families who manage to qualify as independents is re-targeted towards young people from lower-income families who are in greater need of the help. Doing so would almost certainly have a positive impact on access.

Assistance limits are inadequate. As discussed above, in most of the country, single students are currently eligible for a maximum of $275 per week in direct assistance, a figure that has not changed since 1994. Spread over a university-standard 34-week period of study, this translates into $9,350 per year.

Just on *a priori* grounds, if those limits were appropriate in 1994 — which was probably the case, based as they were on the best evidence available at that time — then they cannot be now, after costs, especially tuition, have risen significantly.

Furthermore, although calculations vary, empirical studies indicate that even by conservative estimates at least 25% of all students have need in excess of the lending limits established by the aid system itself.[6] Yet regardless of assessed need (which takes into account the expected contributions of students themselves), students cannot receive more than the $275/week. So we have the rather bizarre spectacle of a need-based program telling students that they need a certain amount of money but then not giving them what they need. Hemingway (2003a,b) makes a compelling case that student assistance maxima are currently inadequate and should be increased to approximately $350/week.

Finally, students are voting with their feet — or at least their bank accounts and borrowing patterns — and have dramatically increased their dependency on private loans in recent years (Junor and Usher, 2002). It is possible that represents "frivolous" or unnecessary borrowing to support life-style spending, but it seems more likely that students are borrowing simply because they need the money to pay basic schooling expenses in a situation where assistance packages are inadequate.

We thus believe that the student financial aid system should increase the maximum amounts available to whatever is required to meet the students' needs. After all, if the system determines that students need a certain amount of money in order to attend postsecondary education, then the student financial aid system should make this amount available. We return to these issues below.

The expectations of parental contributions are wrong. For dependent students whose parents' resources are taken into consideration, there is an income threshold below which no contributions are required and the student is eligible for the full amount of assistance available. This threshold varies by province, according to cost of living and tax rates, but effectively the formula exempts families below about the 40th percentile of family income from making any contributions whatsoever. But by about the 65th percentile of family income, parents are expected to be contributing 75% of marginal after-tax income (if we assume the support of their children comes out of current income), which is extraordinarily steep. Above the 75th percentile, parental contributions are expected to be high enough that virtually no one is eligible for student assistance. Merely at face value, these schedules seem unreasonable.

Furthermore, data on actual parental contributions strongly affirms that the current formulas are wrong on two counts (Ekos Research, 2003). First,

---

[6]See Hemingway (2003a,b) on these and related issues.

they vastly overestimate the parental contributions actually made by parents from the upper two income quartiles. Second, they underestimate the amount of money contributed by families with income just short of the median. As a result, the latter might receive more assistance than they "need", while the former definitely receive less (see Hemingway, 2003a,b). Talks with institutions' student financial award officers provide further ad hoc evidence of these inequities.

We thus believe that the student financial aid system needs to be re-calibrated with respect to parental contributions in order to be fairer and more realistic.

The children of non-paying parents are punished. As explained above, the system simply assumes that parents give their children what it says they should according to its established contribution formulas. There are, however, many parents who do not give their children as much as expected, or provide no support at all — and this will always be the case, even if parental contributions are recalculated along the lines we suggest (i.e., to be more reasonable and realistic). While most Canadian student loan programs do have an appeal system that allows students whose parents are not making the expected contributions to obtain at least some public support, this system is completely unadvertised and hence seldom used.

In most countries, especially those with significant levels of tuition fees, there is some form of loan system that gets at this precise problem. We think Canada should adopt a system of this type for the same reasons as elsewhere.

Loan remission is an inefficient way to help students. Canadian governments spend about a billion dollars in non-repayable assistance annually, but nearly half of this goes to students *after* they have completed a year of studies, or even their entire program, through what is known as loan remission. With this form of assistance, the grant is received not by the student, but by the student's financial institution as a paydown of a portion of an existing student debt. In Alberta and Newfoundland, the loan remission occurs at the end of the program of studies and is based on total accumulated borrowing.[7] In Saskatchewan, Manitoba, Ontario, and Prince

---

[7]Alberta actually has a two-stage remission process. After the first year of study, loans are remitted based on *annual* borrowing. Then, at the end of studies, another remission process reduces outstanding debt based on *total* borrowing. The

Edward Island, it occurs at the end of a given year of studies, based on the amount borrowed that year.

Loan remission is an odd system, and unique to Canada. First, because these programs only pay down existing loans, without putting additional money into the hands of students, to the degree students actually need more money to pay their schooling and associated living costs, they provide no benefit.

Second, by denying students the money up-front, remitting loans after they have been taken out according to certain conditions creates uncertainty about the total assistance packages they will receive, especially in terms of the mix of loans versus grants, which is an important consideration for many, especially those from lower-income families.

Finally, they deliver debt relief with no regard to individuals' actual debt burdens, as measured by debt-to-income ratios in the payback period.

We thus see a need to eliminate existing debt-remission programs and spend more money on (i) up-front grants (or loans) which provide students with the money they need with no uncertainty as to how much of it will be loan or grant, and (ii) debt relief in repayment that is based on actual debt burdens (i.e., a comparison of the payments required in comparison to the individual's income) rather than simply the amount borrowed in a given year or even that accumulated over the student's entire course of studies.[8]

An International Perspective

This section first provides a framework of how student assistance is provided in other countries, then places the Canadian system in that context.

---

stated purpose of the first-year rule — which was introduced in 2001 — was to alleviate concerns about debt among students who had just begun their education.

[8]See Institute of Intergovernmental Relations (2003) for further discussion of these points.

Student Financial Assistance in Other Countries

International practice shows a wide array of ways in which governments and institutions of higher education help students meet their schooling costs, including tuition fees, other mandatory charges, study materials, living expenses, and room and board (see Vossensteyn, 2003b). Figure 1 presents an overview of these different approaches.

Of course there is no single country in which the system includes all of these forms of aid. The precise combination of programs depends on many

Figure 1: The Multitude Ways in which Governments and Higher-education Institutions Subsidize Students

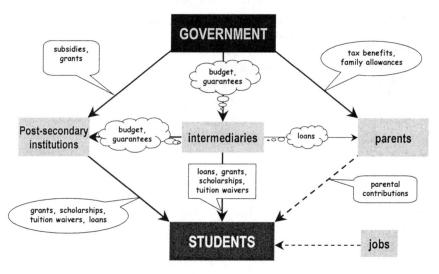

Note: Intermediary institutions include organizations such as banks, student aid agencies, etc. that provide or otherwise deliver student aid. The figure focuses on the ways in which students are supported in meeting their actual out-of-pocket costs, thus ignoring other implicit forms of support, including the direct operating grants made by governments to institutions, which can be thought of as a tuition subsidy. Because we are mainly interested in public forms of support, we also leave funds provided by industry, foundations, and other private sources out of the analysis. The dotted lines represent non-public support, but flows which should nonetheless be considered as part of the system, if only because public support often depends on these other sources.

Ross Finnie, Alex Usher and Hans Vossensteyn

factors, including each country's conception of who is primarily responsible for the costs of an individual's schooling — the student, the parents, the government, or a combination of these — which are in turn determined by its ideologies, traditions, political compromises, and budgetary constraints (see Vossensteyn, 2003a). Here we identify a few broad models that allow us to categorize systems of student support and tuition policies in different countries and to determine which groups of students generally benefit from each system.

The student-centred model. In the student-centred model, students are regarded as having primary responsibility for the costs of study. As such, they often face relatively high tuition fees, implying that public funds to higher-education institutions should not fully cover instruction costs, and financial support is focused on students, not their families (although family contributions are taken into account). Australia, New Zealand, the United Kingdom, Japan, and the United States provide examples of this approach (ICHEFAP, 2003).

In these countries, students are charged considerable tuition fees (sometimes at differential levels by program and institution), while grants, scholarships, and loans are primarily awarded to students on a means-tested basis, thus targeting support to students from low-income families and those who are otherwise needy. This approach reflects the (often implicit) expectation that parents will help their children according to their financial capacity, with parental contributions in some countries facilitated through programs such as tax credits and, in the case of the United States, a parental loan program.

To what extent do students from low- through higher-income backgrounds benefit from these government transfers? The targeting is ostensibly on lower-income (and thus "higher need") families, but this is not always how things work in practice. One problem is that in countries where tax credits figure importantly (e.g., Australia, New Zealand, the United Kingdom), families with high incomes also have the best opportunities to reduce their (taxable) income through those credits. Having higher costs can also increase the amount of support, and in many cases this is again related to family income, such as being enrolled in more expensive programs or at more expensive institutions, living away from the parental home, and being considered independent from one's parents. These factors are particularly relevant to the Canadian system, as mentioned above, and also the United States.

A particularly interesting example of the student-centred model is Australia (see Dobson, 2003). In 1989, tuition fees were reintroduced through the so-called Higher Education Contribution Scheme (HECS). The flat-rate tuition fee, representing approximately one-quarter of average instruction costs, has evolved into three different tariff bands, reflecting cost differences between programs and differences in expected future earnings. Students can pay their tuition up-front with a 25% reduction, or defer payments until after graduation via income-contingent repayments collected through the tax authorities. Because HECS debt has a zero rate of real interest (with only an annual correction for inflation), all students choosing this option are indirectly subsidized (although the absence of the 25% reduction can be considered a substitute for interest fees). Those with low incomes after graduation benefit the most from this interest subsidy because they make lower annual payments and have extended (interest free) repayment periods. A separate system of support for living costs comes from the Youth Allowance program, which provides non-repayable grants, based on parental income and targeted to low-income students, although some funds leak through the income-testing system to arrive in the hands of students from higher-income families. In addition, certain ethnic groups benefit from more specific scholarship programs.

The UK system — at least before a set of reforms being instituted at the time of writing — was much like Australia. The major difference was that student support for living costs came almost fully in the form of student loans, with only a limited number of hardship scholarships. And since loans could be taken up by all students, including those from higher-income families, the benefits from the interest-subsidy of student loans was enjoyed widely. Students from higher-income families had to pay their tuition fees themselves, while those from low- and middle-income groups could get all or part of their tuition waived. Higher-education institutions delivered small amounts of additional assistance to students remaining in financial need.

But in the spring of 2004, the British Parliament passed a bill that will lead to some important changes in tuition and student support. As from September 2004, grants will be reintroduced for full-time students from lower-income households up to an amount of £1,000 per year (approximately CDN$2,500). In 2005, the repayment threshold for student loans (below which no payments are required in that year) will be increased from £10,000 to £15,000 (CDN$37,000) per year. The more important changes will, however, occur in September 2006.

From then onwards, universities will be able to increase tuition fees above the standard rate of £1,150 to a maximum of £3,000 (CDN$7,400)

Ross Finnie, Alex Usher and Hans Vossensteyn

per year. As compensation, the grants for lower-income students will be raised to a maximum £2,700 (CDN$6,600) per year. Universities that want to charge the additional tuition fees must sign an agreement in which they promise to use part of their additional revenues in increase, for example, by offering scholarships for disadvantaged students or actively recruiting students from lower-income families. Finally, the maximum amount students can borrow will be increased, while any unpaid debt remaining after 25 years of repayment will be cancelled.[9]

These changes to a large extent reflect what has been argued by Nicholas Barr for many years. In his view, equity and access can only be promoted through differential tuition fees and predominantly loans (over grants) that have to be repaid when students (graduates) experience the financial benefits of higher education (Barr, 2005). In many ways, the UK system, with its increased role for student loans mixed with targeted grants and generous assistance in repayment through its income-contingent element, has in fact moved in a similar direction to the New Architecture we propose for Canada.

The parents-centred model. In the parents-centred model, parents are morally, and in some cases legally responsible for maintaining their children during postsecondary studies, while there are generally no, or only very low tuition fees. As a result, student grants and loans are available to relatively few students (generally from 15 to 35%) and the amounts awarded tend to be small (Vossensteyn, 1999).

In contrast, parents are substantially subsidized in meeting their maintenance obligations for their children, generally receiving family allowances and/or tax benefits to help them do so. Family allowances typically vary according to family size, particularly the number of children, and go to families from all income categories without a means test. Tax benefits, typically in the form of tax deductions, generally provide more benefits for parents with higher incomes (and hence higher tax rates) than lower-income families in the lower income/tax brackets. Support is thus less need-based than with other systems of support. Such systems can be found in a number of Western-European countries, including Austria, Belgium, France, Germany, Italy, and Spain (ICHEFAP, 2003).

---

[9]For the future of Higher Education Student Funding, Department for Education and Skills, see Web site www.dfes.gov.uk.

Because parents are assumed to make up the difference between the expenses of students and what they get through direct and indirect support, it is usually difficult to say whether total support is sufficient to meet students' costs. However, there is considerable evidence that not all parents make the contributions they are expected to, and students spend considerably more than what they receive through the combination of all forms of public support plus parental contributions and exhibit a trend towards more part-time work (Vossensteyn, 1999, 2003a).

The independent students model. Systems in which students are regarded as fully independent from their families are typically found in countries with the most advanced social welfare systems, including Denmark, Finland, Iceland, Norway, and Sweden (Vossensteyn, 2003a). In these countries, students do not have to make tuition payments, meaning that governments pay all instruction costs. At the same time, these countries have relatively flat wage systems in which higher education graduates do not earn very much more than secondary education graduates.

In addition, public support for students fully covers their living expenses, regardless of whether they live with their parents or away from home. From 40 to 60% of the total support received by the student is provided through student loans, the rest coming in the form of grants, and is in theory fairly evenly available across socio-economic backgrounds. In practice, however, an increasing proportion of students receive contributions from their parents or take part-time jobs in order to avoid incurring debt, while lower-income students lacking family resources remain more dependent on student loans and jobs.

The compromise model. A final approach is where tuition and student support policies reflect a compromise between making students financially independent and having parents share in the costs, as in the Netherlands. All full-time students are eligible for basic study grants, which vary in generosity depending on whether they are living with or away from their parents. In addition, about 30% of all students are eligible for supplementary grants based on a parental income test; for students who do not get a (full) supplementary grant of this type, parents are expected to make up the difference. Students can also take out loans, with those independent from their parents allowed to take up extra loans for the amount their parents are expected to contribute, this option representing a form of protection against parents who do not support their children to that degree. All in all, the three parts (basic grant, supplementary grant/parental contribution, and voluntary loans) each comprise about a third of students' nominal budgets. In practice, however, students have substantially higher expenditure patterns, and as a result are heavily involved in part-time work, which allows them to maintain a higher standard of living and avoid taking out student loans.

Summary and conclusions. This brief survey has demonstrated the different ways in which governments provide financial assistance to students and otherwise help them pay for their postsecondary education. The various approaches result in substantial differences in how different groups of students are assisted. Especially in countries where students are regarded as being financially independent or where support is principally channelled through parents, spending is distributed relatively evenly among individuals from different socio-economic groups. To the degree student financial assistance is meant to open up opportunities for underrepresented groups, the only spending that addresses this objective comes from supplementary programs that target the relevant low-income and minority students. In contrast, systems that focus on students themselves are generally the most successful in helping such disadvantaged groups. With such approaches, however, there is obviously no guarantee that the assistance will be adequate or improve access to postsecondary education for the targeted groups to the degree desired or intended.

This takes us to the issue that different models of student financing have different price-tags for society. All models which, directly or through families, provide public subsidies to all students, tend to carry higher public costs, because students from relatively affluent backgrounds also benefit. More targeted programs can, in contrast, deliver greater amounts of assistance to those most in need, but may be more complicated to implement or go against certain societal values related to government spending generally, and support for postsecondary education in particular. We return to these issues in our discussion below of the proposed New Architecture for Canada.

The Canadian System in International Perspective

The Canadian system for the most part falls in the student-centred model. As we have just seen, the primary characteristic of this system is that students pay considerable tuition fees and are the prime unit for measuring financial need and receiving assistance. That said, the Canadian system also has certain aspects of the parent-centred model, and has been moving increasingly in this direction of late with the increased spending on the tax credits and savings grants from which parents benefit.

That said, a number of specific aspects of the Canadian system stand out in comparative perspective. First, Canada has relatively forgiving criteria for treating students as independent, and thus qualifying for increased amounts of government aid. In most countries, a student is not considered to be independent until age 24 or after the first degree program has been completed, which contrasts to the Canadian rules described above (Quebec's independence criterion is closer to the international norm). As a result, an unusually large proportion of Canadian loans and grants go to moderately older undergraduate students who meet the independence criteria.

Second, the combination of tuition differences (varying across particular programs as well as province of residence) and a need-based student aid system means students in more expensive programs — including those in high-cost professional programs — tend to receive greater amounts of aid than others.

Third, students must take loans before they may receive any grants. In most countries, the criteria for loans and grants are separate, which makes it quite possible to receive both. In the United States, for example, loans are given out on the basis of assessed need, whereas grants are given out on the basis of family income. This aspect of the Canadian system is at least partly related to the fact that it rolls all education-related expenses — including both fees and living costs — into a single financial aid system, whereas most other countries have different systems for these different kinds of expenses.

Fourth, the proportion of assistance that comes in the form of tax expenditures is very high compared to other countries.

Finally, Canada has a great variety of routes through which student aid is delivered, including those at the provincial, federal, and institutional levels. The multiple assistance points approach is similar to the United States, the main differences being that Canadian provincial governments are more important than US state governments in the provision of aid, and the role of institutions is weaker in Canada than in the United States. Furthermore, and again like the United States, Canada delivers aid in a relatively complex mix of loans, grants, tax expenditures, and savings instruments. The result of this complexity is a lack of coherence in terms of the aid delivered, and a lack of transparency for prospective students and their parents in terms of what assistance they are entitled to and what the net cost of their education will be.

A New Architecture for Student Financial Aid

In this section we first describe the basic underlying principles and characteristics of a New Architecture for student financial assistance that addresses these major deficiencies in the current Canadian system as described earlier and otherwise comprises a coherent, effective, and efficient system for delivering student aid where it is needed. We then address various implementation issues and related questions.[10]

A Description of the Proposed New Architecture

The overall design goal is a student financial aid system which ensures that all students have access to the money required to cover the costs of their postsecondary studies without imposing undue hardship on the students themselves or their families or leading to excessive debt loads in the post-schooling period. The system should consist of the following elements.

The first element of the system would consist of arriving at the student's financial aid package. This would begin with the determination of the student's schooling-related costs, including tuition, other fees, equipment, supplies, and living expenses. These calculations would be based on actual expenditures (e.g., tuition fees) or reasonable estimates (e.g., living expenses that cover students' basic needs), much as in the existing loans system. The established formulas should be easily understood and simple to follow in order to be fair and to keep application and administration costs down, but flexible enough to cover students in varying circumstances.[11]

---

[10]The basic elements of this New Architecture were first proposed in Finnie (2003).

[11]In the previous section we mentioned that schooling and living costs are treated separately in many other countries, whereas in Canada they are added together in order to assess the student's overall need and arrive at a single aid package, and we follow that lead here.

Next, similar types of formulas would be used for arriving at what students and their parents were expected to contribute towards these costs — again much like the current system in structure, but with the sorts of adjustments suggested above in order to make them more reasonable and realistic. We would also simplify these formulas in order to make them — and the resulting aid calculations — more transparent and user friendly and less intimidating to those who wanted to know where they stood in terms of the assistance to which they are entitled.

These first elements would be similar to the existing system. Of more radical difference would be that the resulting difference between costs and resources available would be declared the student's financial need, and this full amount would comprise the student's financial aid package.

The composition of the aid package would then be determined, in particular its balance between loans and grants. We propose that the first, say, $5,000 (per year), of assistance be given in the form of a student loan. This "loan up-front" approach would keep incentives right for the most critical first dollars of aid (higher education is an expensive undertaking leading to substantial expected private benefits); it would deliver this first portion of aid in a cost-effective manner (a dollar of government spending on loans goes much further than a dollar spent on grants because the money is effectively recycled as it is paid back); and it would generally limit borrowing to well-defined, reasonable amounts, thus addressing an important element of the "debt aversion" issue.[12]

This loan-first rather than, say, grant-first approach would also be consistent with the existing Canadian system, and thus presumably conform to Canadian's values in this regard. Of course the $5,000 amount could be adjusted according to public debate.

These loans would carry subsidies similar to those that exist in the current student loan system. The money would, therefore, be interest-free while the individual remained in school, the student would be eligible for assistance in the repayment period (see further on this below), and the government would absorb the costs of default in one manner or another (as it has done in different ways over the years).

The balance of the aid would be given in the form of a (non-repayable) grant. This more generous — and expensive — form of assistance would thus be reserved for those who have greater overall need, and would deliver

---

[12] See Finnie (2001, 2002) on the advantages of loans over grants in these and other respects.

Ross Finnie, Alex Usher and Hans Vossensteyn

a price subsidy (the fact that the money does not have to be repaid effectively reduces the cost of the schooling) where it is likely to be most effective in improving access — to individuals from lower income families.[13]

All this said, a grant-first system would be an alternative option, and public debate could help resolve this issue. The rest of the package could remain as proposed.

The second major element of the New Architecture concerns the definition of "dependent" students. We propose that the classification be extended to cover most students not enrolled in graduate or professional programs. In particular, the current rules, which permit many students who take a bit longer to get through their studies because they take time off for work or travel or go to school part-time, would be tightened. A useful starting point might be to consider all single students (i.e., not married, no children) age 25 or younger in any program below graduate school or a second degree professional program to be considered as dependent and thus have their parents contribute towards their schooling. This change would reduce the amount of money going to older students from wealthier families and allow more money to be concentrated on students from lower-income families.

The next element of the system would be focused on the problem of dependent students whose parents could not or would not make the expected contributions. We propose a secondary loan program that would

---

[13]This system means that individuals with greater expenses, including those relating to being in a more costly program or going away to school, will tend to receive more assistance (and more grants), than others, and these decisions (and amounts) may be related to family background as young people from higher-income families incur higher expenses. In this sense the system we propose may have a regressive element. But we believe the proposed approach is the best solution for ensuring that the aid package is complete, and that it opens up opportunities for those from lower-income families, in particular, as they realize they are eligible for financial aid to cover the full cost of their studies — including enrolling in more expensive programs, leaving home to go to school, and so on.

An alternative approach of giving grants based on family income while loans are based on assessed need (which takes *both* family resources *and* the cost side into account) would sacrifice the "single simple program" element of our proposal, while introducing horizontal inequities whereby individuals with the same assessed need would receive different amounts of loan and grant depending on their parents' income.

allow students to borrow an additional amount up to the value of their expected parental contribution (with a maximum value equal to their assessed need). This additional program — like those in existence in many other countries — would not carry the same subsidies as the primary loan system in order to discourage excess and frivolous borrowing, including borrowing by children from higher-income families. In particular, interest should accumulate from the time the loan was taken out. This unsubsidized program could also be made available to students who were unable to meet their own expected contributions out of summer employment.

Further related to the parental non-contribution problem, we would make the expected contributions clearly understood to parents and students alike, thus putting moral pressure on parents to make those contributions to their children's educations.

The fourth element concerns the postschooling period and addresses the problem of excessive debt loads, even though this should be a limited issue in a context where loans are normally capped at $5,000 per year. We propose generous assistance for those who face excessive debt burdens relative to their postschooling incomes in the form of both shorter-term interest relief and, for chronic situations, reduction of the principal owed. Such programs currently exist, but are not heavily subscribed to. They need to be made more generous and better advertised because, while they cost relatively little, they provide a valuable form of insurance to all borrowers. Such programs thus reduce the psychological cost of borrowing even for those who never need to take advantage of the assistance, while obviously providing direct aid to those who do.

Alternatively, a full income-contingent repayment (ICR) system could be adopted, whereby payments were automatically geared to an individual's income in the postschooling period and no payments were required for those with incomes below a certain minimum level, the money collected through the tax system. While ICR systems have a long-standing tradition in the student loans literature, a strong argument could, in the current Canadian context, be made for a simpler fine-tuning (and strengthening) of the present interest and debt-relief programs, thus building on existing structures and conventions in a way that can similarly adjust payments to debt burden in an effective manner.[14]

---

[14]See Finnie and Schwartz (1996) for a discussion of income-contingent student loans in the Canadian context and how the existing interest- and debt-reduction programs make for a "near-ICR" system.

The final element of the New Architecture would be to advertise all elements of this relatively simple, effective, and equitable system so that all potential students were aware of the resources available to them and understood that financial barriers need not stand in the way of their pursuing postsecondary studies.

Consider an example. Suppose a student decided to go away to enter university and that the total cost of doing so — including both direct education-related expenses and living expenses — was $15,000 per year. The student might (by the chosen formulas) be expected to contribute $3,000 out of summer savings and (perhaps) a bit of work during term to those expenses. If the individual came from a low-income family deemed unable to make any contribution to these expenses, the resulting aid package would consist of the full difference between costs and resources available, or $12,000. Of this, $5,000 would come in the form of a loan, $7,000 as a grant. The student would be given the resources to undertake the chosen schooling through what most would probably consider a relatively generous aid package. At the same time, the student would be making a considerable contribution to those costs (the $3,000 in cash and the $5,000 loan), yet without accumulating an excessive amount of debt. And if a significant amount of borrowing did accumulate over the student's full academic career and the individual faced a substantial debt burden relative to his or her postschooling income, further assistance would come in the form of interest and debt relief.

This New Architecture might seem obvious: calculate the student's need, assess the resources available, deliver the difference as the financial aid package, bundle the aid in a judicious combination of loans and grants, provide an alternative source of loans for those whose parents do not provide the assistance expected of them, and help those who have unreasonable debt burdens in the payback period, and make the system well advertised and fully transparent. Such a system should meet the basic goal of removing financial barriers to postsecondary education and undue debt burdens would be avoided. Furthermore, once in place, the system could be fine-tuned in a relatively easy and transparent manner.

All this said, financial considerations are but one barrier to post-secondary education. Others include individuals' perceptions, attitudes, and preparation, and all these need to be addressed if access to postsecondary education is to be made truly open to all, including those from lower-income families. Efforts should, therefore, go beyond the student financial aid system to ensure that prospective students and their parents were abundantly aware of the substantial benefits that typically accrue to higher education. It would be equally worthwhile to institute measures to ensure that potential students were sufficiently well prepared to go on to higher studies when that time came. Other components of a "starting early" strategy should also be considered.[15]

Where Would the Money Come From?

In many circumstances, this new system would deliver increased amounts of aid to students who the current system leaves short-changed because aid limits fall short of the student's needs or expected parental contributions are too high. There will also be a substitution of grants for loans for some high-need students, thus driving aid costs up further. In addition, a greater number of students will likely qualify for assistance as parental contributions are made more realistic. Finally, we propose increased spending on individuals facing hardship in the postschooling period because their earnings are not high enough to comfortably cover their debt loads.

Where would the money come from? Principally from reducing current spending on student financial assistance where it is not needed to ensure access or is otherwise spent relatively ineffectively. As described above, Canada currently spends over $1.7 billion per year in education-related tax credits (37% of all student aid spending), which go to rich and poor alike, with a bias towards the better off, while the delayed nature of the benefits (i.e., tax refunds are received only after a given year's tax form is filed and refund received) further diminishes their effectiveness as a form of student aid. These could be eliminated and the proceeds put into our program. The same goes for the country's various education savings programs, which are taken up disproportionately by higher-income families who have the means of putting money aside for their children's future education costs even as improved aid packages need to be provided to those from lower-income families seeking postsecondary education today. Further savings would come from eliminating the need for existing debt-remission programs, worth another $430 million per year, which would no longer be necessary with the expansions in the up-front grants and assistance in repayment we propose, which would address the related access issues in a more efficient and effective manner. Finally, our tightening of the rules for becoming an

---

[15] See Finnie, Laporte and Lascelles (2003), Looker (2001), and Junor and Usher (2002) on these issues.

"independent" student would reduce spending on those from high-income families who benefit from the system because of the current overly-generous provisions in this regard.

Eliminating spending on these poorly targeted and relatively ineffective forms of student assistance would thus represent at least a large down payment on the funds required by our New Architecture. And while all those currently benefiting from these programs are surely glad to get it, the first goal of the Canadian student financial aid system should be to eliminate financial barriers to access for children from lower- and middle-income families, which the proposed system would do.

That said, many of those currently receiving the forms of support that would be eliminated in the proposed program — tax credits, debt remission, and so on — would receive assistance through the new system, so that what is taken away with one hand would be (at least partially) given back with the other. And most importantly, those who really needed financial support would get it under the New Architecture — and as part of a unified and coherent system that rationally ensured sufficient assistance for all who deserved it rather than giving money to many not in need while delivering to the target populations in only a limited, incomplete, and wasteful fashion.

After those basic needs were met — after the financial barriers to post-secondary education were removed for all — extra money could *then* be directed towards providing subsidies to higher-income families for this clearly costly expenditure. But, to repeat, only after the fundamental goal of assuring access to all was met.

Once costed out in a proper fashion, the parameters of the New Architecture could be adjusted to ensure it met any specific budget limits. For example, the initial $5,000 in borrowing we propose before grants cut in could be increased, thus providing the aid in a more cost-effective manner. Alternatively, it could well be that the savings we propose would provide for more than enough to cover our recommended program, meaning either additional funds could be invested in various kinds of student financial (e.g., targeted grants on specific disadvantaged groups) or the funds otherwise transferred elsewhere.

Contrasting the New Architecture to the Current System

In many ways, the system we propose would be similar to the one currently in place. And we see this as one of its benefits, as it would make its implementation easier than a more radical set of changes. Our New Architecture, would, however, also embody a number of key changes in its structure, as well as some important differences in its detailed workings.

First, while the new system would most resemble the current system of loans and need-based grants, it would represent a single unified and coherent structure that replaced the plethora of existing programs — tax credits, savings grants, debt remission, and so on — effectively doing the job of all these others more simply, thoroughly, and efficiently. In its details, the New Architecture would have the high assistance limits seen in Quebec, the debt limitation limits similar to those in Saskatchewan and Alberta, and the use of up-front grants in much the way that British Columbia uses them.

Second, the full difference between costs and resources available would be declared the student's financial need and this amount of money would comprise the individual's financial aid package. Hence, there would be no unmet need. This is in comparison to the limited aid packages which do not necessarily meet the student's assessed needs currently available.

Third, the full aid package would be delivered up front and in cash through loans and grants instead of months or even years after the fact in the form of tax credits and debt remission and other more ambiguous, uncertain, and delayed forms of assistance.

Fourth, and more in the way of important details rather than structural differences, the formulas used to estimate the student's costs and family contributions would include certain additional expenditures (e.g., computers) on the one side, and fairer, and more realistic, parental contributions on the other. The latter might begin at lower-income levels, requiring modest (nominal?) contributions from low-income parents where currently none are required. But more importantly, the required contribution would rise with income more gradually than in the present system, requiring many middle-class parents to contribute less and allowing more families to benefit from the system.

Fifth, the definition of a dependent student would be extended to include those who simply take a little longer to get into or through their studies. Meanwhile, expected parental contributions would be made clearer and provisions to protect students whose parents did not make those contributions would come in the form of a supplementary loan plan. Aid delivered by institutions would, as now, provide additional help to such students, as well as others who inevitably fell through the cracks of the proposed system (and its appeal procedures).

Sixth, assistance for those facing excessive debt loads would be based on total accumulated debt after leaving school and the individual's income, or ability to service that debt. This approach would resemble an expanded version of current interest and debt-reduction programs, while replacing all existing "debt-remission" programs, which are in most cases based on annual borrowing rather than the total accumulated by the time the individual enters repayment and in no instances take the student's capacity to pay into account.

In short, the New Architecture we propose should be a more effective, more efficient, and less wasteful means of delivering financial aid to those students who need it than the current panoply of overlapping yet incomplete programs, and thus make postsecondary schooling a more viable option for many Canadians from middle- and lower-income families.

Federal-Provincial Considerations

One potential set of complications of such a unified and coherent plan in the Canadian context stems from the associated set of constitutional and jurisdictional issues and the mosaic of different provincial (and territorial) programs currently in place, reflecting the different needs, circumstances, and manner of doing things relating to student financial aid across the country. These differences in turn stem from the fact that postsecondary education is, constitutionally, a provincial jurisdiction, but that the federal government has an established role in the area of student financial assistance, such as their operation of the Canada Student Loan Program since 1964, various grant programs, and the education-related tax credits and savings grants they provide.

Cost-sharing. The short and easy answer to such concerns is that, once the clear advantages of the unified and coherent student financial aid system proposed here are recognized, it would simply be up to the relevant provincial and federal authorities to make it work. They would owe it to their constituents to do so.

And this would not seem an impossible outcome, given the considerable level of federal-provincial cooperation that already exists in the area of student financial assistance. The Canada Student Loans Program, in particular, delivers federal dollars across the country using provincially determined need-assessment procedures and other administrative rules, while coexisting with provincial loan and grant programs, which also differ substantially from jurisdiction to jurisdiction.

A new program could, therefore, presumably function with some level of provincial diversity, rather than a single nationwide set of rules and procedures. There could, for example, be variation in the need-assessment procedures, in the mix of loans and grants, in the amount and type of assistance available in repayment, in the extra aid going to higher-income families, or any of the other specific program parameters as long as the basic characteristics of the New Architecture were maintained (i.e., a single unified program that fully met students' needs).

The federal government and each province could thus agree to a specific form of the sort of unified and comprehensive system described above, and then divide the costs according to a simple formula, such as the benchmark 60/40 split that has come to be the standard for student financial assistance in this country.

Unfortunately, this type of arrangement would have its own problems. Provinces might, most basically, vary in the degree to which they were willing (and able) to provide financial aid to students. Or they might be tempted to push up tuition rates (which they control) and otherwise inflate students' assessed costs in order to increase the amount of federal spending on student aid (even as the provinces took in the resulting increased tuition revenues). Or the federal government might balk at being locked into some sort of cost-sharing arrangement where the provinces were spending only "40–cent dollars", thus distorting spending incentives.

Still, one can imagine a set of federal-provincial agreements pegged as required against a set of reasonably well-defined costs of postsecondary education (including tuition fees) that resolved these problems, with each jurisdiction paying its share.[16] Students would, ideally, see only a single program, thus making it very clear to them the level of assistance for which they were eligible, while making their lives easier at each point of contact with the program, including application procedures, actually taking out the loan, and all aspects of repayment.

---

[16]The federal and provincial governments could, in particular, agree to a single set of need-assessment procedures by which tuition fees and other costs were not pushed up in any such artificial manner. Admissible tuition costs could, for example, be based on average fee levels across the country rather than the actual rates in a given province.

Ross Finnie, Alex Usher and Hans Vossensteyn

Splitting responsibility for the different types of costs. An alternative to this sort of total cost-sharing would be to separate the responsibility for meeting different broad categories of costs. The provinces could, for example, be made responsible for the tuition side of the student's expenses while the federal government took care of living expenses. With tuition fees currently in the $4,000–$6,000 range in most cases (at least for the benchmark bachelor's degree programs in the arts, sciences, and humanities), this would likely work out to represent something close to the traditional/current 40/60 provincial-federal split.

Such an approach would have the additional advantage of keeping the provinces financially, and politically, responsible for the consequences of their tuition policies, thus avoiding the incentive problems described above. In particular, if they raised tuition fees, they would be responsible for providing additional financial aid to those who needed it as a result.

Another variation on the cost-separation idea would be to separate the loans and grants portions of the program, with the provinces being responsible for loans and the federal government being responsible for grants (or vice versa).

Going it alone. In the absence of even limited federal-provincial cooperation of the type just described, any single government — federal or provincial — could, on its own, adopt a formula and set of procedures that *would* work were both levels of government cooperating in a reasonable manner, and then hold up their end of the arrangement.

In the face of provincial intransigence, for example, the federal government could adopt a reasonable need-assessment procedure, guarantee its 60% share of the assessed aid package, and provide that financing in a mix that made sense were the whole package delivered in a unified manner (e.g., the first $5,000 in loans, the rest in grants). Any single province could do the same thing. Students would probably not get their full aid packages as recommended here, and would be similarly denied the other positive elements of our New Architecture in any complete degree and otherwise have their lives complicated by the lack of federal-provincial cooperation. But such unilateralism might represent a credible last resort for a government wanting to improve the student financial aid system.

In such a situation, the responsibility of each level of government would presumably be clear, perhaps creating pressure for greater cooperation — especially if there were other jurisdictions where the system was in fact working in a cooperative manner to students' advantage.

This is, to be sure, very much a second-best scenario. It would likely provide at least a partial improvement in the amount and mix of aid to students and, perhaps most importantly, might prevent one level of government from blocking the move to reform on the part of another — as even the threat of this unilateral option could help bring the parties to the table and provide an additional incentive to reach an agreement. But the existence of two essentially uncoordinated systems would likely lead to various complications, result in a continuation of the problem of unmet need, and otherwise produce only limited gains relative to what a full New Architecture would realize.

Letting the provinces run their own aid programs. One final possibility might be for the federal government to simply transfer funds to the provinces on the condition that they run student financial aid packages that broadly conform to the New Architecture principles and provide sufficient visibility for the contributions made by the federal government. The provinces might then be free to fine-tune their individual approaches within such an overall Education Accord — perhaps each learning from others in the spirit elucidated in the Social Union Framework Agreement of the late 1990s. That said, arriving at the federal government's precise share of total spending (i.e., their transfer to the provinces), perhaps on a province-by-province basis, might present certain challenges, especially in the context of the incentive problems noted above.

Other possibilities and the general principle. Other approaches could be tried. The overarching goal would be to ensure that the federal and provincial governments together committed themselves to delivering student aid packages of the type prescribed by the New Architecture we propose. The driving force should be the understanding that students would not generally care how federal-provincial authorities were divided up or who paid which share of their aid package, only that the program delivered the assistance they needed in the most administratively simple manner possible.

Who Would, and Wouldn't, be Covered by the New Architecture?

We have written this proposal as if it were intended for community college students or those in basic undergraduate (non-professional) university programs; and that is indeed our primary policy target. Other cases include graduate level and professional university programs. These would require special variants of the New Architecture proposed here.

Any plan for graduate students would, in particular, need to take into account the substantial scholarships and teaching/research assistantships available to many candidates, as well as a wider variation in tuition rates. Individuals who go on to these advanced levels are also likely to go on to earn higher salaries than others. In our opinion, the system we propose would comprise a good starting point for devising a graduate assistance program that best served that clientele. We would suggest, most of all, retaining the unified one-system aspect of what we have proposed — while of course taking the other sources of funds for which upper level students are eligible (scholarships, research, and teaching assistantships, etc.) into account.

Professional schools will likely require a substantially different system. Medicine, law, business, and other professional students now commonly face tuition fees of $10,000 per year or more, sometimes many multiples of this, and these trends remain sharply upward. At the same time, most such programs continue to represent good personal investments in terms of future earnings. Student financial aid packages for professional students should reflect these differences, while still recognizing the basic principle of our New Architecture: the need to eliminate financial barriers that stand in the way of postsecondary education opportunities, especially for those from lower-income families, in an effective and efficient manner.

Conclusion

In this paper we have argued that the current system of student financial aid in Canada has a number of major weaknesses. It is complex, delivering many different kinds of support from a variety of sources, and much of the aid is poorly targeted. The result is that it is unnecessarily cumbersome and does not deliver as much assistance to some who need it while providing unneeded benefits to others, including those from the very wealthiest families. We can do better than this.

We have proposed a New Architecture that would replace the plethora of existing programs with a single coherent program that delivered the full amount of aid required to those who needed it in an efficient, effective, and non-wasteful manner. The system would consist of a basic need-based loan/grant support package (with loans capped at $5,000 per year as we propose it), plus a supplementary loan system for those whose parents did not make the contributions expected of them and a relief program for those facing high debt-to-earnings ratios in repayment.

The system should thus effectively provide two critical guarantees to prospective postsecondary students: that financial barriers need not stand in the way of their studies, and that loan burdens will be reasonable and manageable. In doing so, we believe the program would comprise an important advance in terms of enhancing access to postsecondary education in Canada.

Furthermore, the proposed system could be developed without inventing a whole new set of structures and procedures from the ground up — a disruption that would carry its own set of special challenges and costs. Perhaps the best news of all is that we could likely build such a system without spending any new public money.

We acknowledge that any proposed changes would have to reckon with various potentially thorny federal-provincial jurisdictional issues, and that some higher-income Canadians might balk at supporting a change that saw them lose certain tax credits, savings grants or other privileges. But we believe support could be gained for the proposed reform of one of the nation's most important social programs if it allowed its fundamental goal of eliminating financial barriers to postsecondary education to be more effectively and more efficiently realized.

The changes to the Canada Student Loans Program announced in the 2004 federal budget in many ways reflects many of the recommendations made in this paper: increasing loan limits, relaxing parental contributions, directing more money to lower-income students (albeit in the limited form of a dedicated grant for first-year students). The changes to the Canada Education Savings Grants and the new Canada Learning Bond are also in a sense welcome because at least they counter the very definite pro-rich bias of the existing savings incentives.[17]

While these measures are welcome and will likely prove beneficial to students, they constitute only small, unilateral changes to the existing system. Unmet need still exists, parental contributions appear to still be too high, and we continue to waste billions on unneeded tax credits. A more profound re-think of access policy is still required.

---

[17] See Education Policy Institute (2004) for a detailed analysis of these recent budget measures.

Appendix: More Details on the Canadian System

Need-Based Assistance Limits

Need-based aid for single, full-time students with no dependents (and in some cases others) was limited to the following amounts in 2002–03 (based on 34 weeks of study).

Province	Type of Student	Total Maximum Loan	Total Maximum Grants (Up-front)	Source of Up-front Grants	Total Maximum Assistance[a]
BC	All	$275/week	$119/week (35th through 136th week of post-secondary only)	B.C. Grant, millennium bursary	$275/week
AB	Single, no dependents	$10,700/year ($315/week)	$3,000/semester ($88/week)	Alberta Opportunity Grant, millennium bursary	$10,700/year ($315/week)
	Students who have to move	$12,700/year ($374/week)	$4,500/semester ($132/week)	Alberta Opportunity Grant, Supplementary Grant, millennium bursary	$12,700/year ($374/week)
SK	Single, no dependents	$180/week	$95/week	Saskatchewan Grant	$275/week
	Special Incentive Students[b]	$180/week	$205/week	Saskatchewan Grant	$385/week
MB	All	$275/week	$40/week	Manitoba Study Assistance	$315/week
ON	All	$275/week	$3,000 bursary/year ($88/week)	Millennium bursary	$275/week
QC	CEGEP	$2,005/year[c]	$12,451/year	AFE Bursary, millennium bursary	$14,152/year ($416/week)
	Undergraduate	$2,460/year[c]	$14,479/year	AFE Bursary, millennium bursary	$16,619/year ($489/week)
	Graduate	$3,255/year[c]	$14,479/year	AFE Bursary	$17,414/year ($512/week)

(Continued)

Ross Finnie, Alex Usher and Hans Vossensteyn

NB	All	$275/week	$50/week	New Brunswick Bursary	$325/week
PE	All	$275/week	$0	N/A	$275/week
NS	All	$315/week	$0	N/A	$315/week
NF	All	$275/week	Up to $1,750/year ($51/week)	Millennium bursary	$316/week

Notes: [a] The values in the "Total maximum loan" and "Total maximum grants" columns do not necessarily add up to the figure in the final column, "Total maximum assistance", because grants sometimes displace loans.

[b] Special incentive students include Non-Status Indians, Métis, and students residing in northern Saskatchewan.

[c] These totals apply only for students eligible for both loans and grants (students within the normal duration of studies plus one term). If a student is eligible for loans only (students within normal duration of studies plus two or three terms), then the total maximum assistance will be equal to the maximum loan amount.

Debt-Reduction Programs

The following debt-reduction programs are currently in existence.

Jursidiction	Program	Description	Automatic?
BC	None	N/A	N/A
AB	Alberta Student Loan Relief Benefit	Available to first-time, first-year post-secondary students who have been issued more than $5,000 in combined federal/provincial loans and have completed a year of studies. The amount of loan relief is equal to the total value of federal/provincial loans minus $2,500 per semester of study (normally, $5,000). It is paid at the end of the first year and applied against provincial loans.	Yes

(Continued)

	Program Completion Loan Relief	Available to graduating students who have been issued more than $5,000 in combined federal/provincial loans. The amount of loan relief is equal to the total value of federal/provincial loans minus $5,000 per year of study. It is paid upon completion of studies and applied against provincial loans.	Yes
SK	Remission (Special Incentive Students only)	Available to Special Incentive Students whose total student loan assistance exceeds $105 per week of study. Remission is available on the amount between $105 and $180 per week of study, and is only applied to the student's first 60 weeks of post-secondary study. Successful completion of 60% of a full course load is required.	Yes
	Millennium Bursary	Available to undergraduate students who meet minimal merit criteria and are among those with the highest need. The award size varies between $2,000 and $4,000, depending on need.	Yes
MB	Manitoba Millennium Bursary	Given to undergraduate students who do not receive a Canada Millennium Scholarship Foundation bursary and who have loans exceeding $6,000. The award reduces outstanding loans to $6,000.	Yes
	Millennium Bursary	Available to undergraduate students who meet minimal merit criteria and are among those with the highest need. The award size varies between $1,000 and $4,500, depending on need.	Yes
ON	Ontario Student Opportunity Grant	If the student's combined federal/provincial loan exceeds $7,000 for two terms or $10,500 for three terms, a grant will be awarded to reduce debt to those amounts. It is paid at the end of each year and applied against provincial loans.	Yes
QC	Remission	Available to students who have completed studies within a normal period of time and who have received a bursary during each year of study. The amount of remission is 15% of the outstanding loan.	No

(Continued)

Ross Finnie, Alex Usher and Hans Vossensteyn

NB	Millennium Bursary	Available to undergraduate students who meet minimal merit criteria and are among those with the highest need. The award size varies between $2,000 and $4,000, depending on need.	Yes
NS	Millennium Bursary	Available to undergraduate students who meet minimal merit criteria and are among those with the highest need. The award size varies between $2,000 and $3,500, depending on need.	Yes
PE	Debt Reduction Grant	Available to students who complete a year of studies and whose combined federal/provincial loans exceed $6,000. The amount of loan relief is equal to the student's total federal/provincial loans minus $6,000, up to a maximum payment of $2,000. It is paid at the end of each year and applied against provincial loans.	Yes
	Millennium Bursary	Available to undergraduate students who meet minimal merit criteria and are among those with the highest need. The award size varies between $2,000 and $4,000, depending on need.	Yes
NF	Remission	Available to students who have graduated in a timely manner from a program of study in Newfoundland of at least 80 weeks' length. The student's combined federal/provincial debt must exceed $22,016 for programs between 80 and 128 weeks in length or $172 per week for programs that exceed 128 weeks. The amount of loan relief is equal to the total value of the student's federal/provincial loans minus the debt minimums described above. It is paid upon completion of studies and applied against provincial loans.	No
	Millennium Bursary	Available to undergraduate students who meet minimal merit criteria and are among those with the highest need. The award size varies between $2,000 and $3,500, depending on need, and 50% comes in the form of loan remission.	Yes

References

Association of Universities and Colleges in Canada (AUCC). 2002. *Trends*. Ottawa: Association of Universities and Colleges in Canada.

Barr N. 2005. "Financing Higher Education: Commentary on the 2004 UK Higher Education Act", in this volume.

Canada. Human Resources Development Canada. 2002. *Knowledge Matters*. Ottawa.

Dobson, I.R. 2003. "Access to University in Australia: Who Misses Out?" in M. Tight (ed.), *Access and Exclusion*. London: JAI Elsevier Science.

Education Policy Institute. 2004. "Federal Budget Review", *Epicentre* (Spring). Toronto: Education Policy Institute.

Ekos Research. 2003. *Making Ends Meet*. Montreal: Canada Millennium Scholarship Foundation.

Finnie, R. 2001. *Measuring the Load, Easing the Burden: Canada's Student Loan Programs and the Revitalization of Canadian Postsecondary Education*. Commentary No. 155. Toronto: C.D. Howe Institute.

_____. 2002. "Student Financial Assistance in Canada: The Need for More Loans", *Journal of Higher Education and Policy Management* 24(2), 155-170. (See also, Finnie, R. 2001. "Student Loans: The Empirical Record", *Canadian Journal of Higher Education* 31(3), 93-142.)

_____. 2003. "A New Architecture for the Canadian Student Financial Aid System", *Policy Options* 24(8), 50-53.

Finnie, R. and S. Schwartz. 1996. *Student Loans in Canada: Past, Present and Future*. Toronto: C.D. Howe Institute.

Finnie, R., C. Laporte and E. Lascelles. 2003. "Family Background and Access to Post-Secondary Education: What Happened in the 1990s?" Discussion Paper. Kingston: School of Policy Studies, Queen's University.

Finnie, R., S. Schwartz and E. Lascelles. 2003. "Smart Money? Government Spending on Student Financial Aid in Canada", in B. Doern (ed.), *How Ottawa Spends 2003-2004: Regime Change and Policy Shift*. Oxford: Oxford University Press.

Hemingway, F. 2003a. *Assessing Canada's Student Aid Need Assessment Policies*. Montreal: Canada Millennium Scholarship Foundation.

_____. 2003b. "Pressure Points in Student Financial Assistance". Presentation to the Canada Millennium Scholarship Foundation *Pathways to Access* conference, October 2–4, 2003, Ottawa.

The International Comparative Higher Education Finance and Accessibility Project (ICHEFAP). 2003. *Database Student–Parent Cost by Country*. SUNY-Buffalo: Graduate School of Education. At http://www.gse.buffalo.edu/org/inthigheredfinance.

Junor, S. and A. Usher. 2002. *The Price of Knowledge*. Montreal: Canada Millennium Scholarship Foundation.

Looker, D.E. 2001. *Why Don't They Go On? Factors Affecting the Decisions of Canadian Youth Not to Pursue Post-Secondary Education.* Montreal: Canada Millennium Scholarship Foundation.

Milligan, K. 2002. *Tax Preferences for Education Savings: Are RESPs Effective?* Commentary No. 174. Toronto: C.D. Howe Institute.

Institute of Intergovernmental Relations, Queen's University. 2003. *Canada Millennium Scholarship Foundation: Evaluation of the Foundation's Performance, 1998–2002.* Montreal: Canada Millennium Scholarship Foundation.

Shipley L., S. Ouellette and F. Cartwright. 2003. "Planning and Preparation: First Results from the Survey of Approaches to Educational Planning (SAEP) 2002". Ottawa: Statistics Canada.

Usher, A. 2004. *Who Gets What? The Distribution of Government Subsidies for Post-Secondary Education in Canada.* Montreal: Canada Millennium Scholarship Foundation.

Vossensteyn, J.J. 1999, "Where in Europe Would People Like to Study? The Affordability of Higher Education in Nine Western European Countries", in *Higher Education* 37, 159-176.

_____. 2003a. "Fiscal Stress, Worldwide Trends in Higher Education Finance and in Policy Responses to the Condition of Higher Education Austerity". Paper presented at the University Reform and Accessibility of Higher Education conference, June 15-17, Prague, Czech Republic, Enschede: CHEPS.

_____. 2003b. "Models of Student Support, Underlying Principles and Key Examples". Paper presented at the Canada Millennium Scholarship Foundation and CASFA annual conference, Ottawa, September 19-20, 2003, Enschede: CHEPS.

How Best to Fund Postsecondary Education: A Graduate Tax?

H. Lorne Carmichael

When a firm wishes to raise money there are a number of sources it can turn to. The company or its owners may have the capital in hand. If not, there may be public subsidies available, or there may be banks willing to lend the money. Failing this, there may be private investors willing to provide funding in return for a debt obligation or a share of future profits. The structure of these financial instruments can become quite complicated.

The prospects facing a student seeking to pay for postsecondary education are both better and worse. They are better because in many cases the student will have the money or have relatives willing to provide it for no obligation at all. In other cases there may be private scholarships or bursaries available, again for no obligation other than to continue to succeed in the program. And, of course, a large part of the cost is covered by public subsidy. However, if these sources are not sufficient then the only remaining option is to borrow the money through the student loans program, and incur a debt that must be paid back from future earnings.

In recent years in Canada the level of public support for postsecondary education has been declining, and students have had to pay more in tuition. In some cases this financial burden is substantial, and this has led to a new

I would like to thank the Social Sciences and Humanities Research Council of Canada for financial support of this project.

interest in the various ways that students might finance their share of the cost of postsecondary education. Why are we limited in Canada to standard loans with continuing, mortgage style, repayments? This paper will outline and compare some of the alternatives that have been suggested and implemented in Canada and around the world.

There are no new ideas in this paper, and indeed there are very few that can even be called recent. The problem of funding postsecondary education has received steady attention from economists, and the work has been surveyed already in several places (Barr, 1993; Greenaway and Haynes, 2003). My hope is that this paper will make some aspects of the problem and some of the suggested solutions accessible to a wider audience. My overall goal is to promote the discussion of a scheme whereby postsecondary education is funded through a special tax on university graduates. In essence, this program would ask the public to take an equity interest in the success of its most talented scholars.

Background

Currently in Canada about 25% of high-school graduates will go on to take a university degree. Is this the right number? If we look simply at the rate of return to a university degree, the answer would seem to be "no". Postsecondary education is a good investment for those who currently attend and graduate. Estimates of the private rate of return in Canada and elsewhere regularly top 10% as revealed in Table 1.

Of course, money is not the only benefit that is correlated with educational status. University graduates also enjoy better health (Kenkel, 1991), and spend less time in jail (Lochner and Moretti, 2001). As well, there appear to be some external benefits to having an educated population. Higher education is linked to participation in community affairs, the democratic process, and volunteer work (Bynner and Egerton, 2000). As well, low-skilled American workers earn higher wages if they live in cities that have a higher proportion of university graduates (Moretti, 2004). This could be due to complementarities in production among workers, as examined by Johnson (1984). Finally, the effect of higher education on economic growth seems sure to be positive, although estimates are imprecise (Bassanini and Scarpenta, 2001).

Given these benefits it would seem that more and more people should be taking advantage of the opportunity to go to university. However, the

H. Lorne Carmichael

Table 1: Private Rates of Return to University Education in the OECD

	Men %	Women %
Canada	8.7	9.9
Denmark	11.5	11.1
France	14.3	15.4
Germany	9.1	8.4
Italy	6.5	8.4
Japan	7.9	7.2
Netherlands	12.1	12.5
Sweden	11.4	10.8
United Kingdom	18.5	16.1
United States	14.9	14.7
Unweighted average	11.7	11.8

Source: Table is taken from Blondal, Field and Giroard (2002).

numbers above are average monetary returns for those who attend. They do not reflect the expected returns for those individuals who do not attend now but would attend if the system were expanded.

While we have all heard stories of university graduates driving taxis, explicit data on the returns to education for a marginal applicant is hard to find. In one interesting study, Ockert (2003) examined a unique dataset from Sweden. In 1982 college applicants were centrally ranked and admission was granted to those with the highest qualifications. There was a group of students at the bottom of the "acceptable" category who were considered equally qualified and who were randomly assigned admission to the fixed number of places remaining after all the higher ranking applicants were placed. Tuition was free. Ockert had information on the qualifications of each applicant and labour market histories up to 1996. In his sample the rate of return to an acceptance letter was actually negative — most marginal applicants would have earned more money had they not been admitted to university, even though the overall average rate of return was positive.

This data is hardly conclusive, but it is clear that some university graduates earn much more than others, so that the average rate of return to a university education will be significantly higher than the marginal return. It also seems likely that some university graduates whose private returns are below average, say because they have not found work in their preferred fields, would also generate below average social returns. This means that in spite of the high measured rates of return to university education, the social benefit of educating another student may be fairly small. If so, the goal of the university system should not necessarily be to bring in more students. It may well be true that certain students who could benefit are not currently able to attend, but it may also be true that there are some students who are attending who would be better off if they went straight to work or into the college system.[1]

Overall, one inescapable conclusion from this data is that those who attend and graduate from university enjoy a considerable advantage over those who do not. Graduates earn higher incomes, and enjoy better health, longer lives, and higher social status than non-graduates, at least partly due to their experience in university. Unfortunately, the fact that these benefits are not enjoyed by everyone may not reflect just their lack of access. Some people lack the ability to do well at school, and simply will not benefit from a university education.

With this picture in mind it is time to discuss the goals of a program that helps students afford the cost of a university education. I will assume that there is no great need for the overall number of students to be larger or smaller. It is also clear that due to external benefits and in the interest of equalizing the tax treatment of investments in education with investments in capital goods there should be a significant public subsidy to post-secondary education.[2] In what follows, to focus discussion, I will also assume that the size of this current subsidy is about right, and that needed increases in funding should come from higher tuition payments by students.

---

[1] The statement is certainly true *ex post* given that there are always students who do not make it through first year.

[2] I outline the taxation argument in another paper (Carmichael, 1999) and work out some illustrative examples. The required subsidy, which corrects for the fact that opportunity costs are taxed at a lower rate than higher future salaries, is suprisingly large given that there are no external benefits assumed.

The paper will focus on the issue of how best to structure those payments made by students, whatever their size, so as to achieve the important goals of efficiency, accessibility, and equity. We shall see that a major increase in fees need not reduce accessibility.

Goals

Economic efficiency in the context of a student assistance program is similar in concept to accessibility. An important part of each criterion is to make sure that any student with the ability to benefit from a postsecondary education has the opportunity to attend. To achieve efficiency we would also like to be sure that those without this ability do not waste their time in university, but rather enter the college system or the labour market directly. There is another difference as well. To achieve accessibility it must be the case that able students attend even if they do not have the money to pay the costs.

A strong case for accessibility has to do with the desire for equal opportunity. Postsecondary education is a terrific investment for those who attend. It is not fair that some qualified people should be denied access to this opportunity because of the unwillingness or inability of their parents and relatives to pay for them. However, since an education is an investment, this issue might boil down simply to the efficiency of capital markets. If students can borrow money at the going rate of interest, then any investment as profitable as postsecondary education would be accessible to everyone who has the ability. Of course, it is generally not possible to borrow in this way. Students find it difficult to use their future income and good character as collateral on a private commercial loan. Much of the economic literature on student loan programs uses this as a starting point.

A complicating factor is that some of the private benefits of a university education, as discussed above, are not monetary. Apart from better health and other outcomes as discussed above, a university education has important consumption value. Graduates arguably enjoy their experience and most consider it to have improved their lives. The rich are able to consume many goods that the poor cannot, but is it fair that this particular benefit be restricted to those who can afford it?

This issue arises often in the discussion of health care. Suppose there was a cure for a particular disease and the last dose was being auctioned off to two bidders. One is rich and is worried about getting sick in the future while the other is poor and will die soon without the drug. Economic efficiency requires that the good be allocated to the person willing to pay the most. Auctions are an excellent mechanism for this, and in the normal course of bidding the rich person might be expected to submit the highest bid, especially if he or she were unaware of the condition of the opponent.

Even though it is economically efficient, most people would consider this outcome unconscionable. Under the circumstances the drug would be considered a "merit good" — that is, a good that should be allocated (perhaps at no cost) to those individuals who need it without reference to their income. It is clear that most Canadians consider medical care to be a merit good, and this belief underscores much of our health policy. All taxpayers pay for the delivery of health services to those who need them, with the definition of "need" delegated to the medical experts. But should access to a university education also be treated as a merit good in Canada?

The argument here is not so compelling. First, it is clear that students are not sick: by attending university they gain a benefit that is unavailable to the rest of the population. They are not even drawn randomly, but come overwhelmingly from families that already have greater education and higher incomes than the average. This does not seem likely to change. Expansion of the British university system from about 10% of the eligible population to near 20% had virtually no effect on the socio-economic demographics of the student population (Greenaway and Haynes, 2003). Further, there seems to be little that individuals or policymakers can do about the situation. Every trait that psychologists can measure is partly heritable, including intelligence (Turkheimer, 2000), and the impact of the home environment is relatively small. A recent argument that educating parents will lead to better educated children has so far found little empirical support (Black, Devereux and Salvanes, 2003).[3] And, finally, from a practical and moral standpoint it is up to the voters of Canada to decide what they will support, through their taxes, as a merit good. They have clearly made the choice that medical care qualifies, but that postsecondary education does not.

Nonetheless, the argument for universal access to all the benefits of postsecondary education continues to be made, largely by students and professors from within the system. This articulate voice, along with the

---

[3]There is a strong correlation between parental education and children's education, but so far there is little to suggest this is not due largely to the heritability of the ability to do well at school.

H. Lorne Carmichael

tacit but no less powerful consilience of educated middle- and upper-class voters, who want neither higher tuition fees nor higher taxes, has made it politically impossible to raise tuition or taxes in support of education at a time when the university system is in dire need of more resources. In this context, a mechanism that could allow for an increase in tuition fees and at the same time could transparently and obviously maintain or improve accessibility would be most welcome.

Student Loan Programs

In Canada the problem of accessibility is addressed with scholarships and bursaries for poorer students and with the Student Loan Program. This program clearly helps many students to attend university. Nonetheless, some students graduate with high levels of debt, and it has been argued that this debt level, perhaps because the anticipated nominal value is high relative to anything in the student's pre-university experience, will deter enrolment even though it may turn out to be manageable relative to post-graduation income. The empirical importance of this factor has yet to be established (Finnie and Laporte, 2003), but the argument retains some power in public discussions. A second argument is that the desire to pay off a debt will deter some students from entering occupations that have large public benefit but are less well-paid. Examples might include social work and family medicine. If poorer students are more likely to enter these occupations in the first place because of their pre-university experience, the problem will be exacerbated.[4] It is also clear that, if the non-monetary returns to a university degree are seen to be a merit good, then a loan

---

[4]These criticisms of a loan system have been made for many years.

Certainly working class children have little or no experience of financial manoeuvres.... They especially would be unwilling to saddle themselves with future debts, to indenture themselves. The resulting bias on entry into higher education to the sons and daughters of the wealthy ... would lead to a form of social ossification with obvious moral and technical disadvantages. Second, the penalties will be great for those people who after graduation either enter professions which, although of great importance to the community, do not receive such recognition in terms of salary payments, or enter professions in which the risk of low incomes is very significant, such as the writing of poetry. (Merrett, 1967, pp. 292–293)

program will not provide access to those who want to attend purely for these benefits.

An income-contingent student loan program, such as the one in place in Australia (Chapman, 1997) would seem to mitigate these issues somewhat, but perhaps not completely. Under such a system debt payments are geared to income, but the debt remains as a potential claim on future income until it is repaid. Whether this is sufficient to induce "debt aversion" is again an open question, and may depend on the character of the individual. Some may be willing to treat the entire amount as a gift to be repaid (perhaps) with public service, but others may continue to see it as an obligation and this may affect occupational choice.

The classic problem with using private loans to support investments in human capital is that there is nothing to use for collateral. It is easy to borrow money to buy a car because the bank can repossess the vehicle if you stop making payments. If you borrow money for your education the only thing you can offer as collateral is the expectation that you will eventually be earning enough money to repay the loan.

Since it is inevitable that some students will never earn a significant income after graduation, in order to get banks to offer student loans there must be a public subsidy. It follows that a student loan program, income contingent or not, is inequitable because it is not designed to break even. Students who never pay off their debts are subsidized by general taxpayers, including many who did not go to university, and whose children will never attend. Of course, it is always possible to mitigate this inequity by introducing other taxes or subsidies, but the program itself introduces a new subsidy to the more privileged.

A Graduate Tax

There is a program that in principle would provide universal access to university and would require no public subsidy. The earliest version of the idea is probably due to Friedman and Kuznets (1945), who argued that students should consider selling an equity share in their education. This would mean that a student would accept money while in school and pay it back later, but rather than principal plus interest the payment would be a percentage of future income. A version of this idea was tried out by Yale

University in the 1970s[5] and a modified version is still in place at the Yale Law School.[6]

A major issue with this program turned out to be the problem of default. Even though Yale could require participants to allow it to get information on their income from the Internal Revenue Service, it still had to face the problem of getting payment. According to West (1976) this was the most critical issue.

The problem of default is related to the fact that the courts will not allow individuals to sell ownership rights in their human capital. This would amount to slavery, or indentured servitude at best, both of which are illegal. Nonetheless, we are all indentured to the government through our obligation to pay taxes, and every April we all have to settle up. The government also has no difficulty in determining our income for the year, particularly for university graduates who participate for the most part in the above-ground economy. This has led several authors to suggest a version of the equity plan where the government provides the equity and then collects the return through a "graduate tax". Early references include Merrett (1967) and Glennerster, Merrett and Wilson (1968), while much more recently Poutvaara (2003) has proposed such a tax for the European Community.

To fix ideas, suppose that the current direct public subsidy to education is held constant and that tuition payments for a student in an arts and science program at a university were increased to $10,000 per year. Given recent government cutbacks this would restore overall quality of service to

---

[5]Discussions of the Yale Tuition Postponement Option appear in Nerlove (1975) and West (1976). Participants agreed to pay Yale 0.4% of their gross income over a 35-year period per $1,000 advanced to them. In practice, since there was an upper limit on the amount that would have to be paid back, the scheme shared some attributes of an income-contingent loan system. Nonetheless, to "buy out" of the plan the graduate would have to pay back 150% of their initial allocation, plus interest.

[6]This is called the Career Options Assistance Program. The plan is designed to allow graduates to take on lower paying jobs without fear of bankruptcy due to high loan payments. This plan is closer to a pure income-contingent loan plan, and is subsidized by the endowment funds of Yale University.

about the levels of 1990.[7] Total tuition cost to the student over four years would be $40,000.

The idea behind a graduate tax is that there is a cut-off salary below which no graduate would pay any tax. In the simplest case, gross earnings above this rate are taxed at a fixed percentage. Suppose we set a cut-off salary of $35,000, which is close to the average salary of an arts and science grad two years after graduation.[8] A simple spreadsheet calculation shows that, if we assume real income growth of 3%, and also use a discount rate of 3%, then a tax rate of 9% on income in excess of $35,000 over the next 35 years will raise, in current present value, the sum of $40,534.71. Someone who starts at $45,000 under the same assumptions will pay $72,034.71. Someone who starts at $25,000 will pay nothing for the first 12 years, and the present value of all subsequent payments is only $14,330.48. These figures appear in Table 2.

There are many details. Of course, the cut-off income would have to be adjusted for inflation on an ongoing basis. Since the payments reflect the cost of an investment that raises future income, it is clear that they should be deductible from otherwise taxable income, just as the current system allows the deduction of direct tuition payments. It is also clear that universities cannot wait 35 years to be paid in full for the services they provide to students. The only way this system could be useful at all is if the federal government pays the university up front in return for the right to levy a tax on the student.[9] This might require new deficit finance on the part of the government, but such debt would be backed by growth in the

---

[7]This was the conclusion of a committee set up to study the requirements for a quality undergraduate education in the Arts and Science Faculty at Queen's University. The report is available (April 2004) at http://www.queensu.ca/artsci/internal/quality/pdf/A&SQuality_draft_rept010825.pdf.

[8]See Finnie (1999) for a trove of data on earnings of university graduates two and five years post degree.

[9]It is also clear that if the government did not pay up front, it could not be trusted to separate the income from this tax and dutifully send it to the universities. Funding would be set according to political priorities and health care would likely win.

H. Lorne Carmichael

Table 2: Plan 1

Discount rate		3% per year
Earnings growth		3% per year
Tuition	4 years at $10,000	$40,000
Graduate tax payments last		35 years

Payment Formula: $P_t = (Y_t - 35,000) * (0.09)$

Starting income		PDV of payment stream
$25,000	no payments for 12 years	$14,330.48
$35,000		$40,534.71
$45,000		$72,034.71

human capital of Canadians, an asset the government is in a unique position to appropriate.[10]

The calculation of a "break even" tax rate in practice will be a complicated task, and it would take us beyond the scope of this paper to attempt a more precise calculation. In practice salaries for university graduates grow at a much faster rate than 3% in the early years of a career,[11] which might substantially reduce the required tax rate. As well, if the cutoff income is reduced to $30,000 then a tax rate of just over 7% is all that is needed to break even on someone who starts at $35,000. So it

---

[10]Indeed there is nothing to prevent the government from making a market in these claims. This would have the advantage of creating an asset owned by the government to offset the up-front payments made to students.

[11]The data in Finnie (1999) suggest the average growth rate in real earnings between the second and fifth years post degree is at least 5% per year.

might be reasonable to think that the rate could be kept below 10%, or 0.25% per $1,000 advanced.

A huge assumption that underlies these calculations is that participation in the program is required of all students.[12] In practice, if participation is voluntary, a serious problem of adverse selection can be expected to arise. Those students who expect to do well and whose families can afford the direct cost will likely opt out of the program since this is by far the less costly option. In fact there is another problem of adverse selection as well — given that the up-front cost of university has fallen and in particular if the program is expanded to cover some of a student's living expenses, some young people with very weak intentions to study and low expected future income may decide to enter university with no expectation of graduating.

The second of these problems can be handled in the same way that it is now — by requiring students to show academic promise in order to be admitted to university and to continue in their programs. As argued above, there is no strong evidence that the overall number of students attending university is too low. This is perhaps the one area where we should restrict accessibility in order to achieve efficiency. Some students would not be helping themselves, and they might be interfering with the experience of others.

The first issue is more problematic. The Yale Tuition Postponement Option partially addressed it by allowing participants in the plan to cease making payments once their accumulated total exceeded 150% of the advanced amount, plus interest. Nonetheless, participation rates remained below 40%, which may explain why the tax rate under the plan was as high as it was — 0.4% per $1,000 advanced. This would be equivalent to 16% in the example above.

The easiest way to encourage participation by high-income earners in a voluntary plan would be to increase the price of opting-out. So let us continue to list tuition for an arts and science program at $10,000. This payment is covered in full by the government for anyone who joins the graduate tax program. However, anyone who opts out of the graduate tax program would have to pay $15,000 per year. In principle there could be partial participation whereby every $1,500 advanced towards tuition payments leads to a tax of 0.25% (say) on income in excess of $35,000.

---

[12]In contrast, current demands by some students and faculty for increases in funding and zero tuition would force the participation of all taxpayers.

H. Lorne Carmichael

However, for every $1,500 "advanced" to the student for tuition, the university only receives $1,000 from the government.

After graduation participants in the plan could stop making payments once their accumulated total equals 150% of the actual cost — $60,000 plus interest for someone who participated fully. The average graduate would continue to pay the tax over her lifetime, and in present value would still expect to pay about $40,000. This means that there should be a tax rate at which this plan will break even. Those graduates who do better than average will subsidize the ones who do not. In this sense the plan is an improvement over a standard income-contingent loan plan, where graduates who earn little money are subsidized by people who never went to university, and may be earning even less. The details of this scheme are summarized in Table 3.

Table 3: Plan 2

Discount rate		3% per year
Earnings growth		3% per year
Tuition	4 years at $15,000	$60,000
Graduate tax payments last		35 years

Payment Formula: $P_t = (Y_t - 35,000) * (0.09) \sum \dfrac{P_t}{(1+r)^t} \leq 60,000$

Starting income		PDV of payment stream
$25,000	no payments for 12 years	$14,330.48
$35,000		$40,534.71
$45,000	no payments after 30 years	$60,000

Note that under the assumptions above, opting-out of the plan costs $60,000 up front, while participation leads to a cost of *at most* $60,000 in present value. Thus participation rates should be very high. Those people who cannot make the calculation and do opt out will provide a nice subsidy to the university.

One remaining problem is that the plan is beginning to look like a loan program again, given the fixed opt-out level of $60,000. Since the way a program is perceived by students seems to be at the heart of the "debt aversion" issue, this may lead to some of the same problems, even though payments are labelled as extra taxes rather than loan repayments. One way to prevent this without discouraging participation of people who expect to earn high incomes would be to redesign the tax rates so that people earning very high incomes after graduation pay at a lower rate. For example, in the case above where someone starts at a salary of $45,000 and pays 9% of income in excess of $35,000, he or she pays a total of $72,034.71 in present value. If instead, we assume that the person pays 9% of the first 50,000 of income in excess of $35,000, and a fixed amount of $4,500 per year if the income rises above $85,000, then the total payment in present value falls to $63,118.33. The total payment by the "average" student who starts at $35,000 falls to $39,649.89 from $40,534.71. Again it would seem likely that the plan could be designed to break even, although a great deal more effort and data would be needed to determine the appropriate tax rates.

The fact that the program is run by the government through the tax system avoids the problem of default that plagued the Yale Tuition Postponement Option. There is still the problem that some students may emigrate and skip payment. This is a problem for a student loan program as well, and indeed it is a problem for any student support program. In principle it is solved by requiring people to pay up before they leave. In practice there will be people who escape, and this may be a problem that cannot be entirely solved. In the end, some of the extra money paid by more successful students will subsidize the exit of others.

It seems clear that to be most successful the program should be run at the federal level. This will at least avoid problems due to interprovincial migration. However, postsecondary education is a provincial responsibility. One can only hope that the political issues here would turn out to be manageable. There is also the possibility that the costs of administering the program would be too large. This seems unlikely, however, given the experience of Australia in running its income-contingent loan scheme through the tax system.

H. Lorne Carmichael

Finally, one aspect of the current system that has not been adequately discussed in this paper is the student support available through university and private bursaries and federal programs such as the Canada Millennium Foundation. These programs attempt to identify students in financial need and provide support directly. This direct bursary system is a major factor at selective colleges in the United States.

Under a bursary system, just as with a graduate tax, richer students pay a higher price for the same education received by their poorer colleagues. The difference is in the way that "rich" and "poor" are defined. Eligibility for bursaries is determined by the income and wealth of the student and family at the time he or she attends university. Under a graduate tax the student is treated as a single individual, and wealth is determined by actual post-graduation earnings. This has the advantage that identification is automatic, and the remarkably invasive and detailed requirements to report family income in selective US schools are avoided.

Nonetheless, if a graduate tax program were to be implemented in Canada, the bursary money currently available could be used to remove the last remaining barriers to accessibility. For example, the living expenses of those qualified students who are in particular financial need could easily be covered.

Conclusions

A graduate tax, as a program to replace the current student loan program, has some distinct advantages. First, it is more equitable in that it does not require a subsidy from the general taxpayer to make it solvent. Those students who go on to earn high incomes subsidize the ones who do not. Second, it would appear that the program can dramatically enhance the accessibility and the quality of a university education. With no increase in the current public subsidy to education, students would be able to attend university for four years, tuition free, and receive an education that in terms of the quality of the services provided is at the levels available in 1990 — before the long series of cutbacks to postsecondary education in Canada began. In return they agree to an increase in taxes over their lifetime that is certainly manageable, and is itself equitable given the advantages they enjoy as university graduates. There are no constraints on the careers they might choose, and if anything there is a mild encouragement to choose those low salaried occupations that provide public benefits.

The idea of a graduate tax has been around for at least 30 years and to my knowledge it has yet to be implemented in any public jurisdiction. This may mean that the political and practical difficulties are just too great. Nonetheless, even if it is never implemented, public discussion of the graduate tax may help to advance the debate over postsecondary funding within Canada.

It is a puzzle that the Canadian Association of University Teachers and other left-wing voices from within the university system remain adamantly opposed to increases in tuition payments. The evidence, some of which is referenced here, makes it abundantly clear that subsidies to tuition are regressive — they transfer wealth to the middle and upper classes, or to people who will soon enter the middle and upper classes. University graduates are a privileged group in Canada. Policies that benefit the rich by taxing the general public are not normally espoused by the Left.

The argument made is that there are many students who have the ability to benefit from university but who cannot afford to pay tuition. Bursary programs help, but students do not always know about them, and may not think to apply. Loan programs lead to post-graduation debt that some students find frightening. So the only way to really ensure access for everyone is to keep tuition as low as possible. The regressive distributional nature of this policy is ignored or simply disbelieved.

Underlying this attitude is, I believe, a deeper issue. Many academics believe strongly in the ideals of social justice and want to see themselves as contributing to the public good. Their vision is to make the university an egalitarian public space, accessible to anyone who wants to learn. Yet they find themselves in an institution whose role in society, among other things, is to take individuals who are already blessed with ability, give them the additional advantage of further education, and then identify them so as to ease their passage into the upper echelons of the capitalist world. For an academic to acknowledge the regressive nature of tuition subsidies would require them to accept their own complicity in this elite-making process.

A graduate tax will make university as accessible as any program of tuition subsidies. Students are not charged tuition — they do not need to apply for any kind of support and they need not be frightened by the prospect of incurring any debt. Nonetheless, the graduate tax program is designed to recognize the value of a university degree, and indeed it charges more to those students whose degree has particularly high economic value. If a public discussion of the graduate tax can be started, it will be interesting to see what the CAUT and other voices from the Left have to say about it.

In the end, public policy choices towards funding the university system must be based on the broad concerns of efficiency, accessibility, and equity and the very real need within the system for more resources. A graduate tax has the potential to help us achieve all of these goals.

References

Barr, N. 1993. "Alternative Funding Resources for Higher Education", *Economic Journal* 107(418), 718-728.

Bassanini, S. and S. Scarpenta. 2001. "Does Human Capital Matter for Growth in OECD Countries? Evidence from Pooled Mean-Group Estimates". Discussion Paper No. 282. Paris: OECD.

Black, S., P. Devereux and K. Salvanes. 2003. "Why the Apple Doesn't Fall Far: Understanding the Intergenerational Transmission of Human Capital". Discussion Paper No. 926. Bonn, Germany: Institute for the Study of Labor (IZA).

Blondal, S., S. Field and N. Giroard. 2002. *Investment in Human Capital Through Upper Secondary and Tertiary Education*, OECD Economic Studies No. 34. Paris: OECD, 41-89.

Bynner, J. and M. Egerton. 2000. "The Social Benefits of Higher Education: Insights Using Longitudinal Data". Discussion Paper. London: Centre for Longitudinal Studies, Institute of Education.

Carmichael, H.L. 1999. "Restructuring the University System: What Level of Public Support?" *Canadian Public Policy/Analyse de politiques* 25(1), 133-140.

Chapman, B. 1997. "Conceptual Issues and the Australian Experience with Income Contingent Charges for Higher Education", *Economic Journal* 107(442), 738-751.

Finnie, R. 1999. "Fields of Plenty, Fields of Lean: Earnings of University Graduates in Canada". Discussion Paper No. R-99-13E.a. Ottawa: Human Resources Development Canada.

Finnie, R. and C. Laporte. 2003. "Student Loans and Access of Post-Secondary Education: Evidence from the New Post-Secondary Education Survey". Analytical Studies Discussion Paper. Ottawa: Statistics Canada.

Friedman, M. and S. Kuznets. 1945. *Income from Individual Professional Practice*. Cambridge, MA: National Bureau of Economic Research.

Glennerster, H., S. Merrett and G. Wilson. 1968. "A Graduate Tax", *Journal of Higher Education* 1(1), 26-38.

Greenaway, D. and M. Haynes. 2003. "Funding Higher Education in the UK: The Role of Fees and Loans", *Economic Journal* 113(485), 150-166.

Johnson, G.E. 1984. "Subsidies for Higher Education", *Journal of Labor Economics* 2(3), 303-318.

Kenkel, D.S. 1991. "Health Behavior, Health Knowledge, and Schooling", *Journal of Political Economy* 99(2), 287-305.

Lochner, L. and E. Moretti. 2001. "The Effect of Education on Crime: Evidence from Prison Inmates, Arrests, and Self Reports". NBER Discussion Paper No. 8605. Cambridge, MA: National Bureau of Economic Research.

Merrett, S. 1967. "Student Finance in Higher Education", *Economic Journal* 77(306), 288-302.

Moretti, E. 2004. "Estimating the Social Return to Higher Education from Longitudinal and Repeated Cross-Sectional Data", *Journal of Econometrics*, forthcoming.

Nerlove, M. 1975. "Some Problems in the Use of Income Contingent Loans for the Finance of Higher Education", *Journal of Political Economy* 83(1), 157-183.

Ockert, B. 2003. "What's the Value of an Acceptance Letter? Using College Applicants to Estimate the Return to Education". Discussion Paper. Sweden: Institute for Labor Market Policy Evaluation.

Poutvaara, P. 2003. "Educating Europe". Discussion Paper. Copenhagen: Center for Business and Education Research.

Turkheimer, E. 2000. "Three Laws of Behavioral Genetics and What they Mean", *Current Directions in Psychological Science* 9, 160-164.

West, E. 1976. "The Yale Tuition Postponement Plan in the Mid-Seventies", *Higher Education* 5, 169-175.

Section VI

Wrap-Up Panel on Alternative Perspectives, Directions and Innovations

Financing Quality in Ontario Universities

Peter George

This paper is about the work of the Council of Ontario Universities' (COU) Quality and Financing Task Force, which I chair. Those two words, "quality" and "financing", effectively sum up some of the major themes of the conference and the major challenges facing universities in Canada and around the world:

- What is quality in higher education?
- How can it be sustained and enhanced?
- Who should pay for it? and,
- How?

Those are, essentially, the questions that the task force has been asked to tackle, questions that are at the heart of an ongoing public policy debate in Ontario, throughout Canada, and elsewhere, and key elements in what David Cameron has referred to as a "new social contract".

COU's Quality and Financing Task Force includes presidents and vice-presidents from nine Ontario universities and a Quebec university, McGill, and the Association for Universities and Colleges, Canada (AUCC), as well as Chad Gaffield from the University of Ottawa, and Don Drummond of TD Economics. So we have a diverse group that brings a range of perspectives

I am grateful to the members of the COU Quality and Financing Task Force, especially Dr. Paul Davenport, and the COU staff supporting the work of the task force, especially Barb Hauser.

to the issues. We are still at a relatively early stage in our deliberations. My comments here are a progress report; they will not be prescriptive but, rather, I hope, suggestive and inviting of further comments and advice.

Background Context in Ontario

Before touching on the questions that the task force is addressing, it may be helpful to give some context. As you know, the Ontario university scene has been dominated by two preoccupations in recent years: first, preparing for and accommodating the so-called "double cohort", and second, but no less important, securing the funding to ensure our students have access to high-quality education. The first wave of the 90,000 new full-time students who will enrol at universities across Ontario before the end of this decade is now safely ensconced in the classrooms, labs, and residences of our campuses, and another large wave is expected this fall. This has been managed without the crisis that many anticipated.

Ontario universities worked cooperatively with the provincial government over the past five years so that the government's commitment of a place for every qualified student would be met. However, we entered into the negotiations at a time when per student operating funding in Ontario was the lowest among Canadian jurisdictions, and, indeed, among the lowest in North America. And Ontario universities, like their counterparts in other provinces, were challenged by pressing requirements for physical infrastructure expansion and renewal, and by the need to hire thousands of new professors to replace retiring faculty and teach the growing number of students. The Ontario government responded with a substantial infusion of capital funds for new buildings and with commitments for "quality assurance funds" and full funding for enrolment growth. The federal government has also helped in recent years, particularly through new programs like the Canada Research Chairs, which also served to augment instructional resources.

Yet we still face a formidable challenge. Despite the infusion of additional funds, Ontario universities, like other public universities across Canada, do not have access to the level of resources enjoyed by our chief competitors — top-flight American public and private universities. Hence, the mandate of the Quality and Financing Task Force: to ascertain the level of support required for Ontario universities to operate at internationally-competitive levels, and to explore how to achieve that level of support.

In Ontario, as in most other provinces, the government effectively controls tuition revenue through the operating grant funding formula. The tuition freeze in the upcoming two years initiated by the new Liberal government comes after a four-year period in which university governing boards were allowed by the previous Conservative government to set tuition fees in certain "deregulated" professional programs, such as law, dentistry, medicine, engineering, and business, as well as in graduate programs, while fee increases in "regulated" programs, mainly core arts and sciences, were capped at 2% per year. In addition, as a condition for the flexibility that was allowed in the past four years, universities were required to set aside 30% of their revenue from increased fees for student assistance, to help ensure that higher tuition fees were not a barrier to accessibility.

So, Ontario universities are now faced with a significant challenge — we have a government that acknowledges the value of a university education, is committed to expanding access, and wants to ensure that students have access to excellence. We can make a good case for the pressing need for increased resources to ensure that the 320,000+ full-time students who will populate our campuses by 2010 receive a quality education. Yet we know we will be competing with other pressing priorities — health care, elementary and secondary education, and the plight of cities, to name just a few. In the near future, the provincial government is expected to initiate a consultation on the postsecondary funding framework to be implemented following the two-year freeze, in fall 2006. The Quality and Financing Task Force will develop recommendations to inform COU's contribution to this consultation.

Resources for University Excellence

The first variable in the quality-financing equation is, of course, determining what constitutes quality in a university setting. Commonly-accepted indicators of quality include:

* low faculty-student ratios,
* a wide choice of courses and programs,
* well-equipped, up-to-date laboratories and classrooms,
* well-stocked libraries that make use of leading-edge technology,
* highly qualified faculty members,
* adequate support staff and services, and
* well-maintained facilities.

To dissect the impact of just one of these variables — student-faculty ratios — we have an obvious comparison in our American counterparts. On average, the ratio of full-time students to faculty at Ontario universities exceeds 20 to 1, while it is 15 to 1 at comparable American universities (and 13 to 1 at Harvard). On that key indicator alone, American universities have considerable quality advantage, one that is not easily overcome without a significant increase in university revenue.

It is evident that university administrators cannot continue to contend with all the competing budget priorities and with the growing number of students, without an influx of significant new funding.

Some of you are aware of our past efforts to convince previous provincial governments that, on a per-student basis, Ontario universities should be funded at the Canadian average, at least.[1] In recent weeks, however, our efforts to make a convincing case for the need for funding at internationally-competitive levels have been assisted by the work of an objective, government-funded think-tank. Ontario's Task Force on Competitiveness, Productivity and Economic Progress (Martin Task Force) has documented a 10% prosperity gap between Ontario and comparable American states, and a 15% prosperity gap between Canada as a whole and the United States. The task force identified our lower investment in post-secondary education and particularly the underproduction of graduate degree-holders, as a key factor in this prosperity gap. In a report presented to the 2004 annual meeting of the World Economic Forum, the task force observed:

> Investment in education affects productivity and prosperity throughout our society. Most researchers who have analyzed Canada's and Ontario's productivity challenge conclude that education is an important part of the solution. A more educated and better trained labour force creates more value ... Every additional year of school and each additional degree raise income prospects for individuals ... For businesses, the increased availability of skilled workers, researchers, and managers is a critical benefit of postsecondary education. For all of us, the ideas that spill out of colleges and universities improve and create products, services, and processes and lead to new companies and whole new industries. (Ontario. Task Force on Competitiveness, Productivity and Economic Progress, 2003)

---

[1]For 2001/02, grants per full-time equivalent student were $5,948 in Ontario, $7,297 averaged across all ten provinces, and $8,044 averaged across the other nine provinces.

The Martin Task Force noted that Canada's per capita investment in elementary and secondary education and in colleges is comparable to the United States, but that university spending in Canada is much lower — Canada's rate is 50% of US spending per capita. On a per student basis, the spending gap is somewhat lower — Canada's expenditures are 63% of the US rate. The report concludes that "Canada invests substantially less in postsecondary education than the US and this underinvestment reduces our productivity and prosperity" (Institute for Competitiveness and Prosperity, 2004, pp. 17-20).

In the second annual report of the Martin Task Force, which focused on Ontario in relation to 14 competitor states, the difference in funding on a per student basis was examined. The findings: "Over the 1995–99 period, Ontario universities spent a total of $18,334 per student annually, while US universities spent $31,227 per student — a yearly difference of $12,893 per student" (Ontario. Task Force on Competitiveness, Productivity and Economic Progress, 2003, p. 24). While conceding that this gap may have narrowed somewhat in the past few years, this translates into roughly $4 billion annually in additional revenue to bring Ontario universities to those levels. The Martin Task Force looked at the full spectrum of revenue available to public and private American universities, including research and endowment revenue, so the annual "price tag" in terms of operating revenue would be lower, but still very substantial.

These funding gaps — between Ontario and the rest of Canada, and between Ontario and comparable jurisdictions in the United States — are dramatic and significant. The agenda for our task force is clear. We need to articulate a vision for a high-quality Ontario university system, determine the price tag, secure government agreement on that vision and price tag, and decide upon the operating grant and tuition regime that would bring us to that level of excellence.

What is the price tag and can we agree on it? The new Liberal government stated in its election platform that its target would be to increase Ontario university funding to the Canadian average by the end of its first term in office. We must take their commitment at face value. Our task force has tentatively agreed to make Canadian-average university funding for Ontario our working target, our summary quality indicator, our price tag. But we want to propose a stretch goal as well: we will want to press beyond the Canadian average for the average of the 14 states adduced by the Martin Task Force as the appropriate target for the end of a second Liberal mandate.

Another recent study has confirmed the value of university education from a different angle — the private rate of return for students. There have been many such studies, including Herb Emery's paper in this volume. Generally, returns on investment (ROIs) have been high and robust among these studies for graduates of all disciplines. A TD Economics paper released in January estimates that, based on the higher life-time earning potential of university graduates, the after-tax and after-inflation rate of return to a university degree is roughly 12 to 20%. The authors observe that "the outlay still delivers a stellar annual return that far exceeds virtually any financial investment" (TD Bank Financial Group, 2004). Further, the study confirmed that the rate of return is higher for engineering, natural sciences, health sciences, and commerce programs — those very programs for which university boards set tuition rates under Ontario's recent experiment with partial deregulation. So, from two perspectives, the value of universities has been confirmed.

Funding Mix, Tuition Fees and Accessibility

This leads to the second part of the mandate of the Quality and Financing Task Force — we are charged not only with determining the resources necessary to bring Ontario's universities to international levels of excellence, we are also examining how these resources should be split between private and public sources — in other words, what is an appropriate contribution from students through tuition fees and from government through operating grants. I have briefly explained Ontario's current tuition policy, with a mix of regulated programs where tuition levels are controlled by government, and deregulated programs where the governing board of each university sets the tuition rate after considering the price for its programs based on the market place, affordability, and the resource needs of the university. And the new government's tuition freeze, which will begin in 2004/05 and carry through 2005/06, presents a two-year period during which future tuition policy will be decided.

To be frank, there are some philosophical differences on this issue in our task force. There are some diehard deregulationists who believe institutional autonomy means that university boards should set fees. There are some who disagree with this position, and who would prefer a regulated fee regime, especially if government operating grants were high enough. Then there are some who are pragmatists, myself included, for whom a dollar is a dollar, and their major focus is on the target funding level, with the composition of funding a secondary issue.

For the university, I would argue, the source of funds *is* a secondary issue: What does it matter if the marginal dollar comes from operating grants or tuition fees? The government may have a preferred policy goal but must be prepared for the consequences. For government, if fee regulation is a primary policy goal, the trade-off must be increased operating grants; if placing a cap on grants is more important, then regulation of tuition fees must be traded off so they can be set by universities with revenue targets in mind. The government's choice may well matter to students: if the source of the marginal dollar of university revenue is tuition fees, the impact is to lower the ROI for the student, and may even lead to lower participation and retention rates. It is a generally accepted principle in Canada, and in many other jurisdictions worldwide, that the personal benefits derived from post-secondary education are sufficient to justify a direct contribution from students. That is a given, but the question is: What is the appropriate amount?

Universities need additional resources, although this has unfortunately not yet been the subject of spirited public debate in Ontario. And we would not dispute that students, especially low- and some mid-income students, need financial assistance. But it is the public-private mix, and especially tuition fees, that have become the battleground where public attention has been fixed to the neglect of those other important elements.

There are a number of possible solutions. The Ontario government could decide to fund universities at the desired level while maintaining the tuition freeze. Barring this, the solution is *not* to hold tuition fees so low for *all* students that universities do not have adequate resources. If the Ontario government and Ontario's universities can agree on quality funding targets and the requisite level of approved government operating support, then the balance of university revenue needs must come from tuition fees, and the solution is to empower boards to set tuition with those institutional funding targets in mind, and to provide sufficient need-based aid (grants and loans) to prevent qualified low- and mid-income students from being excluded from higher education for financial reasons. Even if the government were to provide universities with all of their needed revenue so that tuition fees were zero, need-based aid would still have to be provided to many students.

The most recent public consultation in Ontario on tuition fees led to the previous government adopting the policy of the current mix of regulated and deregulated tuition. I am referring to the work of the 1996 Advisory Panel on Future Directions for Postsecondary Education, led by the late David C. Smith, former principal of Queen's. His panel advocated a partnership model of funding (government and students) and a return to the legal authority of governing boards to set fees:

The Panel believes it would be more helpful to develop an approach that is characterized by institutional flexibility to determine fees, program by program, based on analysis of the value of programs in a competitive market, and of the revenue that is needed to provide a high-quality learning experience for students ... We agree with those institutions that argue that the flexibility to determine tuition fees would encourage innovation and specialization, and assist institutions in expanding system capacity to meet increased demand. (Smith, 1996, p. 32)

This full deregulation is one approach the Quality and Financing Task Force is considering. A second is what can be termed "selective regulation" with boards setting fees for some programs, particularly graduate and professional programs, and the government setting maximum fees for others, mainly undergraduate programs — a continuation of the recent experiment if you will. A third approach, in some respects less compelling than the others, is a fully regulated regime with government considering the resource needs of the universities in setting fee maximums. And there are several conceivable variations on those three basic options.

From a public policy perspective, determining appropriate fee levels is a challenging proposition. For some commentators (and advocates such as the CFS), tuition rates should be kept low to ensure access for all. Other commentators have long argued that keeping fees artificially low has the perverse impact of mainly benefiting upper-income families — historically more likely to attend university any way and reap the benefits. A recent study by Miles Corak and his colleagues (in this volume) has demonstrated, however, that despite the increase in university tuition rates throughout most of Canada during the past two decades, the participation rate of students from lower-income levels had nearly doubled, and this was the only income group whose participation steadily grew. Application, enrolment, and graduation statistics all demonstrate that higher tuition fees in deregulated programs have not had an adverse effect on recruitment or retention in those programs. And some student groups (e.g., OUSA) and campus student leaders have begun to question the wisdom of keeping tuition fees constrained, at the expense of quality. They want access to excellence, not mediocrity, and they have been prepared to vote for additional ancillary fees, according to the referenda protocol mandated by Ontario government policy (e.g., student-initiated fees to equip engineering labs, construct a new student centre and a new multi-sports complex at McMaster).

Clearly, this is a difficult, multi-faceted issue. A recently-released report by the Montreal Economic Institute questions whether Quebec's university tuition policy — where fees are the lowest in Canada — has actually improved access. The report's conclusion is that, despite low fees — which represent only 9% of total university revenue in Quebec (compared to about 25% in Ontario and 19% for Canada as a whole) — participation rates in Quebec are among the lowest in Canada. Studies in other jurisdictions with low or no fees have also confirmed this finding; low tuition fees do not necessarily ensure access or guarantee high participation rates.

In all the tuition policy scenarios under consideration, however, task force members are adamant that a robust student financial assistance program — that ensures access for lower-income and middle-income students — is a necessity. COU has already identified several improvements to the student loan program that will increase its effectiveness in meeting actual financial need. And I note that Ross Finnie, an expert on student financial assistance, advocates a new "architecture" for student assistance — focusing current federal and provincial expenditures on student assistance into an integrated program that truly meets student needs (see paper in this volume). He considers this to be "one policy area where the solution is not so much new and more money, but rather a matter of doing a better job of allocating the existing resources" (Finnie, 2003, p. 50). In my view, the federal and provincial governments have a responsibility to design and implement targeted programs that guarantee aid to low- and middle-income students, with a larger grant component for the low-income students. The availability of these funds needs to be much better communicated, and be more transparent to low-income families well before their students reach university age, so that perceptions about tuition fees and higher education costs are not barriers to access when crucial educational choices are being made in elementary and secondary school!

Fortunately, steps are already being taken to make improvements to student financial assistance programs. In the 2004 Throne Speech and budget, the Martin government pledged to make the Canada Student Loans Program more effective in ensuring affordability for middle-income families by raising the loan limits so that more of a student's assessed need is met, increasing the family income thresholds and recognizing a broader range of educational expenses. The Throne Speech and budget also promised a new grant for low-income students to cover a portion of the costs of tuition in the first year. The provincial minister of training, colleges and universities has also pledged to review the Ontario Student Assistance Program, so we are moving in the right direction.

We can take heart in the fact that the federal government has acknowledged its responsibility to help make higher education more affordable, not by recommending limits to an institution's ability to charge a fair price for a worthwhile product (in contrast to Ontario's tuition freeze), but by improving the student assistance program. This was the direction the Blair government in the United Kingdom recently took when it introduced flexible tuition fees — lower-income students will receive special grants and tuition subsidies, but those who can afford to contribute to the costs of their education will do so. Loans will be available that provide for repayment rates based on income after graduation, which effectively matches costs to the benefits derived. Nicholas Barr takes us through some of those arguments in his paper. This has been an effective approach in the United States as well, with the federal government contributing substantially to educational costs through the Pell Grant program for lower-income students and a variety of loan programs to serve low- and middle-income families, although there is growing concern that grant funds have not been keeping pace.

It is worth noting here that Ontario universities have already made a substantial commitment to ensuring access. Throughout a decade when government grants as a percentage of operating revenue were steadily decreasing (from 73% in 1992–93 to 51% in 2001–02), Ontario universities were steadily increasing their expenditures on scholarships and bursaries. In 2000–01, these expenditures totaled $278 million, an amount that represented over 8% of total operating expenses. Ten years earlier, the proportion was 2.4%. Notwithstanding that some university representatives object that the Ontario government has been downloading its obligations to the universities, this reflects a movement of Ontario universities towards another American model that is worthy of consideration: the practice of "bundling" various sources of student assistance — federal and state funds as well as private scholarships and bursaries, and institutional aid — into a package specific to the needs of the individual student, so that he or she can see exactly what the "net cost" of tuition and other educational costs will be, and what the debt level will be, and make enrolment decisions accordingly. Researchers like Ron Ehrenberg continue to offer proposals to increase access for low-income students, such as graduated tuition levels, and increasing grants relative to loans, to reduce barriers to access and combat debt-aversion. Considering the higher participation rates of Americans in university education, "bundling" has evidently worked for them.

Concluding Remarks

There is a lot of work to be done to ensure that Ontario universities can fulfill their potential for excellence. A previous COU task force, called the Futures Task Force, identified "shared goals" for the Ontario public, the government, and universities, to ensure that the university system is able to play its part in securing economic and social progress of Ontario. Three of those goals relate directly to the work of the current Quality and Financing Task Force and effectively sum up my message:

- all appropriately qualified Ontario students will have access to a place in an Ontario university;
- no student will be denied access to the program of his or her choice for financial reasons; and
- the education received by Ontario university students will be the best in Canada and on par with that offered at the best public universities worldwide.

This is our working framework!

References

Finnie, R. 2003. "A New Architecture for the Canadian Student Financial Aid System", *Policy Options*, September.

Institute for Competitiveness and Prosperity. 2004. *Partnering for Investment in Canada's Prosperity*. Toronto: The Institute.

Ontario. Task Force on Competitiveness, Productivity and Economic Progress. 2003. *Investing for Prosperity, Second Annual Report*. Toronto: Institute for Competitiveness and Prosperity.

Smith, D. 1996. *Excellence, Accessibility, Responsibility: Report of the Advisory Panel on Future Directions for Postsecondary Education*. Toronto: The Panel.

TD Bank Financial Group. 2004. *Investing in a Post Secondary Education Delivers a Stellar Rate of Return*. TD Economics Topic Paper. Toronto: TD Bank.

The Challenge, the Issues?

Elizabeth Parr-Johnston

I have decided that the best value-added I can provide to this panel will be my personal reflections on a few of the many serious issues facing Canadian universities at this time. My remarks come from my personal experiences and the many joys as well as scars gained from serving as president of two very different Atlantic universities prior to my retirement in July 2002. The issues I would like to put on the table are those with which I am familiar both directly and through broader experience.

- Core funding of universities — federal government's retreat from transfers to provinces in favour of more highly visible funding for research and infrastructure.

It is my firm belief that, no matter how much we wish it were not true, the federal government is now out of the unrestricted transfer field for good. The kind of transfers to provinces for university funding that we once knew is frankly history. To the extent that the federal government chooses to put resources into higher education, we will see the vehicles chosen to be either student aid (Canada Student Loans, Millennium Scholarships...) or a clear focus on research manifest in skewed funding through CFI, SSHRC, NSERC, NIH, Research Chairs, etc.

The corollaries of the federal government's policy decision to alter radically the form in which higher education is funded are that student tuitions have risen rapidly, particularly in certain programs where fees have become differentiated, and that our institutions find themselves faced with a recurring lack of sufficient core operating funds to finance basic undergraduate education. Frankly, in my view, this situation is chronic. Core program funding becomes less and less available and the more research grants that faculties win, the more we are challenged to find requisite overhead funding, which is now provided in part but certainly not in full.

- The growing practice of "tiering" of Canadian universities and the emergence of a few large research institutions who aim to be "world class" as others frankly struggle to maintain or enhance the calibre of their research and their academic programs.

Canada no longer has a uniformly high quality and largely homogeneous university system, but rather one that is increasingly differentiated. At one extreme is a very limited number of large, intensively research-based universities to whom go the lion's share of research resources including particularly those from the federal government. Other smaller and comprehensive universities do an amazing job on their academic programs and produce excellent research, including research that is undeniably world class, yet some find themselves struggling. At the other extreme are medium-sized and smaller, primarily undergraduate institutions that are far more numerous. Many of them offer their students an outstanding education. But it is not easy!

Additionally, we see new universities, a few private, and a growing number of university colleges and colleges with clear ambitions of becoming universities. Where this is going remains to be seen. My hunch is that over time a few of the smaller undergraduate universities will move towards privatization while others will find themselves forced to merge or affiliate in one form or another.

I cannot help but mention the annual *Maclean's* rating along with a growing number of other publications that in one sense provide a form of accountability and information for students and parents, but in another sense force upon institutions participation in the "rating game". In my view, universities have no option but to participate. However, danger arises where decisions as to how a university sets priorities and operates are driven by a desire to raise ratings rather than adhere to internal priorities and plan. Believe me this happens all too often.

- The very real threat of debasing the quality of the undergraduate educational experience concurrent with rapidly rising tuition.

Large classes and video formats, particularly in the first two years of university, are a growing problem. We have research evidence to show that large classes can still provide quality educational experiences, but the growing number of very large classes, many of them via technology, is to me a real concern. Technology can augment the learning experience, but used to handle large numbers it can be detrimental. Indeed, I fret about what I will term a "cash cow" mentality (wherein certain programs attract large number of students and are relatively inexpensive to offer). Our faculty, many of whom are excellent teachers, are driven by the reward structure to focus on research, sometimes to the detriment of teaching and service. To offer complete academic programs, universities of all sizes employ contract and stipendary faculty as well as significant numbers of graduate students. There are both pros and cons to doing this, but I submit the budgetary imperative is a major factor in such decisions and students are not always the winners.

- Intellectual property issues.

Limited space prohibits a full discussion of a complex and critical issue, one that demands growing attention of both faculty and university administrations. Issues like patent rights are often contained in institutional collective agreements, each of which is different and constantly altered as new agreements are concluded. Standardization is not evident in this area! Some agreements set specific limits on the amount of outside consulting that may be conducted by faculty members, others are largely silent. Some share intellectual property rights to a degree, others have no provision. As research grows, particularly applied research, this will be a critical issue to our institutions and our communities.

Related issues include copyright and the skyrocketing cost of academic journals at a time when university libraries are becoming limited by their acquisition budgets. Electronic journals could offer an answer, but to date control of these journals rests in the hands of third parties including, particularly, journal publishers. Some interesting initiatives have been taken jointly by our universities, but the issue will not disappear in the near term.

- A very real lack of resources to address deferred maintenance (our hidden time bomb).

Universities tend to build new buildings rather than address deferred maintenance as it is more feasible to raise funds for a new, named edifice.

However, this is not always the best economic decision. Across Canada, many older buildings continue to leak and crumble. Some provinces have provided targeted funding for renovations, but the multi-billion dollar problem is all too real and it is not going away.

- The growing intrusion of government in establishing its own agenda under the guise of "accountability".

Some of the public priorities I experienced include: (i) a focus on skills versus knowledge; (ii) performance measures/productivity measures which were not well thought out and sometimes counter productive; (iii) government-driven "rationalization", which failed to deliver real savings or improved quality; (iv) graduate program limitations and controls; (v) tuition controls/limits which in the absence of increased government funding impinge upon the institutions' ability to provide students with quality programs; and (vi) student loan and bursary rules and limits that offer insufficient resources to meet student need.

- The stewardship of universities' financial endowments and pensions.

In good times, aggressive and risky management of university financial endowments and pensions can produce rapid rates of growth of the funds and their returns. But, as several of our universities were forced to recall, risk and return are correlated and markets, particularly equity markets, can go down as well as up. In my view, we are the stewards of these resources and our investment policies must be set out clearly to preserve and safely enhance these resources over time. Indeed, our operational budgets as well as scholarships available depend upon having access to the income on these resources over time.

Our universities are nothing less than the future of this nation and we must offer our students the very best possible education and provide our nation with top quality research. There are immense benefits and joys as well as challenges and issues in addressing the above concerns.

It is often said that universities do not change. From my remarks, you can gather that I argue just the opposite. Our universities have changed significantly over the past 20 years and they continue to change in important ways. I offer congratulations to all involved in our universities. What you all do matters greatly and I wish you all the very best!

Higher Education in Canada: Perspectives and Directions for the Future

Douglas Auld

Introduction

This conference is very timely and long overdue. The last major conference examining postsecondary education was the "National Forum on Higher Education" sponsored by the federal secretary of state in 1989. Given the overwhelming importance of higher education to Canada's global competitiveness, a thorough review of the subject is long overdue. As one of the final speakers, I have been asked to provide a summary of the major themes that have unfolded these past two days and provide some concluding remarks of my own.

General Themes

The papers relate to three general topics:

- The structure and efficiency of the postsecondary system in Canada.
- Difficulties associated with access to higher education and the equity implications of those barriers.
- The value of higher education as an investment and rates of return on investments in higher education.

Structure and Efficiency

Several papers address the following topics related to the structure and efficiency of higher education.

- The mix of institutions in the higher education framework.
- The mix of funding, private and public, federal and provincial.
- The interface between higher education and government.

Does Canada have the right mix of colleges, universities, and institutes? Attempting to respond to that question begs the fundamental question: What is meant by the "right" mix? A simple answer would be to let the market decide, but that is impossible since higher education is, in all provinces, controlled by government.[1] Recent reports and announcements have suggested that because the United States has a higher percentage of its population with degrees, Canada needs more university graduates (Government of Ontario, 2003).

In my research, which has not been exhaustive, I have not been able to unearth a single analytical study that attempts to determine the optimal mix of various types of postsecondary institutions. In most jurisdictions, the decisions appear to be political ones with little thought or mention of short- or long-term optimization. If the higher education market is a competitive one, or exhibits strong characteristics of competition, perhaps less reliance should be placed on quotas and funding determined by political decisions.

If one believes in consumer sovereignty and unfettered choice, this could be one step towards a more optimal structure (Auld, 1999).

Structure and Efficiency: The Mix of Funding

A large number of reports and studies have examined the change in the mix of funding sources: how tuition fees, as a share of total operating expenditures, have ebbed and flowed over the past 40 years and the very large increase in private sector funding in the last decade.[2] Today, tuition fees as a share of total expenditure are approximately where they were in

---

[1]Notwithstanding this fact, Skolnik (2005) suggests that community colleges have responded to market demand in spite of government regulation.

[2]For a detailed historical analysis of funding, see Auld and Kitchen (2005).

the mid-1960s. Should tuition, as a share of the cost be relatively fixed over the long run? Should that number be driven by the financial rate of return to higher education? If these rates of return are used as a guideline, more research to refine the methodology is required.

Should the government's share of the cost of higher education be driven by the positive externalities from college and university education? How can these best be internalized to ensure efficient pricing? The difference between subsidizing 25% of the cost of university or 35% has enormous implications for government budgets and the private cost of higher education.

Access and Equity

There appears to be agreement that universal access to higher education has not been achieved, especially as it pertains to those where the capital market fails to recognize the long-term benefits of higher education. Papers at this conference and other research has demonstrated that the federal government's Registered Education Savings Plan (RESP) has failed in a major way: low-income families do not, and cannot, take advantage of the plan (for example, Milligan, this volume and Carmichael, this volume). The plan reduces the debt burden of middle- and upper-income families or their children. The Canada Student Loan Program has also failed in this respect. The Millennium Foundation Bursary Plan does provide some relief across the family income spectrum, but in Ontario such bursaries are immediately applied to the Ontario Student Loan Program.

The 2004 federal budget proposed several reforms to both the Canada Student Loan Plan and the Registered Education Savings Plan (Government of Canada, 2004). One measure provides an initial $500 Education Bond and subsequent increases of $100 per year for children born this year into low-income families. In addition, the 20% matching federal grant for families with Registered Education Savings Plans will be increased for low-income families. While these measures will provide some, albeit small, relief for low-income families, the full benefit will not be reaped for at least 17 years. And, it does not address the fact that low-income families do not have the means to even start an RESP.

Evidence presented at this conference demonstrates that, in spite of higher tuition fees, the demand for higher education continues to rise. Tuition fees are not the overwhelming cost of higher education. For college students living away from home, tuition accounts for only 20% of the cost of education — probably a quarter or even a third — on average for university students.

A conference on higher education would be considered a failure if the subject of income-contingent loan plans (ICLP) was not raised and debated (Finnie, Usher and Vossensteyn, 2005). The subject was mentioned on more than one occasion and, while it is clear there are problems with such a plan, these challenges must be compared to the failure of the status quo. The income-contingent loan plan is, in my view, superior to most of the alternatives that have been advanced to date. The higher education graduate tax also deserves to be examined.

Investment and Rates of Return

Because of the enormous commitments by governments to higher education — probably $20 billion for universities and another $10 billion for colleges and institutes — politicians and taxpayers are demanding more account- ability and measurable returns to higher education.[3] Rates-of-return studies do provide some indication of how people with college or university education contribute by way of higher taxes, lower unemployment, less demand on welfare systems, etc. Even the most conservative estimates suggest that these returns exceed the return on long-term government bonds (Emery, 2005). While not quantifiable in the same manner, the contribution made to business and economic development locally by the presence of higher education cannot be ignored. Most colleges in Canada and some universities are involved in business partnerships to assist local companies to retrain and upgrade the skills of employees.[4]

There are employment opportunities where higher education graduates provide a crucial service to society, but rates of return, in terms of increased earnings, are low. Would society wish to abandon the education of earlier

---

[3]One of the approaches to accountability is the use of key performance quality indicators for higher education. See Leyton-Brown (2005).

[4]Detailed evidence for this in the United States was presented at the conference. See Betts and Lee (2005). In Ontario, the Ontario Small Town and Rural Economic Development Program (OSTAR) provided training rebates to joint college-industry programs in areas deemed important to local economic growth.

childhood education workers just because the salaries in the field are low, resulting in a low rate of return?

Concluding Remarks

I would like to conclude by addressing the more general topic of government control of higher education. There must be in my view a concerted effort to reduce the politicization of higher education which has shackled creativity, forced colleges and universities to operate with rules that result in unwise economic and educational decisions and erode the fundamental purpose of higher education.

The market for higher education is, theoretically, a competitive one. This has been noted by several speakers at this conference. There are many sellers and there are certainly a multitude of buyers: over one million of them on a full-time basis in Canada and another two million as part-time learners. The barriers to entry are not overwhelming. While it would take a considerable capital investment to replicate Queen's University, one could start a small undergraduate arts and science university with $10 million. A more technical institution of higher learning such as the University of Ontario Institute of Technology could be launched with $60 million. A postsecondary community college could be started with a set of core programs for less than $10 million.

Are sums of private money available for higher education? The University of Toronto announced its campaign had reached $1 billion, suggesting that the potential for capital is available.

Are there barriers to obtaining product information in the post-secondary market? Judging by the millions of dollars spent on marketing by colleges and universities and the ease of accessing information through the Web and other sources, product knowledge is readily available. This point was also reinforced at this conference. And, unlike many products, even after you have purchased a product (or program) the customer can change direction.

There is a defensible rationale for government intervention in the presence of externalities. Where social benefits exceed private benefits, a case can be made for financial support by way of lower prices to encourage consumption. There is a widespread consensus that higher education does bestow significant public benefits. A recent study demonstrated that the Province of Ontario enjoys a 12% rate of return on its investment in college education (Robison and Christophersen, 2004).

While a good argument can be made for public sector intervention in higher education, that does not necessarily mean that institutions ought to be subsidized. It makes just as much, perhaps more, sense to subsidize the consumer of higher education, the student.

Are there positive externalities to research? Most would answer "yes" and again, subsidizing scholars to undertake research, both fundamental and applied, is justifiable.

Governments, however, have used the externality argument to create a regulated monopoly. Bureaucracies have been created to approve programs, impose countless and expensive audits on institutions, transfer monies to colleges and universities and generally limit entry into programs. To the extent colleges and universities are silent on this subject, they have implicitly been captured by their regulators.

When asked why government controls higher education, the response is often in terms of having to protect the quality of higher education because the government pays a large share of the bills.

This responsibility could be undertaken by accrediting councils similar to those that are established in other countries and other professions, thus removing or at least reducing the political element in making decisions about higher education.

Reducing the politicization of higher education could be achieved by either allowing new firms to enter the market or, as a more moderate step, replacing direct grants to institutions with vouchers, both federal and provincial, to qualified individuals. The choice of programs to offer and methods of delivery should be the purview of the institution and the board of governors. Public audits could be replaced by a single audit conducted by a reputable accounting firm.

There is no logical support for the control and management of higher education by politicians and bureaucrats. There is, of course, a strong rationale for government support based on equity grounds. Government intervention should therefore focus on providing any qualified student with financial means to enrol in a college or university of her/his choice.

While no one has any expectations that change of this dimension will occur overnight, college and universities should advocate strongly for reform. It will only benefit society in the long run.

References

Auld, D. 1999. *Privatizing Universities*. Toronto: University of Toronto Press.

Auld, D. and H. Kitchen. 2005. *Financing Education and Training in Canada,* 2nd edition. Toronto: Canadian Tax Foundation, forthcoming.

Betts, J.R. and C.W.B. Lee. 2005. "Universities as Drivers of Regional and National Innovation: An Assessment of the Linkages from Universities to Innovation and Economic Growth", in this volume.

Carmichael, H.L. 2005. "How Best to Fund Postsecondary Education: A Graduate Tax?" in this volume.

Emery, H. 2005. "Total and Private Returns to University Education in Canada: 1960 to 2000 and in Comparison to Other Postsecondary Training", in this volume.

Finnie, R., A. Usher and H. Vossensteyn. 2005. "Meeting the Need: A New Architecture for Canada's Student Financial Aid System", in this volume.

Government of Canada. 2004. *Budget 2004: New Agenda for Achievement*. Ottawa: Supply and Services Canada, March 23.

Government of Ontario. 2003. *Task Force on Competitiveness: Interim Report*. Toronto: Government Printers.

Leyton-Brown, D. 2005. "Demystifying Quality Assurance", in this volume.

Milligan, K. 2005. "Who Uses RESPs and Why", in this volume.

Robison, M.H. and K. Christophersen. 2004. *Investing in Ontario Colleges*. CCbenefits Inc. Moscow.

Skolnik, M.L. 2005. "The Case for Giving Greater Attention to Structure in Higher Education Policy-Making", in this volume.

Report on *learn*$ave and the Millennium Pilot Project

John Greenwood

I am pleased to have been invited to participate in this conference. I was asked, in the context of the "innovations and new directions" theme of this session, to speak about two projects — *learn*$ave and the Millennium Pilot Project — that are studying ways of improving access to education. These are two research projects in which the Social Research and Demonstration Corporation (SRDC) is involved. SRDC is a national non-profit social policy research organization that has been pioneering the use in Canada of random assignment designs to evaluate new social policy ideas.

learn$ave is a randomized trial of the use of individual development accounts to encourage adults in low-income families to participate in education and training. The project is being funded by Human Resources and Skills Development Canada and is being operated by a Toronto-based non-profit organization, Social and Enterprise Development Innovations, through a network of local delivery agencies at ten sites across Canada.

Individual development accounts (IDAs) are matched savings accounts designed to help poor families save to acquire assets. Interest in IDAs can be traced to the influential book by Michael Sherraden (1991). Sherraden's view is that assets are different from income. Income maintains consumption, but assets, either by the effect of asset-holding or through the process of asset accumulation, change people's behaviours in positive ways that can lead to long-term improvements in their economic well-being. In the United

States, the "American Dream" IDA demonstration, begun in 1997, is creating 2,000 accounts for low-income Americans; more recently, the federal Assets for Independence Act approved funding for up to 50,000 IDAs that can be used by account-holders to help finance the purchase of a first home, for small business capitalization, or for postsecondary education.

The *learn*$ave demonstration is intended to rigorously test the proposition that low-income people can find a way to save for education or training (a portion of the research sample also has the option of using their savings to start a small business). The catalyst leading to increased savings is the offer to match participants' savings on a three-to-one basis, as long as these savings are spent on the prescribed goals. Attendance at financial management training sessions delivered by local agencies is also expected to help participants achieve their savings goals.

The basic *learn*$ave offer is to provide $3 for every $1 a participant saves up to a maximum of $1,500 (a combined total of $6,000). Participants can accumulate savings over a maximum savings period of three years and have a further year in which to withdraw and use their matched savings.

Between June 2001 and December 2003, close to 5,000 participants were enrolled in the study. The core selection criteria for participants was to be between 21 and 65 years of age, not in school full-time, member of a family with a total annual income not exceeding 125% of the relevant Statistics Canada low-income cut-off, and with financial assets not exceeding the lesser of 10% of annual income or $3,000.

The 3,600 participants who were enrolled at *learn*$ave's three primary sites — Vancouver, Toronto, and Halifax — were randomly assigned to either a basic program group that received the matched-savings offer, or to a "*learn*$ave plus" group that was offered the matched savings together with financial management training, or to a control group. At seven secondary sites — Calgary, Winnipeg, Grey-Bruce Counties (Ontario), Kitchener-Waterloo, Fredericton, Montreal, and Digby County (Nova Scotia) — *learn*$ave's benefits and services vary. At these sites, research is exploring the effects these variations may have on the characteristics of those who choose to enrol and on their savings behaviours.

Participant enrolment only recently ended. Therefore, it will be some time before program impacts can be assessed. The first short-term, in-program impact estimates, based on an 18-month participant follow-up survey, are not scheduled for publication until 2006. However, some results are already known.

First, selling the *learn*$ave offer is harder than might be expected. Enrolment took two and a half years to complete and the original enrolment period had to be extended by six months in order to fill the target sample. Recruitment by the local delivery agencies relied mostly on advertising (community newspapers, transit and bus shelter ads) and word of mouth. It took time for word to spread; even then, many potentially eligible individuals were skeptical of the offer, believed they could not save enough to make it worthwhile, or were uninterested in pursuing education or training. *learn*$ave's limited appeal among the target population suggests that an intervention of this type would likely be a "niche program" rather than a widespread initiative.

Second, the sample recruited by *learn*$ave differs in a number of important ways from the overall low-income population in Canada. *learn*$ave participants tend to be younger and are more likely to be single, and *learn*$ave attracted a population for whom formal education and training appears to be important. About 90% of participants are high-school graduates (compared with under three-quarters of the eligible population) and about 40% have a postsecondary education credential (only about one-quarter of the eligible population is estimated to have an equivalent level of education). A much higher proportion of *learn*$ave participants had recently immigrated to Canada. More than one-third had arrived in Canada since 1998 (less than one-fifth of the equivalent Census population had immigrated between 1996 and the date of the 2001 Census). The *learn*$ave offer has been particularly attractive to Chinese-born immigrants: about one-quarter of participants are Chinese-born. Since many immigrants had to save to finance their move to a new country, they will already have developed money management and saving strategies. This participant data suggests that *learn*$ave may have disproportionately recruited low-income individuals who are predisposed to save and to participate in education and training activities. If so, the ability of the *learn*$ave offer to improve participants' savings behaviours and increase their participation in education could be limited.

Finally, *learn*$ave participants have demonstrated that they are able to save. Participants have been saving an average of just over $50 per month. Collectively they have so far saved $2 million of their own money. With the savings match this means that $8 million is available to these participants to finance their further education and training.

Turning now to the second project, the Millennium Pilot Project is a new initiative of the Canada Millennium Scholarship Foundation designed to better understand how to encourage students — especially students from low-income families — to pursue postsecondary education. The Millennium Pilot Project actually comprises two sub-studies: Future to Discover, which will operate in New Brunswick and Manitoba and will test the impacts of an information strategy and a financial incentive strategy; and, in British Columbia, an evaluation of an academic preparation program called Advancement Via Individual Determination (AVID), which will be implemented on a pilot basis in selected schools.

The Canada Millennium Scholarship Foundation is providing the funding for the Millennium Pilot Project and is arranging for it to be implemented under the terms of Memoranda of Understanding signed with the three participating provincial governments. SRDC has been engaged by the foundation to conduct the evaluation of the projects.

The Future to Discover pilot project will determine whether early interventions with high-school students can help overcome the barriers to pursuing postsecondary education that are associated with a lack of financial resources and a lack of adequate information concerning the benefits of postsecondary education and how to access postsecondary education programs and sources of student financial aid.

The financial intervention in Future to Discover will create individual learning accounts for high-school students from families whose income is below the provincial median. Funds will accumulate in these accounts during a student's high-school years and an amount of $8,000 will be available on high-school graduation to put towards postsecondary education. Participating students will be aware of the availability of these funds as early as Grade 9 and the psychological impact on how they think about the possibility of being destined for postsecondary education may be more important than the money itself.

The information strategy is built on the notion that better information delivered in more effective ways will help students make better choices about postsecondary education. It consists of five components:

- meetings with "postsecondary ambassadors" — current postsecondary education students who will meet with participating high-schools students to provide information about postsecondary education choices and to answer questions about life as a postsecondary education student;
- "career focusing" workshops designed to help students identify meaningful career options and develop courses of action that can lead to satisfying careers;

- "lasting gifts" sessions at which participating students and their parents learn how to access labour market information and make more informed decisions about education and career choices;
- regular mailings of information about postsecondary education and education financing options; and
- access to a website containing information about postsecondary education institutions, academic programs, and student financial assistance.

Participant enrolment for Future to Discover will take place in spring 2004 and 2005. In New Brunswick, 4,000 Grade 9 students will be enrolled in a multiple random assignment study that will evaluate the impacts of the information strategy alone, the financial incentive alone, and the financial incentive offered in combination with the information strategy. Impacts will be measured separately for students from the French- and English-language school systems. In Manitoba, only the information strategy will be tested and 1,000 students will be enrolled (half randomly assigned to the program group and half assigned to the control group).

The AVID evaluation in British Columbia is focused on a somewhat different target group. The AVID pilot project will deliver an enhanced curriculum to students who are "in the middle" academically (generally C-level students in terms of grades but who are judged to be underperforming relative to their potential) as a way of increasing the probability that they will enrol in postsecondary education. The AVID program was originally developed in San Diego, California, and combines advanced academic courses with an elective class focused on writing, inquiry, collaboration, organization, and study and test-taking skills.

The AVID model has already been adopted in one BC school district (Chilliwack) and the Millennium Pilot Project intends to add 19 schools as part of a randomized trial. Participating schools will identify a pool of AVID-eligible students as they exit Grade 8 in June 2005. It is estimated that a little under 1,000 students will be enrolled in the study; they will be randomly assigned either to an AVID class or to the control group. The AVID program begins in Grade 9 and lasts over a student's four years in high school.

The outcomes of primary interest in the Millennium Pilot Project are whether students graduate from high school and apply successfully to a postsecondary education program. The Canada Millennium Scholarship Foundation is committed to funding the study through to at least 2010. SRDC will be using both surveys and data from administrative records to measure outcomes. It may be possible to follow participants longer, for example, through to the completion of postsecondary education.

Both *learn*$ave and the Millennium Pilot Project are long-term research studies. It will be several years before results are available to guide the development of policies to improve access to postsecondary education. I hope to have the opportunity of presenting research results and discussing their implications for policy at conferences such as this one in the future.

References

Sherraden, M.. 1991. *Assets and the Poor: A New American Welfare Policy.* Armonk: M.E. Sharpe Inc.

University Accountability

John Chant

It is not news that Canadian universities have been in a long process of decline. The quality of faculty research has been slipping by international standards. Peers now cite papers of Canadian scholars in the pure, applied and social sciences less frequently than they did in the past. The quality of the undergraduate education has also suffered. The pressure of numbers, the gaps in students' backgrounds, and the ease by which modern technology allows some students to represent the work of others as their own have all contributed to a shrinking role for writing in the undergraduate curriculum. Students can now avoid writing entirely while earning an undergraduate degree.

The forces behind the deterioration of the Canadian university experience are not difficult to understand. The continuing surge in participation has raised the scale of funding needed for universities as other social and economic needs have come forward to compete for the public purse. Universities themselves have responded to shape their offerings to the pressures of increasingly diverse demands of their students and the tightness of their finances. Like Humpty Dumpty, the quality of the university will be hard to put together again. Faculty who have fled to greener and more supportive pastures will be difficult to attract back, or to replace with others. Determination is required to restore curricula once they have been eroded. The solution to our universities' decline through a substantial commitment of more public resources to higher education is neither realistic nor sufficient.

It is unrealistic to expect that the public purse can provide the massive resources needed to overcome the decline. Given the competing demands for funds, universities are not high in the hierarchy of public priorities. Moreover, questions of university funding raise issues that are difficult to reconcile. How can greater public funding be justified for expenditures that yield such substantial benefits to those who will become an economically privileged group? How can broad access to universities be assured without substantial public funding to reduce the barriers to less privileged students? Perhaps as important, how can we avoid the devastating effects of cosmetic solutions that evade the issues by controlling the ability of universities to pass their costs through higher fees to their students. These policies effectively promise the maintenance of access, but access to what? These policies preserve access at the expense of a continuing dilution of the university education that is offered.

Nicholas Barr and Lorne Carmichael in this volume deal with the question of university funding by putting forward schemes that minimize the immediate barriers to student access without increasing the burden on the general taxpayer. Students pay their share for university education after they receive and reap its benefits rather than up-front as at present. More-over, they pay strictly on the basis of their postgraduation income, reducing the uncertainties of the current system of student finance where loans can become a burden to graduates who fail to realize higher incomes by choice or circumstance. Though such a plan could provide a vital element in restoring the health of our universities, it will not be enough to halt their decline and put them on the path to providing the type of higher education needed for our young people.

Increasing funding cannot be the whole solution because finance is only one of the problems plaguing universities. In addition, the system of governance under which universities operate also needs reconsideration. Any governance arrangements must reflect the fact that the public finance of higher education poses a tension between autonomy and accountability. Autonomy is vital for assuring vibrant responses by universities to society's needs for a well-educated populace and for the advancement of knowledge. Accountability is essential because of the substantial resources committed to higher education. Taxpayers need to be assured that their financial con-tribution has been well spent. Similarly, students who provide a substantial share of university funding and commit substantial time to their studies also need to be assured that their time, effort, and money will not be wasted.

Despite the trappings of university autonomy, Canadian universities have operated for a long time under a system of centralized "command and control" that shares the methods of the Soviet planned economies together with their many flaws. This centralization has been justified in the name of accountability. Certainly universities use these public funds and should be accountable through governments to taxpayers for the use of these funds. But accountability can take many forms. In the rest of my comments, I will examine whether the interests of the public and students are well served by this system of centralized control. I will then describe a system that preserves accountability while leaving more autonomy to the universities to control their own destinies.

While many major decisions such as those concerning enrolment, what programs to offer, what fees to charge, and what salaries to pay are nominally decisions of universities, effectively they are made by provincial governments or are subject to their approval. The present system of university governance resolves the tension between autonomy and accountability through a system of centralized control in the hands of ministries of higher education. These ministries have allotted public funds to universities and have often controlled the fees that universities can charge for their programs. At the core of this system is the control of the enrolment quotas that will effectively determine the number of students that will receive funding at each university. Universities failing to meet their quotas lose funding while universities receive no funding or gain funding on a reduced basis for exceeding their enrolment quotas. Ministries have at times managed quotas in a way to push universities to accept more students in order to qualify for their full funding allotment, often without any additional funding to reflect the increased student load.

This system of centralized control failed to work for the planned economies. It suppressed the vital signal and rationing functions of prices that direct activity in a market economy and did not replace them with any adequate substitute. In absence of effective signals, goods and services supplied under planning represent, at best, the planners' views of what the public wants. But planners have only an imperfect knowledge of what their public wants and, indeed, may favour a competing vision. To the extent production decisions fail to reflect demands, they promote lineups and shortages for those things where planners underestimate demand and surpluses where they overestimate demand. Managers in such a centralized system by necessity simplify. The messages from the managers to the producers must be crude, but such crudeness comes at a cost. Producers will meet their instructions in the easiest way possible and will emphasize those characteristics that the planners can most easily observe and reward at the expense of other less measurable characteristics. Yet the unobserved and unmonitored characteristics may be as important to consumers and users as those the planners can control. But planners are fighting a losing battle because attempts to add additional dimensions to the assessment may just lead to greater emphasis on the new dimensions without assurance that it contributes to the more valued dimensions that are difficult to observe and monitor. Central control inevitably leads to a weighting of those features such as quantity that can be readily observed and measured at the expense of those valued dimensions such as quality that are difficult to articulate and quantify. The process is plagued by an uncertainty principle: the use of any indicator for performance monitoring alters its meaning and significance with respect to the desired qualities for which it is a proxy. This problem is especially pronounced for higher education where enrolments, class size, grades, and time to degree are easy to measure, while measures of quality such as faculty-student interaction and increased depth and breadth of knowledge are not.

Is it a stretch to draw parallels between the problems of a "control and command" economy and our system of university governance? Consider the way in which our system of enrolment quotas and student assignment works. Students may prefer one university over another, but will be forced to go to the lesser choice because it will be funded for their enrolment whereas the first choice will not. There is a shortage at the first choice institution, a glut at the lower choice, and unnecessarily disgruntled students. Our system of allocating enrolment quotas to universities creates shortages and surpluses just as certainly as command and control economies. Many students are victims of a system where students are forced to follow finance rather than the other way around.

As often pointed out, mainly by economists, there is an alternative funding arrangement where funding could follow students. Governments could decide, as they do now, that they will provide a specified level of funding per student and also, as now, they could set a ceiling number of students to be funded. The change would occur because government funding to specific universities could be determined by the number of students that they attract, and not by government quotas. Instead of meeting quotas, universities would be funded for as few or as many of the students eligible for funding as they wish within the framework of the total number of students that governments decide to fund. Universities would also be free to set their fees to supplement their government funding.

Such a system would drastically alter the accountability of universities. No longer would they have to satisfy government officials according to their template of performance measures. Rather universities would be accountable to students, the ones who are undergoing the educational processes that universities provide. Students will not have the same arsenal of quantitative measures that can be used to guide universities as the government ministries do at present. Instead, they have qualitative measures of their satisfaction of the enterprise's performance. They would be able to express their satisfaction and provide signals and incentives to universities by voting with their feet. Universities that fail to attract students will suffer cuts in their finances. This change in accountability would shift the balance of the funding criteria from statistical proxies of the university experience to those things that matter to the students whose education, after all, is one of the purposes of universities.

There may be concern that, if students favour a greater emphasis on teaching, such a system lead to a withering of university research. This may occur. Evidence suggests, however, that many students themselves value university research. They still flock into the top research universities in the United States and pay their high fees, even though they know that their faculty is committed primarily to research. Still, students at other institutions may not value their professors' research as much and prefer the faculty to stick more to teaching. A possible outcome could be a greater specialization of universities. Some universities, in the mould of the liberal arts colleges of the United States, will choose to specialize in high-quality undergraduate teaching with small class sizes and close collaboration between students and faculty. Others, much like the top US research universities, will use the visibility of their faculty's research accomplishments to attract students who can, in turn, expect to benefit from this reputation once they graduate.

It is possible that the resulting level of research will prove to be too low relative to the social benefits it provides to the Canadian public. If this is the case, federal and provincial governments can direct additional funds to universities targeted for research.

The system may also reduce the severity of a problem identified by Ehrenberg and Laidler in their papers: the tendency of universities to direct funds towards the sciences and professional schools and away from the humanities and social sciences. Competition for students would put pressures on universities that cross-subsidize some programs at the expenses of others because they run the risk of losing students from their "cash cow" programs to universities that give these students better value for their money. Still, it may be that these present cross-subsidies serve some social purpose or, otherwise, suit the wishes of government officials and their political masters. If they do, these cross-subsidies could be replaced by larger grants that support the students in these programs. The change would have the salutary effect of making the disparity in support for different programs grants more open and subject to public scrutiny.

Universities may do many things from the almost trivial to the fundamental in response to tying funding more closely to the numbers of students attracted. They may resort to advertising — they do that now. But this advertising must be directed to the priorities of students. They may eliminate small vexations and aggravations for students by modernizing procedures for providing services such as parking and library cards. At a more critical level, they may increase the availability of key courses to make timely graduation possible. They may also be forced to re-examine their salary policies to provide greater incentives for professors to meet students' needs. In short, they may treat students as customers. I hesitate to call students "customers", which they are, because these words invariably evoke strong reactions from some quarters. Maybe they are right; most customers have choices among suppliers facing true competition. Students would be better served were universities to appreciate that their well-being depended on meeting students' needs.

The same centralized decision-making that characterizes university governance now appears to be playing an increasingly important role in the funding of research. Canadian research-granting agencies have been transforming themselves from granting agencies to more hands-on research managers directed towards influencing public policy. The distinction between the two is that granting agencies direct their resources to scholars on the basis of research excellence: the probability that the research will produce significant contributions of knowledge in the judgement of the scientific community. Research managers, on the other hand, direct resources to achieve a variety of goals going beyond the contribution to knowledge. In its quest to transform itself from a "granting council" to a "knowledge council", the SSHRC envisions a new and different role for scholars:

> The role of the researcher is not only to develop knowledge, although this is very important in and of itself. They must become more proficient in moving the knowledge from research to action and, in the process, at linking up with a broader range of researchers and stakeholder partners across the country. However big the challenges, researchers have to add new and different connections to those they have already built. (SSHRC, 2004, p. 3)

The SSHRC proposes a new breed of scholar: a researcher, a populiser and publicist, and policy analyst all rolled into one. Each of these tasks involves a different set of skills: the researcher must combine imagination with deliberateness and care, the publicist must simplify, and the analyst must persuade. Certainly there may be some academics who combine these qualities. It is difficult to see this transformation occurring without a downgrading of the values and benefits of basic research.

Funding agencies in this new role have shifted from being supportive of research activity to being more prescriptive of the practice of research and what it entails. They have added goals other than the pursuit of knowledge and criteria other than the achieving of excellence to their mandate. This difference has been captured aptly by John Polanyi, a Nobel prizewinner:

> I have beside me the guidelines for participation in what is called a Canadian Centre of Excellence. These exist ... to foster university research. The reference to "excellence" acknowledges ... that it is the vision (the free enterprise, if that is your line of business) of a small number of researchers that lead to new ideas that matter. So pick the best scientists (excellent, you know) and give them freedom — just so long as they remain the best. This is how it should be done.
>
> But it's not what we do. In our hunger for payoff, our centers of excellence give a miserable 20 per cent weight to excellence. The remaining 80 per cent of the marks in the selection process are for such vogueish things as interdisciplinarity, inter-institutional relations, management structure, relevance, training and socio-economic impact (that was easy to write; I copied it from the form). Applications for funding must address these criteria. They then are sent for evaluation to the scientific peers of the applicant, who pretend to judge worth on this absurd basis. It is absurd, since university research is performed (or should be) in the marketplace for ideas, and not that for devices. (2000, p. D6)

There is another practical aspect of the shift that is disquieting. The motives of the agencies are understandable. They want a bigger, more visible role for their supported research in debates on national issues. They not only want it for its own sake, but they also want it in the belief that it will increase funding for the scholars in their domain. But if the goal of increased visibility and influence is acceptable, they must be careful that they do not win just a pyhrric victory. In the past, government research groups, task forces, royal commissions, and other devices have all brought the knowledge gained from research into the public arena and have drawn out its implications for public policy. Will the re-engineered granting agencies just replace these approaches? Will they bring additional resources to the study of human sciences, or will they merely redirect the resources that formerly served a policy-support function to a new venue? Will the greater funding by the agencies for dissemination and advocacy come at the expense of the basic research that is to be disseminated and its implication advocated?

There is no question that universities and their scholars must be accountable, like every other group that depends on public funding. Accountability can take place in many different ways and through different forms than the present high degree of centralization that limits university autonomy. There is also little question that university autonomy brings benefits in the form of innovation, diversity, and responsiveness to student needs. Accountability and autonomy could both be achieved by allowing funding to chase students rather than the other way around.

References

Polanyi, J. 2000. "Review: The Equation that Rocked the Planet", *The Globe and Mail*, November 4.
Social Sciences and Humanities Research Council of Canada (SSHRC). 2004. *From Granting Council to Knowledge Council: Renewing the Social Sciences and Humanities in Canada*, Volume 1. Ottawa: SSHRC.

Contributors

Douglas Auld is the President at Loyalist College, Belleville.

Nicholas Barr is Professor of Public Economics, European Institute, London School of Economics.

Charles M. Beach is Professor in the Department of Economics and Director of the John Deutsch Institute at Queen's University.

Julian R. Betts is Professor in the Department of Economics at the University of California, San Diego

Robin W. Boadway is Sir Edward Peacock Professor of Economic Theory in the Department of Economics at Queen's University.

John B. Burbidge is Professor in the Department of Economics at the University of Waterloo.

David M. Cameron is Professor in the Department of Political Science at Dalhousie University.

H. Lorne Carmichael is Professor in the Department of Economics at Queen's University.

John Chant is Emeritus Professor in the Department of Economics at Simon Fraser University.

Kirk A. Collins is Assistant Professor in Administrative and Commercial Studies at the University of Western Ontario.

Miles Corak is Director of the Family and Labour Studies Division at Statistics Canada, and is also affiliated with Carleton University as an Adjunct Professor in the Department of Economics.

James B. Davies is Professor and RBC Financial Group Fellow in the Department of Economics at the University of Western Ontario.

Ronald G. Ehrenberg is Irving M. Ives Professor of Industrial and Labor Relations and Economics at Cornell University and Director of the Cornell Higher Education Research Institute (CHERI), Cornell University.

Herb Emery is Associate Professor in the Department of Economics at the University of Calgary.

Ross Finnie is Research Fellow and Adjunct Professor in the School of Policy Studies at Queen's University and a Visiting Fellow at Statistics Canada.

Nicole M. Fortin is Professor in the Department of Economics at the University of British Columbia.

Peter George is President and Vice-Chancellor at McMaster University and is the Chair of the COU Quality and Financing Task Force.

John Greenwood is Executive Director of Social Research and Demonstration Corporation, Ottawa.

David Laidler is Emeritus Professor and Bank of Montreal Professor in the Department of Economics, University of Western Ontario.

Eric Lascelles is a researcher at Statistics Canada and was at the time a graduate student in the Department of Economics at Queen's University.

Carolyn W.B. Lee is Director of Research, Global CONNECT, University of California, San Diego's Division of Extended Studies and Public Programs.

Clément Lemelin is Professor at Département des sciences économiques, Université du Québec à Montréal.

David Leyton-Brown is Executive Director at the Ontario Council on Graduate Studies, Toronto.

Garth Lipps is a Research Analyst with the Family and Labour Studies Division at Statistics Canada.

R. Marvin McInnis is Emeritus Professor in the Department of Economics at Queen's University.

Kevin Milligan is Professor in the Department of Economics at the University of British Columbia and National Bureau of Economic Research (NBER).

Richard E. Mueller is Associate Professor in the Department of Economics at the University of Lethbridge.

Elizabeth Parr-Johnston is retired President of the University of New Brunswick.

Duane W. Rockerbie is Associate Professor in the Department of Economics at the University of Lethbridge.

Michael L. Skolnik is William G. Davis Chair in Community College Leadership at the Ontario Institute for Studies in Education (OISE) of the University of Toronto.

Ken Snowdon is a higher education consultant, Snowdon & Associates Inc.

Arthur Sweetman is Director and Stauffer-Dunning Chair of the School of Policy Studies at Queen's University.

Alex Usher is Vice-President of the Educational Policy Institute, Toronto.

Hans Vossensteyn is Research Associate at the Center for Higher Education Policy Studies (CHEPS) of the University of Twente in the Netherlands.

John Zhao is Research Analyst with the Family and Labour Studies Division at Statistics Canada.

Queen's Policy Studies
Recent Publications

The Queen's Policy Studies Series is dedicated to the exploration of major policy issues that confront governments in Canada and other western nations. McGill-Queen's University Press is the exclusive world representative and distributor of books in the series.

John Deutsch Institute for the Study of Economic Policy

Financial Services and Public Policy, Christopher Waddell (ed.), 2004
Paper ISBN 1-55339-068-7   Cloth ISBN 1-55339-067-9

The 2003 Federal Budget: Conflicting Tensions, Charles M. Beach and Thomas A. Wilson (eds.), Policy Forum Series no. 39, 2004   Paper ISBN 0-88911-958-9
Cloth ISBN 0-88911-956-2

Canadian Immigration Policy for the 21st Century, Charles M. Beach, Alan G. Green and Jeffrey G. Reitz (eds.), 2003   Paper ISBN 0-88911-954-6 Cloth ISBN 0-88911-952-X

Framing Financial Structure in an Information Environment, Thomas J. Courchene and Edwin H. Neave (eds.), Policy Forum Series no. 38, 2003   Paper ISBN 0-88911-950-3
Cloth ISBN 0-88911-948-1

Towards Evidence-Based Policy for Canadian Education/Vers des politiques canadiennes d'éducation fondées sur la recherche, Patrice de Broucker and/et Arthur Sweetman (eds./dirs.), 2002   Paper ISBN 0-88911-946-5 Cloth ISBN 0-88911-944-9

Money, Markets and Mobility: Celebrating the Ideas of Robert A. Mundell, Nobel Laureate in Economic Sciences, Thomas J. Courchene (ed.), 2002
Paper ISBN 0-88911-820-5   Cloth ISBN 0-88911-818-3

School of Policy Studies

Force of Choice: Perspectives on Special Operations, Bernd Horn, J. Paul de B. Taillon and David Last (eds.), 2004 Paper ISBN 1-55339-042-3 Cloth 1-55339-043-1

New Missions, Old Problems, Douglas L. Bland, David Last, Franklin Pinch and Alan Okros (eds.), 2004 Paper ISBN 1-55339-034-2 Cloth 1-55339-035-0

The North American Democratic Peace: Absence of War and Security Institution-Building in Canada-US Relations, 1867-1958, Stéphane Rousse, 2004
Paper ISBN 0-88911-937-6 Cloth 0-88911-932-2

Implementing Primary Care Reform: Barriers and Facilitators, Ruth Wilson, S.E.D. Shortt and John Dorland (eds.), 2004 Paper ISBN 1-55339-040-7 Cloth 1-55339-041-5

Social and Cultural Change, David Last, Franklin Pinch, Douglas L. Bland and Alan Okros (eds.), 2004 Paper ISBN 1-55339-032-6 Cloth 1-55339-033-4

Clusters in a Cold Climate: Innovation Dynamics in a Diverse Economy, David A. Wolfe and Matthew Lucas (eds.), 2004 Paper ISBN 1-55339-038-5 Cloth 1-55339-039-3